They Flew

This seventeenth-century copy of a lost painting by Jusepe de Ribera, previously attributed to Francisco de Zurbarán, depicts Saint Francis receiving the mystical gift of the stigmata while levitating.

They Flew

A History of the Impossible

Carlos M. N. Eire

Yale

UNIVERSITY PRESS

NEW HAVEN AND LONDON

Published with assistance from the Kingsley Trust Association Publication Fund
established by the Scroll and Key Society of Yale College and from the
foundation established in memory of Philip Hamilton McMillan
of the Class of 1894, Yale College.

Yale University Press books may be purchased in quantity for educational,
business, or promotional use. For information, please email sales.press@yale
.edu (U.S. office) or sales@yaleup.co.uk (U.K. office).

Set in PS Fournier Standard Petit Light by Westchester Publishing Services,
Danbury, CT.
Printed in the United States of America.

Library of Congress Control Number: 2023936530
ISBN 978-0-300-25980-3 (hardcover: alk. paper)

A catalogue record for this book is available from the British Library.
This paper meets the requirements of ANSI/NISO Z39.48-1992
(Permanence of Paper).

10 9 8 7 6 5 4 3 2 1

To all my students, past and present,
Who have taught me so much,
And to all those I have yet to meet,
From whom I have so much more to learn

Jesus replied, "What is impossible for humans is possible for God."

—Gospel of Luke 18:27

The truth does not change according to our ability to stomach it.

—Flannery O'Connor,
letter to Betty Hester, September 6, 1955

Contents

PART THREE. MALEVOLENT

Preface

The subject matter of this book is strange stuff, for sure, and there is no predicting how anyone might react to it. Levitation, bilocation, and other such anomalous phenomena that are considered "impossible" have always elicited a wide range of responses, from absolute delight or disbelief to stupefaction or sheer terror. But in a culture such as ours, which tends to reject the concept of a supernatural dimension or not take it seriously, these phenomena can be lightning rods for disagreement. Moreover, not all this disagreeing is purely intellectual. All talk about the supernatural and the impossible, even of the most scholarly kind, can often be emotionally charged.

No surprise, then, that the history of the impossible has an abrasive edge to it, as well as competing approaches, and that writing about it requires making some hard choices. Given the sharp differences of opinion that contend against each other, anyone who writes about the impossible is always forced to pick a side or take a stand of some sort—regardless of which approach one chooses or how objective one tries to be in making that choice—which means, naturally, that whatever is written about this subject is bound to please some readers immensely and also inevitably baffle, bore, offend, or annoy the hell out of everyone else.

So why would anyone venture into this subject? After all, annoying some readers is only one risk involved in writing about the supernatural. Having one's work end up in the crackpot section on bookstore shelves is also highly likely to happen, maybe even a certainty. And that is far worse than annoying readers who might not realize that they need some annoying. A reviewer of the first manuscript draft of this book expressed concern that this book might make the author seem "eccentric." That reviewer was being very kind. To be honest, "eccentric" would be the most polite and least offensive of adjectives that could end up being attached to the name of anyone who dares to write about the impossible, or to my name specifically (and not just because some website has compared me to Satan or because I have been denounced as "very dangerous" and proclaimed an official "enemy of the state" in my native country).[1] So, one must ask again: Why write this book?

The answer is simple enough: Because this important subject has been ignored or sidelined for far too long, and taking it on is something that sorely needs to be done, for various reasons that should become obvious in the following chapters. In addition, it is the right subject to tackle for a historian who has always been intrigued by the ways in which religions and cultures conceive of the relation between the natural and the supernatural. Personal preferences, then, have a lot to do with the writing of this book. This should not surprise anyone. The writing of history is always an intensely personal quest for historians, although some will try to hide this from themselves, their students, and their readers. Ask historians why they write the kind of history they do, and if they are honest, they will tell you that when all is said and done the history they write has everything to do with their life story, their yearnings, and their obsessions. This author is no different. Allow me to switch to first-person mode and show you how this is so by means of a brief narrative.

This project began to take shape unexpectedly, like a proverbial bolt out of the blue, on a bright summer day in 1983 at the Carmelite Convent of the Incarnation, outside the medieval walls of Ávila. The individual responsible for this turn of events could not have been aware of the impact her words would have on me and will never know how much I owe to her.

I and a dozen other pilgrims were being led around the convent by a local tour guide. We were all pilgrims of one sort or another, whether we wanted to admit it or not. The tour was conducted in Spanish, and our guide was young, though not much younger than me. She had been escorting us from room to room, pointing out significant details related to the life of the convent's famous resident, Saint Teresa of Avila. "This was the refectory where the nuns ate. . . . The kitchen is over there. . . . Here is the chapel. . . . This is the staircase where Saint Teresa fell and broke her arm," and so on, room after room. Mundane details. Then we walked into the *locutorio,* the room where the nuns could speak with visitors through a grille-covered opening in the wall. "And this is where Saint Teresa and Saint John of the Cross levitated together for the first time," she said, as if there were no difference between that levitation and the grille, the staircase, the refectory, or the pots and pans in the kitchen (fig. 1). It was simply another detail, that dual levitation. Just another *fact.*

Figure 1. Eyewitness accounts claim that Saint Teresa of Avila and Saint John of the Cross levitated together ecstatically on one occasion while conversing about the Holy Trinity. This painting by José Garcia Hidalgo (1675) seeks to capture the details provided in those accounts.

Whoa.

I knew about levitation, of course. I had heard about it since childhood and had encountered it in fiction, especially in comic books. Superman could levitate. Gravity meant nothing to him. Years later, I encountered it again as a graduate student, in hagiographies and mystical texts, and especially in *The Physical Phenomena of Mysticism* by Montague Summers, which I read with equal measures of amusement, fascination, and suspicion.[2] I had also stumbled into levitation in *A Hundred Years of Solitude,* a novel that sneaks it into the narrative fairly often as a bit of magical realism.[3] But I had never encountered levitation as a fact, as something that was as undeniable as my presence in that room right there and then or as real as any object I could see or touch in that convent. It was a fact in the tour guide's narrative, and I had never before heard a living human being speak of levitation as a fact at the very spot where it had ostensibly happened.

To say that a whole new dimension opened up for me on the spot at that instant is to understate the magnitude of the experience. There was nothing mystical going on. It was a purely rational moment that would have pleased Immanuel Kant immensely.[4] Suddenly, I saw the supernatural and the impossible in a whole new light. It is hard to explain what actually happened, really, but somehow, that very rational moment of clarity immediately sparked some kind of cognitive firestorm that I cannot describe in precise terms. In fact, even after writing this book, I am still tongue-tied. Eureka moments can be like that.[5]

At that instant I knew for sure that I had to venture into the dimension this tour guide had exposed. I knew it would not be an easy journey, or brief. I had been trained to *never, ever* take the supernatural or miraculous as facts in any way, under any circumstances. So the journey of writing this book began with questions. Why was that double levitation a fact for the young tour guide? Had she been coached to speak of it this way? Did she really take it as a fact? Was she being insincere? Was she merely parroting a script written for visitors to the convent, who are normally only devout folk interested in Saint Teresa?

Such questions did not matter too much to me at that moment, however. She had made that specific levitation a fact, and that was that. A discarded and oft-ridiculed mentality from the past had rudely elbowed its way into the present and asserted its survival. As I saw it, what she said and the way she said it—even if insincere—should have been as impossible in 1983 as the levitation she was describing. But it obviously was not for her, and *that* was a fact.

So I started writing this book right then and there, in midsummer 1983. In my head, at least. That is all I could do. I was neck-deep in another project at the time, and my tenure at the University of Virginia was hanging in the balance.

And now this book is being published in 2023. Forty years have passed. That is a big number, freighted with biblical connotations. But I have not been working on this book constantly during these past four decades. I have written other books in the meantime—a couple of them without footnotes—and have only spent the past two years assiduously writing this text you are perusing right now. But the thinking, reading, research, and note-taking condensed into it have been going on since that bright summer day in 1983, on and off, on and off, with many a long pause and occasional spurts of intense archive-diving, library-raiding, and note-shuffling now and then. But as I write this preface, right now, I can recall being in that locutorio at the convent of the Incarnation so vividly that the 3,449 miles between me and Ávila seem to have instantly vanished. I am in two places at once, and I am not bilocating, but this is perhaps as close as I can get to experiencing that impossible feat.

Enlightening moments of insight such as this can transcend language and linear reasoning wonderfully, but they can also exact a high price.

To write a history of the impossible is risky for any scholar nowadays, especially if one suggests, even tentatively, that the assumed impossibility of certain events deserves closer scrutiny and some challenging. This is what I am doing here, in this book. Read on and see. Keep in mind, however, that I will be raising more questions than I dare to answer. The history of the impossible is all about questioning, about being evenhandedly skeptical—that is, being as skeptical about strictly materialist interpretations of seemingly impossible events as about the actual occurrence of the event itself. Counterintuitive as this might seem—given that the impossibility of certain events is deemed unquestionable in our dominant culture and that dogmatic materialists tend to think of themselves as the only truly objective skeptics—this sort of nonconformist skepticism is necessary if one is to claim any kind of genuine objectivity. As Francis Bacon (1561–1626) once suggested, doubting is essential for inductive reasoning: "If a man will begin with certainties," he warned, "he shall end in doubts; but if he will be content to begin with doubts, he shall end in certainties."[6] Nearly four centuries after Bacon's death, his warning applies as much to doubts about the dogmatic scientific materialism he engendered as to doubts about events considered absolutely impossible by that dominant worldview. Bacon might have been peeved or bewildered by this assertion, but it is nonetheless valid.

Bacon's younger contemporary René Descartes (1596–1650) had another way of delivering the same advice. "Everything must be doubted," he suggested.[7] So, please, consider this book a Cartesian exercise in doubt, then, even if the twist it gives to Descartes's method might have annoyed him as much as he annoyed his younger contemporary Blaise Pascal (1623–1662),[8] or as much as he annoyed me in algebra class with his geometric calculus over half a century ago. Annoyance of some sort is as unavoidable when writing about the impossible as it is when dealing with polynomials, simple curves, and differential equations in a final exam.

This book's structure and content have been shaped by questioning. This is why the book is divided into three distinct sections and why saints, frauds, demoniacs, and witches—groups of people that were very different from each other and normally did not mingle—are all examined together, side by side. And this involves both Catholics and Protestants, people who did not just avoid mingling but often hankered to kill each other and did so much too frequently, with excessive zeal. Questions about impossible claims bring all these extremely odd bedfellows into the same book in the same way that such questions brought them face-to-face with official tribunals in their lifetime, civil as well as ecclesiastic, Catholic as well as Protestant. Who is levitating? Who is bilocating? Are they really hovering and flying or suddenly becoming visible in two distinct locations at the same time? If so, then who is causing these phenomena, God or the devil? Or could they be faking everything? If so, then how do they manage to fool people with their trickery, and what are their motives for messing with people's minds? Who is going to examine these impossible events? What criteria will guide their investigations and decisions? In the twenty-first century we can add another question, one which no inquisitor or judge would care to ask: What can we learn from these freakish historical figures and from those in charge of judging them?

Freakish folk are not necessarily ridiculous or dismissible, especially in the study of religion. The impossible events and the aberrant individuals analyzed in this book are essential to religion, even of central significance. They were no sideshow in their own day, as they might seem now, centuries later. They were the main event. One could argue that all encounters with a supernatural reality are the bedrock upon which religions have been built. Such experiences can be called "theophanies," "hierophanies" or "irruptions of the sacred." Those who experience such events do not have to assume the existence of some unseen power beyond the material world that can mess with nature, as well as with their minds. They *know* it exists, most definitely. In the words of one of the most influential historians of religion, such folk enter a "paradoxical point of passage from one mode of being to another."[9] In traditional religious mentalities, these experiences and the narratives they engender generate belief and validate the assumption that the material world we access with our senses and our intellect is only a minute sliver of a much larger and complex reality beyond our ken and that some things that are normally impossible do occasionally happen. Whether one knows it or not, and whether one likes it or not, an essential component of the transition to modernity in the West has been the rejection of this assumption by an ever-increasing number of people and its gradual slippage into near oblivion in the realm of the ridiculous and trivial.

Curiously, this partial eclipse of the supernatural began to creep forward at precisely the same time as the events analyzed in this book were taking place. Was all this levitating and bilocating a reflex of sorts? Maybe, yes. One could argue that the sudden rise in such impossible events might have been some sort of dying gasp of an ancient and fading mentality, a collective rage, or a nearly prophetic expression of the personal sentiments voiced three centuries later by the poet Dylan Thomas: "Do not go gentle into that good night, / Old age should burn and rave at close of day; / Rage, rage against the dying of the light."[10] But the historical truth is that this mentality has not yet died and is still actually thriving and raving in the twenty-first century, here and there, sometimes in unlikely places and even at august institutions of higher learning. This is not to say that some collective "raging against the dying of the light" could not have had something to do with all those levitations and bilocations reported at that time. All of this is certainly possible. But that is not the whole story. Far from it. Such facile reductionism is only applicable to one part of a much greater whole, and it does not get very far into the mystery of these impossible events, or of their meaning back then or now.

The history of the impossible deserves some rationalizing that transcends reductive functionalism, dogmatic materialism, or any other one-dimensional approaches that fail to take belief in a supernatural dimension into account as a very *real* thing for those long-gone folk one is analyzing. After all, these weird events are manifestations of a mentality in which multiple dimensions are believed not only to coexist but to constantly intermingle. (A mentality, incidentally, that bears an eerie resemblance to the multiverse cosmology proposed by some astrophysicists in our own day and age,[11] as well as to philosophical and scientific speculations about our universe being a simulation.[12]) To deal adequately with such a mentality, one must grapple with it, dive deeply into its core and try to think along the same lines, and burrow as deeply as one can into its assumptions, even to the point of suspending disbelief. And above all, one must accept complexity and paradox as givens and involve both of these in one's own reasoning while growing more and more comfortable with unanswerable questions.

Easier said than done, yes, for sure. But this is what I have tried to do in this book and what I hope its readers will try to do too. As I have already said and will say again in the pages to follow, dealing with the impossible requires one to end up with more questions than answers. This can prove unsettling. But the best thing about all things truly unnerving and all things impossible and ostensibly supernatural, such as those that are the focus of this book, is the hard fact that none of these questions are trivial, even though our dominant culture aggressively suggests that they are.

Acknowledgments

Most of this book was written during the great pandemic of 2020–2022. There are many nameless folk who helped me write this book during the crisis, mainly those individuals who scanned and uploaded onto the web so many texts, old and new, all of which would have been otherwise inaccessible. Every now and then I could see their fingertips at the edge of some page, furtively caught by the scanner, and whenever their ghostly presence came into view, I would thank them, whoever they were. The same goes for those here at Yale and other institutions who would retrieve books from library shelves, pack them up, and mail them directly to my plague bunker. Those who delivered these presents need to be thanked too.

Among those with whom I could interact virtually who helped make this impossible book possible, I would first like to thank Alice Martell, my literary agent, whose wise counsel has guided me every step of the way through this journey and many others, whose ability to move mountains astounds me, and whose friendship I treasure. I would also like to thank the following collaborators in this project: Jennifer Banks, my editor, whose perceptive guidance has shaped my thinking and my writing all along the way; Abigail Storch, assistant editor, who has patiently guided me through the labyrinth of manuscript preparation; John Donatich, director at Yale University Press, whose vision has made edgy books like this possible; and the anonymous readers of the first draft of this book and the editors at Westchester Publishing Services, who saved me from entrapment by my own blind spots. I would also like to thank four of my closest and dearest friends and colleagues, Bruce Gordon, Craig Harline, Ron Rittgers, and Victor Triay, for always inspiring me, steering me in the right direction, bringing light into the darkness, and constantly enlightening me in more ways than I could ever count. Most of all, I thank those closest to my heart: my wife, Jane, and our three miraculous offspring, John-Carlos, Grace, and Bruno, who have always proven in infinite ways that love is a supernatural realm and that the impossible is never as impossible as it might seem, or as impossible as so-called experts might imperiously tell us that it is.

They Flew

Introduction

Huge Claims, Vague Proof

While strolling in the garden one day . . . a priest said to him, "Father Joseph, oh, how beautiful God has made heaven!" Then Joseph, as if he had been called to heaven, gave a loud shriek, leapt off the ground, flew through the air, and knelt down atop an olive tree, and—as witnesses declared in his beatification inquest—that branch on which he rested waved as if a bird were perched upon it, and he remained up there about half an hour.

What kind of nonsense is this? Who is this liar quoted above?[1] Human beings can't fly, or kneel on slender tree limbs like little birds, and they have never, ever done so. Such a feat is absolutely impossible, and everyone can agree on this, for certain. Or at least everyone nowadays who doesn't want to be taken for a fool or an unhinged eccentric. So, how is it that in the sixteenth and seventeenth centuries—the very era that gave birth to aggressive skepticism and empirical science—countless people swore that they had witnessed such events? And how is it that some of these sworn testimonies are legal records, archived alongside lawsuits and murder trials, from all sorts of people, not just illiterate, mud-caked peasants but also elites at the apex of the social, intellectual, and political hierarchy? What sense are we to make of this? How does any historian deal with such accounts? How does one write a history of what could never have happened, a history of the impossible?[2]

This book attempts to address these questions and to make sense of what seems nonsensical. Naturally, given the nature of the subject, making sense of it requires accepting the fact that lingering questions are bound to outnumber

Figure 2. This eighteenth-century painting by an unknown artist depicts one of Saint Joseph of Cupertino's most extreme flying ecstasies, which took place when he first laid eyes on the shrine of the Holy House of Loreto and the angels flocking above it.

definitive answers. Its focus is Western Europe at the dawn of modernity, when reports of flying or hovering humans reached a peak, along with reports of other phenomena also deemed impossible by many in our own day and by some doubters back then. Focusing intensely on levitation—the act of rising into the air and remaining aloft—and to a lesser extent on other unnatural phenomena, such as bilocation—the act of being present at two distinct locations simultaneously—this book examines the redrawing of boundaries between the natural and supernatural that marked the transition to modernity. It does so by focusing on some of the most exceptional cases of "holy" levitators and evil "demonic" ones, including witches, as well as on some nuns whose levitations, bilocations, and visions were highly problematic. Because of the richness of source materials available, as well as the exemplary nature of the phenomena involved, our case studies are those of Saint Teresa of Avila (1515–1582); Saint Joseph of Cupertino (1603–1663); the Venerable María de Jesús de Ágreda (1602–1665); and three disgraced nuns, Magdalena de la Cruz (1487–1560),

María de la Visitación (1551–1603), and Luisa de la Ascensión (1565–1636). Cases of impossible miracles involving witchcraft and demonic possession are also analyzed, along with the early modern development of demonology through which such cases were approached. Other unnatural phenomena linked with levitation and bilocation come into view too, but only as ancillary to them and to the process whereby authorities determined whether any such wonder was the work of God or the devil.

The Trouble with Levitation and Bilocation

Unlike spontaneous healing miracles, which really do occur with some frequency and are acknowledged by skeptics and believers alike, including medical professionals who are atheists,[3] levitations and bilocations are extremely rare events that are seldom taken seriously outside certain belief systems. Levitation and bilocation are but two of several physical phenomena that have been linked to mystical ecstasy in various cultures and religions around the world for thousands of years. They are also among the oddest of wonders, everywhere, not just because they seem to happen infrequently but also because by suggesting the presence and power of an unseen force that can toy with nature, they tend not to serve any practical purpose other than confirming the special status of the person who levitates or bilocates. In a religious context—and most accounts of levitations and bilocations have religious origins—the unseen force is usually ascribed to some higher being, but it can also be ascribed to the levitators and bilocators themselves, who are so obviously unlike most of their fellow human beings for whom the tug of gravity within a single location is inescapable. In Christianity, that higher being could be God or the devil, and levitators could be viewed as either holy or diabolical, or, in some cases, as clever frauds. As awesome displays of raw unnatural power, the phenomena of levitation and bilocation have few equals, and this fact alone makes them inherently ambiguous and powerful all at once.

But how is it possible to speak about something that can't possibly happen? Where is the *fact,* that most essential component of history? "Fact" is an English word with many meanings. The *Oxford English Dictionary* lays out dozens of them. But only one of these applies in this case: "A thing that has really occurred or is actually the case; a thing certainly known to be a real occurrence or to represent the truth. Hence: a particular truth known by actual observation or authentic testimony, as opposed to an inference, a conjecture, or a fiction; a datum of experience, as distinguished from the conclusions that may be based on it."[4] So where is the "datum of experience" in any account of levitation or bilocation? What is the *fact* of any levitation or bilocation that anyone can hope to deal with in accounts from the distant past? Acts of levitation or bilocation are "wild facts," to use a term coined by philosopher-psychologist William James over a century ago. As he defined it, a wild fact is any occurrence that has "no stall or pigeonhole" into which "the ordinary and critical mind" can fit it. The alterity of any such phenomenon is so extreme, said James, that it becomes "unclassifiable" as well as an unimaginable "paradoxical absurdity" that must be considered inherently *untrue* as well as impossible. Such wild facts puzzle scientists so much, he observed, that they "always prove more easy to ignore than to attend to." James was intensely interested in psychic and mystical phenomena and greatly pained by the dismissive attitude his fellow scientists displayed toward these phenomena. Most of them, he quipped, thought that passing "from mystical to scientific speculations is like passing from lunacy to sanity."[5]

The situation James described long ago has not changed all that much, and in some respects has worsened for anyone who wants to take wild facts such as levitation and bilocation seriously. This leaves the historian or anyone with a critical mind in a tight spot. If wild facts are "paradoxical absurdities," are there any facts whatsoever left to study? The answer is yes, of course, and this book is proof of it. The fact we can explore is not the act of levitation itself, the wild fact that is inaccessible to us. The fact we can deal with is the testimony. This issue is as brutally simple as it is brutally circumscribed: since we have no films or photographs to analyze for authenticity with the latest cutting-edge technology, all we have is the fact that thousands of testimonies exist in which human beings swore they saw another human being hover or fly, or suddenly materialize in some other location. As one historian has argued, facts can be "hammered into signposts, which point beyond themselves . . . to states of affairs to which we have no direct access." They are "the mercenary soldiers of argument, ready to enlist in yours or mine, wherever the evidentiary fit is best."[6] Testimonies, then, are the only fact—as well as the only *evidence*—upon which any investigation of levitation and bilocation, or history of any "impossible" event that might have occurred in the past, can rest.

Consequently, a history of the impossible is a history of *testimonies* about impossible events. Our dominant culture dismisses these testimonies as unbelievable and merely "anecdotal"—that is, as accounts that have no point of reference beyond themselves, no wider context, and little or no credibility.[7] So why not call it a history of lying, a history of hallucinations, or a history of the ridiculous? The answer to this question is as brutally simple as the issue itself: We need not dismiss all accounts of the impossible as mere anecdotes or falsehoods because the *testimonies* themselves self-consciously accept the impossible event as impossible, as well as bafflingly and utterly real—even terrifying—and of great significance. Moreover, the sheer number of such testimonies is so relatively large, so widespread across time and geographical boundaries, and so closely linked to civil and ecclesiastical institutions that they most certainly *do* have a broader context into which they fit. And that is a very rare and credible kind of evidence, as unique as the events confirmed by it.

Levitation is one of the best of all entry points into the history of the impossible, principally because it is an event for which we have an overabundance of testimonies, not just in Western Christianity but throughout all of world history. Yet levitation is still a subject that attracts disparagement and repels serious inquiry: the very claim that any human being can defy the laws of gravity seems way too absurd nowadays, more than two centuries after Newton, despite the existence of high-speed trains that employ magnetic levitation to hover and fly forward while suspended just a few centimeters above their tracks.[8] Human levitation seems incompatible with seriousness. It's a light subject: weightless, flighty, insubstantial, the quintessence of levity. It smacks of occultism too, or overcredulity, especially if anyone dares to suggest it is possible rather than impossible.[9] And such suggestions can seem shockingly unscholarly.[10] Any study of levitation is difficult to get off the ground, as the pun would have it, for the subject gets little respect and not much has been written about it.[11] Even a crank such as Marcelino Menéndez Pelayo, a Spanish historian who eagerly defended absurd notions—including the claim that Catholic orthodoxy was genetically transmitted among pure-blooded Spaniards—had no patience with levitation and other physical phenomena associated with mystical ecstasy. What this most unreasonable man had to say long ago about levitation and other related phenomena, such as stigmata, is still very much in line with prevailing thought: "Leave all these cases lying in oblivion. Let them be brought to light, in due course, by those who are researching folk customs, or those who wish to satisfy a childish sort of curiosity."[12]

Bilocation is another entry point into the history of the impossible and another subject that Menéndez Pelayo would have wanted to sink into oblivion. Like levitation, it is a phenomenon found in many religions and cultures from ancient times to the present. But, like levitation, it seems incompatible with seriousness, and therefore it receives an equal amount of disrespect and contemptuous dismissals, even though we now have the technology to make bilocation or multilocation possible via the internet. Testimonies of bilocations are fewer in number than those of levitations in Christian history, and the phenomenon is impossible in a double way: not just as something that "cannot" happen but also as something that no one can ever witness in both locations simultaneously. Verifying its occurrence requires matching up eyewitness accounts from different locations ex post facto, something that makes all testimonies less immediate and therefore more open to the likelihood of fraud. But there is no denying the fact that such corroborations have been recorded and accepted as factual, as in the case of the bilocation of Saint Ignatius Loyola to the bedside of the ailing Alexander Petronius (fig. 3).

Circling back to Menéndez Pelayo's dismissal of all such testimonies, we conclude that since this is not a book on folk customs, then, the only other option open to us is a childish one. But what is more childish: to ignore levitation and other such impossible phenomena or to acknowledge their presence in history? If the past itself includes bizarre events and beliefs, are these to be dismissed simply because they seem illogical or because our current frame of reference differs so much from that of previous centuries? The easiest path is to say, yes, of course. But a wiser path to take might be to say, no, of course not. As Lucien Febvre, a very savvy historian, once said: "To comprehend is not to clarify, simplify, or to reduce things to a perfectly clear logical scheme. To comprehend is to complicate, to augment in depth. It is to widen on all sides. It is to vivify."[13] And this vivifying requires not only embracing what might seem strange in the past but accepting the strangeness as an essential rational feature of the past, not as something irrational. As Darren Oldridge has observed, in tandem with Febvre: "However peculiar they now seem, the beliefs of pre-modern people were normally a rational response to the intellectual and social context in which they were expressed."[14]

To bring the past to life in Febvre's sense, then, one must take stock of what might seem outrageously alien, especially if it was once an essential component of a culture's worldview. Yet, what seems alien is only analyzed piecemeal in our day and age. Take witchcraft, for instance. Hardly anyone nowadays would doubt the significance of this subject or the interest it generates in Western cultures. In fact, witchcraft studies *are* very much in vogue. Thanks to historians who have vivified it, we now have so many books and articles on this

Figure 3. This engraving from an illustrated hagiography of Saint Ignatius Loyola depicts his bilocation to the bedside of Alexander Petronius in Rome, who was very ill. Eyewitnesses reported that Ignatius simply showed up unexpectedly, even though the doors were locked, and that the bright glow of his body lit up the whole room.

subject that it has become immensely difficult to gain expertise in it. But many of those who specialize in witchcraft often ignore levitation, a key trait associated with witches, choosing instead to focus on other issues, especially those concerning social, economic, and political factors. So, one needs to ask, why is the study of witchcraft so popular, even though it entails dealing with reports of "evil" human flight, while the study of "holy" levitation is so disdainfully over-looked? Is belief in flying witches worthier of attention than belief in flying saints? This book argues that both deserve equal attention.[15]

In addition to being a light subject that instantly gives rise to punning and joking, levitation also has a shady reputation to overcome, and not just because of its association with demoniacs, witches, and magicians. Levitations are among the most ambiguous of mystical phenomena in Catholic Christian-ity for two reasons: because of the belief that they can be caused by the devil rather than God and because of the fact that they can also be faked, and have been regularly faked for millennia by all sorts of wizards and hucksters. Con-trived acts of levitation performed under tightly controlled conditions can seem real indeed when those performing them are experts at creating illusions and at fooling their audience's senses. It matters little if the illusion is performed on a stage as entertainment or in a chapel or some dimly lit parlor as deceit. A well-faked levitation is still an illusion rather than a miracle. This fact casts a huge dark shadow over all levitations, for it is widely known that anyone who devotes enough time and effort to creating such an illusion might be able to pull it off.

Reports of bilocations are even more vulnerable to dismissal than levita-tions, simply because no single witness can attest to the simultaneous presence of anyone in two different locations. To fake a bilocation seems easy enough. All one needs to do is to recruit or bribe expert liars at both locations. Conse-quently, believing in reports of bilocations requires a more intense leap of faith than believing in levitations.

Nonetheless, religious levitations—that is, those ascribed to supernatural or spiritual causes—can also raise all sorts of questions about the possibility of deceit, especially when they happen in intimate indoor settings. But when they occur unexpectedly in locations where rigging up contraptions to perform a trick or to create mass hallucinations seems more impossible than a miracle, then other sorts of questions pop up concerning their feasibility. In such levitations we are faced with two impossibilities simultaneously, that of the phenomenon itself and that of the lack of hidden contrivances or sensory illusions. And, much more so than bilocation, it is precisely these kinds of levitations—those where deceit itself seems impossible—that are the most puzzling of all and serve as the best of entryways into the history of the impossible.

The likelihood of deceit haunts levitations and bilocations in yet another way, figuratively and literally, for not too long ago these phenomena became intensely linked with ghosts and spirits rather than God or the devil. This happened due to a rise in popularity of the quasi-religious occult movement known as Spiritualism, which spread like wildfire across North and South America, Europe, and other corners of the Western world between the 1860s and the 1920s. Spiritualism had its detractors, for sure, especially among the Christian clergy, professional illusionists, and an array of skeptics,[16] but it was not restricted to quirky outcasts on the margins of respectability. Quite the contrary. As hard as it might be to imagine nowadays, Spiritualism attracted a broad spectrum of devotees, some of whom belonged to the upper echelons of society, such as the eminent chemist and physicist Sir William Crookes; novelist Sir Arthur Conan Doyle, the creator of the hyperrational and immensely popular fictional character Sherlock Holmes; evolutionary biologist Alfred Russel Wallace, Charles Darwin's closest collaborator and competitor; the Nobel laureates Pierre and Marie Curie, pioneers in the study of radiation; and Mary Todd Lincoln, the wife of American president Abraham Lincoln, who attended the séances she held regularly at the White House.

The term "levitation" was coined by spiritualists in the nineteenth century. Although accounts of hovering or flying men and women stretch back to antiquity, no specific term had ever been applied to the phenomenon. But, given its centrality in spiritualist ritual, especially during séances at which mediums levitated objects, their own bodies, or those of others—ostensibly through the agency of spirits—the amazing feat needed a name, and "levitation" seemed to suit the cult's quasi-scientific needs perfectly. Derived as it was from the Latin *levitas,* or "lightness," the exact opposite of "gravitas," or "heaviness," the newly minted term had a distinctly Newtonian feel to it, evoking his law of universal gravitation and empirical objectivity while conveying a sense of the mysteriously spiritual and otherworldly. "Bilocation" was another quasi-scientific term favored by spiritualists, who believed that the human body had an "astral double," a spiritual component that could leave the physical body and appear elsewhere.[17]

Spiritualism never disappeared completely. In fact, the ever-popular Ouija board, still a best-selling game, made and marketed as a toy by Hasbro, the same company that makes Monopoly, is a spiritualist device.[18] But as Spiritualism's heyday waned, so did interest in levitation and bilocation. By 1928, when Olivier Leroy published the one and only comprehensive history of levitation written in the twentieth century, the popularity of Spiritualism was already fading fast. And no comparable effort was ever made to cover the history of bilocation. Doyle, who died in 1930, seemed to embody the cult's decline in his final years. His zealous defense of communication with the dead and of photographs of ghosts and fairies had by then become more of a disposable Victorian curiosity than a set of beliefs to embrace, and since levitation and bilocation were part of the spiritualist package deal, they, too, gradually vanished, except in occultist circles, into the cobwebbed attic of the public's imagination.[19]

The Trouble with Miracles

Levitation and bilocation might have had a shady lineage to overcome, but they nonetheless had—and continue to have—a very different past upon which to claim legitimate significance. Within the Catholic tradition, which shall be our main focus, levitation has an immensely rich history, and so does bilocation, to a lesser extent, especially in the lives of the saints. Although their significance in Catholic culture and devotional life has diminished somewhat, due mostly to the Catholic Church's shift in focus to social and political issues, holy levitation and bilocation are still officially considered genuine miracles that are most definitely *possible.* Demonic levitations and bilocations are still considered possible, too, but have received much less attention since the nineteenth century. Consequently, despite some decline in frequency and in popularity, these miraculous phenomena are still very much alive and far from consigned to oblivion.

Because holy levitation and bilocation are considered miracles in Catholicism—that is, supernatural gifts, or "charisms," that accompany mystical ecstasy and can be markers of exceptional sanctity—they have never completely lost their luster and are not likely to lose it. The Greek term *charisma* denotes any gift bestowed on humans through God's benevolent love (*charis*). Belief in such gifts is as old as Christianity itself and was initially given theological shape by the apostle Paul, who delineated their function in the shaping of the church:

> Everyone has his proper gift [charisma] from God; one after this manner, and another after that. . . . There are different kinds of gifts [*charismaton*], but the same Spirit distributes them. There are different kinds of service, but the same Lord who works all things in all. Now to each one the manifestation of the Spirit is given for the common good. To one there is given through the Spirit a message of wisdom, to another a message of knowledge

by means of the same Spirit, to another faith by the same Spirit, to another
gifts [charismata] of healing by that one Spirit, to another miraculous powers, to another prophecy, to another distinguishing between spirits, to another speaking in different kinds of tongues, and to still another the
interpretation of tongues. All these are the work of one and the same Spirit,
and he distributes them to each one, just as he determines.[20]

Among such extraordinary supernatural gifts, some not mentioned by Paul were
later recognized as legitimate, including levitation, bilocation, and several others
that accompanied mystical ecstasy.

Consequently, because they are deemed divine charisms, extraordinary
gifts of grace, holy levitation and bilocation remain strictly within God's omnipotence and agency in the Catholic tradition. As such, they are never
"achieved"; that is, they can never be willed to happen by the mystic in ecstasy.
An intersection of the natural and supernatural, as well as of the physical and
the spiritual, these are highly charged ambiguous phenomena that always
need to be placed in the context of the life of the levitator. Simply put, for any
levitation to be considered of divine origin in Catholicism, the levitator needs
to be holy, virtuous, and orthodox. Levitation and bilocation are caused by holiness and serve as signs of holiness. And, unlike spiritualist mediums of the
Victorian era for whom these phenomena were absolutely necessary markers of
legitimacy, Catholic saints do not need to display these rare charisms. Their
status as holy individuals does not depend on them. Moreover, these gifts are
only two of the many optional supernatural charisms that sometimes accompany mystical ecstatic states. To contextualize levitation properly, then, it is
essential to consider the full range of these different charisms.

During the Middle Ages, a long list of these divine mystical gifts evolved,
especially through the process of evaluating the holiness of candidates for
sainthood and of writing narratives of their lives as part of that process. The
technical term for any such narrative is "hagiography," derived from the Greek
words *hagios,* meaning "holy," and *graphia,* meaning "writing." Hagiographies
served multiple purposes at once, but their two principal aims were intertwined: to prove someone's sanctity and to encourage the text's readers to imitate and venerate that person. By the thirteenth century, when bilocation and
levitation accounts begin to appear regularly in Western hagiographies, many
supernatural phenomena were believed to be definite signs of sainthood, but
there was no fixed list of the miraculous physical phenomena that could

accompany mystical ecstasy in the life of any saint. Much in the same way that a medical text might contain lists of all the known symptoms for specific maladies, this list of miraculous mystical gifts or charisma would have simply catalogued those known to occur, but the sole undisputed primary characteristic of holiness was always a virtuous life, rather than any miraculous mystical phenomena. Those were always an *ad extra* trait: a bonus. In the seventeenth century this attitude deepened in the Catholic Church as the process of canonization was revamped, and "heroic virtue" came to be emphasized more than miracles.

No holy mystic was ever expected to have all the charisms that could be listed, but it was considered normal for some of these to be inextricably joined to mystical transports in a saint's life. In some cases these phenomena were linked up—such as levitating and emitting an unearthly glow simultaneously— but such pairings were not considered normative, much less essential, in the lives of other levitating saints. Moreover, these charisms could manifest themselves in varying degrees: some saints could levitate more often or higher than others; some might just hover; others might actually fly. All these gifts were wild cards of sorts, and so were the particular combinations any mystic might be dealt by God. The most significant of these charisms could be sorted into two categories: first, those phenomena that were overtly physical and visibly involved the body; second, those phenomena that were not visible but could be conjoined with mystical ecstasy.

In the first category, there were at least fifteen overtly physical phenomena commonly linked with holiness and mystical experiences:

- Visible ecstasies, raptures, and trances: When the body enters a cataleptic state and becomes rigid, insensible, and oblivious to its surroundings.
- Levitation: When the body rises up in the air, hovers, or flies.
- Weightlessness: When the body displays a total or nearly total absence of weight during trances and levitations or after death.
- Transvection: When the body is transported through the air from one location to another in some indeterminate measure of time.
- Mystical transport or teleportation: When the body transverses physical space instantaneously, moving from one place to another without any time having elapsed, sometimes over great distances.
- Bilocation: When the body is present in two places simultaneously.

- Stigmatization: When the body acquires the five wounds of the crucified Christ or other wounds inflicted during his passion.
- Luminous irradiance: When the body glows brightly.
- Supernatural hyperosmia: A heightened sense of smell that allows the mystic to detect the sins of others.
- Supernatural *inedia:* The ability to survive without any food or with very little food at all.
- Supernatural insomnia: The ability to survive without much, if any, sleep.
- Visible demonic molestations: Physical attacks by demons that wound the body.
- Odor of sanctity: When the body emits a unique and immensely pleasant smell.
- Supernatural incorruption: When the corpse of a saint does not decompose but remains unnaturally intact for many years, decades, or centuries.
- Supernatural oozing, or myroblitism: When the corpse of a saint discharges a pleasant-smelling oily substance capable of performing healing miracles directly or through cloths dipped in it.

And in the second category, holy mystics could have at least ten different kinds of otherworldly experiences not visible to others or supernatural powers with which they could be imbued. Some of these were physical gifts, some spiritual, and some mental.

- Visions, locutions, and apparitions: When the mystic has various sorts of encounters with the divine that are not visible to others, and the mystic receives communications from God that are visual, aural, or purely spiritual. These can occur suddenly or during ecstatic states.
- Invisible demonic molestations: When the mystic is assailed by demons spiritually or mentally, sometimes with a visual component that is invisible to others.
- Telekinesis: The ability to move objects at a distance by nonphysical means, without touching them.
- Telepathy: The ability to read the minds and consciences of others or to communicate mentally.
- Prophecy: The ability to know and predict future events accurately, including one's own death.
- Supernatural remote vision: The ability to see events that are occurring elsewhere.
- Supernatural dreams: The ability to receive divine communications while sleeping.
- Infused knowledge: Learning directly from God, without formal education, through ecstasies, visions, locutions, and apparitions.

- Supernatural control over nature: The ability to command the behavior of weather, fauna, and flora and to communicate with animals.
- Discernment of spirits: The ability to distinguish whether any event is of divine or demonic origin.

Tellingly, only one of the phenomena listed above can be called genuinely and exclusively Christian: that of the stigmata, the miraculous duplication of the wounds of Christ on the mystic's hands, feet, and torso, the first recorded instance of which involves Saint Francis of Assisi in the thirteenth century.[21] All other physical phenomena can be found in accounts from other cultures and religions, in which such gifts are linked to individuals with spiritual powers. Curiously, the growth of Western interest in Asian religions, Spiritualism, and the occult cultures in which these marvels are common has led some filmmakers in the late twentieth and early twenty-first centuries to create similarly gifted fictional characters, such as the Jedi knights in the *Star Wars* series, especially Obi-Wan Kenobi and Yoda.[22] Obviously, it is also easy enough to discern how the very concept of "superpowers" reflected in such characters is closely linked to the alternative universes and mythologies created in comic books and the films based on them.[23]

So, obviously, Christian saints who received supernatural gifts were different from ordinary humans. In essence, the charismatic saint could become superhuman—a superhero—at least during those instances when these extraordinary phenomena were manifest. Consequently, these phenomena reflected a certain mind-set or mentality and were simultaneously a confirmation or reification of that mentality. Naturally, fraud and delusion could certainly be involved in claims about such charisma and the miracles associated with them, and the likelihood of that could be obvious to anyone, but in cultures where such phenomena were assumed to be possible, it was *belief* in the charismata that had to be suspended rather than *disbelief*.

The Trouble with Thaumaturgy

Accepting these phenomena as *possible* requires a certain way of thinking about the fabric of reality and of accepting as fact that the cosmos consists of two dimensions, the natural and the supernatural, and that these two dimensions, though distinct, are nevertheless intertwined in such a way that the natural is always subordinate to the supernatural. In this mentality or worldview, which was reinforced culturally by social custom and the political forces of church and state, the natural order could be constantly interrupted and overpowered by the supernatural. Any such irruption of the supernatural was a miracle (*miraculum* or *prodigium*), and the natural world constantly pulsated with the possibility of the miraculous.[24]

By the thirteenth century, scholastic theologians were proposing, analyzing, and dissecting various definitions of a miracle. One of the most influential was Thomas Aquinas, who subdivided miracles into three categories: The highest were those of *substance,* in which "something is done by God which nature never could do," such as levitation and bilocation; next in gradation were those of *subject,* "in which God does something which nature can do, but not in its proper order," such as the power of speech granted to Balaam's ass; and finally there were those of *mode,* in which "God does what is usually done by the working of nature, but without the operation of the principles of nature," such as the healing of illnesses by relics of the saints.[25] Aquinas also stressed the supernatural divine causality of miracles, as well as the fact that their most recognizable feature is the effect they produce in their recipients or witnesses.[26] Miracles, therefore, were an intrusion of the supernatural into the natural realm and always identifiable by their effects.

This binary approach to reality extended to the human being, for humans were believed to have been created in "the image and likeness of God" and to be composed of a mortal material body and an immortal spiritual soul.[27] Saints could tap into the supernatural because they were "holy"—that is, they were more spiritual than other human beings, more attuned to the sacred and divine. As individuals who embraced self-denial and focused intensely on spiritual realities rather than on the needs of their corruptible material bodies, they were able to avoid sinful behavior and live virtuous lives. This made them "holy" and therefore closer to God, and that closeness transformed their mortal bodies, imbuing them with supernatural abilities.[28]

Such abilities were deemed celestial in origin: charisma granted to holy human beings in whom and through whom God worked miracles. Some of these charismata had dark parallels in pagan magic and witchcraft, inherently, so discerning the actual source of the gift was always necessary for Catholic Christians, and that process of discernment could be immensely complicated, awkward, and often painful. In essence, the process involved reckoning the difference between *religion*—that is, whatever was truly supernatural—and *magic,* which was never truly supernatural but rather involved the diabolical agency or some sort of humanly devised trickery.

Given this conundrum, and the inherent instability and ambiguity of the miraculous, every levitation or bilocation—no matter how wondrous—had an unavoidable tragic dimension, and all miracle-workers had to contend with it in various ways. As we shall see, the more extreme the miracle claim, the worse the ordeal that the miracle-worker had to face. Whether it was being grilled by the Inquisition or being confined to a small monastic cell like a prisoner or having one's writings destroyed or hidden away under lock and key, all of the miracle-workers analyzed here had to be refined in some sort of crucible. In essence, achieving the impossible was always potentially dangerous, not just for oneself but for one's community, even if that community was enthralled by the impossible or drawn to it. Magic, religion, and the demonic were too closely intertwined to allow church authorities to approve of miracles instantaneously. Distinctions had to be maintained, and those distinctions were understood in precise terms by educated folk, especially the clergy tasked with the job of doing the discerning. But at street level, among the faithful, the line between religion and magic was anything but precise, especially when it came to popular piety and the ways in which most Christians approached what they believed to be supernatural.

Naturally, the fuzziness of the line between religion and magic in popular piety vexed many a cleric and gave rise to all sorts of tensions and conflicts within late antique and medieval Christianity. That fuzziness attracted the attention of social scientists in the late nineteenth century and throughout the twentieth as well, and various definitions of the distinction between religion and magic eventually seeped into the writing of religious history. Ironically, one result of this social-scientific turn has been the adoption of the term "thaumaturgy" as the favored descriptive term for all miracle-working and of "thaumaturge" for miracle-workers. Etymologically derived from the Greek *thaûma,* meaning "miracle," "wonder," or "marvel," and *érgon,* meaning "work," these terms circumvent the issue of differentiating between *magic* and *religion* by turning all miraculous events into a "scientific" area of study—with a scientific-sounding name—in which transcendent or supernatural forces are not considered whatsoever. Conceptually, the invention and acceptance of thaumaturgy and thaumaturge are derived from Protestant attitudes toward Catholic piety, and whenever these terms are used, they still echo sixteenth-century Protestant polemics, often unknowingly. This quirky epistemological turn requires some explaining.

The Trouble with Protestants

The advent of the Protestant Reformation brought about a sudden redefinition of concepts such as *religion, magic, superstition,* and *idolatry,* as well as of assumptions about the relation between the natural and supernatural realms. Distinctions that had reigned largely uncontested in the Catholic Church of the West and the Orthodox Churches of the East since the first century suddenly began to be challenged in the early 1520s when an earth-shaking paradigm shift took place. The change in thinking resulting from this new Protestant take on reality was similar in scope and significance to the one caused by Copernicus in astronomy, but its impact was much more immediate and widespread. It gave rise to a disparate mentality that still saw reality in binary terms but drew the line between religion and magic differently, rejecting the intense intermingling of the natural and supernatural as well as of the material and the spiritual, thus placing much of Catholic ritual and piety in the realm of magic. Moreover, this Protestant mentality also involved a redefinition of the concepts of *holiness* and *sainthood,* and a rejection of the assumption that self-denial and virtuous behavior could allow human beings to be gifted with supernatural powers.

As if this were not enough of an assault on medieval assumptions about the relation between the natural and the supernatural realms, Protestants of all stripes also rejected the proposition that God had continued to perform miracles beyond the first century, a doctrine that came to be known as "the cessation of miracles" or "the cessation of the charismata."[29] The miracles mentioned in the Bible had really occurred, they argued, but such marvels became unnecessary after the birth of the early church and would never, ever happen again.[30] Consequently, all of those miraculous supernatural phenomena associated with holiness throughout the Middle Ages, including levitation, could not be the work of God. To be more precise, however, by deigning these phenomena "false"— that is, not attributable to God—Protestants did not declare them impossible. Not at all. As most Protestant Reformers and their later disciples saw it, ecstatic seizures, levitations, luminous irradiance, and all such phenomena were still possible indeed and did in fact occur. But they were all diabolical in origin. So, simply put, Protestants stripped God's agency from all such Catholic miracles and gave credit to the devil instead.[31]

Given the religious, social, political, and intellectual turmoil caused by the advent of Protestantism and its great paradigm shift, it is not at all surprising that miracles became a marker of difference between Catholics and Protestants, as well as a flash point of discord and a polemical weapon. And it could be argued that no miracle was more redolent of the odor of "difference" than levitation—a variant on the odor of sanctity—or more freighted with polemical potential. For Catholics, holy levitation could serve as proof of the divine source of their church's authority and of the truth of their teachings and sacraments. If miracles such as this occurred in the Catholic Church, could it really be the seat of the Antichrist, as Protestants argued? Protestants simply countered by insisting that if such weird phenomena were not fraudulent, they could only be demonic, their existence damning evidence of the falsehood of the Catholic Church, which employed the devil's ability to easily fool the unwary. After all, witches hovered and flew too. As Thomas Browne argued in 1646, since Satan was a "natural Magician" he could "perform many acts in ways above our knowledge, though not transcending our natural powers."[32] Meanwhile, however, Protestants and Catholics alike continued to believe that witches hovered and flew and should all be exterminated.

Aye, there's the rub, as Hamlet might say.[33]

Quite an odd rub too, that the phenomenon of levitation should be considered real enough by both Catholics and Protestants. Their interconfessional squabbling was not about the possibility or impossibility of the phenomenon itself but rather about its source. Both opposing camps thought levitation was possible, but their disagreement about its causation had an odd asymmetry to it, for they agreed not only on its possibility but also on the assumption that the phenomenon had an ethical dimension to it that had a lot to do with the agency of the human will. Whereas Catholics believed that levitation was restricted to human beings who chose to surrender their will either to God or to the devil, Protestants believed it was restricted only to those who willed to become allies of the devil.

Something else that makes this difference of opinion seem odd is its timing, for at exactly the same time that Catholics were canonizing levitating saints and burning flying witches and Protestants were busy tossing flying witches into the flames too—by the thousands—modern empirical science was emerging and creating paradigm shifts of its own. For some quirky set of reasons, then, the peak period for flying humans in Western history coincides with the initial development of a new materialistic way of thinking about reality that would reject all this flying as absolutely impossible nonsense.

Consequently, one could also say that the oddest fact about two of the most extreme exemplars of miraculous baroque Catholicism, Joseph of Cupertino (1603–1663), "the Flying Friar," and María de Jesús de Ágreda (1602–1665), the bilocating and levitating nun, is that they walked the earth and ostensibly hovered over it at the same time as Isaac Newton (1642–1727). Although it is unlikely they ever crossed paths with him, it is *not* wholly impossible. If this book were an exercise in counterfactual history, it would be appropriate to suggest the following "what if" scenario: What if Newton had run away from Woolsthorpe Manor, his home in Lincolnshire, England, and traveled to Osimo, Italy, and Ágreda, Spain, in 1659 in a fit of pique after his recently widowed mother removed him from the King's School in Grantham so he could become a yeoman farmer, just like his father?[34] And what if he had caught sight of Joseph and María hovering in the air? Or, at the very least, what if he had run into eyewitnesses who swore they had seen these monastics levitating and glowing? Would that have changed his take on gravity, and if so, how would that have changed history? Or what if he had traveled through Scotland in 1665–1666, when the plague forced him to leave Cambridge temporarily,[35] and had stumbled upon a witch trial or had met people involved in the many Scottish witch trials in which flying was one of the legally valid proofs offered for someone having made a pact with the devil? Or what if he had run into someone who claimed to have seen a flying witch? Might that have changed history too?

These are not idle speculations. Counterfactual history is a valuable thought exercise, and some of its practitioners are quite rigorous about their approach to alternative scenarios and their probable consequences and arguably more attentive to the interplay of specific factors than many historians who never venture to imagine different outcomes. Quirky juxtapositions of facts with alternative scenarios can yield useful insights into the significance of specific details in the unfolding of history, for sure.[36] And juxtapositions of this sort cannot get quirkier or potentially more revealing than linking the potential trajectories of Saint Joseph of Cupertino, the Venerable María de Jesús de Ágreda, and Sir Isaac Newton.

Beyond the factual historical dimension of baroque-era levitators, divine or demonic, one runs into more abstract issues in the metaphysical and epistemological dimension of these accounts. And the questions there, in these conceptual dimensions, make historians very uncomfortable. What about all this hovering and flying? Did these people really float in the air? If so, how and why, and how could it be proved? Could all these testimonies be taken at face value? As soon as these questions begin to pop up, we historians proudly bring out our brackets and wield them with all the epistemological brawn we can muster. "We bracket the question of whether this happened or not," we say, and by that we mean that since we cannot prove that any of this hovering and flying happened, we put those questions aside and instead ask other ones, admitting that all we can analyze is the *fact* that some people believed that such things did happen. So we limit ourselves to analyzing narratives and the beliefs expressed in those narratives but not the events reported in them. Those events remain suspended in an ether of their own, much like some stiff-jointed levitating saint, in that vast limbo where all unprovable and unusable testimonies get squirreled away. And all we are left with is the fact of the testimonies given and of the beliefs reflected in them.

That bracketing will be inescapable in this book: The issue of whether so-and-so *really* flew cannot be addressed. And the same goes for bilocation or any other charisma associated with mystical ecstasy, for there is no way anyone today can prove that someone really hovered or flew or bilocated in the sixteenth or seventeenth century. No one's testimony from the distant past—when photographing or filming did not yet exist—can be taken as absolute proof, not for something as uncommon and unnatural a phenomenon as levitation, even if corroborated by hundreds or thousands of similar testimonies, for a simple reason: Like all miracles, by definition, phenomena such as levitation and bilocation are totally unlike others in history. They are wild facts, as William James would say. If in fact they have taken place, the number of witnesses has been far too small, relatively speaking. And the further back one goes in time, the more difficult it becomes to defend the credibility of those witnesses. The argument made by David Hume in 1748 about the impossibility of proving any miracle solely from testimony is applicable to this project. Hume's argument is still very much in play in contemporary Western culture and worth quoting at this point:

> A miracle is a violation of the laws of nature; and as a firm and unalterable experience has established these laws, the proof against a miracle, from the very nature of the fact, is as entire as any argument from experience can possibly be imagined. . . . Nothing is esteemed a miracle, if it ever happens in the common course of nature. . . . There must, therefore, be a uniform experience against every miraculous event, otherwise the event would not merit that appellation. . . . The plain consequence is (and it is a general maxim worthy of our attention), "That no testimony is sufficient to establish a miracle, unless the testimony be of such a kind, that its falsehood would be more miraculous, than the fact, which it endeavours to establish."[37]

Nonetheless, while it is ultimately impossible for anyone to prove that any levitation or bilocation actually took place, the fact that there are eyewitness testimonies of such instances is easy enough to prove. And those testimonies, which are often rich in details, need no brackets. They can be closely examined as facts as well as evidence, especially because these testimonies tell us something about the past that our present-day culture predisposes many people to overlook or deride. This brings us back to Febvre's observation: "To comprehend is to complicate, to augment in depth. It is to widen on all sides. It is to vivify."[38] As another very wise historian has pointed out, some events force us to face the fact that there are "complexities and ambivalences everywhere." The testimonies of witnesses to impossible events, which are themselves full of complexities and ambivalences, vivify the past. In the absence of ironclad conclusive proof, they allow us at least to obtain "conjectural knowledge and possible truth."[39] One could argue that sometimes they do much more than that, for they can allow us a glimpse of the world as some of those who lived long ago actually saw it.

The Trouble with Modernity

In the Whiggish view of history, phenomena such as witchcraft and levitation are powerful markers of cultural difference, telltale traits of an older, inferior civilization, of the "superstitious" and "magical" culture of the ancient and medieval worlds. In fact, it is precisely these markers that provide one of the most certain boundaries between what is "modern" and what is not.[40] Supernatural phenomena are modernity's foil, significant foci for the articulation of the norms of "modernity" itself.[41] They are also markers that distinguish what is important from what is not. And this is not only true of Whiggish history, which puts forward the Protestant rejection of medieval piety as the first step toward "modernity." It is also true of postmodern history.[42]

Conversely, witchcraft and magic are seen as "important" subjects because they bespeak of Whiggishness itself and of all attempts by elites to dominate their subalterns. Witches and New World natives share the same universe of meaning for postmodern and postcolonial history. Both are victims of the ancien régime writ large—that is, the hyperrationalist, exploitative, moralizing, male-dominated, patriarchal, homophobic, sexist, chauvinist, exploitative, Eurocentric imperialist world order. Nuns and friars who levitate, and, incidentally, reject the central values of Eurocentric hegemony in their monastic vows, somehow do not seem to belong in that same universe of trendy significance. Why not? That is a post-postmodern question waiting for an answer. Perhaps the question itself is a marker of the boundary between the postmodern and whatever may succeed it? The post-postwhatever?

Levitating saints raise questions that no historian should avoid. Never mind the metaphysical questions, that floating ten-ton anvil that historians dare not touch, much less acknowledge. Aside from the fact that they reify social constructions of reality, levitating saints allow us to peer into the very process of cultural change, offering unique insights into an essential component of the transition to modernity. Their flying and hovering reveal complexities about an epistemological revolution that up until very recently was assumed to follow a steep and well-defined upward curve: the triumph of rationality over primitive credulity and superstition. When Max Weber argued in the early twentieth century that the Protestant Reformation was instrumental in the gradual "disenchantment" of the world and the rise of rationalism and empirical science, the miraculous and supernatural had already been stripped of legitimacy.[43] Some bits and pieces of this history have been claimed—as in the case of witchcraft—by those who have found it useful for the promotion of certain social, cultural, and political causes in their own day. Some historians have been an exception to this rule, straining to understand the past on its own terms and accepting the transition to modernity as a very complex process in which the redefinition of the boundaries between the natural and supernatural did not always follow a Whiggish or Weberian upward curve.[44]

Anyone who examines the early modern period carefully should eventually discover that the public sphere in Western Europe was rife with levitating saints and flying witches and other impossible events. This should seem odd, not only because this was the age of Galileo, Descartes, Newton, and Leibniz but also because—as Weber assured us all—Protestantism had already "disenchanted" the world.[45] Under the Weberian formula, how can one explain the Protestant belief in flying witches? How does one account for the fact that Protestants left the devil in full control of his preternatural powers while they stripped God of his supernatural powers on earth? And how does one account for the fact that John Frederick of Saxe-Lüneberg, a Lutheran prince converted to Catholicism as a result of Joseph of Cupertino's levitations, was Leibniz's patron? Or that Newton, born in 1643, could have journeyed to Fossombrone or Osimo as a young man to lay eyes on Saint Joseph, "the Flying Friar"?

In the past few decades, some historians have begun to call attention to the way in which both Catholics and Protestants started redefining the concepts of *natural* and *supernatural*.[46] Much of this work stresses the fact that the epistemological and metaphysical gap between Catholics and Protestants was one of their principal battle lines. Since Protestants tended to reject the miraculous as impossible, most of this recent work has focused on Catholics and on how they tried to identify "real" miracles or on how they tried to argue rationally for their occurrence, relying on the concepts of natural and supernatural or preternatural that were commonly shared by priest, minister, and scientist alike.[47] Precise definitions and boundaries were of immense concern for Protestant and Catholic alike in the early modern period, as were those individuals who seemed to trespass the laws of nature. Levitating saints and flying witches were no sideshow but part of the main act, as essential a component of early modern life as the religious turmoil of the age and as much a part of history as Newton's apple.[48] Distinguishing between the natural and supernatural was as crucial as telling right from wrong and as necessary as classifying the airborne as either "good" or "evil." The shocking truth is that both Protestants and Catholics professed belief in human flight and tried to sort out the airborne among them. No one can deny that the sorting took place at the very same time that calculus, empirical science, and atheism emerged in Western culture.

That is a fact.

But what does this fact tell us about the impossible? What does it tell us about the past and the way we strain to understand it or the present and its concerns and unquestioned assumptions? Why do we have high-speed magnetic levitation trains but feel the need to bracket all reports about hovering saints or witches? How can millions of us humans be in multiple locations simultaneously via the internet, day after day, but still feel the need to scoff at bilocation? Why is the only fact that we can accept about human levitation the fact that others, long ago, thought it was possible? What difference does that make? More than a question mark? Yes. Much more than the question mark missing from the following sentence:

"They flew."

PART ONE

Aloft

There is no impropriety in saying that God does something against nature when it is *contrary to what we know of nature.* For we give the name "nature" to the usual and known courses of nature; and whatever God does contrary to this, we call "prodigies" or "miracles."

—Saint Augustine of Hippo, *Contra Faustum*

1. Hovering, Flying, and All That

A Brief History of Levitation

Like a traveler exploring some distant country, the wonders of which have hitherto been known only through reports and rumors of a vague or distorted character, so for four years I have been occupied in pushing an enquiry into a territory of natural knowledge which offers almost virgin soil to a scientific man.

—William Crookes

So said an eminent scientist in 1874 about his empirical research on unnatural phenomena, such as levitation, which were part and parcel of the cult of Spiritualism very much in vogue at that time.[1] William Crookes, a distinguished chemist and physicist, wanted to unlock the secrets of levitation and of all the other marvels that spiritualists claimed to perform. And after four years of looking into it, he had to admit that he was flummoxed: "The phenomena I am prepared to attest are so extraordinary and so directly oppose the most firmly rooted articles of scientific belief—amongst others, the ubiquity and invariable action of the force of gravitation—that, even now, on recalling the details of what I witnessed, there is an antagonism in my mind between reason, which pronounces it to be scientifically impossible, and the consciousness that my senses, both of touch and sight—and these corroborated, as they were, by the senses of all who were present—are not lying witnesses when they testify against my preconceptions."[2]

Crookes was but one of many in his generation who tried to shine a spotlight on the claims of spiritualists and of those who witnessed their occult unearthly powers. As a skeptical scientist, his investigation involved

Figure 4. Engraving of Daniel Dunglas Home (1833–1886), a Scottish spiritualist medium whose frequent levitations were confirmed by numerous witnesses, including prominent scientists such as William Crookes, who proclaimed them genuine.

digging into the history of these phenomena, and in doing so he was among the first to collect data and come up with an analytical narrative of the phenomenon that spiritualists had dubbed "levitation."[3] And so it was that the history of levitation began to be written, largely by critics and opponents of Spiritualism, and of spiritualists who staged levitations, such as Daniel Dunglas Home (fig. 4). Eventually this trend led to the first comprehensive history of the subject by Olivier Leroy, published in 1928 and still unsurpassed, nearly a century later.

Leroy's book, however, appeared a bit too late. Spiritualism and its phenomena were already waning in popularity. So, tinged as it was with a residual spiritualist glow, the marvel of levitation gradually ceased to attract serious attention in the West. Left in the hands of cultists, illusionists, and magicians, levitation slipped unceremoniously into the realm of the fantastical and trivial, alongside other ostensibly unscientific subjects such as haunted houses, werewolves, vampires, and abductions by aliens from outer space. Among Catholic and Orthodox Christians, however, levitation remained a very serious subject that could not be thrown into the ash heap along with Spiritualism.

Levitating saints continued to be part and parcel of Christian history in non-Protestant churches, even as secularism and skepticism increased, and reports of levitations became more infrequent. In the Orthodox tradition, for instance, two notable post-Enlightenment levitators were the monk Saint Seraphim of Sarov (1754–1833) and Saint John the Wonderworker (1896–1966). In Catholicism, instances of levitation never ceased being reported and accepted as genuine. Four of the best-known Catholic levitators from modernity are Saint Alphonsus Liguori (1696–1787), Blessed Anne Catherine Emmerich (1774–1824), Saint John Vianney (1786–1859), and Saint Gemma Galgani (1878–1903). In the twentieth century, the best-known Catholic levitator was Saint Padre Pio of Pietrelcina (1887–1968), who during the Second World War was credited with intercepting Allied bombers in midair and preventing them from pulverizing the town of San Giovanni Rotondo, where his monastery was located.[4] When he was canonized by Pope John Paul II in 2002, Padre Pio's levitations—though somewhat controversial in some circles—were declared genuine, along with his many other miracles, including his bilocations.[5]

In secular culture, belief in levitation has not died altogether either. In the early twenty-first century, it is still easy enough to find books that claim levitation is possible or even an easily learned skill.[6]

An Ancient Global Phenomenon

Accounts of men and women who hover or fly abound in human history, in many different cultures.[7] Throughout history, levitation has been linked to spiritual power, be it benevolent, indifferent, or malevolent, and in many cultures and religions, down to the present, it tends to be taken for granted as a *fact,* as something which *really* occurs and does not involve deception of any sort. Among Catholic and Orthodox Christians, levitation is believed to have divine or demonic origins. Among Protestant Christians, it has usually been deemed of strictly demonic origin and is most often interpreted as diabolical trickery. In the non-Protestant Christian tradition, "good" or "holy" levitation has always been understood as an involuntary bodily response to intense spiritual experiences. A by-product of mystical ecstasy, always controlled by God rather than the levitator, this phenomenon is only one of several that are associated with a life of asceticism and prayer, along with other phenomena listed in the introduction.[8] Within this same tradition, "evil" or "demonic" levitation is found among those who consort with Satan, and this includes witches, wizards, and sorcerers of all stripes, along with pagan priests and shamans and those who are possessed by demons.[9]

Of course, deception has been as much a part of the history of levitation as belief in its authenticity. In many cultures, especially in the ancient world, the line between the illusionist and the sorcerer or thaumaturge was somewhat blurry, as was the line between what we might call a "trick" and a "miracle." Moreover, given the fact that levitations have been faked for millennia, anyone associated with levitation cannot help but cast a trickster's shadow, as was the case with the spiritualist mediums of the late nineteenth and early twentieth centuries.[10] And levitation is still a common *trick* in the twenty-first century, after all, performed by illusionists around the world, on stages large and small, or on television or the internet.[11] The question here is not how magicians or mediums fool their audiences, however, but how belief in levitation as a *real* miracle flourished among Catholic Christians, especially in the early modern period.

Although the term "levitation" is relatively new, having been coined in late nineteenth-century England, the phenomenon of gravity-defying ecstatics has ancient roots in Asian, Near Eastern, and Western cultures and can also be found in African, American, and Australasian tribal and shamanistic religions. Tracing the origins of Western levitation and, more specifically, of Christian levitation is difficult. This is due to a lack of sources and the absence of any proof for direct lines of transmission. Nonetheless, as far as Asia is concerned, it is well known that various Indian Yogic traditions have accepted levitation as a fact for millennia. We have secondhand testimony of this from a contemporary of Jesus, Apollonius of Tyana (ca. 15–100 AD). Apollonius was a Pythagorean philosopher and wonder-worker from Greece who traveled to India and whose biography was written in the third century. According to his biographer Philostratus (ca. 170–245 AD), levitation is one of the many wonders that Apollonius saw while visiting Indian Brahmans: "He says that he saw them levitating themselves two cubits high from the ground, not for the sake of miraculous display, for they disdain any such ambition; but they regard any rites they perform, in thus quitting earth and walking with the Sun, as acts of homage acceptable to the God."[12] Levitation accounts can also be found in several types of Buddhism, some of which ascribe this power to the Buddha himself.[13] In Tibetan Buddhism belief in levitation is particularly strong and not necessarily linked to Western notions of asceticism, for some levitators in this tradition have female consorts with whom they engage in tantric sex while airborne.[14] Whether Asian traditions influenced developments in the Near East and Europe is a valid question that cannot be answered with definite confidence. The case of Apollonius points to at least some minimal contact. But no one knows for sure how many other Western theurgists might have brought home Asian beliefs and rituals related to levitation.

In the West, some accounts of *aethrobats*—"air walkers"—can be found in Near Eastern and Mediterranean cultures before the advent of Christianity. Among these, two of the most famous are Abaris the Hyperborean, a priest of Apollo, and the Greek mathematician and philosopher Pythagoras (sixth century BC).[15] Although both men were well known in the pre-Christian world, most of what we know about their levitations—which is not much at all—can be found in the work of Iamblichus (ca. 242–325), a Neoplatonist philosopher and mystic whose students believed in his own ability to levitate and glow while in ecstasy.[16] Western pre-Christian levitation accounts are infrequent and skimpy, at best. Nonetheless, it is important to note that in the three cases mentioned above, as in the Yogic and Buddhist traditions, levitation was attributed to the physiological effects of asceticism and meditation. This causal link caught the eye of some interpreters in the late nineteenth century. One of these, Helena Blavatsky, cofounder of the occultist Theosophical Society, made the following observation: "Christian ascetics, through contemplation and self-denial, acquire powers of levitation which, though attributed to the miraculous intervention of

God, are nevertheless real and the result of physiological changes in the human body."[17] Whether or not Madame Blavatsky was correct is a moot question. Her observation makes evident the fact that an undeniable pattern runs like a red thread across time, continents, and traditions: the linkage of levitation, of self-denial, and of the pursuit of intense spiritual activity.

Jewish antecedents are exceedingly rare, not exactly instances of levitation, and not at all linked to asceticism, which suggests that when it comes to levitation, there is probably a greater degree of continuity from paganism to Christianity than from Judaism. The Old Testament contains only two accounts of airborne men, both prophets, neither of whom can be considered a genuine levitator. The first is Elijah, who was snatched up to heaven in a fiery chariot and therefore conveyed off the ground by a vehicle, much like some present-day airline passenger. The second is Habakkuk, who was flown from Judea to Babylon and back to Judea by an angel who grabbed him by the hair, just so he could provide Daniel with lunch in the lion's den (fig. 5).[18] Since his body did not rise off the ground by itself but was in the hands of another being (literally), this cannot be counted as a levitation. Moreover, in the precise terminology of Catholic mystical theology, a flight that long counts as a transvection rather than a levitation.

The New Testament mentions no levitations at all, strictly speaking, but it is full of miracle accounts, all of which upend the laws of nature in some way. A few of these have something to do with the laws of gravity but are not levitations per se. The account of Jesus walking on water is not a levitation since he did not rise into the air,[19] and neither is his ascension to heaven after his resurrection since this was not a case of hovering or flying but of being taken up to heaven, much like Elijah, albeit without a chariot of fire.[20] Yet in both accounts the body of Jesus defies the normal gravitational pull of the earth. The account of the apostle Philip suddenly being carried away by the Spirit of the Lord from one location to another is not a levitation either.[21] Since Philip's relocation was instantaneous rather than a flight in the hands of an angel, like Habbakuk's, this miracle is deemed to be a transvection, spiritual transport, or teleportation. This same criterion applies to the Gospel narratives that speak of Jesus being taken by the devil to the pinnacle of the temple in Jerusalem and to the zenith of a very tall mountain, especially since no mention is made of how Jesus reached these high places.[22] Another New Testament figure associated with levitation is Mary Magdalene, who is mentioned in all four canonical Gospels. The Magdalene is said to have levitated many times later in life, after

Figure 5. Gianlorenzo Bernini's 1661 sculpture of the flight of
Habakkuk, who was transported over great distances by a flying angel
who grabbed him by the hair. This account found in the Book of
Daniel (14:36) is one of the oldest recorded instances of human flight
in the Judeo-Christian tradition.

she left the Holy Land and moved to Gaul, but this claim is nonbiblical, surfaces much later, and can only be found in medieval legends from the area around Marseilles (fig. 6). These local accounts gained a much wider audience through Jacob de Voragine's extremely popular *Golden Legend* (thirteenth century), which told of the Magdalene "being borne aloft by angels every day during the seven canonical hours."[23] The *Golden Legend,* in turn, inspired a good number of artistic representations of this miracle. So, despite popular traditions linking the Magdalene with levitation, it must be kept in mind that we have no such accounts from late antiquity.

Early Christians may not have left behind any record of levitations in the canonical books of the New Testament,[24] but they nonetheless had to face competition and opposition from charismatic miracle-working wizards such as Apollonius of Tyana, previously mentioned, and Simon Magus, who reportedly performed all sorts of wonders, including levitation.[25] Fixing upon a single descriptive term for such figures is difficult. As Simon's name implies, a wonderworker could be called a *magus* (plural *magi*), like the three so-called wise men from the East who visit the infant Jesus in the Gospel of Luke. In its original meaning, the term applied to the priestly caste of ancient Persia, but it evolved to have a broader meaning, signifying those who had occult knowledge, as well as spiritual and magical powers. They were sages who knew how to discover and manipulate the divine secrets hidden in the cosmos, and they could be called wizards, magicians, or sorcerers in English. They could also be called *thaumaturgs* (wonderworkers) or *hierophants* (revealers of the sacred).[26] And there is yet another formal name for them: *theurgists,* which is applicable because these wizards claimed to be engaged in divine work (*theurgia* in Greek). Lines that we might draw in the twenty-first century between philosophy, religion, magic, sorcery, and science were so blurry in the first century that one could say they did not really exist. A theurgist could be a polymath, engaged with all these disciplines at once—and others as well—not just intellectually, but spiritually and practicably. In sum, if some of these theurgists could have time traveled to the twenty-first century, they might have been cheeky enough to claim membership in at least two dozen departments of any university, and in some of its professional schools, including its seminaries and schools of drama and medicine, while serving as chaplains and psychiatrists too. Fortunately, none of them seem to have done so, at least not yet.

The world of the first Christians was teeming with such wonder-workers,[27] and even the miracles of Jesus himself have been interpreted in this context. A sixth-century Hebrew text, *The Life of Jesus,* did precisely this, portraying

Figure 6. Albrecht Dürer, *The Ecstasy of Saint Mary Magdalen* (sixteenth century). Legends that ascribed levitating ecstasies to Mary Magdalene developed during the Middle Ages. Dürer is one of the most prominent artists to have depicted her as an ecstatic levitator, borne aloft by angels.

Jesus as a levitating wizard, and it was published a millennium later in 1681, by Christians, in a collection of texts that ostensibly exposed Jewish anti-Christian blaspheming.[28] Several early Christian texts, written between the second and fourth centuries—some orthodox, some not—focus on Simon Magus, especially, and charge that he clashed with the apostles and challenged them to surpass his "miracles" (fig. 7).[29] The apocryphal *Acts of Peter* (second century) relates how Simon "amazed the multitudes by flying" and how Peter reacted to it:

> And beholding the incredible spectacle, Peter cried to the Lord Jesus Christ: "If thou allow him to do what he has undertaken, all who believed in you shall be overthrown, and the signs and wonders which you have shown to them through me, will not be believed. Make haste, O Lord, show your mercy and let him fall down and become crippled but not die; let him be disabled and break his leg in three places." And he fell down and broke his leg in three places. And they cast stones upon him, and each went to his home having faith in Peter.[30]

The legend of Simon Magus is clear evidence that the earliest Christian community could see levitation in a negative light, as a dark art associated with malevolent spirits. And it was not only the pagan "other" who could levitate— the magus, thaumaturge, or theurgist—but also anyone touched by the devil, whether baptized or not. A case in point is the emperor Julian, known as "the Apostate" (331–363), who renounced his Christian faith and fell under the spell of Neoplatonic philosopher-theurgist Maximus of Ephesus (310–372). The great theologian Gregory Nazienzen (329–370), who had attended school in Athens with Julian, was convinced that his former schoolmate "was bent on one object alone, namely, how to gratify the demons who had often possessed him."[31] Consequently, Gregory and all other like-minded Christians could only attribute Julian's levitations to demonic forces, including the one that took place during his initiation into the mysteries of the goddess Artemis by Maximus of Ephesus: "As if he had embraced an invisible being, Maximus spread out his arms, bent his head backward, rose in the air and remained suspended, motionless, wrapped in a luminous cloud. . . . Julian moved towards him unhesitatingly, as if drawn by an overpowering force. . . . Maximus clutched his hair at once, pulled him up to himself, and they began whirling round the cave, several feet above the ground, with a rapidly increasing speed."[32]

From very early on, Christians drew very sharp binary distinctions between themselves and others: between their religion, which worshiped the only true

Figure 7. The lower half of this fifteenth-century German woodcut depicts Simon Magus and Peter preaching while a demon whispers in Simon's ear. The upper half captures the moment when Saint Peter's prayers cause Simon to plummet to earth as a sword-wielding avenging angel attacks the demons who are keeping him aloft.

God, and all others, which worshiped false gods and demons, and between their miracles, which were divine in origin, and the wonders of all other cults and religions, which were the work of the devil. In essence, then, Christians saw themselves as hemmed in on all sides by the devil, for all religions other than their own worshiped him and did his bidding. Consequently, as far as Christians were concerned, all wonder-working theurgists were the devil's minions, and the warning found in the First Epistle of Peter applied to them as much as it did to the devil himself: "Stay alert! Watch out for your great enemy, the devil. He prowls around like a roaring lion, looking for someone to devour."[33]

By the fourth century, then, belief in the demonic origin of some levitations was well established among Christians and taken for granted among clerics schooled in theology, like Gregory Nazianzen. But belief in the divine origin of levitation was also very much a part of the Christian faith. Threatened as they were by the presence of pagan wonder-workers, Christians naturally came to accept the *fact* of levitation in binary terms, as a phenomenon that was never neutral in value but had to derive either from the devil or from God. Hilary of Poitiers (315–368) and Sulpicius Severus (363–425) were among the first to record accounts of demonic levitation.[34] One of the most vivid accounts comes from Sulpicius, who described one of the exorcisms conducted by Saint Martin of Tours: "I saw a demoniac snatched up into the air as Martin approached him, and he remained suspended there with his hands stretched upwards, and totally unable to touch the ground with his feet. . . . Then, one could plainly see the various torments endured by these wretches. Some of them were suspended in the air upside down, with their feet turned upwards, as if in the clouds, and yet, instead of flapping down over their faces, their garments stayed put, thus preventing their shameful body parts from being exposed."[35]

This binary early Christian approach to levitation was passed on to succeeding generations, throughout the Middle Ages and early modernity, and even down to the present in various traditions, especially in the Roman Catholic Church, where levitation has been considered one of the surest signs of demonic possession since medieval times, along with preternatural strength, unnatural body contortions, and the ability to read minds and speak arcane languages. As an exorcist's manual published in 1651 put it, one of the surest physical signs of possession was "the transporting and uplifting of the body against the patient's will, without it being possible to see whatever is carrying it up."[36]

For Christians, demonic levitation had to have a divine counterpart; God's omnipotence seemed to demand it. So it is not too surprising that at the very same time that Christians were struggling against the levitations of theurgists and demoniacs, a contrary divine phenomenon began to manifest itself within their own society. And it was directly linked to the emergence of monasticism. "Good" or "holy" levitation evolved in the desert, sometime between the second and fourth centuries, among the ascetic Christians who devoted themselves to constant prayer and a life of solitude. And it is there, in that setting, that holy levitation came to be understood as a side effect of contemplation or a physical reaction to an exalted spiritual experience of a supernatural character. It is there, too, that this ecstatic phenomenon came to be understood as wholly involuntary, a gift from above that can never be demanded or controlled.

The great monastic pioneer Saint Antony (ca. 250–350) and a fellow monk, Amun, were among the first to be lifted up in the air.[37] Another early levitator was the monk Shenute (ca. 360–450), who was raised "high into the air by the angels of the Lord" at the tribunal of the governor of Upper Egypt.[38] Women, too, numbered among the earliest levitators, and one of the most exceptional was Mary of Egypt (344–421), a penitent whore who had become a hermit.[39] According to Sophronius of Jerusalem, Mary rose "a forearm's distance from the ground and stood praying in the air" when she met the monk Zozimus in the desert, filling him with terror. Later, she also crossed the River Jordan on foot to receive communion from him, walking on the surface of the water, just as Jesus had done on the Sea of Galilee.[40]

From the fifth century on, accounts of holy levitations can be found in Christian literature, especially in monastic circles and particularly in areas under control of the Byzantine emperor, where after the collapse of the Western Roman Empire literacy levels remained higher, and more hagiographies tended to be written. In some cases, holy miracle-workers such as Theodore of Sykeon (ca. 550–613)—a gifted and very busy exorcist—engage with levitating demoniacs.[41] In most cases, however, it is the holy men and women themselves who levitate. Some of these Byzantine hagiographies made it to the West and can be found in the massive *Acta Sanctorum* published between the seventeenth and twentieth centuries.[42] Among those Eastern monks known for their levitations, three of the most notable lived in the latter part of the first millennium: Joannicus the Great (752–846), Luke of Steiris (896–953), and Andrew Salos, "the Fool" (ca. 870–936). Joannicus was a farmer, swineherd, and soldier before a conversion experience led him to become a hermit at the age of forty. Devoted to a life of extreme asceticism and constant prayer, he is said to have glowed "brighter than the sun" when he levitated.[43] Luke of Steiris, also known as Luke Thaumaturgus, was a

Greek herdsman turned monk, who, according to his hagiography, began levitating as a child, before becoming a monk, much to the astonishment of his mother.[44] Andrew Salos was a one-time slave whose erratic behavior as a "fool for Christ" caused him to be taken for insane, much like Saint Francis of Assisi three centuries later. Unlike Francis, however, Andrew lived in a religious culture in which "fool [*salos*] for Christ" was a venerable hagiographical category like "martyr" or "virgin." His mystical gifts included visions, clairvoyance, telepathy, and levitation, and his suspensions in the air were witnessed by his closest friend Epiphanius, who would eventually become patriarch of Constantinople.[45]

Holy Levitations in the Middle Ages

In the Catholic Christian West, which broke communion with the Orthodox Christian East in the Great Schism of 1054 and developed its own hagiographic traditions, accounts of levitations are relatively infrequent up until the tenth century, when a modest increase in literacy and the writing of hagiographies begins to take place and continues at the same pace until the early thirteenth century, when a dramatic upswing occurs. To a considerable extent this steadily increasing number of recorded levitations corresponds to rising literacy rates and the production of an ever-growing number of hagiographies. In other words, producing more texts for an ever-widening audience has much to do with the increase in levitation accounts. For all we know, innumerable oral accounts of levitations might have circulated during those centuries of low literacy, most of which have been irretrievably lost. Oral histories remain invisible to succeeding generations until they are written down, and this is why the only instances of levitation we can identify or enumerate are those preserved on velum or paper, in a wide array of texts.[46]

Beginning in the tenth century, holy levitations are reported with more regularity and become more closely associated with mystical ecstasy. To this day, however, there is no exact tally of the number of Christian levitators from this or any other period. The only attempt ever made to compile a list of levitating saints was that made by Olivier Leroy in 1928, drawn mostly from the *Acta Sanctorum.* His list, though far from complete, includes many of the better-known holy men and women of medieval Christendom, as well as lesser-known figures. Among the most notable are Bernard of Clairvaux (twelfth century), Christina the Astonishing (twelfth–thirteenth centuries), Dominic de Guzmán (fig. 8), Francis of Assisi, Anthony of Padua (fig. 9), Elizabeth of Hungary, Bonaventure, Albert the Great, Thomas Aquinas (thirteenth century), and Catherine of Siena

Figure 8. As became common in baroque Catholicism, religious orders commissioned artists to depict their saints in ecstasy. This seventeenth-century painting of the founder of the Dominican order shows him hovering over an altar, drawn to an image of the crucified Jesus.

Figure 9. Saint Anthony of Padua was best known in popular piety for his mystical encounters with the Virgin Mary and the infant Jesus. In this seventeenth-century painting, artist Vicente Carducho intermingles the earthly and heavenly dimensions and depicts Saint Anthony hovering, with his shadow clearly visible beneath his feet.

(fourteenth century).[47] Among those missed by Leroy, one of the most impressive is Douceline de Digne (thirteenth century) a levitating Beguine who played a significant role in the court of Charles of Anjou, Count of Provence.[48]

Many of these medieval accounts involve modest hoverings, in which the saint is raised a relatively short distance off the ground. A good number of these levitations occur in private too and are only witnessed by accident, when someone stumbles upon the aethrobat by pure chance. Others, however, are very public and witnessed by more than one person. All of them involve prayer in some way and are interpreted as a by-product of mystical ecstasy. A good number of these medieval levitations involve more than hovering and could almost be classified as flights. The heights reached and the distances traversed in some of the more extreme cases surpass those attributed to any Christian levitators from the first millennium. Three such extreme cases are those of Dunstan of Canterbury, Christina the Astonishing, and Francis of Assisi.

Dunstan (909–998) was an abbot and monastic reformer who served successively as bishop of Worcester, London, and Canterbury and as a minister for several English kings. He is said to have risen all the way to the ceiling of the cathedral at Canterbury, in the presence of many witnesses.[49] The great height of Dunstan's astounding flight is among the first of its kind to be recorded in any Catholic hagiography.

Far more impressive is Christina the Astonishing (1150–1224), a Flemish holy woman of peasant stock who earned the Latin title of Mirabilis because of the many miracles associated with her extreme asceticism. Her wonder-working began at the age of twenty-one, at her own funeral Mass. Taken for dead by her family after she suffered a violent seizure and about to be buried, Christina suddenly came back to life during the singing of the *Agnus Dei,* soared out of her open casket "like a bird" to the roof beams of the church, and stayed perched up there for quite a while in order to escape the stench of common sinners.[50] Filled with terror, everyone fled except for her sister and a priest, who eventually managed to coax her down from the rafters. Given the well-known possibility of demonic levitation, Christina was at first suspected of being a demoniac and imprisoned, but she managed to convince the authorities she was not demon possessed at all and was eventually freed.

From that day forward, Christina embarked on a life of constant penance and prayer, performing outrageously incredible miracles, such as emerging unscathed from blazing furnaces into which she threw herself or surviving total immersion in frozen rivers for very long stretches of time. Constantly shunning human company, she lived in treetops, towers, and church steeples.[51] Her levitations were often spectacular and witnessed by many. Eyewitnesses claimed she could perch like a bird on slender tree branches (as Joseph of Cupertino would do centuries later). Many also claimed to have seen her squatting atop a pole, singing psalms.[52]

Imprisoned a second time because of her family's concern over her bizarre behavior and extreme acts of self-punishment, Christina was freed again and soon recognized as genuinely holy by townsfolk and church authorities alike, including the noted theologian Cardinal Jacques de Vitry (ca. 1165–1240), who met with her and vouched for her genuine holiness. A mere eight years after her death, a hagiography based on eyewitness testimony and written by Thomas de Cantimpré, a Dominican professor of theology, made her outlandish supernatural feats widely known throughout the Catholic world.[53]

Francis of Assisi (1182–1226) is so unique that he has led some experts on levitation to gloss over him dismissively. "Of St. Francis of Assisi's life nothing needs to be said," huffed Olivier Leroy. "Everybody knows something about it."[54] While that might have been true or close to the truth in France a century ago, the same cannot be assumed now. Moreover, then as now, Francis is best known not for his levitations but rather for his nature mysticism and interactions with animals and, most of all, for his stigmata, the miraculous replication of Christ's five wounds on his own body (fig. 10). Since Francis was the first Christian saint ever to receive these wounds, the miracle of the stigmata was sui generis, totally unique, and perhaps more astounding than any other mystical miracle in post-Apostolic Christian history. Its sheer physicality, some have said, "marked a new stage in the history of the miraculous."[55] Yet, it could be argued, Francis's levitations, recorded as they were in multiple hagiographies, would play an immense role in the history of the miraculous too, making this ancient and extremely physical mystical phenomenon more widely known and acceptable and more paradigmatic of sanctity for subsequent generations of mystics and would-be mystics, including the greatest Christian levitator of all time, Joseph of Cupertino, a Franciscan friar wholly devoted to imitating Saint Francis.

The role played by Francis in the history of levitation should never be overlooked. One way of reckoning his immense significance is to consider how quickly he was canonized and how many hagiographies were written within a relatively short time span after his death. Francis died on October 3, 1226, and

Figure 10. In this very unusual depiction of the stigmatization of Saint Francis, artist Vicente Carducho chose to set this mystical rapture up in the air, as a levitation. As is common in many baroque depictions of levitations, Carducho includes an eyewitness in the background.

was canonized a mere twenty-two months later on July 16, 1228, by which time a hagiography commissioned by Pope Gregory IX had already been written by Thomas of Celano, a Franciscan friar who had known Francis. This text came to be known as the *Vita Prima*, or *First Life*. Then, due to frictions within the Franciscan order over the issue of poverty, the Franciscan minister-general commissioned Thomas to write another hagiography in 1244, which he completed in 1247. It came to be known as the *Vita Secunda*, or *Second Life*. And once again a few years later, growing interest in the miracles performed by Francis led the minister-general to commission Thomas to write a detailed account of them. This text, which was completed in 1253—but not printed until 1899—is known as the *Treatise on the Miracles of Saint Francis*.[56] Curiously, Thomas of Celano does not mention levitations directly in either of his hagiographies, but he does say that Francis "dedicated not only his whole heart, but his whole body as well" to Christ and that he "was often suspended in such sweetness of contemplation, caught up out of himself" that he "paid no attention to the things that happened, as though he were a lifeless corpse."[57]

As squabbling among the Franciscans intensified over their interpretation of the rule written for the order by Francis, another hagiographer took up the task of interpreting Francis's life. This was Giovanni di Fidanza (1221–1274), better known as Saint Bonaventure, a brilliant Franciscan theologian-philosopher—and a schoolmate of Thomas Aquinas at the University of Paris—who eventually became minister-general of his order in 1257. Observing a request made of him by the general chapter of the Franciscans that elected him as their leader, Bonaventure wrote two hagiographical texts, the *Legenda Major*, intended for reading, and a shorter *Legenda Minor*, intended primarily for liturgical use in the choir—that is, for the ritual life of Franciscans. Hoping he could bring an end to the extremism and fracturing within his order, Bonaventure synthesized the work of Thomas de Celano and other texts that were in circulation, fashioning an account of Francis's life that tamed the wildness of Francis's commitment to radical poverty without diminishing the intensity of his mysticism, miracles, and supernatural encounters (fig. 11).

Completed in 1261, both *Legenda* quickly eclipsed Thomas of Celano's work, thanks largely to the fact that soon after their completion, a General Chapter of the Franciscan order in 1266 decreed that the *Legenda Major* would henceforth be the official and definitive hagiography.[58] According to one interpreter, the *Legenda Minor* had a profound impact too because the incorporation of the miracle stories in ritual "removed Francis from the category of local thaumaturge

Figure 11. Giotto is one of the first Western artists to depict a levitation. In this fresco, he attempts to faithfully re-create Bonaventure's description of the event.

and reformulated his memory as that of a universal miracle, accessible to all through contemplation, and transferable, so to speak, to any locale."[59] And, unlike Thomas of Celano, Bonaventure does mention levitation explicitly in both *Legenda.* In the *Major,* he writes: "He was occasionally seen raised up from the ground and surrounded with a shining cloud, as he prayed at night with his hands stretched out in the form of a cross." Then he attributes the miracle to the connection between body and soul, adding: "The brilliance that enveloped his body was a sign of the miraculous light which flooded his soul."[60]

About a hundred years after Francis's death, as rancorous divisions over the issue of poverty continued to plague the Franciscan order, a third major hagiography was written by Ugolino di Monte Santa Maria (ca. 1260–1348), a Franciscan friar who belonged to the Observant, or Spiritual, branch of the order, which observed the vow of poverty more strictly than the Conventual branch. This text was an anthology of narratives, some gathered from the earlier hagiographies and others taken from the texts and oral traditions that circulated among the Spiritual Franciscans, many of which had not been collected by Bonaventure or Thomas of Celano. Originally written in Latin,[61] Ugolino's text was condensed and translated into Italian with the title *Fioretti di San Francesco,* or *Little Flowers of Saint Francis,* in reference to the Latin term for anthologies, florilegium, a gathering of flowers.

Whether the narratives in this bouquet of stories were genuine eyewitness accounts that had been circulating orally for a century is unknown, but some experts have argued that they were indeed.[62] What is beyond dispute is that due to the immense popularity of the *Fioretti,* these accounts—regardless of their provenance—became part and parcel of Franciscan lore and gave the world a Francis who levitates dramatically. In contrast to Bonaventure, who in his sole reference to levitation simply says very dryly that Francis "was occasionally seen raised off the ground," the *Fioretti* states: "St. Francis, through constant prayer, began to experience more often the sweet consolations of divine contemplation, as a result of which *he was many times* so rapt in God that he was seen by his companions raised bodily above the ground and absorbed in God."[63] So this text not only indicates that these levitations began to increase toward the end of Francis's life but asserts that they took place very frequently. The *Fioretti* also claims that "because of his purity," Brother Leo, one of Francis's closest companions, "merited *time and time again* to see St. Francis rapt in God and raised above the ground." Leo's access to Francis's ecstasies was apparently constant, and according to the following description of what he often witnessed, these experiences could perhaps be as overwhelming as they were astonishing: "He found him . . . raised up into the air sometimes as high as three feet, sometimes four, at other times *halfway up or at the top of the beech trees—and some of those trees were very high.* At other times he found him *raised so high in the air and surrounded by such radiance that he could hardly see him.* Then Brother Leo would kneel and prostrate himself completely on the ground on the spot from which the holy Father had been lifted into the air while praying."[64]

Making no effort to enumerate these levitations or to distinguish them from one another, the text of the *Fioretti* provides two extremely significant details: first, that Francis could rise to great heights, and second, that the glow he radiated was bright enough to blind observers and conceal his body. We also learn that Brother Leo would respond with a gesture of abject submission by kneeling and then prostrating himself "completely," flat on the ground under the hovering Francis. In another passage, however, we are told that on at least one occasion, Leo *stood* below Francis and tried to touch him: "One time among others, when he was standing there under St. Francis's feet," we read, he was "raised so high above the ground" that he could not be reached.[65]

The most unusual levitation recorded in the *Fioretti* does not involve Leo but rather Brother Masseo, another close companion of Francis. And the phenomenon described is unparalleled in the annals of Christian levitation. While praying in a church with Masseo, Francis went into an ecstasy so intense that "flames of love seemed to issue from his face and mouth." As if this were not extraordinary enough, Francis then involves Masseo in his rapture: "And going out to his companion, all afire with love, he said forcefully: 'Ah! Ah! Ah! Brother, Masseo, give yourself to me!' And he said it three times. And Brother Masseo, greatly amazed at his fervor, threw himself into the holy Father's arms when he said for the third time: 'Give yourself to me!' Then St. Francis, with his mouth wide open and repeating very loudly 'Ah! Ah! Ah,!' by the power of the Holy Spirit lifted Brother Masseo up in the air with his breath and projected him forward the length of a long spear." After returning to the ground, an astounded Masseo would later say that the "spiritual consolation and sweetness" he felt while levitating was the greatest experience of his life.[66]

Francis is unusual in so many ways that it would be wrong to say that his levitations—including the one with Masseo—were a chief distinguishing trait of his mysticism. Levitations were but one of Francis's many mystical gifts. What truly stands out in the case of Francis is the way in which his levitations are *not* explicitly mentioned by Thomas de Celano and then how they barely surface in Bonaventure's hagiography. There is something odd about this silence and restraint and about the way in which the levitation accounts show up a hundred years after his death, and even then, there is no attempt to enumerate or showcase them. And what makes it difficult to dispel the oddness is the fact that we have no definite knowledge of the provenance of the levitation accounts in the *Fioretti*. This void raises questions. On the one hand, if these stories really did circulate for a century before being written down, perhaps some element of fear drove them underground. Why the fear? On the other hand, if these accounts were later inventions, we must assume that someone deemed it useful or necessary to add levitation to Francis's astounding treasure chest of wonders. Why should anyone have felt the need to do so? Despite the oddness of it all, and the questions raised by it, one thing is certain: thanks largely to the *Fioretti,* Francis adds luster to the phenomenon of levitation due to his unquestionable holiness, and on top of this he establishes paradigms subsequently used in the measuring up of future levitators. So, when all is said and done, the oddness of Francis's levitations is eclipsed by the significance bestowed upon them by his ecstatic glow, so to speak, which, as Brother Leo said, could be blindingly bright.

Another peculiar circumstance to consider is that Francis was a trailblazer, a holy man on the cutting edge of the miraculous, for it is during his lifetime and immediately afterward that we begin to see a steadily increasing number of levitations in hagiographies. And while some of these levitations involve relatively minor figures, some involve extremely prominent saints. One of the most spectacular accounts, in fact, involves none other than Francis's hagiographer Bonaventure and the best-known of all medieval theologians, Thomas Aquinas (1225–1274). At the center of this narrative we find Francis himself. As it turns out, in 1260, while he was collecting material in and around Assisi for his hagiography of Francis, Bonaventure spent some time at the friary of La Verna, and by sheer coincidence Aquinas happened to be there too. One day, while Bonaventure was working on his Francis research in his cell, Aquinas went to visit him and found him hovering in the air rapt in ecstasy. According to one account of this rare encounter between two of the greatest doctors of the Catholic Church, Aquinas quickly backed out of Bonaventure's cell, saying as he gingerly closed the door: "Let us leave him alone, this saint is working for a saint."[67] We have reports of Thomas Aquinas levitating, too, on other occasions, although he is certainly not best known for that. According to his hagiographer William of Thoco, who had known him personally, Thomas was seen levitating in ecstasy at Salerno and Naples, about two cubits high (three feet) off the floor.[68]

The list of thirteenth-, fourteenth-, and fifteenth-century levitators gleaned from the *Acta Sanctorum* indicates a marked increase in reports of this phenomenon in the latter part of the Middle Ages. The individuals on this list, however, all made it through the rigorous process of beatification and canonization, which means that we are looking at only a small portion of the total number of men and women deemed holy and worthy of the coveted title of "blessed" or "saint," some—or many—of whom might have had a reputation as levitators. This list, therefore, gives us only a partial glimpse of the possible sum total of levitation accounts from this time period. Yet this glimpse, limited as it is, suggests an increasing number of levitation accounts during these three centuries. In the list of beatified and canonized levitators, we find well-known figures alongside those of various lower levels of fame or obscurity.

And we find some revealing patterns too. First, we can see a high number of female levitators, indicating that this was one rare area in which women could excel alongside men, or perhaps even surpass them: In the three centuries between 1200 and 1400, for instance, nearly half of the levitation accounts in the *Acta Sanctorum*—a full 47 percent—are women. Second, we also note a broad geographical reach for this phenomenon, with representatives from at least a dozen language areas, stretching from Sicily in the south to England and Germany in the north, and Castile in the west to Hungary and Croatia in the east. Third, we can find some extreme levitators who rival Francis when it comes to heights reached, such as Agnes of Montepulciano, who embraced a crucifix that hung high off the ground,[69] and Colette of Corbie, who rose so high that everyone lost sight of her.[70] And, fourth—especially in the fifteenth century—we find a good number of effulgent aethrobats too—that is, levitators who glowed during their ecstasies, such as Venturino of Bergamo, Catherine Colombini, Vincent Ferrer, Peter Regalado, and Antoninus of Florence. In one extreme case of luminance, the Dominican friar Peter Jeremias of Palermo shone so brightly that the light poured out through the cracks in his door, as if his cell were on fire. When an alarmed superior broke down the door, thinking Peter Jeremias needed rescuing, he was surprised to find him hovering and glowing in ecstasy.[71]

Early Modern Mayhem: The Catholic Inflationary Spiral

By the beginning of the sixteenth century, "good" or "holy" levitations had become a common hallmark of genuine sanctity. And it is no mere coincidence that the invention of the printing press in the mid-fifteenth century coincides with a marked increase in the number of recorded levitations. Printed hagiographies, read by both monastics and laypeople, helped raise awareness of all patterns of holiness, including levitation. By the mid-sixteenth century, when the printing industry was already a hundred years old and the reading public had grown in size substantially, the writing and publishing of hagiographies had become a very popular—and profitable—venture. In Spain alone, for instance, the number of hagiographic titles published grew from 23 between 1500 and 1559 to 350 between 1600 and 1639.[72]

In addition, other currents of change had begun to redefine the religious landscape of Christendom, overturning medieval assumptions and enhancing the significance of the miraculous within Catholicism. With the advent of the Protestant Reformation, which denied not only medieval concepts of sainthood but the metaphysical assumptions that shaped them, miraculous phenomena such as levitation became markers of difference. While Protestants denied that anyone could ever become holy through asceticism, or that mystical ecstasy and miracles such as levitation were possible, Catholics responded by seizing upon whatever Protestants denied, augmenting its value. So as Protestants mocked asceticism, monasticism, mysticism, and belief in miracles or, even worse, ascribed such phenomena to the devil, Catholics focused all the more on such things, not just to deny Protestant claims but to strengthen traditional faith from within. Consequently, saints proliferated throughout the sixteenth century, especially in those lands that remained resolutely Catholic, such as Italy and Spain, and the magnitude of the outward signs of their holiness increased in inverse proportion to their extinction in Protestant lands.

Along with the increase in the number of exceptional men and women who accomplished incredible things came an increase in the number of printed hagiographies that extolled what was most distinctively Catholic about them. Sainthood became more formulaic than before and so did the hagiographies, many of which were published under the nearly identical, pro forma, fill-in-the-blank title of *The Life, Virtues, and Miracles of the [Venerable, or Blessed, or Saint] So-and-So,* with a heavy emphasis on the virtues and miracles that Protestants deemed impossible.[73] Spain and Italy, those two regions where Protestantism had made no significant inroads, suddenly seemed full of otherworldly men and women who lived suspended between heaven and earth, figuratively or literally. Credulity was strained by the sheer volume of miracle accounts. In the 1580s, for instance, the Jesuit Pedro de Ribadeneira complained of a "spirit of illusion running rampant" and "the crowd of deceived, evil women whom we have recently seen in many of Spain's most illustrious cities; those who with their trances, revelations, and stigmata have excited and deceived their priests and confessors."[74] By 1600, a prominent Spanish observer could say: "It seems as if one had wished to reduce these kingdoms to a republic of enchanted beings, living outside the natural order of things."[75]

Oddly enough, then, the advent of modernity brought with it to Catholic Europe an increase in precisely the kinds of phenomena that would be dismissed as thoroughly impossible and "medieval" by Protestants and skeptics of all stripes, especially after the Enlightenment of the eighteenth century reduced all religion to mere ethics or sheer nonsense. Olivier Leroy's list of sixteenth-century aethrobats culled from the *Acta Sanctorum* is a veritable who's who of the Catholic Reformation: Francis Xavier, Ignatius Loyola, Peter of Alcántara, Teresa of Avila, John of the Cross, and Philip Neri, to name but a few. The list for the seventeenth century is even longer and the exploits of some of these levitators even more incredible. But these lists do not include the hundreds of others who never came to be well known, such as Saint Hyacintha Mariscotti (1585–1640),[76] or those who never made it to sainthood or whose cases for canonization stalled or were never launched. Perhaps one could even assume that a total listing might number in *thousands* rather than *hundreds,* for it is a case of counting not just those whose canonization fizzled—for whatever reason—but also all those others whose cases were never promoted at all or whose levitations were recorded in manuscripts or simply reported by word of mouth. In addition, one must reckon with all those cases of levitation that were reported to the Inquisition under the rubric of "feigned sanctity," many of which were judged to be demonic or simply deceitful.[77] For, not surprisingly, the religious mayhem of the era brought the devil back into the phenomenon of levitation with a vengeance.

As far as holy levitations were concerned, the most significant figure is Saint Teresa of Avila, whose role in the history of levitation is immense. Teresa reflected and intensified the inflationary spiral in Catholic levitation in unique ways. First, she not only wrote about her own levitations but dissected the miracle from within, giving it an oddly empirical sense of reality as first-person testimony. Second, the number of eyewitness testimonies concerning her levitations is so great, and the descriptions so detailed, as to appear mundane, despite their otherworldliness. Moreover, Teresa did not just experience levitation but objected to it, complaining to God and eventually convincing Him to banish it from her life. To fully understand what holy levitation was *supposed to be,* then, it seems best to devote an entire chapter to her, immediately after this one.

Nonetheless, whatever Teresa reified—as personally intense and unique as it was—can only be understood in a communal or social context, as sharing in a very specific mentality in which certain expectations were commonplace and in which no mystic could be wholly sui generis, totally unlike any others. Like all canonized saints of her age, to be regarded as genuinely holy Teresa had to reflect common expectations while giving them her own personal stamp, for any levitator who did not meet a very specific set of criteria was bound to crash or be brought down quickly.

As one of the many levitators who were under scrutiny around the same time, Teresa needs to be viewed alongside her contemporaries. And among these levitators of her era, some stand out, not just for their leading roles in the Catholic Reformation but also for the characteristics of their ecstasies, which further expanded the marvel of levitation beyond mere hovering in terms of height, duration, location, posture, and accompanying phenomena.

Ignatius Loyola (1491–1556), the founder of the Jesuit order, was observed levitating various times, rapt in ecstasy with his knees bent and his arms outstretched, four or five palms above the floor. He was also known to fill a room with dazzling light when he was aloft.[78] Due to the fact that several illustrated hagiographies of Saint Ignatius were published around the time of his beatification and canonization, we have three different depictions of these events (figs. 12–14).

Francis Xavier (1506–1552), the best known of all Jesuit missionaries, reportedly rose into the air frequently while he celebrated Mass—according to one of his baroque hagiographers—and levitated with his knees bent, his face aglow in a radiant light. And some witnesses in Goa, India, saw him levitating in a kneeling position as he distributed communion.[79]

Tomás de Villanueva (1488–1555), an Augustinian priest and reformer who served as a councilor for Emperor Charles V and was eventually appointed archbishop of Valencia, has the distinction of having stayed aloft for twelve hours while celebrating Mass, far longer than any other levitator of his era.[80]

Pedro de Alcántara (1499–1562), a Franciscan mystic who mentored Teresa of Avila, was an extreme ascetic and exceptional levitator who reportedly soared outdoors, as high as the tallest trees, and was also seen flying ecstatically from a garden to a nearby church.[81] In addition, he could stay aloft for as long as three hours and become as luminous as the sun.[82] Philip Neri (1515–1595), a mystic, reformer, and founder of the Congregation of the Oratory, was another frequent levitator, especially while celebrating Mass, when he would sometimes rise ten or fifteen feet off the ground or as high as the ceiling. His body was often bathed in light too. But Philip felt uncomfortable with such public levitations, and whenever he was in the company of others inside a church or any

Figure 12. Engraving from an illustrated hagiography of Saint Ignatius Loyola that describes one of his levitations, as follows: "He was observed many times at night, his room filled with a bright light; and he was seen raised up in the air, with his knees bent, weeping and sighing, and saying 'My God, how infinitely good You are; You even put up with those who are evil and perverse, which is what I am.'"

other sacred space, he tried to keep his prayers short, fearing that he might become airborne. Philip might have had good reason for keeping his levitating out of view as much as possible, for not everyone was ready or willing to accept any hovering person as holy, as happened with a young girl whose immediate reaction upon seeing him aloft was to tell her mother that Philip must be a demoniac.[83]

Figure 13. Another engraving from a hagiography of Saint Ignatius Loyola depicting him in ecstasy, levitating and glowing, with an eyewitness included in the image for good measure.

Salvador de Orta (1520–1567), a lay Franciscan brother who served as a cook, porter, and designated beggar for his friary during much of his life, was one of many miracle-working holy men and women denounced to the Spanish Inquisition on suspicion of being under demonic influence. Cleared of all charges against him but still viewed by his superiors as something of a problem because of the attention his miracles attracted, Salvador was shuf-

Figure 14. One of the earliest depictions of Saint Ignatius in ecstasy, levitating and glowing.

fled to various friaries here and there and ended up spending his final years in remote Sardinia. His distinction in the history of levitation involves his love of nature—a very Franciscan trait—which could send him into ecstatic levitations. Once, for instance, while he was out begging, a prominent family invited him to join them for dinner and at some point handed him a pomegranate.

Upon slicing it in two, seeing the tightly packed purple grains, and marveling at their beauty and order, Salvador rose up in ecstasy with outstretched arms and remained suspended in the air, much to the surprise of his hosts, who ran out and gathered their neighbors so they could see this miracle with their own eyes.[84]

Early Modern Mayhem: The Protestant Attack

Protestantism created a culture decidedly uneasy with the mixing of heaven and earth or the sacred and the mundane while at the same time retaining early Christian and medieval binary assumptions about the devil's activity in the world. In doing so, Protestantism not only desacralized the world substantially but simultaneously suffused it with an intense demonic presence by ascribing all levitations to the devil, along with all other miracles claimed by the Catholic Church.

This Protestant reconfiguration of the medieval cosmos was a synchronous mixture of desacralizing and demonizing, and this somewhat paradoxical change in worldview and mentality was derived from certain concepts innately central to Protestant thinking. Four essential reconfigurations of reality stand out most starkly—all of them paradigm shifts equal in magnitude to the rejection of the geocentric cosmos by Copernicus and Galileo—each of which concerned some of the most fundamental concepts in the Christian religion: first, how matter relates to spirit; second, how the natural relates to the supernatural; third, how human nature relates to the divine; and fourth, how the living relate to the dead. When it came to levitation, that fourth paradigm shift concerning the living and the dead mattered little, but the first three were of enormous significance. This is not to say that external factors—political, social, economic, or cultural—had no role to play in the evolution of a new Christian viewpoint but rather to emphasize that Protestants, who were themselves affected by these factors, became very aggressive agents of the twin processes of desacralization and demonization.

While this great paradigm shift spearheaded by Protestants affected nearly every aspect of daily life, and especially of the place of symbols and rituals in it, our sole concern here is to gauge the effect it had on conceptions of the miraculous and, more specifically, on levitation. So let us focus on the three concepts that changed the meaning and function of levitation in the eyes of Protestants of all stripes.

First, let us consider the reconfiguration of the relationship between matter and spirit. Ever since the inception of their religion, Christians had accepted a binary understanding of the cosmos: God was spirit, and He had created a material world, ontologically related to Him but metaphysically different and inferior. Humans were the pinnacle of this creation, part matter and part spirit, composed of a mortal body and an immortal soul. Bridging these two essential realms of existence was the role of religion or, more specifically, of the Church and its clergy, and the bridging was effected in myriad ways through rituals and symbols. In sum, the medieval Christian world pulsated with accessibility to the divine, replete as it was with material points of contact with the spiritual realm.

Protestants made matter and spirit much less compatible. And their rejection of material access points to the spiritual realm redrew the boundaries between the sacred and the profane, restructuring the conceptual structure of Christianity as well as its social and cultural realities, turning all Protestants into iconoclasts, literally and figuratively, including those who retained some material aspects of Catholic worship, such as the Lutherans and Anglicans.[85]

This ontological and metaphysical reconfiguration varied among Protestants but found its most extreme expression in the Reformed tradition and in two of their guiding principles: "Finitum non est capax infiniti" (The finite cannot contain the infinite) and "Quantum sensui tribueris tantum spiritui detraxeris" (The physical detracts from the spiritual). These principles, in turn, were derived from three key assumptions. First, the Reformed Protestant tradition assumed that God was radically transcendent and that the supernatural realm was wholly "other," above and beyond the natural and created order. Ulrich Zwingli argued that the things of earth were "carnal" and that they were "enmity against God." He also argued that matter and spirit were incapable of mixing and that "those who trust in any created thing whatsoever are not truly pious."[86] John Calvin was equally adamant: "Whatever holds down and confines the senses to the earth is contrary to the covenant of God; in which, inviting us to himself, He permits us to think of nothing but what is spiritual."[87] Moreover, Reformed metaphysics proposed that matter is not only incapable of bridging the gap between heaven and earth; it actually acts as an obstacle. "The more you focus on material things," said Zwingli, "the more you take away from the spiritual."[88] John Calvin agreed: "Whatever holds down and confines the senses to the earth is contrary to the covenant of God; in which, inviting us to Himself, He permits us to think of nothing but what is spiritual."[89]

The Protestant redefinition of matter and spirit was revolutionary on two fronts. First, it was a theological upheaval and a redefinition of the sacred. Second, it was also a redefinition of the role of the ordained clergy, who were no longer viewed as conduits to the realm of the sacred but rather as ministers of the Word. Religion was no longer a search for the immanence of the divine in this world or an attempt to encounter heaven in the sacraments or in sacred spaces through pilgrimages and the veneration of images and relics. Nor was it a search for the miraculous and otherworldly mediated by priests who enjoyed a higher ontological status than their flocks and through whose agency the transubstantiation of bread and wine into the body and blood of Christ could be effected. Religion was something else, something less immanent and more transcendent, something more focused on an unseen spiritual realm and on a code of ethics, something internalized by individuals and communities, something less tactile and definitely more this-worldly.

Next, let us move on to the second Protestant conceptual shift: the reconfiguring of the interaction between the natural and the supernatural. Overall, despite the many differences and heated squabbles among themselves, Protestants rejected the commonplace irruptions of the sacred that were central to medieval religion. More specifically, Protestants did away with the miraculous phenomena of Catholicism and denied the possibility of merging with God in mystical ecstasy.

In many ways, this second paradigm shift was a desacralization of the world much more intense than that brought about by the Protestant war against idolatry and more profound than that against those non-Christian practices labeled as "magic" or "superstition." This was the ultimate demystification and a Copernican revolution in worldview, even though Max Weber failed to see it as such.

One of the most distinctive traits of Protestantism was its rejection of postbiblical miracles and all those practically oriented supernatural events that historians now classify as thaumaturgy. God could work miracles, certainly, as revealed countless times in the Bible, but as Protestants saw it, the age of miracles had ended long ago, and God's supernatural interventions were a thing of the distant past, strictly limited to biblical times. Luther was blunt about it: "Those visible works are simply signs for the ignorant, unbelieving crowd, and for the sake of those that are yet to be attracted; but as for us who already know what we know, and believe the Gospel, what do we need them for? . . . Consequently, it is not at all surprising that they have now ceased since the Gospel has been sounded everywhere and preached to those who had not known of God before, whom he had to attract with outward miracles, just as when we throw apples and pears to children."[90]

As if this were not enough, Luther added one crowning objection to all the miraculous claims made by Catholics: the devil could manipulate nature and deceive people, and often did, especially in the Catholic Church, which, as he saw it, was led by the Antichrist. This polemically charged Protestant tradition of attributing Catholic miracle claims to the devil was above all an affirmation of their conviction in the inviolability of natural laws. Nature could be manipulated by Satan and humans could certainly be fooled by him, Protestants argued, but genuine supernatural miracles were restricted to God's interventions in biblical times. This assumption about the cessation of miracles was voiced repeatedly among Protestants, as if in a giant echo chamber, and could be found in the work of many of their polemicists. One of these was William Tyndale, the first Protestant translator of the Bible into English, who argued that miracles ceased at the end of the first century, as soon as "the scripture was fully received and authentic."[91]

Ulrich Zwingli also argued against miracles, as did his successor Heinrich Bullinger, who charged that Catholic miracles required "the help of witchcraft,"[92] but it was their French disciple, John Calvin, who gave the Protestant denial of the miraculous its definitive contours. Like Luther before him, Calvin argued that the only function of miracles was to confirm the authority of God's messengers and that they were restricted to those rare occasions when God had something to reveal. But Calvin also took a metaphysical turn, explicitly stating that the ultimate purpose of all biblical miracles was *not* to alter the fabric of the material natural order but simply to authenticate revelation.[93] Moreover, argued Calvin, since Protestants were not revealing anything new, but rather asserting the primacy of the Bible, it was therefore wrong for Catholics to demand miracles from them. Moreover, Calvin also proposed that all the miracles claimed by the Catholic Church came straight from hell. "We should also remember," he pointed out, "that Satan has his miracles."[94]

Accusing the Catholic Church of being possessed by Satan and his Antichrist was a polemical tactic employed by Protestants everywhere, at all levels, by propagandists such as Georg Schwartz in Germany, Philips van Marnix in the Netherlands, and John Bale in England.[95] And this was often done with obsessive zeal. In England—where this zeal kept printers very busy[96]—the mathematician and scientist John Napier drew up a very long list of medieval wonder-workers who were frauds, necromancers, and magicians. This list included the tenth-century levitator Saint Dunstan as well as twenty-one medieval popes.[97]

John Bale was another propagandist who never tired of railing against "the synagogue of Satan" and the "spouse of the devil"—that is, the Catholic Church—and "the devil's unholy vicar at Rome, with all his cursings and conjurings." Bale, too, drew up a list of diabolical magician-popes, and he called one of them, John XII (955–964), "the holy vicar of Satan and successor of Simon Magus."[98] Not to be outdone, the Puritan theologian William Perkins came up with a similar list, adding more popes to it and referring to them as "sundry mal-contented priests of Rome" who "aspired unto the chair of supremacy by Diabolical assistance."[99] In England, in particular, due to the presence of Catholic Dissenters and their clandestine priests within the realm, the association of Catholic rituals and miracles with demonism and witchcraft became common among Protestant polemicists. Denouncing Catholic priests as "a nest of conjuring mass-mongers" who engaged in "magic and conjuration" became a familiar trope.[100] Major treatises on sorcery and the dark arts, such as Reginald Scot's *A Discovery of Witchcraft* or King James I's *Daemonologie,* took every opportunity they could to link Catholicism with demonic magic.[101]

So, even though some Protestants (especially Lutherans) continued to believe in demonic skullduggery and natural signs and portents that conveyed messages, such as cloud formations, astronomical and meteorological anomalies, or monstrous births—wonders (*mirabilia*) rather than miracles (*miraculi*)—and even though supernatural miracles eventually worked their way back into Protestant piety in various limited ways during the late seventeenth and eighteenth centuries,[102] Protestantism might have desacralized and disenchanted the world much more through its take on miracles than through any of its other principles. Ironically, as Bale's quip about Pope John XII being the "successor of Simon Magus" suggests, this desacralization simultaneously increased the devil's presence in the world's history as well as in the present.

Finally, let us turn our attention to the third major Protestant conceptual shift: the redefinition of the relationship between the human and the divine, which naturally led to a new take on levitation and all mystical phenomena. All Protestants—even those few Radical extremists who claimed to have access to the divine realm—shared in a common rejection of the three basic steps of the mystical quest: *purgation, illumination,* and *union.* These hallowed steps and all other enumerations of them had been the bedrock of the mystical tradition of the Catholic and Eastern Orthodox churches since the second century. Now, suddenly, the very idea of becoming ever purer and more godlike seemed repulsively false to Protestants, along with the assumption that anyone could ever have supernatural encounters with God in this life, especially of the sort that caused human bodies to float in the air. The truth, as Protestants saw it, was that no one can truly rise above this world (figuratively and literally) or become a different kind of human being suffused with supernatural gifts. As Luther put it: "What would the nuns and monks do if they heard that in the sight of God they are not a bit better than married people and mud-stained farmers?"[103] So, in one fell swoop, by rejecting what had been the ultimate claims of medieval Christian mysticism, Protestants sought not only the abolition of monasticism but also the relegation of all such outrageous claims to the demonic sphere. The Protestant argument was as clear as it was simple: since God does not levitate bodies or stigmatize them, all such Catholic claims must be either false tricks, or delusions, or nonsense, or—if such things actually do ever happen—the work of the devil, undoubtedly.

The Protestant rejection of monasticism, based as it was on a very different understanding of the perfectibility of human nature and of the way in which humans are redeemed by Christ, figures prominently as a social change effected by theology: it not only caused the largest redistribution of property in Western history before the Bolsheviks came along in the early twentieth century but also brought about a social and economic revolution. Suddenly, an entire social class was eliminated and all their substantial wealth seized. In addition, on both the material and conceptual level, a way of life that focused intensely on otherworldliness was extinguished. The desacralizing impact of the extinction of monasticism seems obvious enough and needs little elaboration. The impact of the rejection of mysticism—the main goal of monasticism—is harder to discern but no less significant. Within Catholicism, men and women who reached the pinnacle of holiness were considered living proof of the divinization of matter. They not only conversed with Christ and the Virgin Mary but had ineffable encounters with the Godhead; they also swooned in rapture, went into trances, levitated, bilocated, read minds, prophesied, manifested the wounds of Christ on their bodies, and healed the sick and lame. And when they died, their corpses could emit a wonderful aroma and remain intact.[104]

Protestants rejected all this intimate commingling with the divine and supernatural. Even Martin Luther, who was influenced by the fourteenth-century mystics John Tauler and Henry Suso, could not abide the ultimate claims made by medieval ecstatics and despised all who claimed direct contact with the divine as *schwärmer*, unhinged fanatics. John Calvin recoiled in horror at the thought that humans might claim any sort of divinization, for his God was "entirely

other" and "as different from flesh as fire is from water."[105] Such a crossing of
boundaries was impossible, argued Calvin, for the human soul "is not only burdened with vices, but is utterly devoid of all good."[106] Protestants sometimes
used the word "saint" to refer to the elect of God, but they had no saints in the
Catholic sense; that is, they denied that anyone could ever reach moral and spiritual perfection in this life, embody supernatural phenomena, work miracles, or
intercede for the living in the next life from their perch in heaven. Protestant
saints lived out their call on earth without otherworldly encounters or miraculous feats. Moreover, they ceased to be links with the numinous and were not to
be venerated or approached as intercessors.

To restrict the supernatural to heaven and the ancient past in this manner was to change the very essence of the Christian religion as it had been lived
for the previous fifteen centuries. Religion was no longer a dimension of life in
which one could encounter the miraculous and mystical—as documented in the
New Testament and all the hagiographies of the previous millennium and a
half—but rather a way of seeking and finding inner and outer conformity to
the Word and will of God. Religion was still definitely focused on a supernatural
reality, but that reality was manifest on earth in a much less intense, direct, or
otherworldly way than in Catholicism. So, as Protestantism made the laws of
nature more fixed and less malleable in the hands of God, religion itself became
something much more natural and more this-worldly. Consequently, it is no great
surprise that by the late seventeenth century, miracles began to be ascribed to
natural causes rather than supernatural intervention in the laws of nature. An
anonymous English author, for instance, published a pamphlet in 1683 in which
he argued that no miracle—not even those recorded in the Bible—had ever
contradicted the laws of nature.[107] And he was not alone in thinking this way.
Nehemiah Grew, a botanist, made the same argument, and so did Edmund Hal-
ley, the famed astronomer after whom the world's best-known comet is named.
Clerics, too, joined this assault on supernatural causes, putting a theological
spin on it. The Anglican Thomas Sprat (1635–1713), bishop of Rochester, proposed that Christianity should be based on reason rather than emotion. Consequently, he also suggested that since God had established the laws of nature
and every event had natural causes, the Christian religion therefore had no
need for the kinds of "extraordinary testimonies from Heaven" favored by "enthusiasts who pollute . . . religion with their own passions."[108]

This is not to say, however, that Protestant attitudes toward the miraculous have ever remained fixed. The miraculous has wound its way back into Prot-

estant piety in various ways and in differing degrees over the past four centuries, especially during the twentieth century. We can catch a glimpse of the subtle changes that began to take place in the eighteenth century, especially in the English colonies of North America, during the spiritual revival known as the Great Awakening. Intense emotional and physical reactions bordering on mystical ecstasy were a distinguishing feature of the fervor generated by this awakening. The wife of Jonathan Edwards, one of the leading lights of the Great Awakening, was among those deeply affected in a physical way by her religious experiences. Sarah Pierpont Edwards wrote a detailed description of an intense period of religious ecstasies she experienced in early 1742. This document, recently discovered, brims over with kinesthetics—agitations, convulsions, fainting, intense elation.[109] And the way she writes about these ecstasies brings her closer to the language found in Catholic mystics than to that of Calvin's *Institutes.* Take this elocution, for instance: "I Knew that what the foretaste of Glory I then had had in my soul came from him & that I certainly should Go to him & should as it were drop into the divine being & be swallowed up in him."[110] Some passages even hint at levitation, at least figuratively. Four of these are startling: "I could not help as it were flying out of my chair without being held down"; "Some verses which still Kept my Body in an Exceeding Agitation Constantly endeavouring as it were to leap & fly"; "My soul was so Exceedingly drawn after God & Heaven that I hoped out of my Chair, I seemed soul & body as it were to be drawn up from the Earth towards Heaven it seemd to me I must naturally & necessarily ascend thither"; "It so exceedingly moved me that I could not avoid Jumping & as it were flying Round the Pew with Exultation of soul."[111]

Obviously, these expressions of ecstatic bliss only make oblique metaphorical references to levitation, but they nonetheless employ language one would not expect to find in a Calvinist. They also clearly indicate that by the eighteenth century the vast gulf created between Catholic and Protestant piety two centuries earlier by the first and second generations of magisterial Reformers was being bridged, at least in some corners of New England.

Miracles as Polemic

But even before such bridging took place, Protestants had never made miracles disappear altogether. Not at all. As Calvin said, Satan had his own miracles, and those would not go away. Helen Parish has observed: "The miracles of the medieval Church were not abandoned, but rather turned into polemical weapons that could be used to condemn Catholicism as a faith which was founded upon deceit, manipulation, and credulity. Miracles that had provided the foundation for the cult of the saints were recast as the tools of its destruction."[112] In an additional polemical maneuver, Protestants went beyond portraying Catholic miracles as products of "deceit, manipulation, and credulity" by giving them a diabolical stench as well. And by arguing that the miracles claimed by the Catholic Church were demonic, Protestants added a very potent weapon to their polemical arsenal: Could any church in which the devil works so freely and constantly really be the true church?

If Protestants could turn the miraculous into polemic, so could Catholics, for the conceptual and polemical mayhem flowed in two directions, naturally and easily. Of the many Catholic polemicists who argued that miracles were an essential proof of the genuine divine origin of the one true church, Thomas More stands out, principally because of the printed debate in which he engaged the English Protestant William Tyndale in the years 1529–1532. The first salvo in this heated exchange was contained in More's "A Dialogue concerning Heresies," which Tyndale replied to in his "Answer to Sir Thomas More's Dialogue," which, in turn, prompted More to write a blistering "Confutation of Tyndale's Answer." More's arguments for the necessity of miracles hinged on their role as proof of divine power and of its presence in the true church. Arguing that God "hath from the beginning joined His Word with wonderful works," More insisted that God still "causeth His church to do miracles still in every age." Pushing his argument further, More added that miracles were the surest proof of the church's divine origin, confirming time and time again "that the doctrine of the same church is revealed and taught unto it by the Spirit of God."[113] Conversely, the lack of miracles among Protestants proved beyond a shadow of a doubt that the only "true" thing about their bickering newfangled churches was their demonic origin.

More was far from alone. Many Catholic hagiographers sharpened the polemical edge of miracles too, even in countries where Protestants were barely a threat, such as Spain. The Dominican theologian Luis de Granada (1504–1588), for one, argued that the continuity of the miraculous in the Catholic Church was proof that it was still under the same divine protection that had assisted all of God's people in the Bible and in Christian history: "It is the same God at work now as then," he said. "One should not think it incredible that He should do now what He did back then."[114]

Not surprisingly, one holy woman whose many miracles provided hagiographers with a golden opportunity to polish, sharpen, and push the argument made by Thomas More and Luis de Granada was none other than Teresa of Avila, that levitator who is the subject of chapter 2. One of her biographers, Diego de Yepes (1530–1616), made no effort to conceal his delight over Teresa's usefulness in anti-Protestant polemics, boasting that she was "an impressive weapon in God's hands."[115] Elaborating on this image, Yepes switched to another metaphor, saying, "It should cause ceaseless admiration to see the birth of a new resplendent sun during these miserable times, in these most wretched centuries during which the darkness of heresy and other sins have seemed intent on blotting out the light of the Church."[116] Leaving metaphors behind, Yepes then moved in for the kill, bluntly: "This, too was planned by God that at almost the same time that the wicked Luther began to plot his lies and deceptions, and to concoct the poison with which he would later kill so many, God should be forming this sainted woman so she could serve as an antidote to his poison, so that whatever was withdrawn from God on one side by Luther should be gathered and collected on another side by her."[117]

Yepes was in good company, as one might expect. In sermons preached throughout Spain on the occasion of Teresa's beatification, this same theme came up several times. Juan de Herrera, a Jesuit, exclaimed that Teresa had crushed Luther's head with the Rock of Christ. Similarly, Juan Gonzalez, a Dominican, crowed that Teresa had effectively won the war against Protestants who scoffed at miracles and profaned sacred spaces and holy objects.[118] In 1588, a mere eight years after her death, the editor of her collected works, Luis de León, wrote in his preface to that massive project: "God willed at this time—when it seems that the devil is triumphant among the throng of infidels who follow him, and in the obstinacy of so many heretical nations who take his side . . . to disgrace and ridicule him by putting before him not some valiant and learned man, but a lone poor woman, to sound the challenge and raise the battle flag, and to openly beget people who can trample, humble, and defeat him."[119]

What are we to make of all this boasting and Protestant bashing, and of the place of the miraculous in it? What light might this polemical melee shed on the history of levitation and especially about its place in early modern Western culture? And what about the issue of credulity and skepticism? What role, if any, did these binary epistemological opposites play in this heated debate on miracles?

It has been argued that belief in miracles was one of the essential components of baroque Catholicism, especially in Spain. As Julio Caro Baroja put it,
"The 'will to miracle'" ruled the day." In hagiography and sermons, miracle was
essential; disbelief an improbable and largely invisible enemy. The few Catholic
clerics who tried to downplay miracles usually met with resistance. Fray Hor-
tensio Félix Paravicino, a preacher famous enough in his day to merit a portrait
by El Greco, found his congregation most unreceptive at the church of San Salvador in Madrid when he told them that miracles might have been important
for the early church but were no longer appropriate for the present.[120]

Official theology and popular piety moved in tandem, propelled by faith
in miracle and guided by hagiography. In this mentality or "social imaginary,"
the natural order was constantly subverted or invaded by the supernatural. The
laws of the physical world were malleable, subject to the supernatural power of
God and his saints. It was commonly believed that supernatural irruptions constantly upended the laws of nature. "Reality" was defined according to such an
understanding: matter and flesh seemed but a gossamer veil that frequently revealed the brilliance of a stronger, brighter force. This was a worldview constructed on faith rather than reason, a perpetual motion machine fueled by
miracles.[121]

Nonetheless, the arguments against skepticism raised by some of those
who wrote about Teresa suggest that not all Catholics were equally ready to believe in the miraculous dimension of her death and afterlife. After publishing his
first edition of Teresa's works, Luis de León found it necessary to write an "apol-
ogy," to be included in subsequent editions, in which he openly challenged doubters and skeptics and in which he stated: "You do not want to believe? Go ahead
and doubt, you are free; you are lord and master of your own judgment; no one is
forcing you; go ahead, then, be skeptical, be know-it-alls, let there be as many of
you unbelievers as you want."[122] Another of Teresa's hagiographers, the Jesuit Francisco de Ribera, also apparently suspected that his testimony might be doubted
and proffered the same disdainful advice when dealing with the subject of Teresa's postmortem miracles: "There will be some who shall ask me why they should
believe what I relate in this chapter, because all of these accounts come only from
certain people who were quite fond of la Madre [Teresa] and could have imagined
it all in order to fulfill their wishes. To these I reply: believe only as much as you
want to believe; I cannot push you any further, and I have no desire to do so
anyway."[123] This literature was not aimed at skeptics but at believers. Obviously,

Ribera was willing to entertain the possibility of doubters picking up his book, but the subject made him bristle impatiently.

In contrast, Teresa's confessor Jerónimo de Gracián seems to have been keenly aware of the shadow of doubt that lurked among the learned, perhaps more attentively than Ribera, and he used this as an artifice in a dialogue he wrote about Teresa's death, in which he sought to contrast belief and unbelief. One of the characters in this text, named Anastasio, personifies skepticism. Acting as a gadfly to two unskeptical characters who are eager to believe in miracles and apparitions, Anastasio constantly tries to cast doubt on their assumptions, usually ascribing such phenomena to natural processes. Anastasio does not disagree that there are different kinds of apparitions but maintains that they are really figments of the imagination. Illness, melancholy, bad humors, and the "thick vapors that rise from the heart to the brain" often produce some of the visions that are mistaken for apparitions. Fantasy and wish fulfillment, combined with overactive imaginations, he argues, are the real cause of many reported apparitions.[124]

And it was not only apparitions that could be explained away: doubt could also be cast on all the other miracles associated with Teresa, including her levitations. "In our ignorance of the way in which many natural things work, they seem miraculous to us," says Anastasio. There could be some natural cause for the fact that Teresa's corpse simply refuses to decompose, for the bodies of some obviously unholy people, such as Cicero's daughter, a pagan, had also remained uncorrupted. Sick people "cured" with relics might have been recovering naturally when the relics were taken to them. Loud knocking noises heard in the night might be caused by unknown natural causes or by overheated imaginations. In this way, says Anastasio, "Miracles are made from nothing." Finally, he raises the same argument leveled against Catholic miracles by Reformed Protestants: they occurred only in the Apostolic Age when they were needed to lend credibility to the Gospel, but they are no longer necessary and therefore never happen anymore.[125] As one might expect, despite its parroting of skeptical arguments, this text is not a primer on unbelief. Gracián employs Anastasio's arguments as a foil. Ultimately, the other two characters Cirilo and Eusebio prevail by raising doubts of their own about Anastasio's logic, making faith and credulity seem more acceptable than disbelief.[126]

Diego de Yepes did not seem too worried about skepticism. On the contrary, he asserted that those who thought that God no longer worked miracles could be easily proved wrong by Teresa's miracles. And he had two arguments against those few who might have doubted Teresa's holiness or ascribed her miracles to the devil. Diabolical causation was out of the question, he said, because the devil would never want to credit and honor any saint and also because it would be impossible for the devil to have sufficient power to delude so many devout, holy, and respectable witnesses.[127]

The potentially self-destructive circularity of these arguments against skepticism suggests that Teresa's hagiographers were painfully aware of the skepticism with which miracle accounts could be met, even by Catholics, but ultimately, they were more interested in bolstering the faith of believers than in changing the minds of skeptics. Ribera, Yepes, Gracián, and Luis de León thought that the evidence they presented could convince any "dispassionate" reader. Reports of Teresa's miracles had to be true because they conformed to hagiographic tradition; anyone who chose to doubt these reports or who thought them to be delusions would also have to disbelieve "many similar things, which fill the histories of ancient and modern saints." This argument was as ancient as the hagiographies used in its construction and as simple as a perfect circle.[128]

Ultimately, then, Catholic polemics that employed miracles and hagiographies could lead polemicists to make a vertiginous wager of the sort made by Luis de León. If one did not believe in the wonders effected by God through Teresa, he huffed, then one would have to doubt it possible for God to work any miracles at all in human history. "Out with revelations, then!" he railed against Catholic skeptics and Bible-thumping, miracle-denying Protestants. "Let us not believe in visions or read about them!"[129] Suspecting that few Protestants, if any, would be willing to carry their skepticism about miracles to its logical conclusion and discard the Bible or that Catholics would turn into atheists, infidels, or pagans, these polemicists wagered that the credibility of Christianity itself depended on belief in the continuity of God's power to perform miracles. Their test case was Teresa, but the scope of their argument was much larger. If one was ready to doubt the truth of Teresa's miracles—including her levitations— then one would also have to concede that the truthfulness of the Christian faith itself was questionable.

Whether or not Teresa would have welcomed knowing that accounts of her levitations could be invested with such a fervid polemical edge is immaterial. Those accounts are among the most surprising in Christian history, as well as in the history of the impossible, and they deserve close scrutiny. Saint Teresa of Avila, perhaps the best-known levitator of her day, reflected and intensified an inflationary spiral in levitations in unique ways. First, she not only wrote about her own levitations but also dissected the miracle from within, giving it a quirky empirical sense of reality, as first-person testimony. Second, the number of external eyewitness testimonies concerning her levitations was so great, and their descriptions so detailed, as to appear mundane, despite their otherworldliness. Moreover, Teresa did not just experience levitation but objected to it, complaining to God and convincing Him to banish it from her life. To fully understand what holy levitation was *supposed to be,* then, one must turn to Saint Teresa.

2. Saint Teresa of Avila, Reluctant Aethrobat

The holy Mother was very humble, and she dearly wished not to be considered
a saint, so she constantly begged me and her other daughters to pull down hard
on her vestments whenever we saw her rising into the air; and whenever she'd
begin to feel that the Lord wanted to elevate her, she'd grab on to floor mats
and the grilles in the choir. At the very same instant, she'd also beg Our
Lord to stop bestowing such favors on her from now on, and one day
she eventually attained this from Our Lord.

One of the best-known levitators of the early modern age, and one of the most
unwilling, is Saint Teresa of Avila. Her resistance to levitation, reflected in the
account above,[1] might seem peculiar at first glance. But in many ways, she is
a quintessential levitator who reflects patterns of holiness set in Christian
hagiography and, in turn, sets patterns for those who follow in her wake. Her
uniqueness is undeniable, too, for many reasons. Three of these are her earthy
approach to things divine, her unease with absolute precision, and her disarm-
ing honesty. For instance, consider her take on mystical terminology: "I would
like, with the help of God, to be able to describe the difference between union
(*unión*) and rapture (*arrobamiento*), or elevation, (*elevamiento*) or what they call
flight of the spirit (*vuelo de espíritu*), or ravishment (*arrebatamiento*)—which are
all really one. I mean that all these different names refer to the same thing, which
is also called ecstasy (*éstasi*)."[2]

So she says in her autobiography, struggling for precision yet dismissing
it, fully aware that inquisitors would be scrutinizing her every word to determine whether her extraordinary trances were of divine origin. Ordered by her
superiors to write about her own life, especially her ecstasies and visions   and

her levitations—Teresa had no choice but to put quill to paper and hope for the best. Given the fact that many in Ávila and beyond were alarmed by her ecstasies and opposed to her reform of the Carmelite order, Teresa was closely scrutinized.[3] Her autobiography, then, was as much a test of her orthodoxy as a testimony of her holiness.[4] Teresa was forced to write her *Vida* (*Life*) because various authorities in the Carmelite order and the Catholic Church wanted to examine her prayer life and her mystical claims in detail.

In Teresa's case, as in many others like hers, raptures, ravishments, and ecstasies occurred at unpredictable times and always had some observable trance-like aspect to them. Since many of these trances produced physical changes in her appearance while she was in the company of other nuns, or of visitors, these trances could not be ignored, and reports of her extraordinary altered states began to circulate rapidly in monastic, clerical, and lay circles throughout Spain and beyond. Nonetheless, gaining a reputation as a mystic or a saint—especially one who falls into trance-like states, or floats in the air miraculously, or claims to commune with God—was somewhat perilous in mid-sixteenth-century Spain, where suspicions of heresy, fraud, or demonic activity ran high.

Certain questions had to be asked by ecclesiastical authorities of anyone who claimed to have experiences such as Teresa's, and these questions were deemed especially necessary in the case of women, for it was widely believed that females were weaker, less intelligent, and less psychologically and emotionally stable than males and much less trustworthy when it came to any claim of supernatural encounters. The great theologian and conciliarist Jean Gerson certainly thought so.[5] And so did the apocalyptic Florentine reformer Girolamo Savonarola and the Spanish cleric Diego Perez de Valdivia.[6] Questions of various sorts arose under this cloud of suspicion. Was Teresa genuinely engaging with the divine, or was she a fraud? Was she "inventing the sacred," a charge that the Inquisition made in cases of fraudulent claims to mystical experience?[7] Could it be that her experiences involved the devil rather than God? Did her behavior in any way contradict or challenge authority? Was her behavior appropriately holy? What kinds of revelations was she claiming? Were her messages orthodox or heretical? Was she in any way linked to any heresy? Had she challenged authority in any way? Was she genuinely holy? Teresa's *Vida* was an attempt to answer all these questions as clearly as possible.

And in this remarkable text, which was really a judicial document, more a forced confession than an autobiography,[8] Teresa had no choice but to confirm what others had already reported numerous times: that she sometimes rose into the air during her ecstasies and that these levitations were not just frequent but also spectacular—and witnessed by many. Some eyewitnesses would later testify under oath that the raptures they saw were so constant and numerous that they "couldn't even dare to count them."[9] And the distraction caused by her raptures was also evident. "Ordinarily, she was so elevated and absorbed in God, and so beside herself," said one of her hagiographers, "that having to handle daily tasks, including writing, was sheer torment for her."[10] Given the fact that eyewitness accounts of her levitations had spread far and wide and that some of these reports were very graphic and even told of efforts to restrain her or pull her down, Teresa had no choice but to dwell on these details in her *Vida,* as in this description of one of her arrobamientos, or raptures, during which she suddenly rose up into the air uncontrollably:

> Once, when we were together in choir, and about to take communion, and I was on my knees, it caused me the greatest anguish, because it seemed to me a most extraordinary thing that would cause people to fuss over it intensely; so, I ordered the nuns not to speak of it. . . . On other occasions, when I have felt that the Lord was about to do this to me again, I have lain on the ground and the sisters have strained to hold down my body, but the rapture has been observed, anyway, as once happened during a sermon, on our patronal festival, when some great ladies were present.[11]

Her analysis of this phenomenon is a cautious interweaving of opinions, questions, and statements of fact, in a voice that has both the ring of authority and a measure of deference. And throughout her texts, her terminology is not always consistent, especially in the case of arrobamiento and arrebatamiento, which sometimes seem to be interchangeable terms.[12] Adding to the lack of clarity in her terminology, Teresa has no specific word for distinguishing her levitations from the states of high ecstasy in which they occur. Although Teresa's levitations are clearly restricted to the most intense ecstasies she reaches in the top two levels (or "mansions") in her text *Libro de las Moradas* (*The Interior Castle*), those ecstasies may or may *not* include levitations. The levitations are an additional physical effect, apparently nonessential, and she has no name for them.

But while her terminology can be fuzzy, her descriptions of her levitations are arguably the most detailed first-person accounts on record, much more so than those provided by any other medieval or early modern Christian mystic.

For instance, in attempting to differentiate between "rapture" (arrobamiento) and "union" (unión) in her autobiography, she explains that what she has experienced in levitations is uncontrollable, precisely because levitation is a divine event and totally beyond her willpower or physical strength. "When I tried to resist these raptures, it seemed to me that I was being lifted up by a force beneath my feet so powerful that I know nothing to which I can compare it, for it came with a much greater intensity than any other spiritual experience and I felt as if I were being torn to shreds, for it is a mighty struggle."[13]

Even more remarkable than the details she provides is her attitude toward her levitations, which she detested and which she begged God to remove from her life. To better understand her unique place in the Christian mystical tradition and in the history of levitation, one must first come to terms with the context in which her story unfolded.

Teresa's Life

Teresa de Ahumada y Cepeda (1515–1582) became a Carmelite nun in her teens, at the Convent of the Incarnation in her native Ávila, a walled city in Old Castile. Her religious name was Teresa de Jesús, but in the English-speaking world she is best known as Teresa of Avila (without an accent on the *A*). During her twenties she was plagued by an illness no doctor could properly diagnose or cure. Brought to death's door, literally, she was taken for dead and readied for burial but regained consciousness only a few hours before being lowered into her grave. Teresa remained paralyzed afterward for quite some time and eventually recovered, albeit slowly and painfully. A lukewarm nun for many years after returning to her convent—according to her own disparaging estimation—Teresa began to experience visions and raptures in her forties, and as these intensified quickly and dramatically, she naturally came under suspicion of being either demonically influenced or a brazen fraud. At the same time, however, many around her were convinced that her experiences were genuinely divine in origin. Consequently, her superiors ordered her to write a detailed account of her life and her ecstasies, under the watchful eye of the Inquisition. That text, which came to be known as her *Vida*, or "autobiography," is an attempt to convince everyone that her remarkable experiences are truly supernatural. And an essential part of the narrative is Teresa's constant emphasis on her own humility and on the pain and embarrassment caused by the ecstasies she experienced in public, or which became public knowledge, especially those ecstasies in which she levitated.

Proving her humility was essential, for nothing could peg an ecstatic nun as a brazen fraud more convincingly than the perception that she might be calling attention to herself or trying to pass herself off as exceptionally holy or spiritually gifted. Since absolute humility was assumed to be inseparable from genuine holiness and one of its chief characteristics, all levitating nuns were trapped in a dilemma, for levitation attracts attention, naturally, and excess attention could easily lead to disaster, or at least to close scrutiny of the sort received by Teresa, which could be a heavy burden to bear, not just for a nun but for the Catholic Church as a whole. Investigations such as the one launched in Teresa's case could end badly, and sometimes did so spectacularly, as in the case of the Dominican nun María de la Visitación, a highly revered mystic similar to Teresa, whose stigmata, levitations, ecstasies, and miracles—accepted and revered for many years by many prominent churchmen as genuinely divine in origin—were eventually declared to be nothing more than "trickery and deceit."[14]

Teresa was painfully aware of the dangers of adulation and the need for humility and spoke openly about her fears: "I was greatly tormented—and still am, even now—to see so much fuss made over me, and so many good things said about me, especially by important people. This has made me suffer a great deal, and still does. . . . And when I thought about how these favors granted to me by the Lord became public knowledge, my torment was so excessive that it greatly disturbed my soul. And this went as far as making me wish, whenever I thought about it, that I could be buried alive."[15]

Such intense fear was not only driven by Teresa's own awareness of the way in which any nun's ecstasies could be her undoing. This fear was also instilled in her by her confessors and spiritual directors, who pressured her to curb her raptures and warned her constantly about the dangers she faced as an ecstatic nun. Speaking in the third person in her *Interior Castle,* Teresa complains: "She is not hurt by what people say about her except when her own confessor blames her, as though she could prevent these raptures. She does nothing but beg everyone to pray for her and beseech His Majesty to lead her by another road, as she is advised to do, since the road she is on is very dangerous."[16] This was not her only problem. An additional danger was far worse than adulation: that of demonic influence.

Belief in the devil's ability to pass himself off as an "angel of light" or even as Jesus Christ Himself was an ancient Christian tenet, deeply embedded in monastic culture. This was an unquestioned assumption, linked to

Figure 15. Saint Teresa's visions of Christ were interpreted by some of her confessors as demonic illusions.

another: a firm belief that the devil always assailed those who aimed for holiness and closeness to God. In Teresa's case, as soon as she began to have visions and other mystical ravishments, her confessors suspected the worst and warned her that her experiences were demonic in origin.[17] As Teresa dutifully confessed that Christ kept appearing to her (fig. 15), the confessors grew increasingly alarmed—and perhaps also peeved—and ordered her to greet her visions of Christ with an obscene hand gesture known as "giving the fig," an equivalent of today's "giving the finger." Dealing with the devil on his own level with obscenities and insults was fairly common advice in monastic culture, as common as the belief that the devil could easily deceive anyone. Teresa dutifully obeyed, despite the pain it caused her to greet Christ in such an offensive way.[18] Years later, in 1622, in his bull of canonization for Teresa, Pope Gregory XV would emphasize the value placed on such obedience: "She was wont to say that she might be deceived in discerning visions and revelations, but could not be in obeying superiors."[19]

Teresa's writing paid off, for her autobiographical account convinced those who scrutinized the text that she was neither a fraud nor a demoniac, thus giving

Figure 16. Saint Teresa claimed she had become quite an expert at driving away the many demons who constantly tormented her. In this image she is vanquishing them with a cross.

her the freedom to write several other extraordinary texts and to establish a new reformed branch of the Carmelite order. Nonetheless, the detailed mystical content of her autobiography was considered so potentially open to misinterpretation that the Inquisition ordered all but one manuscript copy destroyed and then kept what it believed to be the sole surviving text under lock and key for the rest of Teresa's life. And it was not until 1588, six years after her death, that the text was eventually edited and published, in large measure because post-mortem miracles were proving her holiness to be genuine. Yet, despite the Inquisition's positive verdict and the fact that Teresa was credited with miracles and fast-tracked to canonization soon after dying, the Inquisition kept receiving denunciations from some clerics—mostly from the Dominican order—who accused Teresa of heresy and called for the condemnation and destruction of all her printed texts. It was not until 1619, when she was beatified, that such accusations stopped.[20]

By then, ambivalence about her visions, raptures, and levitations had come to seem wrong. Doubt had been triumphantly pushed aside by her own texts, as well as by popular acclaim. Teresa had become a levitating demonslayer and much more of a threat to the devil than any obscene gesture that meek little nuns might flash at him and at the fake visions he used in his attempts to fool them (fig. 16). Luis de León, the editor of her collected works, was well aware of this and of the need to shout it out: "God willed at this time—when it seems that the devil is triumphant among the throng of infidels who follow him, and in the obstinacy of so many heretical nations who take his side . . . to disgrace and ridicule him by putting before him not some valiant and learned man, but a lone poor woman, to sound the challenge and raise the battle flag, and to openly beget people who can trample, humble, and defeat him."[21]

Teresa's Supernatural Encounters

Teresa's raptures and levitations are unique for several reasons, three of which are most significant. First, no other Christian levitator has provided as full a first-person account or described and analyzed the experience in as much detail as Teresa. Second, no other levitator has complained as often and as loudly about levitating as Teresa. And third, few other levitators have brought about an end to levitations as suddenly and dramatically as Teresa. Obviously, her detailed analysis of her own levitations cannot be taken as empirical "proof" of the reality of her levitations, but they do provide an exceptionally clear window into her perceptions, or at least into how she wanted others to understand the phenomenon. And as of yet, no other Christian levitator has ever surpassed Teresa on this account.

When it comes to her description and analysis of her raptures, trances, and levitations, the bulk of it—the mother lode, so to speak—can be found in chapter 20 of her autobiography, which is primarily an account of her attainment of the highest stages of mystical ecstasy. Sorting out her descriptions of various ecstasies is challenging, for it requires grappling with her own terminology and her understanding of the various levels of supernatural encounters with the divine, as well as with her conception of the relation between the natural and the supernatural, the physical and the spiritual, and the divine and the human. Moreover, one must come to terms with her assumptions about the relation between body, mind, and soul, in addition to flesh and spirit and earth and heaven, all of which rely on terms drawn from scholastic and mystical theology and which she never employs in the same precise manner as the *letrados,* those educated male clerics to whom she always deferred.

Teresa's chief assumption, which undergirds her mystical claims, is that human beings can have intimate encounters with the divine and that these involve the whole person and include both the physical and spiritual components: soul, body, mind, and spirit and all the "faculties"—that is, the intellect, the will, and all seven senses. A correlate assumption of hers is that these encounters bridge two dimensions: the heavenly and the earthly, sometimes spoken of as the divine and the created or the spiritual and the material or the eternal and the temporal. This bridging of dimensions, in turn, is assumed to entail— unquestioningly—a highly paradoxical coincidence of opposites beyond normal human cognition, a transcending of binary oppositions in which contradictions dissolve and in which emotional and physical or spiritual and physical opposites such as pain and bliss, logic and emotion, embodiment and disembodiment, materiality and spirituality, and creature and creator become perfectly and blissfully compatible.

And it is this matrix of unquestioned assumptions about what is ultimately real and what is ultimately possible for humans to achieve that governs Teresa's attempts to explain her experiences, all of which, as she constantly reminds her readers, are ineffable and beyond description. Quite often, human language fails, but the failure itself gets a point across, as in her attempt to explain what happens in the highest levels of mystical rapture: "The soul is often engulfed— or, better said—the Lord engulfs it in Himself."[22] This claim is as significant as it is vague, and so is the even vaguer claim that mystical union leads to a "total transformation of the soul in God."[23]

Chapter 20 of Teresa's autobiography deals with these highest levels of rapture, which correspond to the two highest of the seven levels that she identifies in *The Interior Castle,* which she wrote immediately after completing the autobiography, at the urging of many of her fellow nuns and superiors. At this summit of the mystical life, Teresa claims, one begins to shuttle back and forth between earth and heaven, and in all this shuttling the body and the soul take part but are affected in different ways.

In her *Vida* Teresa tends to use the term "arrobamiento," or rapture, for the experiences that take her into the heavenly realm of the divine. Sometimes, however, she also uses "arrebatamiento," or ravishment, for such experiences or suggests that arrebatamiento is in fact a kind of arrobamiento, as she does when she says, "While I was reciting a hymn, there came to me an *arrebatamiento* so sudden that nearly took me out of myself: something I could not doubt, for it was so clear. This was the first time that the Lord had granted me the favor of any kind of *arrobamiento*."[24] Yet in another text written in 1576, eleven years after her *Vida*, Teresa makes a distinction that she did not apply consistently in the *Vida*, asserting that arrebatamientos overtake the mystic more quickly and forcefully: "The difference between *arrobamiento* and *arrebatamiento* is this: In an *arrobamiento* one loses use of one's senses slowly, dying in small increments to external things, step by step; but an *arrebatamiento* arrives suddenly in the innermost recess of the soul without any warning from His Majesty and with such a tremendous speed that it seems as if the soul is rapt to a superior level and one feels as if it is leaving one's body."[25]

In her *Interior Castle*, written in 1577, Teresa adds more uncertainty to her terminology, saying that "there is another kind of *arrobamiento* which I call '*vuelo de espíritu*' (flight of the spirit)—and although these are all the same thing, what they make you feel inside is very different." As she explains it, what makes a *vuelo* feel different is the speed at which it overtakes her, which is much faster and more frightening than that of any other rapture or ravishment.[26]

The Physical Phenomena of Rapture

Regardless of the term used, Teresa makes it clear that whether one levitates or not during an arrobamiento, the body is often affected intensely, even violently, primarily through sense deprivation and paralysis and a lapse into a trance-like state accompanied by physical aftereffects that linger for a while. "Let us now return to raptures (*arrobamientos*), and to their most common traits. I can attest that after a rapture my body often felt so light that it seemed to weigh nothing at all: and sometimes this was so overwhelming that I could hardly tell if my feet were touching the ground. For, during the entire rapture, the body remains as if dead and unable to do anything itself." And in whichever way it was positioned when seized by the rapture, that is how the body stays: whether standing, or sitting, or with the hands open or clasped.[27]

This state of suspended animation brings the body close to death and takes quite a toll on it. In one passage, Teresa says that during these raptures one can feel "like someone who is being strangled, with a rope around their neck, still struggling to catch a breath."[28] Tellingly, Teresa interprets this near-death experience as a sundering of body and soul that is resisted by the human self and which pits lower and higher parts of the self against each other. "What cries out 'help me breathe' at such moments," she says, "is the desire that body and soul have for not being separated, and by saying it, and complaining, and distracting itself, the soul seeks a way to live that is very contrary to the will of the spirit, or of its own higher part, which would prefer not to flee from this suffering."[29]

Again and again, Teresa stresses the physical dimension of her raptures, probably because it was the visibly alarming way her body behaved that drew attention to her mystical experiences. She needed to explain what others were witnessing as something inherently spiritual rather than any of the awful alternatives: demonic fits, mere fakery, mental illness, or a physical malady. Based on her own descriptions of her body's responses to rapture, others could easily mistake such reactions—which would instantly paralyze her and leave her as rigid and insensate as a marble statue--for mere cataleptic seizures:[30] "The hands get freezing cold and sometimes stretched out stiffly like pieces of wood, and the body stays in whatever position it is when the rapture hits, be it standing or kneeling . . . and it seems as if the soul has forgotten to animate the body."[31]

Teresa also claims that all sensory input ceases to function, as if the connection between body and soul is temporarily sundered. At the highest point of rapture, she says, "one will neither see, nor hear, nor perceive," and this is because the soul is then so "closely united with God" that "none of the soul's faculties are able to perceive or know what is taking place."[32] Even if the eyes remain open, she adds, "one neither perceives nor notices what one sees."[33] And in *The Interior Castle,* she comments that to be in such a state requires courage "because the soul truly feels that it is leaving the body when it sees the senses leaving it and it does not know why they are going away."[34] Elsewhere, she also highlights the effects of this near-death experience on the body, not only while the event is unfolding but also afterward: "Occasionally, I come close to losing my pulse altogether, according to those of my sisters who have sometimes found me like this . . . with my ankles disjointed, and my hands so stiff that sometimes I cannot even clasp them together. Until the next day my wrists and my body will continue to hurt, as if my joints had been torn asunder."[35]

These aftereffects are described as profound. "After one regains consciousness, if the rapture has been intense, the faculties might remain absorbed for a day or two, or three, as if in a stupor, so that one seems not to be oneself."[36] Once again in trying to describe what she has experienced repeatedly and how she has felt after any of these bodily raptures, Teresa is at a loss for words. "This favor also leaves a strange detachment (*desasimiento*), the nature of which I'm unable to describe, but I think I can say it differs somewhat from that produced by purely spiritual favors, I mean; for, although those cause a total detachment of spirit, in this favor it seems that the Lord wants it to be shared by the body itself, and it causes one to experience a new estrangement from earthly things, which makes life much more vexing. Afterwards it produces a distress (*pena*) which we cannot ourselves bring about or cast away once it has come. I would like very much to explain this great distress, but I do not think I can possibly do so. If I could say something more about this, I would." Stressing the raw physicality of these experiences alongside their exalted spiritual nature—and again flummoxed by the inadequacy of human language—Teresa also dwells repeatedly on the paradoxical intertwining of pain and bliss, both bodily and spiritual. "These raptures seem like the very threshold of death," she avers, "but the suffering they cause brings such joy with it that I do not know of anything comparable." Consequently, she adds, these raptures are "a violent, delectable martyrdom."[37] Elsewhere, Teresa confesses that during those days when her arrobamientos were constant, she went about "as if stupefied" (*embovada*) and adds: "I did not want to see or speak with anyone, but only to hug my pain, which caused me greater bliss than can be found in the whole of creation."[38]

Resisting the Irresistible Divine Gift

As a paradox within a paradox, Teresa emphasized a strong ambivalence toward her blissful yet painful arrobamientos and arrebatamientos, for they were something to enjoy and fear simultaneously, as well as something one could both crave and detest. A key worry for Teresa was that of agency: Was she willingly bringing these raptures on herself, out of self-indulgence and pride, or was God showering her with irresistible favors? Were these raptures something she could effect at will or control, or were they wholly uncontrollable and irresistible, of divine origin? Not only were such questions being asked by her confessors and superiors, but for quite some time after her raptures began, some of these male clerics commanded her to suppress or resist them. And one of the chief purposes of her autobiographical narrative was to address this question as precisely and fully as possible.

The issue of irresistibility being so crucial, then, forced Teresa to dwell on this subject and to describe the overpowering nature of her arrobamientos—including those that included levitations—in some detail. Moreover, Teresa's handling of this issue is inseparable from her concerns about others witnessing her trances and levitations and about the possible negative repercussions of all the adulation that these phenomena could generate. Consequently, convincing

God that He should stop showering her with physical raptures and, in turn, convincing her confessors and superiors that she was doing her utmost to persuade God of the uselessness and dangerousness of her levitations were one and the same for Teresa.

One way of stressing the irresistible nature of her raptures was for Teresa to emphasize their suddenness and unpredictability, as well as their overpowering force. Relying on metaphor, as usual, Teresa crafted a stunning and very postmedieval description of what it felt like to go into raptures, including those that involved levitations: "When all is said and done, I don't know what I'm saying; but the truth is that, as quickly as a bullet leaves a gun when the trigger is pulled, there begins within the soul a flight—I don't know what else to name it—which, although it is noiseless, is so clearly a movement that it cannot possibly be an illusion."[39] Emphasizing that this "flight" of the soul is no mere fancy or wish-fulfilling illusion (*antojo*), Teresa highlights the vehemence and suddenness of the event, in addition to the fact that what is going on is not something physical but rather spiritual, despite whatever physicality might be involved or whichever bodily phenomena might be witnessed. Teresa also indicates that the event involves an upward motion, a flight. This point is a significant one, especially for the issue of levitation. Over and over, Teresa stresses the futility of resistance alongside references to upward motion, flight, and utter helplessness, as in this passage: "With *arrobamiento,* as a rule, there is no possibility of resisting: almost always, it comes like a powerful and swift force, without any forewarning to your mind, and you are left helpless; you see and feel this cloud, or this mighty eagle, rising and bearing you up with it on its wings. And I say that you then realize and see that you are being carried away, not knowing where."[40]

Discerning when Teresa is speaking of the spiritual effects of rapture rather than the physical ones is often difficult, if not impossible. But in some passages she explains that trying to resist arrobamientos takes intense physical effort, further reinforcing her claim that body and soul share in these events with equal intensity and making it abundantly clear that levitations are nearly as impossible to resist as purely spiritual raptures.

> I have wanted to resist many, many times, and have put all my strength
> behind it, especially with raptures in public, and often also with ones in private,
> when I feared I was being deceived. Sometimes I could resist somewhat, at
> the edge of exhaustion. Afterwards I would be completely worn out, like
> someone who has fought against a powerful giant. At other times resisting

has been impossible, and my soul has been carried away instead, and quite often my head too, along with it, without being able to stop it, and sometimes my whole body too, which has even been lifted off the ground.[41]

In other instances, Teresa explicitly refers to levitations, and what she has to say about her inability to resist these "favors," as well as the physical trauma involved in resisting, is basically identical. A passage previously quoted only partially now deserves to be quoted in full, due to its significance. "When I tried to resist these raptures," she says, "it seemed to me that I was being lifted up by a force beneath my feet so powerful that I know nothing to which I can compare it, for it came with a much greater intensity than any other spiritual experience and I felt as if I were being torn to shreds, for it is a mighty struggle, and, when all is said and done, there is no point to it if this is the Lord's will, for His power can never be overcome by another."[42]

In one of the *Vida*'s longest and most explicit passages about levitation, Teresa draws theological lessons and makes practical observations, and she begins by contrasting God's omnipotence with her helplessness: "Such effects reveal great things. First, they are a display of the Lord's mighty power: as we are unable to resist His Majesty's will, either in soul or in body, and are not our own masters, we realize that, however much this may pain us, there is One stronger than ourselves, and that it is He who grants us these favors, and that we, on our own, can do absolutely nothing. This imprints a great deal of humility in us."[43]

So, once again, we see Teresa returning to the issue of humility, that key virtue she absolutely must always display to prove that her raptures and levitations are of genuinely divine origin. Then, having made it clear that her levitations "imprint" her with the exact opposite of hubris and stressing her humility further, as well as her uncontrollable passivity, she highlights her own fright in the face of her levitations: "Moreover, I must confess that it produced an exceedingly great fear in me at first—a terrible fear, in fact—because *one sees one's body being lifted up from the ground; and although the spirit draws it up after itself,* and it does so very gently if no resistance is offered, one does not lose consciousness and one is able to realize that one is being lifted up. At least, this is what has happened to me."[44]

This passage is mostly self-referential, focused on her own reaction to levitating, but as Teresa often does in her *Vida,* she inserts a very weighty observation as an aside. That key passage, in italics above, is at once theological and "scientific"—if one may stretch the meaning of that term—and it is her personal take on what it is, exactly, that causes the body to rise in the air during a rapture. For lack of a better term, her explanation could be classified as "theological physics," based on that thick bundle of unquestioned metaphysical, ontological, and epistemological assumptions from which mystical theology is spun, especially certain assumptions about the ways in which body and soul relate to one another and how earthbound humans relate to heavenly realities. Simply put, what Teresa says here is that the spirit—or soul—is pulled upward to heaven during arrobamientos, and the body simply follows that upward motion due to the unbreakable bond between body and soul.

Then, returning once again to the issue of the absolute disparity between God's power and human helplessness, Teresa emphasizes divine love as the very essence of all arrobamientos and levitations, and she does so in a way that not only highlights God's love as the bridge linking the chasm between the human and the divine but also reemphasizes the abject loathsomeness of the human self and the human body. "The majesty of Him Who can do this is manifested in such a way that one's hair stands on end, and one cannot help but fear offending so great a God. But this fear is overpowered by the deepest love, newly enkindled, for this God who, as we can see, loves such a foul worm so much that He seems unsatisfied by drawing the soul to Himself so literally, and must also claim the body, mortal though it is, and befouled as its clay is by all the offenses it has committed."[45]

Teresa's stress on the irresistibility of raptures and levitations ultimately needs to be placed in the context of the power relationship between her and her confessors and superiors, as much as in the context of whatever she might have felt or thought about the power relationship between her and God. Urged to resist her raptures when they first began and blamed by her confessors for not preventing them,[46] Teresa needed to highlight this issue of resistance in the autobiographical account she was ordered to write. And she also needed to underscore the point that she continually begged God to refrain from showering her with arrobamientos, especially those in which she levitated in the presence of eyewitnesses who would immediately broadcast news of the wondrous miracle they had just seen. As Teresa saw it, the wider that tales of her levitations spread and the more that adulation of her intensified, the worse for her and the church as a whole. Outlining the experiences that can be expected in the penultimate stage of the mystical ascent—the sixth of the seven mansions in *The Interior Castle*—Teresa has this to say: "In this mansion *arrobamientos* occur continually without any way of avoiding them, even in public, and then the persecutions and murmurings follow, and even though the soul wants to be free from fears, she is never free of them, because so many people foist them on her, especially her confessors."[47]

In a remarkable letter to her brother Lorenzo de Cepeda on January 17, 1577, Teresa lays bare the full extent of her anguish over those uncontrollable levitations:

> Since the last time I wrote to you my *arrobamientos* have been casting me off like a falconer does with a hawk, and it has caused me grief, because sometimes it has happened out in public, and it also during matins with the sisters. Resisting is futile, and it is also impossible to dissemble. These raptures make me feel so intensely ashamed that I would like to hide away somewhere. I continually beg God not to do this while I'm out in public; please, have mercy, ask Him too, because these raptures cause too many problems, and they add nothing to my life of prayer. Lately, I've been walking about like a drunkard.[48]

This letter does not actually employ the Spanish words for "falconers" or "hawks," but its reference to falconry is clear. What Teresa says is "me han *tornado* los arrobamientos." The verb *tornar* is unusual and has several meanings, but one of these comes straight out of the art of falconry, and it is the one that makes the most contextual sense.[49] The English equivalent of this verb is "to cast off," which means "to throw off a bird from a raised glove."[50] So Teresa, the mystic who is close to God and whose levitations leave her feeling ashamed and tottering about like a drunkard, has no recourse but to compare her *enraptured* self to a captive trained *raptor* in the hands of its master and to beg for her brother's prayers because hers are definitely not changing God's mind on the issue of *raptures*. One is left to wonder whether all this densely packed irony is intentional or purely accidental, but there is no mistaking the display of humility and verbal dexterity embedded in it.

Teresa's efforts to control her levitations were much more than purely verbal or limited to prayer. According to eyewitnesses, there was a brute physicality to her resistance. Domingo Bañez, a prominent Dominican theologian who served as one of Teresa's spiritual advisors, said he and many other people once saw Teresa levitate immediately after receiving communion and that she clung to a grille in the church, "greatly distressed," and begged God, out loud: "Lord, for something that is as unimportant as putting an end to these favors with which you shower me, do not allow a woman as wicked as me to be mistaken for one that is good." Others, too, would testify that they saw her clinging to the mats on the choir floor and rising up in the air with them in her hands, which she did to signal the other nuns to pull on her habit and bring her back down.[51]

Turning to *The Interior Castle,* one finds Teresa still speaking about the issue of resistance to raptures, more than ten years after the completion of her *Vida.* What she has to say there is aimed at fellow nuns who might be embarking on the mystical path, and it sheds light on her struggles with raptures. "So," she asks, "is there any possible way to resist?" Her answer is a clear warning to all would-be mystics: "No, there is none at all: on the contrary, resistance only makes things worse." Pretending she has gathered information from someone else, rather than from her own experience, she then goes on to say: "I know this from a certain person who said that it seems that God wants the soul . . . to realize that it is no longer in charge of itself, so, notably, He begins to enrapture it with much greater vehemence." And, once again, as in the *Vida,* she emphasizes the imbalance of power between the human and the divine metaphorically: "This person, then, chose to offer no more resistance than a straw does when it is lifted up by amber—if you have ever seen this—and to surrender herself into the hands of Him Who is so powerful, realizing that it is best to make a virtue of necessity. And, speaking of straw, if a giant can easily snatch up a straw, then, most certainly, so can our great Giant carry away a soul."[52]

Teresa's reference to amber's effect on straws is apt, given what she had to say in the *Vida* about the soul and body being *pulled up* irresistibly in levitations. Though the natural principles involved in the amber-and-straw trick were barely understood in her day, the levitation of very light matter through static electricity and magnetism had been a well-observed and accepted fact since ancient times, and it is obvious that Teresa herself was familiar with this natural phenomenon.[53] Although the term "levitation," which derives from the Latin *levitas,* or "lightness," did not exist in her day, minor instances of this phenomenon in nature were in fact observable. So, as Teresa could not help but levitate, one cannot help but wonder if there was any intentional punning on her mind when she asks peevishly at one point in *The Interior Castle:* "Do you think this is such a *light* thing" [*tan liviana cosa,* meaning a trivial matter], "when it seems to you that the soul is leaving the body and it sees the senses fleeing from it without knowing what is going on?"[54]

When all is said and done, one of the most remarkable aspects of Teresa's levitations is her attitude toward them and how much she complained about them, not just to those around her but to God Himself. As she says in *The Interior Castle,* speaking of herself in the third person: "She does nothing but beg everyone to pray for her and beseech His Majesty to lead her by another road, as she is advised to do, since the road she is on is very dangerous."[55] Much like Saint Catherine of Siena, who received stigmata that were invisible, Teresa preferred to receive raptures that were hidden from others' eyes.[56]

What is truly surprising is not her complaining but the fact that according to her and to those around her, she suddenly stopped levitating, and her nonlevitating public raptures became much less frequent. Although she mentions this in the *Vida* and says that it happened when she was writing the final version of the twentieth chapter,[57] she does not dwell on the subject. In fact, this information is easy to miss, tucked away as it is in a long rambling narrative, somewhat cautiously, almost as an aside. Chances are that Teresa did not want to press her luck, for she would not want her superiors and confessors to think that she was boasting in any way or that she was underestimating God's omnipotence and His absolute control of her ecstasies. "I often begged the Lord not to grant me any more favors with visible external signs," she explains, "for I was weary of having to contend with such worries and, after all, His Majesty could grant me such favors without anyone knowing it. Apparently, He, in His kindness, was inclined to hear my pleas, for up until now—even though in truth it has only been a short while—I have never again received any such favors."[58]

Tracing this issue across time in her other writings is as difficult as following a very sparse trail of crumbs because she continued to skirt the issue. In 1570, five years after she finished the *Vida,* we find her saying that God gave her to understand why her public *arrobamientos* had become so infrequent: "'It is not necessary now,' said God, 'you've received enough credit for what I have intended.'"[59] Turning to the inquests of her beatification and canonization process, we can find corroborating testimonies from those who knew Teresa, such as that of Isabel de Santo Domingo, who had much to say in 1595 about the levitations and their cessation. Sor Isabel was not only an eyewitness to Teresa's levitations, and her efforts to resist them, but also one of the nuns who struggled unsuccessfully to keep her earthbound whenever she rose up in the air. "The sainted Mother was very humble," says Isabel, "and she dearly wished not to be considered a saint, so she constantly begged me and her other daughters to pull down hard on her vestments whenever we saw her rising into the air." She also adds that Teresa would do her utmost not to levitate by grabbing hold of objects that were firmly affixed to the floor or the walls and that she constantly prayed for an end to such public raptures. After being sent by Teresa to the convent she had founded in Seville, Isabel and Teresa kept in touch, and she let Isabel know that the levitations had suddenly stopped and that she was experiencing "greater raptures, but in a much more secret and hidden way."[60]

Additional Accounts

Looking for accounts of Teresa's levitations outside her own texts, one can find additional details, none of which contradict her narrative. Most of these can be found in the beatification and canonization inquests. Others can be found in the two hagiographies published before her beatification and canonization. The first of these was written by the Jesuit Francisco de Ribera, and it appeared in 1590, only eight years after Teresa's death and only one year before his own. Ribera had known Teresa and served as her confessor. The second hagiography was penned by the Hieronymite friar and bishop Diego de Yepes, and it first came off the presses in 1606, when Teresa was well on her way toward beatification. Like Ribera, Yepes had been Teresa's confessor and confidant. Yepes was uniquely poised to further the cause for Teresa's canonization, for in addition to becoming bishop of Tarazona in 1599, Yepes served as confessor to the Spanish king Philip II—at whose deathbed he stood watch—and also to Philip III, his successor. Both Ribera and Yepes rely on Teresa's *Vida* for their narratives, but not exclusively. Their personal acquaintance with Teresa and with others who lived with her or knew her allowed them to add many significant details to the story of her life, and the relatively quick translation of their hagiographies into Latin and several vernacular languages helped to make Teresa and her levitations known throughout the Catholic world.

Among the accounts of Teresa's levitations provided by Ribera, the most surprising and odd, by far, tells of a levitation that overtook Teresa while she was cooking. This incident resembles a parable drawn from Teresa's *Book of Foundations,* in which she says, "So, hey, my daughters, don't get upset when your vow of obedience requires you to do menial external tasks: understand that if you end up in the kitchen, God walks amidst the pots and pans, helping you with what's internal and external at the same time."[61] Ribera's narrative is very brief, but it is so perfect a reification of the pots and pans proverb that it seems tailored to serve as a meditation on it. "One day, upon entering the kitchen," he says, "the nuns found her [Teresa] totally elevated and transfixed, her face beautifully aglow, with the frying pan in her hand, suspended above the flames, and she was gripping the frying pan so tightly that it couldn't be wrested from her hand."[62]

A more detailed version of this story can be found in a hagiography of Teresa's close companion Isabel de Santo Domingo, published in 1638. Relying on accounts left by Isabel, who often did kitchen duty alongside Teresa, the author—Miguel Batista de Lanuza—reveals that Teresa was frying some eggs with the convent's last smidgen of olive oil. Obeying Teresa's orders on how to deal with her levitations, Isabel attempted to pull Teresa down, but failed, and then struggled to remove the frying pan from Teresa's hand because she feared that the oil in it would spill out and be lost. He also adds that this vigorous tug-of-war between Isabel and the enraptured levitating Teresa lasted a while, but the oil did not spill, and the cooking resumed as soon as the rapture ended.[63]

Diego de Yepes also relates some levitation accounts that eventually became well known, not just because his hagiography became very popular but because one of these accounts was included in the graphic hagiography *Vitae Beatae Virginis Teresiae a Iesu* (Antwerp, 1613), which consisted of twenty-five engravings with very brief captions in Latin and may have reached a much wider audience than either of the two lengthy *Vidas* of Yepes and Ribera.[64] This particular levitating episode took place at Teresa's newly founded convent of Saint Joseph, and it involved Alvaro de Mendoza Bishop of Ávila, and several other eyewitnesses (fig. 17). According to Yepes, "The force of this arrobamiento was so tremendous that, without being able to resist it, she [Teresa] rose up higher than the window through which the bishop was about to give her communion."[65]

But Yepes did more than simply recount instances of Teresa's "celestial inebriations," as he called her raptures: He also drew lessons from them and offered his own theological analyses. Some of his efforts to interpret her levitations employed Teresa's theological physics and expanded upon them. For instance, in addition to mentioning Teresa's amber-and-straw levitation analogy, Yepes brings up the magnetic properties of lodestone. Intertwining metaphorical swagger with theological physics, Yepes concludes, "So her soul was so full of this divine fire, that, as if her soul were a flame, it rose up high, and passed on to the body its lightness and agility."[66]

Accounts of Teresa's levitations can also be found in texts related to individuals she knew and interacted with, as we have already seen in the case of Isabel de Santo Domingo. Among such accounts none is more significant than

Figure 17. Engraving from an illustrated hagiography of Saint Teresa of Ávila that depicts her levitating as she is about to receive communion from the Bishop of Ávila.

the one that tells of her joint levitation with her fellow mystic Saint John of the Cross, one of the very few recorded instances of two Christian mystics levitating in unison.

Juan de Yepes y Álvarez (1542–1591), a Carmelite friar who took the religious name Juan de la Cruz (John of the Cross), was educated at the University of Salamanca and was ordained a priest in 1567. By sheer happenstance, his path crossed with Teresa's at Medina del Campo, while Teresa was there on monastic business, and not long after this meeting Teresa recruited John to implement her monastic reform program among the male members of the Carmelite order. In 1570, he became confessor to Teresa and the nuns at the Convent of the Incarnation at Ávila and remained there until 1577, when fellow male Carmelites opposed to his reform program—which was also Teresa's—kidnapped him and took him to Toledo, where he was imprisoned in a tiny cell and abused every day for eight months, simply for trying to reform his order. Although he failed as a reformer and paid dearly for it during the remainder of his brief life, receiving unrelenting mistreatment from his brethren, John would go on to write a series of texts and poems that are among the most sublime and complex in the Christian mystical tradition.

John's indebtedness to Teresa was immense, and the two mystics bonded intensely during his stint as confessor at Ávila. And it was there that one of the most remarkable levitations in Christian history occurred, in the tight space at the Convent of the Incarnation known as the locutorio, or parlor. This space was really two rooms, not one, separated by a thick wall, where the nuns in one room communicated with visitors in the other through a grille-covered window.

Like Teresa, John was prone to raptures and ecstasies and intent on keeping them private. "He tried to hide or to impede his raptures as much as possible," said one of his hagiographers.[67] But on one occasion, while visiting Teresa in the parlor on Trinity Sunday, neither John nor Teresa could control a spectacular arrobamiento that suddenly sent them both up into the air while conversing about the topic of that feast day, the Holy Trinity. Holding on to his chair as he felt the rapture coming, John suddenly shot up in the air, all the way to the ceiling, "still in his chair, as in a chariot of fire, in imitation of his great patron Elijah." Teresa, who was kneeling, immediately shot up too, along with John, her knees stiffly bent. And, as luck or divine Providence would have it, the event was witnessed by one of the convent's nuns, Beatriz de Jesús, who had been tasked with delivering a message to Teresa and happened to walk into the locutorio at the very instant that this dual levitation occurred (fig. 18).[68]

Tidying Up Teresa's Gracious Disorder

Making sense of Teresa's levitations requires assembling widely scattered puzzle pieces, some of which do not fit neatly into the spot where they belong. What she has to say is a bit disorderly, scattered, and full of jagged edges and gaps, and in the end, when all said and done, the picture that emerges after much effort leaves one with some rough and fuzzy spots. Part of the reason for this is Teresa's writing style, which some have called "gracious disorder."[69] In the *Vida*, especially, digressions are frequent, and when she stops digressing, she does not always return to the same topic, or if she does, she might return to some other issue after a few sentences or paragraphs. Quite often, too, she will loop back to a topic previously covered as part of one of her digressions. What this means is that even in a chapter with a substantially narrow focus—such as chapter 20 of the *Vida*, which is mostly about raptures and levitations—issues that belong together are addressed in different contexts or are never fully developed, and

Figure 18. Saint Teresa of Avila and Saint John of the Cross levitate together while conversing about the Holy Trinity.

issues related to a different chapter suddenly pop up unexpectedly. Teresa was aware of this quirk in her writing, which is why she constantly reminds her readers of two of her shortcomings: first, that she lacked a university degree and therefore could not think or write as a scholastic theologian; and second, that what she was straining to explain or illustrate was not just way beyond her capacity as a woman and a nun but beyond the ability of human language and reason as well.

Nonetheless, fuzzy rough spots and all, Teresa's take on levitation does have a great deal of consistency and an impressive measure of theological sophistication. And all of it can be succinctly summarized point by point:

- A life of constant prayer and intense asceticism is absolutely necessary for the mystical quest. Conversely, mystical experiences are supernatural gifts that are never showered at random on the unprepared or the unwilling. Additionally, the mystical quest is understood and explained as an intimate relationship driven by love.
- Those who pursue intimacy with the divine are never in control of whatever supernatural experiences they might have. Mystical experiences—which Teresa calls *mercedes,* or favors—cannot be brought on or halted at will by the mystic, and resisting them is ultimately impossible. God is always in control.
- Mystical experiences vary in intensity and are given by God in gradually increasing increments, usually growing in intensity and complexity as the mystic makes progress. But this progress is not strictly linear or on a straight upward trajectory, and the frequency and intensity of these experiences is never predictable.
- Since all mystical ecstasies involve the convergence of the natural and supernatural— or a crossing over from earth to heaven—they are often spoken of in terms of an upward movement of the human self from lower to higher or, more specifically, from earth to heaven, in both a metaphysical and physical sense.
- Teresa accepts it as a fact that human beings are composed of a soul and a body, which are inextricably united to form a single "self." Moreover, that self is stratified, for as she sees it, a hierarchical relation exists between soul and body, with the soul being the "higher" part. The most intense mystical experiences involve the highest parts of the soul, and at these highest levels, supernatural experiences can also involve the body, robbing it of sensation, sending it into a trance-like state, and lifting it off the ground.
- Teresa maps out her mystical experiences on a spectrum, moving up from the lowest (least supernaturally intense) to the highest (most supernaturally intense), and she employs specific terms for various types of experiences but does not always do so consistently.
- Although the greatest cluster of passages on levitation can be found in chapter 20 of Teresa's *Vida*—a text she wrote under great duress—the narrative and analysis of her experiences found there can only be fully understood by pairing them up with what she says in her *Interior Castle,* written over a decade later, which provides a detailed systematic outline of the various levels of mystical progress.

- When examined in relation to the mystical path that Teresa outlines in her *Interior Castle,* it becomes very clear that the rapture and levitation accounts found in her *Vida* correspond to the two ultimate levels of mystical ecstasy, the sixth and seventh, and that levitation can only begin to happen in the sixth level. Consequently, levitation is a phenomenon reserved for very advanced mystics, and it happens because the body rises up alongside the soul as the soul is drawn toward heaven.

- Despite some inconsistencies, Teresa tends to reserve the terms "arrobamiento" (rapture) and "arrebatamiento" (ravishment) for the highest and most intense levels of mystical ecstasy, and both terms—derived as they are from the Latin verb *rapere,* which means "to seize, snatch, grab, carry off, abduct, or rape"—indicate a loss of control. The body is not always involved in every arrobamiento or arrebatamiento, but when it is, the following altered states can occur: a cataleptic suspension of all five senses, a substantial slowing down of one's pulse and breathing, a loss of body heat, and a severe stiffening of the entire body. Sometimes, in addition to the above, the body can rise into the air uncontrollably and remain suspended above the ground for an indeterminate amount of time.

- Teresa insists that it is impossible to resist arrobamientos or arrebatamientos and the levitations that sometimes accompany them. Resistance can be offered, but it is extremely painful and eventually futile.

- Teresa begged God to take away the physical phenomena that accompanied her raptures, including her levitations, since, as she says, "His Majesty, after all, could grant me such favors without anyone knowing it."[70] And she lets it be known that her pleas were constant and that she asked others to plead on her behalf too.

- Teresa claims that her prayers were answered eventually, and the physical manifestations of rapture ceased—including levitation—even though she continued to experience purely spiritual arrobamientos and arrebatamientos.

Beyond Ambivalence and Fear

Whether or not one believes Teresa or the eyewitnesses who claimed to have seen her levitate is a moot point. The fact remains that we have many such testimonies and that she reified many Catholic beliefs that were being challenged in her day and age. Moreover, it is undeniable that she provided a logical explanation of a strange phenomenon that her culture believed in while avoiding negative judgments by her superiors. Perhaps even more remarkable than her ability to prove the divine origin of her raptures, or her annoyance and embarrassment in the face of such a divine favor, is her successful bargaining with God

Himself, much like that of Abraham, Moses, and Hezekiah.[71] And as a result, she transcended her time and place in yet another way.

What are we to make of Teresa's ambivalence and fear of being seen suspended in the air? Why should it be virtuous for anyone to resist a gift from God, especially one that defies the laws of nature and could be viewed as proof of His existence and power? Perhaps this is as clear a testimony as we can have of the dangers posed by every levitation due to the potential ambiguity of the miraculous and some peculiar wrinkles in the texture of early modern Catholicism. In Teresa's day and age, in a land awash with demoniacs and aspiring saints, the Inquisition looked askance at anyone who drew attention to themselves.[72] The best way not to be found guilty of deviltry or feigned sanctity was to convince the inquisitors that one did not seek to exalt oneself. Teresa summed up the value of levitation in precisely such a way, by complaining about it and counting it as a hard lesson in humility and selflessness rather than as a telltale sign of holiness.

Yet no matter how much Saint Teresa sought to distance herself from levitation, belief in this phenomenon would only intensify among Catholics after her death, thanks in no small measure to her fame. During the seventeenth century, the beginning of the so-called Age of Reason, levitators kept popping up throughout the Catholic world, not just in Europe but also in those places where Spain, Portugal, and France had colonies. And quite a few of them walked the earth—or hovered over it—at the same time as Isaac Newton was using empiricism and inductive reasoning to come up with his law of universal gravitation. Many of these baroque aethrobats followed the paradigms established by the likes of Saint Teresa. Others, however, flew higher and more spectacularly than ever before.[73] To fully appreciate the inflationary spiral that drove seventeenth-century levitating, and to come face-to-face with the history of the truly "impossible," one must turn to its most extreme case, Saint Joseph of Cupertino.

3. Saint Joseph of Cupertino, Shrieking Aerial Ecstatic

This is the life of a great servant of God, who lived so much out of the world rather than in it, that he experienced stupendous elevations of spirit and amazing raptures of body. One could say marvels were his daily routine, prophecy his way of speaking, and miracles the very nature of his being. . . . A man of lowly bloodlines, but of exalted virtue, he lived among men but was familiar with angels and enjoyed God's companionship in constant elevated contemplation.

So begins the *Vita del Venerable Padre Fr. Giuseppe Da Copertino De' Minori Conventuali,* penned by Domenico Bernino, son of the great baroque artist Gianlorenzo Bernini, published in 1722, fifty-nine years after Joseph's death, as the Flying Friar was on his way to beatification and canonization.[1] From the very start, then, the reader is alerted to expect an encounter with unearthly things. Joseph was far from an ordinary man, says Bernino. He was an avatar of the impossible, closer to God and the angels than to other humans. He was a wonder, pure and simple, and miracles were "the very nature of his being." This is a problem.

Most of what we know about Joseph of Cupertino was recorded by men like Bernino who were already convinced that he was a saint and were eager to prove or confirm it. The historical Joseph—that is, the Joseph who lived and breathed in seventeenth-century Italy—is largely inaccessible and irretrievable, save for a few devotional hymns and letters that he left behind, which reveal very little about the details of his life. The only Joseph we can access, then, is *Saint* Joseph, beatified in 1753 and canonized in 1767, who is more of an archetype than a flesh-and-blood individual, as much a myth as a symbol, and more of a paradigm than a human being. As is the case with many saints in the Catholic tradition, the only Joseph accessible to us is a holy man who is painfully aware of his own sinfulness but at the same time nearly perfect, morally and spiritually, and also uniquely capable of tapping supernatural power.

Does this mean that the Joseph available to us is a mere invention, irrelevant and dismissible? Is he little more than a carefully constructed illusion or a projection of early modern Catholic wishful thinking? Not necessarily. The myth of *Saint* Joseph is inseparable from the man who became that myth and from the events that led to the creation of that myth. Even at the most extreme end of the skeptical spectrum, the most hardened of skeptics should have to admit that if *Saint* Joseph is merely an "invention," that invention itself is a real thing, connected to Joseph and his time and place, insofar as it can be attributed to individuals with a commonly shared worldview who knew the historical Joseph, knew people who had known him, or drew upon the testimony of people whose lives had intersected with Joseph's in some way.

Reconstructing Joseph's Life

The chain of testimonies that link saint-making to human beings who somehow crossed paths with the saint-to-be-made is the chief characteristic of the canonization process devised in the early modern era by the Catholic Church, in an effort to adjust to sea changes in thinking brought about by the Renaissance and the Protestant and Catholic Reformations, as well as by the nascent scientific revolution. These changes required the "rationalization" of the supernatural and miraculous, a subject to which we will need to turn later.

Saint Joseph is as much a product of the Catholic Reformation and its baroque culture as he is a reflection of the historical Joseph, a product of baroque Catholicism who was canonized in the Age of Enlightenment. Moreover, Saint Joseph is inseparable from the voluminous records of the beatification and canonization inquests (*processi*) carried out after his death, mostly between 1664 and 1695—when many of those who had interacted with the historical Joseph were still alive—as an essential component of the post-Tridentine saint-making process.

Most of what we know about Joseph of Cupertino comes from the many testimonies in these inquests, which were then painstakingly combed through and turned into narratives by hagiographers intent on broadcasting Joseph's unique story to the world in order to confirm and enhance his status as a saint and intercessor, as well as to prove the supernatural nature of the Catholic Church. The documents produced by these inquests are voluminous and scattered over various archives.[2]

Saint Joseph's beatification and canonization inquests provided much of the material later mined by most of his hagiographers, who relied on the manuscripts themselves or perhaps on much briefer printed summaries and abridgments.[3] On the way to canonization, four hagiographies were published over a span of seventy-five years. The first of these was written by Roberto Nuti, a Conventual Franciscan who had known Joseph and served as his confessor at Assisi. Nuti relied not only on his own memory but also on the testimonies provided for the processi, the beatification and canonization inquests undertaken immediately after Joseph's death. Published in 1678, Nuti's lengthy 736-page hagiography would be heavily used by all subsequent hagiographers. Nuti's *Vita* was followed by that of Domenico Bernino,[4] a lay author who claimed to have witnessed one of Joseph's ecstasies.[5] Relying on Nuti and the processi, Bernino's work was published in 1722, as part of the effort to have Joseph beatified and canonized. Then in 1753, around the time of Joseph's beatification, two more hagiographies appeared, almost simultaneously: one by Paolo Antonio Agelli, a Conventual Franciscan and inquisitor general of Florence, and another by Angelo Pastrovicchi, another Conventual Franciscan. Since Bernino, Agelli, and Pastrovicchi focus more intensely on Joseph's levitations than Nuti, their texts have more to offer on this subject and will therefore be more heavily relied upon here. And these three texts can be compared to a hall of mirrors, wherein one finds multiple reflections of the same details. Pastrovicchi and Agelli relied heavily on Bernino and offer very similar narratives, but the first editions of Bernino and Pastrovicchi provide abundant marginal citations to the inquest processi, while Agelli keeps his sources hidden from the reader.

To date, the most comprehensive narrative account of Saint Joseph's life is Gustavo Parisciani's monumental *San Giuseppe da Copertino alla luce dei nuovi documentti,* over a thousand pages long, thoroughly based on manuscript sources, especially those related to the beatification and canonization inquests, and other texts that had been previously overlooked.[6] Parisciani's meticulous combing of archives has not made all previous hagiographies obsolete, given that the four early ones are now historical documents with merit of their own, worthy of scrutiny. There is no need to duplicate Parisciani here, much less to deconstruct his work. What is needed is a succinct summary of Joseph's life that focuses primarily on his "impossible" levitations and the effects they had on his own life and on the Catholic Church of his day and age. This narrative will take Joseph's hagiographies at face value, for what matters most at this point is not analyzing those hagiographies but laying bare their mindset and whatever facts and observations the authors sought to convey. Analyzing the hagiographical narratives will be the focus of chapter 4.

From Dimwit to Priest

According to tradition, Giuseppe Maria Desa, the man who would come to be known as Saint Joseph of Cupertino, "the Flying Friar," was born in a stable, just like Jesus Christ and Saint Francis of Assisi, his destiny auspiciously foreshadowed by this rare coincidence.[7] As fate, or chance, or divine Providence would have it, Joseph shared another auspicious resemblance to Jesus Christ, for his father, too, was a carpenter.

Joseph was born on June 17, 1603, in Copertino, a town in Apulia, near the southernmost tip of Italy's "heel," a region much closer to Albania and Greece than to Rome. Copertino was under Spanish rule at that time, along with the rest of the Kingdom of Naples—as it had been since 1504 and would be until 1714—and its Spanish overlords preferred to call the town Cupertino, with a "u" as the first vowel rather than an "o," a spelling still used in English-speaking countries, where Giuseppe is known as Joseph of Cupertino.[8]

Joseph's father was Felice Desa, a carpenter and master wainwright by profession, as well as a caretaker of the local castle owned by the Apulian nobleman Galeazzo Francesco Pinelli, who was not only Count of Copertino but also Duke of Acerenza and Marquis of Galatone. Joseph's mother was Francesca Panaca, better known as Franceschina, a strict disciplinarian with a quick temper and a fierce devotion to Catholic piety. Franceschina, a Franciscan tertiary who "worked hard at home, weaving and sewing,"[9] often corrected her son's misdeeds—"even the smallest"—with corporal punishment. According to Roberto Nuti, the earliest of all his hagiographers, young Joseph was "impetuous by nature, ill-tempered and volatile, and easily angered," so perhaps the punctilious and devout Franceschina might have had good reason for feeling a bit overwhelmed by her maternal responsibilities.[10] Joseph had one sister, Livia, who is seldom mentioned by his hagiographers, and four other siblings who died very young and of whom nothing is known. His extended family seemed religiously inclined, and some relatives were clerics, including two who belonged to the

Franciscan order: Father Francesco Desa, a paternal uncle, and Father Giovanni Donato, a maternal uncle.

Some other members of his extended family were relatively well off and educated, but Joseph's own father proved to be somewhat improvident, too easygoing, perhaps a tad too generous or careless, and too easily roped into securing loans taken by friends and neighbors who failed to pay him back. Because these delinquent loans became his responsibility and he lacked the means to pay all of what was owed, Felice feared being thrown into debtor's prison and took to hiding from creditors and lawmen. Eventually, in 1603, he fled to a church, where he avoided arrest by claiming the right of asylum. But this evasion proved disastrous. Frustrated by his escape from their hands, local authorities swooped down on his house and seized it, along with all its contents. As the house was being ransacked, his pregnant wife, Francesca—who was already beyond the normal childbearing age—headed out in a panic for a nearby place of refuge, only to find herself going into labor en route. And so it was that Franceschina delivered Joseph all by herself in a stable, the nearest shelter could find during this emergency.

Joseph endured a difficult childhood, due mainly to his father's negligence, absence, and unpaid debts, which hung like a dark cloud over the family. His austere mother also instilled fear and devotion in him with such great fervor that he could later boast that "he never needed to go through the novitiate in his religious life, having already gone through it effectively under her maternal will."[11] Drawn to spending time in churches and precociously inclined to prayer— perhaps as a way of escaping from his surroundings—Joseph began to exhibit behaviors at a very young age that are normally associated with mature ascetics and mystics, such as praying frequently and falling into trance-like states unexpectedly. Easily distracted at school, where he proved to be a slow learner and something of a class dunce, he would often drop his books and remain immobile for long spells, "with his eyes fixed heavenward and his mouth half open, as if he were listening to the singing and the sound of the angels up there."[12] Soon enough, young Joseph came to be known by his schoolmates and neighbors as Bocca Aperta, or "open mouth," a mocking reference to his trances and his reputation as a dimwit.[13]

Being teased at school proved to be the least of Joseph's worries, for at the age of seven his education was rudely cut short by an illness that lasted several years.[14] Covered from head to toe with sores variously described by his hagiographers as "ulcers," "abscesses," "pustules," "tumors," or "cancers," racked with constant pain, and subjected to ineffective cures that sometimes amounted to torture, Joseph grew increasingly weak. Bedridden and unable to walk yet still impulsively pious, he begged his mother to carry him in her arms to church daily. Finally, at the age of eleven, he was miraculously healed when his mother strapped him to a horse and took him to the shrine of Our Lady of Grace at Galatone, where he was anointed with an unction made by a local holy hermit from the oil of one of the shrine's lamps. Healed instantly, he walked all the way back home to Copertino, about ten miles, aided only by a cane.

Little is known about the remaining years of his childhood, other than his continual absorption in prayer, his extreme fasting, his self-mortification with hair shirts, and his obsessive churchgoing. Although he had learned to read, he was not very proficient at it and remained "mostly untutored in learning."[15] Nonetheless, he became acquainted with some devotional texts—perhaps read to him by his mother—and was drawn to seek the "elevated and sublime mysteries" mentioned in that literature. As he transitioned to adolescence, he began to display an awkward ineptitude for work that would plague him for much of his young adulthood. First, he tried his hand at selling vegetables, somewhat unsuccessfully, and then ventured to serve as an apprentice to a shoemaker, most disastrously. Unable to handle the simplest tasks and lapsing into trances frequently, Joseph proved useless to the cobbler and was quickly dismissed from his shop.

Having failed at simple commerce and menial labor, Joseph set his sights on becoming a Franciscan friar, which he perceived as his true calling, but the ineptitude he had displayed in the secular world proved to be an even more serious obstacle to his admission into monastic life.

Feeling attracted to the Conventual Franciscans, who followed the rule of Saint Francis somewhat loosely, especially on the issue of absolute poverty, Joseph first reached out to two relatives who had probably influenced him and seemed obvious potential patrons, his paternal and maternal uncles, Father Francesco Desa and Father Giovanni Donato, both of whom were well-respected members of that order. These uncles, however, turned Joseph down, closing the door on his dreams of becoming a Franciscan friar. Both of them had long considered their nephew something of an embarrassment and wholly unfit for religious life, not just because of his poor education but also because of his awkwardness and his proven record of failure. Undeterred by this rejection, Joseph kept begging his uncles to find him a place within one of the other branches of the Franciscan order, either the Friars Minor (also known as Observants), who followed the rule of Saint Francis more strictly than the Conventuals, or the relatively new Capuchins, founded in 1525, who were the strictest and most austere of all Franciscans.[16]

Joseph's persistence paid off in due time. Somehow, either through his uncle Francesco directly or through his own initiative, hapless Joseph obtained access to Father Antonio da Francavilla, provincial of the Capuchins, and was accepted into that order as a lay brother.[17] So in August 1620, at the age of seventeen, the ever-incompetent Bocca Aperta entered the Capuchin friary at Martina Franca as a novice, where he donned the much-coveted Franciscan habit and took the religious name of Stefano. But his clumsiness and utter distraction yet again proved his undoing, despite his devotion, humility, and apparent holiness.

Employed in the kitchen and refectory, the novice Stefano created constant mayhem, breaking dishes, spilling the contents of cooking pots, retrieving the wrong items from the pantry, serving food incorrectly, fumbling even the simplest of tasks and stumbling at every turn, or simply ignoring his duties. Although his hagiographers would later ascribe these disasters to his constant mystical raptures, the hard truth seemed obvious to everyone in the friary: this novice was dreadfully "dull-minded, corporeally unsound, spiritually intolerant, and blind to the friary's need for manual labor."[18] Consequently, after eight months of failure upon failure, Brother Stefano, the holy fool, was stripped of his religious name and Franciscan habit and expelled from the Capuchin house at Martina Franca. This rejection was so devastating to him that he would later say: "It seemed to me as if my skin was peeled off with the habit and my flesh rent from my bones."[19]

Returning to the "deceitful world" he had tried to flee was made all the worse for Joseph because his expulsion took place during the penitential season of Lent, a sacred time that emphasized the rejection of everything he now faced unprotected by cloister walls—the world, the flesh, and the devil—and also because some items of secular apparel that he had joyfully shed eight months earlier had been lost or discarded, forcing him to reenter the secular realm bereft of shoes, stockings, or a hat.[20] Worse yet must have been the thought of facing his mother in such disarray, that stern woman whose disappointment and shame he feared would be far worse than his own and whose scoldings and laments he might not have dared to imagine. So, barefoot and bareheaded, hoping to avoid abject humiliation at home, Joseph went straight to his Franciscan paternal uncle Francesco Desa.

Prostrating himself at Uncle Francesco's feet, Joseph cried, "The Capuchin Fathers have taken the habit from me because I am good for nothing." His uncle agreed, scolding him for being "incompetent" and a "vagabond."[21] Since Father Francesco was involved in a Lenten preaching mission at that time, he allowed Joseph to stay with him until Easter, when he accompanied him home to Copertino, where, as Joseph expected, his mother berated him mercilessly. Meanwhile, however, she also pleaded with the authorities not to imprison him for his father's unpaid debts, which had become his responsibility upon his father's death. And she also begged her brother Father Giovanni and her brother-in-law Father Francesco to gain Joseph entrance into some other Franciscan friary. Her pleading paid off, even though both of Joseph's uncles initially turned a deaf ear to her requests. After spending six months hiding from the authorities and bounty hunters in the attic of a chapel, Joseph was admitted as a tertiary novice by the Conventual Franciscan community of La Grotella in Copertino, thanks to his maternal uncle Father Giovanni, who resided at that friary and served as provincial of the Franciscans of Puglia and had by then obviously caved into his sister's incessant appeals.

Placed in charge of the friary's mule and assigned to other menial tasks, Joseph rejoiced. He was a Franciscan once again, admitted back to his true calling. Moreover, his clerical status now gave him immunity from any legal responsibilities for his father's debts. He was not yet a full-fledged Franciscan and still needed to prove himself, but having learned a hard lesson with the Capuchins, he tried to be less incompetent and succeeded, completing tasks fully, even the most difficult ones intentionally thrown his way by superiors wanting to test his mettle. In time, his uncle Giovanni grew more trustful, making him his assistant and assigning him duties beyond the stable, kitchen, and garden, such as begging for alms in the streets of Copertino, where he soon came to be admired by the people he encountered. Within La Grotella, Joseph gave himself over to prayer and asceticism, going barefoot, wearing a hair shirt, wrapping a chain tightly around his lower torso and groin, fasting more than was required, and sleeping only a few hours each night on wooden planks covered by some straw and a worn-out bearskin. During those nighttime hours when he abstained from sleep, he prayed and studied on his own, in secret, trying to make up for his insufficient and haphazard education.

About four years after he entered La Grotella, having won the admiration of his community and his superiors and having also reached the age of twenty-two, Joseph became a full-fledged novice in the Franciscan order in June of 1625.

Taking the vows of poverty, chastity, and obedience, he immediately began preparing for the priesthood, with full support from his uncle Giovanni. Although he was now a shadow of his former bumbling self, learning some basic Latin, memorizing the rules of his order, and acquiring proficiency in doctrine proved difficult for the poorly educated friar previously mocked as Bocca Aperta. Nonetheless, with the help of a patient novice master and of both of his uncles, Joseph made enough progress to move on to the study of dogmatic and moral theology, to receive minor orders in January 1627, and to be ordained as a subdeacon a month later.

Moving up to the next step on the way to the priesthood—becoming a deacon—was an even greater challenge, for all candidates to the diaconate were required to pass a rigorous exam that required them to read, chant, and comment on some randomly chosen Gospel passage. Fully aware of his weak command of Latin and his rather limited acquaintance with the Bible, Joseph prayed to the Madonna of La Grotella for assistance and faced his examiner, Girolamo de Franchi, bishop of Nardo, "as if armed with a formidable shield" given to him by the "Madonna Santissima,"[22] not knowing which Gospel passage he would be asked to wrestle with. Then, to Joseph's delight, and that of his hagiographers, the story quickly veers into the realm of the miraculous as divine Providence rescues him from failure, for the text selected by Bishop Franchi was "Beatus venter qui te portavit" (Luke 11:27, "Blessed is the womb that bore Thee"), the only passage out of the entire Bible that Joseph—still something of a dullard and barely proficient in Latin—had been able to memorize. So, miraculously, Joseph passed his exam.

Ordained a deacon with miraculous assistance from heaven, Joseph had one more hurdle to clear before he could become a priest: an exam more daunting than the previous one. He knew that the examiner this time would be Giovanni Battista Detti, bishop of Castro, who was proud of his reputation for toughness and his zeal for ordaining only the ablest of candidates to serve as priests.[23] After praying for another miracle all through the night to his "Advocate and Protector, the Most Holy Virgin Mother of God," Joseph entered the examination room along with other candidates from the Franciscan friary at Lecce,[24] expecting to fail. And once again, much to his delight and that of his hagiographers, Heaven intervened. That morning, as the exam began, Bishop Detti suddenly learned through an urgent message that he needed to devote his attention to some emergency immediately, and he had no choice but to cut short the exam session. So, after questioning some candidates and being very impressed by their answers, Bishop Nardi decided that everyone else in that room must be equally well prepared, and he passed them all, including Joseph, without asking him a single question.

So, on March 28, 1628, Joseph Desa was ordained a priest.

The seemingly daft and frail son of Felice Desa and Franceschina Panaca had come a long way from his days as Bocca Aperta and Stefano, but he had not yet begun to reach the heights he would eventually reach as Padre Giuseppe da Copertino, the flying saint.

From the Altar to the Inquisition

Joseph's ordination was followed by joy at first and then by desolation. Elated by the "miracle" of his final exam and his consecration as a priest, the first thing he did upon returning to Copertino was to throw himself to the ground at the feet of an image of the Virgin Mary in the chapel of La Grotella and thank her profusely. But soon afterward, after celebrating his first Mass and feeling utterly unworthy to consecrate the Eucharist, a dark night of the soul descended on him, unexpectedly, as happens to many mystics. "Overcome inside by a fierce melancholy, prolonged distrust, and a deep affliction of spirit," Joseph would later confess that he "doubted that he could endure it."[25] During this agonizing time, which lasted for two years, Joseph was deprived of his customary trances and divine consolations. Then, as Joseph would later relate, that dark night lifted as suddenly as it arrived when a friar whom he had never met entered his cell and gave him a new Franciscan habit to replace the tattered one he was wearing. Naturally, Joseph immediately realized that the stranger must have been an angel.[26]

Joseph's awareness of his own sinfulness, enhanced by his experience with the Eucharist and coupled with the melancholy that followed, drove him to take his asceticism to new extremes. Aiming for holiness and more intimacy with God, he devised penances that mirrored a well-established pattern found in many hagiographies with which he was undoubtedly familiar, and one of the chief characteristics of that pattern was excessive fasting that turned into inedia or near-inedia, the feat of surviving without food. Joseph had been abstaining from meat long before he was ordained, and continued to do so, but now he stopped eating bread and drinking wine. Surviving on a meager diet of herbs, dried fruits, and beans, all laced with a bitter powder that repulsed all others who tasted it, he made his punishing diet even worse by eating vegetables on Fridays that were so foul that a fellow friar who dared to sample them remained nauseous for several days. In addition, he strictly observed seven sets of forty-day fasts throughout the year, in imitation of Saint Francis. These 280 days of fasting per year—which involved abstaining from all food for five days each week and eating very small amounts on Sundays and Thursdays—brought Joseph very close to starvation. So, like many other holy men and women one encounters in hagiographies, Joseph could claim he was kept alive by the "Bread of Angels," the Eucharist, which he eagerly consumed every day.

As if all this fasting were not enough, Joseph also waged a brutal war on his own body, "armed for combat against the flesh."[27] He reduced the number of hours he slept even further and scourged himself twice a week with a metal-studded whip that cut deeply into his shoulders and back, leaving the walls of his cell caked with spattered blood. Doing this vigorously seemed essential to him, for whenever he felt too weak to do it himself, he would ask a fellow friar to wield the whip. In addition, Joseph tightened the chain he already wore under his hair shirt, causing it to embed into his skin. The heavy toll taken on his health by all this self-abuse can be easily imagined and must have been obvious to his brethren in the friary, but since asceticism was an essential component of monastic life and unquestioningly assumed to be a pathway to holiness, no one stopped Joseph until he was close to the edge of death. Noticing that Joseph "could barely breathe," his superior took a close look at the emaciated friar and his wounds. Taking off his habit and seeing "his body was one whole single sore" that looked "like a torn cadaver rather than a living man,"[28] the superior immediately ordered him to stop mortifying himself so severely. Joseph, ever the obedient friar, did as he was commanded and moderated his self-punishment, probably saving himself from an early death.

While this excessive self-mortification might seem caused by Joseph's dark night of the soul, which he endured between 1628 to 1630, such an assumption would be wrong, or only partially correct. The hair shirt and chain, the fasting, the scourging, the sleep deprivation, and all such things were part of Joseph's life before the dark night and may have in fact intensified alongside Joseph's melancholy, but they were also part and parcel of a major mystical transformation within Joseph that led to the miraculous feats that gained him a reputation as a very special saint. His levitations and the other supernatural phenomena associated with him were inextricably linked to his self-mortification and his life of prayer. Joseph was "either detached from his senses or disdainful of providing relief for his body," said Agelli, "as if its natural weight aggravated his soul, which only yearned to soar in the upper reaches of Heaven."[29] In this respect, Joseph was no different from any of the great and well-known mystics who preceded him and after whom he modeled himself. They all embodied the paradoxical contradictions that shape the Christian mystical tradition, above all that ultimate paradox in which agony and ecstasy are conjoined ineffably, perhaps most dramatically expressed by Saint Teresa of Avila when she tried to sum up that mystical ecstasy known as the transverberation, in which an angel plunged a spear into her chest: "So great was the pain, that it made me moan; and so utter the sweetness that this sharpest of pains gave me, that there was no wanting it to stop, nor is there any contenting of the soul with anything less than God."[30]

Joseph had been experiencing trances, visions, and ecstasies since the age of eight, and his altered states were not only observed by many but became a defining characteristic of his identity. But it was precisely at the tail end of Joseph's dark night that levitations began to accompany his ecstatic trances. Joseph's mystical transformation began in 1630, at first subtly and indirectly, with seemingly uncontrollable physical reflexes, especially twitching during the reading of sacred texts at meals and also random cries and shrieks that sounded "as if someone had stabbed him with a knife."[31] His trances also began to intensify at the same time, and to last longer, and some of his fellow friars noticed and began to keep a worried eye on him, alarmed by whatever seemed to be developing within Joseph. Then, on the feast of his beloved role model Saint Francis, October 4, 1630, the mystical dam broke, so to speak, and the supernatural torrent that flowed out surprised everyone. While taking part in a procession through the town of Copertino in honor of Saint Francis, Joseph suddenly rose up off the ground and remained suspended in the air, ecstatic, hovering above an astonished crowd of clerics and townspeople.

From this point forward, life would be very different for Joseph, his friary of La Grottella, and the residents of Copertino. Joseph's levitating ecstasies became frequent, and most of them were very public, often witnessed by others. According to eyewitness reports, Joseph would regularly take to the air, always after emitting a loud cry, and hover above the ground anywhere from "one hand" to several "paces" or cubits, even higher than the altar, or over people's heads. Joseph could remain perfectly still in the air, sometimes for hours; he could also gyrate or sing and dance. Many times, at the most unexpected moment, Joseph would let out one of his shrieks—as loud as a cannon blast, by his own description—and take to the air.[32] His levitations were not always predictable but could easily be triggered by anything that affected Joseph spiritually. Simply hearing the names of Jesus or Mary could do it, as could sacred music or the beauty of nature. Prayer, especially, was a common trigger. And saying Mass caused him to rise in the air frequently, especially at the moment of consecration.

Joseph did more than hover or float in the air, transfixed. Sometimes he wept, too, or shouted, or even blurted out a confession of his own sins. So as word of his miraculous levitations spread, the chapel and friary at La Grottella became a magnet for the curious as well as the skeptical and the devout, and the resulting tumult caused by visitors could sometimes turn carnivalesque. Some people would circle around Joseph as he hovered at the altar, gawking, straining to see him from various angles. Others would dare to touch, prod, and jab him with their fingers, poke his open uplifted eyes, or move his arms, trying to make him flinch. Some would dare to test his trances by pricking him with needles or holding candle flames close to his skin.[33] According to numerous eyewitness reports, this prodding and poking never elicited any reaction from Joseph, who remained as still as a marble statue carved by Bernino's father. The only stimulus that could bring him out of his trances was his superior's voice, commanding him to snap out of it. Such was the power of the vow of obedience for Joseph. Consequently, only Joseph's superior could restore decorum when those gathered around the hovering friar acted as childish dolts at a carnival.

Witnesses at Copertino—lay as well as clerical—reported more than seventy feats of levitation for Joseph's beatification inquest, not including his almost daily hovering ecstasies at Mass, which could last two hours. Although these reports tell of miracles that defy the laws of nature and strain credulity with fantastic details that border on farce or cross the line into it, blending the unbelievable and the comical, the stories are told in a matter-of-fact way, with a perfunctory seriousness that one might expect from a police report. Among the many accounts of Joseph's levitations, a handful provide a glimpse of certain patterns, as well as of certain characteristics of the levitations and of the different ways in which the Flying Friar could surprise the people of Copertino.

Holy feast days seem to have been triggers for Joseph's ecstasies, many of which took place within the friary's chapel at La Grottella. One Christmas Eve, at a reenactment celebration of the birth of the Christ child, Joseph began to dance "like David before the ark" when he heard bagpipes and flutes being played by shepherds and, suddenly, with a loud shout, sprang up and flew "like a bird through the air" about forty feet up the nave to the high altar, where he "embraced the tabernacle with both his arms" and remained there for about fifteen minutes without burning himself or his vestments.[34] One Holy Thursday, as he was praying with his brethren, he rose up and flew to the tabernacle at the high altar and remained suspended in midair above a great number of candles and stayed there, in ecstasy, venerating the Eucharist until his superior ordered him to return to the ground. On another occasion, on the feast of Saint Francis, he rose from the ground "about fifteen palms" from the floor and hovered in ecstasy by the pulpit with his arms outstretched and his knees bent, kneeling in midair for a long time.[35]

Rituals, prayers, and sacred music could also be triggers for Joseph's ecstasies. Once, at a veiling ceremony for nuns at a convent of Saint Clare, he heard the choir sing, "Come, you bride of Christ" and hurried over to a nearby priest, taking his hand and rising in the air with him "with a supernatural force." Then, as if this were not amazing enough, Joseph began dancing vigorously with this priest in midair.[36]

Reminding Joseph of something sacred or bringing it to his attention could also cause him to levitate. Once, when a friar was talking to him about the flames that appeared above the heads of the apostles when the Holy Spirit descended on them at Pentecost,[37] Joseph flew up with one of his loud whoops, ecstatic, fixing his gaze on a nearby candle flame. On another occasion, all it took to send him up in the air was to hear a priest say how beautiful heaven must be. This levitation took him up to the top of an olive tree, where he remained perched for about a half hour, kneeling on a slender branch, seemingly weightless. As one account of this event observes, "It was a strange sight to see how the branch which bore him swayed as lightly as if a small bird rested on it."[38]

Some of Joseph's levitations took place outdoors, in public, and some of them served practical purposes. Among these, one of the most remarkable combined flying and superhuman strength. This event occurred when a replica of the calvary was being built on a hill, and the largest of the three crosses proved too heavy for the ten men who were trying to raise it and insert it into a hole in the ground. Seeing the struggle of the laborers and sensing they could be crushed by the cross they were trying to lift, Joseph flew from the friary's gate to the cross, lifted it "as easily as if it were a straw," and dropped it safely in its hole. Once installed, this cross became a special focus of devotion for Joseph, and he would sometimes rise up to the top of it and perch himself on it, in ecstasy, just as he had done previously on an olive tree (fig. 19).[39]

Figure 19. Many of Saint Joseph of Cupertino's levitations supposedly took place outdoors—where it is extremely difficult to deceive witnesses with trickery involving ropes, wires, or other devices—such as this incident involving the installation of a large cross into the ground.

Joseph also worked miracles of a more traditional sort, especially healings, and—in emulation of Saint Francis—miracles involving nature and animals.[40] Joseph could also act as an agent of divine displeasure. Since he could also discern or smell or see the sins of others, he could reprimand people or deny them absolution in confession and predict disasters or illnesses that would befall the unrepentant.[41] But sometimes this harsh side of Joseph was only the flip side of the coin, so to speak. Once, he warned local bigwig Count Cosimo Pinelli, a sexual predator, that he would go blind if he kept abusing a certain girl. Predictably, the count refused to change his behavior, lost his sight, and came begging Joseph for a cure. Then, after showing genuine contrition and repentance in the sacrament of confession, he was miraculously healed by Joseph.[42] So it was that Joseph "became so famous in that land of his, and in the whole province of Apulia, that he was regarded not only as a great saint, but a miracle of sanctity."[43] As one hagiographer put it, "People from far and near flocked to see him, to hear his teachings and implore his prayers, calling him 'the apostle of the country,' and every place he visited tasted the effects of his prodigious goodness."[44]

From the Inquisition to the Papal Court

In Joseph's day and age, being considered a "miracle of sanctity" overflowing with "prodigious goodness" was risky. In fact, the more wondrous the miracles ascribed to you, and the more of a stir you caused, the higher your risk of being closely scrutinized by church authorities. An uneasy binary dialectic was constantly at play in religious life, an arduous struggle to distinguish between the divine and the demonic, the orthodox and heretical, the genuine and the phony, the credible and the incredible. Above all, in this contentious era of reform, religious wars, and rising skepticism—which also happened to be the age of massive witch hunts—the Catholic Church found it necessary to take a cautious approach to claims of sanctity. Holiness had to be contested to winnow out all fakers, heretics, and demoniacs, for the world was full of all three of these. Monastics were especially vulnerable to close examination and to charges of feigned sanctity or heresy.[45] Not even some of the greatest saints of the Catholic Reformation could escape such scrutiny, which is why Ignatius Loyola, founder of the Jesuits, and Teresa of Avila had their own run-ins with the Inquisition and kept being denounced to it even after death, up until the day they were beatified.

So it is not at all surprising that after Joseph's tour of nearby sites in Apulia with his provincial in 1636, which expanded his notoriety considerably, a suspicious cleric denounced Joseph to the Inquisition in Naples.[46] The charge came from apostolic vicar Monsignor Giuseppe Palamolla, who accused Joseph of "abusing the credulity of the people" with his feigned sanctity.[47] The denunciation warned: "There is a thirty-three-year-old man scuttling around this province,

acting like another Messiah, drawing the whole populace to himself with prodigies every step of the way, admired by the simple folk who always believe everything. We must inform our superiors, so they can remedy this and prevent
future evils, especially of the sort that will be unfixable."[48]

After some foot-dragging, Joseph's superiors at La Grottella had no choice
but to hand him over to the Holy Office in Naples in late October 1638. According to his hagiographers, Joseph went to Naples fearlessly, even joyfully, frequently levitating in ecstasy along the way,[49] despite the sadness and worry of
his fellow friars and of the townspeople of Copertino. In Naples, he resided at
the Franciscan friary of San Lorenzo, where he was coldly received. In truth, he
was not a guest, but a prisoner. Detained there for a few weeks and examined
three times by the tribunal of the Holy Office, on November 25, November 27,
and December 1, Joseph was declared to be a genuine holy man, innocent of all
charges leveled against him. This was a relatively quick trial by Inquisition standards, and its brevity lent weight to the verdict.[50]

The questioning was intense enough to leave Joseph a bit shaken, but significantly, the inquisitors never doubted the *facticity* of Joseph's levitations and
miracles. The Inquisition had two concerns: first, whether Joseph's levitations
were of divine or demonic origin and, second, whether he might be intentionally attracting attention to himself out of self-aggrandizing vanity, as Monsignor
Palamolla had charged. Given that his ecstasies were preceded by loud shouts
that interrupted his Masses and drew attention to him rather than the Eucharist, this was a key issue.

Joseph was asked why he did not celebrate Mass in private if he knew it
was highly likely that he would be overtaken by levitating ecstasies. Joseph responded that he would much prefer to celebrate the Eucharist behind closed
doors and had persistently begged his superiors to allow him to do that, but
they had denied all his requests. In sum, his superiors were responsible for his
public levitations during Mass; he was merely fulfilling his vow of obedience.
At one climactic point of the trial, Joseph was also asked whether he derived
pleasure from his *moti,* the physical phenomena that accompanied his levitating ecstasies. Making a crucial distinction, he replied that while the ecstasies
brought him spiritual delight, the physical phenomena caused him nothing
but shame and embarrassment. He had prayed for the levitations to cease, he
said, and had asked his brethren at La Grottella to make the same request from
God, to no avail.[51] His moti were unstoppable. As the inquisitors probed this
subject, Joseph insisted that he had no control whatsoever over his ecstasies,

shouts, hoverings, and flights. Ultimately, Joseph's self-effacing demeanor won over the judges, who might have already been inclined to assume his innocence before the trial had begun. Humility was the key to proving one's innocence in cases like this, along with the ability to make clear distinctions correctly, and nothing else reflected the proper attitude and state of mind more convincingly than being ashamed of one's levitations.[52]

Joseph might have breathed a sigh of relief, but further scrutiny awaited. The tribunal's decision had to be reviewed by the father general of the Conventual Franciscans and the Inquisition in Rome, so he was ordered to go there. Given a few weeks of rest at San Lorenzo in Naples, where he was now an honored guest rather than a prisoner, Joseph immediately received a great deal of attention from clergy and laity alike, especially from the elite of Neapolitan society, including the Spanish viceroy. Consequently, many in Naples also got the chance to witness some spectacular levitations since he could now resume saying Mass in public. At the church of San Gregorio Armeno, where the Inquisition had ordered him to say Mass for the nuns of its cloister, Joseph sprang up with one of his usual shrieks, "rose in flight and placed himself upright at the altar with his hands outstretched as a cross, and he bent forward at the waist among the flowers and the many candles which were burning there." At that point, the nuns began to scream loudly in terror, "He's burning himself, he's burning himself," but as usual, Joseph and his vestments proved fireproof. Then, with another shriek, Joseph "returned in flight to the middle of the church, leaping excitedly, gyrating around very fast, full of inner joy and outward exultation, dancing and singing, 'oh Blessed Virgin, oh Blessed Virgin,' and then, becoming once again immobile and bereft of sensation, he went into ecstasy." Ironically—but true to form—after such a display of miraculous excess, Joseph disparaged himself, telling the nuns that he was nothing more than "a sinner unworthy of living with his devout brethren, fit only for returning to the beasts in the stable." Unconvinced by Joseph's self-deprecation, the nuns flocked around him and snipped off bits and pieces of his habit without him noticing as they asked for blessings, and he regaled them with "pious teachings." And when he finally took off for Rome, he was still wearing that raggedy habit, saying, "I would rather wear this chopped-up habit than a new one."[53]

Once in Rome, Joseph faced his superiors—including the father general of his order, Gianbattista Berardicelli, who greeted him somewhat coldly—as well as inquisitors of the Holy Office, who grilled him anew about his ecstasies.

Lodged at the friary of the Twelve Apostles, he was assigned to a secluded cell. Ordered to celebrate Mass in public, Joseph obeyed, as always, and with his superiors and the inquisitors and some cardinals attending, levitated again during the ritual, giving them all the opportunity to see for themselves why he had caused such a stir. In due time, not surprisingly, even Pope Urban VIII became involved in Joseph's case.

Taken to a papal audience by his Father General, an overwhelmed Joseph bent down to kiss the pope's feet, as everyone was expected to do, but before he could do so, he went into a levitating ecstasy and rose high above Urban VIII's head, hovering there until a command from Father General Berardicelli brought him back down to the ground. Duly astonished, Pope Urban VIII reportedly said to the Father General that if Joseph were to die during his pontificate, he would love to testify as an eyewitness on behalf of his canonization and confirm the sacred reality of Joseph's levitations (fig. 20).[54]

Hovering above the pope's head, however, was not enough to save Joseph from the consequences of his peculiar notoriety and the instability of his status. The Flying Friar was too much of a good thing altogether, too otherworldly, too much of a lightning rod for controversy, and too much of a wild card for Catholic authorities and the Franciscan order. His closeness to the divine and his supernaturally charged ecstasies did not fit easily into the structure of the Catholic Church's hierarchy or into its efforts to Christianize an increasingly skeptical and secular world. Consequently, during his stay in Rome Joseph entered a liminal space in which he remained trapped for the rest of his life, a unique limbo all his own, a state of being that caused his superiors to be simultaneously awed and repelled by him and led to his being ever more sequestered, isolated, stripped of agency, and shuttled to ever more remote locations without regard for his feelings or needs. Given a *monitio*, or warning, by his examiners in Rome, Joseph was marked as someone who would forever remain under constant observation by the Holy Office and his superiors. All saints are "abnormal" by definition, rare human beings whose lives are truly extraordinary. The increasing isolation imposed on Joseph marked him as "hyperabnormal." A prisoner of his own holiness and his supernatural aura, he was turned into a hermit, forced to live a solitary existence though surrounded by fellow Franciscans, and he would spend much of the remainder of his life entombed in his cell, celebrating Mass by himself, eating alone, and going into ecstasy out of view.

Figure 20. This is one of various engravings and paintings that depict Saint Joseph levitating above Pope Urban VIII.

At Assisi with Saint Francis

After meeting Joseph, Pope Urban VIII instructed Father General Berardicelli to assign Joseph to a friary where the Franciscan rule was strictly observed, and Berardicelli sent him to Assisi, the epicenter of the Franciscan world and a place that Joseph had always longed to visit. The Flying Friar arrived there at the end of April 1639, elated, but soon afterward he entered another dark night of the soul, wholly deprived of divine consolation and of his ecstasies. Even worse, Joseph was beleaguered by temptations, nightmares, and demonic attacks that brought him close to the edge of despair. And this situation was made all the worse by the attitude of the guardian of the Assisi Franciscans, Antonio di San Mauro, the former provincial of Bari and a onetime friend of Joseph's who had inexplicably turned against him, treating him contemptuously and often "scolding him for being a disobedient hypocrite and reproving him as such in public."[55] Trapped in an ever-deepening gloom, which lasted for about two years, Joseph longed to leave Assisi. "I would like to return to Our Lady of La Grottella," he said to a fellow friar, "because she is my mother."[56]

Fortunately for Joseph, he was rescued by Father General Berardicelli, who had learned of his situation and summoned him to Rome during the Lenten season of 1644. While in Rome, Joseph suddenly emerged from his dark night and once again began to experience his much-missed ecstasies. His sudden removal from isolation might have had something to do with this improvement. First, he was taken to all seven of Rome's pilgrimage churches,[57] beginning with Saint Peter's, which overwhelmed him so much that he kept his eyes fixed on the floor at all times.[58] He was also taken to meet various cardinals, bishops, and other members of the higher clergy, and many of these encounters caused him to levitate on the spot. Joseph was kept busy in Rome, too much on display, and too much in demand by the elites of the Holy City. In fact, according to Agelli, Joseph was "wearied by the flocking of the great to him, each of whom wanted to have him for himself."[59] Returning to Assisi after Easter as a changed man, Joseph was quickly embraced more warmly by his fellow Franciscans and, in August of that year, was awarded honorary citizenship in Assisi by its city council. True to form, when the council delegates entered his cell to present him with a certificate of this new status of "fellow citizen of St. Francis," Joseph reacted by levitating up to the ceiling.[60]

Despite his intense day-to-day isolation at Assisi and the restrictions placed on him by superiors, the Umbrian hill town proved to be the one place where Joseph interacted most intensely with the elite of church and state. Word of the miraculous "holy friar" who lived in Assisi spread quickly and far and wide in Catholic circles, and before long many high-ranking individuals made a special pilgrimage to visit him, including princes of the church such as Cardinals Facchinetti, Ludovisi, Rapaccioli, Odescalchi, Donghi, Pallotta, Verospi, Paluzi, Sacchetti, and others, many of whom saw him levitate, according to later testimonies. Secular heads of state and titled nobles from all corners of Europe flocked to see him too, such as Prince Leopold of Tuscany, who later became a cardinal; the Duke of Bouillon from France; Mary, daughter of Charles Emmanuel of Savoy; Catherine of Austria; Isabelle, Duchess of Mantua, also from Austria; Princes Radziwill and Lubomirski with their wives and Prince Zamoyski and other grandees from Poland; and also the royal Prince of Poland, John Casimir, who visited the saint repeatedly and corresponded with him.[61] Additionally, two other elite visitors, one from Spain, the other from Germany, figure prominently in Joseph's hagiographies as eyewitnesses to remarkable levitations.[62]

The first of these, Juan Alfonso Enríquez de Cabrera, who visited Joseph in 1645, was arguably the most powerful Spaniard in Italy, a grandee and member of King Philip IV's Royal Council who held multiple titles, including Viceroy of Naples, Viceroy of Sicily, Admiral of Castille, Ambassador to the Papal States, Duke of Medina de Rioseco, and Count of Melgar. After meeting with Joseph in his cell, the count-duke-viceroy reported to his wife, who was traveling with him: "I have seen and spoken with another Saint Francis." Enthralled by such an assessment of Joseph, the wife, Luisa de Sandoval Padilla, begged for an audience with him. Ordered to meet with her and her ladies-in-waiting in the Basilica of Saint Francis, Joseph complied, saying, "I know not whether I will be able to speak" due to his aversion to mingling with females. But as it turned out, Joseph never had to utter a word or come close to any woman, for as soon as he entered the huge church through a side door, he shrieked and flew twelve feet above the heads of his illustrious visitors, hovered for a while in ecstasy before an image of the Virgin Mary, shrieked again, flew back to his takeoff point near the door, and returned to his cell silently, his head bowed, his face hidden from view by his cowl. According to Agelli, the count-duke-viceroy's wife and all the ladies in her retinue fainted, and the count-duke-viceroy simply stood still "in a stupor, with his arms spread wide, bereft of all feeling, as if somewhere between life and death."[63] Meanwhile, the Viceroy's wife had to be revived with smelling salts and a generous amount of holy water sprinkled on her face (fig. 21).[64]

Figure 21. Gioan Antonio Lorenzini's engraving of Saint Joseph's flight over the heads of the Spanish viceroy and his entourage.

Dramatic as this levitation was, it paled in comparison to the one witnessed by the Lutheran Duke Johann Friedrich (1625–1679), ruler of Braunschweig-Lüneberg,[65] who converted to Catholicism after meeting the Flying Friar. This event, which merits closer examination in chapter 4, is perhaps the most symbolically charged of Joseph's miracles.

Johann Friedrich was a descendant of the Saxon princes who championed Martin Luther's Reformation, brother-in-law of King Frederick III of Denmark, and an ancestor of the present-day royal family of England. While on a tour of European courts with two noble companions, this Lutheran duke stopped at Assisi in 1649 so he could visit the famous friar he had heard about in Germany.[66] Taken to the chapel where Joseph was saying Mass through a side door—without Joseph being informed of his presence—the prince and his companions immediately experienced the Flying Friar's supernatural powers. Suddenly, as he was consecrating the Eucharist, Joseph found it impossible to break the host, as required at that moment of the Mass. Staring at the host, he gave a "tearful wail" and "with a very loud shriek, flew about five paces backwards in the air in a kneeling posture, and then back to the altar." Then, after floating back down to the ground and remaining ecstatic for several minutes, he applied all his strength to the sacred host and finally broke it (fig. 22).[67] The Saxon duke was adequately astonished but puzzled by Joseph's weeping and his struggle at the altar, so after Mass, he asked the father superior to question Joseph about it. When asked, Joseph replied that the visitors brought to the chapel must have been heretics with hard hearts because only under such circumstances does the host becomes too hard to break.

Upon learning of Joseph's reply, Johann Friedrich requested a chat with Joseph and, after talking to him for an hour or two, asked permission to attend Mass again the following day. Another miracle occurred at that Mass during consecration: A black cross suddenly appeared on the host, which all could see, and Joseph levitated again, remaining aloft above the altar for fifteen minutes with the host in his hands. As the duke wept openly, one of his companions who was also Lutheran moaned: "Cursed be the instant I set foot in this country; at home my mind was tranquil, but now here I'm rattled by the furies and scruples of conscience."[68]

Johann Friedrich, in contrast, was enthralled. After Mass, Joseph spoke with him until noon and again in the evening after Vespers. Then, after spending another day at Assisi during which he joined the friars in prayer and venerated

Figure 22. This painting by Giuseppe Cades depicts the moment when Joseph's levitation at Mass caused Duke John Frederick of Saxony, a Lutheran, to convert to Catholicism.

the corpse of Saint Francis at his tomb, Johann Friedrich promised to become a Catholic. In 1651, he returned to Assisi and, in the presence of Cardinals Facchinetti and Rapaccioli, abjured his Lutheran beliefs and joined the Catholic Church, making his profession of faith in the hands of Joseph, to whom he would remain devoted for the rest of his life.

But not all of Joseph's elite visitors came to see him out of devotion. He was a curiosity, a spectacle, a miraculous wonder that some in the highest circles wished they could say they had seen. Such was the case of Artemisa, Marchioness dei Medici, who gathered a retinue of ladies and traveled with them to Assisi with the express purpose of seeing Joseph fly during Mass. We know of her—and of her humiliation by Joseph—because of her testimony in Joseph's beatification inquest, in which she reported that he had glowered at her the instant she stepped into the chapel, and said: "Eh, why have you come here out of curiosity? Go away in the name of God!" Years later in that beatification inquest, she would also confess: "I was left like a wet hen, and this made me realize that he could see the secrets of one's heart."[69]

Arguably, the seemingly endless stream of crowned heads, nobles, and princes of the church that flowed through Assisi had more of a painful effect on Joseph's earthly destiny than the demonic assaults and beatings recorded in his hagiographies.[70] Joseph's attractiveness was problematic. Elite visitors were surely welcomed for bringing in extra income, but they must have also been something of a burden for the friars, especially those whose duty it was to cater to their whims with the utmost courtesy. Joseph's celebrity status was problematic for higher church authorities too. On the one hand, he could be seen as living proof of the existence of the divine realities that the church proclaimed. On the other hand, he attracted too much attention and cast a belittling shadow on prelates who lived less than exemplary lives and performed no miracles. Within the Franciscan community there might have also been some fear of Joseph eclipsing the seraphic Saint Francis, their founder, who was buried there at Assisi, for Joseph attracted pilgrims from all walks of life, not just from the upper crust. Then there was the issue of Joseph's spiritual life. If, in fact, he was genuinely close to the divine—as many believed—was it correct or fair to use him as a magnet who attracted constant visitors but had little time left over for his life of prayer? And topping off all such concerns was the issue of the extreme nature of Joseph's ecstatic levitations, which resonated with an instability of their own and therefore remained on the Inquisition's radar even after his holiness had been certified as genuine.

Joseph's expulsion from Assisi was not as predictable as his levitations at Mass, but it proved inevitable, and when it came, it did so just as suddenly as one of those ecstasies, except without any shrieking or whooping. Five weeks after his fiftieth birthday, on the morning of July 23, 1653, Joseph was ordered to go to the visitor's room, where, much to his surprise, the inquisitor general of Umbria was waiting for him, along with his secretary, the chief of Assisi's police, and four soldiers. Father Vincent Maria Pellegrini, the inquisitor, then read a message from Pope Innocent X ordering Joseph to be transferred immediately to the Capuchin friary at Pietrarubbia. Visibly shaken but reminded of the importance of the vow of obedience by his superior, who was also there,[71] Joseph was quickly escorted out of the friary, taken to a carriage, and whisked away from Assisi, wearing only his habit and a pair of slippers. His eyeglasses, breviary, hat, and shoes—his only possessions—were left behind in his cell.[72] They would never be returned to him. The friars, after all, were experts at recognizing good relics when they saw them.

Back with the Capuchins

At the Capuchin friary of Pietrarubbia, Joseph found himself back in that branch of the Franciscans where he had begun his monastic life and from which he had been expelled as totally unfit. That, too, had been an indecorous departure. But now, having been ordered by the Pope to take in Joseph and keep him under wraps, the Capuchins had no choice but to welcome him back. Their friary was somewhat remote and isolated in a mountainous region of northern Italy, on the eastern flank of the Apennines, about fifty miles inland from the port city of Ancona. It seemed perfect for keeping a flying friar out of view.

Joseph was delivered to the Capuchins by Inquisitor Pellegrini, who also brought along strict instructions on how to handle him from Pope Innocent X and Cardinal Francesco Barberini, grand inquisitor of the Holy Office in Rome. Copies of these instructions were posted on the doors of the refectory and of Joseph's cell, as required by the Holy Office itself. The message was clear: Under pain of excommunication, no one at Pietrarubbia was to allow Joseph any contact with the outside world. He was to be totally sequestered, much like a prisoner: no speaking with anyone except the Capuchins of that friary; no writing to anyone, regardless of that person's eminence or rank; no receiving of letters; and no venturing beyond the walls of the friary, ever.[73] Having been read these instructions, Joseph was sent to his cell, which the provincial of the Capuchins would later describe as "the darkest and meanest" of the entire friary.[74]

Despite his sudden dislocation and the severe restrictions placed on him, Joseph continued to levitate "incessantly" at Pietrarubbia, especially during Mass, which could sometimes take him two hours to complete. And despite the Inquisition's clear instructions about keeping Joseph squirreled away, word of his presence at the friary spread quickly and widely, and before long the world from which he was supposed to be shielded invaded Pietrarubbia. And as hordes of people arrived, the Capuchins spotted a gigantic loophole in the Inquisition's instructions, which said nothing about keeping non-Capuchins away from Joseph's Masses and his constant levitating ecstasies.

Through that loophole, thousands of pilgrims flowed into Pietrarubbia.[75] Obviously, the thought had never occurred to the Inquisition that something like this could ever happen at such a remote friary. But it happened, hilariously and with a vengeance, proving that the popular appetite for miracles was insatiable. Father Giovanni Maria di Fossombrone, provincial of the Capuchins, was alarmed by the chaos and later described it in detail:

> Many people, ecclesiastical and secular, and even lay people from distant towns, flocked to our monastery of Pietrarubbia to attend his Masses, which he celebrated publicly in our church. And these throngs who came to ogle and admire his ecstasies and his raptures, or to be aided by his prayers in their needs and infirmities were so numerous that taverns were built around the monastery, along with shelters for the comfort of those who came but couldn't fit into the church where the said father celebrated Mass. To see him, they removed tiles from the roof and punched holes in the very walls of the Church.[76]

Worst of all, some of those who got close enough to Joseph during his ecstasies would prod and poke him, squeeze his hands, or hug him, vainly trying to bring him back to his senses.[77]

This carnivalesque free-for-all could not continue for long, however. On the feast of Saint Augustine, August 28, the crowd at Pietrarubbia was so huge that the vicar of the friary, Giovanni Batista di Santa Agata, brought the chaos to an end by stopping Joseph from saying Mass and ordering "that henceforth he could only be seen by the friars."[78]

By then, it was too late to fix the colossal disaster at Pietrarubbia, which was deemed irreversible by those elite clerics in Rome who acted as Joseph's guardians. In late September 1653, a mere two months after his arrival at Pietrarubbia, Joseph was transferred to an even more inaccessible Capuchin friary at Fossombrone, thirty miles away atop a steep mountain. The command to remove him was given to Ascanio Maffei, the archbishop of Urbino, who passed on the unpleasant task to his vicar-general, Mario Viviani. "Where are you taking me?" asked Joseph when he learned that he was being moved again. But the vicar could not reveal any details to anyone, even Joseph, so without knowing where he was headed, the Flying Friar was spirited away by Vicar Mario Viviani.

Once again, Joseph found himself uprooted without proper explanation, handled as a problem child, traversing unfamiliar territory. Many of the simple folk around Pietrarubbia sought to discover what route he might have taken, but their efforts were in vain. Joseph had simply vanished. The inquisitors were not about to make the same mistake twice. This time their instructions were loophole-proof: the Capuchins at Joseph's new home were to keep his presence an absolute secret, and he was not to be seen by anyone but his brethren at the friary. Father Teodoro da Cingoli, who was charged with keeping Joseph imprisoned, did his best to keep his whereabouts under wraps, but so many people suspected he might be there that the friary had to contend with a steady stream of pilgrims who came in search of Joseph, begging for his prayers. According to Pastrovicchi, these miracle-seekers came "in such great numbers that, for fear of violence, the friars wouldn't go out at all, and hid in the friary."[79]

The throngs vanished gradually, frustrated by the cold response of the friars, and soon enough the friary at Fossombrone slipped back into its usual obscurity. Chaos had been avoided. Joseph would spend three years there in relative calm, during which his fellow friars claimed to have seen him levitate nearly every day, not just at Mass but at random times, whenever something caused him to be enraptured.

Some of these unpredictable ecstasies amazed his confreres. One of these involved a lamb. Overcome by emotion at the sight of a living image of the Lamb of God and the Good Shepherd, Joseph picked up the creature, ran around the garden with it on his shoulders, and then threw it up in the air with "superhuman strength" high above the trees. He then followed after it, catching it in midair and kneeling in ecstasy for two hours on a treetop.[80] Another such impromptu ecstasy verged on comedy. Upon hearing a confrere's praises of the virtues of the Virgin Mary, Joseph lunged at him excitedly and knocked him down. As both of them tumbled to the ground, they screamed simultaneously,

Joseph in ecstasy and the Capuchin in absolute panic. When the other friars rushed to see what had occurred, they found Joseph lying on the ground, enraptured. The Capuchin tackled by him was no longer there, having fled the scene quickly "in great consternation."[81] In contrast, another ecstasy was so intensely powerful that it frightened all the friars. This one was of the predictable sort since it took place while Joseph was saying Mass on Pentecost Sunday, but its magnitude was a bit too surprising. According to Agelli, Joseph flew up "quickly and most impetuously, gyrating like a lightning bolt around the chapel, blasting out a very strange booming scream that shook the whole monastery with its vehemence." At that instant, "suddenly filled with fear," the panicked friars ran outdoors yelling, "Earthquake! earthquake!"[82]

Many other miracles were attributed to Joseph at Fossombrone, such as healing the sick, being able to read the thoughts and consciences of others, having visions, seeing heavenly apparitions, and predicting future events. One of his predictions concerned an event that would have a direct impact on him and his brethren. In early January 1655, on the vigil of the Epiphany, Joseph informed his brethren that he had experienced a revelatory vision of Pope Innocent X lying in bed, on the brink of death. Two days later, Innocent died, as Joseph had predicted. Unbeknownst to him, this change in the leadership of the Catholic Church immediately stirred the leaders of the Conventual Franciscan order to petition for a revision of his imprisonment. This petition to the newly elected Pope Alexander VII was a renewal of previous requests, for the Conventuals had never given up on bringing Joseph back to his branch of the Franciscan order, preferably back to Assisi.[83] This time around, the request received a favorable hearing, but the new pope, who had previously dealt with petitions in Joseph's case as an intermediary, approached it cautiously, well aware of the excesses that had led to his removal from Assisi and Pietrarubbia. His decision, while favorable to the petitioners, was somewhat disappointing to many of them. In June of 1656, Alexander agreed to return Joseph to the Conventual Franciscans, as requested, but ordered that he be sent to their friary at Osimo rather than to Assisi, pointing out that "it is enough to have Saint Francis in that sanctuary."[84]

The pope's decision coincided with an outbreak of the bubonic plague in Italy, however, and the toll taken by this epidemic—which included 15,000 deaths in Rome alone—was serious enough to close most roads and stop traffic between all towns and cities. Consequently, Joseph's move ended up being delayed by a year, but finally, on July 6, 1657, he was removed from the Capuchin friary at Fossombrone and taken to the Conventual Franciscan friary at Osimo, which would prove to be the final stop on his convoluted earthly journey.

From Osimo to Eternal Ecstasy

Pope Alexander VII's orders to the friary at Osimo were funneled through the Inquisition, which was still in charge of monitoring Joseph, and they were as harsh and clearly detailed as they had been upon his transfer from Pietrarubbia to Fossombrone: In essence, Joseph was still a prisoner, to be kept out of sight and in isolation and even forced to eat alone in his cell rather than in the refectory with his brethren. On pain of excommunication, the friars at Osimo were forbidden to grant him contact with anyone outside the friary, in person or through letters, regardless of the rank or eminence of those seeking contact with him, and he was to celebrate Mass in a "private oratory.[85] Pope Alexander and the Inquisition backed up their commitment to these injunctions by denying all pleas from Queen Christina of Sweden, a recent convert to Catholicism who had relinquished the throne and moved to Rome and eagerly longed to meet Joseph in person.

News of Joseph's transfer to Osimo shook his brethren at Fossombrone, some of whom "wept bitterly" as they said farewell.[86] Forced to take back roads to maintain secrecy and avoid crowds, the journey took four days, much longer than expected. Along the way, Joseph and his minders lodged and rested at the Franciscan friary of Saint Victor as well as in some inns and farms. And it was at one of these stops, near his destination, that Joseph had one of his best-known levitations, immortalized many years later in a painting by Ludovico Mazzanti, which now hangs in the friary at Osimo (fig. 23).

At a farm not far from Osimo, while gazing at his surroundings from a balcony with his escort, Joseph spotted the dome of the shrine of the Holy House of Loreto and cried out, "Oh God, I've never seen any such thing! So many angels coming and going from heaven! Don't you see them? . . . Tell me, what is that place?" Informed that he was looking at the shrine that contained the Holy Family's house from Nazareth, which had been brought there miraculously by angels,[87] Joseph cried out again, "No wonder, then, that so many angels come down from paradise to that place; look at it and behold how divine mercy rains down on this spot! Oh, happy place, oh, blessed place!" Then, as ever, an ecstatic Joseph flew immediately off the balcony and perched for a while in a nearby almond tree about twelve feet off the ground (see fig. 2).[88]

Figure 23. This painting by Ludovico Mazzanti is the most widely reproduced image of Saint Joseph's flight upon his encounter with the Holy Shrine of Loreto.

Joseph would spend six years at Osimo, absorbed in prayer, in the strict seclusion mandated by the Inquisition, rarely allowed to venture far from his cell and its adjacent oratory save for those times when he was asked to visit friars who had fallen ill and once, each night, after all the doors of the friary had been locked, when he was allowed to visit the friary's chapel. All intermingling with his brethren was tightly controlled. Assigned one constant companion, Joseph was not allowed to chat with others unless they were "the wisest and most highly esteemed," and those meetings had been arranged ahead of time and approved by his superiors.[89] Joseph's ecstasies continued unabated at Osimo. One friar who was permitted access to Joseph would later testify: "I can say that with my own eyes I have seen his ecstasies take place in his cell *thousands* of times."[90] Given Joseph's isolation, however, there are fewer accounts in his hagiographies of these "thousands" of Osimo ecstasies than one might expect. The local bishop, Antonio Bichi, a nephew of Pope Alexander VII, was among those who did get to see Joseph levitate several times during their conversations. Nonlevitating ecstasies also took place at Osimo. Pastrovicchi writes that sometimes Joseph would be found "deeply in ecstasy" on the floor of his oratory and had to be carried "like a corpse" to his cell next door. He adds that some of these raptures lasted for six or seven hours and that if his eyes remained open, as they often did, gnats and flies alighted on them without the slightest response from Joseph.[91]

Osimo would be the destination in Joseph's constant shuffling and the setting for his ecstatic death. Like many a saint in Christian history, Joseph's clairvoyance allowed him to predict his own death as it approached, and these prophecies intensified as he neared his sixtieth birthday. Much like his role model Saint Francis, Joseph referred to his body as *asino,* or "jackass," and he also abused it through ascetic excesses as vehement as those of Saint Francis. As one might expect, such extreme asceticism took its toll on Joseph's health—so much so that by the time he reached his fifties, he "was always in distress from serious and considerable illnesses," most of which were digestive disorders.[92]

In the summer of 1663, Joseph's health worsened rapidly, as he began to pass blood in his urine and to vomit up blood. On August 10 he developed an unrelenting fever. Although he continued to celebrate Mass for five more days, he was soon incapable of returning to the altar. Having said his last Mass on August 15, the feast of the Assumption of Mary—during which he reportedly had "marvelous ecstasies and raptures," including a levitation—Joseph became too feeble to stand or walk. Allowed to attend Mass and receive communion in his oratory, he continued to have ecstasies and to read the minds and consciences of those around him, as well as to predict the future for them.[93] At this point he also began to say, "The jackass has now begun to climb the mountain," warning his brethren that his own death was near. By early September, despite his constant miracle-working, his health worsened so that those around Joseph gave up whatever hope they might have had of a recovery.[94] Joseph's refrain changed at that point to "The jackass is about to reach the top." Some of Joseph's last miracles involved his own body, which frequently slipped into cataleptic trances and seemed impervious to pain. As was common practice in seventeenth-century medicine, Joseph was subjected to bloodletting, a procedure that required cutting into a vein and cauterizing the wound afterward with a red-hot iron. At one of these sessions, as the surgeon was cauterizing the vein he had opened on Joseph's leg, he noticed that the friar was enraptured, "raised almost a palm's height off the chair," his body so rigid that his limbs could not be moved, his mouth agape, his eyes wide open, staring heavenward, impervious to a fly that kept scuttling back and forth on one of his pupils. When Joseph came out of his ecstasy, after ordered to do so by his superior, he was surprised to find that the bloodletting was over and his leg was bandaged, for his ecstasy had acted like potent anesthesia.[95] And, according to eyewitnesses, the same thing occurred at each of the next three bloodlettings carried out by this surgeon, who—as happened frequently to those who encountered Joseph—had been gently reminded by Joseph of an old and secret sin he had never confessed.[96]

Ecstasies of this sort also often accompanied Joseph's encounters with the Eucharist during these final days, although most of these left him earthbound, spread-eagled on the floor. But Joseph's final communion, brought to him by viaticum from the friary's chapel, occasioned a spectacular levitating ecstasy. Upon hearing the ringing of the bell that announced the arrival of the consecrated host, Joseph flew out of bed, literally, and out of his room—despite the weakness that prevented him from attending Mass—and then fell to his knees to partake of the Eucharist from the friars who were bringing it to him. This would prove to be Joseph's last levitation and also his last communion. Although he appeared "filled with superhuman splendor" when he received the Eucharist, the radiant Joseph collapsed soon thereafter and had to be carried back to his cell. Surrounded by friars who prayed with him and for him, spoke words of comfort, or sang hymns as his condition worsened, Joseph received the sacrament of extreme unction, exclaiming, "Oh what songs, oh what sounds of paradise, oh what fragrances, oh what odors, oh what sweetness of paradise."[97]

The following day, September 18, Joseph had trouble swallowing and could not receive communion. But he spent his remaining hours on earth conscious and in good spirits, changing his refrain to "The jackass has reached the top of the mountain. He can no longer move. He will have to leave his hide here." With some difficulty, due to a swollen tongue and dry mouth, he also began calling on Jesus repeatedly and uttering short prayers such as "Take this heart, Jesus, burn it and maul it" and "May God be praised, may God be thanked, may the will of God be done." That evening, Joseph took the ultimate flight into an eternal ecstasy—this time without one of his shrieks—leaving behind the "jackass" of his body, which he had maltreated since childhood. And, as all hagiographies are expected to say, he left earth "with a placid smile that cheered those around him, with a happy and serene countenance, resplendent with a sudden light."[98]

Joseph was not yet gone from Osimo. On the contrary, he was now more fully present than he had been while alive, for the Inquisition's restrictions on access to Joseph did not apply to his corpse. Finally, Joseph was accessible to the world. His body was now considered a wondrous relic and a point of contact with Joseph himself in heaven. Of course, Joseph could not be venerated as a saint yet, although he had been considered a living saint for decades. The church had yet to certify his saintly status through its long and complex process of canonization. But he could certainly be approached as an intercessor, and according to traditional belief, that intercessory capability was always heightened by nearness to his corpse.

Joseph's body—his "jackass"—was cut open so it could be embalmed with spices and fragrant herbs and so it could be examined by a surgeon, as had been decided the day before he died, to discern the physical effects of his raptures, as in the cases of Saint Carlo Borromeo and Philip Neri.[99] As expected, the surgeon found certain anomalies in Joseph's heart that could be attributed to his ecstasies: his pericardium was shriveled, and the ventricles were devoid of blood and desiccated. According to the surgeon's expert opinion, such unusual deformities were most definitely proof that Joseph's heart had been engulfed by "the supernatural flame of divine love."[100]

Placed on display in a cypress casket within the sacristy of the friary's church on September 19, the body was surrounded by a wooden barrier and guarded by eight priests, eight friars, and eight local noblemen. Such precautions were deemed necessary because of the huge number of people that would surely show up. These expectations proved true, for news of Joseph's interment at Osimo spread very quickly, and "an innumerable throng" flooded the friary as many "who were previously unable to see Joseph alive now came to see him dead." Some lucky few—"those deemed most worthy"—even got to kiss Joseph's hand and feet. At the end of the first day of public viewing, which extended into the night, many people were still arriving and queuing up. Fearing that a riot might ensue if that huge crowd was told to go home without having had a glimpse of Joseph, the friars decided to extend access to his body for an additional day, on September 20, after the funeral rites had taken place.

That extra viewing time might have prevented a riot, but it proved too brief and very disappointing for those who were still waiting in line for their turn when it ended. They "had to be pushed out of the church, either with pleas or with threats." The following day, September 21, the cypress casket containing Joseph's body was nestled inside an oak casket to doubly ensure the preservation of the relic inside. Then, finally, Joseph was buried in a newly created vault at the foot of the altar of the Immaculate Conception, where he had levitated many times.[101]

Immediately, as expected, healing miracles began to take place, all of which were duly recorded in detail, as is fitting for someone already considered a saint years before his death. A few months later, in March 1664, the canonization process was set in motion.[102] The first step was an Episcopal "informative" inquest (*processus auctoritate ordinaria*) that interviewed people in the dioceses of Nardo, Assisi, and Osimo, in which Joseph had lived. Once that inquest was completed, another was set in motion in April 1668, this time from Rome, under the authority of Pope Clement IX. This apostolic inquest (*processus auctoritate apostolica*) took a few more years to complete, and then, as was required, the wheels in the canonization began to slow down as discussion of his case continued, on and off, until 1735, when the Congregation of Rites conferred the title of "Venerable" on Joseph. With more miracles being reported, the process gained some speed again—relatively speaking—as Joseph moved toward the next big step, beatification. Eighteen years later, on February 24, 1753, Pope Benedict XIV issued the brief "Aeternus Dei Filius" in which he elevated Joseph to the rank of "Blessed," thus granting him the right of being venerated by all Catholics. This major change in status, which was accompanied by the two hagiographies of Agelli and Pastrovicchi, increased devotion to Joseph throughout Italy and the world, and with more miracles now being attributed to him, he moved quickly and inexorably toward canonization. Finally, on July 16,

1767, the anniversary of Francis of Assisi's canonization, Joseph was proclaimed a saint by Pope Clement XIII at Saint Peter's Basilica, with all the appropriate pomp.

A century had elapsed since Joseph's death. During those ten decades, twelve different popes had dealt with the issue of his canonization, some more intensely than others. Ironically, Joseph's extravagant miracles did not grant him a sure and easy elevation to sainthood. During Joseph's lifetime, due to the revamping of the canonization process set in motion by the Council of Trent, much more emphasis began to be placed on the "heroic virtue" of candidates for sainthood than on their miracles. By the time of his death, this process was in full tilt. Urban VIII, the pope over whose head he had flown, and Clement XIII, the pope who canonized him, were strongly committed to this change in priorities. Pope Clement had spearheaded the effort of bringing the process of saint-making more in line with rationalist and scientific Enlightenment principles. So it was, then, that Joseph's impossible flights gained a rare degree of credibility within Catholicism at a time when skepticism and caution concerning the miraculous had already crept deeply within that faith's tradition.[103]

In the secular world, immense changes had taken place at an unprecedented pace due to advances in science and technology. In 1709, during that long lull in Joseph's canonization process, Bartolomeu De Gusmão, a Portuguese Jesuit priest who had been filling balloons with hot air and experimenting with them, published a treatise titled "A Short Manifesto for Those Who Are Unaware That Sailing through the Element of Air Is Possible."[104] Experiments with hot-air balloons continued, here and there. Finally, 120 years after Joseph's death and a mere 16 years since his canonization, two French brothers, Joseph-Michel and Jacques-Étienne Montgolfier, successfully launched hot-air balloons in 1783. These balloons, equipped with gondolas in which humans could ride, would initiate a new age in which flight was no longer some "impossible" miracle. We shall return to this wonder later. Ironically—and fittingly—the Montgolfier brothers and their invention eventually relegated Saint Joseph of Cupertino, "the Flying Friar," to the dustbin of history, so to speak, while at the same time making it possible for him to become the potential patron saint of millions of humans flying in aircraft routinely, thinking of it as not much different from flossing one's teeth, taking out the trash, or standing in line for a white mocha cappuccino at some trendy coffee shop.

An ironic twist, for sure, this new role of Joseph's, since it was his flying that had caused his imprisonment. Even more ironic is the fact that some of those who made Joseph's patronage popular in the twentieth century were Catholic American airmen who prayed to him for protection as they dropped bombs on Italy during the Second World War, especially on Monte Cassino, the birthplace of Western monasticism.[105]

And that eerily intense irony, it could be said, borders on the impossible.

4. Making Sense of the Flying Friar

His raptures were continuous, and one can say that he lived more
in ecstasy than in this world.
—Paolo Agelli

Saint Joseph of Cupertino is an enigma begging for deciphering. He was unique in so many ways and so impossibly otherworldly as to defy rational analysis, and his mysticism so extreme as to defy classification.

What are we to make of such a saint or his levitations? And we are referring here to the *saint*, not the man. The saint can be encountered in many documents, but the man himself is much harder to find. Saint Joseph not only levitates more frequently than any other saint in Christian history but also rises higher off the ground. He not only hovers but actually flies—not just indoors, where it is relatively easier to employ wires or other props and fool people, but also outdoors, where such trickery is relatively more difficult or impossible. And he flies forward and backward too. Unlike Saint Teresa of Avila, whose levitations ceased after she complained to God about them, Joseph's gravity-defying ecstasies continued to occur up until the last few days of his life. Moreover, his levitations often point beyond themselves: while they are always carefully described as a side effect of sudden ecstasies brought on by God, rather than as events willed by Joseph himself, they often serve practical purposes and thus are much more than mere wonders. Their instrumentality makes them miracle-working miracles.

Why isn't this common knowledge?

Saint Joseph's relative obscurity is somewhat puzzling. His levitations were ostensibly witnessed by more people than those of any other saint, and the number of lay witnesses—as opposed to clerical ones—is also higher, even though his superiors tried to keep him under wraps and out of public view as much as possible. High clergy and nobility from all corners of Europe went out of their way to visit him and testified that they had beheld his levitations firsthand or begged for the privilege of visiting him, unsuccessfully. And some of these elites were among the most progressive boosters of the so-called Age of Reason, such as the Lutheran Duke John Frederick of Braunschweig-Lüneberg, patron of the very rational mathematician-philosopher Gottfried Wilhelm Leibniz, who served as his privy councillor and librarian, and the Lutheran Queen Christina of Sweden, who employed mathematician René Descartes as her court philosopher, possibly because he advised that "everything must be doubted."[1]

In Joseph's case, then, holy levitation is taken to a higher level, literally and figuratively. Given the extreme nature of his hovering and flying and given the context of his time and place, as well as the impressive number of witnesses, Joseph is truly unique. He reifies and surpasses the expectations of his Catholic culture. And the questions raised by his uniqueness are intensely pointed, sharp edged, and problematic, for even if one dismisses all of his flying as absolutely impossible and nothing more than papistical deceit, trickery, and inanity, one is left with all sorts of questions concerning all that lying, tricking, and unreasoning, not to mention questions about what might have been "really" going on in his life and the lives of those who swore under oath that they had seen him fly.

So, again, one must ask: Why do so few people on earth know about Saint Joseph? Why is the evidence ignored or trivialized? Why has he been relegated to the history of the ridiculous rather than to the history of the impossible, or to the science of antigravitational forces?

Several factors make it difficult to dismiss testimonies about his levitations as lies, sheer nonsense, or mass hysteria. First, the levitations are so extreme as to make the likelihood of trickery seem remote, unlikely, or technologically impossible. The use of wires, ropes, stilts, trampolines, or other contraptions used by illusionists is out of the question for most of his aerial raptures, given their setting and the technology available at that time. Second, the number and status of his witnesses make the accounts seem more credible, paradoxically, even as his levitations become more extreme. Third, those who witness Joseph's flights are not only other monks and nuns, or illiterate rustics, but representatives of the highest echelons of society.[2] Fourth, with Joseph, levitation ceases to be a cloistered *monastic* phenomenon, at least until he is moved to Fossombrone in 1653. His flights thus obliterate distinctions between *high* and *low* culture or *official* and *popular* religion: shepherd and pope, milkmaid and nun, peasant and prince, coachman and duke, page and ambassador. All sorts of witnesses report the same astounding levitations, indoors and outdoors, in candlelit spaces or in the bright light of the noonday Italian sun, over a span of thirty-five years. In many ways, the logical frustration felt by William Crookes when dealing with spiritualist levitation in the late nineteenth century can also arise here, no pun intended. "The supposition that there is a sort of mania or delusion which suddenly attacks a whole room full of intelligent persons who are quite sane elsewhere," he said, "and that they all concur to the minutest particulars, in the details of the occurrences of which they suppose themselves to be witnesses, seems to my mind more incredible than even the facts they attest."[3]

So if one dismisses all eyewitness accounts in this case as fabrications or delusions, one is left with the hard task of explaining why such lies were apparently told and believed or why such delusions took hold as they did within Catholic circles or were convincing enough to elicit conversions from Protestantism. One must still make sense of the Flying Friar as a phenomenon and also make sense of the nature and purpose of such a phenomenon per se on various levels: personal, social, cultural, political, metaphysical, theological, psychological, or medical. And, finally, one must also ask the social-scientific functionalist question, which Saint Teresa also asked—albeit for personal rather than academic reasons—what purpose does a miracle as seemingly useless as levitation serve for any individual or any society?

At the very same time, one must make sense of the unease caused in Catholic circles by Joseph, especially of the undeniable fact that the Inquisition kept a close eye on him while his superiors tried to hide him from the public. For the last three decades of his life—and especially the last ten years of it—Joseph lived much like a prisoner, isolated, unable to join in the ritual life of his monasteries, or even to eat with his brethren. Why? Moreover, he was repeatedly shuffled to various remote locations. Acute ambiguity surrounds him and his ecstasies, not *despite* his reputation as a holy man but *because* of it. Why? The canonization inquests and the hagiographies revel in describing his aethrobatic feats, but at the same time they highlight or bemoan the painful isolation imposed on him.[4] The very Catholic baroque excess of Joseph of Cupertino, then, seems to have been something as troubling as it was marvelous, something to admire and be wary about, something to shout about and something to hide, simultaneously.

Why?

To delve effectively into the ambivalence of Joseph's superiors, one must focus on some of the most significant characteristics of his levitating ecstasies, especially because of the abundance of extraordinary details provided by so many eyewitnesses. God is in the details here, literally and figuratively.[5] The specificity provided in so many of the narratives—so meticulous, so nearly microscopic in focus and quasi-scientific in their attention to minutiae, so unlike previous accounts of levitation—has much to do with the paradoxical wonder of Joseph's miraculousness and with the approach taken to it by the hierarchy of the Catholic Church during the apogee of the so-called Age of Reason, which also happened to be the Age of Religious Wars and the Age of the Witchcraft Craze.

Ecstatic Flight in Context

Levitation was but one in a long list of miracles attributed to Joseph, the vast majority of which were also attributed to other saints, such as healing the sick, controlling natural events, reading the minds and consciences of others, predicting the future, emitting an indescribably pleasant odor, having visions of Christ and the angels, and driving away demons, to name but some of the more impressive ones frequently mentioned in hagiographies and in the *processi* for beatification and canonization. Some other "common" miracles were attributed to him too, but less frequently, such as resurrecting farm animals or knowing what was occurring elsewhere. Some bilocations were also attributed to him; that is, he was seen as physically present in two distinct locations simultaneously. But what made Joseph truly unique—and what shall be our sole focus here—was the miracle of levitation.

At the outset, to fully comprehend the phenomenon of levitation one must address the issue of context. Levitation is contextual. Christian levitators never begin levitating suddenly, out of the blue. They levitate only within a very specific religious context that involves sharing a specific communal view of reality and following certain prescribed paths. This applies to holy levitators as well as to those in league with the devil. And the same could be said to some extent about levitators in other religions. The act of levitation is inseparable from belief in levitation, personally and communally. So one must ask some basic questions. Where did Joseph first learn about levitation? And how did he learn to levitate? Why wasn't it "impossible" for him and for those around him? These questions address a significant analytical issue, that of context and of the complex interrelationship of religious phenomena, especially those of the impossible sort, with time, place, culture, worldviews, beliefs, behavior, and other such variables.

Joseph's levitations are very Catholic, inconceivable outside of his baroque Catholic milieu. His levitations don't just "happen." And the same is true of Saint Teresa's and those of other Catholic levitators. They are constructed out of certain expectations they share with those around them and the complex social processes in which they engage. And this sharing is essential, for levitation does not spring solely out of Joseph's expectations but also those of his culture and religion. For his levitations to happen, they need to fit into a shared web of meaning in which expectations flow in two directions constantly in a reciprocal cycle, from the culture to the individual and from the individual back to the culture. Levitations need to make sense in both ways in this constant cycle, for levitations—to be considered possible—must make sense for all involved in the event (that is, the levitator as well as the community in which the levitator lives). As has been observed, every culture's sense of what is real is determined to a large extent by its social practices and its institutions. In other words, what is considered possible or impossible is delineated, or "set up" by one's culture.[6] And the experiences of mystics are shaped by what is expected within their particular religious tradition.[7] So, one must ask: What was it that Joseph might have seen, heard, or read about levitation?

Joseph undoubtedly encountered accounts of levitation at an early age, and that would not have been unusual, even for a poor boy. Levitation was a rare miracle, but there were plenty of hagiographies that contained stories of levitating saints, as well as oral and written legends. Which accounts or legends crossed his path is anyone's guess; we have no such information. So tracing Joseph's levitations to a specific source or discovering where he might have learned the details of his future "craft"—if one might call it that—is not possible. But baroque Catholicism was abuzz with tales of the miraculous in 1603, the year of Joseph's birth, and that fascination with miracles only increased as his life unfolded. Chances are he might have known something about the levitations of Ignatius Loyola, Philip Neri, and Teresa of Avila, all canonized in 1622 with great fanfare when Joseph was nineteen years old. And he would probably have known of them before that date, for their beatifications, which received a great deal of attention in Italy, took place during his formative years: Ignatius in 1609, when Joseph was six years old; Teresa in 1614, when he was eleven; and Philip when he was twelve. Of these three saints, Teresa of Avila was the one best known for her levitations and the only one to have written about them in detail.

Whether or not Joseph ever read Teresa of Avila's descriptions of her ecstasies and levitations or had any knowledge of them is unknown and probably unlikely. An Italian edition of one of Teresa's hagiographies, written by the Jesuit Francisco de Ribera and translated by Monsignor Giovanni Francesco Bordini, had been published in Rome in 1599. This *Vita* provided a narrative of Teresa's life and work, including accounts of some of her levitations, and Joseph could have conceivably run into it at some point in his youth. Given his poor reading skills, however, he would probably have only heard it read to him or summarized by others who were better educated. And the first Italian translation of her autobiography, in which Teresa dwells on her levitations in detail, was not published until 1636, when Joseph was already in his thirties.[8] By then Joseph had been levitating for several years, so it is highly unlikely that he was influenced by Teresa's *Vita*. Although one can never discount the possibility of someone having translated Teresa's writings orally for Joseph, or at least bits and pieces of her work, but that would be pure speculation. Nonetheless, even without some "smoking gun" sort of evidence linking the two mystics—such as an explicitly clear textual connection between the two of them—it is easy to see that his levitating ecstasies share many of the same assumptions as hers. And it is also possible to observe that the similarities derive from a shared culture.

Mystical experiences could be as varied as the names given to them in monastic culture, so classifying Joseph's supernatural experiences can be troublesome. Sometimes, even those who claimed to have these experiences had trouble classifying them or sorting out the terminology, as was the case with Saint Teresa and her handling of the terms *unión, arrobamiento, elevamiento, vuelo de espíritu, arrebatamiento,* and *éstasi.*[9] Ordered by her superiors to write about her ecstasies and visions, Teresa had no choice but to employ terms with which she was familiar and hope for the best. Joseph himself never engaged with terminology the same way, and neither did those around him or his hagiographers, all of whom employed the terms *estasi* (ecstasies) and *ratti* (raptures) somewhat interchangeably, although sometimes estasi was clearly used in reference to the trance alone while ratti was employed in reference to the levitations.[10] They also sometimes referred to the physical effects of these mystical experiences as *moti* (movements, motions, gestures), distinguishing these from whatever might have been happening to him spiritually and mentally. Following the lead of Joseph's contemporaries, "ecstasy" and "rapture" will be used interchangeably here to refer to his mystical experiences, and since many of Joseph's moti were manifestations of trance-like states, the English term "trance" will be used here to refer to his physical state during his mystical experiences, even though the Italian noun *trance* is not employed in the original documents.

While terminology might have been less than well defined among monastics, certain key assumptions were considered unquestionable. First, the possibility of attaining a powerfully intimate encounter with the divine was assumed to be very real by Joseph and those around him, as was also the case with Teresa. And such ecstasies and raptures—which could vary in intensity—were assumed to involve both the mortal body and the immortal soul. As one of Joseph's hagiographers put it, levitation "is the elevation of the body that follows the flight of the soul to God."[11] Delving into the theological details of this assumption is unnecessary, especially in the case of Joseph, whose ignorance of formal theology was one of his most salient personal traits, even more so than Teresa, who stressed her theological ignorance constantly. Catholic mystics tended to have similar ecstasies because they shared certain assumptions about ecstasies that were widely accepted within Catholic monastic culture in the early modern era. Certain things were expected to happen in ecstasy; understanding the *how* and *why* of these phenomena was unnecessary.[12] A commonsensical awareness of ecstatic trances as *facts* seemed sufficient. The key issue was discerning whether those events were caused by God or the devil.

Another common and widely shared assumption involved metaphysics, even if the ecstatic person was ignorant of philosophy and knew nothing of its constituent branches, including metaphysics, ontology, or epistemology. One of the most basic unquestioned assumptions—understood as a *fact*—was that humans inhabited two realms simultaneously, the material and the spiritual, as we have already seen in the case of Saint Teresa. This *fact* was part and parcel of monastic life and its mystical culture. Mystical ecstasies involved body, mind, and soul because the human self was unquestioningly believed to be composed of matter and spirit. As Bernino put it, ecstasies carry away "the mind and the body, the inner and the outer man."[13] This binary understanding of reality also applied to the location of the mystic, which meant that the *outer man* remained on earth during ecstasies, while *the inner man* was suddenly transported to heaven. As some of Joseph's hagiographers put it, he used to be "more with his soul in heaven than with his body on earth."[14] This constant shuttling between two realms was understood by Joseph and his contemporaries in a pre-Copernican, pre-Newtonian spatial sense, literally, with earth *below* and heaven *above*. Consequently, levitation was also understood and explained in these terms, as a lifting of the spiritualized body in the direction of heaven above, where the mystic's soul had been instantly transported.[15] Teresa of Avila explained her levitations in precisely this way.[16]

Joseph's own understanding of his levitations matched Teresa's, as one might expect, but was much more emotional than rational and more deeply rooted in his ecstatic trances than in theological or metaphysical distinctions. In essence, Joseph had an inchoate perception of the inner/outer and heaven-above/earth-below spatial dichotomies, which he seems to have *felt* deeply, and not at all in a metaphorical way. Although he never wrote much, he did compose some rhymed hymns, and one of them gives us a clear glimpse of his thoroughly existential and somewhat wrenching understanding of the inner/outer, up/down, above/below dimensional dichotomies.

Giesù, Giesù, Giesù,	Jesus, Jesus, Jesus,
deh tirami la sù,	oh, pull me up there,
la sù in paradiso,	into paradise there above,
che là godrò il bel viso,	where I'll enjoy your beautiful face,
là ti posso più amare	where I can love you more
e con angeli lodare.	and with the angels praise you.
Giesù, Giesù, Giesù,	Jesus, Jesus, Jesus,
non vorrei star più quaggiù,	I don't want to stay here below,
vorria venir là sù.[17]	Up there I want to go.

The sense of displacement expressed in these lines is not only intensely spatial but also qualitative, for paradise is "above" and infinitely superior to whatever is "here below," where Joseph feels exiled or imprisoned. The ecstatic upward tug of levitation—evoked in the plaintive "tirami la sù"—is not just some freakish physical anomaly, then, but a redemptive act. This is a view of reality that is passed on and driven into the consciousness of monastics. Such a view produces a specific conception of what is "real" or "possible." It is the matrix in which the experience of levitation is constructed.

Spatial and qualitative distinctions were essential in monastic mystical culture, for they were used to measure the intensity of ecstasies on a scale from low to high. The higher the intensity, the "higher" one's soul was drawn "up" into heaven. Cataleptic trance-like states involving paralysis, aphasia, and insensitivity to physical stimuli were the most common type of "high" ecstasies described in medieval and early modern hagiographies. Consequently, levitation was taken to be a supremely intense kind of ecstatic rapture—a leap into a rarely reached apex of the ecstatic spectrum—in which the cataleptic symptoms of mystical trances could be additionally accompanied by flight.

The Body and the Ecstatic Self

Joseph's raptures came in various levels of intensity, but overall they involved his body in the most extreme ecstatic states conceivable. Whether he remained earthbound, as he sometimes did, or whether he became airborne, his body would go into a total sensory shutdown resembling a catatonic state. And, as one might expect, Joseph's hagiographers provided detailed descriptions of the sensory tests performed on his ecstatic body so they could offer proof of the extreme cataleptic nature of his trances and make some sense of them theologically and rationally.

> During the ecstasies and raptures, one could do anything to his body because there was nothing of him there . . . and he was beyond himself in another world. His eyes usually remained open, but deprived of sight; his ears did not perceive any sound, not even the loudest, unless it came from his superior. . . . All his senses were deprived of their proper functions then. People pricked his feet with needles, seared his hands with fire, poked his eyeballs with their fingers, all in vain, because he was not really there and his body was dead to the world . . . his arms, hands, feet and neck remained so rigid that it would have been easier to break his bones than to move his limbs from the positions into which the rapture had set them.[18]

In modern medical terms, trances of this sort might be diagnosed as *akinetic catatonia* due to four key symptoms of that condition: not responding to other people or one's environment; not speaking; holding one's body in an unusual position; and resisting people who try to adjust one's body.[19] Anachronistic medical and psychiatric diagnoses aside, one of the oddest details embedded in the lengthy quote above is the issue of Joseph's total deafness being overcome by his superior's voice. This significant detail is reiterated often in Joseph's inquest processi and in his hagiographies, and it was instrumental in the Inquisition's approval of his ecstasies, for it served as proof of Joseph's obedience and humility. Asked once how he could hear his superior's commands while totally bereft of his sense of hearing in his ecstasies, Joseph gave an explanation that further convinced the Inquisitors of the divine nature of his raptures: He never heard his superior, he said, but God always did, and at the very instant the superior spoke, the ecstasy would be stopped by none other than God himself, who was most certainly never, ever deaf.[20] This quirky exception embedded in Joseph's ecstasies does not fit the profile of a genuinely physiological cataleptic seizure, making it difficult to diagnose retroactively as pathological, in purely medical terms.[21]

While some aspects of mystical ecstasy might resemble symptoms of a natural diagnosable illness, levitation does not since it is considered an absolute impossibility by modern medical science. As far as modern medicine and science are concerned, no human being in a cataleptic state has ever levitated. Consequently, all talk about levitation in Joseph's day and age stands in stark relief, as a *fact*—that is, as something believed to be as real as catalepsy but attributable solely to supernatural rather than natural causes. Retroactive medical diagnoses are totally irrelevant here. Yet, inexplicably, that supernatural etiology was inseparable from the very specific and extremely rare natural physical fact of levitation, which levitators and those around them had to make intelligible, somehow. All such attempts at explaining levitation were no different from the futile attempts made by mystics to explain their ineffable ecstasies: the ineffability of it all was the thing itself, the mingling of natural and supernatural, begging for comprehensibility.

In Joseph's case, as in Teresa's, the physical force of a levitating ecstasy was often described as overpowering and irresistible, as something beyond the human self. Asked once about what propelled him off the ground, Joseph replied: "It was great, that force; it was a great force, a great force!"[22] At other times, however, that force was described as "a gentle, gentle thing."[23] Like Teresa, who complained of the physical and emotional painfulness of levitating ecstasies, Joseph spoke of his levitations as an "illness" or "malady" he endured,[24] adding, paradoxically, that the ecstasies that accompanied them were "as a taste of the true glory of paradise."[25] But Joseph and Teresa differed as much as they resembled each other. Like Teresa, Joseph is said to have pleaded with God for an end to his levitations, but his pleas, unlike hers, were of no avail.[26] And while Teresa's levitations were silent, Joseph always roared as he went airborne, emitting a loud noise variously described in Italian as *urlo, grido,* or *strillo,* which could mean a scream, shriek, shout, cry, yell, screech, howl, or whoop—a very physical reflex as irrepressible as the levitation itself. One of his attempts to explain these noises employs an explosive metaphor: "As gunpowder explodes when it is ignited in firearms, making a loud bang in the surrounding air, so does the heart of the ecstatic shout out when it's set aflame by the love of God." Curiously, Saint Teresa also used a very similar metaphor.[27] Sometimes the screaming could be perceived as a miracle unto itself, something as supernatural and incredible as the levitation. Such was the case at Fossombrone one Pentecost Sunday, for instance, when Joseph's scream was loud enough to shake the walls and make his fellow friars fear that an earthquake was occurring.[28]

Joseph's levitations were so numerous and so frequent that they became unquantifiable. Tallying them seemed too large a task, apparently, as suggested by the fact that in the Assisi beatification inquest alone—one of several conducted in three different dioceses and over a dozen locations—there are 800 folios dedicated to his trances, ecstasies, raptures, and levitations.[29] Referring specifically to this record in Assisi, Gustavo Parisciani said they were so frequent that "attempting to count and catalogue them would have been a pointless effort." To back up this observation, Parisciani then quotes the diary kept by Abbott Arcangelo Rosmi, where he said: "The ecstasies were frequent, especially at Mass. . . . Consequently, we didn't feel pressed to keep track and number them all."[30] Moreover, this issue of frequency is singled out in most narratives as one of the main reasons for the extreme isolation imposed on Joseph. His constant levitations were too distracting and disruptive, a threat to the rigid rhythms of communal life. And every day was full of triggers that could launch Joseph into ecstasy.

Predictable and Unpredictable Triggers

Joseph was always ready to explode, so to speak. A Jesuit who was granted permission to speak with him said afterward: "He is very intensely united to God and his heart is more disposed to this union than gunpowder is to ignition by the tiniest spark."[31] His world was as full of triggers as of the inexhaustible spiritual meaning he could find in it. This made him epistemologically and mystically volatile, and all his raptures were an explosive response to some meaning encoded in his surroundings. Joseph was constantly reading or decoding the world in a mystical and sacramental way, either investing it with meaning or perceiving the meaning inherent in it.

Celebrating Mass was a constant trigger, day in day out, for all the obvious reasons, and feast days seemed to produce some of his most spectacular levitations. Visual stimuli were constant triggers too. Sacred images, especially icons of the Virgin Mary, crosses, and crucifixes could elicit levitations or become the focal point of his ecstasies (figs. 24 and 25). Joseph had a very fertile and

Figure 24. Saint Joseph was constantly drawn to crosses and other sacred images, which caused him to levitate.

Figure 25. Giambettino Cignaroli's highly spiritualized depiction of Saint Joseph's attraction to images of the Virgin Mary blurs the line between the heavenly and earthly dimensions.

active symbolic imagination that imbued his world with a sacramental dimension. Random encounters with all sorts of things, animate as well as inanimate,
could turn into epiphanies and bring on ecstasies: a lamb could be a manifestation of Jesus, the Agnus Dei or Jesus, the Good Shepherd; a candle could reify the tongues of flame that descended on the twelve apostles at Pentecost.
Auditory triggers were less predictable, and these included sacred music, hymns,
Bible passages, prayers, or even bagpipes or flutes played by shepherds; certain
words or holy names; or the mere mention of one of God's attributes, such as
His goodness or omnipotence.[32] The outcome of conversing with Joseph was
always unpredictable, for one never knew which word or phrase might make
him levitate, and this led many around him to "refrain from conversation" even
though they wanted to speak with him.[33]

Nature itself could have the same potent effect on him, unexpectedly: flowers, plants, animals, and clouds in the sky could all become pathways to ecstasy.
As one of his Franciscan superiors said: "Every natural thing served Joseph as a
stairway to the supernatural."[34] And Joseph's mystical volatility could lead him
as easily to joy as to sorrow. Both emotions were powerful triggers. "On some
occasions," says Agelli, "when the superior ordered him to go into the friary's
garden, he would usually go into a rapture, either when considering the divine
wisdom behind the creation of some plant, or at the song of some little bird.
In his cell, all he did was weep over the passion of Jesus Christ and fly quickly
towards Heaven because of it."[35] No one could ever anticipate the effect their
words or any object in their surroundings might have on Joseph. Tellingly, all his
hagiographers approach Joseph's mystical triggers as logical, thus reinforcing
the correctness of the epistemological matrix that was part and parcel of his
Baroque Catholic culture.

Joseph was also susceptible to an authority trigger, for mingling with
important figures almost always made him levitate. Whether he was taken to
meet with these elites or they had sought him out made no difference. Their
mere presence triggered flights that could have significant repercussions, as happened with Pope Urban VIII, Prince Casimir of Poland, Duke Johann Friedrich
of Braunschweig-Lüneberg, the Admiral of Castille, and many others, including
cardinals, bishops, and authority figures in his own order. The predictability of
Joseph's levitations in the presence of elites counterbalanced the unpredictability of his other frequent levitations. These were utilitarian ecstasies that had
more worldly purpose than others and might seem too good to be true. This
pragmatic fact made his strict isolation something of a sore point among his

brethren and superiors during the last ten years of his life, after he was removed from Assisi in 1653 and kept in strict isolation. The question some might have asked was this: Why should the church hide away someone with so much political potential? But such a question neglected to take into consideration the volatility of that potential, as we shall soon see.

Two of Joseph's meetings with elites stand out for their obvious utility. The first of these involved the most important foreign authority in Italy, Juan Alfonso Enríquez de Cabrera, the Spanish grandee with a long string of titles who served as King Philip IV's ambassador to the Papal States and as his viceroy in Naples and Sicily.[36] The value of impressing someone with so much clout is obvious. Spain was on the wane at that time, but still a mighty world power, and it occupied much of Italy. Courting favor with Philip IV was necessary for every pope, especially at a time when the Thirty Years' War was still being fought and the Papal States were a key player in this religiously charged conflict that pitted Catholics against Protestants. Moreover, Philip IV had his own peculiar religious bent, which included a fascination with miracle-working holy men and women, so having Joseph fly over his representative was something of a spectacular gift for King Philip made all the more valuable for being intangible. Having the grandee's wife faint at the sight of the flying Joseph—and having her relate the whole story to King Philip in person back at court in Madrid—might be considered something of a ribbon on that unusual gift.

An even more spectacular and purposeful levitation was the one that occurred five years later, when Joseph was visited by Duke Johann Friedrich of Braunschweig-Lüneberg. In this case, Joseph was instrumental in convincing this prominent twenty-five-year-old Lutheran to convert to Catholicism. And this conversion can easily lend itself to a functionalist analysis of the polemical use of miracles in the Catholic Reformation.

How the duke was first drawn to Catholicism is uncertain, but it appears that his tour of the leading courts of Europe was not driven solely by political concerns, for when he got to the Italian leg of his journey, he sought out Joseph, whom he had heard about back home. And it was more than mere curiosity, it seems, that brought him to Assisi hoping to meet the fabled Flying Friar, for he had sought support for his request from the highest echelons of the Catholic hierarchy and managed to convince Cardinal Francesco Rapaccioli—who had previously seen Joseph levitate[37]—to write a letter of introduction for him, which he brought along to Assisi. But there was someone else at Rome who was made aware of the duke's wishes. Unbeknownst to Johann Friedrich, Pope Innocent

X had sent a secret missive to the custodian of the friary, ordering him to allow the duke to speak with Joseph "so that the prayers and persuasiveness of the Servant of God Joseph might lead to the conversion of this Lutheran Prince which, if it were to happen, would be very beneficial to religious affairs in that region."[38]

The tone of Pope Innocent's letter to Joseph's superior at Assisi suggests that the pontiff had been led to believe that the Saxon duke was leaning toward conversion and that Joseph might be able to tip him in the right direction. That letter gained Johann Friedrich and his retinue lodgings in the papal apartment at Assisi and full access to Joseph. As previously described, the encounter between the duke and Joseph led not only to two of the most dramatic of Joseph's levitations and eucharistic miracles but also to Johann Friedrich's conversion. Joseph's own glee over the effect he had on Johann Friedrich was hard to hide. "We are overjoyed that the stag is wounded, and have high hopes for his conversion," he said to one of his brethren.[39] Joseph and Pope Innocent were not disappointed: shortly before his departure from Assisi, Johann Friedrich promised to convert and vowed to return there as soon as possible to be formally accepted into the Catholic Church. As the duke planned for the formalities, great consternation swept through Lutheran Germany and Scandinavia, but no one could dissuade Johann Friedrich. Meanwhile, according to his hagiographers, Joseph had to contend with death threats from Germany, as well as ferocious demonic attacks from hell.[40]

Johann Friedrich's conversion puts the polemical dimension of Catholic miracles in high relief. Getting a prominent Lutheran to convert was quite a coup for the Catholic Church, and the fact that his conversion was attributable to the miracles he witnessed at Assisi sharpened the edge of the Catholic argument that its miracles confirmed its legitimacy as the one true church and proved that Protestantism—which had no miracles—was therefore false. The statement attributed to one of the duke's Lutheran companions, "Cursed be the instant I set foot in this country; at home my mind was tranquil, but now here I'm rattled by the furies and scruples of conscience,"[41] sums up the Catholic argument perfectly and makes for a potentially effective parable, especially because that particular companion is said to have converted to Catholicism two years later.[42]

Friedrich's conversion had value beyond polemics. His conversion drove a potentially lethal wedge into Lutheran hegemony in Germany and Scandinavia. The duke's bloodline could be traced back to Friedrich the Wise and all the other Saxon princes who made possible the survival and triumph of Lutheranism, so, consequently, his rejection of the Lutheran faith sent a powerful symbolic signal to all Protestants. Additionally, his principality was a linchpin of the Protestant political and military coalition in Northern Europe, which had just emerged painfully scarred from the Thirty Years' War. Johann Friedrich's conversion also raised fears of a ripple effect at the highest levels of the Protestant world, for his sister Sophie Amalie was queen of Denmark-Norway, consort of King Frederick III of Denmark, and that nation was one of the most powerful Lutheran states of all. Another defection at that high a level—which would have delighted Pope Innocent—could have been disastrous for Lutheranism.

The greatest threat of such a conversion was posed by Johann Friedrich's younger brother, Ernst August, who expressed Catholic leanings loudly enough to worry his entire family. Sister Sophie and her husband, King Frederick III, were so concerned, in fact, that they did their utmost to prevent Ernst August's conversion and to convince Johann Friedrich to return to the Lutheran fold.[43] Ultimately, no one else in the family converted, including Ernst August, but the threat seemed real enough for a while, especially since the wayward duke took steps to re-Catholicize his lands as much as possible and even established a Capuchin friary on his estates. According to his wife, Benedicta Henrietta of the Palatinate, the duke kept portraits of Joseph and spoke of him constantly with "tender devotion."[44] The Catholic fervor of this ducal family remained a thorn in the side of their Lutheran relatives for many years, but their Catholicism would eventually link them to the Hapsburg dynasty through one of their daughters, Wilhelmina Amalia, who married Holy Roman Emperor Joseph I in 1699.[45]

The pious, miracle-believing Catholic duke may have been an embarrassment to his relatives, but he was no foe of reason and science and lured the great polymath Gottfried Wilhelm Leibniz to work for him as counselor and librarian, thus linking the whole family to one of the most illustrious names in the Age of Reason. After Johann Friedrich's death in 1679, Leibniz would continue to serve the House of Braunschweig in various positions, including that of director of the Ducal library at Wolfenbüttel, a job he enjoyed and that prompted him to develop the modern science of cataloging. Unfortunately, Leibniz also had to function as the family's genealogist, a task he detested and deemed worse than the eternal punishment imposed on Sisyphus by Zeus. As one might suspect, Leibniz the mathematical genius who devised calculus was apparently uninterested in the story of his employer's conversion or afraid to speak or write about it. In his brief biography of Johann Friedrich, all that Leibniz cares to say is that the duke became a Roman Catholic under the guidance of the "so-called miracle-worker Father Joseph" at Assisi and that he headed for Loreto as soon as his rites of initiation had taken place.[46]

Patterns in the Narrative

Joseph's levitations are unique for many reasons already mentioned, such as their frequency, the number of eyewitness testimonies, the variety of locations and circumstances in which they took place, the extreme heights and distances involved, and myriad phenomena absent from previous levitation accounts. All things considered, however, one of the most remarkable characteristics of his unique levitations—arguably the most remarkable—is the consistency of the eyewitness testimonies, all of which report the same array of astounding phenomena despite the fact that these witnesses were from disparate locations and different points in time and despite the more puzzling fact that many of these phenomena were unprecedented. Despite the oddness of the details, there is a seamlessness in Joseph's story, a cohesiveness one might not expect to find in narratives of supernatural events, especially those based on accounts from a wide array of witnesses who could not have heard or read about such events in any existing narratives. So assuming that the testimonies were genuine—an assumption based on convincing evidence—the novelty of Joseph's levitations and the cohesiveness of the narrative are both puzzling, for one is left wondering how it is that this unlikely pairing occurred and what it might mean or what it could reveal.

Solving this puzzle to everyone's satisfaction—as if it were in the realm of mathematics, something akin to Fermat's Last Theorem[47]—is as impossible as proving that his levitations took place exactly as all the eyewitnesses asserted. Such is the nature of most religious phenomena of consequence, especially those that involve mystical phenomena. As Rudolf Otto wisely observed over a century ago, "Mysticism is the stressing to a very high degree, indeed the overstressing of the non-rational or supra-rational elements in religion; and it is only intelligible when so understood."[48]

Nonetheless, analyzing the puzzle and coming to grips with its significance helps to make sense of Joseph as a historical event and as a prime exemplar of the history of the impossible. To attempt at least this much, we must examine the details and patterns of his levitation accounts more closely, as conveyed by his hagiographers.

Isolation

One of the most unique characteristics of Joseph's life is the anomalous isolation imposed on him by the hierarchy of the Catholic Church. Normally in his day and age, as in the Middle Ages, miracle-working holy men and women were not shuffled out of view or kept under lock and key. Instead, their holiness and their miracles—which ostensibly proved God's existence and confirmed the power and authority of the church—were on full display, publicly. Granted, many of these holy men and women were carefully scrutinized or even suspected of deviancy, especially from the fifteenth century onward, but once their holiness and their miracles had passed the church's tests, these saintly exemplars were not only allowed to interact with the world but often encouraged to do so, even within a cloistered context.

Joseph was tested by the Inquisition and found innocent of deviancy. In addition, his raptures were deemed to be genuine rather than feigned or of demonic origin, and his nonscholarly theology was declared orthodox. Yet his holiness remained ambiguous and liminal while he was alive, more so than most other saints. All saints in the Catholic tradition live in a liminal state. Those who are holy are suspended continuously on a threshold: still on earth but partially in heaven, still tempted to sin but also uncommonly able to resist.[49] Joseph spent most of his adult life in an extraordinarily intense liminal state, not only because of the characteristics he shared with all saints-in-the-making, especially others prone to mystical raptures, but also because he was at once revered and feared. His own threshold is difficult to describe due to his uniqueness, but one way of identifying it is to say his status was liminal in various ways all at once, suspended immovably, as he himself was in so many of his levitations. In essence, his levitating raptures were themselves a liminal state, for he was neither fully on earth or in heaven but somewhere in between, defying gravity, but only momentarily. And that liminality was the very essence of his raptures, which Joseph himself perceived, even if inchoately, as proven by what he said to a cardinal who saw him in a trance and questioned him about it afterward. It was "the greatness of heavenly things, and the miserable baseness of human things," said Joseph, "that had been the cause of his stupefaction."[50]

Moreover, his miracles were simultaneously affirmative and disruptive: they were theophanies, irruptions of the divine that affirmed the genuine truth of the Catholic Church and its teachings—especially over and against Protestants—while at the same time possibly deemed far too excessive, too much of a good thing, too numinous and ominous all at once.[51] Joseph's trances, shrieks, and flights could be frightening, even terrifying, yet also have a positive effect, as one eyewitness said: "Joseph's ecstasies could be frightful at first, especially his shrieks, but they nonetheless comforted those who watched him, evoking contrition and devotion in them."[52] As is true of many encounters with the supernatural, Joseph's presence could be aptly described as too volatile, as too much exposure to a *mysterium tremendum* and a *mysterium fascinans*—that is, as too much contact with events or forces that evoke dread and awe simultaneously,[53] or simply cause bewilderment,[54] or result in terror,[55] or even make someone faint,[56] or weep,[57] or run away from him screaming.[58] A brush with Joseph could be devastating. In one instance, the witnesses to one of his levitations are described as "overcome by *sacred* terror."[59]

The reasons given for Joseph's isolation by his superiors were purely pragmatic rather than analytical. Concepts such as mysterium tremendum were not on their minds. Moreover, they probably wished to disclose as little as possible about their decision. At the beginning of his narrative, Agelli cites the disruptive potential of Joseph's ecstasies as the cause of his forced isolation. "Joseph was an ecstatic from the time of his priestly ordination until his death," says Agelli, "and for that reason, for more than thirty-five years his superiors would not allow him to join his brethren at choir, or processions, or the refectory, so his raptures and ecstasies wouldn't disrupt those events."[60] Later on, however, he suggests that Joseph's isolation was a compassionate move and a recognition of his unique mystical gifts, designed to allow him and God to achieve greater intimacy with one another: "Pope Urban VIII decided with his enlightened judgment to remove such a great treasure from the public and hide him in a remote spot," he says, "to reserve him intact for God, who would want him for Himself. And it would be up to God whether to display Joseph to others through his secret and wonderful ways."[61] Bernino puts a poetic spin on Joseph's isolation, saying the Inquisition's intention was not to have "such a great treasure" live "like a prisoner in jail" but rather exist "like a reserved relic," an observation that confirms his liminal status as someone suspended between life and death.[62]

The late Gustavo Parisciani, who has carefully examined nearly every extant document related to Joseph, cites some reasons for his imprisonment that never fully surface in the hagiographies. As he sees it, Joseph was as much a lightning rod for intrigues, controversy, and criticism as for adulation, especially when it came to the very touchy political maneuvering involved in deciding which political and ecclesiastical elites would be permitted to visit him and in the equally touchy job of handling the fallout from certain visits. Given the complexity of relations between the papacy and secular rulers in Italy and beyond, as well as the equally complex and often rancorous machinations and intrigues within high ecclesiastical circles, every visit by a secular potentate or ecclesiastical prelate was a potential threat to whatever fragile stability might exist in Rome's internal politics and external relations.

According to Parisciani, Joseph was accused of holding discrete miniconclaves with cardinals—that is, of meddling in the business of papal elections. And he also apparently stirred up all sorts of jealousies and bickering among the nobility who sought to see him, some of whom got the nod, while others did not, much like members or would-be members of today's glitterati who covet admission into exclusive nightspots or social events. In addition, Parisciani claims, Joseph himself was irked by the endless stream of elite visitors who stole precious time from his life of prayer. Apparently, the pope and his inner circle were also well aware of the burden being placed on Joseph and its damaging effect on his spiritual life. All things considered, then, dealing with the constant requests from the prickly elites who clamored to see Joseph could have seemed way too troublesome for those in charge of him, for too many reasons.[63]

Holy Idiot, Holy Fool

Another salient characteristic of Joseph is the way in which his ecstasies are inseparable from his simplemindedness and the way in which he, Bocca Aperta, the open-mouthed "holy fool" from Copertino, transcends and trumps reason. In many ways Joseph reifies the ancient Christian archetype of the holy fool found in both the Orthodox and Catholic traditions, which can be traced back directly to the apostle Paul and his boast that "we are fools for Christ's sake" (1 Corinthians 4:10) and before him to the prophets of the Hebrew Scriptures and also—most significantly—to Jesus himself, who was the paradoxical archetype of unworldly and seemingly unreasonable self-abnegation: the Word of God made flesh who subjects himself willingly and meekly to poverty, harassment, humiliation, extreme suffering, and death.[64]

More significantly, Joseph duplicates or mirrors the foolishness of two of the greatest monastics in the Christian tradition: Saint Antony the Great of Egypt (251–356), with whom he does not appear to have been familiar, and Saint Francis of Assisi (1182–1226), his ultimate role model. Monasticism itself is deeply rooted in holy foolishness because of its rejection of worldly values, which can make every monk or nun seem insane, or even a raving lunatic. The Cistercian luminary Saint Bernard of Clairvaux (1090–1153), who greatly admired Antony the Great, captured the essence of monastic foolishness brilliantly in one of his letters:

> For what else do worldlings think we are doing but playing about, when what they desire most on earth, we flee, and what they flee, we desire? We are like jesters and tumblers, who, with heads down and feet up, exhibit extraordinary behaviour by standing or walking on their hands, and thus draw all eyes to themselves. But ours is not the play of children or of the theatre, which excites lust and represents sordid acts in the effeminate and shameful contortions of the actors. No, ours is a joyous game, decent, grave, and admirable, delighting the gaze of the heavenly onlookers.[65]

The monastic virtue of humility, which is inextricably tied to holy foolishness, was as much of a constant focus for Saint Bernard as it was for Joseph. "Humiliatio est via ad humilitatem," said Saint Bernard in that same letter: humiliation is the way to humility. Joseph knew this, instinctively. And, as we know from his encounter with the Inquisition at Naples, it was ultimately Joseph's humility, not his loquacity or his theological savvy, that convinced the inquisitors of the genuineness of his holiness and orthodoxy. One might say that it was Joseph's foolishness, his all-too-obvious witlessness that disarmed the Inquisition and saved his skin in Naples, and afterward, for the rest of his life. Although he could not have been familiar with the work of Saint Thomas Aquinas (1225–1274), Joseph would have agreed with this passage from his *Summa Theologica:* "One who is strengthened by God professes himself to be an utter fool by human standards, because he despises what the wisdom of men strives for."[66]

Joseph's simplemindedness and lack of education are highlighted in a brutally harsh tone by many sources. This blistering description of him is typical: "Those who knew him would admit that he was an extremely simple person and barely knew how to read, that he wasn't a theologian, or had studied any other subjects, and that he himself was an idiot of low abilities who could barely read or write. Cardinal di Lauria, among others, says Father Joseph was ignorant, had never studied, and could only understand the most basic Latin."[67]

In the monastic tradition, distinguishing between "idiots" and "fools" has never been easy. In fact, "holy idiocy" and "holy foolishness" are often interchangeable. In the Christian East, in Greek, the term *idiōtēs* was used for a man with no special public function or skill. In the Christian West, in Latin, the term *idiota* referred to illiterate rustics without education. Saint Antony the Great of Egypt, the archetypal monastic idiōtēs, whose hagiography was penned by the great theologian Saint Athanasius of Alexandria (296–373), was an "unlettered" ascetic who spent his very long life as a hermit in the desert. Yet his asceticism and his life of prayer allowed him to climb the mystical heights to such an extent that he became an "astute and wise man" who could out argue the cleverest philosophers and heretics. Joseph may not have been aware of his mirroring of this ancient narrative, in which divine wisdom is *infused* into the mystical holy fool, but his hagiographers and many of those who offered testimonies to his canonization inquest would have certainly known of this key paradigm. So it is no surprise that Joseph ends up resembling Saint Antony in the inquest testimonies and the hagiographical narrative.[68] For instance, a fellow friar testified that Joseph "was barely literate, but the way he solved theological problems showed that he had an *infused* knowledge of God that was lofty and deep."[69] Agelli echoed these sentiments: "Father Joseph discoursed on very difficult points of theology like a great theologian, and without preparation he superbly answered any doubts put to him concerning Holy Scripture quickly and excellently in a way that showed clearly that *his knowledge was supernatural and infused,* so that the most learned Father-Master and Regent Antonio di Ponte della Trave, admiring such a depth of understanding, frequently said, 'he knows more than I do.'"[70]

According to some testimonies, Joseph himself seems to have been a bit uncomfortable with his status as idiot savant, most probably because he preferred to emphasize his humility—as he did after his levitations—but this never stopped him from answering questions about his encounters with the divine. When Cardinal Lauria asked, "What might those in ecstasy see during their ecstasy?" Joseph replied, "They find themselves as if within a great gallery of beautiful things in which hangs a highly polished mirror where they can see, all at once, every type of hidden and yearned-for mystery that it pleases God to reveal to them in that great vision."[71] Often, Joseph would answer questions such as this equivocally, mixing self-effacement with vague poetic descriptions of his lofty engagement with the divine. Once, at the end of a particularly intense grilling by the archbishop of Avignon, Joseph begged him not to "take advantage of him" with such questioning "because he was ignorant and didn't know how to converse."[72]

Joseph's foolishness is also often compared to that of his beloved role model Saint Francis, arguably the most exemplary of medieval holy fools.[73] Francis was a countercultural holy man who embraced absolute poverty and homelessness and behaved irrationally in various ways, displaying an absolute horror of money, embracing lepers and beggars, stripping himself naked in the presence of the bishop of Assisi, wandering outdoors in the wilderness, constantly flitting from town to town, courting and relishing humiliation and contempt. In his biography of Saint Francis, G. K. Chesterton summed up his foolishness poetically: "He had made a fool of himself . . . there was not a rag of him left that was not ridiculous. Everybody knew that at the best he had made a fool of himself. It was a solid objective fact, like the stones in the road, that he had made a fool of himself. He saw himself as an object, very small and distinct like a fly walking on a clear windowpane; and it was unmistakably a fool."[74]

Within the Franciscan order, Saint Francis came to be regarded as a mirror image of Jesus Christ, not just because his behavior resembled that of Jesus so closely but also because of the miraculous stigmata he received in a mystical ecstasy that duplicated the wounds of the crucified Christ. Joseph did not receive that same mystical gift, but all of the hagiographies emphasize his love of Christ and crucifixes, especially his obsession with the passion of Christ, his extreme ecstasies during Holy Week, and his exuberance on Easter Sunday. That Joseph was being viewed as another Saint Francis is undeniable. One such piece of evidence—a very telling one—is embedded in the story of the visit to Assisi by the Spanish viceroy who, after meeting with Joseph. ran excitedly to tell his wife, "I have seen and spoken with another Saint Francis."[75]

Such an assessment of Joseph, which was an echo of widely held sentiments, could not be tolerated comfortably at Assisi, where Saint Francis had reigned supreme for over four centuries as the holy man par excellence. There was only room for one Saint Francis at Assisi. So it is highly likely that one of the many reasons Pope Innocent X had for removing Joseph from Assisi was to prevent him from competing with his role model or eclipsing him. Being a living saint can be tricky, for sure.

Distinctive Traits of Joseph's Levitations

Given how often eyewitnesses claimed to have seen Joseph flying or hovering in ecstasy, it is not surprising that testimonies of his levitations contain a wealth of details, some of which are difficult to find in accounts of previous or subsequent levitating saints. As the levitations themselves raise many questions, so do these details. And the details point beyond themselves, establishing a hermeneutic of discernment—that is, a way of making sense of the impossible.

Since many—if not most—of Joseph's levitations occurred while he was celebrating Mass, his *moti*, or movements in that setting, display some specific peculiarities. One of the most extreme of these rare features was the frequency of his raptures at the altar, which interrupted him continually and could make Mass take between two to five hours to complete.[76] "He celebrated Holy Mass more frequently up in the air than on the ground," said his hagiographers.[77] Moreover, we are told that "when celebrating Mass . . . he was incessantly ecstatic" and that "the wonder of it all was that when he came back to his senses, he followed the correct words and the ceremonies so punctiliously that it seemed that an angel was dictating each syllable to him and guiding him through the ritual" (fig. 26).[78]

So, these frequent raptures seem to share one characteristic: the suspension of time. Joseph is not distracted by the raptures or his trance-like states at Mass. He picks up where he left off without missing a beat, much like a film that is paused in which the interrupted dialogue and action resume cleanly and precisely as soon as the playback button is pressed. But this is not all that is peculiar about his eucharistic raptures. These levitations had an assortment of characteristics that are not usually found together in accounts of raptures outside of Mass: "The usual lifting of his body took place like this: As the moment of consecration approached, he would rise on the tips of his toes and stay that way until the consummation of the sacrifice. Then, extraordinary things happened: either he'd take leave of his senses or else he'd fly backwards two paces, or he'd become unconscious or raise himself two palms into the air or else do such things that one could not help but think that he was either wholly absorbed in God or that God was delicately and totally interacting with him."[79]

Only during Mass does Joseph exhibit so many different sorts of *moti* in succession: ascending and descending, hovering, flying, moving backward and forward, rising to the ceiling, remaining inanimate and insentient on the ground or dancing in the air, shrieking as he soars or remaining silent as he holds the host in his hands, entranced; all or some of these are strung together within the celebration of a single ritual. Tellingly, that ritual involved the miracle of transubstantiation, and Joseph mirrors the transcending of the natural order that takes place in that ritual. He, as a priest, is *effecting* a supernatural change in the substance of the bread and wine and is simultaneously *affected* by it, and

Figure 26. One of the many engravings and paintings that show Saint Joseph levitating in ecstasy while celebrating Mass.

his levitation serves to confirm the reality of that supernatural change. The didactic and polemical value of Joseph's eucharistic ecstasies—which "proved" the real presence of Christ in the bread and wine—might have seemed heaven-sent to those clerics who dedicated their lives to enlightening the Catholic faithful or to wrestling with Protestants.

As already mentioned, many of Joseph's trances were different from those just described. He also had seizures that left him bereft of his senses, stiff and motionless. In account after account, Joseph's trances are described as having a freeze-frame effect of sorts, trapping his body in whatever position it happened to be in at the onset of rapture and stopping time, as it were, similar to what would happen to his mind when the celebration of the Mass was interrupted by a rapture. These accounts also describe a glowing effect and weeping, along with a sense of shame or embarrassment in Joseph once the event is over. The following description is typical: "He was frequently seen suspended very still, with his arms outstretched and his eyes upturned, either with his body almost in a sitting position, or his feet in the act of walking, and there was no skill or force that could move him from such a pose. . . . When this ended, his face was tinged with a holy glow and his eyes were full of tears. He would then turn to bystanders and, in order to cover up the divine activity, would ask them to pardon his so-called imperfections and his stupor."[80] The theatricality of these poses—which turn Joseph into a living statue—is all too obvious, but Joseph's display of embarrassment at the end of the raptures, which he dismisses as "drowsiness, infirmities, or a stupor," seems to suggest the exact opposite of an attention-seeking performance.[81]

Many eyewitness testimonies in the beatification inquests (processi) describe something even more dramatic about these freeze-frame poses, for they claim that it was not just Joseph's body that seemed to stiffen completely but also his clothing, as if he were wrapped in some supernatural cocoon that prevented his whole self from being affected by gravity or the drag and flow of the surrounding air. As Cardinal Lorenzo di Lauria Brancati put it in his testimony, despite all of the "sudden and eccentric" motion to which Joseph's body was subjected, "his clothes remained so composed that—with the utmost admiration—I judged it to be humanly impossible for this to be happening."[82] Bernino describes the effects this supernatural cocoon could have on Joseph:

> During his ecstasies and raptures, it was noticed that his clothes—be it his priestly garb or his Franciscan habit—always remained composed as he flew

through the air or hit the ground, propelled by the force of his Spirit. It seemed *as if an invisible hand wrapped itself around him at those moments* and adjusted his clothes according to whatever his position was at any moment. So, when he was celebrating Mass, his vestments always covered his legs and feet. Or, if he was in the act of talking to someone, his head remained covered, or the cowl of his habit remained lowered around his neck. And his Franciscan cord always hung down neatly. In sum, every part of his garb stayed exactly as it should have been, miraculously, despite the many vehement movements of his body.[83]

Here again we find a stress on the freezing of bodily motion at the instant the rapture begins. But the cessation of motion applies only to Joseph's body, not to the ascents or descents of that body or its flights forward or backward, which could be quite energetic or vehement (*vehementi*). So what is being described here is a multifaceted suspension of the laws of nature and the sudden irruption of a supernatural cocoon within nature, that "invisible hand" mentioned by Bernino that envelops an inanimate Joseph and moves him about in the air while keeping his body and his clothing totally motionless, with his head and extremities in various dramatic poses as if he were a statue or a motionless actor in a *tableau vivant*.

Moreover, this same "invisible hand" can move Joseph various heights or change his trajectories. He moves diagonally, not just straight up and down; he can whirl about, dancing; he can gyrate with the speed of lightning; and he can move forward and backward. This flying in reverse direction is another rare levitation phenomenon that makes Joseph unique, and it seems to occur frequently. It could happen with elite visitors, such as Duke Johann Friedrich, at Mass, or it could happen in various other settings. For instance, when he was venerating the veil of the Virgin Mary at Assisi, "He knelt in front of the precious relic but upon moving forward to kiss it, he jumped and flew backwards for eight long paces, and then he reversed that same flight to kiss it, after which once again as before, he flew back eight paces. Then he took to a new flight over the table where the reliquary was resting and there, he went into ecstasy with arms outstretched, with his two hands positioned directly on the flames of two lighted torches.[84] And it also happened when he was handling another relic at Assisi, the habit of Saint Francis: "The Blessed Joseph, in the act of folding the habit of Saint Francis, flew backwards more than three paces and rose so high that he flew over the heads of two deputies who were behind him, and then he fell on his knees in ecstasy on the pavement behind them."[85]

Additionally, the invisible hand seems to influence whatever objects might be in Joseph's flight path or near him. He could fly very close to candles and torches without toppling them or hover directly over them and remain unharmed,[86] his flesh and garments impervious to the flames, as happened at a convent in Naples where the nuns began to scream—needlessly—fearing he would catch on fire.[87] Or he could land on some surface and kneel there without displacing or disturbing whatever items might be on it.[88] Or he could glide between objects and leave them undisturbed, as if they were not even there. This happened at Assisi, when he floated around an elaborate Easter display above the main altar that contained many lamps, ornaments, and wooden structures—on the way up and on the way down—"without harming himself or the display."[89]

The height of his levitations varied. Outdoors, he could sometimes nearly vanish from sight, and indoors the ceiling was his only limit. One time at Assisi while praying before the altar of Saint Francis, Joseph flew up so fast that his fellow friars lost sight of him momentarily, until they looked up at the ceiling and saw him there.[90] Never at a loss for poetic turns of phrase, Agelli had this to say about Joseph's encounters with ceilings: "More than once, Joseph was seen raising the host and his whole person at the same time, carrying himself so high that if his trajectory had not been blocked by the ceiling, he would have been carried along with his consecrated Jesus into the presence of his Eternal Father at the sublime altar of heaven."[91]

That same invisible hand that carried Joseph upward was also powerful enough to create a miracle within a miracle by dragging along anyone Joseph touched. As Agelli put it: "His great union with God not only caused him to be frequently rapt into the air, but as a new and unusual wonder he would also carry others up along with him, to bring them to God."[92] We have various accounts of these double levitations, and the most peculiar thing about them is that those lifted into the air by Joseph are not ecstatic, or even willing to go up with him, but are forcibly taken by him, much like prey in the talons of a raptor. Once, on the feast of the Immaculate Conception—one of Joseph's favorite days of the year—he grabbed a fellow friar and took off with him in tow.[93] Joseph could also engage his unsuspecting levitation partners in dancing up in the air, as he did in the previously mentioned case of the priest with whom he twirled "round and round like David before the Ark."[94]

One of the best-known accounts of a double levitation is that of Baldassare Rossi, "who had fallen into such a furious madness that he treated and abused everyone crazily." Rossi was brought to Joseph for healing, tightly bound to a chair with ropes. What followed after he was untied was a great surprise: "Joseph placed his hand on his head and said: 'Cavaliere Baldassare, don't doubt yourself. Commend yourself to God and to his Most Holy Mother.' Having said this, he then gripped his hair tightly with his hand, and screaming 'oh,' as usual, he rose up in rapture, bringing the madman along with him, high off the ground. After staying afloat in the air for seven or eight minutes, and then returning to the ground Joseph said, 'cheer up, Cavaliere.' The knight regained his sanity and returned home praising God and his blessed liberator."[95]

In this case, miracles are nestled within one another, much like Russian matryoshka dolls: a miracle within a miracle within a miracle—that is, a levitation that causes another levitation and effects a cure (fig. 27).

Finally, one must also puzzle over the screams with which he launched into the air, identified with the Italian words *urlo, grido,* and *strillo.* This odd reflex, one of most distinctive traits of Joseph's raptures, is often described as being very loud and audible from far away.[96] As mentioned previously, Joseph claimed that his shouts were as uncontrollable as his levitations and compared them to the reaction gunpowder always has to a flame or spark.[97] No other levitator in Christian history has howled or whooped this way, but then again, no other levitator has displayed as many unique traits as Joseph. He is sui generis, a rare species of saint, among the rarest of all, uniquely outrageous in his ecstatic excess.

Ironically, Joseph's noisemaking is the least miraculous of his feats, since screaming loudly is a natural phenomenon. But his bellowing is so inseparable from his flying as to seem supernatural, or at least superhuman, loud enough to shake a whole building or to be mistaken for the rumbling of an earthquake.[98] Whether such trembling was really caused by his voice or not, the fact remains that eyewitnesses testified that it was certainly perceived that way. Whether one likes it or not, such a perception reeks of the supernatural, even when attributed to overactive imaginations, bald-faced lying, or the unlikely coincidence that a real earthquake happened to occur at the same instance as his "very strange and powerful booming scream."[99] That seismic coincidence is so unlikely that—if true—it, too, could be called miraculous.

Fittingly, Joseph's distinctive hollering, which everyone around him came to expect and which his hagiographers did not care to dwell on or analyze at

Figure 27. Placido Costanzi's depiction of a miracle within a miracle shows Saint Joseph healing the mentally ill nobleman Baldassarre Rossi by grabbing his hair and lifting him off the ground in an ecstatic levitation, much like the angel who carried Habakkuk through the air from Judaea to Babylon and back (fig. 5).

length, calls attention to his unique oddness. His loud roaring also prompts one to ponder the relation of that oddness to our understanding of past, present, and future. When all is said and done, nonetheless, Paolo Agelli's take on the Flying Friar seems most apt: "The most renowned of Joseph's miracles was his own life itself."[100]

But why did such a remarkable life sink into obscurity? This is one of the weightiest questions raised by the case of Joseph of Cupertino because even among the vast majority of Catholics he has been all but forgotten. He has vanished, his ghostly presence trapped in quirky footnotes or antique prayer cards. How could this happen? Why is he not among the best-known of all saints? Why is he not considered one of the most amazing humans ever? Is it due to the "impossible" factor? Something else? If so, what? Is he trivial, or ridiculous? If so, why? His nearly total obscurity should be jarring, shocking, disturbing. But it is not.

Aye, there's the rub, again.[101]

PART TWO

Here . . . and Here Too

Properly speaking, miracles are works done by God outside the order
usually observed in things.
—Saint Thomas Aquinas, *Summa Contra Gentiles* III, 101.1

5. Transvection, Teleportation, and All That

A Brief History of Bilocation

There are few miracles more amazing than the duplication of the body, which
not only oversteps the forces of nature, but also those of the imagination.

The poetic observation above, made by Domenico Bernino, was meant to enhance the impressiveness of Joseph of Cupertino's miraculous feats, for Joseph
not only floated in midair; occasionally, he could also be in two places at the
same time.[1] Hard as it is to imagine, however, Bernino's remark is more applicable to another Franciscan levitator—an exact contemporary of Joseph—who
made the flying friar seem like a mystical underachiever, too earthbound and
insufficiently amazing.

That other Franciscan who seemed to eclipse him was a Spanish nun,
María Fernández Coronel y Arana (1602–1665), abbess of the convent of the Im-
maculate Conception in Ágreda, who is better known by her monastic name,
María de Jesús de Ágreda, or simply as María de Ágreda. In the Americas, where
she became a folk legend, she is also known as the Lady in Blue or La Dama
Azul (fig. 28).

Sor María (*Sister* María in English) made dealing with impossible claims
much more complicated. Three salient characteristics rarely combined within a
single individual lead her to stand head and shoulders above her contemporaries,
and perhaps above most other Catholic mystics, in the realm of the impossible
in both the natural and the supernatural domains.

First, there is levitation. Sor María became an ecstatic levitating mystic
at the age of eighteen, but much like Teresa of Avila—and unlike Joseph of

Figure 28. A highly stylized depiction of one of Sor María de Ágreda's many bilocations to the New World, where she carried out missionary work among the Jumano natives.

Cupertino—she succeeded in getting the levitations to cease after pleading with God.

Second, her ecstasies also caused her to bilocate. Being in two places simultaneously is a rare mystical gift, most often limited in scope and frequency. But the claims made for Sor María's bilocations are among the most extreme in Christian history, hands down, both in scope and frequency. While most other bilocating Christian mystics normally only manage to appear at relatively nearby locations a handful of times, Sor María ostensibly crossed the Atlantic Ocean repeatedly. While strictly enclosed in her convent at Ágreda—and consistently visible to her sisters there—she boldly claimed to have evangelized the Jumano natives in the northern reaches of New Spain, in the present-day American states of Texas and New Mexico. Moreover, she not only claimed to have done this over 500 times, over the span of several years, but succeeded in convincing many in her day (including examiners from the Spanish Inquisition) that this seemingly impossible miracle had truly occurred.

Third, Sor María's mysticism involved much more than visions, levitations, bilocations, and missionary activity. She also claimed to receive ecstatic revelations and engage in automatic writing that recorded the information revealed to her. Empowered by God Himself and by Mary, the Mother of God, who provided her with privileged information, Sor María wrote a voluminous narrative of the Blessed Virgin's life, about a million words long, in which she not only promoted the doctrine of the Immaculate Conception—which was still disputed in her day and would not be accepted by the Catholic Church until 1854—but also asserted Mary's closeness to the Holy Trinity, emphasizing her role as co-redemptrix of the human race and co-mediatrix, too, along with her son Jesus Christ. In essence, this narrative was ostensibly an autobiography of the Virgin Mary dictated to Sor María, who served as her scribe, in which the Mother of God revealed many intimate details not found in the New Testament or any other early Christian texts. As if this were not impressive enough, Sor María wrote this biography twice, having been forced by one of her confessors to burn the entire first draft, along with all her other writings. Discerning whether this text was truly of supernatural divine origin proved difficult for some of her contemporaries, including officials of the Inquisition and theologians at the Sorbonne.

Moreover, those three extreme claims made by María and by those around her gained her a fourth distinguishing accomplishment which was not in the realm of the impossible but was nonetheless most unusual: she became very influential in worldly affairs as a close confidant and advisor of King Philip IV of Spain. Even though she was a poor nun under a vow of poverty who lacked noble titles and spent her entire adult life locked away in a remote convent, Sor María managed to rise to unprecedented heights in the secular world. She and the troubled Hapsburg king would end up writing over 300 letters to each other over a twenty-year stretch, most of which dealt with intimate details of the king's personal life and his affairs of state. Her influence at the royal court was surprisingly substantial despite her physical absence from it, for King Philip continually relied on her advice and her prayers, not just for personal needs, especially his chronic guilt and his mental and spiritual despair, but also for matters involving domestic and foreign policy. And the speed with which their letters were ferried back and forth was astounding for that day and age, proof positive of the significance the king assigned to this correspondence and to María's role at his court.

Though all four accomplishments deserve attention, her role as advisor to King Philip IV does not really involve the realm of the miraculous, even though it is linked to María's reputation as a miracle-worker. For a nun to become a king's advisor is rare, for sure, but it was hardly impossible or miraculous in and of itself, especially in Spain, as proven by another Conceptionist nun, Luisa de Carrión.[2] Similarly, María's third supernatural claim, though extreme, fails to meet all of the criteria for "impossibility" due to the fact that visions and automatic writing cannot be observed—unlike levitation and bilocation—and can be easily attributed to delusion or willful deceit. Moreover, there are plenty of examples in human history of individuals who have claimed similar sorts of revelations, and there is nothing very unusual about this phenomenon. Consequently, our focus here will be on those two feats that involve the supernatural and the seemingly impossible: María's levitations and bilocations, both of which rank as some of the most audacious and offensive challenges offered to Protestantism in the early modern age. Since her visionary ecstatic writing was viewed in Catholic circles as inseparable from her levitations and bilocations, and therefore also as a challenge to Protestantism, it deserves some scrutiny, but only obliquely. María's polemical edge was as sharp as they came in the baroque age, and all aspects of that edge need to be considered significant, including her "autobiography" of the Virgin Mary. Ironically, although she never met a Protestant in the flesh and most probably never read a single page of Protestant theology, everything about Sor María—absolutely everything, down to her bare feet—was a resounding denial of the central theological and metaphysical assumptions of Protestantism.

Yet, despite their polemical usefulness, these very same accomplishments proved to be problematic, controversial, and divisive—much more than those of Joseph of Cupertino—inspiring devotion among some Catholic authorities but also giving rise to ambivalence and no small measure of suspicion and fear among others, creating a tangled skein of negative responses that ultimately choked María's canonization process. Moreover, in the case of Sor María, more so than in most others of her era, one can also clearly discern the friction created by extreme miracles such as bilocation and divine revelations, especially the uneasy interplay between the miracle-worker's own perception of what has occurred and the claims being made about these miracles by others.

María's case, then, allows us to examine the troublesome roles played by interpretation, embellishment, and exaggeration in the forging of narratives as well as in the creation of doubt and suspicion. Conversely, her case also provides a clear glimpse of the ways in which the Catholic Church sought to maintain a delicate balance between popular piety and official theology and between the affirming and questioning of the seemingly impossible. The fundamental questions raised by María's miracles were immense precisely because of their seemingly outlandish otherworldliness. That excessiveness exposed the fragility of her claims, along with her own vulnerability. Yet, at the very same time, her miracles also reveal the eagerness with which impossible feats could be believed in and embellished, or even suggest the likelihood of pure fabrication. María's case is as tangled a Gordian knot as the history of the impossible can confront, its braided strands woven out of the coincidence of opposites. In it, one can find the convergence of faith and doubt, credulity and skepticism, mystical fervor and sheer invention, self-fashioning and self-abasement, self-promotion and self-censorship, adulation and suspicion, wonderment and fear, truth and falsehood.

As extreme as it is and as messy as it is, the case of Sor María brings us face-to-face with the ways in which impossible claims were made and tested in baroque Catholicism. And among her impossible claims, none was more difficult for the church to handle than her bilocations. Since this phenomenon is so complex, so rare, and so central to Sor María's engagement with the impossible, it needs to be set in context before that engagement of hers can be analyzed. To do this properly, the phenomenon itself and its history within the Catholic tradition need to be examined.

Parsing an Impossible Phenomenon

Bilocation is a mystical phenomenon that defies the known laws of physics, in which a person's body seems to be present in two distinct locations simultaneously. In cases in which more than two locations are involved, the phenomenon is referred to as multilocation.[3] Bilocation and multilocation are not to be confused with other mystical phenomena that involve a sudden shift in location in which there is no duplication of the person. Such nonduplicating instances of relocation can be referred to by various terms, the most common of which is "transvection." These mystical relocations can happen at varying speeds and traverse distances of various lengths. Many transvections are a dynamic form of levitation in which actual flight is the means of conveyance and in which time elapses. In some, however, the shift in location is instantaneous, and the person simply dematerializes in one spot and suddenly materializes in the other, much like teleportation in the science fiction universe of *Star Trek:* "Beam me up, Scotty," and all that, except with the involvement of God—or the devil—rather than a mechanical transporter.[4]

The concepts of mystical relocation, bilocation, multilocation, and transvection have a very long history and a global reach and can be found in folklore and folk magic, shamanistic religions, and many now-extinct ancient religions, as well as in Hinduism, Buddhism, early Greek philosophy, Judaism, Christianity, and Islam. In modern times, they have also appeared in Spiritualism, Theosophy, and New Age spirituality, as well as in parapsychology. Late nineteenth- and early twentieth-century Spiritualism, especially, gave rise to the pseudoscientific field of parapsychology and to plenty of literature on the phenomena claimed by Spiritualism, many of which had their parallels in the world's religions.[5] Bilocation was one of these phenomena, but out of this literature, only one book dedicated solely to bilocation was ever published.[6] In the late twentieth and early twenty-first century, bilocation and mystical relocation became a subject of interest in research on mind-matter interaction, a field of study which seeks a fuller integration of religion and empirical science. In this field, bilocation tends to be considered a fact rather than an illusion or delusion.[7]

In Christianity, bilocation has been much more common than transvection, but its frequency has waxed and waned over time, and its cause has been attributed to two opposing agencies: the divine and the demonic. As was the case with levitation and other Catholic mystical phenomena, Protestant Christianity rejected the belief that God caused bilocation and transvection but continued to believe that the devil could certainly effect it. For Protestants, bilocations and transvections could indeed occur, but if they did, they were exclusively the work of the devil or mere illusions caused by him.

Although a phenomenon vaguely similar to bilocation has been observed at the atomic and subatomic levels in quantum mechanics—a phenomenon commonly referred to as the indeterminacy principle or the Heisenberg uncertainty principle[8]—classical or Newtonian mechanics posits that it is physically *impossible* for a human body completely surrounded by its space and location to be present in another place at the same time. Consequently, in this scientific worldview logic requires that all reports of bilocations be considered either *impossible* or outside the known laws of nature or, in a metaphysical or religious sense, as *supernatural*. For anyone who does not regard the existence of supernatural forces or beings as possible, therefore, every bilocation claim needs to be regarded as an *apparent* or *seeming* bilocation. In fact, the phenomenon itself is so inconceivable—much more so than levitation—that even for believers in the supernatural, a leap of faith is required. As one of Joseph of Cupertino's hagiographers put it: "There are few miracles more amazing than the duplication of the body, which not only oversteps the forces of nature, but also those of the imagination."[9]

Unlike levitation or stigmata, which seem to lack any purpose beyond displaying a divine and supernatural agency as well as the holiness of the levitator, bilocation is a miracle that most often serves some practical purpose. Moreover, in cases in which no overtly obvious pragmatic usefulness seems observable, bilocation can have specific purposes assigned to it.

Another Ancient Global Phenomenon

Bilocation is a universal phenomenon in the history of the world's religions. Mentioning a few examples should suffice to make this fact as obvious as it deserves to be. In Buddhism, it is believed the Buddha himself could be present at two distinct locations simultaneously. Bilocation is one of the *siddhis* of Hinduism and Buddhism—that is, one of the paranormal, supernatural, or magical powers attainable by mystics. And in comparison to some of these siddhis, Christian bilocation seems very lame, even insignificant. In an early Buddhist Yoga text, it is listed as one of the six powers accessible to advanced monks, and it is described as "body-power (kāyavasa), or the power to self-multiply, vanish, fly through walls, even touch the sun or moon."[10]

In ancient Greece, we have the following account of bilocation by third-century philosopher Pythagoras: "Almost unanimous is the report that on one and the same day he was present at both Metapontum in Italy and Tauromenium in Sicily, in each places conversing with friends, though the places are separated by many miles, both at sea and land, demanding a journey of great many days."[11]

In Jewish folklore and rabbinic literature, *kefitzat haderech*, the shortening of the way, or "path jumping," is the ability to travel with unnatural speed, to be in one place and then suddenly appear in another.[12] The term is originally found in Midrashim to explain certain mystical interpretations of travel in the Hebrew Bible, such as Eliezer's seemingly instantaneous journey to faraway Nahor, where he finds Isaac's wife-to-be Rebecca.[13] In East European Jewish folktales, especially those associated with the Hasidic movement, kefitzat haderech was utilized by various revered holy men. Although this phenomenon should be classified as transvection or teleportation rather than bilocation, it does involve bodily displacement.

In Islam, bodily displacement is known as *Tayy al-Ard,* a concept for "traversing the earth without moving," "folding up of the earth," or "covering long distances in the twinkling of an eye." This is a concept of transvection or bilocation familiar to the Shī'īs and Sufis, but each of those traditions has its own interpretation of it. Its roots can be found in the following verses of the Quran: "Solomon said to his own men: 'Ye Chiefs! which of you can bring me the throne of Queen of Sheba before she and her envoys come to me in submission? Said an Ifrit, of the Jinns: 'I will bring it to thee before thou rise from thy council: indeed, I have full strength for the purpose, and may be trusted.' Said one who had knowledge of the Book: 'I will bring it to thee within the twinkling of an eye!' Then when Solomon saw it placed firmly before him, he said: 'This is by the grace of my Lord!'"[14] Some prominent figures in Islam were known for their bilocations, such as the twelfth-century Persian mystic Abusaeid Abolkheir or the thirteenth-century Sufi poet commonly known as Rumi, and medieval Islamic texts contain many accounts of bilocating individuals.[15]

But one need not look solely to the ancient or medieval past to find bilocation accounts in religions other than Christianity or their links to the present. Leaping centuries ahead to 1965, when Paul Twitchell (1909–1971) founded the religious movement of Eckankar, we find him claiming that his inspiration came from "his own bilocation experiences and those of previous saints in various religions."[16]

When it comes to the history of Christianity, not much has been written on instances of bilocation, despite the abundance of such accounts in the lives of the saints. Within the Christian tradition itself, the strangeness of the phenomenon is so intense that bilocation has never attracted significant attention philosophically, theologically, or historically. Given the seemingly impossible nature of the phenomenon, which is ostensibly a shocking violation of the laws of physics, as well as of all notions of the integrity of the human self, it has tended to create confusion and disagreements among philosophers and theologians as well as among the faithful at the popular level. And this confusion has sometimes created problems for those who have claimed any sort of physical mystical relocation.

The chief assumption governing Christian bilocation is that since God is omnipotent, his supernatural power can achieve illogical and baffling miracles with the location of matter, the chief example of which is the Eucharist, in which the body of Christ is believed to be present simultaneously in heaven and in every consecrated host and chalice on earth. However, while the eucharistic theology of the Catholic tradition has always stressed the real, substantial presence of Christ in the Eucharist, ultimately explained in Aristotelian terms as "transubstantiation," it has never sought to explain exactly *how* the flesh and blood of Christ replace the substance of the bread and wine. This point remains a mystery beyond human reason. The same may be said about bilocation, in a way, with an even greater degree of uncertainty involved. While there is agreement on the possibility of a person being in two places simultaneously, there has never been agreement on what happens during a bilocation that is equal in clarity to the doctrine of transubstantiation, much less on *how* it happens, exactly. Until the Middle Ages, there was very little discussion of the issue of bilocating human beings, but as one might expect, scholastic theologians took up this question with differing measures of enthusiasm and hairsplitting. Without delving too deeply into details and terminology, one might say that scholastic opinion divided roughly—and not completely—into two camps.

In one school of thought, the Dominican thinker Thomas Aquinas (1225–1274) and other scholastics who favored Aristotle argued that *location* means that a body is "completely surrounded by its place," so to admit a second location simultaneously is to claim that the body is both *surrounded* and *not surrounded*—a logical contradiction. Moreover, as Aquinas put it, due to the union of body and soul, the human soul can only act upon matter through the body to which it is substantially united. Therefore, the human soul cannot be present in a place in which its body is not present, and this means that if some person is in Rome, he cannot at the same time be elsewhere.[17] With their usual penchant for distinctions, this school of thought explained the real presence of Christ in the Eucharist by speaking of two kinds of presence: *commensurate* and *noncommensurate*. What this difference might entail in the case of bilocation is not as complicated as it seems: Aquinas and others who made this distinction solved the logical difficulties raised by bilocations by proposing that all bilocations are only *apparent* bilocations; that is, the person in the second location is present there miraculously, in a nonphysical way. Bilocation accounts found in hagiographies are to be believed, they argued, but must be explained as "phantasmal replications" or "aerial materializations" of the bilocator's self. In the seventeenth century, the chief proponent of this distinction was the Jesuit theologian Silvanus Maurus (1619–1687).

An opposing school of thought that included the Franciscan thinker John Duns Scotus (1226–1398) and other nominalists who stressed the absolute omnipotence of God rejected the logical necessity of avoiding contradictions regarding miracles, maintaining instead that true bilocation is possible indeed and must be believed in, just like the Catholic doctrine of the Eucharist. This argument, of course, rests on an understanding of God's power as absolute, limitless, and beyond human logic and on an understanding of location as absolute and independent of external place. In the early modern era, the chief proponents of this view were the Jesuit theologians Robert Bellarmine (1542–1621) and Francisco Suárez (1548–1617).[18]

Such differences of opinion reflect the fluidity of the subject of bilocation at the dawn of the modern age and a conceptual instability that permeated theology as well as popular belief. In addition to the scholastic debates just mentioned, there was also plenty of speculation on what to believe concerning bilocations. And the questions raised by the phenomenon seemed innumerable. If the person could be in two places at once, could that person be active in both places? Was it the bilocator's soul that went to the second location, leaving the body soulless, or was the soul still somehow in both locations? Was ecstasy a necessary precondition for bilocation, and if so, how did the ecstatic self interact with its other self and those around that *other*? If the body is physically present in one place and represented in the other place in the form of a vision, as Aquinas and others proposed, did this take place through the instrumentality of angels or through an intellectual, imaginative, or sensible vision caused by God in the witnesses? And if the person in the second location was not a vision of some sort but a physical body, how did the bilocator really get there? Did it happen instantaneously? Was it through transvection or some other sort of flight? And if so, were angels involved? Was it through teleportation? Or was the bilocator's body suddenly given superhuman agility to transport itself back and forth instantly or very quickly? And if so, did angels take on the appearance of the bilocator and stand in as a substitute in the first location so he or she would not be missed? If not, then what, exactly, were people seeing in the first location? Questions abounded, but definitive answers were few. And all these unanswered questions could crop up whenever bilocation claims were made, as shall be seen very clearly in the case of Sor María de Ágreda.

Nonetheless, such questions and differences of opinion aside, late medieval and early modern Catholics could agree on one fundamental assumption: that every bilocation was either the work of God or of the devil. Divine bilocations were genuinely supernatural and true manifestations of the bilocator's person. In contrast, demons could indeed effect *transvections* but not *bilocations.* They could move bodies, for sure, but they could never duplicate the person. Consequently, demonic bilocations—as opposed to those of divine origin—were always illusions, mere trickery on the part of the devil, a created being, a fallen angel whose preternatural powers could alter human perceptions.[19] Discerning the difference between the divine and the demonic was not always easy but was deemed absolutely necessary.

Early Christian Bilocations

The phenomenon of bilocation cannot be found explicitly in the Bible, but there are a few passages that deal with mystical relocation and with human bodies that defy the laws of nature. In the Hebrew Bible, the only passage that alludes to a supernatural relocation is rather vague: "I do not know where the spirit of the Lord may carry you off when I leave you," says Obadiah to the prophet Elijah.[20] In the New Testament, the body of the resurrected Jesus defies physical barriers and suddenly appears in locked rooms or instantly "vanishes from sight" after joining two disciples on the road to Emmaus and conversing with them.[21] Among the apostles, Philip is "snatched away" suddenly after he baptizes an Ethiopian eunuch and instantly reappears in a different location. And after being whisked away, the man he has just baptized "saw him no more."[22] So, strictly speaking, this mystical relocation is not bilocation but an instantaneous transvection or teleportation. All that can be said with certainty about these passages is that they reflect belief in the power of God to do as he wishes with the human body, regardless of the laws of nature, which is the chief unquestioned assumption in all bilocation accounts.

According to an ancient tradition in Spain, the very first bilocation in the church's history supposedly took place in the year 40, when the Virgin Mary—who was in Jerusalem at the time—suddenly appeared in Zaragoza to comfort the apostle James the Greater, who had prayed for help while preaching in Spain. This legend was inseparable from the veneration offered to Our Lady of the Pillar in Zaragoza, which in the late Middle Ages became associated with a wooden image of the Virgin Mary at the Cathedral-Basilica of Nuestra Señora del Pilar, an immensely significant pilgrimage site (fig.29). The origin of this legend cannot be dated precisely but seems to be from early medieval times.

This bilocation story, which claimed to be the oldest in Christianity, was immensely popular in Spain and obviously had a great impact on Sor María de Ágreda, who lived only fifty-five miles from Zaragoza. Her detailed account of this event in her massive *Mystical City of God* tells of the Virgin Mary being ferried to Zaragoza from Jerusalem by angels, so it is not really a bilocation, strictly speaking, but rather a transvection. In her account, the Virgin brings an image of herself crafted by angels, which they mount on a "jasper or marble" pillar they crafted and brought with them, and then instructs the apostle James to build a church in which this image will be venerated. According to Sor María, it is the Virgin Mary who creates a shrine for herself in Zaragoza, the very same shrine that was still being visited by throngs of María's contemporaries.[23] In addition, Sor María tells of a prior visit by the Virgin to the apostle James in Granada—also a transvection rather than a bilocation—where she and her squadron of angels rescue James from being murdered by an angry mob of Jews who are under demonic influence.[24]

In truth, despite the claims made since medieval times, this Spanish legend is not of ancient origin, and we really have no bilocation accounts from the first century. And the same is true of the next twelve centuries, for the most part.[25] Much like the miraculous "gifts" of the stigmata and levitation, this miracle seems to emerge gradually in the Middle Ages. However, since bilocation accounts in late antiquity and the early Middle Ages have been insufficiently researched, this pattern could be more of an illusion than a reality. A relatively rare early account, perhaps among the earliest, comes from the sixth century, and it tells of a bilocation that supposedly took place in the fourth century. It involves Saint Ambrose falling into a trance or a deep sleep at the

Figure 29. An engraving of the bilocation of the Virgin Mary from Jerusalem to Spain. This legend made a deep impression on Sor María de Ágreda, and she incorporated it into her *Mystical City of God*.

altar for three hours during Sunday Mass, in Milan, between the first and second readings of the liturgy, and his being seen at the funeral of Saint Martin at Tours, nearly 600 miles away, at exactly the same time. In this case, as in most others until the late Middle Ages, the author makes no attempt to focus on the testimony of eyewitnesses. Mentioning or describing the event is assumed to be sufficient proof.[26]

Medieval Bilocations

Throughout the remainder of late antiquity and the early Middle Ages, accounts such as this are scarce, In the thirteenth century, however, bilocation suddenly becomes a more prominent marker of holiness in hagiographies. Not surprisingly, Saint Francis of Assisi (1182–1226) leads the way, just as he does with stigmatization. His bilocating begins late in his life, very dramatically, when Francis—who was in Assisi—suddenly appeared at a chapter meeting of his order at Arles, about 500 miles away, while Anthony of Padua was preaching. According to some of the early hagiographers, this bilocation also involved levitation, for Francis appeared "uplifted in the air, his hands outstretched after the manner of a cross, blessing the Brethren," an event immortalized by the artists Giotto and Fra Angelico, both of whom depict Francis floating above the ground (fig. 30).[27] Tellingly, this bilocation was compared to that of Ambrose in the fourth century, revealing that this ancient miracle was indeed a point of reference many centuries later and a significant influence in the development of a medieval bilocation tradition. As Saint Bonaventure's *Life of Francis* put it: "We must verily believe that the almighty power of God, which vouchsafed unto the holy Bishop Ambrose to be present at the burial of the glorious Martin . . . did also make His servant Francis to appear."[28]

Saint Anthony of Padua (1195–1231), one of the most prominent of early Franciscan saints, whose sermon at the chapter meeting of Arles was interrupted when Saint Francis miraculously appeared, also began to bilocate around the same time, and one such event also involved interrupted preaching. A fourteenth-century account relates how while preaching one Holy Thursday at a church in Limoges he suddenly remembered his promise to read one lesson during canonical hours at his friary, about sixteen miles away. Immediately, Anthony stopped preaching and remained silent for a long time at the pulpit. At the very same instant, he appeared in the choir at his friary and read the scheduled lesson. Then, as soon as he had fulfilled that duty, he came back to his senses at the pulpit in Limoges and finished his sermon. Tellingly, again, this bilocation is

Figure 30. Giotto was one of the first artists ever to depict a bilocation, which in this fresco shows Saint Francis visiting Arles while he was still in Assisi.

compared to that of Saint Ambrose at the funeral of Saint Martin, but no mention is made of Saint Francis's sudden appearance at Arles.[29]

Throughout the fourteenth and fifteenth centuries, bilocation accounts begin to increase. Some of these accounts surely provided inspiration to Sor María, especially those that involved Franciscans, especially Spanish ones. One such fellow Franciscan was Pedro Regalado (1390–1456), whose renown as a bilocator has endured for so long in Spanish culture that civic associations in his hometown of Valladolid proposed that the Vatican name him the patron saint of the internet due to his ability to transcend his physical space.[30] In jest, one Spanish newspaper even suggested that his name should henceforth be spelled S@n Pedro Reg@l@do (fig. 31).

Figure 31. This baroque depiction of a bilocation by Saint Peter Regalado interprets the miracle as effected by angels, one of various interpretations of this mystery, which was also voiced by Sor María de Ágreda.

Sixteenth-Century Bilocations

In the sixteenth century, bilocation begins to appear fairly frequently in hagiographies, which could now be printed and circulated much more widely than in the Middle Ages. An unknown number of such accounts also circulated orally but never made it into print, so what we can find in hagiographies might merely be the tip of the iceberg. Among those saints whose bilocations became well known we find a good number of Spaniards and Italians, some of whom also levitated. Among these, we find the Italian saint Francesco di Paola (1416–1507), yet another Franciscan; Ignatius Loyola and Francis Xavier, both Spanish Basques and Jesuits; and Teresa of Avila, a Spanish Carmelite nun.

Francesco di Paola was best known for his prayerfulness, humility, and simplicity, so accounts of his bilocations fit his profile. One such account tells of him of being seen working in the friary's kitchen and serving as an acolyte at Mass simultaneously. Another relates how he was seen praying ecstatically in the chapel and, at the same time, talking to people on the street, just outside the friary. And, according to the record, these events were seen by witnesses who ran back and forth between the two Francescos.[31] Bilocations such as these, which were close enough in distance for the saint to be seen at both locations by the same group of witnesses, are exceedingly rare.

Ignatius Loyola (1491–1556), founder of the Jesuits and a Spanish Basque, was known for his many mystical gifts, including levitation, luminescence, and bilocation. One bilocation account tells of the ever-pragmatic Loyola showing up in Cologne, roughly 870 miles from Rome, to order Leonard Kessel, rector of the Jesuit community, to stay there in Cologne instead of returning to Rome, as he was planning (fig. 32).[32] Another account that seems to have been interpreted as a short-distance transvection in Rome has him appearing suddenly in a sick man's room and healing him, even though the windows and doors were all locked. To top off this miracle, his luminescence also lit up the whole room (see fig. 3).[33]

Another Spanish Basque and Jesuit bilocator who probably had a deeper influence on Sor María was Francis Xavier (1506–1552), the most celebrated and venerated missionary of early modern times. Xavier was an indefatigable pioneer of missionary ventures into Asia and as well known for his miracles as for the thousands of conversions he claimed to have made in India, the East Indies, and Japan. His bilocations were so frequent and amazing that some

Figure 32. Engraving from an illustrated hagiography of Saint Ignatius Loyola depicting his bilocation from Rome to Cologne, during which he ordered Father Leonard Kessel not to leave that German city.

critics might be tempted to say they were almost banal. Among the most famous of these bilocations is the one in which he rescued some sailors from certain death during a violent storm by suddenly appearing in their launch while never leaving the ship he was on and then piloting those terrified sailors back aboard, where he had remained visible during this miraculous rescue.

Ever pragmatic, like his superior, mentor, and fellow Basque Ignatius Loyola, Xavier managed not only to save some lives through this bilocation but also to convert two Muslims who were on the imperiled launch.[34] This miracle is not mentioned in Xavier's letters or any early hagiographies, however, and first appears in 1596, in Orazio Torsellino's hagiography.[35] The same is true of other miracles too. This has led some critics to argue that Xavier's case proves that miracle accounts could be exaggerated or invented ex post facto as a means of ensuring someone's canonization.[36]

Sor María could have also drawn inspiration from Teresa of Avila, whose texts she certainly read and whose bilocations she might have heard about. Teresa's own texts do not say much about bilocation, nor do her early hagiographies, but her canonization inquests do contain some bilocation accounts. While María could not have read these manuscripts, it is possible that—given Teresa's great renown—some of the stories found in them could have become part of the oral culture shared by monks and nuns in Spain. Three such accounts give us a glimpse of Teresa the bilocator. Ana de San Agustín, a Carmelite nun at Malagón, testified that she was awakened one night by Teresa, who ordered her to go to the chapel and relight the sanctuary light near the tabernacle, which must always be lit but had gone out. When Ana entered the chapel, she was surprised to see that Teresa was already there, waiting for her, but as soon as she had relit the lamp and turned around, Teresa had vanished. And at that moment she realized that Teresa was at Ávila, about 145 miles away. As she saw it, Teresa had done this to inspire her to be a more vigilant sacristan.[37] Father Enrique Enriquez, a Jesuit, related a bilocation story involving a confrere, Gaspar de Salazar, who had known Teresa intimately. Salazar, he said, once told him how Teresa suddenly appeared in his locked room to comfort and advise him, even though she was "many leagues away." When Salazar had the chance sometime later to ask Teresa in person about this visit, she said "with humble modesty" that God had indeed sent her to help him.[38] Sor Ana de Jesús Lobera, another Carmelite nun, testified that she knew of many occasions when Teresa had bilocated to offer spiritual advice and comfort to those in need. She related the story of how Teresa—who was in Segovia, about ninety-five miles away—visited a nun on her deathbed in Salamanca. Soon after Teresa's visit, said Ana de Jesús, the ailing nun died joyfully, her face all aglow with a "heavenly and supernatural light." When the nuns who had been with Teresa in Segovia that day were asked if Teresa had really been there, they confirmed it, adding that at the exact time Teresa was comforting the dying Isabel in Salamanca, she was in a cataleptic ecstasy in Segovia, looking "as if she were dead."[39]

Yet another sixteenth-century mystic who could have impressed María was Philip Neri (1515–1595), founder of the Congregation of the Oratory. On March 12, 1622, three weeks before María's twentieth birthday, when she was in the thick of her levitating and bilocating ecstasies, Loyola, Xavier, Neri, and Teresa—all bilocators—were canonized on the same day. Spanish celebrations of this quadruple canonization were of epic proportions and generated a large number of texts related to these saints and their miracles, some or many of which could have reached Ágreda. María might also have read or heard about the bilocations of Catherine dei Ricci (1522–1590), a Dominican nun in Prato, near Florence, who struck up a correspondence with Philip Neri and visited him in Rome, about 185 miles away, without ever leaving her convent. A stigmatic who underwent the agony of Christ's Passion every week, beginning at noon on Thursday and ending at four o'clock on Friday, Catherine reportedly had frequent conversations with Neri during her visits. Neri would attest to this, along with five other witnesses, and he, too, was reported to have visited her at least once without ever leaving Rome.[40]

Seventeenth-Century Bilocations

By the time Sor María was born in 1605, bilocation had become a certain *possibility* for Catholic mystics. Consequently, bilocators were popping up all over the map, figuratively and literally. But, given that bilocations were much easier to fake or "invent" than levitations or stigmata and harder to disprove, too, testing the veracity of such events was challenging for the church. And as the winnowing of the wheat and the chaff went on, María had many accounts of bilocation to hear or read about, and to be inspired by, as did all her contemporaries, especially those in monastic life. Her century had many bilocators, including some who were deemed frauds, such as Luisa de Carrión and Francisco de la Fuente, but also many who were not, as will be detailed in chapter 8. María, therefore, was not an isolated phenomenon but very much a part of a religio-cultural world in which bilocation had become not only something possible but expected of those who were exceptionally holy.[41] This was especially true of Italy and Spain and its colonies, where bilocation seemed to thrive. What made María unique was not her bilocations in and of themselves but the extremes to which she took the bilocating paradigm, which tested the limits of belief and credulity, as well as of reason. Comparing her to some of her contemporary levitators should help to place her claims in context and to bring her uniqueness into high relief.

María de Ágreda and the aforementioned Luisa de Carrión were not the only nuns who claimed to have engaged in missionary work in distant lands through miraculous bilocations. Although we shall never know for sure how many nuns made such claims by mere word of mouth, which have been irretrievably lost, we do have evidence of several whose claims were preserved in manuscript and in print. In many of these seventeenth- and eighteenth-century accounts, however, it is not always clear that the visits to distant lands were bilocations, strictly speaking, or transvections, or some wholly spiritual visionary experience. In fact, the medieval concept of bilocation becomes somewhat unstable in the seventeenth century, especially in Spanish colonies, turning into a phenomenon that could be called *mystical displacement,* or *mystical journeying,* in which the protagonists leave their home locations—usually a cloister—and rapidly or suddenly find themselves present elsewhere.[42] Descriptions of the displacement can vary. Some accounts involve transvection of some sort, some speak of teleportation, and others describe purely spiritual journeys. Some mention physical displacement, but sometimes the event seems to resemble the extrasensory phenomenon of remote *viewing,* which involves the psychic "seeing" other locations near and far.[43] Moreover, establishing that the mystic is visible in both locations simultaneously—especially the place of origin—becomes less common in many of these baroque accounts. Sometimes no effort at all is made to mention witnesses. But in all cases, regardless of the fuzziness with which the visits are explained, all those involved claimed to have been "present" elsewhere in some miraculous way.

One such nun was Ana María de San José (1581–1632), a Discalced Franciscan from Salamanca who claimed to have visited pagans in the Indies and other lands many times. Ordered by her confessor Juanentín del Niño to write an autobiography, Ana María did so, and soon after her death he published it, adding copious hagiographic flourishes, hoping to kick-start her beatification inquest.[44] In it, she speaks of visiting other lands "in spirit" or "in her heart"[45] because of her anguish over the number of souls headed for damnation and the lack of missionary priests available for the task of converting them, much like María de Ágreda would do.[46] Juana de Jesús María (1564–1650), a Carmelite

Figure 33. Saint Joseph bilocates from Assisi to his mother's deathbed at Copertino.

tertiary from Burgos, claimed to have made numerous visits to distant lands, including Turkey, Algeria, Brazil, and the Philippines, as reported by her hagiographer Francisco de Ameyugo. And she also claimed to have sometimes visited North America, where Indians shot arrows at her as she flew above them.[47] In addition, she insisted that Luisa de Carrión accompanied her on some of these visits, a clear indication that oral accounts of bilocations or transvections to distant lands were definitely in circulation. Nonetheless, these claims ultimately struck the Inquisition the wrong way, for in 1679 it banned her biography.[48] Isabel de Jesús (1630–1677), a nun from Miedes de Aragón, a mere sixty miles from Ágreda, claimed to have visited Japan and the Indies. Some claims stretched beyond the mission field to the battlefield. Martina de los Angeles claimed to have killed the Lutheran Swedish king Gustavus Adolphus "with her own hand" in 1632 at the Battle of Lützen,[49] and Antonia Jacinta de Navarra claimed to have battled the Turks physically, alongside Christian warriors.[50]

In Italy, Joseph of Cupertino (1603–1663) was an exact contemporary of Sor María, and it is tempting to wonder what might have transpired if the two had ever met. Both were bilocators, so such counterfactual speculation is not wholly idle. Both were ecstatic Franciscan mystics showered with mystical "gifts" from above, and both took those gifts to extremes: Joseph with levitation, María with bilocation. But Joseph's recorded bilocations in his hagiographies were few in number and much more limited in scope than María's, confined as they were to two deathbed visits. The first of these was a visit to a former neighbor in Copertino, Ottavio Piccino, "an old decrepit man" who had made Joseph promise that he would comfort him at the hour of his death. Although he was in Rome when Ottavio's death approached, Joseph knew the time had come, and he suddenly turned up at Ottavio's bedside as promised, surprising everyone in town before vanishing as soon as Ottavio died. His second bilocation served the same purpose for his mother, to whom he had promised the same kind of aid. Although he was in Assisi at the time, he appeared in Copertino instantly, bathed in a bright light, immediately after hearing his mother's plea for help. At that same time, his brethren in Assisi saw him weeping, and when asked about the reason for his tears, he replied, "My poor mother has just died" (fig. 33).[51] Whether or not María de Ágreda ever heard of Joseph matters little. Both shared in the same assumptions about the seemingly impossible, and both redefined the impossible in their own way, as part of a common mentality within Catholicism and their Franciscan order.

New World Colonial Bilocations

Due to the colonizing and missionizing efforts of Spain, this common Catholic mentality shared by María de Ágreda and Joseph of Cupertino had become global by the seventeenth century. No one reified this global reach and this common mentality more intensely than Martín de Porres (1579–1639), a Dominican lay brother in Lima, Peru. An unlikely prospect for clerical life or sainthood at birth, Martín was the natural son of a Spanish colonist and a freed African slave who was a *curandera,* or natural healer. Consequently, due to the social and racial prejudices of his age he was denied a formal education as well as the opportunity of becoming a priest or of rising within his order above lay status.[52] Against all odds, however, this humble biracial servant who served as cook, custodian, barber, and nurse for his friary gained fame in Lima and beyond as a miracle-worker, a great healer, and a holy man with many mystical gifts, including luminescence, levitation, and bilocation. According to accounts from many witnesses, his levitations were frequent, and his bilocations were extreme enough to range over four continents, with visits to other locations in South America, North America (Mexico), Africa (the Barbary Coast), Asia (the Philippine Islands, China, and Japan), and Europe (France). These accounts would be among the first to involve transoceanic distances as well as a biracial bilocator. The accounts from Japan and North Africa also involved repeated visits—just like María's missionary journeys. But in Martín's case, he not only served as a missionary but also offered care and solace to Christian missionaries and to captives taken hostage by Muslims.[53] In addition to these extraordinary miracles, Martín was said to have the power to communicate with animals and to convince them to alter their behavior for the sake of harmony.[54] Despite such remarkable miracles, as well as a life of heroic virtue, Martín would not be canonized until 1962 by Pope John XXIII, over three centuries after his death.

Martín also befriended another local saint and Dominican tertiary, Isabel Flores de Oliva (1586–1616), who he sometimes counseled and aided and whose canonization trajectory was the opposite of his in terms of speed. Known in Lima by her religious name of Rose and after her canonization as Saint Rose of Lima, she was an extreme ascetic and ecstatic mystic. Although she is not known for bilocating, she claimed to have received the gift of the stigmata and holds the distinction of being the first American-born person to be canonized.[55] She was eventually given the title of Patroness of the Indies, America, and the

Philippines, and was beatified in 1668 and canonized in 1671, a mere fifty-five years after her death.

The transmission of culture, piety, and mentalities from the Old World to the New was intensely reified in Rose of Lima, who patterned her life after that of Saint Catherine of Siena (1347–1380), with whom she was intimately familiar. All one must do to see the resemblance between these two female saints is to read Raymond of Capua's *Life of Saint Catherine,* which Rose of Lima sought to mimic and surpass. Likewise, although there is no easily identifiable moment for the acceptance of bilocation or transvection as normative, it is relatively easy to spot the emergence of a bilocating mentality among New World nuns, who amplified mystical relocation with unequaled intensity, making the European bilocators seem like underachievers in comparison.

Again, as in the case of Old World bilocators, we have no way of knowing how many oral accounts of bilocations, which are no longer accessible, might have circulated. But we do have enough written accounts to suggest that bilocation not only ceased to be *impossible* in the monastic mentality of the New World between 1550 and 1750 but became somewhat commonplace, especially among nuns. And María de Ágreda, it could be argued, might have played a significant role in this paradigm shift, especially in the New World, where her *Mystical City of God* and the hagiography of Jiménez Samaniego usually appended to it became immensely popular.[56] Identifying American bilocating nuns is still a work in progress, but in the past few decades, an impressive list has been compiled.[57] Among the most significant of these are at least thirteen who deserve close attention, all of whom identified very intensely with the paradigm of a mystically relocated female missionary. Since all these colonial New World nuns stretched the boundaries of the *possible* in ways that their European counterparts seldom did, if ever, they brought the phenomenon of Catholic bilocation into a distinct phase of development and deserve more attention than this brief chapter on the history of bilocation. For the sake of comparison, brief summaries of their cases have been included in appendix 1.

In sum, the claims of these thirteen levitators from the Spanish colonies shared common traits, including two salient ones: first, that of being involved in missionary work through mystical relocation; and, second, that of transcending the walls of their cloisters or communities in extreme ways, including engaging in battles with pirates. Whether the feats they claimed were deemed impossible or not seemed to matter little to them, their hagiographers, or their devotees at the time when those claims were made. And, given that some of these nuns and their hagiographers were contemporaries of Enlightenment skeptics and atheists in the Old World as well as in the New, those claims reflect the endurance of certain beliefs and mentalities. Back in the Old World, meanwhile, mystical relocations continued in the face of increasing doubt and even of ridicule and hostility. They continued at a slower pace, for sure, but refused to stop. A brief review of this most recent part of the history of bilocation should help place the phenomenon and its interpretation in a fuller context.

Bilocations in a Skeptical World

After María of Agreda's death in 1665, bilocations continued to be reported in Catholic Europe, especially in Italy, which began to overtake and surpass Spain in the number of impossible feats attributed to saints. Quantifying this phenomenon is difficult, if not impossible, for there is no way of knowing how many oral accounts circulated or how many of these simply disappeared with the passage of time. All we can count is the number of bilocation accounts that made it to print, and of these some of the most prominent, as before, were those connected to the exceptional men and women put up for canonization.

In the nineteenth century, as secularism gained increasing supremacy in Western cultures, bilocation seemed to become increasingly rare among Catholic saints, or perhaps less well publicized, as the genre of hagiography diminished in prominence among Catholic publishers. A rare exception during this time was John Bosco (1815–1888), priest, educator, preacher, writer, social activist, and founder of the Salesian order, which dedicates itself to helping the poor, disadvantaged, and the ill in many countries throughout the world. Don Bosco—as he was known—took on the many dire problems created by rapid urbanization and industrialization in the northern Italian city of Turin. Don Bosco's bilocations, reported from various places, tended to be as pragmatic as those of his many predecessors. The difference between him and them is the setting and the circumstances, which are fully modern, with acrid climate-changing smoke and aggressive skepticism flooding the air he supposedly miraculously traversed.[58] He was canonized in 1934.

The twentieth century, too, had relatively few well-known bilocators, although researchers in the field of parapsychology seemed to have had little trouble finding many who lived in obscurity.[59] One amazing Catholic bilocator who has escaped notice outside France is Yvonne Beauvais (1901–1951), an Augustinian nun and superior general also known as Yvonne-Aimée de Malestroit. This remarkable mystic who exhibited many supernatural gifts, including bilocation, was also intensely engaged in practical matters such as the creation and supervision of a medical clinic and was even awarded the French Croix de Guerre and Légion d'Honneur medals in 1945—that second one by General Charles de Gaulle himself[60]—for the clandestine assistance she offered French resistance fighters and Allied soldiers during World War II, which sometimes involved disguising airmen as nuns. Her bilocations, which number over 200 and stretch over a span of twenty-five years, are among the most meticulously charted of all time and include locations within France and other countries in Europe, Asia, Africa, and North and South America.[61]

Mother Yvonne-Aimée might not have attracted much attention with her seemingly baroque miracles, but the twentieth century did have one bilocator who set back the clock and shattered complacency toward the miraculous with a vengeance, so to speak. Pio of Pietrelcina (1887–1968), better known as Padre Pio, a Capuchin friar from southern Italy, continuously exhibited all of the major miraculous phenomena associated with mystical ecstasy—including stigmata, levitation, bilocation, and clairvoyance—through two world wars and into the Cold War and the space age.[62] Although he lived under a cloud of suspicion like so many of his bilocating predecessors,[63] he eventually prevailed and was canonized in 2002 by Pope John Paul II, who was one of his devotees.[64] That Polish pontiff had not only visited Padre Pio in 1947—long before he became pope—to have his confession heard by him, but had also credited him with miraculously curing a friend's cancer in 1962. Padre Pio was controversial in his day and continues to be as much of a target for vituperation in the secular sphere as he is a magnet for veneration among some of the faithful. Padre Pio was a throwback to the Middle Ages and the baroque age: an affront to the secular values and mentality of his day, a ray of light to traditionalist Catholics, and something of an embarrassment to Catholics who prefer to think of themselves as modern and progressive.

In many ways, Padre Pio mirrors María de Ágreda, not just because of his mystical gifts but also because of the controversial nature of those seemingly impossible phenomena attributed to both of them. Although María's era and culture approached the supernatural and the impossible in ways that differed from those of the twentieth or twenty-first century, she nonetheless proved troublesome. And the trouble she caused—which is inseparable from her life story—allows one to delve into some of the most fundamental questions surrounding the interpretation of the history of the impossible, in her day as well as in our own.

Having set the context for Sor María, let us move on to her impossible feats.

6. María de Ágreda, Avatar of the Impossible

> Having been enraptured in ecstasy by the Lord, without knowing exactly how,
> it seemed to her that she was suddenly in some other part of the world, with a
> much different climate, among people she recognized as Indians from previous
> abstract visions. . . . And as soon as her rapture came to an end, she found
> herself in the same spot where she had been when it began.
>
> —José Jiménez Samaniego

Born in 1602 in Ágreda, a frontier village in the northeastern corner of Old Castile near the border of Aragón, Sor María was destined never to leave her isolated hometown or the convent she joined at the age of fifteen. Save for her
alleged bilocations, she never ventured very far at all, spending her entire life in
the same quarter of Ágreda, in two dwellings. The first of these was the house in
which she had been born and reared, which her mother turned into a nunnery
and where she resided until 1633. The second was a new and larger convent
nearby, on the edge of town, expressly built to accommodate more nuns. She
would die in that second cloister in May 1665 in an aura of sanctity, seemingly
a prime candidate for a speedy canonization. Her hagiographer, quoted above,
was certain of it.[1] And although many others agreed back then, it has yet to
happen, more than three centuries later.

The Coronel family claimed hidalgo status—the lowest rung of nobility—
but were probably of partial Jewish ancestry, and they were far from wealthy or
socially prominent.[2] Of the eleven children born in that household, only four
would survive: two boys, Francisco and José, and two girls, María and Jéronima.
Much of what we know about María's childhood comes from two sources. The
first is an autobiography she began writing but never completed, which contains

Figure 34. Sor María de Ágreda is depicted in this engraving as the Virgin Mary's scribe.

abundant details about her family, childhood, and adolescence.[3] The second is the hagiography written by José Jiménez Samaniego, bishop of Plasencia, her Franciscan superior and great admirer, who worked diligently for her canonization. As hagiographer, he is far from an impartial source, given his chief aim, but much of what he includes in his *Life of Sor María,* first published in Barcelona in 1687, can also be found in the testimonies collected for her canonization inquests and can thus be regarded as a fairly accurate account of major features of her character and of events of her life. In addition, since his hagiography was included as an appendix in many editions of her most significant text, *The Mystical City of God,* his interpretation of basic facts—including miracles— became so definitive and so foundational in the creation of Sor María's persona that it needs to be taken into consideration as a portrait or mirror image of Sor María the "legend."

Jiménez Samaniego stressed the heightened spiritual atmosphere of María's household, as did María herself, in her unfinished autobiography. According to both accounts, Francisco Coronel and Catalina Arana were very devout parents, wholly given over to ascetical extremes. Her father, Francisco, awoke before dawn to pray and spent at least three or four hours a day praying, carrying a heavy cross around and sometimes laying on it as if crucified, and engaging in various forms of self-mortification. María described him as a man who hated leisure and as someone "naturally intense and choleric, but able to restrain his passions so excellently that what remained of them was just exactly what he needed for his valiant efforts to be virtuous, to rid himself of his imperfections, and to never be angry."[4] Not to be outdone, her mother, Catalina, also spent several hours a day praying, contemplating a human skull, focusing on Christ's crucifixion—just like her husband—whipping herself, and rehearsing her own death. María described her as "blessed with the qualities of a strong woman, as described by Solomon," as "magnanimous, big hearted, always very energetic,"[5] and as driven by a "manly vigor."[6] Moreover, María's parents encouraged imitation. "For from the age of nine or ten," María would later say, "they made their children pray in constant devotions and had us engage in mental prayer, for which they withdrew into their bedrooms and indicated for me to do the same in another room."[7] María needed no prodding. She was precociously spiritual but something of a worry for her parents due to her frequent illnesses and pronounced mystical tendencies. She prayed ceaselessly, more than her parents, and often heard voices, saw visions, entered trance-like states, and talked to invisible beings.

At the mere age of four, María was granted permission to receive the sacrament of confirmation, which was administered by none other than Diego de Yepes, bishop of Tarazona and hagiographer of Saint Teresa of Avila, who, after conversing with the young girl, had recognized her as spiritually gifted and precociously mature. According to Jiménez Samaniego, young María was "enlightened by divine illuminations" and "captivated by the goodness and the infinite beauty of God, and sweetly absorbed in His Sacred love."[8] According to María, she began to experience the presence and illumination of God as soon as she began to think.[9] At the age of six, however, María began to experience a dark night of the soul. "I wept and grew sad. . . . I was left alone, surrounded by gloom, bereaved; and the hardest thing of all was to lack very soft sweetness of the Lord's gifts."[10] Stripped of her encounters with the divine—a painful experience normally reserved for advanced adult mystics—María became moody, irritable, and overly scrupulous about her sins. Yet, despite the darkness that enveloped her, María's prayer life became so intense that her parents turned one of the rooms in the Coronel house into her private oratory, where she spent hours and hours by herself. At the tender age of eight, she took a vow of celibacy.[11] As she approached puberty, María's health declined sharply, and at one point, when she was thirteen, fearing that death was imminent, she received the sacrament of extreme unction, and arrangements were made for her funeral and burial.

Much to everyone's surprise, however, María made an astonishing recovery, both physical and spiritual, and as her health returned and her dark night faded, she regained her intimacy with the divine and supernatural. At this time, she also began to display a penchant for ecstatic writing of a highly imaginative sort, penning a travelogue of a flight she had made around the earth and into the heavens during a mystical vision. The earthly part of this account included descriptions of strange undiscovered lands and fantastic beings such as those represented in some early modern maps and texts, including headless, one-eyed, and dog-headed men, as well as the obligatory cannibals so feared by European explorers. The heavenly portion of the account shows that she was familiar with classical and Christian cosmology.[12]

When María was fifteen, her entire family left "the world" to become monastics after her mother had a vision in which God ordered her to become a nun. Her father, then in his fifties, and her two young brothers joined the Franciscan order and moved to Burgos. Then María, her mother, and her only sister turned their house into a Discalced Franciscan nunnery belonging to the Order of the Immaculate Conception, and they were soon joined by three nuns from Burgos.[13] During her first years in this small cloister, María embraced a life of prayer and self-mortification with zeal and was given her own cell and allowed more privacy than the other nuns.[14]

Though still in her teens and a mere novice, María quickly achieved the high mystical states of "recollection" and "the prayer of quiet," during which she would "forget everything terrestrial" and feel "annihilated" by her "Divine Spouse."[15] Whenever she was not absorbed in prayer, she would read "spiritual books," perform tasks in the convent, as demanded by her superior—who happened to be her mother—and engage in "acts of charity."[16] Constantly, she also mortified her body, and this penitential asceticism was not just rigorous but extreme. In addition to fasting constantly and observing a vegan diet,[17] María wore a hair shirt under her habit, along with a girdle studded with spiked rings and a heavy abrasive vest of chain mail. To top off her self-punishment, she also wrapped her body in chains and fetters, scourged herself daily, and wore a crucifix riddled with needles that she could press into her breast when she prayed. Nighttime brought no relief. In addition to sleeping for only a few hours, she did so without a mattress or pillow, on a hard wooden pallet which "resembled a torture rack."[18] Much like many other mystics, María's ecstasies were inextricably interwoven with horrific suffering. Illnesses plagued her constantly, along with the pain, wounds, and weakness caused by her austerities. She was also constantly assailed by angry demons who tormented her spiritually, mentally, and physically. Hell-bent on enhancing the pain caused by her self-torments and ailments, these demons also "tortured her constantly with dreadful words and imaginary visions, and smothered her with tribulations," tempting her to despair and making her think that "she was on the wrong path, on the way to perdition."[19] Every night, she said, she felt as if the demons were about to snuff out her life.[20]

The full perplexing marvel of Sor María was not yet in full bloom, however. Far from it. As astounding as her ecstasies, her austerities, her illnesses, and her encounters with demons might seem, they were only part of a much more complex engagement with the supernatural and the impossible. The bare facts of the rest of her life could seem humdrum in contrast, especially since she never left home. When she was only twenty-five, María was named abbess of her convent—after receiving a papal dispensation due to her young age—and she would serve in this post for the rest of her life, save for a three-year sabbatical between 1652 and 1655. But such a summary falls woefully short of conveying the full measure of María's life, her achievements, and her uniqueness. Much more was already happening in her life before she became an abbess, and even more would happen after she reluctantly but obediently assumed that role.

Sor María, Ecstatic Levitator

Sor María's austerities were accompanied by raptures. In 1620, at the age of eighteen, she began to experience frequent and prolonged ecstasies, at first in her isolated cell and soon afterward in the presence of her fellow nuns. It did not take long for her arrobamientos to take place in view of the other nuns, despite her many efforts to conceal and resist them.[21] Many of these raptures would occur immediately after she partook of the Eucharist, which she did daily. While rapt in ecstasy, María became cataleptic, much like Joseph of Cupertino, totally oblivious to her own body and her surroundings.[22] She also began to levitate during these raptures and to attract attention in her convent and beyond its walls.

María's levitations, which began when she was only eighteen years old, were described by Samaniego as follows: "Her body was elevated a short distance above the ground; its natural heaviness so diminished, that it seemed weightless and could be blown around with just one puff of breath, as if it were merely a leaf from a tree or a light feather." Such raptures could last between two and three hours, he added, and turn her face radiant. And much like Joseph of Cupertino, her ecstatic levitations could be triggered instantly by certain stimuli: communion, spiritual texts, sacred music, the mere mention of any of God's attributes. During these levitating raptures, "her external composure was so modest and so devout, she seemed like a Seraphim incarnate."[23]

The convent's sisters watched in amazement at first and "experimented" with María's body when it was aloft—especially by testing her weightlessness—to confirm the raptures were genuine and of divine origin. To allay all suspicions of demonic influence, they called in the provincial of their order, who determined after testing her obedience that he could find "no evidence whatsoever "of demonic involvement."[24] After his visit, María's levitations became "more frequent and more marvelous."[25] Sometimes, other phenomena were witnessed during her levitating raptures. Once, for instance, "a resplendent globe of light descended from above, extremely clear and beautiful, and it hovered for a long time, and it was seen by everyone, and taken to be a heavenly prodigy."[26]

Before long, word of these levitations spread beyond the convent of the Immaculate Conception and beyond Ágreda too. As Samaniego observed, "It is not at all easy for any such admirable and noteworthy thing to remain contained in any community; news of it will inevitably leak out."[27] Consequently, between 1620 and 1623, many curious visitors streamed through María's convent, eager to see the ecstatic levitating nun with their own eyes. Many of them, however, including all the nuns, did more than simply gawk. As happened with Joseph of Cupertino, María's levitating body was constantly poked and prodded, unceremoniously. "Her body remained so deprived of sensation," said Samaniego, "that it seemed dead, and no amount of maltreatment or torment could be felt by it."[28]

Shockingly, Sor María the levitating nun had become a spectacle without being aware of it at all, due to the cataleptic state caused by her raptures. Throngs of curious onlookers, clerical, monastic, and lay, flowed through Ágreda to view María through the convent's *comulgatorio,* the window through which the cloistered nuns received communion from the hands of a priest. All this took place without María's permission or, even worse, without her knowledge of it. Samaniego speaks disapprovingly of the "imprudent and dangerous disorder" of this spectacle. Anyone who wished to see María was allowed to do so, regardless of their status. The nuns would move María's cataleptic, levitating body close to the comulgatorio—as it floated in the air—remove the veil from her face so its miraculous glow could be seen, and then allow viewers to take their turn at peering through that opening or even blowing on María and "moving her body with a single puff of their breath,"[29] as if she were a feather or some other wispy plaything.

For three years, this carnivalesque display of supernatural power drew visitors to the Convent of the Immaculate Conception, day in and day out, with the encouragement of ecclesiastical authorities and not a single word of censure, according to the accounts that have survived. Worse yet, María's Franciscan superiors ordered the nuns at the convent and all visitors to never reveal to her that she was being displayed and manhandled in such a disrespectful way.

According to her own account and those of some eyewitnesses, when María finally learned that this was happening, she was horrified. The moment of truth arrived in early 1623, quite by chance, when a mentally unstable beggar she greeted at the convent door—a "loco," or madman, who had previously taken part in a viewing at the comulgatorio—inadvertently blurted out the awful secret. In shock, María quickly confirmed the veracity of the beggar's account, only to discover, much to her horror and dismay, that no one at the convent, not even her mother and sister, wanted to bring an end to the spectacle. In a letter written years later, she would say: "If secular justice had found me guilty of some great crime and paraded me on a donkey to shame me in public, it would not have grieved me as much as knowing that I was observed having those ecstasies and levitations of mine."[30]

Her immediate response was one of sheer desperation, and her community's reaction to it was far from gracious. First, María found a lock with which she could prevent the comulgatorio shutters from being opened. But she was ordered to turn in the key to the lock, and her vow of obedience forced her to do so. Then, since her daily levitations were prompted by communion, she sought a way of avoiding that sacrament, although she loathed doing so, and devised a way of breaking the fast required before communion by ingesting a medicinal syrup shortly before Mass, claiming her illnesses made this necessary. Reprimanded for doing this, she stopped doing it and begged her abbess for permission to take communion in private. Her request was granted, but the abbess and some of the nuns found a way of thwarting María's wishes by removing a panel from the choir door and carrying her from her cell—in ecstasy—to the comulgatorio, where she would be put on display to anyone who wished to see her levitating, without her being aware of it. Shuttling her weightless body to and fro was very easy, say the sources, for she was "as light as a feather." Once the public viewing by "everyone who wanted to see her" had taken place, she would then be returned to her cell, and the panel on the door would be replaced to keep her from suspecting that anything was amiss.[31]

María's abhorrence of her public levitations stemmed from several interconnected factors, and all of these—which were also in play for Teresa of Avila and Joseph of Cupertino—had to do with fear of the perceptions that levitation might elicit. As we have seen before, levitating was as inherently dangerous as it was wondrous, principally for three reasons. First, a marvel such as levitation could make people venerate the levitator and hold her in high esteem, a phenomenon fraught with danger, for it naturally casts doubt on any such person's humility. Genuine saints are supposed to eschew adulation and avoid any behavior that could make them susceptible to the sin of pride. Second, the issue of possible demonic influence was also at play since the devil was believed capable of causing levitations. Third, levitators ran the risk of being perceived as frauds or tricksters, and raised questions about their purported holiness. The answers to those questions, in turn, determined their reputation and identity. María the would-be saint and bride of Christ was therefore as fearful as she was ashamed and mortified. "The Lord willed it that she would find out" about her public levitations, said Samaniego, "so she could suffer the martyrdom of finding herself helpless in the face of such an awful assault on her humility and modesty." As he saw it, María was devastated not only because of "her fear of the danger" involved in her public levitations but also because of "the horror of all that publicity" generated by her levitations, which basically made her an easy target for the Inquisition.[32]

Seeking help from her abbess, her confessor, or her other superiors proved useless, for all of them wished to keep her on display. Seeking help from God proved fruitless too. Despite constant pleas to God "from the core of her soul," in which she implored for her ecstatic levitations to cease, the miracle continued taking place regularly.[33] Reconciling her intense disgust over being turned into a spectacle with her desire to fulfill her vow of obedience, which forced her to take communion daily, seemed impossible to María. Driven to despair, she contemplated pretending that she had lost the power of speech, or even that she had gone mad, but her conscience—and perhaps also her common sense—prevented her from attempting any such brazen deceit.[34] Meanwhile, as this drama unfolded and her ecstasies and levitations continued, her illnesses worsened, and her demonic attacks intensified.

Then, as the absolute limits of María's endurance were being tested, help came unexpectedly when two notable visitors arrived in Ágreda: Antonio de Villalacre, who had just ended his term as Franciscan provincial—and who was complicit in the staging and promoting of María's spectacle—accompanied by his brother, Juan de Villalacre, who had just assumed that same post. Knowing that Father Juan now had authority over her convent as provincial, María rushed to speak to him. Weeping uncontrollably, she related what was happening to her and begged for help, stressing the "dangerous and unseemly nature" of the role she had been forced to play. Father Juan responded by ordering her to pray directly to God for the cessation of her ecstasies and all the external favors (*exterioridades*) that accompanied them. Although she had already asked God for this repeatedly, to no avail, she obeyed the provincial immediately. This time, "armed with faith and obedience," she "threw herself at God's feet," praying with all the fervor she could muster, and God finally granted what she sought. Instantly, all her ecstasies and exterioridades ceased, much to her delight.[35] And they would never again occur. No more levitating for Sor María, ever. Praying as an act of obedience to a superior's orders had apparently made all the difference.

Predictably, María's fellow nuns reacted to this abrupt change with dismay, anger, and suspicion. "They abandoned sound judgement and loosened their tongues," said Samaniego. It seemed wrong to them that God would suddenly put an end to such a great marvel. Now that the levitations had ceased, some said they should never have occurred, and everyone tried to pinpoint the cause of their disappearance. Surely, some thought, this must prove that the levitations were diabolical. Others said María must have committed some hidden sins for which she was now being punished or that it was all due to inconstancy or weakness on her part, simply attributable to the fact that she was a woman.[36]

Much like Teresa of Avila, and totally unlike Joseph of Cupertino, Sor María made her ecstatic levitations cease through prayer, the very act that had caused them in the first place. What María's contemporaries made of this impossible feat and its sudden and seemingly premature truncation differed from what was made of those two other cases. The circumstances were as different as the personalities involved. María had begun levitating and ceased doing so very early in life, between the ages of eighteen and twenty-one. Teresa had started and stopped levitating in early middle age and then became involved in the reform of her religious order and the establishment of seventeen new convents, among other things. Joseph had begun young and never, ever ceased levitating but ended up living like a prisoner in remote friaries, hidden from view.

As we have already seen, levitation was paradoxical: it had an unearthly glow, an aura of ambivalence and ambiguity surrounding it as well as one of wonder, fascination, and fear; it was both necessary and unnecessary, an awesome gift and an awful burden, something to publicize and hide all at once. It was a definitive affront to Protestants but also a puzzling and irksome quirk. In the case of Sor María, however, unlike those of Teresa and Joseph, this quirk was only part of a much larger and more perplexing cluster of impossible feats. When María's levitations ceased, much grander impossible feats became manifest, and they were so colossal that they turned the levitations into a mere footnote often overlooked in succeeding centuries.

Sor María, the Bilocating "Lady in Blue"

One of María's impossible feats was linked to the levitations but ultimately eclipsed them in significance. While in ecstasy in Ágreda, as her cataleptic, levitating body was being gawked at, or blown about like a leaf, or being shuttled to and from the comulgatorio, Sor María claimed to be elsewhere at the same time, thousands of miles away, across the Atlantic Ocean, working as a missionary among North American Indians. But this was not all. The Indians themselves and Spanish Franciscan missionaries in New Mexico would later corroborate her incredible claim and give rise to the legend of the Lady in Blue, a reference to the blue cloak that was part of María's Conceptionist Franciscan habit.

Bilocation accounts pose an inevitable challenge to those who investigate them, insofar as they always require the matching up of eyewitness testimonies from two different locations: one set from the original and permanent spot where the person remains—usually in ecstasy—and the other from the distant and temporary spot where that person suddenly appears and eventually disappears. Proving that any bilocation has taken place is always awfully difficult, if not impossible. In fact, to be convinced that any bilocation has taken place requires a leap of faith, even for those who offer their eyewitness testimony, for the simple reason that no witnesses to any such miracle can ever see what is going on beyond their own location at the original point where the levitator is supposedly visible. In an era without instant communications, the time lag in the reporting and matching of accounts could be considerable, so constructing a single narrative out of any bilocation could take years, as was the case here with María de Ágreda. Several contemporary accounts of her miraculous bilocations exist, and they overlap and intertwine over a period that spans three decades. These accounts provide a tangled yet congruent pair of narratives: one generated in Spain, the other in the New World.

Sources of the Legend

The first account was purely oral, and it came from María herself, who spoke to her confessors about these experiences, as well as to her sisters in the convent. This account surfaced between 1620 and 1623, as these events were ostensibly unfolding, and no written record of it is known to exist. Naturally, as with any such ostensible miracle, tales of María's adventures in the New World began to circulate rapidly by word of mouth, especially in Franciscan circles. How the tale was told, exactly, and how its details could have morphed as it passed from person to person is something hidden from view. But we do know that tales of a Spanish nun who visited New World natives did eventually reach Mexico, where the Franciscans were very active in mission work. Then, as one would expect, Franciscan superiors in Mexico began an investigation since the mission field involved in these tales—present-day Texas and New Mexico—was under their supervision. Written accounts began to surface soon thereafter, and these would link María's own narrative with that of the natives and missionaries in the New World.

This first written account never made it into print and did not play much of a role in the development of the Lady in Blue legend. It consists of two brief

paragraphs at the end of a chronicle of the Spanish exploration and coloniza-
tion of New Mexico, which was penned in the late 1620s in the colonial capital
of Mexico by Gerónimo Zárate Salmerón, a Franciscan missionary. Although
sketchy, this account tells of a local narrative circulating by word of mouth in the
New Mexico Territory about numerous visits paid to native tribes by a Spanish
nun. Although the nun is not named in the narrative itself, the subtitle that
precedes it makes her identity explicit: "Account of the Holy Mother María de
Jesús, abbess of the convent of Santa Clara de Ágreda." Without a doubt, then, by
1628, when this manuscript was written, Franciscans in Mexico were already
crediting Sor María with missionary activity in the New World.[37]

In 1630, seven years after María's levitations and bilocations had ceased,
a second account of her visits to America was written and quickly appeared in
print. Its author was Alonso de Benavides, a Franciscan friar who had spent five
years as a missionary in New Mexico. This account, which does not identify
María as the missionary nun, was very brief, merely one chapter in a long detailed report on the "temporal and spiritual treasures" of the New Mexico missions written for King Philip IV, which has come to be known simply as the 1630
Memorial of Alonso Benavides.[38] As sparse in details about the identity of the
nun as it was replete with extravagant claims about her feats, this seminal text
would become the foundation of the Lady in Blue legend and a focal point of
reference for all subsequent accounts of María's bilocations.

Benavides would also play a major role in two more accounts. In 1631,
after returning to Spain, Benavides met with María at her convent in Ágreda,
along with two other Franciscans, Andrés de la Torre, her confessor, and Sebastián
Marcilla, head of the Burgos Province. After this meeting, Benavides would write
a letter to the missionaries in New Mexico about María's bilocations and also
attach a letter ostensibly penned by María herself—that he forced her to write
under her vow of obedience—in which she confirmed that she had indeed evangelized the Jumano Indians. This text, which would not be published until a
century later, is the third account and the first to contain direct testimony from
María.[39] In her later brushes with the Inquisition, this document would play a
large role.

Due to the stir made in Catholic circles by tales of María's extreme bilocations and to the Franciscan order's desire to promote the success of their
missions, Benavides penned yet another report in 1634, this one addressed to
Pope Urban VIII, in which he included details not found in his previous two
accounts.[40] The original text of this fourth account, known as Benavides's 1634

Memorial, appears to have never been published and thus has had a greater impact on modern scholars that gained access to it than on those responsible for creating the Lady in Blue legend.[41] The chief purpose of the second *Memorial,* much like the earlier one, was not so much to call attention to the Lady in Blue as to highlight the supernatural prowess of the Franciscan order and to position it favorably for royal patronage. Benavides also had ecclesiastical ambitions of his own that cannot be overlooked. Naturally, the caution or skepticism with which these texts have been approached can vary.[42]

The fifth account to be written came from María herself, who penned it in 1650, after she had been questioned by the Inquisition for the second time in her life. This remarkable text, addressed to Father Pedro Manero, the superior general of the Franciscan order in Spain, seeks to correct or even deny many of the details found in earlier accounts, including some that she had earlier declared to be accurate. Her brush with the Inquisition behind her, her close relationship with King Philip IV unbroken, the mature María was no longer afraid to safeguard her orthodoxy and her reputation by contradicting Benavides, his sources of information, or the legends spawned by his reports. "They are accurate about some things," she says about Benavides's accounts, "but other things have been added and exaggerated." Carefully muffling her grievances and refusing to lay blame directly on any single individual, María nonetheless confesses that much had gone awry in the telling and retelling of her story back in 1629–1634. These distortions, she observes, "stemmed from the fact that the information was gathered from nuns and friars" and that because the story was transmitted through so many friars and nuns, "it was unavoidable that the truth of it would be adulterated, especially on a subject where imprudent religious enthusiasts feel one is doing something grand by adding on more, but what gets added on is usually illegitimate, dangerous, harmful, and offensive to the truly pious. I have been unlucky because they have raised up many testimonies about me, saying more than has really occurred and happened to me; throughout my life it has caused anguish and suffering."[43]

Keenly aware of the danger involved in denying the veracity of some details that she had verified twenty years before by affixing her signature to Benavides's 1631 letter and by confirming his report in a letter of her own, the middle-aged María tried to distance herself as much as possible—and as humbly and deferentially as possible—from the young and "inexperienced" María, who had been too easily cowed by her male superiors into approving their half-truths, fables, and exaggerations.[44] "The truth," she says, "is that I went along with the

Figure 35. Antonio de Castro's depiction of María de Ágreda preaching to American natives, frontispiece from the 1730 Mexican edition of Benavides's correspondence with the Franciscan missionaries.

reports passively, not actively, and that I was horribly pained by what was written up." And that truth, she argues, absolves her of any wrongdoing. "I was trembling, beside myself with anxiety, and never realized what I was signing; I did not even pay attention to it. The truth is that I left everything in the hands of those highly responsible fathers, entrusting the success of my affairs to them more than to myself, for they were prelates and scholars."[45] This important document would never be published and has only survived in a handful of manuscript copies. Consequently, its impact on the legend of María's bilocations was not as significant as it should have been.

The sixth and definitive account appeared in 1670, five years after María's death, in the twelfth chapter of the hagiography written by José Jiménez Samaniego. Longer than any of the previous accounts on which it relied, this one consolidated the merging of María's identity with the Lady in Blue legend and also lent an authoritative seamlessness to the narrative of her miraculous missionary feats. The hagiographer's achievement can be attributed in part to his skill as a writer; in part to his main goal, which was to promote María's canonization; in part to the close personal relationship he had with María, which provided him with privileged information; and in part to the access he had to multiple other accounts in the beatification and canonization inquests that took place shortly after her death—documents that few other people could access. Whether he also had access to Inquisition documents is uncertain. The seamless narrative of the hagiography is tidier than the accounts that preceded it and naturally takes for granted the miraculous nature of all the improbable events involved, including some that María herself exposed as fictive or incorrect in her report to Father Manero. Moreover, since this hagiography was appended to many editions of María's immensely popular text *The Mystical City of God*, it gained the widest readership, eclipsed all other accounts, and became definitive.

Conflating Narratives from Two Continents

One of the most distinct features of the Lady in Blue legend is how long it took for events in a remote corner of Spain to be linked with events in an even more remote corner of Spain's New World empire. Another distinct feature is how a single master narrative was eventually crafted out of different and sometimes conflicting accounts. That narrative is a blending of stories, some of which do not agree and all of which tell of an astounding miracle that could never be conclusively proven. To trace the unfolding of the Lady in Blue legend, one cannot assume the accuracy or veracity of all available accounts. As with any miracle, even those that do not involve conflicting accounts, all the serious historian can do is to bracket the question of whether the miracle "really" occurred as the accounts state and to focus instead on how those involved became convinced that a miracle had indeed taken place or how a miracle was simply invented or inflated.

Coming up with a master narrative in María's day and age was far from quick or easy for those involved in this ostensible miracle, given the distance between Ágreda and New Mexico, the remoteness of the missionary outpost she claimed to have visited, and the extreme nature of the miracle involved. And that master narrative would end up having several kinks in it, some of which were substantial. Tracing the construction of that narrative is not easy either, but it is certainly possible, especially if one pays close attention to the chronological sequence of the events in question and the assumptions that guided the authors of that narrative. This process, then, involves the interweaving of stories and events in both Spain and America, and it is perhaps best laid out in the present tense to give a greater sense of immediacy. Naturally, the narrative itself assumes that the testimony and chronology provided by all the individuals involved in this miracle story are accurate and that events unfolded exactly as the testimony states. But historians cannot overlook kinks in that narrative—obvious or subtle—that suggest alternative possibilities.

According to María, the bilocations begin in 1620, as a component of her "external favors" (exterioridades)—that is, those cataleptic trances that caused her to levitate. As these bilocations begin, she speaks to her confessors about her visits to America and her missionary work with Indians. The specificity of her accounts is startling. She can describe the landscape and climate as well as the people she encounters, and she can pinpoint the location as New Mexico. Later in life, in her 1650 report to Father Manero, María would explain her fascination with mission work and with that region, specifically. It all began with her ecstasies, she says. "At this time and in this state of mind," she reveals, "the Lord would let me know occasionally that he wanted me to work on behalf of his creatures and for the welfare of their souls." While in ecstasy, she claims, God would often show her all the souls in the world who were ignorant of Him and headed for damnation, and her reaction was intense: "My heart would break when I saw that God's abundant redemption did not fall on more than just a very few," she says, "and seeing this caused me bitter and unbearable pain." As her grief intensified with every such vision of specific peoples around the globe, the Lord then let her know that among all the pagans and infidels He had shown to her, "the ones toward whom His compassion was then most inclined, were the New Mexicans and the inhabitants of other remote kingdoms in that part of the world."[46]

According to María, her engagement with the New Mexican tribes expands gradually. First, she begins to have visions in which she observes the New Mexicans and their environment passively. Then her desire to teach them the Catholic faith grows as her visions become increasingly more vivid: "Those kingdoms were shown to me in detail," her account says, "with the features and properties of that part of the world, the appearance of the men and women ... and other circumstances." Before long, she claims, she finds herself sliding into a more active role with the New Mexicans: "It seemed to me I addressed them and begged them to go seek ministers of the Gospel to teach them the catechism and baptize them, and I came to know them too." But when it came to understanding or remembering how all of this became possible during her ecstasies at the age of nineteen or twenty, the middle-aged María claims to be stumped: "The way this happened is something I do not feel I can explain nor do I remember clearly."[47] While María attributes her knowledge of the people of New Mexico to divine revelation, one should not overlook the fact that her own Franciscan order was engaged in mission work in that remote frontier of the Spanish Empire and that it is highly likely that she had heard about those missions and the natives who were being Christianized. In addition, one cannot overlook the fact that other members of her order were at that very same time gaining fame throughout Spain as bilocating miracle-workers and that some of the bilocations attributed to them involved mission activity in the New World.

One of these bilocators was a Franciscan nun, previously mentioned, Sor Luisa de la Ascensión (1565–1636), also known as Luisa de Carrión because of the location of her convent.[48] Sor Luisa not only gained fame for her extreme fasting, ecstasies, visions, prophecies, and healings but also for her numerous bilocations. Visited by King Philip III in 1613, she maintained a close relationship with him and was said to have bilocated to Madrid in 1621 to assist him at the time of his death. She was also said to have bilocated to Japan, where she offered comfort to Juan de Santa Marta, a Franciscan missionary, at the time of his martyrdom in 1615; to Rome, where she supposedly smashed a vial full of poison intended for Pope Gregory XV (1621–1623); to Assisi, where she venerated the corpse of Saint Francis; and, most notably, to New Mexico, where she catechized the Jumano Indians. In 1633, Luisa was accused of fraud and pacts with the devil and denounced to the Inquisition.[49] After an intense investigation within Luisa's convent, the Inquisition moved her in 1635 to an Augustinian convent in Valladolid, about 100 kilometers away, before any decision had been reached in her case, and she died there as a virtual prisoner sixteen months after her arrival. Eventually, the Inquisition would declare in 1648 that none of the accusations were true, and her corpse would be returned to her convent in Carrión. Although she had been pronounced innocent, her long brush with the Inquisition proved to be too much of a stain on her character, and the once famous and revered nun slipped into obscurity.[50]

The other bilocator was a Franciscan friar, Francisco de la Fuente, who ended up being condemned by the Inquisition in 1632 for falsely claiming he had bilocated to the New World to evangelize some natives.[51] This friar was found guilty of fraud and of making a pact with the devil, and was sentenced to serve as a galley slave for four years and—should he survive that potentially lethal stint as a rower—to remain permanently exiled from the Inquisition districts of the Toledo and Logroño tribunals. A mere twenty-five years old at the time of his sentencing—five years younger than María—he was one of over four dozen individuals ritually condemned at an auto de fé staged in Madrid's Plaza Mayor in 1632, at which six unrepentant Judaizers and one heretic were executed.[52] Unfortunately, after this event he disappeared from the historical record.

Meanwhile—according to other accounts that would surface several years later—around the same time that María says she began to travel to New Mexico mystically, the Franciscan friars at the remote mission of San Antonio de Isleta in New Mexico, near Albuquerque, begin to get visits from Jumano Indians who beg for baptism for all their people, hundreds of miles away. Unable to spare any missionaries to send on a long trek to the land of the Jumanos, in present-day Texas, the Franciscans turn down their request.[53] Whether or not these two series of events occurred simultaneously is impossible to prove, due to the fact that there are no original records that confirm the visits of the Jumano natives to the San Antonio mission. But there is no denying that this conjunction of events became an integral part of the master narrative.

Meanwhile, back in Ágreda, María continues to talk to her confessors, Fathers Juan de Torrecilla and Sebastián Marcilla, about her visits with primitive tribes in a faraway land. She also speaks about this marvel with her fellow nuns, and tales of her visits to America begin to circulate in Spain. In 1622, two years into the saga of her ecstasies, the minister-general of the Franciscans, Father Bernardino de la Sena, meets with María to learn the details of her bilocations. Satisfied that the miracle is genuine and of divine origin, he approves of it but refrains from publicizing it in print, therefore keeping the story out of public view. According to testimony María will provide many years later, her constant bilocations continue to occur until 1623, along with her ecstatic levitations,[54] but other accounts will later claim that she kept visiting New Mexico for several years, although perhaps with less frequency. Benavides will clearly state that in 1629 "the same nun" was still visiting the Jumanos,[55] and elsewhere he says she was still visiting New Mexico in 1631.[56] Jiménez Samaniego will write of visits as late as 1625, for certain, and perhaps even later.[57] María herself will say in 1631, in the statement Benavides ordered her to write to the missionaries, that she was still visiting the Jumanos,[58] but two decades later she will deny this was true and blame the exaggeration on Benavides. This discrepancy is one of the more obvious kinks in the master narrative.

Throughout the early 1620s, according to Benavides, the Jumanos coming regularly to that area of the San Antonio mission to trade buffalo hides keep making the same request every time they show up, but Father Esteban de Perea, the superior of the mission (*padre custodio* or custos), repeatedly turns down their requests. In late 1625, two years after María's ecstasies ceased, the San Antonio mission receives a new custos sent from Spain, Father Alonso de Benavides, along with twelve additional friars. Benavides will claim that he learned immediately of the Jumanos and their request for baptism and that he would listen to their pleas every time they showed up. But he, just like his predecessor, disappointed the Indians. "For lack of friars, we did not send anyone to preach to them," Benavides would say in 1634, "nor did they tell us who had advised them to do this, nor did we ask them, convinced that they were just like many other Indian nations who were also asking for baptism."[59]

In 1626, not long after the arrival of Benavides at the San Antonio mission, back at Ágreda, one of María's confessors, Sebastián Marcilla, sends a letter to the archbishop of Mexico, Francisco de Manso y Zúñiga, containing an account of María's bilocations and of her miraculous missionary efforts in the New World, which she, of course, has told him about. Marcilla mentions placenames as well as certain tribes, including the Jumanos, hoping these details will catch Archbishop Manso's eye. Marcilla also begs Archbishop Manso to send Franciscan missionaries to the Jumanos to investigate María's claims: "An effort should be made," he says, "to ascertain whether or not there is any knowledge of our holy faith in them, and in what manner our Lord has manifested it."[60] It is at this point in time, and through this letter, that María's claims are first revealed in the New World, or so it seems. Whether or not these events occurred in the chronological order laid out in surviving records is impossible to prove or deny, as in the case of the earliest visits of the Jumanos to the San Antonio mission.

Two years later, in late 1628, Archbishop Manso finally gets around to conveying this information about María to his Franciscan missionaries in New Mexico, and he does so by sending a fresh contingent of missionaries to New Mexico, who arrive at San Antonio de Isleta in July 1629, led by Father Esteban de Perea, the previous custos of the mission. Perea hands Benavides a letter from the archbishop that commands him to investigate María's claims about what has been occurring in the land of the Jumanos "with the exactness, faith, and devotion that the case demands."[61] So, nearly a decade after María's visits to New Mexico became known in Spain and nearly three years after her identity as a missionary to the Jumanos was revealed to Archbishop Manso in Mexico, the bilocations are finally about to be officially examined at the American spot where they have ostensibly occurred.

Benavides is shocked. Years later he would say: "When the news reached New Mexico in 1629, we were totally ignorant of what was being reported, nor had we ever heard of Mother María de Jesús. But we eventually realized that the great care and solicitude with which the Jumano Indians came to us every summer pleading for friars to go and baptize them must have been something set in motion in Heaven."[62] Since some Jumanos happen to be on one of their regular trading jaunts, encamped there at the mission at exactly the same time as Archbishop Manso's letter arrives, Benavides asks them for details about the nameless woman who supposedly visits them but of whose existence he is totally unaware. Since Benavides's account is the only record we have of the exchange between the Jumanos and the Franciscans, it is impossible to know whether or not he and the other missionaries posed leading questions or made suggestions that influenced their responses.[63] In fact, due to the absence of any other eyewitness testimony of this exchange, there is really no way of knowing how much of the legend of María's bilocations was revealed to the Jumanos there and then and no way of denying the possibility that the Franciscans grafted the claims made by María onto their New Mexican setting and onto the Jumanos themselves. At present, due to the absence of documentation, there is no way to convincingly verify this account of the "discovery" of the visiting missionary woman's identity.

One detail mentioned by Benavides strongly suggests that the Franciscans were eager to prove that María's claims were true and that a bit of projecting and suggesting did take place. Asked to describe the woman's appearance, all the Jumanos can do is to comment on her clothing, and the details they provide, especially about her blue cloak, suggests to the friars that she might indeed be a nun. That suggestion leads one of them to bring out an image of the aforementioned Franciscan nun Luisa de Carrión, whose reputation as a miracle-worker and bilocator was still untainted by any questioning from the Inquisition. When this image is shown to the Jumanos, they exclaim that the woman who visits them dresses in exactly the same way—a gray habit with a blue cloak— but is much prettier and younger.[64] When asked why they have never revealed these details before, the Jumanos simply say: "Because you didn't ask us before, and we assumed that she was around here too."[65]

Benavides sends two missionaries to the Jumano lands immediately, according to his own account, along with the visiting natives, who were about to return home anyway. Whether he was amazed, intrigued, or perhaps a bit pinched by guilt for not granting the previous requests of the Jumanos is something he keeps to himself. And much of what happens next is unclear due to significant differences in the accounts of Benavides, Jiménez Samaniego, and María de Ágreda. Benavides says that when these two investigators, Fathers Juan de Salas and Diego Lopez, finally reach their destination, they are greeted by a procession of Jumanos carrying a flower-bedecked cross—something they claim was suggested by the young missionary in the blue cloak—and are then regaled with stories about how frequent her visits were, how she taught them in their own tongue, and how she reprimanded them for not being able to convince the Franciscans to baptize them.[66] However, since María stridently denied in 1650 that she paid any visits to the Jumanos after 1623, her insertion into this account is highly questionable.

According to Benavides, the Jumanos also venerate crosses and images of Jesus with great fervor, "as if they had been Christians for a very long time" and also impress Fathers Juan and Diego with their detailed knowledge of the Catholic faith bequeathed to them by their blue-cloaked missionary.[67] Much to their surprise, natives from neighboring tribes begin to arrive, begging for baptism, claiming to have been visited by the same woman.[68] After a few days, according to Jiménez Samaniego, the Jumanos and their neighbors finally receive their long-awaited baptism. Benavides, however, makes no mention of any baptisms taking place. All he says is that Fathers Juan and Diego return to San Antonio de Isleta, convinced that the Jumanos have been properly instructed in the Catholic faith, and that they give a full report to Benavides, replete with details about María's wondrous feats.[69] At this point, then, the Spanish and the New World narratives merge. As Benavides puts it: "Thus we were persuaded that this nun was the Mother María de Jesús mentioned in the Archbishop's letter, the very one miraculously turned into an apostle by God."[70]

Having been relieved of his post at San Antonio de Isleta, Benavides returns to Mexico in late 1629, where he is ordered to write a report on the New Mexico missions for his Franciscan superiors, King Philip IV, and the Council of the Indies. As previously mentioned, this *Memorial*, published in Madrid in 1630, contains one chapter on the miraculous conversion of the Jumanos. Benavides sails back to Spain and delivers his report to the minister-general of the Franciscans, Father Bernardino de la Sena, and to King Philip. He then travels to remote Ágreda to interview Sor María in person in 1631, under orders from his superior Father Sena to determine the accuracy of her descriptions of New Mexico and the veracity of her account. At that meeting, María confirms that she is indeed the nun with the blue cloak who visited the Jumanos, and Benavides establishes her bilocations as a certain "fact" then and there. "She convinced me totally," he says, "by describing to me things in New Mexico just as I saw them myself, along with other details. . . . She left me with no doubts whatsoever."[71]

In his 1634 *Memorial,* however, Benavides would add a twist to his narrative by bringing in testimony from Father Juan de Santander, commissary general of the Indies. According to Benavides, Father Juan became convinced that the missionary nun was not María de Ágreda but Luisa de Carrión. Eager to prove his hunch, Father Juan traveled to Carrión and met with Luisa's confessor, Domingo de Aspe—"a friar of great merit and zeal"—who showed him a book he was writing about Luisa in which one chapter "described how . . . Mother Luisa had been miraculously carried to the conversions in New Mexico." Father Juan also told Benavides that Father Domingo "showed him the actual passage from the book but didn't allow him to copy it."[72] So, according to Domingo de Aspe and Juan de Santander, there were really two Ladies in Blue, María and Luisa, converting Indians in separate regions of New Mexico. Somehow, this twist in the narrative, a mere paragraph in the 1634 *Memorial,* failed to become part of the Lady in Blue legend.

Given the circumstances in which the Lady in Blue legend emerged, and given the evidence available, it is certainly possible that much of the legend was fabricated by overeager Franciscan missionaries who were intent on proving the veracity of María's claims, and perhaps also those of Luisa de Carrión. And it is also likely that both of these Conceptionist Franciscan nuns had heard stories about the Franciscan missions in New Mexico and were inspired to insert themselves into that setting mystically and imaginatively, as the hapless friar Francisco de la Fuente had tried to do before he was hauled in by the Inquisition. Moreover, since Luisa de Carrión was older than María de Ágreda and Francisco de la Fuente, and tales of her bilocations to the New World were circulating in Spain at the time that María's bilocating and levitating ecstasies began, one should not discount the possibility that Luisa begat María, and perhaps also Francisco de la Fuente.

Moreover, since Benavides published at least 400 copies of his 1630 *Memorial* in Spain before he traveled to Ágreda to meet with María in 1631 and that text doubtlessly circulated among Franciscans, it is indeed possible that María might have read it before meeting with Benavides. This text might have provided her with many of the details with which she managed to convince Benavides that she had indeed visited the Jumanos and was therefore the Lady in Blue.[73]

No one should ever discount any such possibilities, especially because Luisa and María were Franciscans, and proving their miraculous bilocations added luster to their order and to their missions. One must wonder, after all, whether Benavides and his missionaries would have shown equal enthusiasm for identifying a bilocating nun who happened to be a Carmelite, a Dominican, or an Ursuline. At the same time, nonetheless, one must also wonder about the how and why of it all; that is, one must ask why something as impossible as bilocation was thought to be possible, at least in some cases, and how anyone could ever seek to prove it or believe it.

But in the case of Sor María, suspending one's disbelief was often necessary, for bilocation was only one of her incredibly impossible achievements.

7. The Trouble with María

Since the regions she visited were so barbarous that the people have no language
and can only grunt, how could she preach to them and teach them?
How could she and they understand one another?

—Inquisitor Antonio González del Moral

The "fact" established by Benavides—that María was the nun who would come to be known in New Mexico lore as "the Lady in Blue"—solved a mystery but also gave rise to the troublesome questions that surrounded all miracle-workers in baroque Spain, where the possibility of fraud or demonic activity was always suspected and needed to be disproved. The magnitude of María's claims was immense and unparalleled. Certainly, a miracle involving over 500 bilocations, each traversing over 5,000 miles, gave church authorities cause for concern. Bilocation accounts were part and parcel of the Catholic imagination, as well as of hagiographic traditions, but they were relatively rare and infrequent in comparison to other sorts of miracles. María's bilocating feats dwarfed those of any other saint, including the founder of her own order, Francis of Assisi. Naturally, then, her claims raised suspicions that needed to be disproved and questions such as the one in the epigraph above.[1] Since such issues could only be handled by the Inquisition, it was therefore inevitable that this tribunal would get involved. In 1635, therefore, inquisitors came to Ágreda to probe into María's bilocations and to interrogate her in person, carrying out a fact-finding inquest rather than a *proceso,* or formal trial.[2] Ascertaining whether María's bilocations really occurred or whether they were of diabolical origin was a difficult task that many inquisitors were well equipped to handle, for such inquests followed a well-mapped and familiar routine.[3] As inquisitors saw it, the devil was in the details, literally, and so was deceit, and this required them to examine all miracle claims meticulously. In María's case, the possibility of demonic agency could be dismissed by probing her own understanding of what had occurred and by testing her humility and submission to authority. The possibility of fraud was harder to handle. Due to its innate anchoring on eyewitness testimony and the inquisitor's absolute reliance on the trustworthiness of those eyewitnesses, bilocation was as tough to prove as to disprove. All the inquisitors could do was to assess María's character, compare her testimony with those of eyewitnesses at both spots involved, and reckon the credibility of the miracle being claimed.

Sor María under Scrutiny

María's first encounter with the Inquisition was brief, somewhat cordial, and inconclusive. It was carried out by the Logroño tribunal, at the request of the Suprema, or Supreme tribunal in Madrid. This was not a local inquest, then, but one generated at the highest echelons of the Inquisition. The *Suprema* ordered the Logroño inquisitors to investigate various items in the life of "the nun at Ágreda, who is called María de Jesús." First, they were to determine whether "she has ecstasies in public, and whether she gives people crosses and rosary beads, and what divine graces she assigns to these items." On the surface, at least, this request was not as odd as it might seem. The issue of crosses and beads being distributed by nuns who had a reputation for holiness could lead inquisitors to discover greater sins and evils than mere vanity. Second, they were to inquire into claims that she was "taken away to the very remote kingdoms of the Indies to convert and catechize the Indians there so they could convert and receive baptism." This issue was the most important of all, as the Suprema pointed out, since the Inquisition had recently processed and condemned a certain Francisco de la Fuente, a Franciscan friar who had made similar claims and fooled many into believing him, including "the same provincial minister who is now so strongly defending and backing all those aforementioned claims of the aforementioned María de Jesús." The greatest concern of those at the Suprema was that "the nun at Ágreda" might have fallen prey to "the same deceit and illusion of the devil" as Francisco de la Fuente and the Franciscan superior in charge of both. In addition, the Suprema requested all of the Logroño tribunal's files on the case of Francisco de la Fuente and instructed the tribunal to collect all the documents they could lay their hands on that had been written by María or had anything to do with her "so they could be examined."[4]

Although most of the Inquisition records for María's encounters with the Inquisition have been lost, letters sent to the Suprema about her case have survived—including some from the first inquest of 1635—all of which allow us to peer into the inner workings of the first inquest obliquely.[5] In 1635, statements were collected from four individuals, including one who was bound to treat her gently: her confessor Andrés de la Torre, who also happened to be an examiner (*calificador*) for the Inquisition. The issue of her very public ecstasies and levitations was deemed unoffensive, especially since they had ceased in 1623. As far as the bilocations were concerned, however, the Logroño inquisitors skirted the issue by deeming themselves unable to pass judgment: "We have no examiners here who are qualified to handle this," they observed.[6] Tellingly, they also felt it necessary to suggest that María could have been influenced by Francisco de la Fuente, who had made similar claims about being carried to the Indies by angels only to end up condemned by the Inquisition. It was Francisco, they charged, who was personally responsible for convincing the director of María's province to believe her bilocations were genuine.[7] Having shifted considerable blame to a known fraud and unable or unwilling to pass judgment on the veracity of María's bilocations, the inquisitors decided not to charge her with any wrongdoing or diabolical engagement. Their report was duly archived so it could remain available if needed in the future. For all practical purposes, then, María was cleared, but only temporarily, and her case remained open indefinitely. And the specter of such lingering suspicions would haunt her for the next fifteen years.

Her fears were not unreasonable. The Inquisition had a very long memory. One might say that it had an indelible memory in its archives that extended indefinitely into both the past and the future. For instance, in December 1648 the Suprema in Madrid requested that the Logroño tribunal send it all of the files of María's 1635 inquest, along with all of the files for the 1632 proceso of Francisco de la Fuente, the Franciscan friar condemned as a fraud in 1632 for claiming the same kind of missionary bilocations to the New World. This 1648 letter specifies that the request is for the reexamination of claims made about María by Friar Francisco to two prominent Franciscans who were now deceased, one of whom was the provincial minister who oversaw both María and Francisco. The claims in question could be highly damaging for María, for according to this letter, Francisco had told the provincial that she had accompanied him on some of his missionary visits to New Mexico, along with Saint Inés, and that on one occasion María had brought along some consecrated hosts so he could give communion to the Indians he had converted and baptized. In addition, the letter mentions a notebook that Francisco de la Fuente had shown to his superior that supposedly contained "other things concerning the life of María de Jesús."[8]

That letter was a prelude to the reopening of María's case in 1649. This time, the immediate cause for suspicion came from her involvement in the political arena rather than her mysticism or bilocations. Ever since 1643, María had become a close confidant of King Philip IV, with whom she corresponded regularly. That relationship granted her a certain degree of immunity—certainly more than she had in 1635—but it also inevitably made her vulnerable to fallout from the constant intrigues that plagued the royal court. An unsuccessful conspiracy against King Philip IV hatched in 1648 by the Duke of Hijar was the dramatic event that drew the Inquisition's attention to her anew. Although she was not part of this conspiracy, which involved plans to wrest the kingdom of Aragón from Philip IV and crown the Duke of Hijar as its king, she had made the mistake of replying to a letter from the duke.[9] The fact that the plot failed and the guilty parties were duly punished made no difference. The mere fact that María had corresponded with the leading figure of this failed coup made many at court suspicious of her, especially because of her close relationship with King Philip.

So in September 1649, the Supreme tribunal of the Inquisition ordered that María's 1635 case be reopened. The main objective of this inquest was to determine if she had played any role in the Duke of Hijar's plot, but as always happened with the Inquisition, all fresh allegations of misconduct immediately dragged up whatever dirt had been collected before. Consequently, it was inevitable that her ecstasies and bilocations would be included in this investigation too, especially since her case had never been formally closed.

Preparations for this reopening of her case began in January 1649, when some calificadores collected various testimonies. Her confessor Andrés de la Torre was once again involved in presenting evidence and analyzing María's life and writings, but this did not deter the calificadores from requesting that all previous documents pertaining to María be dug out of the archives, along with whatever texts she had written. Eager to display their objectivity and impartiality, these examiners insisted that María be interrogated in person again, especially because her case contained "many improbable things" (*muchas cosas inverosímiles*). Skepticism about her miraculous claims rose to the surface among the examiners. According to one report, "They found it very hard to convince themselves that it was God's doing and not a passive or active illusion, or both together, along with some credulity on the part of those who have governed her."[10]

Once the inquisitors had all the necessary documents and texts in their hands, they commissioned three new calificadores to submit their opinions. Their reports bristled with suspicion and hostility. One of them, Lucas Guadín, a Jesuit, found plenty of reason for concern. Even though he abstained from openly declaring her "either a good or evil spirit," he nonetheless thought there was reason to suspect "that her path was not safe, and her spirit was evil." Her raptures and ecstasies were probably not genuine or holy, he argued. He also condemned the terminology used by María in a litany she had written to the Virgin Mary. Even worse, he deemed her a victim of demonic delusions. Refusing to lay all the blame on her, Guadín wagged his finger at the Franciscan order, too, for coddling María and encouraging such error to flourish. In his opinion, it would be best for the Inquisition to assign a non-Franciscan confessor to María and to appoint non-Franciscan calificadores to her case. In closing, he suggested that all the attention-seeking nuns involved in promoting María's highly question-able miracles needed reprimanding and silencing, coldly remarking that their confessors needed "to humiliate them" and "bury deeply all the mystical favors they mention in confession" and make them realize that "they should live con-vinced that no one in the world is ever going to recall their existence."[11]

The other two examiners, Alonso de Herrera and Tomás de Herrera, were only slightly less caustic in expressing their displeasure with María. Tomás de Herrera thought that her visions were attributable to the effect of demonic delusions on her overheated imagination, something that was very common with all women, "especially those seeking to be highly esteemed." Alonso de Herrera agreed, adding that the devil had probably blocked her senses with his delusions and that she had allowed those diabolical hallucinations and her deep desire to work as a missionary to fool her into believing that she had visited the Jumanos.[12]

Taking these three reports to heart, the inquisitor general ordered the Logroño tribunal to send "one of the most learned, intelligent, and satisfactory" examiners to Ágreda to pay María a surprise visit and grill her as intensely as possible. The man chosen for this job, Antonio González del Moral, a Trini-tarian priest, and his notary Juan Rubio arrived at Ágreda on January 18, 1650, armed with a long list of eighty questions, some of which had numerous subsections.[13] María, now an abbess and well known in the highest circles of

Spanish society, was not totally unprepared to respond to an inquisitorial barrage, but being ill and bedridden—as was often the case with her—and having just been bled with leeches, she was in no shape to endure the torturous grilling imposed on her by these unexpected visitors, which dragged on for ten days in bitter midwinter cold for several hours each morning and then several more each afternoon, save for one Sunday off. As an additional ordeal, the febrile María was required to kneel constantly during every session, with nary a momentary respite. Two months later, in a letter to King Philip IV, she would say: "When those visitors arrived, I found myself so alone and so bereft of advice . . . subjected to constant questioning . . . at a time when I had no confessor or priest who knew 'my inner self' because those who had known me and counseled me were now dead."[14]

Although this inquest had been triggered by the botched coup led by the Duke of Híjar, very few of the questions on the examiner's list had anything to do with her role in that affair. Instead, María was questioned extensively on the nature of her ecstasies, visions, and revelations and on her bilocations to the New World. The fact that María was on intimate terms with King Philip might have made her examiner a bit more cautious, for sure, but it did not seem to have tempered his inquisitorial enthusiasm all that much. Father Antonio González del Moral was relentless in his probing of María on all sorts of sensitive points, both great and small, day in and day out. The questions all aimed, in one way or another, to test María's mettle, as well as her orthodoxy, obedience, and humility, and to ascertain whether any diabolical influence was involved.

Although the original transcript of this inquest has unfortunately vanished, it is possible to reconstruct it in some detail through two summaries. The first of these comes directly from María's hand: the report she sent to Father Pedro Manero immediately after the inquest in 1650, which gives a detailed account of the questions she was asked, as well as of her responses to them. The second is an extract of the original transcript published by Eduardo Royo in 1914, which, in turn, was summarized extensively in 1979 by José Pérez Villanueva.[15] María's report to Manero and Royo's extract match up so well that one can confidently rely on both for a reconstruction of what transpired during those very tense, very cold ten days.

Father Antonio was most interested in hearing María explain how the bilocations began and what she experienced. In addition, he wanted her to interpret what had happened and how she thought it could be possible to be in two places simultaneously. Was she present physically in both locations? If not, then how could her dual presence be explained? He also spent a good deal of time quizzing María on the nature of the raptures and mystical experiences that were an integral component of her bilocations. Other questions were less theologically volatile and merely addressed practical issues. One, the thirty-seventh, gives a good sense of Spanish prejudices about American Indians as well as of the sorts of details on which she was grilled: "Since the regions she visited were so barbarous that the people have no language and can only grunt, how could she preach to them and teach them? How could she and they understand one another?"[16] What did she teach them? Did she use a pulpit? How much time did she spend with them each day? Could she describe their way of life, their food, or their weapons? "Did she get wet when it rained on the way to those other kingdoms or when she was there, and, if so, did she return to the convent was her habit still wet?"[17] And so on. Then Father Antonio quizzed her at length on some of the more extravagant details of Benavides's two *Memorials* and on her own verification of those details back in 1631. Had she been flown to New Mexico by angels or by Saint Francis of Assisi? Had she continued to visit New Mexico after her ecstasies ceased in 1623? Had she taken rosaries and crosses from Spain or personal objects and given them away to the Jumanos or brought back objects from the New World? Had she been killed by Indians who were enemies of the Jumanos? Had she died there more than once? Had she accompanied the Jumanos to the San Antonio mission and remained invisible to the friars?

Her answers to all these questions were guarded and very carefully phrased. Outlandish claims, such as her martyrdom at the hands of the Indians or her being borne aloft to the Indies by the archangel Michael and Saint Francis, were bluntly dismissed as false or as misunderstandings or exaggerations of things she might have said. Theological and metaphysical questions were all dodged with great skill and equal measures of deference and humility. She was unable to explain how any of this happened, she said. All she knew is that she felt it happen and that it felt very real. "In the way He thought best, The Lord gave me reason to believe," she explained, "that some souls were, in fact, converting and would convert." In addition, these bilocations had taken place too many years ago, she insisted, when she was still too young and inexperienced. "Drawing on the better understanding of things I have now that I am older," she explained to Father Manero, as she probably also did to Father Antonio, the Inquisition's calificador, "it seems to me that either it was all the work of my imagination or that God showed me those things by means of abstract images of the kingdoms and what was going on there, or perhaps that they were shown to me there. Neither then, nor now was I, or am I capable of knowing the way it happened."[18]

María then turned to the Bible for proof that her inability to explain her experience was to be expected. "Whether or not I really and truly went in my body is something about which I cannot be certain," she confessed, just as had happened to Saint Paul the Apostle.[19] "What I can assure you beyond any doubt," she continued, "is that the case did in fact happen, and that as far as I know it had nothing to do with the devil or wrong desires. This I will affirm once, twice, or many times."[20]

Then, with all the proper reverence and caution she could muster, María offered two hypotheses about her bilocations, refusing to commit herself to one or the other, emphasizing her own doubts about each. The first was that she had bilocated bodily, as some thought; the second was that an angel had assumed her likeness in New Mexico while she was in ecstasy in Ágreda. In support of bodily bilocation, she argued that she definitely saw everything in New Mexico clearly, learned the names of people and places, and experienced the weather in a sensory manner. She also saw the Jumanos eating their primitive food, lighting their torches at night, bowing in gratitude when she taught them the catechism, and accepting the rosaries she brought to them. Nonetheless, these sensory experiences could be deceiving. "I have always questioned the idea that it happened to me in my body," she admitted, "and for that reason, in the statements I have made, I express doubts and distrust." Pivoting to an alternative hypothesis, María also had this to say: "The way in which I am most inclined to believe this happened and that seems most credible to me was, or is, that an angel, taking on my looks, appeared there and preached and taught them the catechism, while here the Lord showed me what was going on there as an answer to my prayers. For the Indians seeing me there was true, according to Father Benavides, and that is the reason I feel it was an angel who looked like me." With the right kind of self-deprecatory bravado, she went on to admit that she sometimes doubted the reality of her bilocations altogether. "Still, when all is said and done, I must ask myself why the Most High would have chosen an instrument as base and low as myself. When I take a look at myself, I feel it must have been only in my mind, that, yes, all this is imaginary."[21] To suggest such an intense level of doubt was perilous, however, since it would make liars out of Benavides and her superiors and make her complicit in their fraud. So

María pivoted again, reemphasizing points she had already made. "My considered opinion of this whole case is that it really happened," she affirmed, "but the way and the 'how' are not easily known since it happened so many years ago: since the Indians said that they had seen me, either myself or some angel who looked like me did go there."[22]

Father Antonio, the examiner, had many other questions about specific details. One of the most significant involved the frequency of her bilocations. Had she really visited the Jumanos 500 times? Her answer once again dodged the issue of explaining how it happened while at the same time affirming the reality of it all: "I have already said that I do not know whether I really went or some angel for me," she carefully noted. "But if the number five hundred is taken to represent all the times I became aware of those kingdoms, in one way or another, or all the times I prayed for or wanted their conversion, in that sense it is true, and the number would be even more than five hundred."[23] This internalization of the bilocations, which focused on her "becoming aware" of them "in one way or another," allowed her to lend sufficient fuzziness to these events while simultaneously establishing their reality. When all was said and done, the 500 visits were "true" in a very specific mystical sense, and María was leaving it up to Father Antonio to call into question the veracity of all her mystical trances, something he really could not do without stepping over the line into heresy himself. Consequently, Father Antonio found it necessary to ask questions about her mystical experiences. Two questions were potential trapdoors. First, "Had she ever seen God clearly and distinctly, and, if so, on what times and occasions?"[24] Of course not, she replied. Human eyes are incapable of any such thing. God can only be perceived spiritually and intellectually in an ineffable way through an "intuitive vision."[25] Second, had she made physical contact with angels or been carried aloft by them? Of course not, she said again. Angels are spirits. "I have never seen them do anything other than stand at a distance, serious, severe, and pure," she huffed, respectfully.[26]

Having dealt with the issue of the bilocations, which brought out discrepancies between the accounts of Benavides and María, the interrogation moved on to the 1631 document and letter in which María made no mention of any disagreement with Benavides. The main question was why she had agreed to confirm things which were not true? This was perhaps the trickiest of all questions, for answering it involved confessing deceitfulness while at the same time deflecting some of the blame to Benavides and her superiors with a proper balance of humility, respect, and contrition. What she had to say involved a masterful blending of self-criticism, self-praise of her obedience, and transference of the ultimate responsibility to others. Her final statement in the report to Manero encapsulates what she said in response to Father Antonio, her examiner: "That the truth was adulterated, the facts embroidered or changed, is nothing to marvel at, for the grave fathers who gathered the information and prepared the statement had not been my confessors when the case happened, and Father Fray Francisco Andrés had only recently come. Being timid, I said little. They got their information from people who knew nothing more than a few words they had heard here and there, so it was impossible to purify the truth; they could only adulterate it." As for her complicity in promoting falsehoods, María excused herself adroitly by insisting that she was cowed into doing so and that she was too flummoxed at the time to pay attention to all the details that she was confirming with her signature. "I signed without thinking about or paying attention to what I was doing," she said. "I have already said what was invented. All those names, those things that happened to Indians and friars, and all the rest . . . is not true. About how this happened, I have already said what I think."[27]

Two other issues still needed to be covered by Father Antonio, and these took up less time than the issue of the bilocations. One was the event that had precipitated this inquest: the role María might have played in the conspiracy of the Duke of Híjar. Determining María's innocence on this issue took relatively little time. Her friendship with Philip IV and the king's own testimony eclipsed whatever suspicions had been spawned by her correspondence with the treasonous duke. The remaining issue was a bit trickier: her biography of the Virgin Mary, which she had burned after being commanded to do so by a priest who was temporarily substituting for her trusted confessor Andrés de la Torre.

As if claiming hundreds of bilocations across a wide ocean and advising the king through a constant exchange of letters were not audacious enough, Sor María also dared to claim an intimate relationship with the Virgin Mary and to assume the mantle of a heavenly scribe, not much different from that of the four evangelists. Her *History of the Virgin Mary,* which she claimed the Mother of God had revealed to her, was a very detailed biography many times longer than the four canonical Gospels combined. This text proclaimed that the Virgin Mary had been immaculately conceived, a hotly contested theological proposition that would not be declared dogma until the nineteenth century. It also proclaimed the Virgin Mary to be co-redemptrix and co-mediatrix of the human race—along with her son Jesus—and, in addition, portrayed her as the head of the infant church during the interval between the resurrection of Jesus and the time of her own death. Such a text could not help but be controversial and be included in Father Antonio's questionnaire.

María had claimed all along, ever since she had begun to write this text in 1637, that her confessors and superiors had encouraged her to do it. But the text did not please everyone who read it, and she knew it could cause trouble for her. In 1645, while her beloved confessor Andrés de la Torre was away, a temporary confessor was so scandalized by this text that he ordered María to burn her original autograph copy. Unbeknownst to that confessor and most other people, however, a copy had been sent to King Philip earlier, and it survived in his hands, hidden from view. Ordered by her superiors to write the book again, María had taken on the task obediently, but as soon as her name was linked to the Duke of Hijar conspiracy, she burned what she had recently produced in a panic. Once again, however, she was ordered to start for a third time, and when Father Antonio arrived in January of 1650, she had some pages she immediately handed over to him. The examiner found nothing to criticize or condemn in that text but did question her about adjectives and honorific terms such as "immaculate and most perfect mirror of divinity" and "complement of the ineffable and most holy Trinity" that she had used in writing about the Virgin Mary, not just in the biography but in a litany she had penned some years before. María's answers were an impressive display of her command of Catholic theology, her erudition, and her familiarity with the Bible and the church fathers.[28] Satisfied that her Marian adjectives were correct and that the Virgin Mary's biography was the result of direct divine inspiration, Father Antonio confirmed its orthodoxy. What he did not know—and María never revealed to him—was the fact that the king had a complete version of this immense text.

As the inquest wound down and she finished answering the final question, María was asked if she had anything else to say or declare. In response, María launched into the issue of her "weak and fragile" memory and all her "illnesses and ailments," which had made it difficult for her "to be examined and to be questioned and re-questioned over many different days about things that happened so many years ago."[29] Then she immediately began to express her high regard for the Inquisition, which she claimed to "respect and venerate as a daughter of the Church." To prove this point, and to make sure that Father Antonio could perceive the full measure of her orthodoxy and her submission to the Inquisition, she begged for the chance to declare her adherence to "the faith that the Holy Tribunal defends so steadfastly." Granted her request, María proceeded to recite a detailed and expanded version of the Nicene Creed that filled several folios and must have caused some serious cramping in the hands of notary Juan Rubio.[30] Doubling down on the issue of her fidelity to the Inquisition and her admiration of it, María kept the notary Juan Rubio very busy filling more folios with proclamations of her eagerness to submit herself to the church's guidance in all things. "Prostrated in the presence of the Holy Tribunal of the faith and at the feet of all the *señores Inquisidores*," she declared, "I thank you humbly for examining me and for educating and enlightening my ignorance, for no other earthly creature is in greater need of correction and advice than me." Tugging at the heartstrings of Father Antonio and his notary Juan Rubio and reinforcing her submissiveness to them, she then ended her profession of faith by emphasizing again that her gratefulness for the inquest was made all the more profound by the fact that she felt very much alone and without guidance—given that her confessors had all passed away—and that she now had no one to "govern" her who really knew her inner self.[31]

All in all, the inquest was a great victory for María, for instead of being reprimanded or having her case left open—as had happened in 1635—she had now managed to overwhelm her inquisitors, both of whom not only called her "a treasure," declaring their admiration for her and their satisfaction with her answers and her conduct, but also actually requested that she give them crosses and other personal articles that they could take back to Logroño. Father Antonio's final assessment was as splendid as anyone could have hoped, including María herself and King Philip IV, and it contradicted everything suspected by her three initial calificadores Lucas Guadín, Alonso de Herrera, and Tomás de Herrera back in 1649, when they had urged the Inquisition to probe deeply into her case due to the high likelihood that she was deluded and under demonic influence: "I have recognized great virtue and great intelligence in her," said Father Antonio, "and in her knowledge of Sacred Scripture, which has been acquired more through prayer and constant interior engagement with God than through formal studies." In addition, Father Antonio also reprimanded Benavides and those responsible for the *Carta* of 1631 for "adding much and inventing much too much" and for forcing María to confirm their exaggerations and affix her signature to their report under her vow of obedience. She could not be blamed for her "indiscreet obedience" to her superiors, continued the calificador, because she had been just a very young girl at the time. "She is a good Catholic and a faithful Christian, well-versed in our sacred faith" concluded Father Antonio, "and she is free from any fictional inventions or demonic delusions."[32] Shortly after this report reached the inquisitor general, he approved it.

María had not only survived her brush with the Inquisition but prevailed, at least for now. Her bilocations had been approved as genuine. Questions about how they took place, exactly, were left unanswered, but their reality and divine origin were confirmed. She had indeed achieved the seemingly impossible, at least in the eyes of those who could easily have branded her a fraud or a demoniac: she not only had become a genuine holy bilocator but had managed to earn praise for it, unlike her two contemporaries and fellow Franciscans Luisa de Carrión and Francisco de la Fuente. A few weeks after her ordeal, she wrote to King Philip: "The Inquisition came . . . and they examined me concerning events from my early years . . . and they have proceeded with great piety and discretion. . . . I have come away exceedingly fond of the Holy Tribunal and the purity of their proceedings; I only worry about my answers, for I don't know if they were correct, due to my solitude and to not being able to get some advice."[33] A week later, King Philip replied: "I am most grateful for the secret with which you have entrusted me, and feel sorry for the hardships God gives you, but the truth never fails, and all these dark clouds are only there to allow the light of your virtue to shine more clearly." Then he let María know that he was in touch with her superior general, Father Manero, and that he had already informed him of the visit paid to her by the Inquisition and was very pleased with her.[34] Knowing that she had the support of not only the crown but also the Franciscan order was something María needed badly at this time.

She had just gained acceptance for her bilocations, but doing the same for her other impossible feat—serving as the Virgin Mary's scribe—would not be so easy. Her massive manuscript of *The Mystical City of God,* which she had been ordered to burn, could easily become a greater problem than her bilocations. In that same letter to the king just cited, she closed by saying: "The Inquisitors said nothing about my history of the Queen of Heaven." Then, referring to a copy of that text secretly owned by the king, she said with some relief: "They must not know about it." Her final lines bristle with anxiety about her *Mystical City:* "Until this storm calms down, it's best for it to remain hidden. May God's will be done in all things, and may He guard me and favor Your Highness."[35]

But how was it that King Philip IV came to have that copy of María's book, and why should he have chosen to keep it hidden? To fully appreciate the significance of Sor María's boldness and her escape from condemnation despite all her impossible claims, one must consider how those claims affected King

Philip IV, the highest authority in María's Spain, and how he drew the line between the possible and the impossible.

The King's Spiritual Advisor

Sor María's account of her bilocations to New Spain did more than attract the Inquisition's attention: it also captured King Philip IV's imagination. The monarch was in dire straits when he first heard of Sor María.[36] His personal life was a disaster: he was an insatiable adulterer who eventually fathered at least thirty illegitimate children and had sired two heirs to the throne who had died in childhood. Philip was haunted by his sins. His reign was an even worse mess than his personal life. Constantly at war—this was the period of the Thirty Years' War—he had seen Spain go bankrupt several times, despite the constant flow of gold and silver from America.[37] Controlled by his chief advisor and mentor, the Count-Duke of Olivares, Philip was ambivalent toward his failures yet felt incapable of assuming charge.[38] To make matters worse, Catalonia and Portugal had both rebelled against his rule in 1640, and soon enough dissidents in Andalusia, Aragon, and Naples would attempt to follow the same path.[39]

Philip IV would be enthralled by Sor María in a profound way, and he established a most unusual relationship with her. In 1643, on his way to the front against the French and the Catalans, still reeling from the recent resignation of his prime minister and alter ego the Count-Duke of Olivares, Philip IV made a detour and went to see Sor María in person. From that moment until their deaths—which occurred only four months apart—the king and the nun would engage in constant contact, writing 300 letters to each other. In essence, Sor María became a nonsacramental confessor. Though she could not absolve him of his many sins, she became a therapist of sorts, a compassionate listener, a wise yet powerless and totally unthreatening advisor. He poured out his heart and soul to her; she counseled him and assured him of her constant prayers. He would leave a wide blank right margin in his letters. She would fill in that margin with her response and send the letter back to him. Over and over.

As Philip neared death, he inserted into his will the following instructions about the book into which all the letters were bound: "Since I maintained a long-term correspondence with Mother Sor María de Ágreda, finding in her venerable letters immense consolation and perhaps discovering through them things unattainable by human intelligence . . . I entrust as much as possible to my successor the protection and conservation of the said book wherever it may be, for it is full of sacred doctrine, love, wisdom, advice, and celestial documents."[40]

No one has ever considered it an exaggeration to say that Sor María had the best connections possible. Her relationship with the king not only assured that the Inquisition would approach her with great caution but also gave her the utmost clout. Ultimately, she could hound the king into pressuring Pope Alexander VII to issue a decree defending the Immaculate Conception in 1661. Ultimately, she could act with the utmost daring in the spiritual realm and claim that she was the conduit for special revelations from the Virgin Mary, especially concerning that much-contested issue of the Immaculate Conception. Her biography of the Virgin Mary—ostensibly a revelation from on high—could easily have been interpreted as a fifth Gospel and the ultimate affront to Catholic orthodoxy. Some at that time might have thought it impossible for it not to be resoundingly condemned and consigned to oblivion. But it never was. And how that was possible needs some explaining.

Sor María, Ecstatic Scribe, Fifth Evangelist

As if claiming hundreds of transcontinental and transoceanic bilocations and writing hundreds of letters to the king was not audacious enough, Sor María dared to claim an intimate relationship with the Mother of God. Even more audacious, she dared to assume the mantle of a heavenly scribe like the four evangelists Matthew, Mark, Luke, and John and to write a history of salvation—a fifth Gospel of sorts—massively longer than the four canonical Gospels combined (over 710,000 words versus 64,427). This text, which María called *The History and Life of the Virgin Mary*—and some Franciscans came to call a "second Bible"[41]—was published five years after her death, in 1670, and given an elaborate baroque title, the short version of which is

> *The Mystical City of God, Miracle of his Omnipotence, and Mystery of his Grace,*
> *Divine History and Life of the Virgin Mother of God, Our Queen and Mistress,*
> *the Most Holy, Restorer of Eve's Fault and Mediatrix of Grace, Revealed in these*
> *Latter Centuries by the Same Lady to her Servant, Sor María de Jesús, Abbess of*
> *the Convent of the Immaculate Conception in the Town of Ágreda.*[42]

This multivolume behemoth of a text eclipsed all other biographies of the Virgin Mary, a type of devotional literature that was very popular at the time.[43] It gained instant notoriety, eliciting mixed responses ranging from praise and devotion to puzzlement and condemnation. Translated into Latin and every major European vernacular language, it would eventually run into over a hundred editions but prove as troublesome to church authorities as María's bilocations—and even more controversial.[44]

The premise of this book, which could justifiably be called *The Gospel of the Virgin Mary,* is that the Mother of God has chosen to reveal to the world through María de Ágreda many things that were intentionally left out of the New Testament, thus granting her a unique status alongside the four evangelists, especially the apostle John, the author of the gospel that bears his name as well as of the Book of Revelation that promises the arrival of the Heavenly Jerusalem[45] at the end of history (fig. 36). Sor María's book is an all-out assault on Protestant theology, ontology, metaphysics, epistemology, and hermeneutics and could easily horrify all Lutheran, Reformed, or Radical divines or drive them mad with rage. In it, she declares that God sent six angels to guide her, followed by eight others, who purified her and led her into His presence, and that she then beheld the Blessed Virgin, as she is described in the Book of Revelation,[46] and was able to glimpse the broad sweep of the Virgin's life, from conception to her assumption into heaven.

This massive biography covers the lives of the Virgin's parents, Joachim and Anne; the conception and birth of the Virgin; her childhood; her betrothal to Joseph; the birth of Jesus; the childhood of Jesus and his ministry, passion, death, and resurrection; the birth of the Christian church and the first fifty or sixty years of its history, in which the Virgin Mary plays a leading role; and, finally, the Virgin's death and her triumphal reception in heaven. The book abounds in details large and small, many of which cannot be found anywhere in Christian literature, such as the exact number of angels who escorted the Virgin Mary during every major event in her life, the transcript of the sentence pronounced by Pontius Pilate at the trial of Jesus,[47] and the text of a letter written by Saint Peter to the Virgin Mary.[48] *The Mystical City* is more than a mere narrative: it also includes copious lessons and exhortations ostensibly provided by the Virgin Mary herself through her faithful scribe, María de Ágreda. Obviously, Sor María was not at all respectful of the Protestant principle of *sola scriptura.* Literally and figuratively, she embodied its denial.

While María's book does not contradict the four Gospels and in fact employs them as the basic framework of much of her narrative, she does claim that the Virgin Mary has revealed many details not contained in them. Many of these concern the life of Jesus and the apostles, but the vast majority concern the Virgin

Figure 36. Sor María de Ágreda is paired up with Saint John the Evangelist, who was also traditionally believed to be the author of the Book of Revelation in the New Testament, in which the arrival of the New Jerusalem is prophesied. This image seeks to establish the Virgin Mary's status as co-redemptrix of humanity and Sor María's status as a fifth evangelist.

Mary herself, and the main thrust of the narrative is the proclamation of the Virgin's intense and indispensable role in salvation history. In brief, the revelations contained in the 2,800 pages of *The Mystical City* could be summed up in one proposition: "The Virgin Mary is coredeemer of the human race." Simply put: "No Mary, no salvation."

Sor María's text is a historical narrative, but its context is theological, and its intent and horizon are quasi-apocalyptic: the title itself, *The Mystical City of God,* is an allusion to the New Jerusalem that descends from the new heavens to the new earth in the Book of Revelation 21:1–3, "God's dwelling place with people." The New Jerusalem, then, is a metaphor for the body of the Virgin Mary—a divinized human body that gave birth to the redeeming God incarnate—which makes her co-redemptrix of all humanity or, as the title of the book proclaims, the very "mystical" city of God herself, in whom God dwells in his fullness.

Moreover, the reason given by God and the Virgin to Sor María for suddenly revealing truths about the distant past 1,600 years after Jesus Christ walked the earth is also apocalyptical in dimension. María's world, God declares, is worse off than it was when He became incarnate in the Virgin Mary's womb: it is a world on the brink of annihilation and sorely in need of redemption. "For now, this is the hour and the opportune time to let men know the just cause of my anger," says God to Sor María, "and they are now justly charged and convinced of their guilt . . . now that the world has reached this wretched century . . . when eternal night approaches for the wicked."[49]

Significantly, the remedy that God proposes to María is not turning to Christ or paying closer attention to the Gospels—as Protestants would expect to hear—but turning to the Virgin Mary and relying more intensely than ever on her intercession. Quoting God the Father directly, Sor María writes: "I want to make known to mortals how much her intercession is worth, who brought them redemption from their sins by giving mortal life in her womb to the immortal God."[50] This is an aggressive Mariology, defiantly anti-Protestant even if not consciously so. It is an exaltation of the Virgin Mary that reflects her place in popular and monastic Catholic piety and also enhances it, providing a theological matrix for that enhancement. And it is a Mariology that springs from within, so to speak, from the very depths of female monastic spirituality and mysticism, rather than from the battlefield of scholarly male-dominated clerical polemics. This Mariology is theologically sophisticated, in its own way, but as Teresa of Avila might have put it, it is definitely not the work of *letrados,* learned men, although some critics would later contest the book's authorship, arguing that its handling of biblical texts and scholastic theology is far too dexterous for any woman.[51] Its wellspring is mystical rather than scholastic, and its conduit is a nun from the boondocks with no formal education. It matters little—or not at all—that she has never met a Protestant, much less debated with one. Her message is thoroughly Catholic and, whether she knows it or not, devastatingly anti-Protestant.

Sor María's message is at once historical and ahistorical. A post-Renaissance woman who has obviously received a good education beyond the confines of any school—although she was once described as a "simple rustic" by a dismissive priest—María shows ample acquaintance with the Bible, some apocryphal texts and some of the fathers, some scholastic theology, and a fair amount of early church history, and she is painfully aware of how essential it is for her revelations to be set in a historical perspective. Nonetheless, she does so by denying one of the central tenets of the Renaissance and the Protestant Reformation: the privileging of the New Testament and the Apostolic Age. That was a special time, she admits, but so is her own day and age. Revelation is not limited to the Bible or the early church. God speaks to her, and Sor María quotes him:

> I did not reveal these mysteries in the primitive Church because they are so magnificent, that the faithful would have been lost in scrutinizing and admiring them at a time when it was more necessary to establish firmly the law of grace and of the Gospel. Although all such mysteries and the Gospel are in perfect harmony with each other, human ignorance might have recoiled at their magnitude and suffered doubt, when faith in the incarnation and redemption and the precepts of the new law of the Gospel were still in their infancy. . . . If the world was then not yet capable of fully obeying the law of grace and fully assenting to faith in the Son, so much less was it prepared to be introduced into the mysteries of His Mother and to faith in her. And now the need for these mysteries is so much greater, that I am compelled to reveal them.[52]

Lest anyone doubt Sor María's role in conveying previously hidden mysteries about the Virgin Mary's role in redemption, God adds: "I do not intend that your descriptions and declarations of the life of the Blessed Virgin shall be mere opinions or contemplations, but certain truth. . . . Thus speaks the Lord, God Almighty!" And what is revealed by God and the Virgin Mary to María is astounding. Relatively little of the narrative of María's text—which begins before the birth of the Virgin Mary and extends past her life on earth—can be found in the New Testament. The amount of detail provided by María is overwhelming but perhaps a clear reflection of how much nonbiblical tradition and legends from apocryphal texts could be fused with biblical accounts and lively, imaginative piety in a convent. Throughout the entire text, the Virgin Mary is the main focus, naturally, and the main thrust of the narrative is to highlight the crucial role she played as co-redemptrix with her son, the God-man Jesus.

María claimed she began to receive the inspiration for her *History and Life of the Virgin Mary* in 1627, shortly before she was elected abbess. But she did not begin writing until 1637 and did so somewhat reluctantly, she said, in obedience to the command of her confessor Francisco Andrés de la Torre and other superiors. "I dragged my feet and resisted obeying everyone for many years; not daring to undertake a task that was so far above my powers."[53] As soon as she began writing, all self-doubt seemed to vanish. In the first twenty days, we are told, she wrote enough text to fill 326 printed pages. This writing spree was inseparable from her mystical ecstasies, which began to intensify as revelations poured forth from heaven. "I felt a change within me and a highly spiritualized state of being," she explained. "A new light was given to my understanding, which communicated and infused into it a knowledge of all things in God. . . . This knowledge is a light that illumines: holy, sweet, pure, subtle, penetrating, splendid, steady, and clear, causing love of good and hatred of evil."[54] Publication was not the immediate objective. This was a risky venture in Spain, a land where the Inquisition kept a close eye on anyone who might be in league with the devil or bent on "inventing the sacred," as the Holy Office preferred to call the nasty business of fraudulent mysticism. María's very careful insertion of the statement about the "love of the good and hatred of evil" infused by her visions was a shield against any such suspicions about her and perhaps also against apprehensions of her own. As she would confess much later, she was often assailed by doubts, which she attributed to demons. "There isn't a single word I wrote down that the Devil didn't contradict with his relentless and obstinate temptations," she said, adding, "His most common trick was to tell me that I imagined everything I wrote or merely invented it, naturally; at other times he would say that what I wrote was false and simply crafted to deceive others. His hatred for this book was so great that in order to obliterate it, that dragon stooped to saying that it was nothing more than my meditations, at best, or a mere side effect of my ordinary prayers."[55]

María's initial burst of ecstatic writing slowed down in the following months, but she kept writing in fits and starts over the next six years, whenever she could, under the direction of her confessor Francisco Andrés de la Torre. All along, she claimed to be assailed by demons who filled her with self-doubt and shaken by fellow nuns and some priests who urged her to stop. By 1643, when she began her relationship with King Philip IV, Sor María had finished the work. It was unlike anything ever written by any Christian since the first century, either male or female, and in the very tight monastic circles in which it was read it caused as much consternation as excitement. Fortunately for María, King Philip was among those who were enthralled by the text, which was copied and sent to him in three installments between October 1643 and July 1646. Unfortunately, not everyone agreed with the king. Sometime in late 1646, while Father de la Torre was away attending a meeting in Toledo, María was assigned a temporary confessor who thought nuns should never be allowed to write and ordered her to burn everything she had written. Ever the obedient nun, and ever worried about the trouble this book could cause for her and her convent, María inciner-ated the whole manuscript, along with other writings of hers. When Father de la Torre returned, he was angered by what had happened, reprimanded María, and ordered her to begin writing the whole text again from scratch.[56] María obeyed, as always, but Father de la Torre died in March 1647, before she could make much headway. No longer under his direction and feeling bereft, María paused her writing. Then, fearful of what might ensue when her alleged involve-ment in the conspiracy of the Duke of Hijar brought her under the Inquisition's watchful eye again in 1649, she burned whatever she had written.[57]

Of course, María knew that a copy of her text had been sent to King Philip and that it survived. That copy would remain in the king's hands until his death as a well-kept secret out of everyone's reach, including Sor María's. And know-ing how fond the king was of María and of her *History of the Virgin Mary*—which he claimed to have read many times—those rare few who knew of its existence never dared to ask for its destruction while Philip was alive. Late in her life, however, María apparently asked her hagiographer José Jiménez Sa-maniego to swear that he would get rid of it, if possible. In 1682, seventeen years after María's and King Philip's passing, fearing that keeping the manuscript hidden from the Inquisition would hurt María's chances of being canonized, he kept his promise and burned all of it, save for the title page.[58]

For ten years after this traumatic event, Sor María pressed on, living her life as if she had never written an earthshaking sacred text, balancing her ecstatic trances with her duties as abbess, and enduring that brief second encounter with the Inquisition in 1650, which placed a stamp of approval on her impossible miracles. After a well-deserved but all too brief sabbatical leave from her duties as abbess, during which she sought to deepen her mystical life, she was reelected to the post in 1655 and assigned a new confessor, Andrés de Fuenmayor, who immediately ordered her to rewrite her *History of the Virgin Mary.*

So the obedient Sor María began writing this book for a third time and wrote feverishly for the next five years, in part from memory—simply rewriting what she had burned—and in part from her constant encounters with the Virgin Mary, which, according to her, had not only continued but actually intensified. On May 6, 1660, she finished writing it. And she managed to do this while struggling with her frail health, writing other texts, advising the king, and running her convent of the Purísima Concepción as efficiently as ever. To ensure that everyone knew why she had dared to write this text, to reiterate her obedience and abject submission to the church, and to proclaim its heavenly origins, she had this to say in its final paragraph:

> I have written this Divine History under obedience to the prelates and confessors who govern my soul, assuring myself by this means that it is God's will that I should write it and obey his Most Blessed Mother who for many years has ordered me to do so. And though everything written has been submitted to my confessors' censorship and judgement, though there is not a single word that they have not seen and discussed with me, even so I now submit it again to their better judgement, and above all, to the correction of the Holy Roman Church to whose censorship and teachings I declare myself subject as her daughter . . . because I want to live and die obedient to it.[59]

Yet after proclaiming such profound humility and submission to the church, María penned a missive to her sisters in which she boasted of having a vision in which she received ultimate approval for her impossible book from God Himself. In this vision María found herself raised to the highest level any human can ever hope to reach, facing the royal throne of the divine Trinity, where she beheld God the Father, Son, and Holy Spirit, as well as the Virgin Mary, who sat at the right hand of the Son, all surrounded by angels. Then she saw the Father pull out from his chest an "immensely beautiful" closed book that he handed over to the Son, to whom He said, "This book is mine and everything it contains pleases me and has my approval." Then, after showing great appreciation for it, the Son and the Holy Spirit passed the book on to the Virgin Mary, who received it with "incomparable gladness and pleasure." As all this was unfolding, María was overwhelmed by the dazzling beauty of the book and wondered what its contents might be. Aware of María's curiosity, the Virgin Mary then asked her: "Do you want to know what book this is which you have just seen?" The Virgin then opened the book and showed it to María, and she was able to see that it was none other than the history of the Virgin's life that she, María, had penned. "You most certainly will not have to worry anymore," the Virgin said to María, reassuringly.[60] Once again, as she had done continually throughout her multivolume *History,* María abased and exalted herself simultaneously, expressing a paradoxical mix of fear, humility, submission, confidence, and well-camouflaged pride, for one final time.

During the final five years of Sor María's life, this second complete manuscript version of her massive *History of the Virgin Mary* began to make the rounds within learned theological circles, especially among Franciscans. As her health deteriorated and death approached, Sor María had no inkling of what would become of this remarkable yet potentially alarming text. For all she knew, right up to the moment of death, she could have been commanded to burn the manuscript again for a third time. And although she was certain that King Philip would jealously guard his copy of the first version, she also knew that he, like her, did not have long to live and that once dead, the fate of his belongings would become uncertain.

On March 3, 1665, María received a letter from King Philip. Her failing health prevented her from replying until the 27th of March. This would be the last exchange between them. Nearly two months later, on May 24, Sor María would die, after predicting her own death and preparing for it rigorously and perfectly. Her whole life had been dedicated to perfection and sinlessness—that goal so fiercely deemed impossible by Protestants—and according to eyewitnesses, her death was as perfect as one might expect from someone who was headed straight for heaven. The fact that her corpse would resist decomposition and remain intact for centuries would be interpreted as confirmation of that judgment. Less than four months later, on September 17, King Philip would die at the palace complex of the Escorial, in the same austere bedchamber in which his grandfather had died, adjacent to the main altar of the royal basilica. He would be entombed beneath that bedchamber and altar, along with his immediate ancestors, in that remote hideaway where he had spent long hours ruing his sins, fretting over his kingdom's steep decline, and begging for Sor María's prayers and advice.

Reception of "The Mystical City of God"

In 1668, three years after the deaths of María and King Philip IV, King Charles II—Philip's severely handicapped son—took a significant step in the promotion of María's canonization by asking two prominent theologians to review *The Mystical City.* One of them, Bishop Diego de Silva, said he "marveled at its excellence," confessing, "I began as a critic, but I finished as an admirer." The second examiner, Andrés Mendo, a Jesuit, was equally enthusiastic: "Sor María's writing," he said, "enlightens the mind with a knowledge of the most sublime truths and inflames the heart with divine love."[61] Their opinions helped launch the publication of the book in 1670, a mere five years after María's death. This first edition included the biography of María written by José Jiménez Samaniego, along with all the requisite ecclesiastical permissions and lavish praise from several theologians, including Fathers Silva and Mendo. The process of canonizing María began in earnest in 1673, when Pope Clement X declared her "venerable" and called for the creation of a commission to handle her case.

María's canonization seemed assured to her devotees, especially because her corpse—like those of many saints, including Teresa of Avila—refused to decompose.[62] But her *Mystical City,* which had to be taken into account for her canonization, proved to be a polarizing text, evincing praise and veneration from some readers and vitriolic opposition from others.[63] Objections to its publication were numerous, not just because of its central claim of being a special revelation from the Virgin Mary herself, but also because of specific issues in the text itself, including the one found most offensive by many theologians—especially Dominicans—who were opposed to accepting the Immaculate Conception as sound doctrine. These "Maculists," as opponents of the doctrine were known (as opposed to the "Immaculists" who promoted it), wasted no time denouncing María to the Inquisition.

In 1672, about the same time that her canonization process was launched, the inquisitor general in Spain ordered that all copies of *The Mystical City* be removed from circulation to reexamine its contents, due to these denunciations and the fact that some early editions had been published without the requisite permissions. At the same time, Maculist opponents of the book denounced it to the Roman Inquisition as well, setting yet another investigation in motion outside of Spain.[64] The end result of this Roman inquiry was a huge setback for María's cause: in June 1681 Pope Innocent XI condemned *The Mystical City* and placed it on the *Index Librorum Prohibitorum*. The response from Spain was predictable. Thanks largely to the efforts of María's hagiographer Samaniego, who defended the text's orthodoxy, and to the pressure put on Pope Innocent by King Charles II of Spain, the book was removed from the *Index* a few months later. But the damage inflicted on María's reputation was difficult to ignore, especially because a version of the *Index* printed in Venice continued to include her book until 1713, when the lapse finally caught Rome's attention, and the publisher was forced to retract its inclusion.[65]

Meanwhile, after 1681 the Supreme Council of the Inquisition in Spain and the Roman Inquisition continued to receive denunciations about *The Mystical City*'s content and pleas to stop its circulation on the grounds that there were "impediments" to consider. These impediments fell into two categories. The first were *reparos,* or questions about specific doctrinal issues in the text; the second were *fundamentos,* or objections to its claim of being a revelation written by a woman who was divinely appointed for the task. Unsurprisingly, most of the fundamentos were issued by Dominicans who objected to the doctrine of the Immaculate Conception. Nonetheless, in late December 1685 the Inquisition decreed that *The Mystical City* was free of error and could be circulated and read as a "private revelation," the contents of which no faithful Catholic was obligated to believe.[66] As the Supreme Council put it, "The work is judged to be worthy of being read, as are others of a similar quality and those that treat the private revelations of men of exceeding virtue." And when it came to the author herself, the Inquisition ruled that María was "incapable of active or passive deceit, due to the worthiness of her many virtues." In addition, however, the Inquisition decreed that only the first edition of 1670 was acceptable since all others lacked the proper permissions.[67]

Having been removed from the Roman *Index* and approved by the Inquisition, publication of new editions of *The Mystical City* intensified, along with translations, but the text continued to be closely examined by clerics in Spain and elsewhere, as well as by several prominent theological faculties. The French translation gave rise to a heated discussion at the Sorbonne in Paris, which led to a vote on its orthodoxy. In 1696, a majority of those who examined it (102 out of 152), voted to condemn it. This condemnation stressed the following points: that it gave too much weight to the revelations ostensibly received by its author;[68] that many of its revelations were new and contrary to what the apostles of Jesus would have supported; that it upheld the "adoration" of the Virgin Mary, which should only be given to God, rather than the "veneration" that is proper for human saints; that it referred all of the Virgin Mary's virtues and graces to her Immaculate Conception; that it attributed too much power and control over the church to her; that it overstressed her role as coredemptrix, Mother of Mercy, and mediatrix of grace; that it gave a too graphic and "indecent" description of the sexual intercourse between the Virgin Mary's parents; and that it contained too many other imaginary and scandalous details.[69] "This book does not lead to edification," complained the Sorbonne theologians opposed to it, linking it to heretics old and new: "It leads instead to the destruction of Christian piety; it resurrects the errors of Arius, Nestorius, Pelagius, Vigilantius, Photius, Baius, Jansen, and the Predestinarians; and its author is impudent, sacrilegious, blasphemous, idolatrous, a Pelagian, a Quietist, and a Lutheran."[70]

In contrast, and in response to such charges, several universities approved the text, including those of Salamanca, Alcalá, and Oviedo in Spain; Louvain in the Spanish Netherlands; Coimbra in Portugal; and Toulouse in France. One of the closing statements in its defense by the Louvain faculty in 1715 echoes the previous approvals by other universities and sums up its position by simply emphasizing the heroic virtues of Sor María rather than her theology: "Finally, this text cannot be attributed to the devil because from start to finish it breathes nothing but humility, patience, love, and the suffering of hardships."[71]

Despite the weight carried by all its supporters, the text's opponents could not be silenced, however, and it continued to elicit condemnations, especially because of its claims about new private revelations and its strident confirmation of the doctrine of the Immaculate Conception, which was attributed to the controversial medieval Franciscan theologian John Duns Scotus rather than to María herself.[72] Some critics even argued that María could not be the sole author of the text due to its theological sophistication. No woman could ever handle complex subjects so expertly, they argued. It was simply *impossible*.[73] Consequently, *The Mystical City* was denounced in innumerable ways, perhaps most aptly abridged into a single paragraph by a modern biographer of Sor María: "False, erroneous; presumptuous; scandalous; containing matter contrary to the Church's teaching; fostering heterodoxy; in part downright heretical . . . derogatory to the Church's authority; betraying anachronisms in religious thought; telling of revelations contradicting those of other mystics; and also revelations that are demonstrably improbable; smelling of legendary nonsense; disfigured by passages offensive to chaste persons."[74] By the end of the seventeenth century, bickering over Sor María's texts had created two opposing camps within the Catholic Church, each equally tenacious in its support or condemnation but also equally unable to achieve total victory. And this fracturing had a negative effect not only on the status of the text—despite its many editions and translations—but also on the cause of María's canonization.[75]

The Sorbonne's condemnation might have been deemed excessive by some, but there is no denying that *The Mystical City* worried some clerics and theologians in Spain and the rest of the Catholic world as well. Four years before the Sorbonne's condemnation, as part of the procedures for the cause of María's canonization, Pope Innocent XII had already ordered a review of the condemnation issued in 1681 by his predecessor Pope Innocent XI. Then, in 1729, those in charge of María's canonization erred on the side of caution by requesting yet another review of *The Mystical City,* hoping a new positive verdict would clear the path for her cause definitively. Their plan backfired, however. Pope Benedict XIII approved a new commission to examine the book but died in 1730 before he could appoint its members. His successor, Clement XII, named six cardinals and three theologians to carry out the review, but these men never completed their task before Clement's death in 1740, and all their voluminous paperwork was passed on to his successor, Benedict XIV, who extended the review.[76]

Meanwhile, the bitter squabble between supporters and opponents of María and her text intensified, and the ceaseless printing of pro-María (*Agredista*) and anti-María (*Antiagredista*) texts only served to place *The Mystical City* in a poor light. What is arguably the most ardent and influential of all Antiagredista texts appeared in 1744. "On Private Revelations, Visions and Apparitions," written by German theologian Eusebius Amort, eviscerated María's claims of private revelations and stirred up a torrent of responses from Agredistas.[77] In return, Amort continued firing away at them,[78] and they kept firing back ad nauseam.[79] Consequently, as Benedict XIV's review crawled forward, new issues intensified the controversy, including the question of whether or not María was the sole author of *The Mystical City.* This question was raised by critics who found it totally impossible for an uneducated nun, or any woman whatsoever, to engage in sophisticated theological arguments in favor of the Immaculate Conception. The text, they charged, surely must have been authored—at least in part—by some male theologian familiar with scholastic theology and the work of John Duns Scotus.[80]

In 1757, the outcome of Benedict XIV's lengthy review process was a disappointment to Agredistas. Even though it decreed that María was indeed the author of this text and others attributed to her, it failed to settle the issue of its orthodoxy conclusively. Even worse, shortly before he died in 1758, Benedict XIV wrote a confidential "Judicium," or judgment, which was to be passed on to his successors. In this document, Pope Benedict advised future pontiffs to withhold approval or disapproval of *The Mystical City* and to keep closed the cause of María's canonization. In 1773, Pope Clement XIV—a Franciscan and staunch supporter of the Immaculate Conception—made one more attempt to dispel all suspicion about María and her book by appointing yet another commission to examine the text, but its members could not agree on a verdict. Consequently, Clement XIV chose to reiterate the advice given by his predecessor Benedict XIV, ordering that total silence be observed on the issue of María's *Mystical City* and that her canonization process be halted indefinitely. Ironically, several witnesses reported that Clement XIV was visited and comforted at his deathbed in Rome on September 22, 1744, by Alphonsus Liguori, founder of the Redemptorist order, who on that day also happened to be in ecstasy at the episcopal palace of Sant'Agata de'Goti, in Campania, about 120 miles to the south, in the presence of several other witnesses. In other words, the dying pope who consigned Sor María's canonization to limbo was supposedly visited by a bilocating saint who would be canonized relatively quickly, a mere ninety-five years later.[81]

Unwilling to abandon their cause, María's devotees challenged this papal decision. King Charles III of Spain and the Franciscan order pressured Rome to keep the canonization process alive and to separate it from the seemingly endless bickering over *The Mystical City,* but Pope Clement's successor, Pius VI, refused to cave in to their demands. In 1778, the Spanish ambassador to Rome reported that Pope Pius found such a suggestion illogical, for the "two branches"—that is, the text and its author—were "indivisible" and "in and of themselves should be seen as essentially connected."[82]

Skepticism about María's *impossible* claims was inevitable, even among people of faith, due to their enormity, and this is why skeptics of various stripes had irritated María's Catholic devotees ever since she had first faced the Inquisition in 1635. But by 1778, those devotees had plenty of reason for viewing Pope Pius VI as an ally rather than an enemy. His skepticism was tame compared to that of all sorts of irreligious materialists who considered María's claims outrageously impossible. Such skeptics could do much more than simply poke fun at the simple-minded credulity of Agredistas; they could also denounce their beliefs offensive, or even dangerous. One such skeptic who had once embraced a clerical career—Giacomo de Casanova—gives us a good glimpse into this new world.

When the Venetian Inquisition hauled in the infamous womanizer Casanova in 1755 for his offenses against religion and common decency, the jailers handed him a copy of the first volume of Sor María's *Mystical City,* hoping it would help him see the error of his ways. Although he was a former seminarian, Casanova had never heard of this book or its author, but he was curious enough to read some of it. After escaping from prison, he would say that it gave him nightmares and that all he could find in it was "everything that could be created by the extravagant and overheated imagination of an extremely devout Spanish virgin who was given to melancholy, trapped in a convent, and guided by ignorant and flattering confessors." Even worse, he added: "She tried to cloak all of her chimerical and monstrous visions with respectability by calling them 'revelations.'"[83]

Oddly enough, a few years later the coach in which Casanova was riding on his way to Madrid unexpectedly made a rest stop in Ágreda.[84] But this unplanned visit to María's hometown did not change his opinion about her or *The Mystical City.* Instead, he sneered at the coincidence of finding himself there: "The Spanish woman's book is just perfect for driving any man insane, especially if he is given this poison while he is imprisoned in solitary confinement, with nothing else to do," he said.[85] "Far from increasing or exciting in my mind a fervor or a zeal for religion, the work tempted me to regard as nonsense everything that pertains to mysticism, and to dogma too."[86]

Casanova and many of his contemporaries now weighed all impossible claims on a different scale, for faith itself was under siege, along with the belief system that made that faith possible. Yet attempts to restart the cause for María's canonization continued for many generations beyond Casanova's. And resistance to them within the Catholic Church continued to be driven by the same internal skepticism as before, only now more intense and painfully aware of the possibility of ridicule as Western culture became less and less receptive to religion. Unsurprisingly, all subsequent attempts to resurrect the cause for María failed, even after 1854 when Pope Pius IX proclaimed the Immaculate Conception to be dogma that all Catholics should believe. Much to the dismay of María's devotees, the next pope, Leo XIII, continued to insist that no pronouncements should be made about María and her *Mystical City,* and as pleas for a reopening of her case intensified, he doggedly renewed that ban in 1887.

In the twentieth century, despite continued papal opposition to María's canonization, devotion to her continued to increase worldwide.[87] In 1912, the publication of George Blatter's English translation of *The Mystical City* sparked a revitalization of interest in María's cause among Catholics in the United States. By 1954, on the one hundredth anniversary of the proclamation of the Immaculate Conception, some dedicated American Agredistas began to push aggressively for a reopening of her case. These efforts received a boost in 1992, when medieval theologian John Duns Scotus—who had always been linked to María and her *Mystical City*—was beatified by Pope John Paul II. Emboldened by this turn of events, Agredistas in the United States and Spain, especially, redoubled their efforts to move forward her canonization and the recognition of her *Mystical City* as thoroughly orthodox.

These efforts have yet to succeed. The cardinal in charge of canonizations, Joseph Ratzinger, who would go on to assume the papacy as Benedict XVI, issued an ambiguous ruling in 1999 requiring further review of the case. Since canonizations can move at a glacial pace—especially if they involve anyone who might spark controversy—not much has happened since, despite many renewed efforts by Agredistas.[88] The review never seems to end.

But Sor María's twenty-first-century devotees refuse to consider it *impossible* for her *not* to be canonized. After all, as they see it, Sor María knew how to astonish the world all too well and how to overcome impossibility better than anyone else in her day.

PART THREE

Malevolent

Angels can perform prodigies, they cannot perform miracles.
—Saint Thomas Aquinas,
Quaestiones Disputatae de Potentia Dei

8. Tricksters of the Impossible

A nun who meddles in politics cannot be a saint.
—King Philip II of Spain

Too much of a good thing, as everyone knows, can be bad. Especially too much of the miraculous, for when the impossible becomes constantly possible, the boundary between the sacred and the mundane can easily blur, divine splendor can dwindle, and the awesome can become banal, or even trivial. Worse yet, when belief in the possibility of the impossible reaches fever pitch, posing as a miracle-worker can become easier and may be a tempting option for attention seekers and tricksters. And discerning the difference between the natural and the supernatural or between genuine and fraudulent miracle claims can become immensely difficult, if not impossible, for the clerical elites in charge of ensuring the purity of the faith, as well as for the laity, including crowned monarchs. Inevitably, given the devil's reputation as the ultimate trickster—the fact that he was "a liar and the father of lies,"[1] ever eager to cause trouble—he, too, could more easily wheedle his way into the picture.

Such was the dilemma faced by early modern Catholicism when miracles became a highly valued feature of Catholic identity as well as a polemical weapon to wield against Protestants and skeptics of all stripes. It was a vexing conundrum, and a painful one, for it required doubting, and doubt always rubs faith raw. Sorting the genuinely divine from the fraudulent or demonic was an ordeal that also required intellectual, emotional, psychological, and spiritual fortitude on the part of all involved in the process. Teresa of Avila, Joseph of Cupertino, and María de Ágreda were liminal avatars of the impossible, suspended between the divine and demonic, their sanctity revered and questioned simultaneously, perfectly poised to play the role of tricksters acting as agents of the devil, the ultimate trickster.[2] All three bore the brunt of doubt and survived their ordeal. But many other liminal "living saints" who claimed similar impossible feats did not survive intense scrutiny. We will never know how many, exactly, since so many of the Inquisition's records have been lost, but it is undeniable that in the surviving records, those found guilty of fraud or diabolical mischief do outnumber those who were not. Consequently, to fully understand the context in which belief in impossible feats was forged, one must also consider cases of ostensibly holy individuals whose impossible feats failed to be recognized as genuinely divine; that is, one must take into account cases in which doubt and reason trumped faith. Cases of failure, therefore, can shed light on the larger questions that lurked behind belief in impossible miracles, and they can also help reveal how the boundaries of belief were drawn in a contentious age. Additionally, failures add texture and depth to both narrative and analysis, allowing us to pay attention to structural issues, such as negotiations of status, relations between elites and subalterns, issues of liminality, questions of gender, and even metaphysical questions involving social and political issues, such as where the line is to be drawn between the world of the senses and that of the spirit, who gets to draw that line, and what difference it might make for them to draw it one way rather than another.

Three spectacular and extremely well-documented cases of failure lend themselves nicely to the task at hand. One might even say that they do so splendidly, for these three individuals had all achieved status before they fell from grace as charismatic living saints equal to that of Teresa of Avila, Joseph of Cupertino, and María of Ágreda. In fact, one could argue that in some respects the meteoric rise of their reputation as miracle-workers was more impressive than that of Teresa, Joseph, and María. Moreover, their dramatic exposure as tricksters by the Inquisition makes the success of those three other mystics seem even more remarkable.

Our three failed saints are all Iberian nuns who came to be known by the location of their convents and ended up being imprisoned by the Inquisition in convents other than their own. Each of their cases represents a different type of disgrace. All three reportedly levitated and bilocated; two claimed to survive without eating at all; and one claimed to have bleeding stigmata on her head, hands, feet, and torso. The first, Magdalena de la Cruz, "the Nun of Córdoba" (1487–1560), eventually confessed to being in league with the devil and ascribed her unnatural charisma to him. The second, María de la Visitación, "the Nun of

Lisbon," who was born in 1551 and died sometime after 1603, eventually confessed to being a total fraud who cleverly tricked everyone into thinking her miracles were real. The third, Luisa de la Ascensión, "the Nun of Carrión" (1565–1636), was eventually declared innocent of fraud by the Inquisition twelve years after her death but nonetheless ended up forever disgraced and consigned to oblivion through her humiliation.

Before delving into these three cases, several points need to be made clear. First, although the Inquisition examined those suspected of fraud with a strict either/or dichotomy in mind (either a fraud or a genuinely holy person; either a feigned miracle or a genuine one), inquisitors were very much aware that discerning the difference was often extremely difficult and that many shades of gray stood between black and white. Consequently, before any denunciations were made and then during the entire investigation, until sentence was pronounced, everyone involved was mired in ambiguity. As William Christian has observed, "Much religious excitement occurs precisely during the ambiguous period . . . in the margins of the known and the approved, around persons whose works, visions, or organizations are not yet validated, at places that are in doubt."[3] Second, inquisitors often had to take the issues of sincerity and illusion into consideration, which is why the issue of motivation was a key point. Had the suspects sincerely believed in their claims, even if they were deluded, or had they willfully misled others in order to gain saintly status for themselves? Here, again, Christian's observations seem very perceptive, for the ambiguity created by the accusations and the investigation could often lead to mere conjectures or "possibilities" rather than proof. Third, inquisitors always needed to determine causality: If the miracles in question were not feigned, were they of divine origin or demonic origin? Was the suspect mentally ill or not? Here, too, were many shades of gray with which to contend. Finally, inquisitors needed to determine whether the accusations leveled against anyone were legitimate or motivated by spite, envy, or some other kind of vindictiveness. So, quite often, investigations into spiritual fraud were communal events that involved entire convents and monasteries. Simply put: every fraudulence case was complex and required great patience and sensitivity on the part of the investigators and the accused.

One more issue that needs to be addressed at the outset is that of gender, especially since our three stellar frauds are women. Given that "learned" opinion warned that women were much less stable than men, spiritually and mentally, the number of women investigated as frauds tended to be higher than that of men. Unfortunately, we do not have precise statistics on this disparity. In her work with sixteen feigned holiness cases from Venetian Inquisition records, Anne Schutte discovered certain gender patterns. First, women accused of feigned holiness tended to be nonelites who fit into a "distinct sociocultural group": unmarried, illiterate or poorly educated, and generally unfamiliar with books. The men, in contrast, tended to be clerics, overwhelmingly: two friars, three secular priests, and a friar-turned-bishop. Only one of the men in her sample was a layman. Second, at all stages of the investigations, she says, and at all times, the Inquisition "treated men and women differently," usually assigning greater guilt to the men and imposing harsher sentences on them (since they were ostensibly stronger and smarter), even in cases in which a female suspect had influenced a male being prosecuted along with her.[4] Whether these patterns reflect the totality of all feigned holiness cases in Venice or in Spain or anywhere else remains to be seen. Much more statistical research is needed.

Iberia, Land of Enchanted Beings

No one has yet to come up with a cogent explanation for it, but impossible miracles were not evenly distributed in the early modern Catholic world. Despite its many manifestations of deep fervor, Catholicism in Northern, Central, and Eastern Europe lagged far behind Catholicism in Southern Europe with regard to the miracle claims being examined here. France had its fair share of such claims in the early modern era, especially as the chaos created by the Wars of Religion receded in memory and the 1600s became le grand siècle for mystical theology,[5] but the presence of Calvinists in its midst and various lingering ecclesiastic instabilities made France pale in comparison to monolithically Catholic Italy and Iberia when it came to miracle claims. Italy certainly had its share of miracle-workers and of the burden of sifting out the frauds, well into the eighteenth century,[6] but of these two miracle-claiming hot spots on the map, Iberia was the hottest, so to speak, and Spain was downright incandescent, undisputedly boiling over. And, due to its infamously vigilant Inquisition, Spain was also superbly equipped to hunt down anyone suspected of fraud or diabolical influence and to leave behind for posterity copious records of its entanglements with such vexing folk.

This is not to say that credulity was more prevalent in Spain than anywhere else. Not at all. Inquisition records prove that there were plenty of skeptics.[7] But there is no denying the evidence for an intense desire for encounters with the supernatural in early modern Spain. And that abundance of evidence is due to the Inquisition and its record-keeping, which have allowed us to know more about all aspects of piety in Spain than in other places that were less efficient in their control of religious misbehavior, error, and deception. We also have plenty of other evidence that Spain was awash in religiosity, brimming over with miracle seekers and miracle claims in which the lines between the natural and supernatural and the possible and impossible were constantly crossed.

As early as 1600 some Spaniards, such as Martín González de Cellorigo, realized something odd was afoot. "It seems," he said, "as if one had wished to reduce these kingdoms to a republic of enchanted beings, living outside the natural order of things."[8] Don Martín was not referring to monks and nuns, specifically, but to the wider culture in which he lived, in which the supernatural claims of monks and nuns ran riot and in which an intense interest in the supernatural affected Spanish religiosity as a whole, across class lines and regional boundaries. This proliferation of mystics and miracle-workers—and of miracle-seeking Spaniards—was openly acknowledged by the clergy, some of whom wrote guides for monastic confessors on how best to approach all miracle claims. Books such as *A Treatise on the Examination of True and False Revelations and Raptures* by Father Geronimo Planes, a Discalced Franciscan, tackled the increase in miracle claims and frauds head-on, blaming it on the devil, urging readers not to lose faith in God's power to achieve the impossible simply because of an overabundance of fraudsters.[9]

Awareness of this peculiar baroque quirk ran deep in Spanish culture long after it had vanished and eventually caused no small measure of embarrassment among some nineteenth-century intellectuals who were eager to banish it from view. Marcelino Menéndez Pelayo, that testy Spanish historian previously quoted in the first few pages of this book, had much more to say about early modern Spain's fascination with the miraculous than what has already been mentioned. This is how he dismissed that era's overabundance of miracle claims and spiritual fraudsters with utter disdain: "Throughout the seventeenth century, there were a great number of cases of false devotion; but if you've seen one, you've seen them all. There isn't even any variety in the details. . . . It would be vain and useless verbosity to pay much attention to cases of this sort . . . all of which correspond to the reigns of Felipe III and Felipe IV, in which the flood of frauds was immense . . . but in such cases, dogma was never an issue."[10]

In the twentieth and twenty-first centuries, fortunately, many Hispanists have chosen to highlight precisely what Menéndez Pelayo wanted to bury deeply, interpreting it in various ways.

José Antonio Maravall has summed up the essence of Spain's baroque religiosity with a Weberian spin, portraying it as the exact reverse of the Protestant "disenchantment" of the world. The early modern age was "most certainly
a time of faith . . . frequently veering into superstitious behavior."[11] Stephen Haliczer has approached this phenomenon from a gender perspective, pointing out
that Spanish society was intensely affected "by an upsurge of feminine religious
enthusiasm without parallel since medieval times" and that this enthusiasm
focused on mystical phenomena and miracles.[12] Patrocinio García Barriúso, a
Franciscan priest and historian, has described early modern Spanish religiosity
as far too credulous for its own good, "easily inclined to admire and acclaim as
holy and as miraculously gifted all those who presented themselves as bearers of
new divine messages . . . and dazzling and astonishing miracles."[13] Teófanes
Egido López has taken a functionalist approach, depicting early modern Spain
as a society gripped "by an enthusiasm for the marvelous" and "deeply in need
of the supernatural."[14] Social and cultural historian José Luis Sánchez Lora, another functionalist, has suggested that Spain's hunger for miracles was driven
by a despair shared by elites and common folk in the face of inept rulers, plagues,
famines, constant warfare, rebellions, and rising skepticism.[15] The imprecision
of these assessments does not necessarily make them any less perceptive. A subject as amorphous as religiosity eludes exactness. And there is no denying that
functionalist claims about a hunger for the miraculous do ring true, especially
in the face of undeniable decline and disasters.

Given this widely acknowledged propensity of Spanish Catholics to accept the miraculous as commonplace, one of the most difficult tasks faced by
the clergy in Spain was that of dealing with excess fervor not only among the
laity but also among some of the most intensely devout members of their own
class—that is, among monks and nuns who claimed to have tapped into the
supernatural realm and gained the ability to achieve the impossible. But belief
in miracles created a space for imposture as much as it did for hope in the impossible. By the end of the sixteenth century, on the cusp of the slippery slope
to decline, Spain was already full of ersatz saints and miracle-workers who served
a much-needed function. One cleric described the fraudsters he observed with
as much contempt as the elite sycophants they attracted: "Ordinarily they pre-
tend to be spiritual and say that they are swept up in ecstasies and mortal raptures and claim to have the spirit of prophecy; and they love to become rich
because of the virtue they completely lack, receiving great gifts and hefty donations from nobles and devotees. Oh, how many of these frauds I know who make

the rounds from palace to palace and fool the lords and ladies into thinking that their mere presence sanctifies their homes and redeems their guilt."[16] Not all clerics dispensed scorn so evenhandedly, however. Some, such as Gaspar Navarro, preferred to assign all the blame for clueless credulity strictly to "vulgar and barbarous people, and idiotic common folk lacking in discernment and incapable of reasoning."[17]

The number of potential spiritual frauds was so high that it led the Spanish Inquisition to investigate feigned sanctity as an especially dangerous category of religious deviancy. Various terms were employed by the Inquisition for this type of wrongdoing: the crime itself was called "feigning" (*fingir*), "fooling" or "deceiving" (*embaucar*), and "imposture" (*impostura*); the offenders themselves were called "tricksters" (*embaucadores* or *embaucadoras*) or "deluded" (*ilusos* or *ilusas*); and the phenomenon as a whole came to be known as "inventing the sacred" (*haciendo invención del sagrado*).[18] Naturally, given the Inquisition's deep-seated loathing of the devil and his wiles, its handling of such misfits often involved wrestling with two tricksters simultaneously: one human and the other demonic.

Discerning the difference between a genuine saint who engaged with the sacred, such as Teresa of Avila, and an impostor who "invented" the sacred—as the inquisitors put it—was seldom easy, for the very process of discernment involved scrutinizing some of the most distinctive teachings of the Catholic Church, especially those that distinguished it from Protestantism, such as the value of asceticism and prayer, the possibility of mystical encounters with the divine, the accessibility of the miraculous, and the permeability of the boundaries between the spiritual and the material, as well as the demonic and the divine. Consequently, every case of suspected fraudulence or demonic activity perched all inquisitors on the edge of a slippery slope.

By the mid-seventeenth century, the criteria for discerning who was "inventing" the sacred were well established.[19] More often than not, those who ended up under investigation were found guilty, but it is well known that many who were later canonized as saints passed through the same ordeal, including Teresa of Avila, Ignatius Loyola, and Joseph of Cupertino. Maintaining certain standards was deemed necessary, not just as a question of authority or as a concern with charismatic claims outside the church hierarchy but also as a pastoral issue. Those accused of feigned sanctity were examined for signs of delusion, excessive pride, mental illness, or demonic influence. They were also screened to prevent the spread of false teachings and social disorder. Questioning the authenticity of popular holy men and women, however, was sometimes the same as questioning belief itself.

It could be argued that the relative obscurity of most Inquisition cases of feigned sanctity does not matter much, or even that such cases were not a side-show at all but rather the main event, at street level, as far as religious elites were concerned. In the end, they prove that questions of discerning the differ-ence between genuine and false, or spiritual and material—what Andrew Keitt calls "boundary issues"[20]—were of immense concern for Catholics and at the heart of their religious life. It could also be argued that questions of this sort were also of immense concern for Protestants and Western culture as a whole, for a complex set of dialectical relationships were engendered by them, pitting believers against one another and fueling the rise of skepticism. When all is said and done, as shall be seen in chapter 9, when it came to belief in "impossible" feats, Catholics and Protestants were closer to each other than it might seem at first glance due to their shared belief in the power of demonic forces. Moreover, as Keitt has also argued, the seventeenth century was a period of "profound con-ceptual turmoil and epistemological uncertainty," in which "rationalism was employed as often to shore up belief in the miraculous as to challenge it."[21]

And amid all this turmoil and uncertainty, few individuals challenged be-lief more intensely than living saints suspected of fraud, for many of the most astounding miracle claims came from men and women who were revered as saints in their own lifetimes. A common occurrence throughout Christian his-tory, such cases began to intensify in the early modern period, especially in the wake of the Protestant Reformation.[22] After 1563, when the Council of Trent sealed its reforming dictates, the process of identifying and canonizing saints after their death underwent a gradual and uneven tightening in the Catholic Church. Eventually, the process of canonization was carefully codified and reg-ulated, and new standards of proof for sanctity were established,[23] and in 1588, the task of processing all sainthood cases was placed in the hands of the newly created Congregation of Sacred Rites and Ceremonies in Rome. Nonetheless, as the new process for identifying saints was being set in place, rules for moni-toring the veneration of holy men and women who were still alive remained somewhat unclear. In 1634, as a response to the fact that so many living saints were being venerated and sought out for miracles in the Catholic world, espe-cially in Spain and Italy, Pope Urban VIII—the very same pontiff over whose head Joseph of Cupertino flew—ordered local church authorities to stamp out any such devotion. In other words, no living human being was to be venerated, even if he or she was considered an astounding miracle-worker.[24] This new policy was to be strictly enforced and is one of the major reasons that Joseph of Cupertino kept being shuffled to ever more remote and inaccessible locations as his fame increased.

In Spain, the veneration of living saints began to intensify and to acquire peculiar characteristics in the sixteenth century, and the three "failed" miracle-working nuns about to be examined here were all engendered by this phenomenon as well as representatives of it. Among the many holy men and women of this sort that emerged in Golden Age Spain, none shaped the cult of the living saint more intensely than the mystic Sor Juana de la Cruz (1481–1534), abbess at the third-order Franciscan convent of Santa María de la Cruz, in Cubas de la Sagra, not far from Madrid, who seems to have been a role model for María de Ágreda.[25] An ascetic, visionary, and frequent ecstatic who claimed to have undergone a mystical marriage to Christ, Sor Juana gained renown as a preacher through whom Christ spoke while she was enraptured. Having won the admiration and support of Cardinal Francisco Jiménez de Cisneros, the most powerful churchman in Spain, as well as of the young King Charles V, who attended some of her "sermons,"[26] Juana became one of the most admired religious figures of her day. More significantly, as far as the cult of living saints is concerned, Sor Juana acquired a reputation as an extraordinary miracle-worker, especially as a healer and a rescuer of souls from purgatory, and as a distributor of blessed and indulgenced rosary beads (*cuentas benditas*), rosaries, crosses, medals, and other objects that she claimed had been taken to heaven and returned to earth. These were prized in the same way as relics and believed to convey divine blessings.[27] Occurrences of this phenomenon soon began to multiply in Spain and to be expected of extraordinarily holy women mystics.[28]

While Juana was still alive, as could sometimes happen before the Council of Trent extinguished such local expressions of popular piety, her beatification process was begun in 1515 by the archbishop of Toledo, Bernardo de Sandoval y Rojas, and from 1519 to 1521, an official diocesan inquest (*proceso*) into her virtues and miracles was carried out in anticipation of her eventual canonization.[29] In 1530, four years before her death, she was officially given the title of "Venerable," which validated her cult and placed her on the first rung of the ladder to canonization. During this time, one narrative of Juana's life was written, along with a record of her devotions and visions at her convent,[30] plus two hagiographical accounts of her extraordinary virtues and miracles, all published while she was still alive. The first of these, written by Father Antonio Daza, was reedited and republished twice,[31] and the first version was turned into a trilogy of plays by the great dramatist Tirso de Molina.[32] A second hagiography was written by Pedro Navarro, who was ordered to do so by the vicar-general of the Franciscan order.[33] Both of these texts unabashedly referred to her as "Santa Juana" and spurred the expansion of her cult. Veneration of Sor Juana spread far and wide in Spain and its New World colonies, as well as elsewhere in Europe.[34] In addition to becoming a revered saintly figure among the faithful, elites as well as commoners, Juana also became a role model for many other Spanish nuns, including all three of the notorious frauds who are featured in this chapter. Tellingly, Father Antonio Daza, the author of Juana's first protohagiography, would become confessor to one of these three nuns, Luisa de Carrión, and write an account of her life which would end up being suppressed by the Inquisition.

The fate of Juana's canonization—which seemed so certain while she was alive—is perhaps indicative of the negative effect that some of her fraudulent imitators had on her reputation. Despite the fact that Juana was already Venerable at the time of her death in 1534 and that many of Spain's clerical and secular elites flocked to the tomb at her convent in which her incorruptible corpse was buried, her canonization process stalled due to a convergence of factors, such as the loss of some of the documents, the somewhat chaotic progress of the Council of Trent (1545–1563), and the reorganization of the canonization system set in place by it. Three other attempts to get her case back on track in 1664, 1702, and 1980 have stalled too, and the only positive result thus far has been the reaffirmation of her "heroic virtue" and her status as Venerable by Pope Francis in 2015.

Magdalena de la Cruz, "the Nun of Córdoba": Diabolical Abbess

Magdalena de la Cruz was born in the Andalusian village of Aguilar de la Frontera in 1487, to a poor family of humble lineage. In 1504, at the age of seventeen, after a childhood reportedly full of supernatural encounters, she entered the Franciscan cloister of Santa Isabel de los Ángeles in Córdoba, one of the few convents in her region that did not require the dowry her parents could not provide. Eventually, she would serve as its abbess from 1533 to 1542. From the very start, she earned a reputation in her convent as an extreme ascetic and living saint, principally because of her frequent mystical ecstasies and the externalidades that accompanied them, especially her trances, visions, prophecies, levitations, bilocations, and stigmata, as well as her gift of healing and her inedia—that is, her apparent ability to survive without consuming any food whatsoever other than the consecrated host she received at communion.[35]

For nearly forty years, the authenticity of Sor Magdalena's supernatural gifts went largely unquestioned, and she attracted admirers at the highest levels of society, such as Francisco de los Ángeles Quiñones, the superior general of the Franciscan order, who visited her more than once; Francisco de Osuna, the mystic whose texts had a profound influence on Teresa of Avila; and Alonso Manrique, archbishop of Seville and inquisitor general, who called her "his most precious daughter."[36] Even the Spanish royal family became fervent devotees. In 1527, when Empress Isabella was about to give birth to the future king Philip II, some of Sor Magdalena's garments were taken to Valladolid, over 300 miles to the north, so the royal infant could be wrapped in them and thus shielded from the devil's wrath.[37] According to some accounts, Magdalena was also asked to bless the infant prince's layette, a request that was apparently very much in vogue among the other ladies at court. Likewise, before embarking on a military campaign against the Ottoman Turks at Tunis in 1535, Emperor Charles V sent his battle standard to Córdoba to be blessed by Magdalena.[38]

As one would expect, Magdalena's fame attracted many visitors, wealthy patrons, and donations to the convent of Santa Isabel. Her supernatural feats turned heads, made her a celebrity, put her convent on the map, and gave it financial security, allowing for major physical renovations.[39] Luis Zapata de Chaves, a court gossiper who had served as a page to Empress Isabella and the young Prince Philip II, attributed Sor Magdalena's fame to her miracles and described her rise to prominence as follows: "She sparked astonishment and admiration among her fellow nuns first, then among her neighbors in Córdoba, then, later, in all of Spain, and even in Rome and the whole world. She went without food or drink for days on end; slept on a rough mat on the floor; could tell what was going on in other places; wore a hairshirt constantly; could be seen levitating a foot above the ground while praying; and could be whisked away to other locations every now and then, and say where she had gone and who had requested her presence." According to Zapata, Magdalena had even bilocated to the Battle of Pavia on February 24, 1525, and on that same day revealed to everyone at her convent that King Francis I of France had been defeated and taken prisoner by Emperor Charles V.[40]

Magdalena had turned herself into a living saint and a "walking, living relic," as one scholar has put it.[41] This self-fashioning began early in her life, before she became a nun, and stories told later about her precocious holiness amplified its effect. One such story told of a demon expelled from a possessed man's body that refused to come near her because, as the demon himself put it, "She has been a saint since she was in her mother's womb."[42] Another story related how she began to have visions at the age of four.[43] Yet another told of how, at the age of five, she tried to imitate Christ's crucifixion by nailing herself to a wall.[44]

Magdalena's self-fashioning was assiduously methodical, and something she pursued with uncommon zeal, mostly by taking all the behaviors associated with holiness to extremes. Magdalena did not simply fast. She refused to eat altogether, claiming that all the nourishment she needed came from the Eucharist. She did not simply wear a hair shirt or sleep on the floor. She mortified her body in even more severe ways. She not only levitated and bilocated but also received the stigmata, one of the rarest of mystical gifts.[45] Her trances were frequent, deep, and prolonged, and even when stabbed in her feet and limbs with long needles, she would never flinch.[46] Her miraculous cures were numerous, and her prophesies seemed astonishingly accurate.[47] She claimed to free many souls from purgatory not only through her intercessory prayers but also by taking on the suffering of those entrusted to her, which sometimes involved voyaging to purgatory itself and returning from it with her body so superheated that it could instantly turn water coming in contact with it to steam.[48] In addition, the anguished moans of the suffering souls in purgatory could often be heard emanating from her cell.[49] She received visits, visions, and messages from Jesus Christ, the Virgin Mary, Saint Jerome, Saint Francis, Saint Dominic, and other saints and angels.[50] And, as was becoming increasingly common in her day,[51] Magdalena, the living saint, distributed pieces of herself—hair, skin, and blood-stained cloths—as well as myriad items that had come in contact with her body or had been blessed by her,[52] including the skin that peeled off her feet whenever she dunked them in water after one of her visits to purgatory.[53]

Not everyone was favorably impressed by Sor Magdalena, however. Two future saints cast doubt on her ecstasies, visions, and miracles and warned others not to venerate her. Juan de Ávila refused to get carried away by the wave of adulation created by Magdalena, "which was sweeping the world." He also predicted that she would come to a bad end and was denied access to her when he visited Córdoba.[54] Ignatius Loyola, too, viewed her with suspicion. Once, when regaled with accounts of her mystical gifts by a young Jesuit novice who had recently met with her and called her "one of the holiest and most prudent women in the world," Ignatius reproved the novice for jumping to such conclusions about "any such woman" and for measuring sanctity by "any such things" as her alleged ecstasies and miracles.[55]

Ultimately, it was not the opinions of such prominent skeptics that brought Magdalena under closer scrutiny but rather her own claims and her behavior, plus her hubris, which began to alarm her sisters. Having been elected abbess three times, in 1533, 1536, and 1539, Magdalena became increasingly authoritarian and vindictive. She not only seemed to delight in humiliating those nuns at her convent who came from privileged or noble families but also segregated the "good" nuns who had bright auras from the "bad" ones who had dark auras.[56] Then, from the circle of these "good" nuns she created a clique of acolytes—"reared in her cell"—who were constantly at her side to do her bidding and were in charge of keeping skeptics such as Juan de Ávila away from the convent.[57] Even worse, she issued threats to anyone who dared to challenge or question her sanctity, telling them that God would punish them in the hereafter as well as in the here and now.[58] And to reinforce these threats, she would attribute the deaths of all who doubted her miracles to the disrespect they had shown to her, claiming that the suffering souls of those dead skeptics came to visit her at night to repent of their insolence.[59] She also insisted that the nuns confess their sins to her, and although she had no sacramental power to absolve them, she warned them that if they disobeyed this command, they would never be forgiven by God.[60] At the same time, in contrast, she stopped going to confession, claiming that her own sinlessness made her participation in that sacrament superfluous.[61]

Aiming to remain abbess as another election approached in 1542, Magdalena brought her miraculous mystical claims to new heights, telling the nuns that she had become pregnant through the agency of the Holy Spirit, just as the Virgin Mary had, and that this miracle had taken place on the feast of the Annunciation. According to some accounts, the pregnancy seemed real because her abdomen swelled visibly during the next nine months, until Christmas day, when she claimed to have given birth to none other than Jesus himself. This was no mere vision of the infant Jesus, she boasted, but a flesh-and-blood divine baby boy. In other words, this was a second incarnation of Jesus, as astonishingly miraculous as his first, for Magdalena also affirmed that she had been granted the gift of perpetual virginity by Christ himself when she was a young girl.[62] Unlike the first incarnation of the second person of the Holy Trinity, however, this one did not last long. After giving birth, breastfeeding him, and wrapping

him up in her hair, Magdalena said, the baby Jesus suddenly vanished, causing her locks to turn from black to blonde.[63] Afterward, strands of this blonde
hair became highly prized relics that were given to a select number of Magdalena's devotees.[64] And if anyone doubted that this had really happened, Magdalena offered to show them her nipples, which she claimed were as heavily
chapped as those of any mother who had recently given birth.[65] No record exists of anyone daring to ask for this proof.

Given the extremity of this claim and that of her survival without food
for many years, as well as her severe authoritarian bent, Magdalena approached
the next abbatial election of 1542 in a weakened position. Friction had been
building among the convent's nuns, especially between those Magdalena favored
and those she constantly reprimanded and marginalized, and this election only
served to heighten tensions. Meanwhile, Magdalena soon found herself under
intense scrutiny from above by Franciscan superiors to whom her disgruntled
nuns had complained. Those superiors first homed in on one of her more
extreme claims, that of inedia. Consequently, she was forced to prove that she
actually could survive without eating, as she claimed to have done for over a
decade. To do this, her superiors locked her in a cell with some friars posted
near it as around-the-clock sentries to ensure that the only sustenance she received was one communion wafer per day. This test failed, for Magdalena managed to escape through a window. Although this evasion could easily have been
taken as an admission of fraud on her part, Magdalena turned the tables on the
skeptics by claiming that the escape was miraculous and that the test she was
undergoing was no longer necessary because the Virgin Mary had given her permission in a vision to stop her extreme fasting altogether.

While she convinced some of the genuineness of her sanctity through this
ruse, Magdalena failed to win the support of most of her nuns and was not
reelected as abbess in 1542. From that point forward, her fall from grace was
swift, and it did not take long for Magdalena, the living saint, to find herself in
deep trouble. In 1543, not long after losing the election, some strange and alarming phenomena began to arouse more suspicion. First, a pair of nuns who kept
watch over her at night claimed they had seen some large black goats surrounding her bed, which Magdalena identified as souls from purgatory who were seeking her assistance. On another occasion, a nun saw a shadowy figure standing
near Magdalena's bed, ran out of the room screaming, and immediately described
what she had just seen to all the other nuns.[66] Magdalena claimed that this visitor was an angel, but the nuns at Santa Isabel were not fooled. They knew bet-

ter: That visitor had to be a demon, as they saw it, because good angels were never dark. So, they immediately reported this incident to their Franciscan superiors, as they were expected to do, and Magdalena was quickly locked away.

Before a full investigation could begin, however, Magdalena fell critically ill. As her condition worsened and her doctor advised her to prepare for death and confess her sins, all hell broke loose, literally and figuratively, when Magdalena made a horrifying confession: She was not a saint, she revealed, but a brazen fraud, and many of her so-called miracles were mere trickery, made possible by her own devious ingenuity and the help of some accomplices in the convent. Even worse, some of her miracles—especially her levitations, bilocations, and prophecies—had been the work of the devil, specifically of two demons to whom she had given her soul when she was about twelve years old: one named Balban, the other named Patonio. When Magdalena's confessor asked about these demons, they took total control of Magdalena and spoke directly to him, insisting that they would never leave her body because their pact meant she was theirs to keep and drag down to hell. One of the demons revealed that he was always at her side; the other said he was in charge of spreading news about her miracles and making people believe she was a saint and that whenever she was whisked away to another location, as she often was, he took her place at the convent, in her image and likeness, so no one could tell she was absent.[67]

Eventually, Magdalena finally admitted in her own voice that all of the demons' statements were indeed true, including the revelation that every day for the past forty years she had engaged in "carnal delights" with one of those demons. Magdalena was then forced to confess all these sins publicly to her fellow nuns and to beg their forgiveness, but when she was asked to sign a document that detailed her wrongdoing, she started to shake violently. Deeming her possessed, the priest overseeing this event exorcized her successfully, and her fellow nuns got to listen to the heated exchange between him and Magdalena's demon, during which, at one point, the demon spoke in "the Chaldean tongue" (Aramaic), as demons are wont to do.[68] Freed from her demons, Magdalena signed this document but still had much more to endure, including another public confession of guilt in the presence of the Franciscan provincial and three other witnesses, followed by lengthy questioning by the Inquisition. All the nuns in the convent, too, were interrogated.

The tale told by Magdalena and her demons, as summarized in the final sentence pronounced by the Inquisition, reveals an intricate braiding of deception and preternatural activity carefully aimed at creating a false aura of sanctity.

Tellingly, Magdalena's demons revealed that it was her burning desire to be regarded as a saint that had made it easy for them to lure her into making a pact with them. As the Inquisition's sentence put it: "Her demon told her to do whatever he asked and in return he promised to make everyone think she was a saint . . . and the demon assured her she would not need to worry about their pact being discovered."[69] Such was the allure of saintliness for Magdalena, and such was her awareness of the benefits which a reputation as a saint and a pact with the devil could provide.

Magdalena's confession is proof positive that she and those around her were well aware of the seemingly impossible feats that could be ascribed to demons as well as of those which could easily be faked, such as her stigmata, which she admitted were self-inflicted wounds,[70] or her visions and visits to purgatory, which were totally fabricated,[71] or her inedia, which required the help of accomplices who procured food for her secretly, out of view.[72] Moreover, the very fact that she could find collaborators is the best proof we have of how feigned sanctity could become a communal effort within a convent and of how relatively easy it could be for deception to remain undetected or unreported for a long time, especially when the fraud is the work of a shrewd abbess with a coterie of zealous acolytes. Ultimately, it was Magdalena's overreach, her "vainglory" and vindictiveness as abbess,[73] and her promotion of ever more outrageous claims, such as her inedia and her birthing anew of Jesus, that caused her carefully crafted saintly persona to turn suddenly into its demonic opposite.[74]

It makes little difference whether it was the demons speaking or Magdalena, or perhaps even the Inquisitors superimposing a demonic template on her deception. The testimony summed up in the Inquisition's sentence makes it clear that Magdalena's self-fashioning involved a deep familiarity with the patterns of sanctity found in medieval hagiographies and an equally deep acquaintance with medieval demonology. And one should not reject the possibility that Magdalena's confession might have been her last great fraud, an expertly performed attempt to shift blame from herself to the devil so she could seem less culpable and more deserving of mercy.

Ultimately, after examining many witnesses and weighing the potentially negative effects that a harsh sentence might have on the reputation of the Franciscan order, the Inquisition was merciful indeed. At an auto de fé in the Cathedral of Córdoba on the May 3, 1546, the public reading of her crimes and her sentence took ten hours to complete, from six in the morning until four in the afternoon, followed by a Mass and a sermon.[75] With her mouth gagged, a rope tied around her neck, and a burning candle in her hand, Magdalena was forced to stand on a scaffold through this ordeal, elevated for all to see, dressed in her Franciscan habit but without her veil. Admitting that they could have sentenced her to death for "having offended God our Lord so greatly and abominably" but reminding the assembled throng that God "never desires the death of sinners, but rather their conversion and their chance to survive and save their souls," the Inquisitors condemned Magdalena to perpetual seclusion in the convent of Santa Clara, at Andujar, where she would always have the lowliest possible status, perform the most unpleasant tasks, and have no contact whatsoever with the outside world.[76] For the next fourteen years, until her death in 1560, she reportedly lived a life of constant penance in total obscurity. The nun who had once been revered as a living saint totally vanished from view, but not from memory. Her sudden fall from grace, her appalling imposture, and her lurid dalliance with the devil would become legendary and haunt all discourse on mystical claims and demonic deception for generations to come, in Spain and beyond.[77] "May God remove such horrors from the spirits and memories of all people," said one observer, perhaps too keenly aware of how impossible it would be for that to happen.[78]

María de la Visitación, "the Nun of Lisbon": Total Fraud

Portugal, too, produced the case of a living saint who exhibited all the signs of holiness and high ecstasies, including the impossible feat of levitation, but was eventually unmasked as a fraud. In this case, the feigned sanctity rested mainly on the "gift" of the stigmata.[79]

María Lobo de Meneses was born in 1551, to a noble Portuguese family that moved in the highest circles.[80] Her father, Francisco Lobo, served as ambassador for King John III at the court of Emperor Charles V; her mother, Blanca de Meneses, was also of noble lineage. Orphaned while still a young girl, she entered the Dominican convent of La Anunciada in Lisbon as a novice in 1562, at the age of eleven. Five years later she took her final vows and became a full-fledged member of this large nunnery, which housed many noble women.[81] Deeply influenced by the Dominican mystic Catherine of Siena (1347–1380), who had herself experienced a mystical marriage with Jesus Christ,[82] Sor María claimed that she, too, had become Christ's bride and began to refer to him as her husband (el Esposo).[83] María combined her bridal mysticism with an intense focus on the suffering Christ and went as far as to keep a life-sized cross on her bed, which she called "my wife" (*mi Esposa*). She slept with it every night and often stretched herself upon it as she prayed.[84] Sometimes she would enter a cataleptic state, levitate, and glow while praying.[85] She also began to have visions in which she was visited by Jesus Christ and the Virgin Mary, as well as by Mary Magdalene, Saint Dominic, Saint Thomas Aquinas, and Saint Catherine of Siena.[86]

In 1575 her ecstasies, visions, and levitations began to intensify and become more frequent. During one of these raptures, she claimed, Jesus had removed the crown of thorns from his head and placed it on hers, causing her to bleed profusely. The wounds caused by the crown, which remained visible thereafter and caused her great pain every Friday, were only the first step in the gradual transformation of her body into a living, bleeding, pain-riddled image of the suffering Christ.[87] In 1578, on Wednesday of Holy Week, she claimed she saw a vision of the crucified Christ hovering in the air in the convent's chapel, and as she levitated off the ground to meet up with him in midair, a bright-red ray of light shot out of the wound on Christ's chest and pierced her heart, leaving a vermilion gash on her own torso, which would bleed every Friday thereafter.[88] Finally, in 1584, shortly after her election as prioress of her convent, the transformation of María's body was made complete in two separate ecstasies. In March, on the feast of the great Dominican theologian Saint Thomas Aquinas, shortly before dawn, in the privacy of her cell, Christ crucified appeared again, and this time five bright flaming rays shot out from his wounds—one from each hand and foot, plus one from his side—piercing the corresponding spots on María's body "with great force" and causing wounds to appear.[89] In September, on the feast of the Exaltation of the Cross, dark nubs that looked like rusty nails (*clavos*) began to form on the wounds on her hands and feet, and shortly afterward, ruby red circles appeared around these clavos, surrounding them like "gorgeous roses."[90]

María was now fully stigmatized. Unlike Saint Francis, whose stigmatization took place in a single event in the presence of eyewitnesses, María's stigmatization not only occurred in four distinct phases over a period of nine years but had also taken place privately each of these times, without any eyewitnesses. Moreover, unlike her role model, Catherine of Siena, whose stigmata were invisible,[91] María's wounds were not only highly visible and a constant focus of attention but also painful and bled regularly, like clockwork, on specific days, at specific times, with unique distinguishing features.[92] The wound on her side bled only on Fridays and when touched with a cloth would produce an imprint of five small bloody stains in the shape of a cross.[93] These cloths were produced every Friday and distributed as miracle-working relics throughout the Catholic world, not only in Europe but even in the Americas and Japan.[94] The wounds on her hands and feet were so painful, she claimed, that she could not tolerate having them touched by anyone, especially on Wednesdays, Thursdays, and—worst of all—on Fridays.[95] Those on her hands were constantly in view, while those on her feet were rarely seen.[96]

As significant as María's visions, miraculous healings, and levitations were—and many eyewitnesses claimed they saw her hovering "two palms" or half a foot above the floor numerous times[97]—it was her stigmata that attracted the most attention and made her well known as a living saint throughout the Catholic world. Much of the credit for María's fame can be attributed to one of her confessors, the mystical writer Luis de Granada (1505–1588), a Dominican friar whose devotional books were immensely popular.[98] Beginning in 1584, after her final stigmatization event, Fray Luis wrote to several authorities in the Catholic Church, including Carlo Borromeo, archbishop of Milan, and Juan de Ribera, bishop of Valencia, praising Sor María and describing her as "another Saint Catherine of Siena."[99] He also published a short hagiographic text and wrote a much longer hagiography,[100] which remained unpublished for a very long time, in which he portrays her as a living saint and as the embodiment of the divine character of the Catholic Church, as well as living proof that God continues to perform miracles through it.[101] Reports of Sor María's miracles even made their way into the newsletters of the powerful German banking family the Fuggers, in which the argument was made that her stigmata had to be genuinely supernatural because they were "far above the possibilities and artfulness of human nature."[102] By 1588, four years after receiving her final stigmatization, Sor María the living saint had come to be so well known throughout the Catholic world that a constant stream of curious visitors kept flowing in and out of the convent of the Anunciada, all of them eager to ogle the Nun of Lisbon—as María came to be known—and her miraculous stigmata or to seek her intercession for some miraculous cure.

As her fame increased, so did the number of skeptical or hostile accusations made against María and her "phantasmagorical castle of heavenly charisms."[103] However, the great number of prominent ecclesiastics who believed in her made it difficult for these accusations to be taken seriously, especially because none of her detractors could back up their accusations with conclusive proof of deceit on her part.

Nonetheless, one group of powerful detractors within the convent, led by the sisters and daughters of the Count of Linares, caught the ear of their Dominican superiors and of the Inquisition. Eager to silence all skeptics and confident that an investigation would serve that purpose, the Inquisition commissioned two prominent Dominicans to scrutinize these allegations of fraud: Fray Luis de Granada—who had known María since she had entered the convent at the age of eleven—and Fray Gaspar d'Aveiro. These two friars arrived at the convent on November 1, 1587, and after spending one hour washing her hands with soap and water—haltingly, as she begged them to stop, wailing in pain, crying out, "O wounds of Our Lord Jesus Christ"—they determined that the stigmata had to be genuine, since their efforts to wash them off had failed.[104] Two and a half weeks later, Sixto Fabri de Luca, the master general of the Dominican order, closely inspected María's wounds again and declared her stigmata as well as her visions and ecstasies to be of divine origin. Yet, despite his own ringing endorsement of María, Fabri ordered a third investigation to be conducted by Luis de Granada, María's longtime acquaintance and confessor, Fray Juan de las Cuevas, confessor to Cardinal Archduke Albert, and Fray Gaspar d'Aveiro, confessor to all the nuns at the Anunciada convent.

This third investigation took place over the span of three days—November 25–27—and involved all the nuns at La Anunciada, each of whom were enjoined to relate whatever they knew about María and her miracles. Naturally, those who had denounced María as a fraud renewed their accusations. But, as it turned out, these skeptics were a small minority, and their damning complaints against María were eclipsed by the praise heaped upon her by most of the other nuns. The three investigators also examined each and every one of María's wounds with great care under bright candlelight. According to their report, María allowed them to poke and prod her stigmata "like a lamb . . . with great meekness," despite her constant expressions of pain and discomfort. And while her feet were being examined, they reported, she went into two ecstatic trances, the second of which "made her whole body shudder and left her transfixed for a long time."[105] The examination of her chest wound, which was carried out on a Friday when it normally bled, left the investigators "in awe and grateful to God" that they had been allowed to see "such an evident miracle and such a sacred testimony of the passion and wounds of our Redeemer." All in all, they concluded, María's wounds were a miracle of "supernatural origin and beyond the ability of all human artifice." The chief lesson to be learned from their report, they concluded, was that the miracles made possible by the Catholic faith testify to its genuinely divine character and that Sor María's miracles had been ordained by God "to awaken those who are asleep during these times when malice reigns supreme."[106]

María had prevailed once again. After receiving this report, Master General Sixto Fabri declared all the accusations against María to be false. She was no fraud, after all, but a genuinely holy stigmatic and worthy of admiration. Shortly after this pronouncement was made, María was reelected prioress of La Anunciada, apparently well on her way to heaven, ultimately, and to a privileged place of honor in the Catholic Church. But Fabri had made one decision that undermined the results of the past three investigations: he refused to punish or expel those nuns who had "falsely" accused María of fraud.[107] With her enemies still surrounding her, María had no real chance of avoiding conflict. Complaints kept flowing, many of which had more to do with her lack of humility and her poor leadership than with feigned miracles. Ultimately, however, it was not complaints of this sort—or even claims that she had been secretly observed painting on her stigmata—that would lead to María's undoing but issues of nationalism, politics, and secular authority.

María happened to live during a highly volatile time in Portugal's history, and as a member of a prominent noble family—and as a living saint and source of immense national pride—she was inevitably drawn into the political arena. The main issue at stake was Portugal's sovereignty, which became highly unstable when the childless King Sebastian died in battle in 1578, and the throne passed to his uncle Henry, a celibate cardinal who died in 1580 without a legitimate heir. Much to the dismay of many in Portugal, the succession crisis that ensued led to the annexation of their kingdom by King Philip II of Spain. Philip had legitimate dynastic claims since his mother was Empress Isabella, daughter of King Manuel I of Portugal, but other claimants to the throne who championed Portugal's independence were a constant threat to Philip.

Even though some elites in Portugal suspected that María favored independence from Spain, she had managed to stay away from politics throughout the succession crisis and King Philip's seizure of the throne. She had very cordial relations with King Philip and his viceroy—who consulted her often—and Philip was so captivated by her claims that he asked her to bless the Spanish Armada that set sail from Lisbon in May of 1588 for the invasion and conquest of England.[108] If the Spanish Armada blessed by María had been successful rather than a humiliating disaster, she might have escaped further scrutiny, at least for a few years. But the Armada's annihilation was doubly harmful for her.

First, it raised new questions about her holiness and miracle-working powers since her blessing of the armada had obviously failed. Then, by giving the Portuguese some hope for their own cause—including the possibility of a successful English invasion led by the contender Antonio—that colossal defeat pulled María into the realm of conspiracies, willingly and unwillingly. Rumors circulated that she had said after the Armada's failure that "the Kingdom of Portugal does not belong to Philip II, but to the Braganza family" (to which the contender Antonio belonged). Even worse, she had also predicted that "if the king of Spain does not restore the throne that he unjustly usurped, then God will punish him severely." Moreover, Sor María reportedly dared to speak of herself as the living incarnation of Portugal and of her wounds as symbols of Portugal's repression by Spain.[109] To make matters worse, knowing what her sentiments were, some Portuguese nationalists brazenly invoked her name in support of their rebellious cause without her knowledge.[110] Some also gave credence to the rumor that María's main intention all along had been to free Portugal from Spain's yoke. As one contemporary put it in November 1588, it was certain that all her miracles "were faked and designed to favor the party of don Antonio."[111]

As soon as word of María's political advocacy reached Philip II, her reputation as a saint ceased to matter. According to one account, Philip curtly observed: "A nun who meddles in politics and stirs up the people cannot be a true saint."[112] On August 9, 1588, her close friend Cardinal-Archduke Albert, King Philip's nephew and viceroy in Lisbon, following instructions from Philip himself, ordered the Inquisition to investigate Sor María and her alleged miracles.[113] After collecting fifteen folios full of accusations against María and interrogating fifty-nine witnesses—a process that took two months—the inquisitors were now ready to interrogate María herself, who had been stripped of her position as prioress. At first she claimed the high ground, maintaining her innocence, repeating all of the same accounts she had previously given concerning her miraculous ecstasies.[114] But this team of inquisitors, which included the archbishop of Lisbon, the bishop-elect of Braga, one Jesuit priest, one Augustinian canon, and one Dominican friar, dared to be much less deferential and lenient than previous investigators and much less sensitive about the pain she claimed to feel when her wounds were examined.

Having listened to her denials—somewhat impatiently, one must assume— they scrubbed her hands with a rough cloth, water, and black soap. As María wailed, feigning pain, the stigmata slowly began to fade. Within a half hour, her stigmata had totally vanished, leaving the water bowl full of paint residue and her pearly white hands perfectly clean and wound-free. They were not real wounds after all, as many believed, but expertly executed miniaturist paintings of wounds that had fooled far too many experts.

Ordered to confess, a shaken María begged to be left alone for a day to collect her thoughts. The next morning, after spending the night under the watchful gaze of four nuns, María made a dramatic confession. Falling to her knees, groveling at the feet of the inquisitors, she expressed remorse, begged for mercy, and admitted that every aspect of her vaunted sanctity had been a lie, down to the smallest details. All of her prolonged ecstasies and trances had been faked; the stigmata on her head were small self-inflicted wounds; the stigmata on her hands, feet, and chest had been painted on; the cross-shaped bloodstains she produced were carefully crafted using blood from self-inflicted wounds; her levitations had been accomplished with the aid of thick-soled footgear known as *chapines* and wooden poles hidden from view under her habit; and her halos and luminescence had all been produced through the manipulation of lamps and mirrors. And so on. Not a single miracle had been genuine, even those healings that had supposedly occurred through her agency, which she now attributed to the faith of those who believed in her.[115] In addition, she also confessed that she had feigned her pain during previous inspections of her wounds, knowing that this ruse would prevent the examiners from scouring them vigorously enough to take off the paint, and that she never thought anyone would ever dare to give her a scrubbing such as the one that revealed her duplicity.[116]

Unlike Magdalena de la Cruz, who had immediately blamed the devil for her duplicity as soon as her fraudulence was discovered, Sor María insisted that she alone deserved blame. When pressed to ferret out the devil, she repeatedly held firm: nothing she had done whatsoever was demonically induced or the result of some pact with the devil. All she would admit was that she had excelled as an actress and illusionist and that her sole aim had been to gain admiration as a saint and mystic, for purely selfish reasons.[117]

On November 7, 1588, the Inquisition passed sentence on María, declaring her guilty of "trickery and deceit" through her own "artifice and invention."[118] Consigning her to "perpetual incarceration" at a convent outside Lisbon, the inquisitors ordered her to spend the rest of her life continually doing penance, shut off from contact with the outside world. In addition, they decreed that all physical objects and pseudo-sacramentalia related to her were to be destroyed— images, books, manuscripts, crosses, beads, cloths, and any such items—to make it seem "as if they had never existed."[119] Given the seriousness of her offenses, this was a relatively benign sentence, which the inquisitors said was based on the lack of demonic involvement in her deceit as well as her own expressions of remorse, which were considered genuine. Political motives might have also influenced the Inquisition's leniency.[120]

A public announcement of María's sentence was delayed until December 8, when it was read out to a great throng assembled at Lisbon's cathedral and, over the next few days, throughout all other churches in Lisbon, one by one. Before long, news of María's shocking unmasking had spread throughout Europe and Iberia's overseas colonies. The magnitude of this scandal was too great to keep contained, especially because of the individuals involved. King Philip II remained silent, but his viceroy in Lisbon, Cardinal-Archduke Albert, had to admit his role in creating the scandal to Pope Sixtus V in a full report. Some other leading figures involved paid a heavy price for being so easily duped. The Papal Nuncio Bongiovanni was immediately recalled to Rome and replaced, and Sixto Fabri, superior general of the Dominican order, who had repeatedly vouched for María's sanctity, was quickly removed from his post.[121] Fray Luis de Granada, who had not only admired her for a long time but also written a hagiography in which he praised her virtues and miracles as equal to those of canonized saints, was hit the hardest. A mystic himself, also revered as a living saint by many, the eighty-eight-year-old Fray Luis, in failing health, hurried to address the scandal in two texts.[122]

In the first of these, afterward published as a pamphlet, Fray Luis attempted to explain how so many prominent and learned men could have been so easily fooled. As he saw it, Sor María's virtuous life—her prayer life, her devotion to the sacraments, her outward humility and charity—made him and many others assume that her miracle claims were true. At bottom, he argued, it was still a mystery how she could be virtuous in some respects but not others. Her deceitfulness and the scandal caused by it were hard lessons from which all believers had something to learn,[123] including Sor María herself, who seemed to have fully repented. In the final analysis, then, her duplicity was a test of faith.[124]

In the second treatise, which was much longer, Fray Luis wrestled with his own dismay and the potential damage María's duplicity and his own blindness to it could cause to the Catholic faithful. This text, "A Sermon on Scandals Caused by Public Disgraces," was much more than an admission of his own shortcomings or an attempt to refurbish his own reputation.[125] It was also an anguished plea for calm, a sharp-edged polemical weapon, and a mystically inclined theological meditation. A fall from grace such as Sor María's was very dangerous for the faithful, for it made "good people weep, bad people laugh, and weak people faint." Even worse, in the long run it had the potential to "scandalize nearly everyone, and make them lose faith in the virtue of good people."[126] But losing one's faith over such an incident would be a great mistake, he argued, because the human propensity for sin affects everyone equally, and frauds such as María have a way of sorting out "those who truly love God from those who do not."[127] Ultimately, then, a key lesson to be learned in this case was that God does not allow frauds to go undetected and that the Inquisition was a perfect instrument guided by His hand. As Fray Luis put it: "The truth is, that if this affair is prudently examined, we will find in it the marvel of the Holy Office, which is run by virtuous and righteous men who have no respect for this world; but consider it their principal responsibility to confront deceivers, scoffers, and hypocrites, and wolves dressed in sheep's clothing, all of whom they punish. And this punishment should not give rise to fear among good people, but rather joy and confidence, seeing that they have a good shepherd who defends them from the wolves and keeps them safe."[128]

Fray Luis died shortly after writing these two texts, and some would attribute his death to the pain María's betrayal had caused him. But while Fray Luis spent his last days on earth drawing positive lessons from this scandal, one Protestant polemicist turned the scandal into a potent weapon with which to attack the Catholic Church and highlight its demonic nature. Cipriano de Valera (1531–1602), a former Hieronymite monk from southern Spain who had turned Protestant and fled to Geneva—and was subsequently burned in effigy at an auto de fé in Seville in 1559—collected various published texts that praised María's holiness and used them as ammunition to take aim against Catholic corruption, duplicity, and hypocrisy. In 1594, a few years after news of María's fraud had become well known throughout Europe, Valera published a brief treatise in Spanish aimed at convincing his fellow countrymen that they should turn away from their horribly idolatrous Catholic faith.

The title of his brief treatise—like so many of that age—was a concise summary of his argument: "The swarm of false miracles and demonic illusions with which María de la Visitación, prioress of the convent of the Anunciada in Lisbon, fooled many people; and how she was exposed and condemned in the year 1588."[129] Valera's main argument was simple enough and very much in keeping with Protestant anti-Catholic polemic: María was no fraud at all but rather in league with the devil, for it was Satan himself who caused all of the miracles claimed by the Catholic Church.[130]

So, ironically, in a case in which blatant fraud had been exposed and in which the Catholic Church had declared the *impossible* feats claimed by a miracle-worker to be mere trickery, stripped of all supernatural or preternatural agency, Valera, the Protestant who had translated Calvin's *Institutes* into Spanish and revised the 1602 translation of the Bible by Casiodoro de la Reina, argued that such miracles were *possible* indeed and that the devil had used his powers to make the impossible happen.[131] Simply put, since it was impossible for genuine miracles to occur, all observable miracles, such as those claimed by María, had to be the work of the devil.[132]

After being sent to a convent in Abrantes, Sor María spent the remainder of her life doing penance in obscurity, apparently impressing her new sisters with her conduct and gradually having the rigors of that penance lightened, always at the request of the prioress and her fellow nuns. The last glimpse we have of María is from March 1603, when a new inquisitor general lifted the remaining penances that had been imposed on her in 1588. After this date she vanishes from view, dying in obscurity but never erased from memory.

Luisa de la Ascensión, "the Nun of Carrión": *Extreme Ascetic Bilocator*

Another mystic whose impossible feats earned her a reputation as a living saint was Sor Luisa de la Ascensión (1565–1636), a Franciscan nun who has already been mentioned in connection with Sor María de Ágreda. Much like the Nun of Lisbon, Sor Luisa came to be known simply as the Nun of Carrión due to the location of her convent of Saint Clare, which was in northern Castile, in the town of Carrión de los Condes.[133] The Nun of Lisbon and the Nun of Carrión shared many traits in common, and the fame won by both was as extreme as their falls from grace were dramatic. Both were famously effective miracle-workers and healers. Sor Luisa, however, outshone Magdalena de la Cruz when it came to the intensity of her mystical charisms. Unlike Magdalena, Luisa was not visibly stigmatized, but the bilocations she supposedly achieved were among the most extreme ever reported, and her inedia—her ability to survive without eating—was as extreme as that of María de la Visitación, the diabolical abbess of Córdoba. Curiously, as in the case of María de la Visitación, it was the claim of inedia that eventually brought ruin to the Nun of Carrión, not any of her other claims, even those of multiple far-flung bilocations.

Sor Luisa and María de Ágreda both belonged to the same branch of the Franciscan Conceptionist Poor Clares,[134] befriended Kings of Spain (Philip III and Philip IV), and were enthusiastic promoters of the doctrine of the Immaculate Conception of the Virgin Mary.[135] Both were authors, although Sor Luisa's writings were limited to mystical love poetry.[136] Both levitated, too, and gained fame for their ecstasies, visions, prophecies, and their numerous bilocations. After receiving a visit from King Philip III in 1613, Luisa remained in touch with him, and in return he showered her convent and the town of Carrión with favors. In addition to supposedly bilocating to Philip's deathbed in Madrid in 1621, she also ostensibly bilocated to Japan in 1615 to comfort a martyr; to Rome to save Pope Gregory XV from poisoning; to Assisi to venerate Saint Francis at his tomb; to a battlefield in Flanders to cheer Catholic soldiers fighting Protestants; to the Battle of White Mountain near Prague to encourage Catholic troops to a pivotal victory over Protestants;[137] and, most amazingly, to New Mexico many times, where she served as a missionary to the Jumano Indians. Some reports would even pair her up with María de Ágreda, as co-missionaries,[138] and initially, the Franciscans in New Mexico assumed that the so-called Lady in Blue mentioned by the Jumanos must have been Sor Luisa, rather than Sor María.[139] Due to her fame, it is highly likely that Luisa inspired María of Ágreda, who was thirty-seven years younger and undoubtedly familiar with her miraculous exploits, especially her bilocations.[140]

Luisa Colmenares Cabezón was born in 1565 in Madrid, which had recently been designated as the capital city of Spain by King Philip II. Her parents were Juan Colmenares and Jerónima Cabezón, both courtiers in the service of the crown. Her maternal grandfather, Félix Antonio de Cabezón, was a prominent composer and organist who had served as chamber musician for Emperor Charles V and later became chapel musician for King Philip II. Intensely pious from an early age, Luisa was sent to live with a widowed aunt in Carrión in 1582, at the age of seventeen. Gradually attracted by the contemplative life of the nuns at the Franciscan convent of Santa Clara, which she visited often, Luisa joined that community in 1584, taking the religious name of Luisa de la Ascensión.

At the convent of Santa Clara, Luisa quickly impressed everyone with her intense devotion and austerities. From the very start, Luisa displayed a penchant for eating as little as possible and doing so on the floor rather than at a table. Sometime around 1595, she stopped eating altogether—or seemed to—except for the communion wafer offered to her daily at Mass,[141] as well as morsels of heavenly food provided to her by angels.[142] In addition to fasting, Luisa scourged herself bloody every day, wore tight iron rings around her neck, along with prickly hair shirts and metal breastplates studded with sharp barbs, and slept for only a few hours each night on a wooden plank on the floor. Sometimes she would prostrate herself on the floor at doorways and ask the other nuns to step on her as they entered or left the room. In addition, she spent many hours in her cell at night stretched out on the floor, on a life-size cross, praying, and carrying that fifty-pound cross around, too, dragging it up and down the stairs on her bare knees. She also claimed that she was constantly attacked by demons who pummeled her with iron bars and chains, knocked out her teeth, and ripped out her fingernails and toenails.[143] Witnesses who would later testify to the Inquisition said that demons had thrown her down the stairs, knocked her off her choir seat, tossed her from one room to another, and bitten off pieces of her flesh. Apparently, the nuns at Santa Clara came to view her as a very useful decoy for deflecting demonic assaults on others, especially at the moment of death, when she would often be placed under the deathbeds of fellow nuns so that she would be assaulted by demons instead of the nun who was dying.[144] As one might expect, Sor Luisa became something of an expert demonologist as a result of these encounters and also a successful exorcist.[145]

As could often happen with ascetic nuns, Luisa also began to experience prolonged cataleptic ecstasies and raptures, during which she was impervious to pain, even when pricked with pins or singed by flames. Her ecstasies could occur anywhere and leave her frozen in strange awkward poses. Her levitations were slight, but, as in the case of other levitators, her body seemed to become weightless and could be blown about easily. Sometimes, she was seen levitating along with her life-size cross, giving viewers the impression that she was actually nailed to it, as if crucified.[146] Cataleptic raptures also occurred in chapel every day after she took communion, and these could be witnessed by outside visitors, some of whom traveled from faraway locations just to view her in ecstasy through the comulgatorio window.[147] Luisa also claimed to have received invisible stigmata when she was only four or five years old that caused her intense pain every Thursday and Friday, as well as other constant pains that rivaled those of many martyrs.[148]

Luisa's reputation as a miracle-working mystic and living saint grew gradually, first within the convent and, eventually, beyond its walls. By 1604, her saintliness was so well established that it led to the publication of a brief protohagiography and to the circulation of a legend that Luisa's sainthood had been predicted before birth to her parents and that she had received a special blessing in her mother's womb.[149] By this point, she was also well known for having established a popular confraternity, the Defenders of the Most Pure Conception of the Virgin, which was dedicated to promoting the doctrine of the Immaculate Conception. King Philip III himself was among the first to join, along with the rest of the royal family and many other nobles and significant figures. By 1621, this confraternity would have over 80,000 members throughout Spain and its empire, with Luisa as its undisputed leader.[150]

The most impressive proof of Luisa's widespread reputation as a living saint, by far, could be found scattered throughout the Catholic world in innumerable small objects connected to her—sacramentalia—which were highly sought after and fervently collected as divine talismans: small crosses, rosary beads, medals and cards imprinted with her image, cloth patches, and other trinkets that she had supposedly touched and blessed and which she claimed had been taken up to heaven by angels and brought back to earth loaded with divine graces.[151] Some of the crosses had her name inscribed on them, and some of the images depicted Sor Luisa trampling on a large reptilian beast resembling a serpent or dragon, an allusion to similar images of the Immaculate Conception.[152] All sorts of wondrous feats and miracles would be attributed to Luisa through such objects, and through her intercession, including innumerable healing cures, some resurrections from the dead, and the release of countless souls from purgatory.[153]

Luisa generated many of these talismans herself and was behind their distribution, ostensibly as an act of obedience to her confessors, who had ordered her to do this.[154] According to her, the divine graces conferred by her crosses and beads were a gift that came directly from God, assured by promises made to her while she was enraptured.[155] These sacred objects were in high demand. A priest at the parish church of San Miguel in Madrid boasted of a shrine he had filled with Luisa's crosses, rosary beads, medals, images, and cloths. And a duke claimed to have 2,000 crosses he had obtained from Luisa herself. Obviously, these sacramentalia had acquired a value similar to that of relics, or identical to them, for their ostensibly heavenly provenance imbued them with the power to convey indulgences and divine favors—some very specific—as outlined in the printed texts that sometimes accompanied them. One such text, collected and filed away by the Inquisition, made the following claims about rosary beads ostensibly blessed in heaven at Sor Luisa's request:

> Be advised that Our Lord has granted these beads all the indulgences and graces that every Supreme Pontiff since Saint Peter has granted to all religious orders, and to churches in Rome, Jerusalem, and Santiago in Galicia. . . .
>
> —They have the same power as an image of the Agnus Dei.
> —They have power over all dangers posed by water and fire.
> —They have power over all storms on land and sea.
> —They have power over all plagues and all illnesses.
> —They have power over all demons. . . .

Apparently, whoever composed this text knew that some Luisan objects being peddled were not genuine, for the final line of the text reads as follows: "None of the original ones of these will ever be lost because their owner, or some other person will always find them. Why this is so is a great mystery that will be revealed after her death."[156]

In 1609, at the age of forty-four, as her fame kept increasing, Luisa was elected abbess of her convent, a post she would hold until 1617, and it seemed she was on her way to rivaling or eclipsing the feats of many previous saints, including Saint Teresa of Avila. King Philip III held her in high esteem, as did Pope Gregory XV and many other luminaries of church and state. Pilgrims flocked to the convent of Santa Clara from all corners of Iberia and from other lands as well. Then, suddenly, in 1611, as a bolt out of the blue, six nuns at Santa Clara denounced her as a fraud to the inquisitor general, Bernardo Sandoval de Rojas (uncle of the Duke of Lerma, King Philip III's most powerful minister). Their charge was very specific and limited solely to her claim that all she ever consumed were the consecrated hosts she received in communion, the heavenly morsels provided by angels, and an occasional sip of water. These six nuns accused their abbess Luisa of eating in secret and swore they could prove it.[157] The convent of Santa Clara immediately became a vortex of recriminations: most of the nuns came to Luisa's defense and pleaded with their Franciscan superiors to punish the six "liars" who had denounced Luisa as a fraud.

Fearing the worst sort of implosion within the convent and anticipating nothing but disaster for the Franciscan order if the Inquisition were to get in-

volved, the provincial general of the Spanish Franciscans acted quickly, placing
Father Antonio Daza, the confessor of the Santa Clara nuns, in charge of an
immediate investigation in the hope of keeping the Inquisition at bay. Father
Daza was far from impartial, however. He not only venerated Sor Luisa but had
also begun to write a history of her life in anticipation of her eventual canonization. Not surprisingly, Father Daza ruled after a brief inquest that the accusations were false, driven by jealousy and anger. Powerful relatives of some
of the six nuns reacted to this exoneration by contacting the Inquisition, but
that tribunal declared in October 1611 that it had no jurisdiction over this
case and that all accusations against Luisa should be handled by a tribunal of
the Franciscan order.[158]

The Inquisition had been kept out of the unpleasant mess at Santa Clara
for the time being, but keeping it away would prove impossible. Accusations of
fraudulence, once made, almost always left a cloud of suspicion over the accused,
and that was certainly true in the case of Sor Luisa. Even though she had been
found innocent, and even though her popularity as a living saint kept increasing, rumors of her deceit continued to circulate in the world beyond the convent, intermixed with her eagerly collected beads and crosses. In 1614, hoping
to squelch all talk of fraud once and for all, Father Antonio de Trejo, vicar-general
of the Spanish Franciscans, took it upon himself to question Sor Luisa. Asked
to tell the truth, on pain of excommunication, Luisa denied any wrongdoing
and affirmed that "in the previous twenty years . . . her stomach could not accept any food whatsoever," adding that on those rare occasions when she had
tried to eat, she could never consume any amount of food larger than a single
hazelnut.[159] The vicar-general pronounced Sor Luisa innocent once again and
condemned all rumors of fraud as false and libelous, and this verdict seemed to
dispel the clouds of suspicion that enveloped her. Or so it seemed for the next
two decades.

Eclipsed by Luisa's ever-increasing reputation as a saint, the accusations
disappeared from view. In 1623, her saintliness more highly regarded than ever,
Luisa even received a special visit from Charles, Prince of Wales, son of the English king James I, who had come to Spain to negotiate his proposed marriage
to Infanta Maria Ana, the daughter of King Philip III. Luisa's pull was so irresistible that the Protestant heir to the throne of England had felt compelled to
go out of his way to meet her.[160] Many other elites came to see her too. After all,
she was a living saint. But in 1633, as her halo kept growing ever brighter, un-
stoppably, the Inquisition unexpectedly announced that it would investigate new

and old accusations made against her. As it turned out, unseen by the public's eye, the Inquisition had been collecting denunciations against Luisa for many years, slowly building up a very detailed case against her, which added up to 162 folios.[161]

The thoroughness and slowness with which the Inquisition approached this case would become legendary. After months and months of interminably sustained questioning of Luisa and many others—as their investigation intensified—the Inquisition decided to remove her from Santa Clara and the Franciscans and to seclude her at the Augustinian convent of the Incarnation in Valladolid. On March 28, 1635, the transfer of Luisa took place. Local authorities and people from all walks of life bid a lengthy farewell, kissing her feet, expressing their dismay. The whole town was up in arms, "resolutely committed to not losing such a gem, swearing they would risk their lives, honor, property, wives, and children" to prevent her from being taken away. After recovering from a rapture— her final one in Carrión—Sor Luisa quietly cajoled the crowd into accepting her fate. Then, in the late afternoon, as Sor Luisa was taken out of town by carriage, a mob poured out into the streets, wailing and weeping, mobbing her coach, straining to touch it, aching for a final glimpse of their holy nun as she departed. Popular piety had collided with official religion, and the result was a resounding rejection at the local level of the Inquisition's decision. As King Philip IV's *corregidor* reported: "It is astounding that even though it was announced that Sor Luisa was being taken away by order of the Inquisition, instead of running away from her and abandoning their devotion, the people actually became more fervent, creating such a mad rush to revere and proclaim her a saint that her coach crushed many people, without anyone being hurt, and the same people said that they had never heard so much applause."[162]

While Luisa was secluded at the Valladolid convent, the Inquisition pursued its investigation vigorously, questioning and requestioning Luisa repeatedly from May to August 1635 and reviewing statements found in various documents, especially a biography of Luisa written by her confessor Father Domingo de Aspe, to which Luisa herself had contributed orally. Father Aspe's biography, which was riddled with exaggerations and which Luisa claimed to have never read but nonetheless approved with her signature, as an act of obedience to Father Aspe, was the source of many of the worst suspicions the inquisitors had about her.[163] So Luisa was now meticulously examined on the meaning of many passages and words in these documents and asked to comment upon or to affirm or deny the veracity of hundreds of issues.[164] Not content solely with examining her, the inquisitors also continued to question others and to search for additional information, even after they were done with Luisa.[165] They forbid everyone from speaking about her as long as her trial lasted, demanding that the thousands of crosses, beads, and relics of Luisa that were in circulation be surrendered to church authorities or the Inquisition, under penalty of excommunication.

Nonetheless, to ban conversation on any subject is one thing; to stop it is quite another. Many devotees kept writing and talking to each other about Luisa, including King Philip IV, who exchanged letters about the progress of the Inquisition's case against the Nun of Carrión with her fellow Franciscan bilocator Sor María de Ágreda, even as late as 1646. Given the similarities between their profiles, Sor María the bilocator had a keen interest in Luisa, worried about her fate, and gently nudged her friend and confidant King Philip IV to steer the Inquisition in a favorable direction. The king, in response, assured the Nun of Ágreda that he was badgering the inquisitor general "to speed up everything and pay close attention to this matter," for he, too, desired "what was most convenient and just" for the Nun of Carrión, whose case was still in limbo ten years after her death.[166]

By all accounts, Luisa endured her quiet penitential life gracefully at the convent in Valladolid, cut off from the world, living among strangers who were initially suspicious of her. The bishop of Valladolid, a devotee of Luisa, expected her to be cleared of all charges and to be eventually canonized, so with that end in mind, he requested frequent reports on Luisa's behavior from her fellow nuns. According to these texts, which the nuns later ratified in person before the inquisitors, Luisa was an exemplary nun who never once complained about her situation or spoke about the accusations that had brought her there.[167] The bishop also tried to keep track of miracles attributed to her during this period, but according to the record he kept, they dwindled to a mere handful.[168] Her exile from Santa Clara lasted less than two years. At dawn on October 28, 1636, Luisa died of quartan fever (malaria) and was immediately buried there, at the Augustinian convent in Valladolid. Meanwhile, the Inquisition continued its investigation as if she were still alive, and the nuns who had initially denounced her kept insisting that Luisa was a fraud. Their distinguished relatives, too, continued to vilify Luisa and the convent of Santa Clara.[169] In November of 1637, in fact, Inquisitor Francisco Antonio Diaz de Cabrera recommended that Luisa be found guilty of all the charges leveled against her and that her corpse be removed from hallowed ground and burned publicly, "as punishment for her and as an example for all others."[170] Not everyone in the tribunal agreed, however, so the case dragged on.

In 1640, as the Inquisition continued its slow, plodding investigations, it received a letter containing a stunning confession from Inés Manrique, the chief ringleader of the accusing nuns, in which she admitted that all of her accusations had been false, driven by envy and resentment.[171] As soon as this confession arrived, the inquisitors interrogated the surviving nuns again, creating a new vortex of accusations, counteraccusations, confessions, and recriminations.[172] Faced with this new evidence, the Inquisition chose to reconsider all of its previous deliberations, assigning Fray Pedro de Balbás the difficult task of drafting a review, which he completed in 1643.[173] Moving at a snail's pace, the Inquisition finally issued a definitive sentence on May 23, 1648, declaring Luisa innocent of any fraudulence or wrongdoing and, at the very same time, ordering "in totum" the annihilation of all objects connected to her, including beads, crosses, images, relics, and such, as well as all books and other texts on her life and miracles and anything else linked to her, including the two biographies written by Father Antonio Daza and Father Domingo de Aspe. In addition, it prohibited any further mention of her, ever, as well as the publication of any texts about her. In essence, Luisa had been absolved but relegated to oblivion and denied any veneration as a saint. Naturally, this ambivalent ruling irked Luisa's devotees who had never lost hope in her eventual canonization. One such disgruntled defender of her holiness wrote to the president of the Supreme Council of the Inquisition: "With this sentence, you have left the said Sor Luisa with a worse reputation than she already had while she was being imprisoned and processed. . . . This sentence brands her as a fraud and a schemer . . . and the notary who informed me of it said the sentence was only slightly less awful than ordering Luisa to be burned in effigy."[174] Such complaints fell on deaf ears, however. On October 12, 1648, after five months of sifting through all sorts of appeals, the Inquisition let it be known that it stood firmly behind its previous sentence: every physical object connected to Sor Luisa and every word written about her had to vanish from the earth, forever.[175] All in all, it had taken the Inquisition fifteen years to reach a final verdict on the Nun of Carrión, during twelve of which she was already dead and buried. In 1550, as a small token of mercy, the Inquisition finally allowed Sor Luisa's corpse to be moved from Valladolid to the convent of Santa Clara in Carrión, under strict orders forbidding any veneration of it whatsoever.

In an impossible situation, ambivalence, caution, restraint, and some measure of doubt had trumped faith.

9. Protestants, Deviltry, and the Impossible

One Evening when we were in the Chamber where Margaret Rule
then lay, in her late Affliction, we observed her to be, by an Invisible Force,
lifted up from the Bed whereon she lay . . . while yet neither her Feet,
nor any other part of her Body rested either on the Bed, or any other support,
but were also by the same force, lifted up from all that was under her,
and all this for a considerable while . . . and it was as much as
several of us could do, with all our strength, to pull her down.

When it came to impossible feats in the early modern era, the devil was always involved in some way, as in the Protestant exorcism described above, which took place in 1693 in Puritan Boston.[1] The devil was omnipresent then, not only because Catholics and Protestants constantly demonized one another but also because both camps believed it possible for Satan and his minions to manipulate the laws of nature and achieve the seemingly impossible.[2] Curiously, Catholics and Protestants shared what historian Stuart Clark calls "the principal aim of demonological enquiry," which was precisely "establishing what was supernatural and what was not."[3]

More specifically, the basic principle of late medieval and early modern demonology shared by Catholics and Protestants was the assumption that demons were incapable of altering the laws of nature. Only God could do that, these two Christian rivals agreed. But since demons were spiritual beings, incredibly ancient and clever, they were endowed with capabilities that surpassed those of any human, such as vastly superior intelligence, strength, and speed and an intimate knowledge of the workings of nature. Consequently, demons could perform feats that seemed supernatural but were, in fact, not truly supernatural since they simply involved the manipulation of entirely natural means, much like the feats effected by proficient twenty-first-century scientists or engineers. This distinction was subtle yet significant: it meant that the amazing feats performed by demons on earth were not "supernatural," that is, above or beyond the natural, but rather "preternatural," or simply besides the natural yet still within it (L. *praeter*), "suspended between the mundane and the miraculous," as a historian of science has aptly put it.[4] Catholics and Protestants agreed that the astounding, seemingly impossible feats of demons were not really miracles, although they could often be indistinguishable from the real thing. So, curiously, while they rejected the possibility of divine miracles, Protestants continued to believe that the devil could perform "impossible" feats that might easily be mistaken for miracles wrought by God.

These criteria, seemingly unquestionable, led early modern demonologists— Protestant as well as Catholic—to intensely scrutinize all claims of impossible feats, hoping to discern whether they were divine or demonic in origin. It was a messy enterprise, however, due to a lack of consensus on how much demons could ultimately achieve and due also to the disturbing fact that they could create illusions that could easily fool anyone. To make discernment even more difficult, experts believed that one could also have nondemonic illusions or encounter totally natural events that could easily be mistakenly attributed to demons. Catholic and Protestant demonologists alike puzzled over such conundrums, not in some abstract theological realm but in full engagement with real-world concerns and events that tested the mettle of all Christians, elite or not, learned or unschooled.[5] And, of course, Catholics and Protestants eagerly turned their often contrary assessments into polemical ammunition to fire against each other, making the theory and practice of discerning the demonic "contested, in flux, and essential."[6]

Polemics and issues of causation aside, the surprising fact is that Protestants and Catholics could agree that seemingly impossible feats, such as levitation and bilocation, were indeed possible and did, in fact, occur. This point of agreement between Catholics and Protestants is one of the oddest wrinkles in early modern history, and one of the most significant too, because it reveals a continuity—a shared mentality—that rubs awkwardly against all the other discontinuities and core disagreements between these two competing branches of Western Christianity. Even more significant, this agreement also runs against the grain of the era's increasing skepticism and of the new worldview created by the rise of rationalism and modern empirical science.

Oddly, then, although Protestants denied the possibility of divinely ordained supernatural miracles such as levitation and bilocation, they continued to believe that such seemingly impossible feats were indeed possible and were in fact the work of the devil and his preternatural powers, either through his mastery of the laws of nature or through his craftiness, which allowed him to easily fool humans, much like an extremely clever illusionist. What the Calvinist Cipriano de Valera had to say about the Nun of Lisbon's miracles also applied to all Catholic miracles: "They have no foundation in the Word of God, but rather in dreams, false miracles . . . and in illusions of the devil, who feigns being Christ's equal."[7] Catholic miracles were "true indeed," he added, "but only of the sort that are worked by Satan in order to fool humans."[8] Valera summed up the paradox in Protestant thinking succinctly: Catholic miracles were simultaneously "false" insofar as they were performed by the devil rather than God, but they were also very "real," insofar as they actually took place, either through very convincing illusions or through the bending of the laws of nature.

Demonizing one's enemies or placing them in league with Satan was nothing new. Neither was the inclination to entwine the natural, preternatural, and supernatural. That braiding was one of the chief characteristics of the transition to modernity, which was no clean, straight, steep ascent to empiricism and pure reason. Demonizing could be metaphorical at times, certainly, but even in such instances, the imagery employed reified deeply held beliefs that affirmed the reality of the devil and of his preternatural powers. Valera's argument was not new but merely an echo of beliefs passed on to him by the great Protestant leaders of the previous generation, most of whom, surprisingly, adopted medieval Catholic demonology virtually unchanged and wielded it as a weapon against the Catholic Church, along with the equally lethal weapon of the "cessation-of-miracles" argument. Briefly examining the beliefs of Martin Luther (1484–1546) and John Calvin (1509–1564), the most influential leaders of the two major Protestant traditions—the Lutheran and the Reformed—should provide a revealing glimpse of the core beliefs guiding Protestant metaphysical assumptions and attitudes toward the devil's role in seemingly impossible feats that trumped the laws of nature.

The Devil, Martin Luther, and John Calvin

Luther's devil had distinctly biblical features, some of which were sometimes transmuted by the spin he put on them, as he did in his commentary on Paul's letter to the Galatians, where his exegesis turns the devil into a monstrous absolutist monarch who is totally in charge of a fallen world: "It cannot be denied that . . . the devil lives and surely rules the world. And his power is such, that we are all his subjects, not just in terms of our bodies and our all things, and the bread we eat. So, all of us who are flesh are under his rulership, and he can injure children through his witches, or blind them and steal them and take their place, as I heard happened in Saxony where he drained all the milk from the breasts of five women."[9]

Despite his core principle of *scripture alone,* Martin Luther—like many of his contemporaries—ascribed many functions to the devil which are not explicitly found in the Bible.[10] Luther's devil was a *Tausendkünstler,* a prolific and very creative artist capable of thousands of tricks, each a masterpiece of evil.[11] This devil was an odd amalgam of German folklore, monastic traditions, and Christian beliefs, and Luther himself made no attempt to sort out these different strands when speaking about him. For instance, Luther once claimed the devil had kept him awake at night by throwing nuts at the ceiling.[12] "It is not a unique, unheard-of thing for the devil to bang around and haunt houses," he affirmed. "In our monastery in Wittenberg I heard him for sure. . . . The devil came and knocked three times in the storage chamber as if dragging a bushel away."[13] Similarly, the devil could cause quarrels between people or fool them into seeing or hearing the most preposterous things.[14] He could trick hunters into thinking he was a hare or show up as almost any animal[15]—especially an ape.[16] Once, Luther told of a man who was attacked by the devil in the form of a goat. The man wrestled with the beast, ripped off its horns, and watched it disappear.[17] On another occasion, Luther found a dog in his bed at the Wartburg castle and flung it out the window, convinced that it was a demon.[18]

Luther's devil could be much more than a mere prankster. He also caused sickness, either directly or through witches. Luther once complained, "I believe that my illnesses aren't natural but are sheer sorcery."[19] Yet another time, Luther argued that *all* illnesses came from Satan.[20] Sometimes, the devil manipulated the weather too: "There are many demons in the forests, water, swamps, and deserted places. . . . Others are in dense clouds and cause storms, lightning, thunder, and hail and poison the air."[21] Luther's folksy devil did worse things, too, as a fiend who haunted the landscape. "Many regions are inhabited by devils," he said, "and Prussia is full of them." Luther also claimed that a certain lake near Eisleben was "the abode of captive demons" who could cause storms.[22] Luther's devil could also drown experienced swimmers, and he once advised his congregation never to swim alone and to always bathe at home rather than in any stream, pond, lake, or river.[23]

At times, Luther came close to sounding like a Manichean or a Cathar, though he never espoused outright dualism. He summed it all up by saying: "Our Lord God sends no misfortune or evil into the world other than through the devil, from whom come all sorrow, misery, and sickness."[24] Despite the fact that all evils, including temptation, came indirectly from God through the devil, Luther argued that all evil itself was attributable to Satan. Once, when someone asked Luther whether the devil's power was commanded by God, Luther quickly replied: "Oh, no! The power he uses is not commanded. No way, no! But our Lord God doesn't stop him. . . . It's as if a great lord saw someone lighting a blaze and did nothing to prevent it, but merely looked through his fingers. This is what God does with the devil."[25] And, naturally, this nearly free rein of the devil over humankind included the miracles performed by him that the Catholic Church claimed to be of divine origin. Convinced as he was that the Catholic Church was "the seat of the Antichrist," Luther attributed all its miracle-working to the devil. And all that diabolical mischief was on the same spectrum of evildoing as witchcraft, magic, and other occult practices, which were as real to him as the devil.[26]

Luther's devil was no mere theological concept. He was a very real fiend who had to be warded off, preferably with as much crudeness as possible because Luther was convinced that the Evil One should be attacked with his own weapons. Consequently, he fought his very medieval Catholic devil with his own quirky methods, often saying the most outrageous things and boasting about them afterward. "The devil seeks me out when I am at home in bed," he said, "and I always have one or two devils waiting to pounce on me. They are smart devils. If they can't overwhelm my heart, they grab my head and plague me there, and when that proves useless, I show them my ass, for that's where they belong.[27] Taunts such as "Lick my ass" and "Eat my shit" were hurled at the devil by Luther with abandon.[28] Flatulence topped all this scatology, much like frosting on some cake from hell. Once, after farting loudly, he said: "Take this, devil! Here is a crozier for you; go to Rome and give it to your idol! [the Pope]."[29]

Pious Christians who are offended by scatological crudeness have had some trouble accepting this kind of talk, but the truth is that Luther's scatological humor cannot be easily isolated or ignored. It is deeply woven into his diabology and therefore also into his soteriology and eschatology. Sometimes, theological issues and farts are intertwined. "Almost every night when I wake up the devil is there, itching to argue with me," he boasted, pointing out that the arguing often involved his central doctrine of salvation by faith alone. "I have come to this conclusion," he added. "When the argument that the Christian is without the law and above the law doesn't help, I chase him away with a fart."[30] And whenever his conscience was troubled by particular sins, he would say: "Hey, devil, I just shit in my pants too; have you added that to your list of sins yet?"[31] Luther elaborated on this approach of his: "Tonight when I woke up the devil came, wanting to argue with me, objecting and throwing it up to me that I was a sinner. So, I said to him: Tell me something new, devil! I already know that very well; as always, I have committed many real and true sins . . . but all these sins are no longer mine, instead they've been taken by Christ. . . . If this isn't enough for you, devil, I just happened to shit and piss: wipe your mouth with that and take a big bite!"[32]

Luther's behavior toward the devil was much more than a carnivalesque gesture or coarse buffoonery.[33] It was the ultimate proof of the validity of his doctrine of salvation by faith alone and of the challenge he had issued to the Catholic Church and to the devil who held sway over it. By showing contempt for the devil on the devil's own terms, Luther hoped others could see that he had no fear of damnation and that he was claiming leadership in a cosmic struggle, along with Christ, his savior.[34] And that struggle included wrestling with Luther's devil as well as arguing that the miracles claimed by the Catholic Church and all his other enemies were truly the devil's work.[35]

John Calvin, the second-generation French Reformer who became the leading voice of the Reformed Protestant tradition and who influenced Valera most intensely, did not have as much to say as Luther did about his personal encounters with the devil or about the specific effects of diabolical power, but he nonetheless promoted the same argument against Catholic miracles as his Saxon predecessor.[36] Comparing Catholic priests to Egyptian magicians, Calvin attributed all contemporary miracles to "sheer delusions of Satan."[37] Convinced of the omnipotence of God, as well as of His providential direction of every event on earth, Calvin insisted that genuinely divine miracles had always been scarce and that on the rare occasions when God had chosen to alter the laws of nature—as recorded in the Bible—He had done so with only one end in mind: "So that we may know that what he really confers is exclusively determined by his will."[38] Such a mentality was passed on to the various sorts of Reformed Protestants who followed Calvin's lead, including Valera.[39]

Catholics argued that Protestantism could be proven wrong through its lack of miracles, and Calvin answered this charge by reinterpreting the role played by miracles in the Christian religion and by denying that there was any real substance to Catholic claims.[40] The only purpose of genuine miracles was to strengthen the authority of God's messengers, said Calvin, not to make them the focus of attention or to alter the laws of nature or the fabric of material reality.[41] Consequently, he argued that it was wrong for Catholics to demand miracles from Protestants because they were not forging some new gospel or conveying some new revelation but were instead "retaining that very Gospel whose truth all the miracles that Jesus Christ and his disciples ever wrought serve to confirm."[42] Insisting that miracles had totally ceased to occur by the end of the Apostolic Age, sometime around the year 100, Calvin declared invalid all of the miracle claims made by the Catholic Church beyond that date. Those "miracles," he argued, are not at all genuine but rather diabolical in origin: "We may also fitly remember that Satan has his miracles, which, though they are deceitful tricks rather than true powers, are such a sort as to mislead the simple-minded and untutored. . . . Idolatry has been nourished by wonderful miracles, yet these are not sufficient to sanction the superstition either of magicians or idolaters."[43]

Calvin, then, would not attribute any postapostolic miracles to God and, consequently, could only grant them to the devil. The gift of miracles was restricted to the first century of Christian history, he argued, and its only purpose was to spread the truth of the Gospel among the heathen of antiquity.[44] The miracles claimed by Catholics were therefore utterly false and demonic, and all they accomplished was to lead humanity away from the true worship of God.[45]

Calvin's denial of postbiblical miracles was the capstone of his polemic against Catholic claims about seemingly impossible phenomena, including levitation and bilocation. True religion, as he saw it—and as his followers would too—should never seek to change the laws of nature or the way the material world functions but rather to accept the world as it is: as eternally subject to God's will and as always incapable of transmitting any spiritual power in and of itself through any human being, dead or alive. Calvin's influence spread far and wide in his own day and for generations after his death. And one can hear an echo of his voice in his contemporary the Englishman John Bale, who saw the devil at work as much in Catholic ritual as in all the dark arts. The Catholic Eucharist, he said, "serveth all witches in their witchery, all sorcerers, charmers, enchanters, dreamers, soothsayers, necromancers, conjurers, cross diggers, devil-raisers, miracle-doers, dog-leeches, and bawds; for without a mass they cannot well work their feats."[46]

But how and why did the devil come to play such a significant role in early modern European mentalities? And why was it that despite all their profound theological differences, Protestants and Catholics shared an extremely similar set of beliefs concerning the absolute reality of preternatural diabolical feats? And why was Protestant diabology so closely dependent on medieval Catholic diabology? Why is such continuity embedded amid so many discontinuities? Many of the pieces of this puzzle can be found in the late Middle Ages, and some can be found much further back in time, too, even before the birth of Christianity. The devil is very old, after all, and that makes a hell of a difference. As a Spanish proverb has it, "Más sabe el diablo por viejo que por diablo." Loosely translated into plain English, "It's not the fact that he's the devil that makes the devil so smart; it's simply the fact that he's so old."

Religion, Superstition, Magic, and the Devil

All things diabolical in early modern Europe were inseparably connected to a belief system in which pre-Christian and Christian elements were thoroughly mixed and thus linked to an extrabiblical matrix. This was especially true in the case of miracles, the diabolical, and the many behaviors that could be deemed "magic" and "superstition." A murky haze hung over the devil, especially, clouding all beliefs and rites associated with him, and this can be attributed to two factors. First, since the Christian devil was an amalgam of ancient Jewish, Near Eastern, and European folklore and since much of the demonological lore was extrabiblical, clear definitions did not begin to emerge until the fifteenth century. And even then there was much disagreement on the part of experts. Second, much the same could be said about all of popular piety, many elements of which were also an alloy of Christian and pre-Christian elements, into which the devil was inextricably woven. By the sixteenth century, elites such as Erasmus of Rotterdam and Guillaume Briçonnet were inveighing against this intermingling, calling for a return to a "pure" Christianity stripped bare of all traces of superstition and heathenism. The Protestant goal of restoring the Church to ancient pristine forms through *scripture alone* flowed naturally from this late medieval Reformist thrust: *ad fontes* (returning to the original sources of the faith) and *sola scriptura* (adhering strictly to the Bible alone) were but two sides of the same coin. All Reformers committed to this goal faced a daunting challenge, for many of these rites and beliefs that came to be associated with the devil—and to be rejected by the Church as magic and superstition—were deeply embedded in

European culture and most often concerned mundane vicissitudes of life (health, fertility, love, finances) rather than spiritual issues. Discerning the difference between what was truly divine or neutral or demonic or between religion and certain ancient problem-solving strategies deemed magical or superstitious was never simple and required some hermeneutic, that is, some set of guidelines for interpreting phenomena according to specific preconceived assumptions. The same was true when it came to determining where the line should be drawn between magic and religion, or magic and superstition, or religion and superstition. To further complicate matters, sorcery and witchcraft were also added to the mix in the fifteenth century and linked to the devil, adding yet more distinctions to make and more areas of aberrant piety to eradicate. By the dawn of the sixteenth century, the devil came to be linked to three very murky categories of deviancy: magic, superstition, and witchcraft. Yet the exact meaning of these concepts and terms remained a contentious issue into the eve of the Reformation era, even as campaigns were mounted to combat magic, superstition, witchcraft, and the devil. And, not surprisingly, with the advent of the Protestant Reformation disagreements became even more intense and numerous.

In the sixteenth century, binary oppositions such as magic/religion, superstition/religion, and demonic/heavenly gained intensity, and their meaning grew ever more unstable and divisive. Ironically, though they could not agree on how to combat the devil, magic, and superstition, Catholics and Protestants alike agreed that such combat was always necessary. So it came to pass that as Catholics launched campaigns against the devil, magic, superstition, and witchcraft, Protestants waged a similar war but at the very same time railed constantly against much of Catholic ritual and piety as demonic, magical, and superstitious. Though the primary sources themselves sometimes blur distinctions when dealing with practices condemned by both Catholics and Protestants—making it difficult for us to deal with them in isolation from one another—they can nonetheless be subdivided into four categories, in each of which the devil played some part.

The first and most nebulous deviant category is that of superstition. It is an ancient Latin term, which pagan Romans employed in reference to any beliefs or practices which *falsely* and *foolishly* placed faith in supernatural causes. Ever since the early days of the Christian religion, pagan rites and beliefs that were condemned as superstitions were linked to the devil. Saint Augustine, the most revered and oft cited of the Latin Church fathers, bequeathed this thinking to the West. In the fifth century, Pope Leo I would affirm it, proposing that the devil gained control of humanity through superstitions.[47] Adopting such a teaching meant, in practical terms, that whether one was aware of it or not, all rites and observances not sanctioned by the Church put one in league with the devil—or worse, were de facto acts of demonic veneration. In the thirteenth century, Thomas Aquinas would define superstition as "a vice contrary to religion by excess, not because it offers more to the divine worship than true religion, but because it offers divine worship either to beings who should not be worshiped, or to God in an improper way."[48]

The second category, closely related to superstition, was that of magic, or of the occult, or of the hidden arts. For Augustine, who died in 430 as the Vandals were ravaging the Roman Empire, magic was all about incantations, signs, divinations, auguries, amulets, cures, and "consultations and arrangements about signs and leagues with devils." It was all demonically induced delusion and "fornication of the soul."[49] For Pope Leo I, merely one generation after Augustine, the practice of magic was the ultimate outcome of superstition and of commerce with demons. In the seventh century, Isidore of Seville would further codify magic, providing medieval theologians with a long, detailed list of the various types of illicit practices "supported by demons."[50] This conception of magic as an inherently demonic and pragmatic attempt to effect changes on the world or to gain knowledge of its workings or foreknowledge of future events would become Church doctrine and guide its policies toward European folk beliefs in the Middle Ages.

By the thirteenth century, the Church's duty to combat magic as something dangerous was widely recognized by elite authorities. Thomas Aquinas summed it up as follows: "Man has not been entrusted with power over the demons, to employ them to whatsoever purpose he will; on the contrary, it is appointed that he should wage war against the demons. Hence in no way is it lawful for man to make use of the demons' help by compacts either tacit or express."[51]

Under this rubric of magic fell a long list of practices, many of them inseparable from folk customs or even from folk medicine. In the late Middle Ages, the gap between theology and popular piety widened in the minds of learned elites, leading many to think that a great deal of popular piety was in the hands of the devil. By the sixteenth century, Erasmus would be complaining that all pilgrimages and the veneration of relics were not much different from the magical arts. And the Protestant Reformers would take one step beyond Erasmus and dismiss nearly all Catholic ritual as devilish magic.

The third category, narrower than superstition and magic, was that of sorcery or witchcraft. Although the ultimate definition of witchcraft was not fully developed until the fifteenth century, it had ancient antecedents, older than Christianity itself. In essence, what ended up being known as witchcraft was an amalgam of three disparate traditions: first, the ancient, pre-Christian practice of malevolent magic, *maleficium* (literally, "evilmaking" or "evildoing"), which the Romans had turned into a punishable crime; second, various European folk traditions; and third, learned Christian views on the demonic origins of all unsanctioned rites. This amalgam proved to be a lethal mix for anyone suspected of the crime of maleficium from the fifteenth to the eighteenth century, for the Age of Devils was, above all, the age of witches and of their persecution. Catholics and Protestants persecuted maleficium with equal ferocity. Estimates for the number of men, women, and children prosecuted as witches for the crime of maleficium during this period range from between 100,000 and 200,000. Few scholars doubt the existence of sorcerers or of the practice of maleficium—that is, of the attempted manipulation of natural, preternatural, and supernatural forces by sorcerers who sought to inflict harm on others. What is still a matter of much debate is whether those accused and convicted of witchcraft engaged in the very specific diabolical acts that the various churches of the Reformation era came to link with maleficium, a question we shall explore later in this chapter.

The fourth category, which was distinct from superstition, magic, and witchcraft but not altogether divorced from them—was the narrowest of all: direct personal encounters with the devil. This level of deviance was the ultimate possible outcome of all three demonically centered activities, and it involved two distinct sets of phenomena. The first set had to do with all apparitions of the devil and of the exchanges between demons and humans, which led to all sorts of abominable consequences, such as the signing of pacts with the devil. Most such engagements led to charges of witchcraft, but the pact alone was a heinous enough crime. Catholics and Protestants alike waged war on these encounters and all diabolical pacts.

The second set of phenomena concerned demonic possessions, or cases of human beings whose bodies had been completely taken over by demons, and also with obsession, or cases of individuals whose minds and wills underwent severe and very focused temptations by demons. Possession was an ancient phenomenon, and a biblical one too, for the Gospel narratives are full of accounts of demon-possessed people who were freed of this affliction by Jesus and his apostles. Catholics and Lutherans believed in possession but had radically different approaches to dealing with it; the Reformed were divided on its possibility and on the ways of handling it.

In addition to confronting these four categories of diabolically inclined misbehavior—superstition, magic, witchcraft, and direct encounters with the devil—church elites also had to contend with two "sciences" that had an aura of respectability and enjoyed the support of powerful patrons: astrology and alchemy.[52] Churchmen of all denominations were prone to tie both of these sciences to the devil, too, but found it hard to prove that connection. Some practitioners of astrology and alchemy were also physicians who dabbled in the other occult and magical arts. One of these polymaths, Heinrich Cornelius Agrippa von Nettesheim (1486–1535), author of *Three Books of Occult Philosophy*, was a complex thinker who prospered and eluded persecution in his own day but would probably have fallen victim to the war against the devil if he had lived a generation or two later.[53] In this nebulous borderland between ancient sciences and the occult arts lie not just the furthest reaches of the devil as imagined by any inquisition or church court but also the lowly origins of modern empirical science.

Established authorities—both Catholic and Protestant—dealt with each of these four demonically linked aberrant behaviors in various ways, according to time and place, but tolerance was never an option. The contours of persecution were determined by the perceived aberrances themselves, as well as by local circumstances, so let us examine each of the four categories of deviance, one by one.

Superstition

For Catholics, any rite or practice unsanctioned by the church that aimed at gaining supernatural favors could be deemed superstitious. Protestant churches followed this guideline too but added many of the rites of the Catholic Church to their list of superstitions. The two confessions shared a narrower understanding of superstition firmly limited by two distinguishing traits: passivity and ignorance. This most simple realm of superstition, more mundane than any other, consisted of all attitudes, behaviors, and devotions that were passively and ignorantly accepted and unquestioningly engaged in. This kind of superstition required no special knowledge or training, other than that provided by mere exposure to one's culture.

Among Catholics, the campaign against this kind of mundane superstition had begun in the late Middle Ages, but it was conducted at a learned level, by elite reformists, rather than at the parish level. Intellectuals such as Jean Gerson (1363–1429), chancellor of the University of Paris, could decry the many superstitions that existed in his day but lacked the means to put an end to them. "There are many things introduced under the appearance of religion among simple Christians," he said, "which it would have been more holy to have omitted."[54] He thus brought the critique of superstition inside the church, so to speak, calling attention to offenses within it. Others, in particular Erasmus of Rotterdam, Jacques Lefèvre d'Étaples, and Guillaume Briçonnet, followed suit, further developing this internal scrutiny along humanist lines and pushing for an ad fontes housecleaning that would bring the church back to its pristine first-century state.[55]

All Protestants agreed that the Roman Catholic Church was thoroughly corrupted by superstition from top to bottom, and much of their war on superstition consisted of their rejection of Catholic piety. Luther retained much more medieval folk religion than any other major Reformers—especially when it came to all things diabolical—but nonetheless rejected much of Catholic ritual as useless works righteousness, especially those rites, for example, that gave the impression of guaranteeing a predictable outcome: pilgrimages, the blessing of objects, the use of holy water, the veneration of saints and their relics, and the wearing of holy medals. In the Reformed camp, superstition was a much greater concern than the delusion of works righteousness, and the attack on Catholic piety was more severe. As Reformed Protestants saw it, the central miracle of the Catholic faith—transubstantiation—was no more than "hocus-pocus," literally, the mumbled "hoc est corpus meum" of eucharistic consecration transformed into a magical incantation every bit as mystifying as "abracadabra."[56] In response to Protestantism, the Catholic Church reaffirmed the absolute legitimacy of its rituals and, at the very same time, initiated a campaign to fight superstition on two fronts: internally, in regard to valid rituals, and externally, in regard to practices it deemed un-Christian. Relying on scholastic theology, the Catholic Church took a more methodical approach to the issue of superstition, subdividing it into four different types: the *improper worship* of the true God, *idolatry, divination,* and *vain observances,* which include magic and the occult arts. Concerning the one area of Catholic piety where reformists had detected the most intense superstition, the directives of Trent were clear but not very specific: "In the invocation of saints, the veneration of relics, and the sacred use of images," ordered the council, "every superstition shall be removed."[57] In a similar vein, but with more detailed instructions, Trent demanded that all of the superstitious abuses that surrounded the Mass be eliminated.[58] These reforms were quickly implemented in some places, such as Spain, and more gradually in others, such as Germany. By the early 1600s, much of what had offended purists such as Erasmus was still in place, but the more blatant superstitions surrounding Catholic worship had in many places been greatly reduced.

Magic

Beyond the "vain observances" and mundane superstitions that Catholics tried to eliminate and beyond the Protestant attack on Catholic "idolatry" and "superstition," reformers of both traditions aimed to eradicate a worse sort of commerce with the devil, that of the magical arts. Unlike superstition, magic was not mired in ignorance or passivity: it required some skill, knowledge, and expertise, and it concerned rites other than those sanctioned by the Catholic Church. At this level, the devil became much more actively involved, even if no evildoing was involved, and no explicit pacts were made with him, and no one was aware of his presence and participation. Though the line between magic and witchcraft could be blurry at times, distinctions were nonetheless made by experts, and a certain range of practices that did not necessarily involve *explicit* pacts with demons or inflicting harm on others came to be identified as magic. This magic tended to fall into two categories: divination and the manufacture and use of special substances.

Divination was the attempt to discern what is hidden, especially in the future, and it was practiced in a vast number of ways through specialists of various sorts, many of whom claimed special supernatural gifts. These different paths to hidden knowledge were of ancient origin and derived from the assumption that all of nature was encoded with secrets and that these secrets could be accessed with the right skill or supernatural gift. And there were as many kinds of divination as there were substances and objects to plumb for secrets. These sundry ways of accessing what was hidden from view were classified by the learned according to the means through which the knowledge was sought, with the Greek suffix *manteía* (prophecy or determining the will of the gods)—"mancy" in English—appended to the root word. Even a partial list can seem too long in our day and age, despite the continued presence of some of these arts in our midst:

aeromancy, by means of the air and winds

chiromancy, or palmistry, by the lines of the hand

capnomancy, by the ascent or motion of smoke

catroptomancy, by mirrors

alomancy, by salt

cartomancy, by playing cards

anthropomancy, by inspection of human viscera

belomancy, by the shuffling of arrows

geomancy, by points, lines, or figures traced on the ground

hydromancy, by water

necromancy, by the evocation of the dead

oneiromancy, by the interpretation of dreams

pyromancy, by fire[59]

Catholics and Protestants condemned all such practices as diabolical and tried to wipe them out. Yet the illicit divining survived, as court records prove. The desire to interpret nature as a messenger was so strong, and the struggle against it so complex, that sometimes the oddest twists in divination could be deemed orthodox and completely free of demonic ties. This was also true among Protestants, especially German Lutherans, who developed a penchant for reading unusual natural events as divine messages and turned wonder-decoding into one of their most distinctive traits. These "wonders" (*Wunder*) that conveyed divine messages were as numerous and varied as all freakish events: astronomical anomalies, strange lights in the sky, cloud formations, unusual weather, earthquakes, beached whales, deformed animals, and shockingly abnormal human births. Such aberrant *Wunder* never predicted the future but did convey warnings about worse things to come, and most often they also revealed that something was awfully wrong with the moral order of the locale where they occurred. Wonder-decoding fell into a category of its own among Protestants, as distinct from that of active magic and of belief in miracles.[60]

Nothing points as convincingly to this distinction as another misdeed attacked along with active divination: the manufacture and use of potions, elixirs, philters, and other magical substances. This was an ancient practice that had continued to evolve in Christian Europe alongside advances in medicine and science.[61] Concoctions prepared by experts were as innumerable as human needs in a world where empirical science had not yet fully developed. These confections stretched on an ethical spectrum from good to evil. Many of these substances were remedies for illness prepared by healers who had learned their craft from some elder and would pass it on to apprentices. This kind of pharmaceutical practice could be found at various levels, from the illiterate village wise woman to learned scholars who practiced what they called natural magic.[62] All such work was considered good, or "white," magic.[63] Then there were concoctions not intended for healing but rather for producing certain effects: to make someone fall in love or out of love; to ensnare, enchant, and entrance; and to induce altered states of mind. Among these, love philters were most common. These potions were not necessarily considered injurious, though those on the receiving end might not have always agreed. At the other extreme of the spectrum were malevolent substances, the sole purpose of which was to inflict harm or suffering, even death. These were regarded as maleficium, or literally, "evildoing," and were feared and outlawed. Belief in the effectiveness of these substances ran deep at all levels of society, and we have plenty of evidence that such substances were concocted and used.

That was not all. Early modern Europeans also relied on unsanctioned non-Christian rituals to effect good, indifferent, or malevolent changes in the world around them. Incantations, hexes, and spells were verbal magic, which could be put to all sorts of uses, both good and evil. They could be spoken, sung, or written. A vast array of practices fell into this category, from spells cast in elaborate arcane rituals to incantations written on parchment and worn as an amulet around the neck. And then there were objects transformed by spells into talismans, which were believed to have some magical agency, usually to ward off evil. But harm could also be caused through hexed objects. The most common form of maleficium, which required no expertise, was that of the evil eye, and the most ubiquitous talismans were those that ostensibly deflected it. Christianity had never fully extinguished this ancient belief that simply involved looking at someone and wishing them harm or misfortune, usually out of envy, spite, or resentment.

All these beliefs and practices existed in a nebulous gray area throughout the Middle Ages, up until the fifteenth century. White magic, though formally condemned as diabolical, was not always easily identifiable and thus thrived in the face of illness and disease. The natural magic of the learned could blend with herbal therapies, alchemy, and medicine, and some forms of it would eventually evolve into empirical science. Both neutral and black magic were outlawed and persecuted in many places but survived through apathy, secrecy, and dissimulation and sometimes through the complicity of clerics who could easily be deemed as superstitious as their flocks. By the late fifteenth century, however, as the church became much less tolerant of such practices, all magic would turn pitch black and explicitly demonic in its eyes, and all who performed it would be regarded as diabolical sorcerers who had to be hunted down and exterminated. And as this great change was taking place, along came the Protestant Reformation and, in its wake, the age of the great witch hunts.[64]

Sorcery

Witchcraft, also known as sorcery, was related to magic, but in the late Middle Ages it acquired a distinct character. Though both magic and sorcery aimed to produce effects beyond natural human powers, and though both were officially believed to do so through the agency of the devil, what came to be known as sorcery, or witchcraft, was identified as a distinct form of maleficium, or evilmaking, that required very intimate relations with the devil. The performance of maleficium itself had been condemned since time immemorial, long before it acquired the characteristics ascribed to it in the late medieval period. And the punishment had always been extreme. The key biblical text that guided all medieval and early modern thinking on how best to deal with sorcery was Exodus 22:18, which read in Latin: "Maleficos non patieris vivere." Most Protestant translations of this passage tended to agree, even after the original Hebrew was consulted: "Those who practice sorcery should not be allowed to live." But Luther's German Bible and Calvin's Geneva Bible employed the feminine noun for the sorcery worker: *Zauberinnen* and *sorciere*. The King James English Bible chose a neutral noun: "Thou shalt not suffer a *witch* to live" (emphasis added).

The witch hunts that unfolded in the late sixteenth century had long and ancient roots. A key development in the ninth century, which would become part of canon law, was the legal definition of sorcery as apostasy and heresy, a spiritual crime punishable by the church. Maleficium was now an offense that straddled church and state: as the act of inflicting harm on others, it was a civil crime; as apostasy and heresy, it was a spiritual crime. This influential legal text, known as the *Canon Episcopi,* pronounced "the pernicious art of sorcery and magic" to be "invented by the devil" and called on all bishops to chase away from the church all followers of such "wickedness."[65] The most immediate origins of early modern witch-hunting can be traced to 1320, when Pope John XXII authorized the prosecution of sorcerers by the Inquisition on the grounds that all sorcery was demonic, and its practitioners were therefore to be dealt with as heretics.

In his day, maleficium had already begun to assume certain diabolical characteristics, which he described in his 1326 decretal *Super illius specula*. "Grievingly we observe . . . that many who are Christians in name only . . . sacrifice to demons, adore them, make images, rings, mirrors, phials, or other things for magic purposes, and bind themselves to demons. They ask and receive responses from them and to fulfill their most depraved lusts ask them for aid. Binding themselves to the most shameful slavery for the most shameful of things, they ally themselves with death and make a pact with hell. By their means a most pestilential disease . . . grievously infests the flock of Christ throughout the world."[66]

The prosecution of sorcerers was sporadic from 1320 on, but as these trials evolved, the notion that sorcerers belonged to an organized satanic cult increased in popularity, especially among the learned. Popular preachers such as Bernardino of Siena (1380–1440) helped to spread this belief among the laity, too, and sparked many a local persecution along the way. In his own native Siena, in 1427, he called on everyone to turn in these evildoers: "Whether within the city or outside its walls, accuse . . . every witch, every wizard, every sorcerer or sorceress, or worker of charms and spells."[67] In 1435–1437, as Bernardino and others preached against witches and as tribunals prosecuted them, Johann Nider wrote his *Formicarius,* the first detailed description of a witch cult. Shortly thereafter, systematic witch hunts began to take place in the Alpine regions of Switzerland, Savoy, and Dauphiné.

Nider's *Formicarius* could only be distributed in manuscript form and would not be printed until 1479. By then, however, it had stiff competition from about thirty other manuals, including one written in 1489, *On Witches,* by Ulrich Molitor, which enjoyed a robust printing history during those early days of book publishing. The most important of these newer books, by far, was the *Malleus Maleficarum* (Hammer of witches), attributed to Heinrich Kramer (1430–1505) and Jacob Sprenger (1436–1495), two Dominican inquisitors who had prosecuted witches and were commissioned directly by Pope Innocent VIII in 1484 to write the definitive book on witchcraft.[68] Experts now attribute the writing to Kramer (also known by his Latin humanist name Institoris), who had been chased out of Innsbruck by the local authorities for being too extreme in his witch-hunting and felt compelled to defend his approach. First published in 1486, the *Malleus* was reprinted fourteen times between 1487 and 1520 and sixteen times between 1574 and 1669, and it would teach many an inquisitor and magistrate how to identify, prosecute, and convict witches.

Its very title—which employed the feminine noun *maleficarum,* or "of sorceresses"—reflected one of the main propositions of the *Malleus:* that most of those involved in satanic maleficium were women and that "all witchcraft came from carnal lust." Assuming that females had a much greater sex drive than males, as was commonly believed in their day, the authors of the *Malleus* argued that the devil could easily lure women to serve him through their "insatiable" lust. It also claimed that having sex with the devil was the first step to becoming a witch and that those who became witches of the highest rank had to make a pact with the devil, abjure their Christian faith, and seal their devotion to Satan with an oath of homage and a total, eternal surrender of their bodies and souls. Sometimes these pacts were made in private but more often in solemn ceremonies attended by other witches. The diabolical power granted to witches by this pact was immense:

> These sorceresses . . . stir up hailstorms and harmful winds with lightning; . . .
> cause sterility in humans and domestic animals; . . . offer to demons or kill
> the babies whom they do not devour. . . . They also know how to make horses
> go crazy under their riders; how to move from place to place through the air,
> either in body or imagination; how to change the attitudes of judges and
> governmental authorities so that they cannot harm them; how to bring
> about silence for themselves and others during torture . . . how to reveal hid-
> den things and to foretell certain future events; . . . how to turn human
> minds to irregular love or hatred; on many occasions, how to kill someone
> they wish to with lightning, . . . how to take away the force of procreation or
> the ability to copulate; how to kill infants in the mother's womb with only
> a touch on the outside; also on occasion how to affect humans and domes-
> tic animals with sorcery or inflict death upon them by sight alone without
> touch; and how to dedicate their own infants to demons.[69]

This was just the tip of the proverbial iceberg. Any mundane misfortune could be blamed on witches, along with unspeakable crimes such as infanticide and cannibalism. The factual claims of the *Malleus* concerning the power of witches made it relatively easy to try anyone for witchcraft, which is why so many experts on the history of witchcraft have assigned it such significance. From a legal standpoint—and the *Malleus* was above all a manual for identifying and trying witches in court—this seemingly limitless evil power meant that nearly every misfortune could be attributed to witches and that the evidence needed to convict someone for the crime of maleficium tended to be purely circumstantial. Moreover, since curses were commonly used in premodern culture and since belief in their efficacy ran deep, the potential was always high for any quarrel in which curses had been uttered to turn into a witchcraft accusation. A strained relationship between individuals or any prior verbal threats or insults were all that was needed to establish a likely motive for maleficium, and the misfortune itself—be it a lightning strike, or an illness, or an obsessive attraction to someone, or the death of a child or a cow—could easily serve as the ultimate proof.

Almost any accusation could therefore be taken seriously, and in many cases, proving that someone was a witch could be relatively easy, especially if torture was employed to extract a confession from the accused. Even worse, the *Malleus* set up the witch as supernaturally endowed to lie, resist torture, and plant doubts in the minds of judges and civil officials, making it all that much easier for the courts to disregard all denials made by the accused and whatever misgivings might arise from a lack of solid evidence.

The publishing success of the *Malleus* and its influence should not be mistaken for wholesale acceptance. Even before it was written, disagreements about witchcraft were common, so as soon as the *Malleus* was published, there were dissenting voices. In fact, one of the purposes of the book was to refute skeptics who denied the existence of witchcraft and stood in the way of its prosecution. That the University of Cologne ultimately refused to approve the book—although the authors claimed to have its endorsement—points to the lack of agreement that surrounded witch-hunting. While some found the *Malleus* too extreme, others found it lacking, especially regarding its coverage of the widely held belief that witches worshiped the devil together in wild ceremonies known as sabbats, which were an inversion of Christian ritual and in which they danced naked, kissed the devil's rear end, engaged in sexual orgies, sacrificed children, ate human flesh, and flew through the air. In exchange they received preternatural powers that allowed them to change shapes and perform other wonders and were also assigned an "imp" or "familiar spirit," a demonic sidekick who obeyed their commands.

Disagreements over details such as these were never fully resolved, and scholars in our own day disagree on how to best interpret that fact. But experts do tend to agree on two points: first, that the *Malleus* figured prominently in all debates over witchcraft for a long time, as well as in many a witch hunt, and

second, that differences of opinion among those who believed in witchcraft seldom gave them pause or prevented witch-hunting.

Exterminating the Devil's Minions

The Protestant Reformation did not cause massive witch hunts, at least not initially. In fact, the advent of Protestantism slowed down the persecution of
witches, as Catholics focused their energies on combating Protestants, and the
Protestants, in turn, concentrated on surviving and on expanding their reach.
However, while the publication of witchcraft texts ceased between 1520 and
1570 and the number of persecutions declined, witch-hunting never stopped altogether. Strange as it may seem, one of the few things that Catholics and
Protestants agreed on was the need to exterminate witchcraft.

On a purely civil secular level, in 1532 the Holy Roman Empire adopted
a unified criminal code, known as the *Constitutio Criminalis Carolina,* in which
the practice of maleficium through sorcery was designated a capital crime, punishable by death. The *Carolina* also called for the extraction of confessions
through torture. Meanwhile, the nascent Protestant churches began to prosecute witches. In Zurich, under Bullinger's leadership, witchcraft trials began
in 1533. Luther, who claimed to have constant confrontations with the devil,
praised the execution of four witches in Wittenberg in 1541. Calvin, likewise,
called for the "extirpation" of all witches in 1545 when plague broke out in
Geneva, and in that year alone forty-three witch trials were held in that relatively small city, resulting in twenty-nine executions.[70]

These Protestant outbursts against witchcraft were a sign of things to
come. By the late 1550s, as the era of orthodoxy, confessionalization, and social disciplining dawned, persecutions intensified. In Geneva around 90 people
were tried for witchcraft between 1556 and 1570, and 30 of these were executed.
The year 1571 was the worst of all in Geneva, when over 100 witchcraft trials
were held, and 36 of them led to executions. Similarly, Lutherans in Wiesensteig—
with a population of only 5,000—convicted and killed 63 witches in 1563 and
then broadcast the news in a pamphlet titled *The True and Horrifying Death of
Sixty-Three Witches.*[71] For the next century or so, from the 1560s on, the situation only worsened. In the Swiss canton of Neuchâtel, for instance, 360 witchcraft trials would be held between 1588 and 1677, with 243 people executed, a
conviction rate of almost 68 percent. In the nearby canton of Luzern, between

1550 and 1675, the conviction rate was nearly 50 percent, with 505 trials and 254 executions.[72]

Catholics turned on witches with equal ferocity. In one of the most intense witch hunts of the age, in the lands of the archbishop-elector of Trier, 368 people were burned as witches in twenty-two villages in the six years between 1587 and 1593; two of those villages were left with only one female inhabitant apiece. The Trier witch hunt did not target women, however. Its net caught men, women, and children from all classes, even from the governing elite, including burgomasters, councilors and judges, canons of various collegiate churches, and even parish priests. Of those executed, 108 came from the aristocracy. Among the elite victims was Dietrich Flade, chief judge of the electoral court and rector of the university, who had opposed the witch hunt and spoken out against the use of torture. The death of Flade, whose leniency had aroused suspicion, gave even greater license to the witch-hunters.[73]

Trier was only a prelude to greater horrors on both sides of the confessional divide. In Lutheran Quedlinburg, for instance, about 133 witches were executed in a single day in 1589. At Catholic Fulda, about 200 were burned between 1603 and 1605. Hunts of this sort, as well as many smaller ones, were repeated many times over, in many places throughout Europe, even into the eighteenth century. Experts estimate that 100,000 to 200,000 witch trials were conducted between the 1560s and 1680s and that these led to somewhere around 50,000 to 60,000 executions. The most notorious persecutions were those chain-reaction hunts in which the accused were asked to name their fellow witches under torture. In these massive hunts, accusations would spiral out of control, and stereotypes would break down. Instead of focusing on women—as the *Malleus* and other treatises advised—these hunts would drag in anyone who was accused. Such persecutions peaked in the 1620s and 1630s, mostly within the Holy Roman Empire, in areas where local courts had no higher authority to restrain them. The highest tolls were at the Catholic prince-bishoprics of Bamberg (1623–1633), where 600 witches were killed, and Würzburg (1626–1631), where among the 900 killed were a nephew of the bishop, a score of priests, and several small children. In Bonn, which endured a similar persecution at that same time, an eyewitness described the havoc in detail:

> There must be half the city implicated: for already professors, law-students, pastors, canons, vicars, and monks have here been arrested and burned. His Princely Grace the Elector-Archbishop of Cologne has seventy wards who

are to become pastors, one of whom, eminent as a musician, was yesterday arrested; two others were sought for, but have fled. The Chancellor and his wife and the Private Secretary's wife are already executed. . . . A canon of the cathedral, named Rotenhahn, I saw beheaded and burned. Children of three or four years have devils for their paramours. Students and boys of noble birth, of nine, ten, eleven, twelve, thirteen, fourteen years have been burned. In fine, things are in such a pitiful state that one does not know with what people one may talk and associate.[74]

How the process could reach such ferocity was described in heartbreaking detail by Johannes Junius, mayor of the city of Bamberg, who managed to smuggle out a letter to his daughter while he awaited execution in 1628: "Innocent I have come into prison, innocent have I been tortured, innocent must I die. For whosoever comes into the witch prison must become a witch or be tortured until he invents something out of his head. . . . And so I made my confession . . . but it was all a lie."[75]

Trier, Bamberg, Bonn, and Würzburg were extreme cases. And so was Germany as a whole, which racked up about 25,000 executions—by both Catholics and Protestants—half of the total for all of Europe. Exact statistics are difficult to calculate, and experts can disagree on the numbers, but it seems clear that there was a great unevenness in the number of trials held in different regions and also in their execution rates. At the low end of the spectrum, according to Wolfgang Behringer's calculations, the regions with the least intense witch hunts were Ireland, Portugal, Iceland, Croatia, and Lithuania. At the high end, the areas most deeply scarred by witch-hunting were Germany (especially in the south and west), the south of France, Switzerland, Poland, Belgium/Luxembourg, Italy, Britain, and Denmark. Execution rates varied immensely too. Spain and its notorious Inquisition, for instance, not only had relatively few witch trials but also a low execution rate of single-digit percentages. In contrast, some German, French, and Swiss areas killed around 90 percent of those tried for witchcraft.[76] The disparities can be as surprising as they are revealing: Scotland, which had only one-quarter as many people as England, killed over three times more witches than its southern neighbor and, according to Julian Goodare, had one of "the most severe witch hunts in Protestant Europe," with an extremely high rate of executions per capita.[77] In contrast, in other areas such as England witch persecution was steady and prolonged, but it involved relatively low numbers year after year, save for an intense spike in the 1640s and 1650s during the civil war and the era of the Puritan Commonwealth.[78] More or less is also true of eastern Europe. Many trials in areas with fewer trials tended to be generated from below, by neighbors, and to focus on specific individuals and their alleged acts of maleficium rather than on the wholesale extermination of anti-Christian demon-worshiping misfits whose perversions fit the profiles outlined in learned witchcraft manuals. For instance, in Finland about 1,500 to 2,000 witch accusations during this period involved maleficium but made no mention of the Sabbat or of pacts with demons. In these areas, the fiercest persecutions were those carried out by local authorities who could not be easily reined in by any higher power. Finally, the most salient statistical disparity of all throughout Europe is that, overall, about 75 percent of those executed as witches were women. But in Finland the majority were men.[79]

Flying witches, male and female, eventually disappeared from Christian skies due to rising skepticism. Nowadays, they emerge once a year at the end of October, mostly as harmless props, mere caricatures of old hags, but they only do so in nations that observe a secular sanitized version of the old feast of All Hallows' Eve, better known as Halloween. The devil who supposedly made their flights possible has largely vanished from that festival, but during the transition to modernity, he was all too real. Even pioneering skeptics who opposed witch hunts, such as Johann Weyer (1515–1588), who argued that most witches were poor, deluded old women who should not be persecuted, never let go of the conviction that the devil was very real indeed and that he was largely responsible for the mayhem of the witch craze. "This sly old fox," he said about the devil, "needs no one's help, being abundantly capable on his own of mocking men, blinding them mentally and physically, torturing them with unnatural maladies, striking them with ulcers, and disturbing the air in many ways." Fooling people into believing that their misfortunes were caused by witches, rather than by him, was one of his favorite tricks. After all, Weyer warned: "It is the principal aim of that blood-thirsty scoundrel to promote strife and devise slaughter."[80]

By the late seventeenth century, flying witches had begun to disappear, but one could still find "experts" such as Joseph Glanvill (1636–1680), a member of the Royal Society who published a massive tome in which he argued for the reality of witchcraft and provided scores of accounts of individuals affected by their demonic power. His *Saducismus triumphatus* (1681) compared those who refused to believe in witchcraft with the Sadducees of the New Testament who refused to believe in spirits (fig. 37).[81]

Figure 37. Frontispiece to Joseph Glanvill's Protestant exposé on the many ways in which the devil could work wonders and deceive the faithful.

Figure 38. Detail of the butler in Glanvill's account who flew with assistance from the devil.

Reprinted numerous times, Glanvill's text contained two accounts of demonic levitations. One account involved a bewitched butler who was "carried in the air to and fro" over the heads of several men who had tried unsuccessfully to hold him down, with several of them "still running under him to prevent his receiving hurt if he should fall." Fortunately, when the butler suddenly plummeted to the ground, those men were able to catch him in their arms (fig. 38).[82] The other account involved a young boy who "passed in the air over a garden wall, and was carried so above ground more than thirty yards" and on another occasion was also seen by nine people inside his house "strangely hanging above the ground; his hands being flat against a great beam in the top of the room, and all his body two or three foot from ground" for "a quarter of an hour" (fig. 39). Young Richard Brown claimed that his flights and hoverings had

Figure 39. Detail of the boy in Glanvill's account who hovered near the ceiling and could not be restrained or pulled down.

been caused by a neighbor, Jane Brooks, who was a witch. Brooks was tried and executed in March 1658.[83] Images of both stories were prominently displayed on the title page of several editions. Glanvill's fiercest opponent in the public sphere was John Webster (1610–1682), a physician and skeptical rationalist. Their intense debate was a last great gasp of sorts, as skepticism increased and witch persecutions gradually dwindled.[84]

Across the Atlantic Ocean in New England, Increase Mather (1639–1723), a Puritan minister, theologian, and president of Harvard College, continued to believe in witches' flight. "It is not usual for Devils to be permitted to come and violently carry away persons through the Air, several Miles from their Habitations," he said, adding: "Nevertheless, this was done in Sweedland about Twenty

Years ago, by means of a cursed Knot of Witches There."[85] Mather also believed that God could grant permission to the devil to "change himself into what Form or Figure he pleaseth." In essence, Mather's devil was still identical to Luther's Tausendkünstler: "He has perfect skill in Opticks and can therefore cause that to be visible to one, which is not so to another; and things also to appear far otherwise than they are." Moreover, it was "most certain," he warned, "that bewitched Persons are many times really possessed with evil Spirits."[86]

Ironically, such intense belief in the devil's power to deceive probably played a large role in bringing the witch hunts to an end, out of fear that perhaps too many of those accused of witchcraft could be innocent folk falsely accused by witnesses in the grip of the devil's wiles. That was Mather's ultimate argument. If one cannot trust the devil, especially because he loves mayhem and finds it so easy to deceive humans, then why trust the testimony of those who denounce witches? But for anyone to argue as Mather did, and for such arguments to be convincing, there had to be many shared assumptions about the devil. And those shared assumptions—whether put to the test in a court of law or on the streets—had to be part of "an intellectually sophisticated society" in which, as Sarah Ferber has pointed out, "educated people exposed to sceptical views" could still believe in phenomena that modern science would deem impossible.[87] Grappling with that intellectual sophistication is our next crucial step.

10. The Devil Himself

Faced with a case of supposed possession a sixteenth-century observer had the choice of three possible kinds of explanation: first, a supernatural cause, a devil; second, disease; third, fraud. . . . Now, as an historian (which is what I am trying to be), the first possibility, a devil, must be excluded. Whatever their personal beliefs, historians should not ask their readers to accept supernatural phenomena. I think this is a sound principle and a widely accepted one.

—D. P. Walker

That the devil was considered real in the early modern world cannot be denied. One may relativize "real" by placing quotation marks around the word to suggest that, yes, the concept of the devil—rather than the devil himself—played a role in abstract theology and in the lives of early modern men and women. But they themselves would have objected to such a relativist dilution of the devil's reality, and many would have surely mocked British historian D. P. Walker, quoted above.[1]

Excluding the devil from history, as Walker advises, was not as viable an option in early modern times as it is today, and assuming that the devil cannot be real would not have been considered a "sound principle" either. Back then way too many people, whether learned or ignorant, Protestant or Catholic, thought that the devil was very real and that he knew how to make the impossible possible. Levitation and bilocation were definitely in his bag of tricks, much like the rabbits and pigeons usually hidden in the top hats of twentieth-century stage magicians.

The devil might not have been deemed omnipotent since only God can have total control of creation, but it was widely believed that demons could still perform impossible marvels. A hell of a lot of them. After all, hadn't Jesus called the devil the "ruler of this world"?[2]

Ignoring the distinction between *preternatural* and *supernatural,* as Walker does, would have been considered unsound, and highly risky too. After all, demonology became a science in the sixteenth century, and that science was all about fine distinctions of this sort. In fact, mistakenly calling the devil a supernatural cause rather than a preternatural one might have caused many an early modern student to fail certain kinds of exams, at many schools. A fine distinction, yes, but immensely significant, especially for those who dealt with two groups of dangerous people who levitated and bilocated and were considered agents of chaos: demoniacs and witches. The early modern world was full of both of these people, or at least full of learned men who were convinced that such people did exist and posed a threat to society. And dealing with them required making fine distinctions.

Let us deal with the demoniacs first. While relatively fewer in number than witches, the demonically possessed were considered more frightening in various ways and their impossible feats more disturbing and more revealing of the devil's preternatural powers. In addition, cases of demonic possessions could become lightning rods for polemics on both sides of the Catholic-Protestant divide.

Demoniacs and the Impossible

A relatively little-known fact in the history of Western civilization is that as witch hunts waxed and waned in early modern Europe, printers throughout the continent cranked out title after title on demonology and witchcraft for nearly three centuries, the vast majority of which were authored by immensely learned men. And this is such a notable characteristic of the transition to modernity—alongside that of the birth of modern empirical science—that one could argue that the creation of demonology is a parallel scientific revolution, unjustly and imprudently ignored.[3]

Though ancient and medieval Christians had dealt with the devil head-on since the Apostolic Age, up until the fifteenth century all codification of this subject was somewhat haphazard, with no definitive systematic treatment of the devil and his work on earth through his diabolical and human minions. And it was not until the sixteenth century that demonology per se—the systematic study of all things diabolical—became a thriving branch of theology and of jurisprudence. Statistics speak for themselves. While at the start of the sixteenth century all the existing books dedicated solely to demonology could easily be contained within a single bookshelf, by 1799 a large room might not be enough, for by then, over 1,000 titles on subjects related to the devil and sorcery had been published. Demonology had come into its own as a bona fide science, alongside the works of Copernicus and Galileo.[4]

We shall return to these books in the second half of this chapter. For now, let us turn our attention to the demoniacs, those unlucky human beings ostensibly possessed by the devil who could make the subject of all those texts seem very, very real.

Belief in demonic possession was widespread among Catholics and Protestants. Why this is so is difficult to determine from the perspective of social history and to some extent that of intellectual history. Its cause is ultimately impossible to gauge, as is the veracity of possession events, for all religious belief encompasses doubt, and belief does not necessarily cancel out a whole range of behaviors, from the cold, insincere, calculated manipulation of others to the manifestation of bizarre, seemingly unexplainable phenomena. In the early modern age, then, the devil could be used to serve certain purposes, but he could also become manifest in many other ways, some predictable and others not at all.

Christian diabology is rooted in the New Testament, which is full of accounts of demonic possession and of warnings about the devil's evil power and his insatiable appetite for mayhem. It is also deeply rooted in the monastic tradition. From its inception, monasticism had been a way of life built out of dualities, its very structures and dimensions devised cosmically as an extension on earth of the struggle between God and Satan. As monasticism grew in popularity and the monks' struggles with demons became part of Christian lore, evil spirits became an ever-growing preoccupation for the church at large. By the fourth century, the Roman emperor Julian the Apostate could say of Christians: "These two things are the quintessence of their theology, to hiss at demons and make the sign of the cross on their foreheads."[5]

Throughout late antiquity and the Middle Ages, the devil was a constant presence to Christians, and accounts of personal encounters with the devil and of demonic possessions were plentiful. In the sixteenth and seventeenth centuries, as Christendom splintered and the printing press made the circulation of these testimonies much easier and widespread, such accounts multiplied exponentially. Naturally, given the differences among the various competing religious camps at that time, the devil's doings could vary in accordance with beliefs, as did the ways in which he was handled. But no matter how different his profile was in each church, there is no denying that he did show up often, and not only in theological texts and sermons.

As previously mentioned, Martin Luther provided his followers with detailed descriptions of his encounters with the devil, as well as advice on how best to deal with him. This Lutheran preoccupation with the devil gave rise to a new genre of devotional texts in the 1550s: the *Teufelsbuch,* or "devil book." Though these books were intended to call for repentance and to warn the faithful about the dangers of specific sins, they also managed to sustain the devil's prominence and to instill fear of him. Closely related to social disciplining and to the attempt to instill the Reformation ethic of "decency, diligence, gravity, modesty, orderliness, prudence, reason, self-control, sobriety, and thrift,"[6] the Lutheran devil books mirrored the Catholic cult of the saints in which each saint had his or her specialty, with specific devils being assigned mastery over certain sins. Some of these texts addressed the central Lutheran issue of faith, such as Andreas Fabricius's *Holy, Clever, and Learned Devil,* Simon Musaeus's *Melancholy Devil,* and Andreas Lange's *The Worry Devil.* Others focused on individual sins that affected everyone: the drunkenness devil, the gluttony devil, the lust devil, and so on. Some introduced devils who were highly specialized, such as Johann Ellinger's "walk-about devil who loiters on the street" and the "frivolous, voluptuous, hopping and skipping dance devil who is an intimate companion of the walk-about devil." Some devil books singled out sins that were specific to one class. Andreas Musculus's *Trousers Devil,* for instance, condemned rich young men who wore sexually suggestive garb. Cyriakus Spangenberg's *Hunt Devil* blasted away at the nobility's obsession with hunting.[7] These devil books proved to be so popular that the Catholic Church began producing their own versions, eventually publishing thirty-nine such texts.[8] The most famous devil book of all, perhaps, is the *Historia von Dr. Johann Fausten,* first published in 1587, which tells the cautionary tale of Faustus, a learned man who allowed his insatiable curiosity to get the best of him and sold his soul to the devil. While these texts portrayed the sinner as responsible for breaking God's Law, they nonetheless stressed the power of the devil and the cosmic struggle between humans and the spiritual forces of Satan and his minions. With an estimated 250,000 of these Teufelsbücher in circulation by the 1590s, the devil certainly gained much exposure thanks to the Lutheran clergy.

Among the Reformed, no leading light spoke of the devil as frequently, or on such intimate terms, as Luther. Nonetheless, the devil played a significant role in Reformed theology. Zwingli believed that the devil was very active in the world and a masterful deceiver and that he had to be actively opposed. "Ye know well what work the devil has sometimes done in many places," he said, "which if it had not been obstructed would have resulted in great deception and injury of all Christendom."[9] Zwingli also tended to demonize his opponents and to blame their errors on the devil, especially in the case of Catholics and Anabaptists. In addition, Zwingli was convinced that many of the miracles claimed by the Catholic Church were demonic in origin.

Calvin agreed with Zwingli on all these points but spoke of the devil much more often, elaborating on his many fiendish roles. Calvin's devil was a liar, a trickster, and a tempter. Above all, the devil was a "constant presence" and "the most daring, the most powerful, the most crafty, the most indefatigable, the most completely equipped" of all enemies, as well as the best armed, "with all the engines," and, to top it off, "the most expert in the science of war."[10] Fortunately, especially for the elect, this mighty enemy was constantly reined in by God: whatever he did, he could only carry out with God's permission. This meant that the devil acted much like an executioner who fulfilled sentences imposed by God, the supreme judge. As Calvin put it, the devil was the "minister" of the wrath of God.[11] Moreover, Calvin also stressed that without the gift of God's grace, human beings were not much different from devils.

Ever pragmatic, Calvin stressed that being aware of the devil's power was necessary for two reasons: first, it made the elect realize how much grace and protection they needed from God, and second, it made them grateful for being rescued from such a great, wicked power. This very providential take on the devil, so closely linked to the doctrine of election, placed all those who were not among the elect in the devil's camp. By the same token, this view of the devil also made it the responsibility of the elect to wage war against him and his human minions, especially the sorcerers. For the Reformed, then, the devil was very real and very active, constrained by God but always there to be fought against. Unlike Luther, however, none of the Reformed leaders put much stress on apparitions of the devil or personal scuffles with him. Unlike Lutherans, Calvinists also tended to remove the rite of exorcism that had long been attached to the sacrament of baptism. This practice became controversial and caused much division in some places, such as in Saxony, when the Crypto-Calvinist chancellor Krell introduced this change in ritual. Given the Reformed influence on England, the devil found in the Anglican Church had Reformed features, but others, too, marked him as distinctly English, unmistakably ambivalent, and as given to puritan restraint as to popish excess.

Among Catholics, all medieval diabolism remained in place, both among monastics and layfolk. But, as the devil's presence was intensified by the ever-growing number of Protestant heretics, so was the church's vigilance and its response to all things demonic. Among monastics, the devil seemed to become ever more active and more aggressive, especially as the mystical streak deepened in response to Protestantism. As previously detailed several times, in convents and monasteries all over Catholic Europe and even in the New World, monks and nuns who claimed extraordinary spiritual experiences were subjected to rigorous questioning and often processed by the Inquisition. And the monastics themselves grew ever more conscious of the devil and his infinite capacity for deception. For those mystics and would-be mystics who crossed over to the spiritual dimension, especially women, becoming a demonologist was essential.

A case in point is Teresa of Avila (fig. 40), who mentioned the devil regularly in her works and described her encounters with demons as if she were discussing the pots and pans in her convent's kitchen.[12] While many of these passages refer to demonic temptation, the number that deal with demonic apparitions is also high. Sometimes the devil appeared in "physical form" and also in "formless" visions. Once, for instance, she claimed she saw two demons wrap themselves around the throat of a priest who was living in a state of mortal sin. On another occasion at a funeral, she saw the corpse being mauled by demons. Sometimes the demons attacked her. "One night," she said, "I thought they were choking me."[13] Teresa was not alone, or that unusual. By the mid-sixteenth century, convents suddenly seemed full of devils and of nuns like Teresa, who resisted them, and of nuns who did not (fig. 41).

Teresa herself was subjected to painfully meticulous scrutiny, and her confessors tried to convince her that all of her raptures and visions—including those in which she saw Jesus Christ—were straight from the devil. At one point, she was even ordered to respond to her visions of Jesus with obscene gestures. And she also came close to being exorcised of the demons that her superiors suspected had taken control of her body and mind. Cases of nuns who were easily deceived by the devil and of nuns who were possessed by him began to multiply rapidly in the 1550s and 1560s, as did Inquisition trials and exorcisms. One

Figure 40. Medieval demonology reified: a baroque depiction of Saint Dominic under demonic attack during a levitating ecstasy.

such case involving John of the Cross, who was called upon to deal with a possessed nun, was typical: "The exorcisms are accompanied by terrible convulsions in the poor girl: she furiously insults Friar John, foams at the mouth, screams, thrashes about in a frenzy on the floor, and even tries to attack the Friar and his companions.... The young exorcist holds a cross before her...."

Figure 41. Saint Teresa under attack from demons during prayer and penitential scourging.

The demoniac throws the cross to the ground; but the friar orders her to take it up and kiss, and she obeys, while bellowing."[14]

Exorcisms could turn into titanic struggles that took weeks or months to complete, some of which became public spectacles, with huge audiences. In most cases, the devil—or devils—would eventually be vanquished. The Catholic Church had well-established rituals to deal with demoniacs, and they involved the use of both verbal and physical components: adjurations, prayers, commands, questions—all in the name of Christ—along with the use of crosses, images, consecrated hosts, and holy water. Distinctions were also made between various degrees of demonic influence: infestation (when devils congregate in a certain location), obsession (when devils assail someone constantly), and possession (when devils take over someone's body and mind).

In the sixteenth century, this rite had yet to be standardized, so there were local as well as personal variations, some of which came to be viewed as corrupt and too reliant on superstition and magic. In the 1530s Pedro Ciruelo had already warned that the devil himself had corrupted the rite and that many priests employed "gross expressions as well as superstitious formulas" that were mixed with "holy and pious words."[15] To do away with such abuses, the rite of exorcism would be standardized in the *Rituale Romanum,* the definitive liturgical compendium issued by Pope Paul V in 1614. This new rite, which replaced all others, prescribed set firm guidelines concerning the identification of genuine possessions and their treatment.[16]

By 1614, as possession cases continued to proliferate, this codification was more than a reform: it was an affirmation of the power and authority of the rites, sacraments, and sacramentals of the Catholic Church. In other words, by 1614, exorcisms had become one of the strongest proofs the Catholic Church had to offer of its authenticity and its superiority to all Protestant churches. Moreover, exorcism acquired a polemical dimension because possessions were not limited to convents and monasteries, or even to Catholics. As in the case of witchcraft, demonic possession crossed religious boundaries. And some of the most salient differences between the religion of Catholics and Protestants stood in sharpest contrast when it came to possession, for while Catholics had an elaborate rite that was physically grounded in the use of images, sacraments, and the sacramentals of holy water and oil, Protestants employed prayer alone and the reading of Scripture. These differences applied to all phenomena involving the devil.

As possessions increased among laypeople, Catholics found a distinct advantage in their rite of exorcism, especially in areas where religious allegiance was contested. Successful exorcisms became part of the Catholic polemical arsenal, not just on the local level, or in monolithically Catholic places such as Italy,[17] but throughout Europe, thanks to the printing press. Among those who capitalized on the polemical dimension of exorcism, one of the earliest—and one of the most impressive—was the Jesuit Peter Canisius (1521–1597), whose successful exorcisms were credited with effecting many conversions back to Catholicism. His exorcism in 1570 of the young noblewoman Anna von Bernhausen was among the most dramatic and the most publicly acclaimed.[18]

In France, especially, the polemical use of exorcism acquired an unparalleled intensity.[19] Among the most celebrated, or infamous, is the case of Nicole Obry in 1566, which came to be known as the Miracle of Laon. The demoniac in this case was a married adolescent, about fifteen or sixteen years old, who at first was exorcized by both Huguenots and Catholics. While the Huguenots seemed to be getting nowhere with their prayers, the Catholics gained access to the demons through their rites, and the fallen angels began to speak through Obry. Not surprisingly, these demons openly expressed allegiance to Geneva and the Calvinist cause. The first six demons to be expelled from her body reportedly headed straight for Geneva, and the seventh and most powerful identified himself as Beelzebub, the Prince of the Huguenots. After a series of public debates with the bishop at the cathedral of Laon, in which the remaining demon inside Obry constantly boasted of his success among the Huguenots, the bishop finally vanquished the devil by holding a consecrated host above the girl's body.

The attention paid to this case in print was enormous. On the Catholic side, the Miracle of Laon was promoted as proof positive of the real presence of Christ in the Eucharist and of the divine power inherent in the Catholic Church. Among the Huguenots—who had been unsuccessful with these demons—Obry's possession was portrayed as a fraud, the very embodiment of Catholic superstition and deception, as well as of the diabolical nature of Catholic rituals. Some Huguenots attributed all these events to witchcraft too.[20]

The Miracle of Laon was no isolated case: dozens of such well-attended spectacles dotted the map of war-torn France. As with the case of would-be mystics, many frauds also attracted attention and caused discord. One of the most extraordinary of such exorcisms was that of Marthe Brossier in 1598–1599, who was publicly exorcized in several different towns and cities. Though Brossier was pronounced a fake in Paris, not all Catholics agreed with this verdict, and she continued to have very public demonic fits outside France for a few years and to attract much attention.[21]

Brossier was only one of many such demonically possessed exhibitionists. For the next century, the devil continued to vex religiously divided France, and every public exorcism, genuine or not, elicited polemical responses. In seventeenth-century France, over twenty nunneries were hard-hit with a series of mass possessions.[22] Three convents received a great deal of attention due to their communal possessions, in which many nuns were simultaneously possessed and in which the exorcisms became public spectacles as well as polemical causes.

The first such case involved the Ursuline convent at Aix-en-Provence in 1611, where eight nuns became demon possessed, and a priest, Louis Gaufridi, was eventually convicted of causing this demonic invasion through a pact with the devil.[23] The second and most celebrated diabolical invasion of an entire convent took place in 1632–1634, at Loudun.[24] Once again, a priest, Urbain Grandier, was found guilty of unleashing all of these devils on the nuns, and the exorcisms were held in public. The wild gyrations, lewd contortions, and obscene speech of the possessed Ursuline nuns, as well as the exhausting efforts of the exorcists, were witnessed by huge crowds, numbering up to 7,000. Nicolas Aubin, who identified himself as an eyewitness, described what he saw:

> When the exorcist gave some order to the Devil, the nuns . . . struck their chests and backs with their heads, as if they had their necks broken, and with inconceivable rapidity; they twisted their arms at the joints of the shoulder, the elbow, or the wrist, two or three times around. Lying on their stomachs, they joined the palms of their hands to the soles of their feet; their faces became so frightful one could not bear to look at them; their eyes remained open without winking. Their tongues issued suddenly from their mouths, horribly swollen, black, hard, and covered with pimples, and yet while in this state they spoke distinctly. They threw themselves back till their heads touched their feet, and walked in this position with wonderful rapidity, and for a long time. They uttered cries so horrible and so loud that nothing like it was ever heard before. They made use of expressions so indecent as to shame the most debauched of men, while their acts, both in exposing themselves and inviting lewd behavior from those present would have astonished the inmates of the lowest brothels in the country.

Levitation was part of the spectacle too. According to Aubin, the mother superior, Jean des Anges, "was carried off her feet and remained suspended in the air at the height of twenty-four inches." Then, he added, "A report of this was drawn up and sent to the Sorbonne, signed by a great number of witnesses, ecclesiastics and doctors, and . . . the Bishop of Poitiers who was also a witness. . . . Both she and other nuns lying flat, without moving foot, hand, or body, were suddenly lifted to their feet like statues. In another exorcism the Mother Superior was suspended in the air, only touching the ground with her elbow."[25]

Thousands of readers were made aware of all the bizarre events through printed accounts that expressed conflicting points of view, with Catholics touting their church's power over the demons and Huguenots denouncing the entire spectacle as a hoax.[26] But Catholics had a polemical advantage over the Huguenots. All the Huguenots could do is argue that the possessions were faked, the result of madness, or the work of the devil. Some Protestants in England found the Catholic account of Aubin (quoted above) so ludicrous that they published a verbatim translation under a misleading title, convinced that the sheer outrageousness of the claims would itself unmask the fraud: *The cheats and illusions of Romish priests and exorcists. Discover'd in the history of the devils of*

Loudun.[27] Unconvinced that the title was sufficiently polemical, the same text was reissued in 1710 as *The devil in disguise: or, Rome run a roving: Being a wonderful discovery of many monstrous cheats and impostors that the popish clergy in France designed to impose upon mankind, under the mask of singular piety and holiness, but have thereby exposed themselves to all men as the very original of villany and wickedness. A narrative of extraordinary use to all Protestants who intend to continue steadfast in the reformed religion.*

Proving fraudulence was difficult, nonetheless, especially in the face of public spectacles such as this. Moreover, to accept the possessions as genuine rather than fraudulent would be to give credit to Catholic rituals, given that so many of these exorcisms resulted in victories over the devils. Catholics, in contrast, could use the exorcisms as proof of the power of their church and their rituals.[28] Additionally, in those cases where priests were convicted of sending the devil into nuns, Catholics could also boast of the efficacy of their reforms. Few other events could prove that the Catholic Church would not tolerate bad priests better than the public execution of some of them.

Loudon was not the last spectacular possession event. A third such case arose at Louviers in 1647, where two priests were convicted of causing a diabolical infestation.[29] And one of the largest of all mass possessions, which affected at least fifty nuns, occurred forty years later in Lyons, between 1687 and 1690. By that time, however, such events attracted much less attention, and this mass possession in Lyons—though larger than the one in Loudon—received much less coverage. In the long run, however, the events at Loudun could not be easily buried. Four centuries later, during the Cold War, the devils, nuns, and exorcists of Loudun attracted unexpected attention from novelists, playwrights, musicians, and filmmakers, as well as scholars, as no possession story ever had or perhaps ever will.[30]

Moreover, while these French outbursts of mass possession may have attracted more attention than any others in print, they were only part of a larger phenomenon. We have no definitive list, but we do know that mass possession was something rarely seen before the fifteenth century, while there were at least twenty such events in the sixteenth century, in Italy, Germany, Spain, France, and the Netherlands, and twenty or more in the seventeenth century, in the very same lands and also in far-off Peru. We also know of two outbreaks in the eighteenth century: one in Italy in 1721 and one in Germany in 1750.[31] The vast majority of these cases, unlike the three French ones mentioned above, did not involve charges of witchcraft. These mass outbreaks, along with smaller ones, proved divisive, not only in Catholic–Protestant relations but also within the Catholic community itself.

In the Puritan English colony of Massachusetts, demonic possessions could be linked to witch hunts, as happened in 1693, around the time of the infamous Salem witch trials. Cotton Mather (1663–1728), son of Harvard president Increase Mather, an eminent Puritan divine who had played a role in the Salem witch hunt, became involved in the attempt to rid a possessed girl named Margaret Rule of her demons. In many respects, Mather's description of her diabolical fits reads much like the accounts from Loudun, especially regarding her contortions. "She would also be strangely distorted in her Joynts," wrote Mather, "and thrown into such exorbitant convulsions as were astonishing unto the spectators."[32] In addition, Margaret Rule also levitated, and on one occasion "her tormentors [the demons] pulled her up to the ceiling of the chamber, and held her there, before a very numerous company of spectators, who found it as much as they could all do to pull her down again."[33] Five eyewitnesses who submitted affidavits to Mather confirmed the levitations. One of these, Samuel Aves, wrote:

> I do Testifie that I have seen Margaret Rule in her Afflictions from the Invisible World, lifted up from her bed, wholly by an Invisible force, a great way toward the top of the Room where she lay. In her being so lifted she had no Assistance from any use of her own Arms or Hands or any other part of her Body, not so much as her Heels touching her Bed, or resting on any support whatsoever. And I have seen her thus lifted, when not only a strong Person hath thrown his whole weight across her to pull her down, but several other Persons have endeavored with all their might to hinder her from being so raised up; which I suppose that several others will testify as well as myself when called unto it.[34]

Two other Puritans involved in this demonic levitation had this to say:

> One Evening when we were in the Chamber where Margaret Rule then lay, in her late Affliction, we observed her to be, by an Invisible Force, lifted up from the Bed whereon she lay, so as to touch the Garret Floor [the ceiling of the room], while yet neither her Feet, nor any other part of her Body rested either on the Bed, or any other support, but were also by the same force, lifted up from all that was under her, and all this for a considerable while, we judged it several Minutes; and it was as much as several of us could do, with all our strength, to pull her down. All which happened when there

was not only we two in the Chamber, but we suppose ten or a dozen more whose Names we have forgotten.[35]

According to these affidavits, then, Margaret Rule's levitating body behaved exactly as did Saint Teresa's, which resisted all the efforts of her nuns to hold or pull her down.[36] The huge difference, of course, is that Teresa was a Catholic nun levitating in divine ecstasy, and Margaret Rule was a Protestant Calvinist demoniac being raised up in the air by devils. Robert Calef, a skeptical Boston merchant who was opposed to witch hunts and belief in demonic wonder-working, wrote to Mather after reading the levitation affidavits, pointing out that if demonic levitation were indeed possible, then the Catholic position on miracles would be proved correct. Calef wrote: "I suppose you expect I should believe it [Rule's levitation], and if so, the only advantage gained is that what has so long been controverted between Protestants and Papists, whether miracles are ceast, will hereby seem to be decided for the latter; it being, for aught I can see, if so, as true a Miracle as for Iron to swim; and the Devil can work such Miracles."[37]

Eventually, all these demonic spectacles, Catholic as well as Protestant, would cast too large a shadow over religion in general, especially in certain elite intellectual circles. By the mid-eighteenth century, the devil would come to be viewed by many Enlightenment thinkers as the worst of all superstitions and the ultimate proof of the absurdity and danger of all traditional religion. Such thinking would turn practical too, and judges would eventually begin to chase the devil out of courtrooms and to exile him from official records. Mr. Justice Powell in Hertford, England, deserves much "far-reaching" credit for this development, simply for supposedly refusing to accept testimony in 1712 from a witness who claimed to have seen accused witch Jane Wenham flying, ruling that it was inadmissible because "there is no law against flying."[38] But such elite conceptions of what was possible or impossible, no matter how cheeky or progressive, did not stop the devil from possessing thousands of people or deter exorcists and hypnotists from trying to expel them from human bodies.[39]

Witches, the Impossible, and the Science of Demonology

Interest in demonology began to blossom in the 1530s, a period of relative calm in witch-hunting, with the publication of two texts that elaborated further on questions of magic, superstition, and witchcraft. Both were written by Spanish theologians. The first of these, Martín de Castañega's *Treatise on Superstitions and Sorceries* (1529), stressed the reality of the diabolical dimension through a stark duality: "There are two churches in this world," Castañega wrote, "one Catholic, and one demonic . . . and, just as the Catholic Church has sacraments . . . the Diabolical Church has its execraments, which, in everyday speech we call superstitions and sorceries."[40] The second, *A Treatise Reproving All Superstitions and Forms of Witchcraft* (1530), enjoyed a much wider circulation and was reprinted numerous times over the next century. Its author, Pedro Ciruelo, was a biblical scholar and professor of theology at the University of Alcalá. Ciruelo's treatise, a veritable encyclopedia of unsanctioned popular piety, further reinforced the notion that witchcraft was a demonic counterreligion: "Necromancy is one of the arts taught by the devil to witches, who are men or women that have made a pact with the devil, and who, after rubbing certain ointments on their bodies and saying certain words, they fly through the sky at night and travel to far-off lands to perform their malevolent acts."[41]

Ciruelo emphasized that the devil allowed witches to traverse distances by carrying them physically through the air but that, more often than not, witches simply fell into trances, and the devil made them imagine they had gone somewhere and done all sorts of things that seemed so real that they would afterward be convinced that the illusory events had really taken place. On this point, as on so many others, Ciruelo said nothing new, but he lent his authority to many of the beliefs that became entrenched among the learned and those who carried out witch hunts.

Though skeptics who rejected such beliefs could be found here and there, the first major challenge to dominant witchcraft theories, to witches' flight, and to witch-hunting came from a Calvinist Protestant physician, Johann Weyer (1515–1588), a disciple of the learned occultist Heinrich Cornelius Agrippa, mentioned in chapter 9. Weyer was convinced of the reality of the devil and of his power to deceive human beings but refused to believe that witchcraft was a demonic counterreligion of the sort described by the *Malleus* or experts such as Ciruelo. Witches were not evil humans endowed with preternatural powers by the devil, he argued, but wretched melancholics who were mentally ill. Most of them, he affirmed, were "stupid, worn-out, unstable old women" who had been seduced by the devil's deceptions and by the constant use of hallucinogenics.[42] Consequently, he argued, to persecute witches was not only wrong but unnecessary, illegal, and illogical because their alleged crimes had not actually taken place. Weyer opposed the use of torture, especially the extraction of confessions.

The real solution to the problem of witchcraft, as he saw it, lay in treating the madness of the accused rather than in killing them.

In 1563, Weyer put forward this radically new medical interpretation in a massive book titled *De Praestigiis Daemonum* (On the deceptions of demons), which also contained medical advice on how to treat those who thought they were victims of sorcery. This work was followed in 1577 by a condensed version, *De Lamiis* (On witches). While Weyer's take on witchcraft as insanity may seem ahead of its time, his thinking was still guided by belief in demons and their power. He also thought that some sorcerers he called *magi infames*—disreputable magicians—really did knowingly deal with the devil and should be persecuted. In an appendix to *De Praestigiis* published in 1577 titled *Pseudo-monarchia Daemonum* (The false kingdom of the demons), Weyer provided a catalogue of demons, complete with the instructions that "disreputable magicians" used in their approach to them. Weyer's *Pseudomonarchia* was not a manual but an exposé of what he deemed to be the real threat to society: those occultists who conjured demons while whispering secrets to one another. So to ensure that the *Pseudomonarchia* would not be used to summon demons, Weyer left the incantations incomplete.

Weyer's books enjoyed a wide circulation but had no discernible effect on witch-hunting. Those who agreed with him tended to have little impact too. Among these, Michel de Montaigne (1533–1592), the great French statesman and essayist, was perhaps the best known. But Montaigne wrote no treatise on witchcraft, only an essay, "On Cripples" (1588), in which he echoed Weyer's sentiments, arguing that medical prescriptions were the real solution to the witchcraft problem, not executions. Two followers of Weyer who did seem to have some influence on policy were the jurist Franz Balduin and the mathematician Hermann Witekind. Balduin was opposed to witch trials on legal grounds. Witekind, who published an antipersecution treatise in 1585 under the pen name Augustin Lercheimer, reiterated Weyer's pleas for the more compassionate treatment of deluded old women who confessed their pacts with the devil. As a Calvinist, he also emphasized the supremacy of God's providence and turned this teaching into an argument against witch-hunting: all misfortunes are really nothing other than punishments inflicted by God. And the devil is clever enough, he added, to fool people—including the accused—into thinking that a witch has caused whatever harm is in question. In England, Weyer influenced Reginald Scot, who put an anti-Catholic spin on his treatise *The Discoverie of Witchcraft,* first published in 1584. Scot sought to prove, much like Weyer, that most of those prosecuted as

THE DEVIL HIMSELF 333

witches were "poor, aged, deformed, ignorant people" whose dreary lives had been twisted by illusions. Scot argued that the irrational and un-Christian practices of witch-hunters—or "witchmoongers," as he called them—stemmed from the superstitious beliefs of the Roman Catholic Church. He bemoaned the fact that while all the "popish charmes, conjurations, exorcismes, benedictions, and curses" were now totally discredited in England as "ridiculous, and of none effect," "witches, charms, and conjurors," which were just as ludicrous, were "yet thought effectuall" by his fellow Englishmen. And he also made it clear that his purpose was to ensure that "the massemoonger [papist] for his part, as the witchmoonger for his, shall both be ashamed of their professions."[43] His information on witchcraft was gleaned not just from books like Weyer's but also from his own observations in rural courts and from his personal experiences with neighbors who believed in witches and leveled accusations against them. Though banned by King James I in 1603, Scot's *Discoverie* was published abroad, in translations, and would later be reprinted numerous times in England.

Skepticism and moderation could not compete with the devil, however, at least not for another century or so. Those who called for restraint were drowned out by a loud and persistent chorus of experts who never tired of calling for more vigilance and more persecutions. After 1570, a slew of texts on witchcraft poured forth from presses everywhere, the vast majority of which upheld the traditional line. Curiously, this crusade against witchcraft may have been the most intensely ecumenical event of the Reformation era, for Lutheran, Reformed, Anglican, and Catholic pounced on the witches with equal fervor and read each other's books.

The Reformed churches led the way in this publishing boom with three books. First, in Zurich in 1571, Heinrich Bullinger wrote and published *On Witches,* which outlined the Reformed position very carefully.[44] In Geneva, only one year later, theologian Lambert Daneau came out with a dialogue, *Les Sorciers,*[45] which was quickly translated into Latin. An English translation, *A Dialogue of Witches,* was published in London in 1575, and a German one was published in 1576. Daneau, like Bullinger, called for the harshest possible prosecution of witches. In Heidelberg, where witch-hunting was banned, Thomas Erastus attacked Weyer and all lenient skeptics head-on in his *Disputation on Witches,* published in 1572 and expanded in 1578, adding yet another well-respected voice to the Reformed chorus.[46]

Among Lutherans, the Danish theologian Nils Hemmingsen published his *Admonishment to Avoid Magical Superstitions* in 1575, during an outburst of

witch-hunting in Denmark.[47] In 1583, Paul Frisius dedicated his highly anecdotal *The Devil's Hoodwink* to Landgrave George I of Hesse-Darmstadt, in support
of witch-hunting. Arguing that witches were "poor whores of the devil," Frisius
insisted that they had no power of their own. Their maleficium, which was real
enough, came straight from the devil, though they themselves and those around
them failed to grasp that. This was the "devil's hoodwink," which simultaneously
blinded the witches to their real powerlessness and cloaked the devil in invisi-
bility. Ultimately, Frisius sought to instill belief in the reality of the devil, who
worked his evil in disguise. His devil was a "master conjurer," an "arch-trickster,"
a "master magician," and an "artist with a thousand skills."[48] The witches, though
puppets of the devil, were still blameworthy and more than deserving of death,
for their intention was evil to the core, and they allowed themselves to become
diabolical instruments. All in all, thanks in large measure to Luther's own intense and complex emphasis on the power of the devil, Lutherans produced a
substantial number of texts on witchcraft and demonology, including "devil
books," that genre of literature previously mentioned.

In England and Scotland, many treatises on witchcraft were published
after 1570, including translations of continental works, but all were eclipsed by
Daemonologie, written by King James VI of Scotland in 1597, six years before
he assumed the English throne as James I.[49] The king's interest in witchcraft
stemmed largely from his wedding trip to Denmark in 1590, where he met Nils
Hemmingsen, just mentioned above, the author of *Admonishment to Avoid
Magical Superstitions.* By coincidence—or by design, as James would come to
believe—this voyage was plagued by mishaps, including some ferocious storms
at sea on the way back to England. Suspecting sorcery, a witch hunt was launched
in Copenhagen, and as expected, several of the women who were rounded up
confessed to having raised the storms with the aid of the devil. A corresponding
witch hunt in Scotland, where King James himself did some of the questioning,
yielded similar testimony. Touched in such a personal way by maleficium, inspired
by Hemmingsen's work, and angered by that of the skeptics Johann Weyer and
Reginald Scot, who needed to be refuted, King James felt compelled to warn all
his subjects as no monarch had ever done before. And in his preface, he laid all
his cards on the table in the opening sentence: "The fearefull aboundinge at
this time in this countrie, of these detestable slaves of the Devill, the Witches
or enchanters, hath moved me (beloved reader) to dispatch in post, this following treatise of mine, not in any way (as I protest) to serve for a shew of my
learning and ingine, but onely (mooved of conscience) to preasse thereby, so

farre as I can, to resolve the doubting harts of many; both that such assaultes of Sathan are most certainly practized, and that the instrumentes thereof, merits most severely to be punished."[50]

The North Berwick witch hunt of 1590, in which over 100 suspects were rounded up, including some nobility, was the first of many large-scale witch hunts in Scotland. In the same year that *Daemonologie* was published, from March to October 1597, around 400 suspected witches were brought to trial in Scotland, and about half of them were executed. Other witch hunts would follow, some of them very intense, especially those of 1628–1631, 1649, 1661–1662, and 1697–1700. The exact number of witch trials and executions is not known, due to incomplete records, but it is estimated that the total number of witches killed in Scotland during the Reformation era is about 1,500. Calvinist demonology provided the framework for these persecutions, not only in Scotland but also in New England, where a century after King James's *Daemonologie* was published, Puritan divines such as Cotton Mather—son of Increase Mather, cited in chapter 9—would still be cranking out texts such as *Wonders of the Invisible World,* which argued for the necessity of the infamous Salem witch trials in Massachusetts.[51]

Within the Catholic fold, the learned response to the witchcraft issue was just as severe. One of the most significant texts on the subject appeared in 1580: *On the Demon-Mania of Witches.*[52] Authored by French jurist and statesman Jean Bodin (1530–1596), this text was a long and detailed refutation of Johann Weyer and all other skeptics. Convinced of the reality of witches, their flights, and their pacts with the devil, as well as of the danger they posed to society, Bodin proposed that normal trial procedures concerning evidence, witnesses, testimony, and torture be relaxed or set aside in witchcraft trials since, as he saw it, the existing regulations made it hard to convict anyone, and most rumors about witches were true, anyway.[53] His aim was to streamline the trials so that courts could eliminate witches more quickly and efficiently, for, as he said, "anyone accused of being a witch ought never to be fully acquitted and set free unless the calumny of the accuser is clearer than the sun, inasmuch as the proof of such crimes is so obscure and so difficult that not one witch in a million would be accused or punished."[54] Bodin's *Démonomanie* would be reprinted numerous times, just like Weyer's *De Praestigiis,* not just in French but also in Latin, Italian, and German.

As persecutions intensified, more and more learned treatises were published. Some were written by scholars, others by witch-hunters. Peter Binsfeld, episcopal vicar of Trier, the man responsible for one of the largest of all witch hunts, published a Latin treatise in 1589 titled *Of the Confessions of Warlocks and Witches,* which was based on his own experiences with sorcerers.[55] Another expert author was Nicholas Remy, a magistrate and witch-hunter in the Duchy of Lorraine who boasted of having sentenced at least 900 sorcerers to death. Remy's *Daemonolatreiae,* published in 1595 and dedicated to his sovereign Duke Charles III, was translated into German and reprinted often.[56] It would eventually compete with the *Malleus* for the top spot on the list of definitive witch-hunting textbooks. Since it was based on experience, like Binsfeld's *Confessions,* it had an air of gritty authenticity that was lacking in more scholarly texts. Remy was well aware of this advantage: "It may be that some will accuse me of being nothing but a retailer of marvelous stories, seeing that I speak of witches raising up clouds and traveling through the air, penetrating through the narrowest openings, eating, dancing, and lying with Demons, and performing many other such prodigies and portents. But I would have them know first that it was from no scattered rumours, but from the independent and concordant testimony of many witnesses that, as I have said, I have reported these things as certain facts."[57]

Remy's *Daemonolatraie* earned its renown and longevity by being many things at once: an engaging collection of bizarre, fantastic tales; an encyclopedia of witchcraft; a proof of the devil's existence and power; and a vindication of witch-hunting.

A third experienced judge who chose to write about his personal encounters with witchcraft was Pierre de Lancre, who in 1609 conducted a witch hunt in southwestern France among the Basque people. Like Remy, de Lancre boasted of having executed many witches (around 600, he claimed) and of having gained intimate knowledge of their crimes and their infernal rituals. Sent by King Henry IV to the town of Labourd, where residents had complained of being overrun with witches, de Lancre was given full authority over witchcraft cases. The result was a chain-reaction panic, like those in many other places where a local court handled witch-hunting. After he had finished his work at Labourd, de Lancre penned three treatises based on his experiences as a witch-hunter. The most influential of these books was his first, *On the Inconstancy of Evil Angels and Demons.*[58] Filled with lurid accounts of the diabolical activities of the Basque witches, including a very detailed description of a witches' Sabbat, this sensational book was translated into German in 1630. De Lancre's two other books, which had less of an impact, expanded on what he had covered in his *Inconstancy.*[59]

The most significant Catholic text—which would eventually eclipse the *Malleus* and Remy's *Daemonolatreiae*—was written not by a prosecutor but by a learned Jesuit priest, Martin del Rio (1551–1608). Born in Antwerp of Spanish descent, this polymath who was fluent in at least nine languages and wrote on many different subjects would be called "the wonder of the century" by the Flemish humanist Justus Lipsius (1547–1606). But he is best remembered—and not too fondly—for his *Investigations into Magic,*[60] a nearly encyclopedic study of all things diabolical and occult. This work, first published in three parts in 1599–1600, was reprinted at least twenty times. And its influence would cross religious boundaries and oceans and would eventually be used in 1692 by the Puritan judges of Salem in their witch hunt. The last reprint was in 1755, at Cologne.

Del Rio dealt with witchcraft and magic as a scholar rather than a jurist, linking the subject to other disciplines such as mathematics, astrology, and alchemy. In doing so, he gave his work an edge that most others lacked, synthesizing theology and law, philosophy, and what was then the cutting edge of science. His explanation for the surge in witches experienced in the sixteenth century was that heresy leads to diabolism, magic, and witchcraft. The thesis itself was not novel, for it had already been proposed by his fellow Jesuit Juan de Maldonado (1533–1583), but his rendering of it struck a deep chord among Catholics, especially those who had to deal with the witchcraft issue. "Magic follows heresy, as plague follows famine," he said. "We have seen heresy flourishing in Belgium and we see swarms of witches laying waste the whole of the North, like locusts. The heretics are strongly opposed by the Jesuits. This book is a weapon in that war."[61]

Unlike Binsfeld, Remy, and De Lancre, who had prosecuted witches and heard their confessions, Martin del Rio obtained his information secondhand, through research. Ironically, his derivative description of the witches' Sabbat became definitive. And it doubtlessly played a role in shaping the assumptions of many a judge and prosecutor. Absurd as the rites described may seem in our day and age, they seemed all too real in their own day.

> There, on most occasions, once a foul, disgusting fire has been lit, an evil spirit
> sits on a throne as president of the assembly. His appearance is terrifying,

almost always that of a male goat or a dog. The witches come forward to worship him in different ways. Sometimes they supplicate him on bended knee; sometimes they stand with their back turned to him. They offer candles made of pitch or a child's umbilical cord and kiss him on the anal orifice as a sign of homage. Sometimes they imitate the sacrifice of the Mass (the greatest of all their crimes) . . . and similar Catholic ceremonies. After the feast, each evil spirit takes by the hand the disciple of whom he has charge, and so that they may do everything with the most absurd kind of ritual. . . . They sing very obscene songs in his [Satan's] honour. They behave ridiculously in every way . . . and then their demon-lovers copulate with them in the most repulsive fashion.[62]

Not surprisingly, experts disagree on how to interpret this text, and every approach offers its own theory, so consequently, economic, social, political, psychological, anthropological, and even biological interpretations compete for attention. Since the total number of women executed in witch hunts was three times greater than that of men, many experts have focused on issues of gender. Despite all the disagreement, however, there seems to be some consensus on four points.

First, it is clear that the increase in witch-hunting in the sixteenth and seventeenth centuries really did take place and is no exaggeration, even though the number of trials and executions was lower than previously believed.

Second, it is also clear that witch hunts were *not* all alike, due to competing ideologies and vast regional differences. For instance, we know that some witch hunts were generated from above, by elites, and others from below, by the common people. Another notable difference, now highlighted, is that between the older tradition of maleficium, or simple harming through magic, and a newer diabolical tradition—developed in the fifteenth century—that focused on the pact, demonic worship, the Sabbat, demonic sex, aerial flight, infanticide, cannibalism, shapeshifting, and the use of imps and familiars. We now know that these two traditions existed simultaneously; sometimes they mixed, but often they did not.

Third, it is becoming increasingly clear that early modern witch hunts should not be thought of as a "panic" or a "craze"—that is, as some irrational blip in Western civilization or some form of temporary insanity. After all, not every witch was burned in a chain-reaction hunt like those of Trier or Bamberg. A steadier sort of persecution was always there, bubbling up from below alongside the massive witch hunts, and many witch trials were strictly about malefi-cium and not about devil worship. In other words, in many cases witch trials were pragmatic solutions to everyday problems, approached according to an un-derstanding of the world and premises and assumptions that not only made sense but were considered rational even by the most learned savants.

Finally, a fourth point—which is seldom discussed openly—concerns the devil's absence, or, more precisely, his nonbeing. In other words, it is taken for granted that the devil is *not* and *never* has been a "real" being, much less a causal agent, and that the only acceptable way to study witchcraft is to share in that assumption. In addition, that shared assumption is most often viewed *not* as a mere conjecture, or a hypothesis, but rather as an incontestable *fact,* accepted with a strong degree of conviction that resembles that of the inquisitors who assumed that all magic involved *implicit* dealings with the devil. As a result, those who study witchcraft nowadays face the daunting task of explaining why so many early modern Europeans believed in the devil and why he was so real to so many of them. This is a thorny problem, for sure: so thorny that most scholars prefer it to remain as invisible as the devil himself.

Levitation, Transvection, and Witches on Pitchforks

Maleficium might have been the main concern everyone had with witchcraft, but there were other issues connected to it that vexed churchmen and jurists, and one of these was whether or not witches flew through the air to attend their diabolical Sabbat rituals (fig. 42). In his *Compendium Maleficarum* (1608), Cath-olic demonologist Francesco Maria Guazzo said: "Many of the followers of Luther and Melanchthon maintained that witches went to their Sabbats in imag-ination only, and that there was some diabolical illusion in the matter, alleging that their bodies had often been found lying at home in their beds and had never moved from them."[63]

Guazzo was not really addressing some new disagreement caused by Prot-estant Reformation. The issue in question—whether the devil really made witches fly or merely caused them to imagine that they flew—had been hotly contested since the early tenth century, when a legal text known as the *Canon Episcopi* decreed it a heresy to believe in the claims of "some wicked women, who have given themselves back to Satan and been seduced by the illusions and phantasms of demons" and insisted that they rode in the air "upon certain beasts with Diana, the goddess of pagans . . . and in the silence of the night traverse

Figure 42. A Calvinist representation of witches' demonic flight on brooms, from Cotton Mather's *Wonders of the Invisible World.*

great spaces of earth" (fig. 43). Addressed to bishops in the barely Christianized Frankish Empire, where "an innumerable multitude" believed this to be true, this decree commanded that "the priests in all their churches should preach with all insistence to the people that they may know this to be in every way false and that such phantasms are imposed on the minds of infidels and not by the divine but by the malignant spirit . . . Satan himself." In addition, the *Canon* also denied that the devil could really transform humans into animals, as was also commonly believed. It was all an illusion, but such illusions *really* did happen, in the spirit. "Who is so stupid and foolish as to think that all these things which are only done in spirit happen in the body?" asked the *Canon* impatiently, while affirming the reality of spiritual illusions and of the devil's power and arguing for the annihilation of witchcraft.[64]

Even though the *Canon Episcopi* was eventually included in Gratian's *Corpus Juris Canonici* in the twelfth century and thus became part of the church's canon law, its position on the flight of Satanists and the transformation of witches into animals was contested and circumvented in various ways through-

Figure 43. Albrecht Dürer, one of the greatest German Renaissance artists, reflects popular beliefs by depicting a witch riding backward on a flying goat.

out the Middle Ages by several prominent churchmen and theologians, especially as concern over witchcraft began to increase in the thirteenth century.
Some argued that the witches mentioned in the *Canon* were totally different from
those of the thirteenth century; some claimed that the *Canon* was not binding
because it had not been approved by a church council; some complained that
following the *Canon* would interfere with the extermination of witches; and
others cleverly pointed out that the *Canon* did not explicitly say that flying was
impossible.

Curiously, disagreements about witches' flight led to the development of a
cluster of positions on the issue of flying that combined elements of flight, transvection, illusion, and bilocation, an amalgam of propositions that basically defended the possibility of someone going airborne and of being in two places at
the same time. What Ulrich Molitor—a proponent of the idea that witches' flight
and the Sabbat were illusions—had to say in 1489 about such illusions was very
similar to what would be said to explain the bilocations of Luisa de Carrión
and María de Ágreda in the seventeenth century, save for the fact that Molitor
was speaking about demonic rather than divine or angelic agency. "During sleep
as well as during a waking state, devils can produce impressions so vivid that
men believe they see or act in actuality," he argued, adding that "at the precise
moment that a man is one place, nevertheless he is able to appear in spirit in
another."[65] Tellingly, Molitor's text *On Witches* contained images depicting what
the witches imagined, representing the illusion as real, including one of the first
images of witches in flight to appear in a printed book, in the original Latin
edition, depicting three witches who have been transformed into animals riding on pitchforks (fig. 44). A different version of this image was used in a later
German translation, and a totally different image appeared in another later
German translation, showing a witch on a pitchfork being borne aloft by a
demon (fig. 45).[66]

By 1489, when Molitor was writing, belief in witches' flight had gained
considerable ground but was nonetheless in flux. In addition, many demonologists had by then linked the issue of flying to that of the witches' Satanic ritual
of the Sabbat. And this intertwining was itself in flux, necessarily, as evidenced
by the fact that the magisterial and definitive book on witchcraft, the *Malleus
Maleficarum*—which codified the idea of the Sabbat—did not elaborate on
witches' flight.[67]

But belief in the Sabbat and in witches' flight had become common among
inquisitors before Molitor and the *Malleus* came along. One fifteenth-century

Figure 44. One of the earliest printed depictions of witches as changelings with animal heads, flying on a crude pitchfork, from Ulrich Molitor's *On Witches,* 1489.

Figure 45. A very early printed depiction of a devil carrying a witch aloft on a pitchfork, from Ulrich Molitor's *On Witches,* 1489.

document that predates the *Malleus*—*The Vauderie of Lyon*—painted a vivid picture of the Sabbat that included flying witches. Referring to "apostates from the faith" who "have or acquire great familiarity with demons," this text written by an anonymous inquisitor describes how "they go out at night, following after Satan—some walking, some riding on a malign spirit . . . others on a staff . . . and they go to an assembly, sometimes quite far and distant." The descriptive narrative continues, focusing on the staff "on which some of these faithless people say and declare that they are borne through the air and also over great distances" and on the "abominable ointment" derived from the body parts of slain children with which the witches anoint themselves and their staffs, "directed by the demon's craft and instruction" (fig. 46). The Sabbat itself is described as follows, ostensibly based on confessions made by the witches themselves:

> Whenever they gather at the synagogue of Satan, these perverse, blind, and wretched people worship that demon . . . as if it were a god. They do this with suppliant prostration and kneeling or genuflection with clasped and clapping hands, and by kissing the demon on some part of his body, usually his backside or posterior. . . . Also, after the aforesaid impious apostates have done homage . . . with all possible reverence, they give themselves to the demon whom they worship. And some receive that one as their master, others truly and more commonly as their god, promising under oath that they will not worship or have any other god thereafter. . . . Also, at that assembly, immediately after doing homage . . . they begin to dance to the sound of a faint horn or pipes. . . . During this dance, at a signal known to them, every man and woman lies down and mingles together in the manner of brutes or sodomites. And even the devil, as an incubus or succubus, takes whatever man or woman he wishes and has carnal knowledge of them, although brutishly.[68]

This description contains all the basic elements of the Sabbat: A nighttime assembly at a remote site; witches' flight; ointments that involve child killing; devil worship; pacts with the devil; unbridled feasting, dancing, and sex; and a renunciation of the Christian God. But belief in such assemblies or in any of their components was not univocal or universal among clerics, scholars, or the unschooled. This was one realm of belief with considerable room for disagreement on the details, as well as on the chief premises. So it is not surprising that major Protestant Reformers such as Luther, Melanchthon, Zwingli, and Calvin

Figure 46. Belief in the witches' Sabbat and in their malevolent activities also included belief in their ability to fly, depicted here—before the advent of Protestantism—by Hans Baldung Grien, one of Germany's most prominent artists.

should have appropriated different strands of medieval demonology and different positions on what sorts of impossible feats the devil could perform. What is surprising is that the strands and attitudes they adopted were still fundamentally identical to those found in Catholicism. Luther and Melanchthon's denial of physical witches' flight was based principally on what was found in the *Canon Episcopi* and in the writings of those who accepted its take on flying. For instance, despite his absolute belief in the reality of the devil and his powers, Luther had this to say in 1518, a year before he was excommunicated by the pope: "Many believe that they ride on a broom or a goat, still others on other things, to some place, where they celebrate strange rites with others, which is not only forbidden to be done, but even to be believed in . . . or that old women are transformed into cats or other beasts and wander at night, and this, too, must not be believed. . . . These are illusions of the devil, not true things."[69]

Similarly, Calvin, who thought that the devil was God's powerful avenger against the reprobate, argued as follows about the illusions with which the devil—at God's command—fools humans in a very real way:

> The devil has such dominion over the unbelievers that although a thing may not be done in actual deed, yet the illusion is such that it makes men believe that they see that which they do not see. And so it is a kind of enchantment, that is to say of devilish illusion, when a man shall be made to think that one is transformed into a wolf, or that he sees the shape of a thing that has no actual substance or truth in fact. . . . If we are faithless, it is a just reward for our quenching of the light that should have shone into us and of our turning of our backs on God. And when we will not be ruled by him, then we no longer discern between white and black, but men seem to us to be wolves, and all things are out of order, and justly so.[70]

Yet not all Calvinists felt the need to agree with Calvin. A case in point is the French Huguenot Lambert Daneau, whose *De Veneficiis* was translated into English in 1575 and had a profound influence on the development of witchcraft beliefs in England, giving credence there to the absolute physical reality of witches' flight. Stressing the significance of evidence gathered in witchcraft trials, Daneau denied that the Sabbat and witches' flight were "onely in cogitation of mind and illusion of the devil." Admitting that "this matter hath bin in great controversie," he argued on logical grounds that "the constant confessions of sorcerers themselves, along with other infinite testimonies," could not be easily dismissed, "for they confesse this when they are neare their death, and when

Figure 47. Witches flying on a goat and a crude pitchfork in the background of this 1591 illustration from Peter Binsfeld's *On the Confessions of Magicians and Witches* drive home the point that witches' flight was inseparable from all their other malevolent activities, such as the ritual murder of infants.

they are condemned and lead to execution for that offence, and when they bee tormented, when such talke can help them no longer."[71] In other words, the scenes malevolent sorcery depicted in Peter Binsfeld's *Of the Confessions of Warlocks and Witches* were most definitely accurate (fig. 47).

So when we find Francesco Guazzo, a Catholic, arguing against skeptics on the issue of witches' flight, condemning Luther and Melanchthon, what we see is not necessarily anti-Protestant polemic, for belief in witches' flight was not required of Catholics, and some of them actually preferred to agree with the *Canon Episcopi*. Consequently, Guazzo's description of the Sabbat, which is nearly identical to that of *The Vauderie of Lyon,* was aimed at some fellow Catholics as much as at Protestants he singled out for criticism. In fact, his conjuring of the names of two Protestant heresiarchs could have very well been a way of shaming fellow Catholics who refused to believe in the reality of witches' flight.

> I hold it to be very true that sometimes witches are really transported from place to place by the devil, who in the shape of a goat or some other fantastic animal carries them bodily to the Sabbat. . . . This is the general opinion of the theologians and Jurists of Italy, Spain, and Catholic Germany, while a great many others are of a like opinion. . . . But it must be known that before they go to the Sabbat they anoint themselves upon some part of their

Figure 48. A Catholic depiction of a witch flying through storm clouds on a goat, from Francesco Maria Guazzo's *Compendium Maleficarum* (1608).

bodies with an unguent made from various foul and filthy ingredients, but chiefly from murdered children; and so anointed they are carried away on a cowl-staff, or a broom, or a reed, a cleft stick or a distaff, or even a shovel, which things they ride.[72]

As Guazzo pointed out, many authorities believed that witches did indeed fly to their Sabbats (fig. 48). As he put it, "This is the *general* opinion," which he very well knew was not at all the same as a "universal opinion," much less a doctrine. Moreover, he was painfully aware of the fact that there were many who disagreed with him, both Catholic and Protestant. Moreover, he surely must have known that not every Protestant agreed with Luther, either, and that the issue of flight, levitation, or transvection of witches was an ambiguous and hotly contested issue within confessional boundaries as well as across them.

What relatively few Catholics or Protestants dared to openly challenge, however, was the necessity of wiping out witches and their *maleficium*. And much of the effort to wipe out the witches involved having no patience with ambiguities, among Protestants as much as among Catholics. So, as some historians of witchcraft have pointed out, there was a vicious cycle, or "chain of causality," established by witch-hunters, which made witches' flight necessary for them: "No flight, then no searching for a Sabbat, no Sabbat, then no questioning of 'accomplices,' and no confessions from them, and then no new charges to be made. And this is why the question of witches' flight assumed central significance."[73]

Due to the demonology they shared, Lutherans, Reformed Protestants, and Catholics could persecute witches with equal ferocity, regardless of ambiguities and disagreements surrounding belief in witches' flight. As mentioned in chapter 9, witches were burned alive in Luther's Wittenberg. They were also burned in Denmark and Württemberg, which were also Lutheran, and in Calvin's Reformed city of Geneva—including some who confessed to flying to a Sabbat and having sex with the devil—and witch trials and executions continued to be carried out by that city-state well into the seventeenth century.[74] Meanwhile, in Zurich, where witch trials would be held until 1714, Heinrich Bullinger wrote against witches and other "black arts" and argued that God was pleased by the execution of sorcerers.[75] Witchcraft literature and persecution spread across the map, along with Protestantism, to England, Scotland, Scandinavia, Transylvania, and other lands. And, naturally, Protestants everywhere continued to believe that Catholicism and witchcraft were linked due to the stranglehold the devil had on it, especially when it came to its "idolatry and superstition." As far as witches' flight was concerned, it has been argued that after 1590 Protestants began to see witches' flight as a demonic illusion rather than a physical act, but this shift in thinking did not necessarily lead to a reduction in witchcraft persecutions.[76] The persecutions wound down for various other reasons, both among Catholics and Protestants, as skepticism gained ground among educated elites and churchmen.

Belief in the demonic nature of witchcraft and in its existence underwent many permutations in the seventeenth century, as did belief in the "impossible" phenomenon of witches' flight. Some of these changes can seem startling, and one of the most startling of all is the seemingly "modern" attitude taken by Alonso de Salazar Frías, a Spanish inquisitor in the Basque region of Navarre, in Spain, where an outbreak of witchcraft caused much commotion. Salazar began his investigation of witchcraft confessions and accusations in 1611, and after reviewing what he had found, he declared in 1612 that the witch trials should be stopped immediately. What Salazar reported to the Supreme Council in Madrid stunned them: as he saw it, the witches' confessions were too full of contradictions, and he could not find any physical evidence of devil worship or maleficium.[77]

In 1614, due largely to Salazar's recommendations, the Spanish Inquisition pardoned all those who had already been condemned for witchcraft in Navarre—an incredibly rare admission of error—and established new rules that ended all witch-hunting in Spain. These rules required distinguishing between reality and illusion, proving intent to cause harm, avoiding forced confessions, and searching for natural causes of the illnesses, injuries, deaths, and disasters reported in accusations. So, even in ultra-Catholic Spain, during the height of witch persecutions that led to the slaughter of thousands of suspected witches elsewhere, a major rejection of the leading witchcraft theories occurred in an unlikely place.[78] When it came to the devil and his flying witches, then, there could be significant disagreement and surprising turns in any narrative.

The Devil in the Details

Political, social, economic, and cultural circumstances had a lot to do with every diabolical manifestation, and the phenomenon can certainly be better understood when all of these various perspectives are taken into account. But none of these approaches in isolation can explain the phenomenon in its complex totality. Luther referred to the devil as a *Tausendkünstler* (an artist with a thousand skills). If the thousand skills were to be ascribed instead to the men and women who used the devil for their own purposes, then Luther might seem even more perceptive in our own day and age. Whether the devil was really there four centuries ago, employing his thousand skills, is no easier to prove or disprove now than it was then. The fact remains that whether it was the devil himself or men and women who employed him for their own purposes, the devil played one hell of a role in the birth of modernity during the sixteenth and seventeenth centuries, that era also known as the Age of Reason.

Ironically, the devil continues to cause trouble in our own day and age for anyone who thinks of the ascent from "medieval" to "modern" or from "superstition" to "reason" as one neat upward line on a graph with no downward dips, or just a few, at most. But the devil is not at fault. The problem is not the devil's presence in the early modern age, which is undeniable, whether folk believe in him or not. The real problem is that some definitions of "modernity" cannot take him and his thousand tricks into account. Epochal transitions can be slow

Figure 49. The Enlightenment did little to stifle popular beliefs in witches and their ability to overcome gravity, as depicted here by Spanish artist Francisco Goya in one of several witchcraft paintings commissioned by a Spanish nobleman in the late 1790s.

and messy and cannot really be charted neatly, especially with single lines that always curve upward. Protestants put into motion many changes that can easily be identified as modern—changes that ushered in new mentalities and worldviews—but they also prized traits that do not lend themselves to categorizing as "modern" or "*not* modern." Simply put, Protestants did not make a clean break with the medieval past. The devil proves this conclusively, and so do some other curious Protestant beliefs and practices.

Protestants continued to believe in a world peopled by evil spirits and in divinely crafted natural signs and in impossible events such as levitation and bilocation, even if only as demonically induced illusions. Consistory and visitation records show that many Protestants did not abandon the "magical" or "superstitious" world of their forebears and had to be constantly reprimanded for their lapses.[79] Some Protestants even ascribed enchanted qualities to their leaders: some Zurichers, for instance, spread a rumor that Zwingli's heart had remained intact when Catholics burned his corpse,[80] and some Lutherans came to believe that pictures of Luther could not burn.[81] These parallel beliefs in incombustibility should not be ignored or squirreled away out of sight as endnotes. When all is said and done, they are facts to be reckoned with: details that should make everyone acknowledge that the past is as complex as the present and that the usefulness of concepts such as "modernity" or "post-modernity" can sometimes be very limited. When it comes to tracing transitions to modernity, as well as seemingly impossible feats, the devil is always in the details, ever ready to pounce on the unaware and the ill-informed, as well as on anyone who encounters Francisco Goya's witchcraft paintings[82] for the first time, one of which depicts a frightful demonic levitation. (fig. 49). Goya, after all, has been "venerated as the first modern artist,"[83] and far too often heralded as a harbinger of "modernity."[84] Surprise! Modernity, post-modernity, and post-post-modernity have many dimensions, some of which tend to be ignored or summarily dismissed, often at an undetected cost.

Epilogue

Vague Logic, Leaps of Faith

> Gravity must be caused by an agent acting constantly according
> to certain laws, but whether this agent be material or immaterial
> I have left to the consideration of my readers.
>
> —Isaac Newton

The world's first certifiable levitator was no saint, thaumaturge, witch, or demo-niac. He was Jean-François Pilâtre de Rozier (1754–1785),[1] a young physicist, chemist, and inventor, a genuine child of the Enlightenment who moved with great ease in elite scientific and social circles, despite having been dismissed by his Benedictine teachers as "scatterbrained, dissipated, keen on pleasure and unamenable to studies."[2] As much a showman as a scientist, Pilâtre would de-light his bewigged audiences by performing flashy experiments, such as inhal-ing hydrogen and setting it ablaze as he exhaled it through a glass tube, much like some fire-breathing dragon (fig. 50). He also once convinced the Academy of Science and the Royal Society of Medicine to approve a respirator he had invented by donning a rubberized suit, strapping on his contraption—a snorkel-like device connected to an air tank—and immersing himself in excrement in a Paris sewer for over half an hour, under three feet of lethal mephitic gas, and then emerging hale and hearty from the stygian depths thanks to empirical sci-ence and his ingenuity.

His first levitation took place on October 15, 1783, in the gondola of a tethered hot-air balloon crafted by brothers Joseph-Michel and Jacques-Étienne Montgolfier, which rose into the air at the Château de la Muette, near the outskirts

354

Figure 50. The world's first certifiable levitator, Jean-François Pilâtre de Rozier, blowing hydrogen into a flame.

of Paris, and allowed him to hover aloft for about four minutes, a far shorter time than some of the levitating saints of old but certainly at a much, much higher altitude than any of them had ever reached (fig. 51).[3] Climbing onto this *machine aérostatique* was riskier than any of his previous stunts since no human being had ever reached such heights and the highly flammable varnish-glazed cloth balloon was propelled upward by a burner that consumed straw and wool as fuel, but Pilâtre had been given some measure of assurance by three aeronauts who had preceded him.

Figure 51. Jean-François Pilâtre de Rozier's first balloon levitation at the Château de la Muette, October 15, 1783.

About a month earlier at the Palace of Versailles, on September 19, a lamb, a duck, and a rooster had gone up in a balloon, confined in a cage. Much like the mid-twentieth-century Russian dog Laika and the American chimp Ham, who were launched into space before any humans had ever ventured so far beyond the earth's atmosphere, these three barnyard critters were test subjects. If their blood vessels could withstand the high altitude, it was assumed, then humans might also survive such a levitation. Their flight lasted eight minutes, and they landed safely about two miles away. After being examined by Pilâtre de Rozier, who declared them to be perfectly healthy, the beasts were declared "heroes of the air" and granted a place of honor in the royal menagerie at Versailles. Their takeoff had been viewed by the ill-fated King Louis XVI and Queen Marie Antoinette, as well as by a tightly packed crowd of 120,000 to 130,000 that included "the greatest, the most illustrious, and the most knowledgeable in the nation gathered to pay a solemn homage to the sciences under the eyes of the august court that protected and encouraged them."[4] King Louis had suggested sending condemned criminals up in the balloon rather than animals but ultimately relented in the face of pressure. There were simply too many eager

elite volunteers who objected to the possibility of having any such honor bestowed on any low-born miscreants who might survive.[5]

Pilâtre de Rozier extended the range of his levitating on November 21,
1783, along with the Marquis d'Arlandes, a French military officer, when both
of them flew in an untethered hot-air balloon, traversing about five and a half
miles in twenty-five minutes and ultimately landing safely outside Paris.[6] One
eyewitness wrote: "The emotion, the surprise and the kind of anxiety caused by
a spectacle so rare and so new was carried to the point that several ladies were
taken ill."[7] Having just negotiated the Treaty of Paris with Great Britain that
ended the American Revolutionary War, Benjamin Franklin was there too, along
with "a vast concourse of gentry" and thousands of other witnesses: "We observed it lift off in the most majestic manner," wrote Franklin, adding some
details: "When it reached around 250 feet in altitude, the intrepid voyagers lowered their hats to salute the spectators. We could not help feeling a certain
[crossed out: "religious"] mixture of awe and admiration. Soon the navigators
of the skies were out of sight, but the machine, gliding on the horizon and op-
erating at its best, rose to at least 3,000 feet, where it remained visible. It crossed
the Seine just beyond the Conference toll house. Passing between the military school and the Royal Hospital of the Invalids, it was carried into full view
of all Paris."[8] Meanwhile, a French noblewoman sat in her carriage near the
Seine River observing for the first time a hot-air balloon rise into the sky, confirming what many believed: that modern science could make the impossible
possible. "Oh yes, now it's certain!" she cried with mixed emotions, reflecting
the materialist optimism of her day, as well as the many disappointments it
would engender. "One day they'll learn to keep people alive forever, but I shall
already be dead!"[9]

Whether this story about the noblewoman is apocryphal or not is immaterial. It reflects the spirit of the times. By 1783 the so-called Age of Reason
and the Enlightenment, along with advancements in empirical science and technology, had created a new way of seeing and interpreting the world, reflected as
much in the noblewoman's anguished optimism as in the ingenuity and daring
of the Montgolfier brothers and Pilâtre de Rozier. Call it a "worldview," "mind-
set," "mentality," or "social imaginary." Throw in the German *weltanschauung* or
the French *mentalité* too. Any of these terms will do. A new way of thinking had
emerged, an epistemic revolution, and in the minds and hearts of myriad philosophers, scientists, inventors, atheists, freethinkers, and even churchmen and
theologians, the supernatural had been expelled from earth, relegated to some

unseen, utterly unreachable dimension or declared an infantile and useless concept. Hence Benjamin Franklin's decision to scratch out the word "religious" in reference to his impressions about the balloon flight he witnessed. It was a very revealing slip of the pen: It was no longer proper or wise to speak of "a *religious* mixture of awe and admiration." Much better to say, he obviously thought, "a *certain* mixture of awe and admiration." The boundaries of the impossible, too, had been reconfigured. Levitation was no longer a rare supernatural or preternatural wonder. It was definitely possible, with the proper equipment, and it could be achieved naturally. But it was still dangerous, whether one was carried aloft in a cloth balloon propelled by flames or whether one was leaning over a dying saint in his wheelchair.

Tragically, the pioneering aeronaut Pilâtre de Rozier died while attempting to cross the English Channel on June 15, 1785, when his balloon caught fire at an altitude of 1,500 feet and plummeted to earth near the Pas-de-Calais. The clever and fearless Pilâtre was done in by a malfunction in one of his own inventions, a hybrid balloon with two chambers: one for heated air and another for nonheated lighter-than-air hydrogen gas. He and his companion, Pierre Romain, hold the unenviable distinction of being the first known victims of an aviation disaster.

So much for the predictable dangers of early ballooning. Now for the unpredictable. What could possibly be dangerous about levitating in a wheelchair?

Two years after Pilâtre's fatal crash, ninety-year-old Bishop Alphonsus Liguori was near death, confined to a wheelchair, struggling to cope with his loss of eyesight, hearing, and mobility. Born in 1696, Liguori was a contemporary of many of the leading figures of the Enlightenment and had outlived several of them, including Voltaire, Julien Offray de La Mettrie, David Hume, and Denis Diderot. While they and others had been busy doing away with the supernatural realm, Bishop Liguori had spent his long life tending his flock as a dedicated shepherd and establishing a new religious order, the Redemptorists. A musician, painter, poet, and prolific writer, the author of over 100 titles in theology and spirituality, some of which were best sellers, he was revered as holy by many who knew him, and he was a miracle-worker too, well known for spectacular levitations and bilocations. The fact that so many leading lights of his day had done away with God and the supernatural realm did not seem to inhibit his mysticism or its physical side effects.

One testimony relates how in 1787, near the end of his life, while being wheeled about by his caretaker, a certain Father Volpicelli, Alphonsus said that he was extremely distressed by his physical disabilities and the way they prevented him from fulfilling his obligations as a priest. Eager to cheer up the nearly deaf bishop, Father Volpicelli stooped down to speak some words of comfort directly into his ear. "Given your limitations," suggested Volpicelli, "all you need to do is to say, 'My God, I love you with all my heart!'" Immensely cheered by this, Alphonsus repeated the words and went into ecstasy instantly, springing about a palm's length into the air—about nine or ten inches—and ramming his head very hard into Volpicelli's chin. Some days later, Alphonsus asked the bruised Volpicelli to remind him again of the brief prayer he had previously recited into his ear. This time around, we are told, "Volpicelli took the precaution of not leaning down so closely" when repeating the formula, to avoid another collision. "And he was right to do so," it turned out, "for the old saint was again raised in the air the same way."[10]

So it was at the dawn of modernity. Two very different kinds of levitation coexisted in 1787, a mere twenty years after the canonization of Joseph of Cupertino: a supernatural or preternatural one rarely seen and limited to folk who surrendered their wills either to God or the devil and another purely natural, readily visible to thousands and available to anyone with access to the proper equipment. These two forms of levitation were based on conflicting and seemingly irreconcilable conceptions of reality and of what is deemed possible and impossible. They were also based on different belief systems: an older one that included God, a supernatural realm, and levitating saints and which kept shrinking and losing influence as time passed, and a newer one that had little or no need for God, the supernatural, or miracles and which kept expanding and gaining an ever-widening influence. In this newer belief system governed by empiricism and the "ironclad rules of cause and effect," God was left with little to do, if anything.[11] Or, as the biblical scholar David Strauss would put it in the nineteenth century, those ironclad deterministic rules created a "housing problem" for God.[12]

But these belief systems have never coexisted as a pure and simple dichotomy. There has always been—and one might argue there always might be—a third way of believing, a vast polymorphous variegated middle between those two extreme poles, abounding in myriad attitudes and convictions, which include open-mindedness and compromise as well as confusion, skepticism, indifference, and apathy, ever in flux according to time, place, and circumstances. Within this third way there has always been ample room for empirical science and religion to interact rather than contradict or repel one another and for creative inspiration and influences to flow in both directions. This is why Isaac Newton wrote as much about theology, spirituality, alchemy, and prophecy as he did about science, penning about 1.3 million words on biblical subjects alone, an astonishing legacy that languished in nearly total obscurity until 1936 when his nonscientific writings were auctioned.[13]

Newton was not the only scientist of his day intrigued by the interrelationship between the natural and the supernatural. Robert Boyle (1627–1691) was also very interested in what he called "Phaenomena that are, or seem to be, of a Supernatural Kind of Order" and had even begun to write a book on this subject shortly before he died.[14] In the preface to this unfinished and unpublished treatise, he said:

> I am well aware that we live in an age when men of judgment consider it their part to greet a report of supernatural phenomena with contempt and derision . . . but if the natural philosopher observes some phenomena that are above nature, there will arise the humbler consideration that there are objects beyond the grasp even of a philosopher in this life, and that some truths are not explicable by the powers of matter and motion, which truth is indeed of great importance in this age, when the Epicureans use the notions of their philosophy to reject everything that is contrary to it.[15]

Newton and Boyle are stellar examples of an attitude that was prevalent among a fairly large number of scientists. Emanuel Swedenborg (1688–1772) is a more extreme and astounding example of an Enlightenment scientist drawn to the supernatural. Swedenborg, the son of a Swedish Lutheran bishop, was an anatomist, physiologist, chemist, metallurgist, geometrician, engineer, and inventor credited with several pathfinding discoveries in neurology.[16] In the 1730s, Swedenborg was drawn to spiritual matters and set out to find theories for the relationship between matter and spirit, soul and body, the finite and the infinite, and the order and purpose of creation. In the 1740s he began having dreams and visions and writing texts based on these mystical experiences, including his magnum opus, *Arcana Celestia,* or *Heavenly Mysteries.* Swedenborg quickly gained a reputation as a mystic and prophet, and eventually, his followers established a church based on his revelations. Among those who were initially drawn to him was hyperrational philosopher Immanuel Kant, who purchased all eight volumes of the *Arcana Celestia*—which he could barely afford on his professor's salary—and pored through them with his usual obsessive intensity. Although initially impressed, Kant would soon afterward publish an anonymous refutation of Swedenborg's spiritual and psychic "nonsense."[17] Privately, Kant ridiculed himself for getting caught up in such "metaphysical daydreaming," saying that his interest in Swedenborg's stories only proved to him how far over the edge one can go with philosophical fabrications when one's thinking is completely unhindered by empirical data. Yet, even in his dismissal of the scientist-turned-mystic, Kant admitted privately that things spiritual had a tug of their own on him. "I can't help but feel a little attraction to nonsensical things of this sort, as well as to their rational underpinnings, and to suspect they have some legitimacy," he said, "despite all the absurdities involved in the stories about them, and the inconsistencies and incomprehensible concepts which rob them of their value."[18]

Within the Catholic Church were many clerics in positions of authority who were also aware of this new way of addressing the issue of the relationship between the natural and the supernatural and of the negative effect that advances in science were having on religion. One of the responses of the Catholic Church to this changing intellectual climate—as shall be soon discussed—was the establishment of very strict scientific guidelines for the verification of miracles.[19] These guidelines were a clear indication that the miracle-rich Catholic Church was painfully aware of the need to keep up with changes in the wider world. Ultimately, as an institution based on truth claims, it simply could not afford to bury its head in the sand. And the same was true of most other churches in Western Europe. Readjusting perspectives became an absolute necessity. After all, as has been observed, if it is true that "scientific and religious ideas always come braided together," it is also true that they "influence and shape each other to a degree that has gone unnoticed for several reasons, including the fact that until recently cultural elites and other commentators have held simplistic, reified views about science and religion and have often understood them as implacable enemies."[20]

This vast expanse of specific beliefs, opinions, and uncertainties that existed and still exists alongside the religious and scientific belief systems is not to be mistaken for unbelief, for belief of one sort or another is always inescapable for anyone who is not an omniscient being. This welter of perspectives, objective and subjective, was the result of an epistemic revolution, a seismic rift in thinking, a paradigm shift in belief, which has been interpreted in various ways. Brad Gregory has referred to it as "hyperpluralism," and Charles Taylor has called it "the great disembedding," both of them identifying the Protestant Reformation as its efficient cause.[21] Ethan Shagan has argued that it is a "transformation of belief" which can be credited with having "propelled Western thought into modernity" independently of Protestantism.[22]

This third way of believing can rightfully be called a belief system, untidy, fuzzy, and mutable as it can be. The word that comes to mind when dealing with this vast jumble is bricolage, because ever since the dawn of modernity it has been a realm of belief that mixes a diverse range of available ideas, possibilities, mentalities, and attitudes and whatever configuration those mixtures take. That configuration can always vary from individual to individual and institution to institution, and it is always susceptible to change too. This way of believing, which Shagan identifies as "modern belief" or "sovereign belief," creates a framework for credulity but leaves a huge space for private judgment and every individual's perception of what could or should be believed. In other words, specific beliefs are malleable, even interchangeable, in this modern way of believing, but its chief assumptions are relatively solid and stable and anchored in private judgment.[23]

Ultimately, this means that "every era is credulous, but they are credulous in different ways," which is why modern-day unbelief is, in fact, a form of belief, and why phenomena such as levitation end up being dismissed as impossible in modern and postmodern materialistic culture.[24] Every age and culture has its own unquestionable beliefs, and our own tends to prize the rationality and superiority of unbelief as one of its core beliefs, especially in regard to denying the existence of a supernatural dimension. Such unquestionable pervasive beliefs—Troelstch's "social facts"—which William Blake called "mind-forged manacles" in 1794 and Max Weber spoke of as the "steel-hard casing" or an "iron cage" a century later, are difficult to detect and acknowledge, for they frame our thinking and are very much like the air we breathe, which we take for granted as much as an octopus takes water for granted. And even when perceived for what they are—as difficult as that is to do—these manacles and cages are even harder to discard or annihilate.[25]

The old premodern way of viewing the possible and impossible, the new modern scientific way, and the myriad ways to do so in between those two poles have now coexisted for at least five centuries, with varying degrees of friction and always—always—with extremists at either pole shouting loudly at each other and at everyone in between. Such occurred in "a brisker than usual" debate at the Metaphysical Society in London in 1875, where Frederic Harrison, a Positivist, dismissed belief in miracles as "the commencement of insanity," and Henry Edward Manning, Archbishop of Westminster, retorted that an inability to believe in the supernatural was "a commencement of the ossification of the brain."[26]

Yet it is obvious that despite all the shouting, the older belief system has never been fully eclipsed by the new one. Reports of supernatural levitations and bilocations gradually shrank in numbers in the Western world after 1787 but have never ceased surfacing altogether. Nearly a century ago, Olivier Leroy identified nineteen levitators in the period between 1700 and 1800 and the same number between 1800 and 1912. Since Leroy was the only researcher to have ever compiled lists of levitators—and he admitted his lists were far from complete—we have no reliable statistics on modern or postmodern cases of supernatural levitations.[27] Finding statistics on bilocation is even more difficult, and the same is true when it comes to demonic phenomena, be it levitation, bilocation, transvection, or witches' flight. Nonetheless, it is possible to find reports of all such phenomena, supernatural as well as demonic, occurring constantly all the way into the present day. Two previously mentioned levitating and bilocating twentieth-century monastics offer ample proof of the persistence of belief in these phenomena: Yvonne-Aimée de Malestroit (1901–1951), whose reported bilocations were among the most extreme in all of Christian history, and Saint Pio of Pietrelcina, also known as Padre Pio (1887–1968), canonized in 2002, whose frequent levitations and bilocations were acknowledged by many eyewitnesses, along with many other charisms associated with mystical ecstasy, including the stigmata (fig. 52).[28] One could also cite the case of Sister Maria Teresa Carloni (1919–1983), whose frequent bilocations were said to comfort persecuted leaders of the Catholic Church in the satellite states of the Soviet Union at the height of the Cold War, as well as that of Sister Rita Montella (1920–1992), who is believed to have bilocated numerous times alongside Padre Pio and also has been credited with saving Pope John Paul II's life through bilocation by suddenly showing up at St. Peter's Square in Rome and pulling on the arm of assassin Ali Agca as he fired his gun.[29]

Then, on the preternatural side of the impossible—which is still as inseparable from the supernatural nowadays as it has ever been—reports of demonic levitations have continued to surface well into the present day, usually in connection with exorcisms. And such stories have made their way into contemporary popular culture with a vengeance through films such as William Friedkin's *The Exorcist*—which was based on a true story—and others of the same genre.[30] Catholic literature on this subject continues to thrive and flourish in spite of the theologians who eliminated the devil and bid farewell to him,[31]

Figure 52. Two twentieth-century avatars of the impossible: Padre Pio of Pietrelcina, levitator, bilocator, and stigmatist, and Sister Yvonne-Aimée de Malestroit, extraordinary bilocator.

as well as the Second Vatican Council's deemphasizing of the devil.[32] Even more surprising is the resurgence of possession stories involving levitation among Protestants and the veritable flood of texts published by nonmainstream Protestants on "spiritual deliverance."[33]

That such beliefs should be thriving among nonmainstream Protestants at the start of the third millennium is not too surprising, given the fact that this segment of the Protestant spectrum is deeply rooted in dissenting traditions that have rejected various tenets of the magisterial Reformations of the sixteenth century and the major denominations that stem from them. Moreover, the revivalist movements of the nineteenth century that spawned evangelical Protestantism, especially of the Pentecostalist strain in the twentieth century, have passed on their rejection of the cessation-of-miracles doctrine to their followers, all the way down to the present.[34]

That such beliefs are still thriving among Catholics should surprise no one. These have always been core beliefs of Catholicism. Although a good number of Catholics in North America and Europe no longer pay much attention to this marker of Catholic identity—and some might even express embarrassment and dismay at its robust survival—these core beliefs remain embedded in global Catholicism as well as in the official teaching of the Catholic Church.[35] Because these beliefs are still a cornerstone of the cult of the saints and this cult is itself an essential component of Catholic piety and identity, it is very difficult to imagine them being jettisoned.[36] Simply put: no miracles, no Catholicism. Not *real* Catholicism, anyway, or at least not the traditional sort of Catholicism depicted by Bartolomé Esteban Murillo in his painting *The Angels' Kitchen,* which bewilders most visitors to the Louvre Museum (fig. 53).

The endurance of these beliefs among Catholics can be attributed to many different factors, a major one of which is the creation of a strong link between empirical science and the supernatural. This process of "rationalizing" the miraculous began in 1588 with the creation of the Congregation of Sacred Rites (Congregatio Sacrorum Rituum), which was placed in charge of handling the canonization of saints, among other things. Through a gradual process of reform that stretched from its founding to 1642, the Congregatio established new criteria for assessing the veracity of miracle accounts through a process of empirical fact-checking, much of which required the participation of medical and scientific experts. As a result, the Congregatio assumed the dual role of assuring Catholics of the veracity of miracles through scientific criteria and of simultaneously refuting Protestant dismissals of miracles as demonic or fraudulent.

Figure 53: In this 1646 painting commissioned by the Franciscan friars of Seville, Spanish artist Bartolomé Murillo intertwines the mundane and the supernatural. The event depicted here is the ecstasy of a friar whose kitchen duties—which he was obligated to carry out due to his vow of obedience—are being miraculously fulfilled by angels while he is ecstatic, suspended motionless in midair. Tellingly, Murillo's depiction of this event places as much emphasis on the presence of witnesses as on the angels and the levitation itself. The identity of the levitating friar has been disputed for centuries, but the Louvre Museum, which owns the painting, guesses that it could have been a lay brother named Francisco Dirraquio.

In addition, by serving in these two roles the Congregatio could naturally claim to uphold the new criteria set in Western culture by the emerging empirical sciences. As Paolo Parigi has argued, the work of the Congregatio enabled the Catholic Church to ensure that "a rational space for miracles could therefore always exist."

Creating this rational space was a masterful adaptation to the great epistemic paradigm shift of the era, Parigi avers, for rather than abdicating control of the supernatural to the scientists, "Rome created an institutional mechanism that, while allowing for the impossible to change depending on the level of scientific knowledge, firmly maintained the power of proclaiming miracles in the hands of religious authorities."[37] Moreover, others have argued that the benefits of this move toward empiricism extended beyond the Catholic Church itself to the emerging natural sciences. Bradford Bouley goes as far as to propose that through its collaboration with science and medicine the Catholic Church became "a major contributor in early modern attempts to understand the natural world."[38]

A key feature of the empiricism injected into the canonization process by the Congregatio was the creation in 1631 by Pope Urban VIII of the position of the *promotor fidei,* or promoter of the faith. Ironically, Urban was the pope above whose head Joseph of Copertino had ostensibly levitated and who had supposedly vowed to testify about this miracle were he to live long enough to take part in Joseph's canonization inquest.[39] The *promotor fidei* came to be better known as the "devil's advocate" (*advocatus diaboli*) due to the chief task assigned to whoever held this post, which was to ferret out errors in the proceedings of the Congregatio, find reasons for denying canonization to candidates, and cast doubt on the testimony presented in their favor, especially on all claims being made for supernatural activity.

Casting doubt had a method and a purpose. To be judged legitimately supernatural in origin, the phenomenon involved in any miracle claim had to be deemed totally impossible—that is, beyond nature according to empirical medical and scientific principles. As Parigi explains, "The task of the Devil's Advocate was not to deny the existence of miracles but to create space for false miracles—that is, for the occurrence of events, or facts that, although inexplicable by science or medicine, were nevertheless not true miracles. Doing so legitimized the claim of the Church to be the guardian of the supernatural."[40] In other words, by denying that many miracle claims did not involve supernatural agency, which the advocate often did, even in the case of some of Joseph of

Cupertino's levitations,[41] Catholic religious authorities were able not only to maintain control of the boundary between the possible and the impossible but also to suffuse that control and every earthly event they deemed truly supernatural with a lustrous rational sheen.

One devil's advocate in particular did much to make the rationality of that sheen even more lustrous: Prospero Lambertini (1675–1758), who would go on to become Pope Benedict XIV in 1740 and ended up approving Joseph of Cupertino's beatification in 1753 and his canonization in 1767.[42] While he was serving in the Congregatio, the future Benedict XIV, who was very deeply influenced by the intellectual and scientific currents of the Enlightenment, took up the challenge of bringing more empirical scientific rigor to the canonization process, especially its evaluation of miracle claims.[43] His effort culminated in the publication of an enormous multivolume book, *On the Beatification of the Servants of God and the Canonization of the Blessed*,[44] which set stricter empirical standards for distinguishing between natural and supernatural phenomena.

One category of miracle on which Lambertini's book focused very intensely was that of medical oddities found in the corpses of saints, ranging from incorruption, to the oozing of substances, to peculiar anatomical abnormalities, such as the extraordinarily large heart of Philip Neri, which had apparently broken some ribs due to its size, and the total absence of body fat or a penis in Charles Borromeo.[45] Autopsying and examining the corpses of holy men and women had become routine in the late sixteenth century, and this practice had assumed an increasingly larger role in proving the genuine holiness of those who were on the path to canonization. One of the first prospective saints to undergo several autopsies was Teresa of Avila, whose corpse refused to decompose, emitted a wondrously pleasant aroma, and oozed a substance that could effect healing miracles.[46] Lambertini's book was full of guidelines for judging signs of genuine holiness in the corpses of individuals who had acquired a reputation as holy. Anatomical abnormalities and asceticism, for instance, were among some of the traditional markers of holiness he targeted for deemphasizing. An extreme lack of body fat, such as found in Borromeo's corpse, for instance, could be attributed entirely to the natural effects of fasting. In the case of stigmata, he warned that the human imagination could have too intense an effect on perceptions and that some of the wounds taken to be of supernatural origin could merely be the result of psychosomatic autosuggestion.[47]

When it came to physical phenomena associated with mystical ecstasy, Lambertini found a way of affirming their absolute possibility through an interweaving traditional theology and philosophy with the science of his day and age. Focusing on the relationship between soul and body—and even citing ancient authorities such as Plato—he set down criteria for distinguishing different levels of ecstasy, rapture, or elevation and of determining whether they had genuine supernatural origins. Supernatural raptures, such as those experienced by Joseph of Cupertino, were a more extreme form of ecstasy in which the body was affected so profoundly by the soul's presence in the divine realm that it, too, became thoroughly spiritualized and immune to gravity. Simply put, a metaphysical transformation canceled out the laws of physics. In the case of Joseph, then, according to Lambertini, "in an intimate union with God, his heart aflame with the love of God, nearly torn asunder by this sweet love, he went into ecstasies and raptures."[48]

Nowadays, nearly three centuries after the publication of Lambertini's book, belief in the supernatural and the seemingly impossible still endures among Catholics and some Protestants, and the survival of this belief defies the empiricism and the hegemonic cultural tendencies that declare these phenomena impossible, nonsensical, absurd, ridiculous, and worthy of scorn. This brings us full circle, back to a question raised at the very start, slightly amended. How does one sum up a history of what could never have happened, a history of the impossible? Obviously, there is no denying the existence of testimonies, and these accounts are not just a *fact* but also evidence of what Émile Durkheim called a *social fact,* which he defined as follows: "In reality, there is in every society a clearly determined group of phenomena separable, because of their distinct characteristics, from those that form the subject matter of other sciences of nature. . . . Here, then, is a category of facts which present very special characteristics: they consist of manners of acting, thinking, and feeling external to the individual, which are invested with a coercive power by virtue of which they exercise control over him. . . . Thus, they constitute a new species and to them must be exclusively assigned the term social."[49]

Belief in impossible phenomena such as levitation and bilocation was a social fact in the early modern age, especially in Catholic enclaves, large and small, but also in Protestant ones, where such belief involved the devil rather than God. It was a belief "invested with a coercive power" that exerted control over members of these societies. Simply put, such belief was an inescapable reality that determined what was possible or impossible.[50] Whether one assented to these beliefs or not was immaterial. One was expected to accept it, and many did so, to some extent, because rejecting it involved being punished or ostracized in myriad ways. Among Catholics, denying a saint's ability to levitate might prompt accusations of heresy; among Protestants, denying the reality of witches' flight might cause the skeptic to be denounced as a witch. Skepticism often exacted a high price during the transition to modernity.

Whether levitations and bilocations were actually happening and being witnessed—thereby giving rise to the belief and the social fact of the belief—is ultimately unprovable, given the surviving evidence at our disposal, but the social fact is easy enough to verify, convincingly, as is the undeniable admixture of belief and skepticism and various epistemic stances that marked the passage to modernity.

The impossible miracles of the early modern age can be approached in various ways, some of which are incompatible and each of which provides its own valuable perspective.

The oldest approach is the original one, which comes from within the phenomenon and is also its wellspring, so to speak: the perspective of faith. From this perspective, God's supernatural agency—or the devil's preternatural one—can make the impossible possible. Another approach is that of purely materialist empirical science, which excludes the existence of supernatural or preternatural agency and has traditionally denied the possibility of anything it deems naturally impossible. This perspective is now hegemonic in Western culture. A third approach is that taken by the Catholic Church after the Council of Trent, which involves employing medical and scientific knowledge in the investigation of miracle claims. This perspective is still an essential component of the Catholic Church's take on impossible phenomena, especially in its canonization process and in its approach to all miracle claims.

A fourth and relatively more recent approach is that taken by social scientists and other scholars influenced by social science. This approach, which ignores the metaphysical issue of the supernatural altogether, focuses on the social matrix in which impossible miracles occur and has multiple perspectives. Overall, such studies tend to be functionalist; that is, their analysis is guided by the theory that all aspects of society serve a pragmatic purpose or role and can best be understood in the context of the needs and goals they fulfill for the social organism in question.[51]

Examples of this functionalist approach abound, but one of the best-known and most influential functionalist scholars is historian Keith Thomas, who has argued that belief in magic and miracles was an absolute necessity in premodern times due to "a preoccupation with the explanation and relief of human misfortune" due to all the concerns raised by "the hazards of an intensely insecure environment."[52] A nearly identical functionalist interpretation of miracles can be found in Paolo Parigi's analysis: "Miracles are reducers of uncertainty," he declares. "They give a sense of meaning to life's hardships and mitigate life's vicissitudes."[53] Parigi's work is also representative of another social-scientific perspective, previously mentioned, in which all wonder-working tends to be identified as magic or thaumaturgy, thus echoing Protestant polemics from a bygone era. Rather than saving the miraculous, he concludes, "Rome succeeded in saving magic."[54]

A focus on institutional and political structures also pervades social-scientific approaches to miracles. This is especially true of studies that analyze the canonization process and the work of the Inquisition and, quite intensely, the persecution of witches. Since all charismatic Catholic miracle-workers intrinsically pose a threat to the stability of church authority and so many of them end up being placed under investigation, it could be argued that analysis of this dimension of the miraculous is necessary for a full understanding of any miraculous phenomena associated with holy men and women. This is also true in the case of witches, even though the threat they pose is to all of society rather than any specific church authorities. As far as gender is concerned, the same could be said, given that so many levitators and bilocators were women and that most witches were also female.

Such a pronounced gender imbalance cries out for analysis. Issues of class also enter into consideration when the social matrix of miracles is being analyzed, for obvious reasons. A case in point is that of Magdalena de la Cruz, who stirred up class frictions within her convent as abbess. But class issues attract less attention than gender when it comes to Catholic miracles, principally because class imbalances are not as pronounced as those in gender when it comes to this subject and have therefore been considered less significant to the interpretation of the miraculous. When it comes to witches, however, class issues do loom large in much of the scholarship due to the marginal social status of so many of those who were persecuted.

A fifth approach to the miraculous is that of *postsecular* interpretation, the underlying assumption of which is that the spheres of faith and reason, religion and science, or the natural and supernatural are not at all incompatible, as many intellectual elites have been saying since the dawn of modernity. Although there is plenty of disagreement over the exact meaning of the term "postsecular," it is generally applied to a perspective that challenges the chief premises of the scientific revolution and the Enlightenment—and of the materialist secularism they engendered—and therefore seeks to dethrone them.[55] The concept and term "postsecular" has a combative edge to it as well as a pragmatic one. Much like the terms "postmodern," "poststructural," "postfeminist," and "postcolonial," the term "postsecularism" is rooted in the conviction that Western culture has arrived at some sort of apogee (or nadir) that needs to be transcended. Consequently, postsecular and all the other various "posts" share in a common epistemological and historical conceit, as well as in a triumphalist and quasi-apocalyptic claim to finality, each proclaiming itself an interpretive end point, a "post" after which there could be no more "posts." Unlike all the other "posts," however, which tend to ignore metaphysical issues, the postsecular approach has less of a triumphalist streak and a much greater degree of tolerance and appreciation for the miraculous—perhaps even a yen for those impossible phenomena discarded so flippantly by benighted materialists.

Not everyone who fits into the postsecularist mold would accept the term as an adequate label for themselves, and if all who do fit the mold were herded into a room, there would surely be many who would feel uncomfortable being near one another and bolt for the nearest doorway or window, but that is ultimately immaterial. It is their perspective that links postsecularists, not the term, much less any membership in some specific academic society. Consequently, there are various types of postsecularist approaches to the miraculous, some of which overlap in perspective and methodology. One type is rooted in religious belief itself and in personal encounters with spiritual and otherworldly phenomena.[56] Another type in particular has generated the most serious and challenging scholarly approach. This approach has a firm grounding in the discipline of the history of religions and comparative religion. Its credentials are impeccable, and its methodology is academically sound. But its daring leap beyond the boundaries of traditional religious studies puts it in a category of its own.

It would be foolish to try to name this approach, or to pigeonhole it, especially because it is still evolving, and the individuals involved are a very diverse group. Some of these daring scholars have issued a rallying cry against the "dogmatic secularism" that permeates the academic study of religion. Calling for a new kind of skepticism—one that questions the validity of dogmatic secularism—they state their goals clearly, as follows: "Taking a cue from their less-than-marginal place in scholarship today, we call supernatural beings the 'Unbelieved' and the explicit or implicit denial of them 'Dogmatic Secularism.' We argue that objective historians should not discount, in advance, evidence that points to the existence or involvement of the 'Unbelieved' in history; instead, we should cultivate a sceptical attitude towards all sources."[57] Their rallying cry drew a spirited response by several other scholars, the contents of which clearly indicate that there are various ways to challenge dogmatic secularism, and no single approach is likely to nudge it aside, much less replace it.[58]

Meanwhile, a group of scholars associated with medievalist Sylvain Piron at L'École des Hautes Études en Sciences Sociales in Paris have created a new publishing house dedicated to exploring the significance of the *impossible* as well as "ways of living with the *invisible*."[59] In his recent study of Christina the Astonishing, Piron avers that the most important question is not what Christina's contemporaries might have thought of levitation as some sort of trope but rather what the obstacle might be against levitation in our own day and age.[60] In his concluding remarks he calls for the creation of a "social science of the activities of the invisible," avoiding terms such as "religion" and "magic," which, he avers, are "excessively burdened with value judgments." For this scientific approach to move forward, he boldly advises, what is needed is "a suspension of disbelief which neither affirms nor judges, but simply allows itself and invites us to observe, to listen, possibly to admit that the worlds of the spirit are undoubtedly even richer and more surprising than we think or could imagine."[61]

Another approach is best reified in the scholarship of Jeffrey Kripal, a University of Chicago-trained historian of religion who constantly dares to cross boundaries and venture into subjects that fall outside the purview of traditional academic religious studies, such as encounters with extraterrestrial beings or the religious dimension of science fiction literature. Kripal is brutally honest about his openness to the possible existence of dimensions and phenomena beyond the ken of present-day science while exemplifying to the fullest all the scholarly rigor demanded of a professional academic. He wears his passion for alternate possibilities on his sleeve with as much boldness as he refuses to hide his impatience with the limitations of the "iron cage" of secularist materialism into which all scholarship on the seemingly impossible is imprisoned.

As a historian of religion, Kripal calls attention to the fact that "although there is a fundamental base to what human beings experience as reality, this reality behaves differently in different historical periods and linguistic registers" and that "things that are possible in one place and time are impossible in another, and vice versa."[62] Intensely aware of what scholars of religion have been trained to do and to say, Kripal challenges the dogmatic materialism that guides scholarly research on religion and, more specifically, research on ostensibly impossible miracles. His reaction to the functionalist evasiveness drummed into all scholarship on the history of the impossible is eloquently summed up in the following outburst, which deserves to be quoted at length, especially because of its points of reference.

> I cannot tell you how many times I have heard an otherwise admired colleague say something like, "Well, it does not really matter if Joseph of Cupertino flew up into the tree after a scream, or if Teresa of Avila floated off the floor as her sisters piled on top of her to avoid a social embarrassment. What matters is how the popular belief in such presumed levitations was disciplined, controlled, and maintained by the church and later constructed as sanctity and as a saint. . . . Really? I want to pull my hair out in such moments. . . . A super-pious Italian man ecstatically flies into a tree and has to be retrieved with a ladder, or a raptured Spanish nun cannot keep herself on the floor in front of some visiting noblewomen, and these physical events do not matter to you? Uh, excuse me, if either of those things actually happened (and our historical records suggest strongly that they did), such anomalous events change pretty much everything we thought we knew about human consciousness and its relationship to physics, gravity, and material reality. Either single event would fundamentally change our entire order of knowledge. And you don't care? Don't you find that disinterest just a little bit perverse?[63]

Kripal's approach ruffles feathers in academia. But he has also touched a raw nerve in today's ostensibly secularist culture and has won over many a reader. Despite a lingering fear of the COVID-19 pandemic, an international conference hosted by Kripal at Rice University in 2022 attracted 200 in-person attendees along with 1,700 online registrants.[64]

Another type of postsecularist approach, less scholarly, has generated the greatest amount of literature. This approach focuses on the human mind and its relation to the physical world and could be aptly described as psychophysiological. It evolved gradually, mostly within the field of psychology in the early twentieth century, but ultimately coalesced at a 1998 conference at the Center for Theory and Research of the Esalen Institute,[65] where discussions eventually led to the following realization, as expressed nine years later in a groundbreaking coauthored book, *Irreducible Mind:* "By the year 2000 our discussions had advanced to the point where we believed we could demonstrate, empirically, that the materialistic consensus which undergirds practically all of current mainstream psychology, neuroscience, and philosophy of mind is fundamentally flawed."[66] Much of the literature generated within this perspective argues for hidden powers inherent in the human mind and the reality of many phenomena deemed impossible by empirical science, with an eclectic blending of perspectives from empirical science, psychology, medicine, and liminal branches of these materialist disciplines that shade off into the psychical, the parascientific, and the occult.[67] A central assumption of some of this work is that human minds do not emerge from brains but are rather an expression of an elemental force: "Mind is a fundamental process in its own right, as widespread and deeply embedded in nature as light or electricity."[68] The observations and arguments made from within this perspective can sometimes be dizzying, as in the following case: "There is no doubt that hints of large changes in cosmology are on the horizon. Perhaps the most startling claim to come from some quantum physicists is that consciousness creates reality. This inverts the metaphysics of classical physics, in which mind is a passive onlooker, as it were hanging on to matter by its shirttails, in quantum mechanics, mind makes a comeback onto the stage of reality, this time as a sovereign performer."[69]

That "performer," of course, can bring about levitation and bilocation, and that is precisely what went on every time Joseph of Cupertino rose aloft into the air with one of his shrieks. "To make sense of Joseph's phenomena," says this author, "then, we need to upgrade our view of human mental potential."[70] Needless to say, this perspective on the possibility of the impossible has difficulty finding acceptance in academia precisely because it calls into question too many of its assumptions and guiding principles. And by dismissing the supernatural and preternatural and ascribing levitation to "mind," it also runs against the grain of traditional Christianity, both Catholic and Protestant.

Beyond the fringe of academia there exist various approaches to the miraculous that should not be classified as postsecular, for even if they refer to empirical science or claim to be parascientific, their main intent is not to reconcile faith and reason or religion and science but to explore the paranormal with elements of pseudoscience and in some cases even to revive ancient occult traditions or to blend them with nineteenth-century Spiritualism. At this end of the interpretive spectrum, academic historians can easily lose their bearings as well as their wits and perhaps any chance of being taken seriously by their colleagues.

When all is said and done, phenomena deemed impossible in the twenty-first century remain a risky liminal field of study, suspended between legitimacy and illegitimacy. Rooted as they are in belief and closely tied as they are to a worldview directly derived from ancient and medieval times, these phenomena are markers of alterity; that is, they reify a premodern "otherness" that is at once marginal, primitive, and somewhat unsettling to many in modern society who, like D. P. Walker, prefer to keep the supernatural safely encased in amber like one of the Mesozoic insects used to clone dinosaurs in the fictional world of *Jurassic Park*.[71] One might even say that the cognitive and epistemic dissonance created by levitation, bilocation, and all such "impossible" miracles is extreme enough to make them radically different from modernity, even grotesque, and to imbue them with that "hard edged alterity" that so many modern elites attribute to all things medieval.[72]

Nonetheless, for all of their hard-edged alterity, these impossible phenomena are unavoidable for anyone who ventures into the early modern age or even into some corners of our secular world, where people can be found who believe not just in the levitations and bilocations of saints long dead but also in those of men and women who lived fairly recently, such as Gemma Galgani (d. 1903), Faustyna Kowalska (d. 1938), Yvonne-Aimée de Malestroit (d.1950), and Pio of Pietrelcina (d. 1968). The Durkheimian social fact that makes these impossible phenomena possible in certain settings is still with us—as unavoidable as mountains in Tibet—along with the "fact" of the testimonies of those who claim to have witnessed such things. When all is said and done, the levitations and bilocations of the early modern age are no different from the miraculous apparitions of Christ or the Virgin Mary in the nineteenth and twentieth centuries, which scholars have deftly analyzed as undeniable "facts" that were not only inextricable from the social and political matrix of their time and place but also profoundly affected history, locally as well as globally; which is why now, in the early twenty-first century, over five million pilgrims still flock to the Marian shrine at Lourdes every year.[73] As the titles of relatively recent books on apparitions in Germany, Spain, France, and Portugal make clear,[74] the miracles being analyzed in them are approached as a component of secular history, politics, and culture rather than as some "lingering cultural manifestation of a remote, impoverished and illiterate world."[75] One of these scholars, William Christian Jr., trained as a sociologist, has proven through his work that late medieval and early modern apparitions are in essence no different from those of the twentieth century, insofar as they occur in specific time- and place-bound matrices that can be analyzed in very similar ways.[76] Belief, after all, has as much of a political or socioeconomic context as unbelief.[77] Time and place make for different contexts, but context itself is always a constant reality. And that context, social scientists tend to say, determines the appeal as well as the function of miracles, even those deemed most impossible. In turn, those miracles, which tend to be viewed primarily from a functionalist perspective, become phenomena that inevitably "teach us much about the ways social realities are variously constructed, contested, and transformed,"[78] even when those social realities include belief in saints who can resurrect dismembered infants.[79]

As valuable as such insights are in a utilitarian sense—usefulness being the very telos or purpose of social science—they cannot shed light on the totality of the miraculous. No currently acceptable scholarly perspective can do that either, for the supernatural element of the miraculous eludes academic scrutiny. Miracles take place in the realm of faith, and that realm, by definition, transcends ordinary experience, as do the testimonies of the eyewitnesses who avouch for their occurrence and the social facts that make those testimonies possible. Miracles, it could be said, are not just puzzling for historians but also immensely frustrating. The further one goes back in time, the more difficult it becomes *not* to bump into them, or into their preternatural demonic counterparts. The testimonies are simply there in the historical record, cluttering it up abundantly, and their existence cannot be denied. But ironically, it is ultimately impossible to prove that what is claimed in these testimonies happened exactly as recorded. Beyond the realm of faith, the evidence can seem insufficient despite its sheer volume. Hence the frustration.

Yet levitation and bilocation accounts are as hard to dismiss as to prove true. By raising questions about our perception of the past, these accounts of the impossible also force us to confront our assumptions in the present and perhaps even to confront our own unreflective enmeshment in the social facts that govern our thinking and behaving and our own role in the construction of social facts for our time and place. Moreover, these accounts do more than raise significant questions. They also reveal the power of belief to shape mentalities and the power of social facts to shape thought and behavior or to determine the limits we place on what might be possible.

Funny thing, how the word "suspend" in the expression "to suspend disbelief" is also the same word used to describe the condition of "being held aloft without attachment,"[80] a semantic coincidence that places disbelief in the same situation as any levitator, including both Joseph of Cupertino and Jean-François Pilâtre de Rozier: *Suspended*. Strange stuff, this bit of poetic justice, as strange as levitation itself. Disbelief is the opposite of belief, of course, but both modes of thinking are opposite sides of the same coin that most of us call "reality." We live in an era in which disbelief is so powerful it seems almighty, principally because "reality" is conceived of as one-dimensional, not as some two-dimensional coin or multidimensional universe. Suspending disbelief has become difficult, even impossible. But that might be a misperception, a mirage of sorts, caused by our constant immersion in our own zeitgeist or dominant worldview. History itself teaches us that the power of belief should never be underestimated, neither in the present nor in the past nor perhaps in the future as well. Belief is real. Its power is a constant, always there in the profane as much as in the sacred, ever on the edge of surging, ever ready to be tapped, for good or for ill. Even as the content of belief evolves and specific beliefs go extinct and others arise, belief itself remains an inescapable reality for all individuals and societies, even the most materialistic—as any former subject of the Third Reich or the Soviet Empire will confirm—and its potential power endures, undimmed by the passage of time or whatever kind of slippage eventually brings revered orthodoxies to their doom. Belief is the immortal soul of the imagination, as well as of all mentalities, mindsets, worldviews, epistemic regimes, discourses, social imaginaries, and social facts. And when it comes to things supernatural—that inexhaustible fuel of the fires of faith—the power of belief can be limitless. Anything is possible. One might even dare to add an exclamation point at the end of the following sentence:

They flew!

Appendix 1
Seventeenth- and Eighteenth-Century Bilocators
in America and Europe

Bilocating Nuns from the Spanish Colonies

María de Jesús Tomellín (1582–1637), also known as Lily of Puebla, a Conceptionist Mexican nun who claimed to have visited Europe and several pagan lands and to have been present at the funeral of Spanish king Philip III. As with other nuns of her age, she attributed her journeys to "spiritual flights" or supernatural "agility" rather than *bilocation* per se. She was so well known in her day that she was the subject of three hagiographies and is second only to Rose of Lima in the amount of attention paid to her in the early modern era. Despite much lobbying for her beatification and canonization, however, her case stalled, much like that of María de Ágreda.[1]

Francisca de la Natividad (d. 1658), a Discalced Carmelite nun from Puebla, Mexico, claimed to visit several heathen lands in the autobiography she was ordered to write by her male superiors. Francisca claimed to have taught the pagans she visited to make the sign of the cross and recite the paternoster, the Ave Maria, and the Credo, as well as the Ten Commandments, "most efficaciously and tenderly with my heart and soul, as if she had them visibly present and saw them with her corporeal eyes."[2] As in the case of María of Ágreda and Ana María de San José in Spain, Francisca attributed her missionary journeys to the deep anguish she felt about the souls who were headed for certain damnation. Additionally, she said she wished she had been a male so she could have been a missionary physically instead of spiritually.[3]

Catarina de San Juan (1607–1688), also known as the China Poblana, a beata, or intensely devout laywoman from Puebla, Mexico, claimed to have made frequent journeys to various continents. Born in India, kidnapped by Portuguese pirates, converted to Christianity by Jesuits, and taken as a slave to the Philippines and afterward to Mexico, she was eventually freed and became a prominent figure in the religious life of Puebla, where she remained close to the Jesuits of that city. Her visits to her native India, the Philippines, Japan, China, and the Mariana Islands, as well as to North America, were described by her Jesuit hagiographer Alonso Ramos.[4] Quite often, her "spiritual presence" in these distant lands served as scouting trips for the Jesuits, during which she would find the most suitable mission fields and potential converts. Sometimes she would act as a missionary herself, as she claimed she did with none other than the emperor of China, to whom she preached the words placed in her mouth by Christ and the Virgin Mary.[5] Additionally, as if all this were not impressive enough, she claimed to have taken part in some battles in Europe and to have braved pirates in the Caribbean.[6] Given such claims, it is not too surprising, then, that the Inquisition banned the circulation of Catarina's images in 1690 and censured her biographies in 1695, including the massive multivolume work by Alonso Ramos, "for containing useless revelations, visions, and apparitions that are implausible as well as full of contradictions and indecent, reckless, and improper comparisons that are knowingly blasphemous."[7]

Despite such reversals, accounts of bilocating or transvecting American nuns continued to surface well into the eighteenth century, as the Enlightenment was sweeping through Europe.

Ana Guerra de Jesús (1639–1713), a Guatemalan beata whose hagiography was written by her Jesuit confessor Antonio de Siria, claimed to have visited the rebellious region of Petén, one of the last Maya strongholds in Central America.[8]

Ursula Suárez (1666–1749), a Chilean nun, wrote an autobiography in which she claimed to have visited an unidentified land, and perhaps also Arabia.[9]

Jéronima del Espiritu Santo (1669–1749), a Colombian from Bogotá, told of visiting Asia and the Indies in her autobiographical diary.[10] Jacinta María Ana de San Antonio (1674–1720), from Oaxaca, Mexico, told of numerous visits to other local, regional, and international locations, including Jerusalem.[11]

Francisca de los Ángeles (1674–1744), a nun from Queréntaro, Mexico, claimed in her letters that she had visited Texas and New Mexico, accompanied by Christ, her guardian angels, and Saint Rose of Viterbo (the patroness of her convent). During one such visit, she claimed she met two old Indians who remembered having seen María de Ágreda, a clear indication of the influence of the so-called Lady in Blue in colonial monastic circles. She also explained that she got there by flying and walking "with supernatural speed."[12]

María Manuela de Santa Ana (1695–1793), a nun from Lima, Peru, detailed in her autobiography how she had visited many locations around the world, including China, Guinea, and Turkey, and how she had gone to Rome with Saint

Paul and Saint Augustine. She also expressed great sorrow for not being able to "travel the world and catechize Jews, heretics, and pagans, especially blacks, for whose conversion and baptism I beg God constantly."[13]

Similar late seventeenth- and eighteenth-century claims of nearby or far-flung visits to other locations can be found in the lives of numerous nuns, including Antonia de la Madre de Dios, a Mexican Augustinian;[14] María de Jesús, from Colombia;[15] Inés de la Cruz, from Mexico;[16] and Dolores Peña y Lillo, from Chile.[17] And in the nineteenth century, one can still find nuns, such as María Ignacia del Niño Jesús, claiming to have visited Spain and Rome.[18]

Bilocating Saints and Aspiring Saints from the Baroque and Enlightenment Eras

In the Age of Reason and the Enlightenment, several bilocators were exceptionally prominent, but relatively little scholarly attention has been paid to their bilocations.

Ursula Micaela Morata (1628–1703), a Capuchin Poor Clare nun and abbess in Alicante, Spain, who claimed many mystical gifts, including that of bilocation to distant lands and incorruptibility, and whose canonization is still pending.[19]

María de Jesús de León y Delgado (1643–1731), a Spanish Dominican lay sister known as La Siervita (The Little Servant) who lived in the Canary Islands and reportedly exhibited all the major physical phenomena associated with mystical ecstasy, including bilocation, levitation, the stigmata, and incorruptibility, but has yet to be canonized.[20]

John Joseph of the Cross (1654–1739), a Discalced Franciscan from the island of Ischia who was canonized in 1839.[21]

Angelo of Acri (1669–1739), a Capuchin priest and spellbinding preacher who was active in southern Italy and hailed as a saint in his own day but was not canonized until 2017 by Pope Francis.[22]

Paul of the Cross (1694–1775), from Savoy, founder of the Passionist order, canonized in 1867.[23]

Alphonsus Liguori (1696–1787) is the best-known and most significant of this band of bilocators. Founder of the Redemptorist order that Geraldo Majella joined, Alphonsus was a multitalented musician, artist, lawyer, theologian, philosopher, and writer of extremely popular devotional literature who was appointed bishop of Sant'Agata dei Goti in 1762, much to his own dismay. A levitator as well as a bilocator, he was observed by various witnesses at two locations simultaneously several times, most notably when seen aiding Pope Clement XIV at his deathbed in Rome in September 1774 while others witnessed him rapt in a cataleptic ecstasy in his episcopal residence near Naples. Alphonsus was canonized in 1839, on the same day as fellow bilocator John Joseph of the Cross.[24]

Felice Amoroso of Nicosia (1715–1787), a Capuchin friar, beatified in 1888.[25]

Geraldo Majella (1726–1755), a Redemptorist lay brother from the Kingdom of Naples canonized in 1904, who not only bilocated but also reportedly walked on water to rescue some fishermen during a storm.[26]

Appendix 2
The Emergence of the "Lady in Blue" Legend
A Chronology

1610s: Luisa de Carrión claims she bilocates to various distant locations, such as Rome, Japan, New Mexico. She begins to be revered as a "living saint."

1611: Luisa de Carrión is accused of feigning inedia by some fellow nuns; the Inquisition passes the investigation of this case to the Franciscan order.

1614: Father Antonio de Trejo, the vicar general of the Spanish Franciscans, pronounces Luisa de Carrión innocent of all the charges against her.

1620: In Ágreda, Sor María begins to experience ecstatic raptures during which she ostensibly bilocates and interacts with natives in the New World. She speaks with her confessors and fellow nuns in Ágreda about her visits to America and her missionary work with Indians, providing many details of the New Mexican landscape, climate, flora, fauna, and people.

1620s: According to later accounts, Franciscan friars at the mission of San Antonio de Isleta in New Mexico receive visits from Jumano Indians from hundreds of miles away, begging for baptism for all their people. Father Esteban de Perea, the superior of the mission, repeatedly turns down their requests.

1620s: Bilocations by Luisa de Carrión continue.

1622: Sor María meets with the minister-general of the Franciscans, Father Bernardino de la Sena, and gives him a detailed account of her bilocations. Satisfied that the miracle is genuine and of divine origin, he approves of it but refrains from publicizing it in print, therefore keeping the story out of public view.

1623: Sor María's raptures, levitations, and bilocations cease, according to later testimony from her, but other accounts will later claim that she kept visiting New Mexico for several years, although perhaps with less frequency.

1625: According to José Jiménez Samaniego, her hagiographer, Sor María is still visiting New Mexico.

1625: The San Antonio mission receives a new custos sent from Spain, Father Alonso de Benavides, along with twelve additional friars. Benavides will later claim that he learned immediately of the Jumanos and their request for baptism and that the Indians failed to mention visits from a nun.

1626: One of María's confessors, Sebastián Marcilla, sends a letter to the archbishop of Mexico, Francisco de Manso y Zúñiga, which contains an account of María's bilocations and of her miraculous missionary efforts in the New World. Marcilla mentions place-names as well as certain tribes, including the Jumanos, hoping these details will catch Archbishop Manso's eye. Marcilla also begs Archbishop Manso to send Franciscan missionaries to the Jumanos to investigate María's claims. Manso sits on this information and does nothing.

1628: First written account of the Lady in Blue. Gerónimo Zárate Salmerón, a Franciscan missionary, writes a chronicle about his missionary work in New Mexico. This account—though sketchy—tells of a local narrative circulating by word of mouth in the New Mexico Territory about numerous visits paid to native tribes by a Spanish nun. Although the nun is not named in the narrative itself, the subtitle that precedes it makes her identity explicit: "Account of the Holy Mother María de Jesús, abbess of the convent of Santa Clara de Ágreda."

1629: According to Alonso de Benavides, "the same nun" is still visiting New Mexico.

1629: A fresh contingent of missionaries arrive at San Antonio de Isleta in July, led by Father Esteban de Perea, the previous custos of the mission. Perea hands Benavides a letter from Archbishop Manso conveying the information he received about Sor María's bilocations from her confessor and commands him to investigate María's claims about what has been occurring in the land of the Jumanos.

1629: According to Alonso de Benavides, he interrogates some visiting Jumanos, and they reveal that a nun in a blue cloak has indeed been visiting them. When shown an image of Luisa de Carrión, they say the garb is identical, but their visitor is much younger and prettier. Benavides sends two missionaries to the Jumano lands, and they find evidence of Catholic piety, especially the veneration of crosses and of images of Christ.

1629: Narratives from Spain and New Mexico merge during this encounter between missionaries and Jumanos. Sor María becomes the most likely match for the Lady in Blue.

1630: Second written account of the Lady in Blue. Relieved of his post after five years at the San Antonio de Isleta mission, Alonso de Benavides heads back to Spain via Mexico and writes a lengthy report on those missions for King Philip IV that includes one chapter on the "temporal and spiritual treasures" of New Mexico. In this chapter, Benavides relates the story of a nun who has visited local natives.

This account, which does *not* identify María as the missionary nun, has come to be known simply as the *1630 Memorial of Alonso Benavides.*

1631: According to Alonso de Benavides, "the same nun" is still visiting New Mexico.

1631: Third written account of the Lady in Blue. Alonso de Benavides meets with María at her convent in Ágreda and afterward writes a letter to the missionaries in New Mexico about María's bilocations. He attaches a letter ostensibly penned by María herself—that he forced her to write under her vow of obedience—in which she confirms that she had indeed evangelized the Jumano Indians. This text, which would not be published until a century later, is the third account and the first to contain direct testimony from María.

1632: Francisco de la Fuente is condemned by the Inquisition for falsely claiming he had bilocated to the New World to evangelize some natives.

1633: Luisa de Carrión is accused of fraud and pacts with the devil and denounced to the Inquisition.

1634: Fourth written account of the Lady in Blue. Alonso de Benavides pens yet another report, this one addressed to Pope Urban VIII, in which he includes details not found in his previous two accounts. This fourth manuscript, known as *Benavides's 1634 Memorial,* appears to have never been published.

1634: Benavides suggests in his *Memorial* that there were really two Ladies in Blue, Sor María and Luisa de Carrión, according to testimony he received from Father Juan de Santander, commissary general of the Indies, and Domingo de Aspe, Sor Luisa's confessor. But this information does not become part of the Lady in Blue legend.

1635: Luisa de Carrión is moved by the Inquisition to an Augustinian convent in Valladolid.

1636: Luisa de Carrión dies sixteenth months later, still under suspicion of fraud.

1648: The Inquisition finds Luisa de Carrión innocent of all charges, posthumously.

1650: Fifth written Lady in Blue account. After being questioned by the Inquisition for the second time in her life, Sor María writes a new account of her bilocations for Father Pedro Manero, the superior general of the Franciscan order in Spain. In this manuscript, Sor María seeks to correct or even deny many of the details found in earlier accounts, including some that she had earlier declared to be accurate.

1670: Sixth written account of the Lady in Blue. José Jiménez Samaniego includes a new account in chapter 12 of his hagiography of Sor María. This account consolidates the merging of María's identity with the Lady in Blue legend.

Notes

Abbreviations Used in the Notes

Archives

AHN   Archivo Histórico Nacional, Madrid
ASV   Archivio Segreto Vaticano, Rome
BNE   Biblioteca Nacional de España, Madrid
BNF   Bibliothèque nationale de France, Paris

Collected Works

AS   *Acta Sanctorum quotquot toto orbe coluntur,* 69 vols. (Brussels: Alphonsum Greise, 1863–1940)

CO   E. Cunitz, J.-W. Baum, and E. W. E. Reuss, eds., *Joannis Calvini Opera Quae Supersunt Omnia,* 59 vols. (Braunschweig: C. A. Schwetschke, 1863–1900)

LW   Martin Luther, *Luther's Works,* 55 vols., edited by Jaroslav Pelikan et al. (St. Louis: Concordia, 1955–1986)

Migne, *PL*   Jaques-Paul Migne, ed., *Patrologiae Cursus Completus / Series Latina,* 221 vols. (Paris: Migne, 1844–1864)

O.C.   Santa Teresa de Jesús, *Obras Completas,* edited by Efrén de la Madre de Dios and Otger Steggink, 9th ed. (Madrid: Biblioteca de Autores Cristianos, 1997)

OCLG   Fray Luis de Granada, *Obras Completas,* 51 vols. (Madrid: Fundación Universitaria Española, 1994–2008)

WA   D. Martin, *Luthers Werke: Kritische Gesamtausgabe,* 136 vols. (Weimar: Hermann Böhlau, 1883–2009)

WAT   D. Martin, *Luthers Werke: Kritische Gesamtausgabe, Tischreden,* 6 vols. (Weimar: Hermann Böhlau, 1912–1921)

Hagiographies and Biographies

Agelli · Paolo Agelli, *Vita del Beato Giuseppe di Copertino* (Livorno, 1753)

Bernino · Domenico Bernino, *Vita del Venerable Padre Fr. Giuseppe Da Copertino De' Minori Conventuali* (Rome, 1722)

JSRV · José Jiménez Samaniego, *Relación de la vida de la Venerable Madre Sor María de Jesús* (Madrid, 1727)

Nuti · Roberto Nuti, *Vita del servo di Dio P. Giuseppe da Copertino* (Palermo, 1678)

Parisciani, *ND* · Gustavo Parisciani, *San Giuseppe Da Copertino a la luce dei nuovi documenti,* 2nd ed. (Osimo, Italy: Donare Pace e Bene, 2009)

Pastrovicchi · Angelo Pastrovicchi, *Compendio della vita, virtù e miracoli del Beato Giuseppe di Copertino* (Rome, 1753)

Texts

Ayer MS · Benavides Memorial of 1634, Ayer MS 1044, Newberry Library, Chicago

HIEA · Joaquín Pérez Villanueva and Bartolomé Escandell Bonet, eds., *Historia de la Inquisición en España y America,* 3 vols. (Madrid: Biblioteca de Autores Cristianos, 1984)

Institutes · John Calvin, *Institutes of the Christian Religion,* edited by J. T. McNeill, translated by F. L. Battles, 2 vols. (1559; repr., Philadelphia: Westminster Press, 1960)

MCD · The Venerable María de Agreda, *Mystica Ciudad de Dios* (Madrid: Bernardo de Villa-Diego, 1670)

P1807 · María de Agreda, *Mystica Ciudad de Dios* (Pamplona, 1807)

Procesos · *Procesos de beatificación y canonización de Santa Teresa de Jesús,* edited by Silverio de Santa Teresa, 3 vols. (Burgos: Bibloteca Mística Carmelitana, 1934–1935)

All translations of non-Biblical texts are my own, unless otherwise indicated. The English translation of the Bible quoted here is the New International Version.

Preface

1. On the comparison to Satan, see J. Parnell McCarter, "Book Review: Carlos Eire's *War against the Idols,*" accessed January 21, 2023, http://www.puritans .net/bookreviewwaragainstidols.htm. On the other accusations: unfortunately,

all the vitriol spewed online by the Socialist utopia of Cuba has vanished from view, as often happens with totalitarian regimes that have trouble maintaining their websites or excelling at anything other than imprisoning those who disagree with them.

2. Montague Summers, *The Physical Phenomena of Mysticism, with Especial Reference to the Stigmata, Divine and Diabolic* (New York: Barnes and Noble, 1950).

3. Gabriel García Márquez, *Cien Años de Soledad* (Havana: Casa de las Américas, 1968); translated by Gregory Rabassa as *A Hundred Years of Solitude* (New York: Harper and Row, 1970).

4. Immanuel Kant, *Die Religion innerhalb der Grenzen der bloßen Vernunft* (1793); translated by Theodore M. Greene and Hoyt H. Hudson as *Religion within the Limits of Reason Alone* (New York: Harper Torchbooks, 1960).

5. Scientists do take this phenomenon seriously. See David Burkus, "How to Have a Eureka Moment," *Harvard Business Review,* March 11, 2014, https://hbr.org/2014/03/how-to-have-a-eureka-moment; and Hannah England, "The Science of Eureka Moments," Ness Labs, accessed January 21, 2023, https://nesslabs.com/eureka-moments.

6. Francis Bacon, *The Advancement of Learning* (1605), bk. 1, chap. 5, sec. 8.

7. René Descartes, *Meditations on First Philosophy,* translated by Donald Cress, 3rd ed. (Indianapolis: Hackett, 1993), Meditation I, pp. 13–17. See also Diego Morillo-Velarde, *René Descartes: De omnibus dubitandum* (Madrid: EDAF, 2001).

8. Blaise Pascal, *Pensées,* translated by W. F. Trotter (Mineola, NY: Dover, 2018), p. 23.

9. Mircea Eliade, *The Sacred and the Profane: The Nature of Religion,* translated by Willard R. Trask (New York: Harcourt Brace, 1959), p. 26.

10. Dylan Thomas, "Do Not Go Gentle into That Good Night," in *Dylan Thomas: Selected Poems 1934–1952* (New York: New Directions, 2003), p. 122.

11. See Adam Frank, "The Discover Interview: Max Tegmark," *Discover,* July 2008, pp. 38–43. For an introduction to multiverse cosmology and theories other than Tegmark's, see Alex Vilenkin, *Many Worlds in One: The Search for Other Universes* (New York: Hill and Wang, 2007). See also Carlos Eire, *A Very Brief History of Eternity* (Princeton, NJ: Princeton University Press, 2010), pp. 211–16.

12. See Fouad Khan, "Confirmed! We Live in a Simulation," *Scientific American,* April 1, 2021, https://www.scientificamerican.com/article/confirmed-we-live-in-a-simulation/. See also Michael Talbot, *The Holographic Universe: The Revolutionary Theory of Reality* (New York: Harper Perennial, 2011).

Introduction

1. Agelli, pt. 2, chap. 3, p. 198.
2. One historian of religion who has engaged with the impossible and very eloquently argued for its validity as a scholarly subject is Jeffrey Kripal, whose focus is on the recent past and the present. See his *The Super Humanities: Historical Precedents, Moral Objections, New Realities* (University of Chicago Press, 2022); *Authors of the Impossible: The Paranormal and the Sacred* (University of Chicago Press, 2010); and (with Whitley Strieber) *Super Natural: Why the Unexplained Is Real* (New York: Tarcher Perigree, 2016).
3. See Jacalyn Duffin, *Medical Miracles: Doctors, Saints, and Healing in the Modern World* (Oxford University Press, 2009).
4. *The Compact Edition of the Oxford English Dictionary,* 2 vols. (Oxford University Press, 1971), 1:947.
5. William James, "What Psychical Research Has Accomplished," in *The Will to Believe and Other Essays in Popular Philosophy* (New York: Longmans Green, 1905), pp. 299–302.
6. Lorraine Daston, "Marvelous Facts and Miraculous Evidence in Early Modern Europe," *Critical Inquiry* 18, no. 1 (1991): 93–124. Daston argues that during the early modern age, facts came to be regarded as "evidence *in potentia*" and takes up the question: "How did our current conceptions of neutral facts and enlisted evidence, and the distinction between come to be?" (pp. 93–94).
7. The *Compact Edition of the Oxford English Dictionary* defines "anecdote" as "the narrative of a detached single event, told as being in itself interesting or striking" (p. 80). As Jeffrey Kripal has observed, to categorize certain testimonies as "anecdotal" is to argue that they have no broader context and are therefore "pure anomalies that can be fully explained (away) as local constructions of a single human psyche and so should not concern us as either meaningful or real in the sense that other things are real. . . . No 'broader context' equals 'unreal.' These anomalies are best left ignored, then, as meaningless blips, as statistical flukes, or as neurological hiccups." Kripal and Strieber, *Super Natural,* p. 84.
8. See Louise and Richard Spilsbury, *Maglev Trains* (New York: Gareth Stevens, 2017); or Hyung-Suk Han and Dong-Sung Kim, *Magnetic Levitation: Maglev Technology and Applications* (Dordrecht: Springer Netherlands, 2016).
9. A few authors, such as Michael Grosso in his study of Saint Joseph of Cupertino, *The Man Who Could Fly* (Lanham, MD: Rowman and Littlefield, 2016), try to promote rational acceptance of levitation and other such phenomena.

For more on this approach, see E. F. Kelly, E. W. Kelly, M. Grosso, et al., eds., *Irreducible Mind: Toward a Psychology for the 21st Century* (Lanham, MD: Rowman and Littlefield, 2007); and E. F. Kelly, A. Crabtree, and P. Marshall, eds., *Beyond Physicalism: Toward Reconciliation of Science and Spirituality* (Lanham, MD: Rowman and Littlefield, 2015).

10. Most scholars avoid the subject, but nonscholarly studies abound, such as Steve Richards, *Levitation: What It Is, How It Works, How to Do It* (Wellingborough, UK: Aquarian Press, 1980). And some have examined it as a cultural phenomenon, especially Peter Adey, *Levitation: The Science, Myth, and Magic of Suspension* (London: Reaktion Books, 2017). For my review of Adey's book, see *Annals of Science* 75, no. 4 (2018): 368–69.

11. The most thorough study of Christian levitation is that of Olivier Leroy, *La Lévitation* (Paris: Librairie Valois, 1928); translated as *Levitation* (London: Burns Oates & Washbourne, 1928). Joachim Bouflet, *La lévitation chez les mystiques* (Paris: Le jardin des Livres, 2006) relies on Olivier but also ventures beyond Christianity and into the twentieth century. Albert de Rochas D'Aiglun's *Recueil de Documents Relatifs à La Lévitation du Corps Humain [Suspension Magnétique]* (Paris: P. G. Leymarie, 1897) is a relic of late nineteenth-century occult and pseudo-scientific approaches to the subject.

12. Marcelino Menéndez Pelayo, *Historia de los heterodoxos españoles,* 8 vols. (Madrid: C.S.I.C., 1947), 4:249–50.

13. Lucien Febvre, *Combats pour l'histoire* (Paris: A. Colin, 1952), p. 96.

14. Darren Oldridge, *Strange Histories: The Trial of the Pig, the Walking Dead, and Other Matters of Fact from the Medieval and Renaissance Worlds,* 2nd ed. (London: Routledge, 2018), p. 3. Oldridge adds that "to view them [premodern people] as irrational is no less insulting—or mistaken—than to view African tribespeople as 'savages.'"

15. As historian of witchcraft Erik Midelfort has said: "When we ignore the awkward realities and contradictions of this or any period, we shortchange the past. We shortchange ourselves as well. If we choose to remember only the 'progressive' parts of history, the ones that readily 'make sense' to us, we oversimplify the past and our own lives. We cultivate an artificially naive view of the world." Midelfort, *Exorcism and Enlightenment: Johann Joseph Gassner and the Demons of Eighteenth-Century Germany* (New Haven, CT: Yale University Press, 2005), p. 6.

16. See David Walker, "The Humbug in American Religion: Ritual Theories of Nineteenth-Century Spiritualism," *Religion and American Culture: A Journal of Interpretation* 23, no. 1 (Winter 2013): 30–74.

17. See Oliver Fox, *Astral Projection* (New York: Citadel Press, 1993); Robert Monroe, *Journeys out of the Body* (New York: Doubleday, 1973).

18. See Linda Rodriguez McRobbie, "The Strange and Mysterious History of the Ouija Board," *Smithsonian Magazine,* October 27, 2013.

19. See Stefan Bechtel, *Through a Glass, Darkly: Sir Arthur Conan Doyle and the Quest to Solve the Greatest Mystery of All* (New York: St. Martin's Press, 2017); and Erika White Dyson, "Gentleman Mountebanks and Spiritualists: Legal, Stage and Media Contest between Magicians and Spirit Mediums in the United States and England," in *The Ashgate Research Companion to Nineteenth-Century Spiritualism and the Occult,* edited by Tatiana Kontou and Sarah Willburn (London: Ashgate, 2012), pp. 231–66.

20. 1 Cor. 7:7, 12:4–11.

21. See Arnold I. Davidson, "Miracles of Bodily Transformation, or How St. Francis Received the Stigmata," *Critical Inquiry* 35, no. 3 (2009): 451–80.

22. Protestantism and skepticism have all but driven the history of Christian mysticism out of view in Western culture. See Karen Wetmore, *The Empire Triumphant: Race, Religion and Rebellion in the* Star Wars *Films* (Jefferson, NC: McFarland, 2005), especially chap. 2; and Stephen Teo, *Eastern Approaches to Western Film: Asian Reception and Aesthetics in Cinema* (London: Bloomsbury Academic, 2019), especially chap. 1.

23. See Jeffrey Kripal, *Mutants and Mystics: Science Fiction, Superhero Comics, and the Paranormal* (University of Chicago Press, 2015); Christopher Knowles, *Our Gods Wear Spandex: The Secret History of Comic Book Heroes* (Newburyport, MA: Weiser Books, 2007); and Stephanie Burt, "Who Really Created the Marvel Universe?," *New Yorker,* February 15, 2021.

24. For a masterful analysis of this mentality, see Caroline Walker Bynum, *Christian Materiality: An Essay on Religion in Late Medieval Europe* (Brooklyn, NY: Zone Books, 2011).

25. Thomas Aquinas, "On Miracles," in *Summa Contra Gentiles,* bk. 3, chap. 101, translated by Fathers of the English Dominican Province, 4 vols. (London, 1928), vol. 3, pt. 2, pp. 60–61. For Balaam's talking ass, see Num. 22:2–25:9.

26. "Now a miracle is so called as being full of wonder, as having a cause absolutely hidden from all: and this cause is God. Wherefore those things which God does outside those causes which we know, are called miracles." Thomas Aquinas, *Summa Theologica,* translated by Fathers of the English Dominican Province, 3 vols. (New York: Burns, Oates & Washbourne, 1947), vol. 1, pt. 1, question 105, article 7, objection 3, p. 520.

27. Gen. 1:26.

28. For a brilliant and concise introduction to this subject, see Peter Brown, *The Cult of the Saints: Its Rise and Function in Latin Christianity* (University of Chicago Press, 1981).

29. See D. P. Walker, "The Cessation of Miracles," in *Hermeticism and the Renaissance: Intellectual History and the Occult in Early Modern Europe,* edited by Ingrid Merkel and Allen G. Debus (Washington, DC: Folger Shakespeare Library, 1988), pp. 111–24; Alexandra Walsham, "Miracles in Post-Reformation England," in *Signs, Wonders, Miracles: Representations of Divine Power in the Life of the Church,* edited by Kate Cooper and Jeremy Gregory (London: Boydell Press, 2005), pp. 273–306; Moshe Sluhovsky, "Calvinist Miracles and the Concept of the Miraculous in Sixteenth-Century Huguenot Thought," *Renaissance and Reformation / Renaissance et Réforme* 19, no. 2 (1995): 5–25; and Philip Soergel, *Miracles and the Protestant Imagination* (Oxford University Press, 2012), pp. 33–46.

30. See, for instance, William Whiston, *Account of the exact time when the miraculous gifts ceas'd in the church* (London, 1749). This belief has waxed and waned in significance throughout the history of Protestantism and was intensely analyzed a century ago by the Calvinist scholar Benjamin Warfield in *Counterfit Miracles* (New York: Charles Scribner's Sons, 1918).

31. Martin Luther began attributing Catholic miracles to the devil in 1520 in his *Address to the German Nobility* (WA 6:447) and continued to do so thereafter. All the magisterial Protestant Reformers agreed on this point, including the influential John Calvin, who dismissed Catholic miracles as "mere illusions of Satan" in the prefatory letter to King Francis in his *Institutes of the Christian Religion* (CO 2.17). English translation by Ford Lewis Battles in *Institutes.*

32. Thomas Browne, *Pseudodoxia Epidemica or Enquiries into very many received tenents and commonly presumed truths* (1646), in *The Works of Thomas Browne,* edited by Charles Sayle, 3 vols. (Edinburgh: Grant, 1912), 1:188.

33. William Shakespeare, *Hamlet,* act 3, scene 1.

34. James Weatherall, *Void: The Strange Physics of Nothing* (New Haven, CT: Yale University Press, 2013), p. 13.

35. Gillian Brockell, "During a Pandemic, Isaac Newton Had to Work from Home, Too. He Used the Time Wisely," *Washington Post,* March 12, 2020.

36. See Philip E. Tetlock, Richard Ned Lebow, and Geoffrey Parker, eds., *Unmaking the West: "What-if" Scenarios That Rewrite World History* (Ann Arbor: University of Michigan Press, 2006), esp. chap. 1, "Counterfactual Thought Experiments: Why We Can't Live without Them and Must Learn to Live with Them," by Geoffrey Parker and Philip Tetlock.

37. David Hume, *An Enquiry concerning Human Understanding,* pt. 1, sec. 10, "Of Miracles," in *The Clarendon Edition of the Works of David Hume,* edited by Tom L. Beauchamp (Oxford University Press, 2000), pp. 86–87.

38. Febvre, *Combats pour l'histoire,* p. 96.

39. Natalie Zemon Davis, "On the Lame," *American Historical Review* 93, no. 3 (1988): 574.

40. "Whiggish" historians hail the Protestant Reformation as the beginning of modernity and of the upward march of science, progress, and freedom. See Herbert Butterfield, *The Whig Interpretation of History* (London: Bell, 1931). Butterfield uses the terms "Protestant history" and "Whiggish history" interchangeably. See pp. 5–20.

41. This assumption is brilliantly questioned by Fabián Alejandro Campagne in "Witchcraft and the Sense-of-the-Impossible in Early Modern Spain: Some Reflections Based on the Literature of Superstition (ca. 1500–1800)," *Harvard Theological Review* 96, no. 1 (January 2003): 25–62.

42. See Anthony Cascardi, *The Subject of Modernity* (Cambridge University Press, 1992); Stanley Jeyaraja Tambiah, *Magic, Science, Religion, and the Scope of Rationality* (Cambridge University Press, 1990).

43. Max Weber, "Science as a Vocation," in *Max Weber: Essays in Sociology,* edited by Hans Heinrich Gerth and C. Wright Mills (New York: Oxford University Press, 1946). This "disenchantment" thesis is an essential component of one of the most influential books on early modern religion: Keith Thomas, *Religion and the Decline of Magic* (Oxford University Press, 1971). For a revisionist take on this classic text, see Michael Hunter, *The Decline of Magic: Britain in the Enlightenment* (New Haven, CT: Yale University Press, 2020).

44. See Stuart Clark, *Thinking with Demons* (Oxford University Press, 1997); Midelfort, *Exorcism and Enlightenment.*

45. See Robert Scribner, "The Reformation, Popular Magic, and the 'Disenchantment of the World,'" *Journal of Interdisciplinary History* 23 (1993): 484, 487.

46. In addition to the work of Andrew Keitt and Fabián Alejandro Campagne, see Julie Crawford, *Marvelous Protestantism* (Baltimore: Johns Hopkins University Press, 2005); Daston, "Marvelous Facts and Miraculous Evidence"; and Lorraine Daston and Katharine Park, *Wonders and the Order of Nature* (New York: Zone Books, 1998).

47. For an insightful summary and analysis of the development of these concepts in medieval and early modern thought, see Daston, "Marvelous Facts and Miraculous Evidence," pp. 95–100.

48. Andrew Keitt argues in *Inventing the Sacred: Imposture, Inquisition, and the Boundaries of the Supernatural in Golden Age Spain* (Leiden: Brill, 2005) that the seventeenth century was "a period in which rationalism was employed as often to shore up belief in the miraculous as to challenge it" (p. 7). For a concise summary of Keitt's views, see his article "Religious Enthusiasm, the Spanish Inquisition, and the Disenchantment of the World," *Journal of the History of Ideas* 65, no. 2 (2004): 243–44.

1. Hovering, Flying, and All That

1. William Crookes, "Notes of an Enquiry into the Phenomena Called Spiritual during the Years 1870–1873," *Quarterly Journal of Science,* 2nd ser., 41 (January 1874): 77.

2. Crookes, "Notes of an Enquiry," p. 77.

3. "Human Levitation," a history of the phenomenon, appeared in Crookes's *Quarterly Journal of Science,* 2nd ser., 45 (January 1875): 31–61.

4. Naturally, this claim has been contested. See Sergio Luzzatto, *Padre Pio: Miracles and Politics in a Secular Age* (New York: Metropolitan Books, 2010), p. 212; and Claudia Baldoli, "Religion and Bombing in Italy," in *Bombing, States and Peoples in Western Europe, 1940–1945,* edited by C. Baldoli, A. Knapp, and R. Overy (London: Continuum International, 2011), p. 147.

5. See Luzzatto, *Padre Pio.*

6. Michael Grosso, *The Man Who Could Fly: St. Joseph of Copertino and the Mystery of Levitation* (Lanham, MD: Rowman and Littlefield, 2015); Steve Richards, *Levitation: What It Is, How It Works, How to Do It* (Newburyport, MA: Weiser Books, 2015).

7. See Wolfgang Behringer and Constance Ott-Koptschalijski, *Der Traum vom Fliegen* (Frankfurt: S. Fischer, 1991); Wolfgang Behringer and Dieter Bauer, *Fliegen und Schweben* (München: Deutscher Taschenbuch, 1997); Constance Ott-Koptschalijski, ed., *Märchen und Mythen vom Fliegen* (Frankfurt: Fischer-Taschenbuch, 1992); Clive Hart, *Images of Flight* (University of California Press, 1988); Serenity Young, *Women Who Fly: Goddesses, Witches, Mystics, and Other Airborne Females* (Oxford University Press, 2018).

8. See Montague Summers, *The Physical Phenomena of Mysticism* (London: Rider, 1950), esp. chap. 2.

9. Pope Benedict XIV, *De Servorum Dei Beatificatione et Beatorum Canonizatione,* 4 vols. (Rome, 1743), vol. 3, chap. 49.3.

10. See W. J. Crawford, *Experiments in Psychical Science, Levitation, Contact, and the Direct Voice* (New York: E. P. Dutton, 1919).

11. David Blaine, "Levitation," accessed January 21, 2023, https://www.youtube .com/watch?v=w6CNvFnlPL0; Criss Angel, "Levitation," accessed January 21, 2023, https://www.youtube.com/watch?v=WKedVgotoJk; "How to Levitate Like Criss Angel," Wikihow, December 21, 2022, https://www.wikihow.com /Levitate-Like-Criss-Angel.

12. Philostratus, *Life of Apollonius of Tyana,* translated by F. C. Conybeare (Loeb Classical Library, Harvard University Press, 1912), I.3.15.

13. Kenneth L. Woodward, *The Book of Miracles: The Meaning of the Miracle Stories in Christianity, Judaism, Buddhism, Hinduism, and Islam* (New York: Simon and Schuster, 2001), p. 317.

14. See Glenn H. Mullin, *The Flying Mystics of Tibetan Buddhism* (Chicago: Serindia, 2006), pp. 48, 50, with graphic illustrations on pp. 103, 106, 119, 120, 128, 138, 150, 155, 181, and 206.

15. Anonymous, "Human Levitation," *Quarterly Journal of Science* 45 (January 1875): 41–42. See also Olivier Leroy, *La Lévitation* (Paris: Librairie Valois, 1928), pp. 4–13.

16. Gillian Clark, introduction to *Iamblichus: On the Pythagorean Life* (Liverpool University Press, 1989), p. xvi.

17. Helena Blavatsky, comments on "A Treatise on the Yoga Philosophy," in *Collected Writings,* 15 vols. (Wheaton, IL: Theosophical Press, 1966–1968), 2:466–67.

18. 2 Kings 2.11; Dan. 14:36.

19. Matt. 14:22–36; Mark 6:45–56; John 6:16–24.

20. Luke 24:50–53; Acts of the Apostles 1:9–12.

21. Acts of the Apostles 8:26–40.

22. Matt. 4:1–11; Mark 1:12–13; Luke 4:1–13.

23. Jacobus de Voragine, *The Golden Legend,* translated by William Granger Ryan, 2 vols. (Princeton University Press, 1993), 1:380.

24. For mention of some apocryphal second- and third-century noncanonical texts with references to apostolic ascents to heaven, see Xavier Yvanoff, *La Chair des Anges: Les phénomènes corporels du mysticisme* (Paris: Editions Seuil, 2002), pp. 146–50. Unfortunately, Yvanoff provides no footnotes or citations.

25. See Robert Knapp, *The Dawn of Christianity: People and Gods in a Time of Magic and Miracles* (Cambridge, MA: Harvard University Press, 2017); Harold Remus, *Pagan-Christian Conflict over Miracle in the Second Century* (Phila-

delphia: Philadelphia Patristic Foundation, 1983); and Howard Clark Kee, *Miracle in the Early Christian World* (New Haven, CT: Yale University Press, 1983).

26. From the Greek: *thauma* = marvel or wonder + *ergos* = working; from the Greek: *hieros* = sacred + *pharein* = to reveal. Basically, an intercessor with the divine, who can make it present.

27. See Matthew W. Dickie, *Magic and Magicians in the Greco-Roman World* (London: Routledge, 2001), chaps. 9 and 10.

28. Johann Christoph Wagenseil, ed., *Tela Ignea Satanae: Arcani, et horribiles Judaeorum adversus Christum Deum et Christianam Relgionem Libri* (Altdorf, 1681). For much more recent attempts to explore this dimension of the miracles of Jesus, see Bertrand Méheust, *Jesus Thaumaturge: Enquête sur l'homme et ses miracles* (Paris: Intereditions, 2015).

29. Acts 8:9–11. There are various legends about Simon Magus, and not all of them agree. See Florent Heintz, *Simon "le magicien"* (Paris: J. Gabalda, 1997); and Alberto Ferreiro, *Simon Magus in Patristic, Medieval, and Early Modern Traditions* (Leiden: Brill, 2005).

30. Acts of Peter 31–32, in *The Apocryphal New Testament,* translated by J. K. Elliott (Oxford: Clarendon Press, 1993), in *Lost Scriptures: Books That Did Not Make It into the New Testament,* edited by Bart Ehrman (Oxford University Press, 2003), pp. 150–51.

31. Nazianzen, *First Invective against Julian,* sec. 74; see also secs. 54–56; *Julian the Emperor, Containing Gregory Nazianzen's Two Invectives,* translated by C. W. King (London: Bohn's Classical Library, 1888), pp. 43, 30–32.

32. Émile Lamé, *Julien L'Apostat* (Paris: Charpentier, 1861 pp. 51–52.

33. 1 Peter 5:8.

34. For Hilary, see *Contra Constantium,* in Migne, *PL,* vol. 10, cols. 584–85.

35. Sulpicius Severus, *Dialogues,* 3.6; Migne, *PL,* vol. 20, col. 215.

36. Candido Brognoli, *Manuale Exorcistarum ac Parochorum* (Bergamo, 1651), p. 90, item 26.

37. St. Athanasius, *Life of Antony,* translated by Robert Gregg (Mahwah, NJ: Paulist Press, 1980), pp. 76, 78–79.

38. E. Amélineau, *Les moines égyptiens: Vie de Schnoudi* (Paris: Leroux, 1889), pp. 318–19.

39. See Benedicta Ward, *Harlots of the Desert* (Kalamazoo, MI: Cistercian, 1987).

40. Sophronius of Jerusalem, "Sancta Maria Aegyptiaca," *AS,* April, 1:79, 83.

41. *Vie de Théodore de Sykéon,* translated by A. J. Festugière (Brussels: Société des Bollandistes, 1970), chaps. 15–16.

42. The 68-volume hagiographical collection of the *AS,* cited in note 40, is the result of a monumental project launched in 1643 and completed in 1940 by the Bollandist Society, originally a Jesuit enterprise. The volumes and entries are organized according to the months of the year and each saint's feast day.

43. *AS,* November, 2:352, 398: "Suspensum a terra in aere quasi duobus cubitis totum illuminatum et supra solem splendentem."

44. *AS,* February, 2:85; translated by Walter Connor and Carolyn Loessel as *The Life and Miracles of Saint Luke of Steiris* (Brookline, MA: Holy Cross Orthodox Press, 1994), chap. 7.

45. *AS,* May, vol. 6, Corollarium ad XVIII Maii, pp. 15–16 (supplement at the back of the volume, with its own pagination). For more on holy fools in Orthodox Christianity, see John Saward, *Perfect Fools: Folly for Christ's Sake in Catholic and Orthodox Spirituality* (Oxford University Press, 1980), esp. chap 2; translated by Lennart Rydén as *The Life of St. Andrew the Fool* (Uppsala: Uppsala University, 1995).

46. Perfunctory levitation accounts can sometimes be found in devotional texts such as Thomas of Cantimpré's *Bonum universale de apibus* (thirteenth century), or in sermon exempla such as Caesarius of Heisterbach's *Dialogus Miraculorum* (thirteenth century), or in letters from prominent churchmen such as Peter Damian (eleventh century). For exact references to these texts, see the entries under the keyword "levitation" in *Thesaurus Exemplorum Medii Aevi,* accessed February 24, 2023, http://thema.huma-num.fr/keywords/KW0663.

47. Leroy, *La Lévitation,* pp. 39–49.

48. Saint Douceline is not as well known as the other thirteenth-century levitators listed here, but she has been receiving more attention since her hagiography was translated into English by Kathleen Garay and Madeleine Jeay, *The Life of Saint Douceline, Beguine of Provence* (Woodbridge, UK: Boydell and Brewer, 2001). The original Occitan text by Felipa Porcelet, *Vida de la Benhaurada Sancta Douceline,* was first translated into French by J. H. Albanés (Marseille: Camoin, 1879) and again, nearly a century ago, by R. Gout, *La Vie de Sainte Douceline* (Paris: Bloud et Gay, 1927). See Sean Field, *Courting Sanctity: Holy Women and the Capetians* (Ithaca, NY: Cornell University Press, 2019), chap. 2, "Douceline of Digne, Co-mother to the Capetians"; and Madeleine Jeay and Kathleen Garay, "Douceline de Digne: De l'usage politique de l'extase mystique," *Revue des Langues Romanes* 106, no. 2 (2002): 475–92.

49. *AS,* May, 4:374.

50. *AS,* July, 5:651.5 C–D.

51. *AS,* July, 5:652 B.

52. *AS,* July, 5:653 A. "In subtilissimis arborum ramusculis dependeret."

53. Translated by Margot King as *The Life of Christina Mirabilis* (Toronto: Peregrina, 1986); Latin original and French translation, with abundant commentary and analysis, by Sylvain Piron, *Christine l'Admirable: Vie, chants et merveilles* (Brussels: Vues de l'Espirit, 2021).

54. Leroy, *La Lévitation,* p. 42.

55. Arnold Davidson and Maggie Fritz-Morkin, "Miracles of Bodily Transformation, or How St. Francis Received the Stigmata," *Critical Inquiry* 35, no. 3 (Spring 2009): 456.

56. See Gilbert Wdzieczny, "The Life and Works of Thomas of Celano," *Franciscan Studies,* n.s., 5, no. 1 (March 1945): 55–68.

57. *Second Life,* chap. 61, translated by Placid Hermann, in *St. Francis of Assisi: Writings and Early Biographies,* edited by Marion A. Habig (Chicago: Franciscan Herald Press, 1973), pp. 439, 443.

58. See Jay M. Hammond, "Bonaventure's *Legenda Major,*" in *A Companion to Bonaventure,* edited by Jay M. Hammond, J. A. Wayne Hellmann, and Jared Goff (Leiden: Brill, 2014), pp. 453–507.

59. Timothy J. Johnson, "The Legenda Minor," in Hammond, Hellmann, and Goff, *A Companion to Bonaventure,* p. 435.

60. *Legenda Major,* chap. 10, translated by Benen Fahy, in Habig, *St. Francis of Assisi,* pp. 705–6. This passage is nearly identical in *Legenda Minor,* chap. 4, p. 812.

61. A more recent edition is available: *Actus Beati Francisci et Sociorum,* edited by Marino Bigaroni and Giovanni Boccali (Assisi: Edizioni Porziuncola, 1988).

62. Translator Raphael Brown thinks that this text "represents not folklore, but a direct oral tradition transmitted by several of the Saint's closest friends … through a few intermediaries to the author, and that this oral tradition, although occasionally inaccurate in chronology and topography, is in the main reliable, unless disproved by earlier evidence." *Brown* then provides a long list of eminent experts who share this opinion. See Brown's introduction to his translation of Ugolino di Monte Santa Maria's *The Little Flowers of Saint Francis* (Garden City, NY: Image Books / Doubleday, 1958), p. 27.

63. Brown, *Little Flowers,* "Considerations on the Holy Stigmata," p. 1438.

64. Brown, p. 1439.

65. Brown, pp. 1439–40.

66. Brown, pp. 1328–29.

67. *AS,* July, 3:791 E: "Sinamus, inquit, Sanctum qui laborat pro Sancto."

68. *AS,* March, 1:669 A–B: "Duobus cubitis elevatus a terra." French translation of William de Thoco's hagiography, *Saint Thomas d'Aquin: Sa vie* (Paris: Téqui, 1924).

69. *AS,* April, 2:792.

70. *AS,* March, 1:558.

71. *AS,* March, 1:295 A.

72. Figure cited by José Luis Sánchez Lora, *Mujeres, conventos, y formas de la religiosidad barroca* (Madrid: Fundación Universitaria Española, 1988), p. 374.

73. See Peter Burke, "How to Be a Counter-Reformation Saint," in *Religion and Society in Early Modern Europe, 1500–1800,* edited by Kaspar von Greyerz (London: George Allen and Unwyn, 1984), pp. 45–55.

74. Pedro de Rivadeneyra, *Tratado de la tribulación,* quoted in Richard Kagan, *Lucrecia's Dreams* (Berkeley: University of California Press, 1990), p. 115.

75. Martín Gonzalez de Cellorigo, *Memorial de la política necesaria y util restauración a la república de España,* quoted in J. H. Elliott, *Spain and Its World, 1500–1700* (New Haven, CT: Yale University Press, 1989), pp. 262–86.

76. Hyacintha was beatified in 1726 and canonized in 1807, and is depicted levitating in various engravings. Her hagiographer was the Theatine priest Girolamo Ventimiglia. See his *Vita della beata Giacinta Marescotti* (Brescia: Turlino, 1729), pp. 187–88.

77. See Jesús Imirizaldu, *Monjas y Beatas Embaucadoras* (Madrid: Editora Nacional, 1977).

78. *AS,* July, 7:441 D, n111.

79. Dominique Bouhours, SJ, *La vie de S. François Xavier, apôtre des Indes et de Japon,* 2 vols. (Louvain, 1683–88), vol. 2, bk. 6, pp. 348–49.

80. *AS,* September, 5:832 F.

81. *AS,* October, 8:764 F: "Aliquando ab horto ad ecclesiam subito per aera ducebatur." See also pp. 755 F, 756 A.

82. *AS,* October, 8:734 A (three hours); p. 764 EF (luminosity): "Candidisima nube radios solis imitante caput ipsius circumdari, totamque splendore viciniam illustrari."

83. *AS,* May, 6:584 DE.

84. *AS,* March, 2:679 AB.

85. The awkward term "social imaginary" has been used by various philosophers and social scientists to describe this complex relation between conceptual structures and social realities. For a brilliant analysis of the changes in the social imaginary brought about by the Protestant Reformation, see Charles

Taylor, *A Secular Age* (Cambridge, MA: Belknap Press of Harvard University Press, 2007), pp. 146–211.

86. Zwingli, "Commentary on the True and False Religion" (1525), in *The Latin Works and the Correspondence of Huldreich Zwingli,* edited by S. M. Jackson, 3 vols. (London: G. P. Putnam's Sons, 1912–1929), 2:92.

87. Calvin, "Commentary on the Four Books of Moses," *CO* 24:387.

88. *Huldrych Zwinglis Sämtliche Werke,* 21 vols. (Berlin: C. A. Schwetschke und Sohn, 1905), 8:194–95.

89. Calvin, "Commentary on the Four Books of Moses," *CO* 24:387.

90. "Denn jene sichtbare Werk sind allein Zeichen für den unverständigen, ungläubigen haufen. . . . Darumb ist nicht Wunder, dass sie nu aufgehöret." Third Sermon for Pentecost, John 13:23–31, *Dr. Martin Luther's Sämmtliche Werke,* edited by Ernst Ludwig Enders, 2nd ed., 67 vols. (Erlangen, 1862–1885), 12:236–37.

91. William Tyndale, *An Answer to Sir Thomas More's Dialogue,* edited by Henry Walter (Cambridge University Press, 1850), p. 130.

92. Heinrich Bullinger, *A Commentary upon the Second Epistle of Saint Paul to the Thessalonians,* translated by R. H. (London, 1538), fol. 51.

93. *Institutes* I.8. 5–6, *CO* 2.63; see also Commentary on Acts 5:15, *CO* 48.104.

94. "Et nous doit aussi souvenir que Satan a ses miracles." *Institutes,* Prefatory Address to King Francis I, *CO* 3.18, pp. 16–17.

95. Georg Nigrinus (Schwartz), *Papistiche Inquisition und gulden flus der Römischen Kirchen* (1582); Philips van Marnix, *The bee hive of the Romishe Church* (1579); John Bale, *The Pageant of Popes* (1574).

96. See Helen Parish, "Magic and Priestcraft: Reformers and Reformation," in *The Cambridge History of Magic and Witchcraft in the West,* edited by David Collins, SJ (Cambridge University Press, 2015), chap. 13.

97. John Napier, *A Plaine Discovery of the Whole Revelation of St. John* (Edinburgh, 1594).

98. John Bale, *A mysterye of inyquyte contayned within the hereticall genealogye of Ponce Pantolabus* (1545), fols. B2r–v, B5v, C8r. See also Helen Parish, *Monks, Miracles, and Magic: Reformation Representations of the Medieval Church* (London: Routledge, 2005), chap. 6.

99. William Perkins, *A Discourse of the Damned Art of Witchcraft* (Cambridge, 1608), p. 5r.

100. Quoted in Parish, *Monks, Miracles and Magic,* p. 146.

101. See Keith Thomas, *Religion and the Decline of Magic* (Oxford University Press, 1971), p. 78; and Parish, *Monks, Miracles, and Magic,* pp. 140–46.

102. See Philip Soergel, *Miracles and the Protestant Imagination* (Oxford University Press, 2012), pp. 33–46; and Jane Shaw, *Miracles in Enlightenment England* (New Haven, CT: Yale University Press, 2006).

103. "De votis monasticis Martini Lutheri iudicium," *WA* 8:573–669; translated as "Judgment of Martin Luther on Monastic Vows," *LW* 44:305.

104. See Bradford Bouley, *Pious Postmortems: Anatomy, Sanctity, and the Catholic Church in Early Modern Europe* (Philadelphia: University of Pennsylvania Press, 2017); and Paolo Parigi, *The Rationalization of Miracles* (New York: Cambridge University Press, 2012).

105. Calvin, "Commentary on John's Gospel," *CO* 47.90.

106. "Mais l'ame estant abysmée nc e gouffre d'iniquité, non seulement est vicieuse, mais aussi vuide de tout bien." *Institutes* II.3.2, *CO* 3.335, p. 292.

107. Thomas, *Religion and the Decline of Magic,* pp. 107–8.

108. Thomas Sprat, *The History of the Royal-Society of London, For the Improving of Natural Knowledge* (London, 1667), pp. 360–61.

109. Kenneth P. Minkema, Catherine A. Brekus, and Harry S. Stout, "Agitations, Convulsions, Leaping, and Loud Talking: The 'Experiences' of Sarah Pierpont Edwards," *William and Mary Quarterly,* 3rd ser., 78, no. 3 (July 2021): 491–536.

110. Minkema, Brekus, and Stout, "Agitations," p. 530.

111. Minkema, Brekus, and Stout, "Agitations," pp. 524, 525, 530.

112. Parish, *Monks, Miracles, and Magic,* p. 46.

113. Thomas More, "Confutation of Tyndale's Answer," in *The Complete Works of St. Thomas More,* 21 vols. (New Haven, CT: Yale University Press, 1973), 8:244–47. Original spelling modernized. The argument about miracles was but one of many in this nearly encyclopedic exchange over points of doctrine and ecclesiology.

114. Luis de Granada, *Historia de Sor María de la Visitación y Sermón de las caídas públicas* (Barcelona: J. Flors, 1962), p. 154. Similar statements can be found on pp. 26, 148–49, and 156.

115. Diego de Yepes, *Vida, Virtudes, y Milagros de la Bienaventurada Virgen Teresa de Jesús* (Madrid, 1599); modern edition published under the title *Vida de Santa Teresa de Jesús* (Buenos Aires: Emecé, 1946), p. 17.

116. Yepes, *Vida, Virtudes, y Milagros,* p. 14.

117. Yepes, pp. 17–18.

118. *Sermones Predicados en la Beatificación de la B.M. Teresa de Jesús* (Madrid, 1615), fol. 172r (Juan de Herrera, SJ); fol. 123 r–v (Juan Gonzalez OP).

119. Fray Luis de León, *Obras Completas Castellanas de Fray Luis de León,* edited by Félix Garcia, OSA, 4th ed., 2 vols. (Madrid: Biblioteca de Autores Cristianos, 1967), 1:905–6.

120. Julio Caro Baroja, *Las formas complejas de la vida religiosa: Religión, sociedad y carácter en la España de los siglos XVI y XVII* (Madrid: Akal, 1978), p. 92.

121. See Sánchez Lora, *Mujeres, conventos y formas de la religiosidad barroca,* p. 258.

122. Fray Luis de León, *Obras Completas,* 1:915–20.

123. Francisco de Ribera, SJ, *Vida de la Madre Teresa de Jesús* (Salamanca, 1590). Modern edition edited by Jaime Pons, SJ (Barcelona: Gustavo Gili, 1908), p. 543.

124. Jerónimo de Gracián de la Madre de Dios, "Dialogos del tránsito de la Madre Teresa de Jesús" (1584), in *Fuentes históricas sobre la muerte y cuerpo de Santa Teresa de Jesús (1582–1596),* edited by J. L. Astigarrage, E. Pacho, and O. Rodriguez (Rome: Teresianum, 1982), pp. 43–44, 46.

125. Gracián, "Dialogos," pp. 77–78.

126. Gracián, p. 44.

127. Yepes, *Vida, Virtudes, y Milagros,* pp. 18, 423.

128. Ribera, *Vida de la Madre Teresa de Jesús,* p. 543. Ribera's circular reasoning can be found in Gregory of Tours (sixth century): "For, as Gregory frequently repeats, if healing and mercy did not happen in his own days, who would believe that they had ever happened or ever would happen again?" Peter Brown, *The Cult of the Saints* (University of Chicago Press, 1981), p. 82.

129. Luis de León, *Obras Completas Castellanas,* 1:920.

2. Saint Teresa of Avila, Reluctant Aethrobat

1. Testimony of Sister Isabel de Santo Domingo, in *Procesos,* 2:463.

2. *Libro de la Vida* 20.1, *O.C.,* p. 108.

3. See Jodi Bilinkoff, *The Avila of Saint Teresa* (Ithaca, NY: Cornell University Press, 1989); and Alison Weber, *Teresa of Avila and the Rhetoric of Femininity* (Princeton University Press, 1990).

4. See Alison Weber, "Saint Teresa, Demonologist," in *Culture and Control in Counter-Reformation Spain*, edited by Anne J. Cruz and Mary Elizabeth Perry (Minneapolis: University of Minnesota Press, 1991).

5. Medieval women mystics were often suspected of greater spiritual and mental instability than men, but it is Jean Gerson, theologian and chancellor of the University of Paris, who is often credited with intensifying this

suspicion and lending it greater intensity in his 1415 treatise *De probatione spirituum,* in Jean Gerson, *Opera omnia,* edited by Louis Ellies Du Pin, SJ, 5 vols. (Antwerp, 1706), 1:37–43. See Wendy Love Anderson, "Gerson's Stance on Women," in *A Companion to Jean Gerson,* edited by Brian Patrick McGuire (Leiden: Brill, 2006), pp. 293–316. For attitudes toward women mystics in Teresa's day and age, see Weber, *Teresa of Avila and the Rhetoric of Femininity,* esp. chap. 1, "Little Women: Counter-Reformation Misogyny," pp. 17–41.

6. Girolamo Savonarola, *Trattato della revelazione della Chiesa divinitus fatta / Compendio di rivelazioni* (Venice, 1536), fols. 16r–16v; Diego Perez de Valdivia, *Aviso de gente recogida,* edited by Alvaro Huergo and Juan Esquerda Bifet (Universidad de Salamanca, 1977), pp. 17–21, 55–104; Alison Weber, "Between Ecstasy and Exorcism: Religious Negotiation in Sixteeenth-Century Spain," *Journal of Medieval and Renaissance Studies* 23 (1993): 221–34.

7. See Andrew Keitt, *Inventing the Sacred: Imposture, Inquisition, and the Boundaries of the Supernatural in Golden Age Spain* (Leiden: Brill, 2005).

8. See Carlos Eire, *The Life of Saint Teresa of Avila: A Biography* (Princeton University Press, 2019), esp. chaps. 1 and 2.

9. Diego de Yepes, *Vida, Virtudes, y Milagros de la Bienaventurada Teresa de Jesús* (Madrid, 1797), chap. 15, p. 112. All subsequent page references will be to this edition.

10. Yepes, *Vida, Virtudes, y Milagros,* chap. 15, p. 113.

11. *Vida* 20.5, *O.C.,* p. 109, where she uses "arrebatamiento" to describe a purely spiritual vision with no accompanying physical phenomena.

12. As in *Vida* 38.1, *O.C.,* p. 207.

13. *Vida* 20.6, *O.C.,* p. 109. Teresa also complained that they left her wracked with pain, as if all her joints had been pulled apart. *Vida* 20.12, *O.C.,* pp. 111–12.

14. For Sor María, see Richard Kagan, "Politics, Prophecy, and the Inquisition in Late Sixteenth-Century Spain," in *Cultural Encounters: The Impact of the Inquisition in Spain and the New World,* edited by Mary Elizabeth Perry and Anne J. Cruz (University of California Press, 1991), pp. 105–20, and esp. note 50 for further reading.

15. *Vida* 31.12, *O.C.,* p. 168.

16. *Moradas* 6.6.2, *O.C.,* p. 544.

17. For an incisive analysis of the direct effect of such beliefs on Teresa, see Weber, "Saint Teresa, Demonologist," pp. 171–95.

18. *Vida* 29:5–6, *O.C.,* pp. 155–56.

19. Pope Gregory XV, "Bula de canonización de Santa Teresa de Jesús," in *Biblioteca mística carmelitana*, edited by Silverio de Santa Teresa, 35 vols. (Burgos: El Monte Carmelo, 1934–1949), 2:219–21.

20. For details, see Eire, *Life of Saint Teresa*, pp. 50–54, 150–55.

21. Fray Luis de León, *Obras Completas Castellanas de Fray Luis de León*, edited by Félix Garcia, OSA, 4th ed., 2 vols. (Madrid: Biblioteca de Autores Cristianos, 1967), 1:905–6.

22. *Vida* 20.19, *O.C.*, p. 113: "Muchas veces se engolfa el alma u la engolfa el Señor en si, por mijor decir."

23. *Vida* 20.18, *O.C.*, p. 113: "Este transformamiento de el alma de el todo en Dios."

24. *Vida* 24.5, *O.C.*, p. 133.

25. *Cuentas de conciencia* 58.8, *O.C.*, p. 626.

26. *Moradas* 6.5.1, *O.C.*, p. 540.

27. *Vida* 20.18, *O.C.*, p. 113. Teresa adds: "Although one rarely loses consciousness, it has happened to me sometimes, totally, but only infrequently and briefly. Ordinarily, one's consciousness does get disturbed, but despite one's inability to do anything outwardly, one is still able to hear and understand everything, as if it were taking place far away."

28. *Vida* 20.13, *O.C.*, p. 112.

29. *Vida* 20.14, *O.C.*, p. 112.

30. Catalepsy (from Greek for "seizing, grasping") is a neurological condition that causes muscular rigidity, fixity of posture, and unresponsiveness to external stimuli, as well as decreased sensitivity to pain. Teresa of Avila has been diagnosed with temporal lobe epilepsy. See Marcella Biro Barton, "Saint Teresa of Avila: Did She Have Epilepsy?," *Catholic Historical Review* 68, no. 4 (October 1982): 581–98; and Encarnación Juárez-Almendros, "Historical Testimony of Female Disability: The Neurological Impairment of Teresa de Ávila," in *Disabled Bodies in Early Modern Spanish Literature* (Liverpool University Press, 2017), pp. 116–66.

31. *Cuentas de conciencia* 58.7, *O.C*, p. 626. In the *Vida* 20.4, she says, "The soul seems to stop animating the body, and thus the natural heat of the body diminishes very sensibly, and it grows colder gradually, though with the greatest sweetness and delight." *O.C.*, p. 109.

32. *Vida* 20.18, *O.C.*, p. 113.

33. *Vida* 20.19, *O.C.*, p. 113.

34. *Moradas* 6.5.12, *O.C.*, p. 543.

35. *Vida* 20.12, *O.C.*, pp. 111-12: "Que parece me han desconyuntado."

36. *Vida* 20.21, *O.C.*, p. 114.

37. *Vida* 20.11, *O.C.*, p. 111: "Un recio martirio sabroso."

38. *Vida* 29.14, *O.C.*, p. 158.

39. *Moradas* 6.5.9, *O.C.*, p. 543: "Con la presteza que sale la pelota de un arcabuz, cuando le ponen el fuego." Teresa uses terms from her own century: an arquebus that shoots balls rather than bullets and a fuse that is lit and ignites gunpowder rather than a trigger.

40. *Vida* 20.3-4, *O.C.*, p. 109.

41. *Vida* 20.4, *O.C.*, p. 109.

42. *Vida* 20.6, *O.C.*, p. 109.

43. *Vida,* 20.7, *O.C.*, pp. 109-10.

44. *Vida* 20.7, *O.C.*, p. 110; emphasis added.

45. *Vida* 20.7, *O.C.*, p. 110.

46. *Moradas* 6.6.2, *O.C.*, p. 544.

47. *Moradas* 6.6.1, *O.C.*, p. 544.

48. *O.C.*, p. 1074.

49. According to the ultimate Spanish lexicographical authority, "tornar" means "to rotate the arm a fraction of a circle in order to launch the bird of prey on one's wrist." "Girar el brazo una fracción de círculo para lanzar al aire el ave de cetrería posada en el puño," *Diccionario de la Lengua Española,* 2 vols., 21st ed. (Madrid: La Real Academia Española, 1992), 2:1997.

50. See Breck Falconry, "Falconry Glossary," accessed January 5, 2023, https://sites.google.com/site/breckfalconry/glossary. See also *The Compact Edition of the Oxford English Dictionary,* 2 vols. (Oxford University Press, 1971), 1:350.

51. Yepes, *Vida, Virtudes, y Milagros,* chap. 15, p. 110.

52. *Moradas* 6.5.2, *O.C.*, p. 541.

53. In the first century AD, Pliny the Elder mentions in his *Natural History:* "When rubbing with the fingers draws forth the *caloris anima* (heat of the soul), amber attracts straw, dry leaves, and linden bark, just as the magnet attracts iron." See Yoshitaka Yamamoto, *The Pull of History: Human Understanding of Magnetism and Gravity through the Ages* (Singapore: World Scientific Publishing, 2018), p. 94.

54. *Moradas* 6.5.12, *O.C.*, p. 543.

55. *Moradas* 6.6.2, *O.C.*, p. 544.

56. One need not puzzle much over this, given that Teresa consistently explains why she wanted her levitating raptures to cease: they attracted too much of

the wrong kind of attention, they left her feeling like a stupefied drunkard, and worst of all, as far as she could tell, they were unnecessary.

57. Her hagiographer Diego de Yepes (*Vida, Virtudes, y Milagros,* chap. 15, p. 114) says the levitations stopped "fifteen years before her death," which would be the year 1567. Teresa finished writing her *Vida* in 1565.

58. *Vida* 20.5, *O.C.,* p. 109.

59. *Cuentas de conciencia* 9, *O.C.,* p. 597: "No conviene ahora; bastante crédito tienes para lo que yo pretendo."

60. *Procesos,* 2:463.

61. *Fundaciones* 5.8, *O.C.,* p. 690.

62. Francisco Ribera, *Vida de Santa Teresa de Jesús* (Barcelona: Gustavo Gili, 1908), p. 465.

63. Miguel Batista de Lanuza, *Vida de la bendita madre Isabel de Santo Domingo, compañera de Santa Teresa de Iesus, coadjutora de la santa en la nueua reforma de la Orden* (Madrid, 1638), p. 33.

64. The artists involved were Adriaen Collaert and Cornelis Galle. For more on this graphic hagiography, see Eire, *Life of Saint Teresa,* pp. 136–41.

65. Yepes, *Vida, Virtudes, y Milagros,* chap. 15, p. 112.

66. Yepes, chap. 15, p. 110.

67. Jeronimo de San José, *Historia del Venerable Padre Fr. Juan de la Cruz, Pimer Descalzo Carmelita, Compañero y Coadjutor de Santa Teresa de Jesus en la Fundación de su Reforma* (Madrid, 1641), bk. 2, chap. 9, p. 183.

68. De San José, *Historia,* bk. 2, chap. 9, p. 185. Carmelites believed that they could trace the origins of their monastic rule all the way back to the prophet Elijah, who was taken up to heaven in a fiery chariot (2 Kings 2:3–9). Teresa and John were attempting to reinstate the "ancient rule" among the Carmelites that they claimed was based on Elijah's.

69. E. Allison Peers, introduction to *The Autobiography of Teresa of Jesus* (New York: Image Books, 1991), p. xlix: "Her methods of exposition are not rigidly logical. . . . Her books have a *gracioso desorden* [Herrick's 'sweet disorder']." (*Note:* Peers's parenthetical reference is to a poem by Robert Herrick, "Delight in Disorder.")

70. *Vida* 20.5, *O.C.,* p. 109.

71. Gen. 18:16–33; Exod. 32:9–14; 2 Kings 20:1–11.

72. See Gillian Ahlgren, *Teresa of Avila and the Politics of Sanctity* (Ithaca, NY: Cornell University Press, 1996).

73. See José Luis Sánchez Lora, *Mujeres, conventos, y formas de la religiosidad rarroca* (Madrid: Fundación Universitaria Española, 1988).

3. Saint Joseph of Cupertino, Shrieking Aerial Ecstatic

1. Bernino, pp. 1–2.

2. Parisciani has compiled the most complete listing of all these manuscript sources in his *ND*, pp. xix–xxvii.

3. Such as Pastrovicci, and *Beatificationis et canonizationis Josephi a Cupertino* (Rome, 1751).

4. Bernino/Bernini also wrote a history of heresies and a biography of his own father. For a documented discussion of Domenico's biography and professional career, see Franco Mormando, *Domenico Bernini: The Life of Gian Lorenzo Bernini; A Translation and Critical Edition, with Introduction and Commentary* (University Park: Pennsylvania State University Press, 2011), pp. 4–14.

5. "Immobile in estasi in presenza mia." Bernino, p. 345.

6. See note 1.

7. Agelli, p. 2. The legend that Saint Francis was born in a stable—accepted as a fact by several of Saint Joseph's biographers—has been traced to Bartholomew of Pisa's *De Conformitate Vitae B. P. Francisci ad Vitam Domini Nostri Jesu Christi,* which was approved by the Observant Franciscan order in 1399.

8. Cupertino, California, was named after Arroyo San José de Cupertino, now known as Stevens Creek, a stream named after Saint Joseph of Cupertino in 1776 by Spanish explorers.

9. Parisciani, *ND*, p. 5.

10. Nuti, p. 2. Gustavo Parisciani, however, points out in *ND*, p. 11, that others remembered young Joseph as very good natured, "di buona indole e di buona inclinazione."

11. Agelli, p. 2.

12. Agelli, p. 3.

13. Bernino shortens the name to Boccaperta, p. 5.

14. The earliest hagiography (Nutti, p. 4) says six years; later ones say four (Agelli, p. 4), or five (Pastrovicchi, p. 2).

15. Agelli, p. 3: "Massime non ammaestrato nelle scienze."

16. Agelli (pp. 5–7) and Pastrovicchi (pp. 3–4) disagree on these details. Pastrovicchi only mentions Uncle Francesco, but Agelli says that Uncle Giovanni also partook in this rejection and that both uncles considered Joseph totally unfit for monastic life or the priesthood.

17. Pastrovicchi (pp. 3–4) attributes the contact with the Capuchin provincial to Uncle Francesco Desa's patronage, but Nuti (p. 8), Bernino (p. 13), and Agelli (pp. 7–8) say that Joseph approached him on his own initiative.

18. Agelli, p. 8: "Stolido di mente, o malsano di corpo, o insofferente d'animo, o mancate di vista per gli esercizi manuali del Convento."

19. Agelli, p. 8: "Sentirsi cavar la pella e distaccare la carne dalle ossa."

20. "Secolo ingannevole," a term employed by Pastrovicchi, p. 3.

21. Pastrovicchi, p. 5.

22. Bernino, p. 27.

23. Bernino, p. 28.

24. Nuti, p. 15.

25. Agelli, p. 16.

26. Pastrovicchi, p. 9.

27. Bernino, p. 41. Like Saint Francis, Joseph also took to calling his own body Brother Ass (Frà Asino), p. 46.

28. Agelli, p. 21.

29. "O come alienato da' sensi, o come disdegnosoi porgere sollievo a quel corpo." Agelli, p. 122.

30. *Vida* 29.13, *O.C.,* p. 158.

31. Gustavo Parisciani, *Ecstasy, Jail, and Sanctity* (Osimo, Italy: Pax et Bonum, 1964), p. 12.

32. Pastrovicchi, pp. 30–32. For an attempt to distinguish Joseph's levitations as "holy" rather than demonic, see Antonio Blasucci, "Il fenomeno dell'estasi in San Giuseppe da Copertino," in *San Giuseppe da Copertino tra storia ed attualità*, edited by Gustavo Parisciani and Giancarlo Galeazzi (Padua: Messagero, 1984), pp. 93–118.

33. Such callous testing of cataleptic saints in ecstasy was nothing new. Saint Douceline was subjected to even worse treatment in the thirteenth century. See Philippine De Porcelet, *La Vie de Sainte Douceline fondatrice des béguines de Marseille, Composée Au Treizième Siècle En Langue Provençale,* translated by J. H. Albanés (Marseille: Camoin, 1879), pp. 81, 93.

34. Agelli, pp. 25–26.

35. Pastrovicchi, pp. 20–21.

36. Pastrovicchi, p. 22; Agelli, p. 90.

37. Acts of the Apostles 2:1–4.

38. Pastrovicchi, p. 22.

39. Pastrovicchi, pp. 21–22.

40. Bernino, pp. 56–70.

41. Bernino, p. 81.

42. ASV, Riti, 2045, fol. 119v, cited in Parisciani, *ND,* p. 169.

43. Agelli, p. 28: "Miracolo di Santità."

44. Pastrovicchi, p. 11: "Prodigiosa beneficenza."

45. See Andrew W. Keitt, *Inventing the Sacred: Imposture, Inquisition, and the Boundaries of the Supernatural in Golden Age Spain* (Leiden: Brill, 2005).

46. For a thorough account of Joseph's brush with the Inquisition, accompanied by original documents, see Gustavo Parisciani, *L'Inquisizione e il caso S. Giuseppe da Copertino* (Padua: Edizioni Messaggero Padova, 1996).

47. Parisciani, *ND*, p. 202.

48. ASV, Riti, 2039, fol. 77, cited by Agelli, p. 45; Parisciani, *L'Inquisizione,* pp. 50–51. Bernino, p. 84, has slightly different wording.

49. Agelli, p. 47.

50. This narrative is based on Prospero Bottini's *Relation to the Holy Office in Rome,* app. I in Parisciani, *L'Inquisizione,* pp. 285–90, as well as Parisciani's own summary of the proceedings, pp. 43–80.

51. Saint Teresa of Avila also begged God to stop her levitations, but in her case—in contrast to Joseph's—God granted her request. *Vida* 20.5, *O.C.,* p. 109.

52. As one of Joseph's accusers put it, "La santità si deve occultare, e non andarsi publicando per le piazze." Parisciani, *L'Inquisizione,* app. 1, "Relazione di Prospero Bottini," p. 286.

53. Agelli, pp. 50–52; Bernino, pp. 92–94.

54. Pastrovicchi, p. 24; Agelli, p. 57; Bernino, p. 103.

55. Pastrovicchi, p. 15; Agelli, p. 64.

56. Agelli, p. 65; Pastrovicchi, p. 16.

57. San Giovanni Laterano, San Pietro, San Paolo fuori le mura, Santa Maria Maggiore, San Lorenzo fuori le mura, San Sebastiano, and Santa Croce in Gerusalemme.

58. Bernino, p. 128.

59. Agelli, p. 69.

60. Pastrovicchi, p. 17.

61. For more on Joseph's impact in Poland, see Gustavo Parisciani, *San Giuseppe da Copertino e la Polonia* (Padua: Edizione Messaggero, 1988).

62. Bernino, pp. 170–76.

63. Agelli, p. 102; Nuti, pp. 572–73.

64. Bernino, pp. 176–77.

65. *Allgemeine deutsche Biographie,* 56 vols. (Leipzig: Jetzer-Kähler, 1881), 14:177–80.

66. The diary of the Franciscan abbot of Assisi suggests that Johann Friedrich was already leaning toward Catholicism at the time of his visit. See *I Tre Diari (1645–1652) dell'abate Arcangelo Rosmi su San Giuseppe da Copertino,* edited by Gustavo Parisciani (Padua: Messagero, 1991), pp. 199–201.

67. Bernino, p. 181; Agelli, p. 105.
68. Pastrovicchi, pp. 29–30. "Sia maledetto quando son venuto in questi paesi; stavo nella mia patria quieto d'animo, ed ora qui mi agitano furie, e scrupoli di coscienza."
69. Agelli, pp. 113–14.
70. Agelli, pp. 109–11.
71. "Alquanto disturbato in quel punto." Pastrovicchi, p. 69.
72. Parisciani, *Ecstasy, Jail, and Sanctity*, p. 45.
73. The full text of the instructions can be found in Parisciani, *ND*, p. 1012.
74. "Era la più oscura e cattiva di quel Convento." Agelli, p. 121.
75. "Migliaja di persone." Father Giovanni Battista, Capuchin Vicar of Pietrarubbia, quoted in Agelli, p. 125.
76. Quoted by Agelli, p. 126. Pastrovicchi also mentions *capanne* (huts), p. 70.
77. Bernino, p. 344.
78. Quoted in Agelli, p. 125.
79. Pastrovicchi, pp. 70–71.
80. "Con forza sovrumana." Agelli, p. 135.
81. "Con grande sbigottimento." Agelli, p. 134.
82. Agelli, pp. 135–36; Pastrovicchi, p. 71.
83. See petition dated May 26, 1656, in Parisciani, *ND*, p. 1014.
84. "In quel santuario basta un San Francesco." Agelli, p. 139.
85. See document 18 in Parisciani, *ND*, pp. 1014–15.
86. Agelli, p. 140.
87. For more on this shrine, see Karin Vélez, *The Miraculous Flying House of Loreto: Spreading Catholicism in the Early Modern World* (Princeton, NJ: Princeton University Press, 2018).
88. Agelli, p. 143; Pastrovicchi, pp. 75–76.
89. "Soli religiosi più accreditati e più savi." Agelli, p. 147.
90. Father Eugenio Maccatelli, quoted in Parisciani, *Ecstasy, Jail, and Sanctity*, p. 55.
91. Pastrovicchi, p. 77.
92. Agelli, p. 155; Nuti, p. 661. Parisciani, *ND*, p. 917, adds hemorrhoids to his list of ailments.
93. Agelli, p. 158.
94. Nuti, pp. 667–68.
95. Agelli, p. 160; Nuti, p. 666.
96. Pastrovicchi, pp. 81–82.
97. Agelli, p. 162; Pastrovicchi, p. 82; Nuti, p. 669.
98. Agelli, pp. 163–65.

99. Nuti, p. 676. The practice of performing autopsies on the corpses of holy men and women became common in this era. See Bradford A. Bouley, *Pious Post-mortems: Anatomy, Sanctity, and the Catholic Church in Early Modern Europe* (Philadelphia: University of Pennsylvania Press, 2017).

100. "Fiamma sovrannaturale d'amor divino." Agelli, p. 166; Pastrovicchi, p. 84.

101. Agelli, pp. 167–68; Pastrovicchi, pp. 84–85; Nuti, pp. 678–79.

102. Parisciani, *ND,* pp. 965–1003, provides a detailed account of Joseph's canonization process.

103. A development well documented and analyzed by Paolo Parigi, *The Rationalization of Miracles* (Cambridge University Press, 2012).

104. *Manifesto summário para os que ignoram poderse navegar pelo elemento do ar.* See Adílio Jorge Marques, ed., *Bartolomeu Lourenço de Gusmão: O padre inventor* (Rio de Janeiro: Andrea Jakobsson Estúdio, 2011).

105. For a different sort of miracle account connected to this patronage, see "A Feud with Saint Joseph Cupertino," *From the Housetops,* vol. 3.1, 1948, reproduced at https://catholicism.org/a-feud-with-st-joseph-cupertino.html.

4. Making Sense of the Flying Friar

Epigraph: Agelli, p. 154.

1. For a long list of witnesses and visitors, see Parisciani, *L'Inquisizione e il caso S. Giuseppe da Copertino* (Padua: Edizioni Messaggero Padova, 1996), pp. 202–11; Pastrovicchi, p. 87. See also Gustavo Parisciani, *San Giuseppe da Copertino e la Polonia* (Padua: Messagero, 1988).

2. Agelli (pp. 198–99) stresses this fact, emphasizing that the authenticity of these elite testimonies was confirmed by the authority of the papacy ("Formatti coll' autorità della Sede Apostolica").

3. William Crookes, "Notes of an Enquiry into the Phenomena Called Spiritual during the Years 1870–1873," *Quarterly Journal of Science,* 2nd ser., 3 (January 1874): 77.

4. Joseph's transfer from Assisi to Pietrarubia was "cum ordine praeciso et ei non permitteretur allocutio cum saecularibus." Parisciani, *L'Inquisizione,* appx. I, pp. 289–90.

5. But not at all as architect Ludwig Mies van der Rohe meant it when he coined this expression. See Jeremy Till and Sarah Wigglesworth, "The Future Is Hairy," in *Architecture—the Subject Is Matter,* edited by Jonathan Hill (Milton Park, UK: Routledge, 2001), p. 12.

6. Bertrand Méheust, *Somnambulisme et médiumnité*, 2 vols. (Le Plessis-Robinson: Empecheurs, 1999), 2:271–73. For more on this insight, see Jeffrey Kripal, *Authors of the Impossible: The Paranormal and the Sacred* (University of Chicago Press, 2010), p. 224.

7. Jure Kristo, "The Interpretation of Religious Experience: What Do Mystics Intend When They Talk about Their Experiences?," *Journal of Religion* 62, no. 1 (January 1982): 21–38.

8. For a more detailed account of editions and translations of Teresa's texts, see Carlos Eire, *The Life of Saint Teresa of Avila: A Biography* (Princeton University Press, 2019), pp. 99–131.

9. *Libro de la Vida* 20.1, *O.C.*, p. 108.

10. "Questo fortunato stato di Estasi, o Ratti" is but one example: Bernino, p. 334.

11. Agelli, pp. 188–89.

12. See Kristo, "Interpretation of Religious Experience."

13. "La mente, e il corpo, l'huomo interno, e'l esterno." Bernino, p. 323.

14. Nuti, p. 516; Bernino, p. 287. See also Parisciani, *ND,* p. 326.

15. Bernino, p. 334: "Perche di lui allora non v'era altro, che l'Anima, che tutta stava fuori di sè in altro Mondo."

16. *Vida* 20, *O.C.* For more on this subject, see Olivier Leroy, *La Lévitation* (Paris: Librairie Valois, 1928), pp. 190–202, and the entry "Lévitation" in *Dictionnaire de spiritualité, ascétique et mystique,* 17 vols. (Paris: Beauchesne, 1933–1995), 9:738–41.

17. Nuti, p. 156.

18. Bernino, p. 334.

19. See Edward Shorter and Max Fink, *The Madness of Fear: A History of Catatonia* (Oxford University Press, 2018); and Stanley Caroff, Stephan Mann, and Andrew Francis, eds., *Catatonia: From Psychopathology to Neurobiology* (Washington, DC: American Psychiatric Publishing, 2007).

20. Agelli, pp. 134–35.

21. This is not to say that some retroactive diagnosis is impossible. Other mystics have had their ecstasies and visions attributed to some kind of pathology. Hildegard of Bingen was diagnosed as suffering from visual migraines over 100 years ago. See Charles Singer, "The Scientific Views and Visions of Saint Hildegard (1098–1180)," in his *Studies in the History and Method of Science* (Oxford: Clarendon Press, 1917), pp. 1–58. As previously mentioned, Teresa of Avila has been retroactively diagnosed with temporal lobe epilepsy (see chapter 2, note 30).

22. "Fu una gran forza quella, fu una gran forza, fu una gran forza!" Parisciani, *ND,* p. 438. Teresa writes: "Desde debajo de los pies me levantavan fuerzas tan grandes que no sé como lo comparar." *Vida* 20.6, *O.C.,* p. 109.
23. "Mi venne una cosa soave, soave." Nuti, p. 570.
24. "Oh, questa mia infermità!" Bernino, p. 339.
25. "Come un assaggio della vera gloria del paradiso." Parisciani, *ND,* p. 440.
26. Agelli, p. 181.
27. Agelli, p. 189; Bernino, pp. 329–30. Saint Teresa said: "As quickly as a bullet leaves a gun when the trigger is pulled, there begins within the soul a flight." *Moradas* 6.5.9, *O.C.,* p. 543. Could this coincidence suggest this metaphor was commonly used in monastic circles?
28. Agelli, pp. 135–36; Pastrovicchi, p. 71. Joseph's ecstatic screaming is totally unique.
29. ASV Riti 2044. See Catrien Santing, "Tira mi sù: Pope Benedict XIV and the Beatification of the Flying Saint Giuseppe da Copertino," in *Medicine and Religion in Enlightenment Europe,* edited by Ole Peter Grell and Andrew Cunningham (Farnham, UK: Ashgate, 2007), p. 97.
30. Parisciani, *ND,* p. 442n12. The number of Joseph's levitations is unique too, as is their frequency. No other levitator on record comes close to matching him.
31. Pastrovicchi, p. 27. Yet another use of the gunpowder metaphor.
32. Once, for instance, merely hearing a girl sing made him rise a few feet off the ground "higher than a table." Agelli, p. 40.
33. Bernino, p. 343.
34. Agelli, p. 184.
35. Agelli, p. 123.
36. Agelli, p. 102; Nuti, pp. 572–73; Bernino, pp. 176–77.
37. Agelli, p. 97; Bernino, pp. 172, 180.
38. Agelli, p. 104; Bernino, p. 181.
39. Bernino, p. 184; Agelli, pp. 106–7.
40. Bernino, pp. 195–96; Agelli, pp. 109–11.
41. Pastrovicchi, pp. 29–30; Agelli, p. 107; Bernino, pp. 183–84.
42. Eric John Dingwall, *Some Human Oddities: Studies in the Queer, the Uncanny and the Fanatical* (London: Home & Van Thal, 1947), p. 20.
43. For a brief account of his family's machinations, see Oskar Garstein, *Rome and the Counter-Reformation in Scandinavia: The Age of Gustavus Adolphus and Queen Christina of Sweden* (Leiden: Brill, 1992), p. 461.
44. "Tenerissima divozione." Agelli, p. 108.

45. For a brief account of this horrifically unhappy marriage, see Charles Ingrao, *The Habsburg Monarchy, 1618–1815,* 2nd ed. (Cambridge University Press, 2003), p. 128.

46. Georg Heinrich Pertz, ed., "Bey dem so genandten wunderübenden Pater Joseph," *Leibnizens Geschichtliche Aufsätze und Gedichte Gesammelte Werke. Aus den Handschriften der Königlichen Bibliothek zu Hannover,* 4 vols. (Hannover, 1843), vol. 1, p. 9.

47. For more on this mathematical puzzle that remained unsolved for three and a half centuries, see Simon Singh, *Fermat's Last Theorem* (London: Fourth Estate, 1997).

48. Rudolf Otto, *The Idea of the Holy: An Inquiry into the Non-rational Factor in the Idea of the Divine and Its Relation to the Rational,* translated by John W. Harvey (Oxford University Press, 1936), p. 22.

49. "The attributes of liminality or of *liminal personae* ('threshold people') are necessarily ambiguous." See Victor Turner, *The Ritual Process* (London: Penguin, 1969), p. 81. Anthropologist Victor Turner developed the concept of liminality in the twentieth century, relying on the work of Arnold Van Gennep, *Rites of Passage* (1909). See also Victor Turner, "Betwixt and Between: The Liminal Period in Rites de Passage," in *The Forest of Symbols* (Ithaca, NY: Cornell University Press, 1967).

50. Agelli, p. 154.

51. Otto, *Idea of the Holy,* p. 7. "Numinous" derives from the Latin "numen" ("god," "spirit," or "divine"); "ominous" from the Latin "omen" (potentially foreboding event). These terms, as used in the study of religion, were developed by Rudolph Otto in his *Das Heilige* (Breslau: Trewendt and Granier, 1917).

52. Agelli, p. 161.

53. Otto, *Idea of the Holy,* pp. 12–30.

54. As in the case of some painters at Assisi: Pastrovicchi, p. 25.

55. As in the case of the congregation at Nardo: Pastrovicchi, p. 23.

56. As in the case of the Spanish viceroy's wife: Bernino, pp. 176–77.

57. Bernino (p. 178) lists weeping as a common response to Joseph's levitations.

58. As in the case of one of the Capuchin friars at Fossombrone: Agelli, p. 134.

59. Bernino, p. 341: "Oppressi da sacro terrore"; emphasis added.

60. Agelli, p. 27: "Disturbandosi co' suoi ratti ed estasi le funzioni."

61. Agelli, pp. 115–16.

62. Bernino, pp. 169–70.

63. Gustavo Parisciani, *Ecstasy, Jail, and Sanctity* (Osimo, Italy: Pax et Bonum, 1964), pp. 43–44.

64. For a superb summary and analysis of this archetype, see John Saward, *Perfect Fools: Folly for Christ's Sake in Catholic and Orthodox Spirituality* (Oxford University Press, 1980).

65. Saint Bernard of Clairvaux, *The Letters of St Bernard of Clairvaux,* translated by B. Scott James (London: Burns and Oates, 1953), p. 130.

66. Thomas Aquinas, *Summa Theologica* II–II, Q. 113, Art. 1 ad 1, translated by T. R. Heath, accessed January 22, 2023, https://www.newadvent.org/summa/3113.htm.

67. Agelli, p. 91.

68. Nuti (pp. 369–401), devotes an entire chapter (33) to the marvel of Joseph's supernatural wisdom.

69. Another cleric who was a theologian agreed, saying "Brother Giuseppe discoursed on Divine Attributes very learnedly because of his *infused* supernatural knowledge, and left me stunned and amazed." Bernino, pp. 166–67.

70. "Si vedeva chiaramente che la sua scienza erea soprannaturale ed infusa." Agelli, p. 95; Bernino, p. 167.

71. Agelli, p. 26.

72. "E qui pregollo a non interrogarlo di vantaggio, perchè era ignorante, e non sapeva discorrere." Agelli, p. 118.

73. Recognizing Saint Francis as a holy fool is a centuries-old tradition stretching back to his own day, but in the late twentieth century, it began to receive increasing attention, as evidenced by the publication of books that linked Francis with foolishness in their titles, such as Julien Green, *God's Fool: The Life and Times of Francis of Assisi* (Harper San Francisco, 1987); Christopher Coelho, *A New Kind of Fool: Meditations on St. Francis and His Values* (London: Bloomsbury, 1991); and Jon Sweeney, *The St. Francis Holy Fool Prayer Book* (Brewster, MA: Paraclete Press, 2017). Curiously, *Fools for Christ: Essays on the True, the Good and the Beautiful* (Eugene, OR: Wipf and Stock, 2001), by the eminent theological historian Jaroslav Pelikan, does not include Saint Francis or any Catholic figures.

74. *The Collected Works of G. K. Chesterton,* 37 vols. (San Francisco: Ignatius Press, 1986), 2:71.

75. "Hò veduto, e parlato con un altro San Francesco": Bernino, p. 176; Agelli, p. 102.

76. Nuti, p. 246.

77. Bernino, p. 332: "La celebrava più in aria, che in terra"; Agelli, p. 193.

78. Agelli, p. 123; Bernino, pp. 334–35, 346.

79. Agelli, p. 193; Bernino, pp. 332–33; Nuti, p. 247.

80. Agelli, pp. 24–25; Nuti describes an instance of clasped hands (p. 570): "Con le mani giunte."

81. "Sonnolenza, Infermità, e Sbalordimento suo": Bernino, p. 335. Displays such as this are numerous: see Agelli, p. 196.

82. "Con somma mia ammirazzione giudicai impossibile che umanamente ciò accadesse." *Summarium,* pp. 8, 11, cited in Parisciani, *ND,* p. 448.

83. Bernino pp. 333–34; emphasis added.

84. Agelli, p. 195; Bernino, p. 340.

85. Agelli, p. 196; Bernino, pp. 340–41.

86. Agelli, p. 195; Bernino, p. 340.

87. Pastrovicchi, pp. 20–21.

88. Bernino, p. 339.

89. Bernino, p. 332.

90. Bernino, p. 341; Agelli, p. 196.

91. Agelli, p. 197.

92. Agelli, p. 88.

93. Agelli, pp. 88–89; Pastrovicchi, p. 26.

94. Pastrovicchi, p. 22; Agelli, p. 90.

95. Agelli, pp. 89–90; Pastrovicchi, p. 26.

96. Nuti, p. 247: "Un grido grande, che si sentiva molto lontano."

97. Agelli, p. 189; Bernino, pp. 329–30.

98. Pastrovicchi, p. 71.

99. "Urlo sì strano di veemente rimbombante voce." Agelli, pp. 135–36.

100. Agelli, p. 22.

101. William Shakespeare, *Hamlet,* act 3, scene 1.

5. Transvection, Teleportation, and All That

1. Saint Joseph did bilocate, according to some accounts, but only a few times. One such account can be found in Bernino, p. 103.

2. King Philip IV's father, Philip III, had established a similar relationship with the nun Sor Luisa de Carrión, who ended up being denounced to the Inquisition and died under a cloud of suspicion. For more on her, see the two studies by Patrocinio García Barriúso, OFM: *La monja de Carrión: Sor Luisa de la Ascensión Colmenares Cabezón* (Zamora, Spain: Ediciones Monte Casino, 1986) and *Sor Luisa de la Ascensión: Una contemplativa del Siglo xvii* (Madrid: self-published, 1993). See also Teófanes Egido López, "Religiosidad Popular y Taumaturgia del Barroco: Los milagros de la Monja de Carrión," in *Actas del II*

418 NOTES TO PAGES 176-178

Congreso de Historia de Palencia, 4 vols., edited by María Valentina Calleja González (Palencia, Spain: Departamento de Cultura, 1990), 3:11–40.

3. To read about bilocation in the *Dictionnaire de spiritualité ascétique et mystique* (Paris, 1937–1995), one must do so in the article titled "Multilocation."

4. For more on the science of teleportation, see Michio Kaku, *Physics of the Impossible* (New York: Doubleday, 2008), chap. 4, pp. 55–69; and Chad Orzel, "The Physics of Star Trek: Quantum Teleportation versus Transporters," *Forbes,* August 15, 2015.

5. See Charles Richet, *Traité de métapsychique* (Paris: Alcan, 1923), pp. 700–710; Jean Lhermitte, *Le problème des miracles* (Paris, 1956), pp. 179–212. On the pseudo-philosophical subject of *métapsychique,* see J. de Tonquédec, *Merveilleux et miracle chrétien* (Paris: Centre d'étude Laennec, 1955); and Yvonne Castellan, *La métapsychique* (Paris: Presses Universitaires de France, 1955; later editions have the title *La parapsychologie*).

6. At least in Western European languages. See Ernest Bozzano, *Considerazioni ed ipotesi sui fenomeni di bilocazione* (Rome: Tipografia Dante, 1911); translated into French as *Les phénomènes de bilocation* (Paris: Éditions Jean Meyer, 1937).

7. See Pamela Rae Heath, *Mind-Matter Interaction: A Review of Historical Reports, Theory, and Research* (London: McFarland, 2011), esp. pp. 28–32; and the essays in Edward Kelly, Adam Crabtree, and Paul Marshall, eds., *Beyond Physicalism: Toward Reconciliation of Science and Spirituality* (New York: Rowman and Littlefield, 2015).

8. Defined in the *Encyclopedia Britannica* as "Uncertainty principle, also called Heisenberg uncertainty principle or indeterminacy principle, statement, articulated (1927) by the German physicist Werner Heisenberg, that the position and the velocity of an object cannot both be measured exactly, at the same time, even in theory. The very concepts of exact position and exact velocity together, in fact, have no meaning in nature."

9. Bernino, p. 103.

10. Dominik Wujastyk, "The Path to Liberation through Yogic Mindfulness in Early Āyurveda," in *Yoga in Practice,* edited by David Gordon White (Princeton University Press, 2012), p. 34.

11. Quote from Porphyry cited in Christoph Riedweg, *Pythagoras: His Life, Teaching, and Influence,* translated by Steven Rendall (Ithaca, NY: Cornell University Press, 2002), p. 4.

12. See Mark Verman and Shulamit H. Adler, "Path Jumping in the Jewish Magical Tradition," *Jewish Studies Quarterly* 1, no. 2 (1993/1994): 131–48.

13. Gen. 24:42: "I came today to the spring, and I said: O Lord, God of my master Abraham, if You would indeed grant success to the errand on which I am engaged." A mystical Talmudic reading of this passage interprets the usage of "I came today" as indicating that "the land contracted" so Eliezer could "miraculously reach his destination quickly," and that his intention "was to say to the members of Rebecca's family that on that day he left Canaan and on the same day he arrived, to underscore the miraculous nature of his undertaking on behalf of Abraham." See Sefaria, "The William Davidson Talmud," Sanhedrin 95a, accessed January 3, 2023, https://www.sefaria.org/Sanhedrin.95a .16?ven=William_Davidson_Edition_-_English&vhe=Wikisource_Talmud _Bavli&lang=bi&with=all&lang2=en.

14. Qur'an, sura 27 (An-Naml), ayat 38–40.

15. See Reynold A. Nicholson, *The Mystics of Islam* (London: G. Bell, 1914).

16. Oxford Bibliographies, October 25, 2018, https://www.oxfordbibliographies .com/view/document/obo-9780195399318/obo-9780195399318-0208.xml.

17. Thomas Aquinas, *Summa Theologica*, I.76.8: "But since the soul is united to the body as its form, it must of necessity be within the entire body, and within each of its parts. For it is not an accidental form of the body, but rather its substantial form." (Sed quia anima unitur corpori ut forma, necesse est quod sit in toto, et in qualibet parte corporis. Non enim est forma corporis accidentalis, sed substantialis.)

18. Francis Siegfried, "Bilocation," in *The Catholic Encyclopedia,* vol. 2 (New York: Robert Appleton, 1907).

19. Walter Stephens, *Demon Lovers: Witchcraft, Sex, and the Crisis of Belief* (Chicago: University of Chicago Press, 2002), pp. 291–92.

20. 1 Kings 18:12. This is not to say that other passages that do not explicitly suggest bilocation cannot be subjected to mystical interpretations that read bilocation into the narrative. See notes 12 and 13 in this chapter.

21. John 20:26; Luke 24:13–35.

22. Acts of the Apostles 8:39–40.

23. *MCD* IV.7.17.347–56. For a glimpse of the attention lavished on this shrine in Sor María's day, see Antonio de Fuertes y Biota, *Historia de Nuestra Señora del Pilar de Caragoza* (Brussels, 1654); and Joseph Felix de Amada, *Conpendio de los Milagros de Nuestra Señora del Pilar de Zaragoza, Primer Templo del Mundo Edificado en la Ley de Gracia, consagrado con asistencia personal de la Virgen Santissima, viviendo en carne mortal* (Zaragoza, Spain, 1680).

24. *MCD* IV.7.16.319–26.

25. Some lists of bilocators include Pope Clement I (d. 99 AD), but whatever legend is behind this listing is not mentioned as a point of reference in subsequent early Christian accounts of other bilocating saints.

26. Gregory of Tours, *De miraculis S. Martini* I, 5, Migne, *PL,* vol. 71, 918c–919b. The chronology of this account is problematic since Ambrose died in April of 397, seven months before Martin, who died in November of that year.

27. See Bruce Cole, "Giotto's Apparition of St. Francis at Arles: The Case of the Missing Crucifix?," *Simiolus: Netherlands Quarterly for the History of Art* 7, no. 4 (1974): 163–65.

28. Bonaventure, *Legenda Major,* pp. 4, 10; translated by Emma Gurney Salter as *The Life of Saint Francis by Saint Bonaventura* (London: J. M. Dent, 1904), p. 42. This bilocation is also described by Thomas de Celano in his *Vita Prima* I.18.48. See *St. Francis of Assisi: Writings and Early Biographies,* edited by Marion A. Habig (Chicago: Franciscan Herald Press, 1972), pp. 269–70.

29. Jean Rigauld, *The Life of St. Antony of Padua* (London, 1904), pp. 47–48. English translation from a French translation by "An English Franciscan." Edited and translated in French by Ferdinand-Marie d'Araules as *Vie de Saint Antoine de Padoue* (Bordeaux, 1899), pp. 44–46. There are various versions of this story.

30. "San Pedro Regalado, patrón de los internautas," *El Mundo,* December 14, 1999; and "The Internet's Open-Source Patron Saint," *Economist,* April 22, 2000, https://www.economist.com/science-and-technology/2000/04/20/the-internets-open-source-patron-saint.

31. See *AS,* April 1, pp. 103–234, which includes material collected for his canonization. See also Giuseppe Roberti, *San Francesco di Paola: Storia della sua Vita,* 2nd ed. (Rome: Curia Generalizia dell'Ordine dei Minimi, 1963).

32. Christoph Genelli, *Das Leben des heiligen Ignatius von Loyola, Stifters der Gesellschaft Jesu* (Innsbruck, 1848), pp. 358–59; Genelli, *The Life of St. Ignatius of Loyola,* translated by Thomas Meyrick (London: Burns, Oates, and Co., 1871), pp. 309–10.

33. Mikolaj Leczycki, *The glory of the B. Father S. Ignatius of Loyola, founder of the Society of Jesus* (Rouen, 1633), p. 188.

34. Dominique Bouhours, *La Vie de Saint François Xavier de la Compagnie de Jesus, Apostre des Indes et du Japon* (Paris, 1682), bk. 5, pp. 444–54. This miracle is not mentioned in early hagiographies and only begins to appear in 1596, in that of Orazio Torsellino, *De Vita Francisci Xaverii.*

35. Horatii Tursellini, *De Vita Francisci Xaverii, Qui primus è Societate Iesu in Indiam et Japoniam Evangelium inuexit* (Antwerp, 1596).

36. See Andrew Dickson White, *A History of the Warfare of Science with Theology in Christendom,* 2 vols. (New York: D. Appleton, 1896), 2:5–15.

37. *Procesos* 3:444.

38. *Procesos* 1:17.

39. *Procesos* 1:477.

40. Pietro Giacomo Bacci, *Vita di San Filippo Neri* (Rome, 1622), bk. 3, chap. 11; Filippo Guidi, *Vita della venerabile Madre Suor Caterina De Ricci* (Florence, 1622), chap. 43, pp. 132–33; F. X. Schouppe, *Instruction Religieuse en Examples Suivant l'ordre du Catéchisme* (Paris, 1883), p. 199; Florence Mary Capes, *St. Catherine de' Ricci: Her Life, Her Letters, Her Community* (London: Burns and Oates, 1905), p. 251.

41. See Jane Tar, "Flying through the Empire: The Visionary Journeys of Early Modern Nuns," in *Women's Voices and Politics of the Spanish Empire,* edited by Jennifer Eich, Jeanne Gillespie, and Lucia Harrison (New Orleans: University Press of the South, 2008), pp. 263–302; and Magnus Lundberg, *Mission and Ecstasy: Contemplative Women and Salvation in Colonial Spanish America and the Philippines* (Uppsala: University of Uppsala, 2015), esp. pp. 183–214.

42. The terms "mystical displacement" and "mystical journey" are employed by Silvia Evangelisti in "Religious Women, Mystic Journeys and Agency in Early Modern Spain," *Journal of Early Modern History* 22 (2018): 9–27.

43. Pseudoscientific experiments in remote viewing were carried out by the US and Soviet governments during the Cold War. See M. Srinivasan, "Clairvoyant Remote Viewing: The US Sponsored Psychic Spying," *Strategic Analysis* 26, no. 1 (January–March 2002): 131–39.

44. On nun's autobiographies, see James S. Amelang, "Women's Spiritual Autobiography in Early Modern Spain: From Sacred Conversation to Mistero Buffo," *Dimensioni e Problemi della Ricerca Storica* 2 (2002): 63–74.

45. *A la Serenísima Señora Infanta Sor Margarita de la Cruz, Religiosa Descalça de su Real Convento de Descalças Franciscas de Madrid, en Razón del Interrogatorio en la Causa de la Venerable Virgen Sor Ana Maria de San Ioseph, Abadessa de la mesma Orden* (Salamanca, 1632), chap. XLI, pp. 110–11.

46. See Sonja Herpoel, "L'autobiographie de Sor Ana María de San José, un sermon volé?," *Neophilologus* 70 (1986): 539–46; and Lundberg, *Mission and Ecstasy,* pp. 187–88.

47. Francisco de Ameyugo, *Nueva maravilla de la Gracia descubierta en la vida de la venerable madre Sor Juana de Jesús Maria* (Barcelona, 1676), pp. 426–29.

48. Evangelisti, "Religious Women, Mystic Journeys," p. 19.

49. Andrés de Maya y Salaberria, *Vida prodigiosa y exercicio admirable de virtudes de la V.M. sor Martina de Los Ángeles y Arrilla* (Zaragoza, 1678), pp. 176–78.

50. Isabelle Poutrin, *Le voile et la plume: Autobiographie et sainteté féminine dans l'Espagne moderne* (Madrid: Casa Velazquezz, 1995), pp. 83–84; Stephen Haliczer, *Between Exaltation and Infamy: Female Mystics in the Golden Age of Spain* (Oxford University Press, 2002), pp. 259–63.

51. Bernino, p. 140.

52. On the impact of race on Martín's life, ministry, and canonization process, see Celia Cussen, *Black Saint of the Americas: The Life and Afterlife of Martín de Porres* (Cambridge University Press, 2014). For an analysis of the context of race in Martín's role as a baroque saint, see Erin Rowe, *Black Saints in Early Modern Global Catholicism* (Cambridge University Press, 2019), esp. pp. 77, 172, 180, 185–90, 206–10.

53. For an early summary of these accounts, see Bernardo de Medina, *Vida Prodigiosa del Venerable Siervo de Dios Fr. Martin de Porras* (Lima, 1673), pp. 68–79; for a summary from the time of his beatification, see Alberto M. Valdés, *Vida Admirable del Bienaventurado Martín de Porres,* 3rd ed. (Lima: La Providencia, 1907), esp. pp. 189–253.

54. On this point, especially, see Alex García-Rivera, *St. Martin de Porres: The "Little Stories" and the Semiotics of Culture* (Maryknoll, NY: Orbis Books, 1995), chaps. 5, 7, 8.

55. See Frank Graziano, *Wounds of Love: The Mystical Marriage of Saint Rose of Lima* (Oxford University Press, 2004).

56. See Anna Nogar, *Quill and Cross in the Borderlands: Sor María de Ágreda and the Lady in Blue, 1628 to the Present* (University of Notre Dame Press, 2018), chaps. 3–5.

57. For a glimpse of the pioneering work on colonial nuns carried out two decades ago, see the review essay by Asunción Lavin, "The Church: Institution and Spirituality in New Spain," *Mexican Studies/Estudios Mexicanos* 17, no. 2 (Summer 2001): 403–12.

58. On Don Bosco's spiritual side, see Cristina Siccardi, *Don Bosco mistico: Una vita tra cielo e terra* (Turin: La Fontana di Siloe, 2013); on his pragmatic side, see Pier Luigi Guiducci, *Senza aggredire, senza indietreggiare: Don Bosco e il mondo del lavoro: La difesa dei giovani* (Turin: Elledici, 2012).

59. Ernest Bozzano wrote about forty-eight such cases in his *Considerazioni ed ipotesi sui fenomeni di bilocazione* (Rome: (Luce e Ombra, 1911); translated in French as *Les phénomènes de bilocation* (Paris: J. Meyer, 1937).

60. Philippe Barthelet and Olivier Germain-Thomas, *Charles de Gaulle jour après jour: Chronologie détaillée* (Paris: F.-X. de Guibert, 2000), p. 96.

61. See Patrick Mahéo and René Laurentin, *Bilocations de Mère Yvonne-Aimée: Étude critique en référence á ses missions* (Paris: O.E.I.L., 1990), esp. the charts on pp. 137–57.

62. See Gerald Messadié, *Padre Pio, ou, Les prodiges du mysticisme* (Paris: Presses du Châtelet, 2008); and Bernard Ruffin, *Padre Pio: The True Story,* rev. 3rd ed. (Huntington, IN: Our Sunday Visitor, 2018), esp. chap. 30 on bilocation; and Sergio Luzzatto, *Padre Pio: Miracoli e politica nell'Italia del Novecento* (Turin, 2007).

63. See Francesco Castelli, *Padre Pio under Investigation: The Secret Vatican Files* (San Francisco: Ignatius Press, 2008); and Sergio Luzzatto, *Padre Pio: Miracles and Politics in a Secular Age,* translated by Frederika Randall (New York: Picador, 2010; original Italian edition Turin, 2007).

64. See Andrea Tornielli, *Il segreto di Padre Pio e Karol Wojtyla* (Segrate, Italy: Piemme, 2006).

6. María de Ágreda, Avatar of the Impossible

1. *JSRV,* pp. 82–83.

2. See Marilyn H. Fedewa, *María of Ágreda, Mystical Lady in Blue* (Albuquerque: University of New Mexico Press, 2009), pp. 14–15.

3. This document is available in Eduardo Royo, ed., *Autenticidad de la Mística ciudad de Dios y biografía de su autora,* vol. 5 of María de Ágreda's *Ciudad Mística de Dios* (Barcelona: Herederos de Juan Gili, 1914), pp. 18–101.

4. Royo, *Autenticidad,* p. 43.

5. Royo, p. 44. No information is given on how and where her mother acquired a human skull for her meditations.

6. Royo, p. 53: "Animo varonil."

7. Clark Colahan, trans., *The Visions of Sor María de Ágreda: Writing Knowledge and Power* (Albuquerque: University of New Mexico Press, 1994), report to Father Manero, p. 115. See also María's unfinished autobiography in Royo, *Autenticidad,* p. 41.

8. *JSRV,* p. 8.

9. Royo, *Autenticidad,* p. 86. María provides a detailed account of her precocious mysticism in pp. 81–94.

10. Royo, p. 97. Her dark night is vividly described in pp. 95–101, which are the last pages she was able to write before dying.

11. *JSRV,* chaps. 1–4; quotes from p. 8.

12. *Redondez de la tierra y mapa de los orbes celestes.* An English translation of most of this remarkable document, titled "Face of the Earth," can be found in Colahan, *Visions of Sor María de Agreda,* pp. 41–97. Colahan attributes this text to the young María but argues that she revised it later in life.

13. Royo, *Autenticidad,* pp. 44–76.

14. *JSRV,* p. 55.

15. *JSRV,* p. 48.

16. *JSRV,* pp. 51–52.

17. *JSRV,* p. 105. "Además del perpetuo ayuno referido, ayunaba tres dias en la semana a pan, y agua"; *JSRV,* p. 104. "Nunca comía carne, ni lacticinios. . . . Su ordinaria comida era legumbres, y yerbas; y de esto solo lo que bastaba para sustentarse."

18. *JSRV,* pp. 98–100; also Fedewa, *María of Agreda,* p. 33.

19. *JSRV,* p. 62; also p. 56.

20. *JSRV,* p. 102: "Cada noche le parecía le avían de acabar la vida."

21. *JSRV,* pp. 72, 74.

22. *JSRV,* p. 77.

23. *JSRV,* pp. 80–81.

24. *JSRV,* pp. 81–83.

25. *JSRV,* p. 85.

26. *JSRV,* pp. 85–86.

27. *JSRV,* p. 129.

28. *JSRV,* p. 80.

29. *JSRV,* p. 130.

30. *JSRV,* p. 133; Colahan, *Visions of Sor María de Ágreda,* report to Father Manero, p. 118.

31. *JSRV,* pp. 131–33. For María's own account of these events, see her letter to Father Manero in Colahan, *Visions of Sor María de Ágreda,* pp. 117–18.

32. *JSRV,* p. 133.

33. *JSRV,* p. 134.

34. *JSRV,* pp. 134–35.

35. *JSRV,* pp. 136–37.

36. *JSRV,* pp. 138–39.

37. Father Gerónimo's chronicle was titled *Relaciónes de todas las cosas que en el Nuevo-Mexico se han visto y sabido, asi por mar como por tierra, desde el año 1538 hasta el de 1626.* For more on this text, see Anna Nogar, *Quill and Cross in the Borderlands: Sor María de Ágreda and the Lady in Blue, 1628 to the Present* (University of Notre Dame Press, 2018), pp. 14–18.

38. *Memorial que Fray Juan de Santander de la Orden de San Francisco, Comissario General de Indias, presenta a la Magestad Catolica del Rey don Felipe Quarto, nuestro Señor. Hecho por el Padre Fray Alonso de Benavides, Comissario del Santo Oficio, y Custodio que ha sido de las Provincias y conversiones del Nuevo Mexico. Tratase en el de los Tesoros espirituales, y temporales, que la divina Majestad ha manifestado en aquellas conversiones y nuevos descubrimentos, por medio de los Padres desta serafica Religion* (Madrid: Imprenta Real, 1630).

39. *Tanto que se sacó de una carta que el Reverendo Padre Fray Alonso de Benavides, custodio que fue del Nuevo Mexico, embió a los religiosos de la Santa custodia de la conversión de San Pablo de dicho reyno, desde Madrid, el año de 1631.* Included in Francisco Palóu, *Evangelista del Mar Pacifico: Fray Junípero Serra* (Mexico, 1730). Available in a modern edition (Madrid: Aguilar, 1944), pp. 308–17; translated by Colahan in *Visions of Sor María de Agreda,* pp. 104–14.

40. Alonso de Benavides, *Memorial a la Sanctidad de Urbano VIII nuestro señor açerca de las conuerçiones del Nueuo Mexico hechas en el felicissimo tiempo del govierno de su pontificado, 1634,* Congregatio de Propaganda Fide, Vatican Archives, Rome, Ayer MS.

41. The manuscript has yet to be published in Spanish. An English translation was published by the University of New Mexico Press in 1945 with the title *Fray Alonso de Benavides' Revised Memorial of 1634.* Colahan also provides an English translation in *Visions of Sor María de Agreda,* pp. 101–10.

42. One social scientist has observed: "Benavides's *Memorials* have the appearance of a curious mixture of ethnography, fiction, and fable." See Daniel Reff, "Contextualizing Missionary Discourse: The Benavides 'Memorials' of 1630 and 1634," *Journal of Anthropological Research* 50, no. 1 (1994): 52; for a different analysis, see Anthony J. Cárdenas-Rotunno, "Fray Alonso de Benavides's Memoriales of 1630 and 1634: Preliminary Observations," *University of New Mexico Latin American Institute Research Paper Series* 45 (July 2007): 5–23.

43. Colahan, *Visions of Sor María de Ágreda,* report to Father Manero, p. 120.

44. Colahan, p. 121.

45. Colahan, p. 124.

46. Colahan, pp. 118–19.

47. Colahan, p. 119.

48. For more on her, see Patrocinio García Barriúso, *La monja de Carrión* (Madrid: Monte Casino, 1986); and P. García Barriuso, *Sor Luisa de la Ascensión: Una contemplativa del Siglo xvii* (Madrid, self-published, 1993).

49. For very detailed accounts of the accusations leveled against Sor Luisa, see *Relación de la causa de Sor Luisa de la Ascensión, monja del Conuento de Santa Clara de Carrión que se da para calificar* (1633); and Pedro de Balbas, OFM,

Memorial informativo en defensa de sor Luisa de la Ascensión, monja professa de Santa Clara de Carrión (Madrid, 1643).

50. See Francisco Luis Rico Callado, "La Inquisición y las visionarias clarisas del siglo XVII: El caso de sor Luisa de la Ascensión," *Bulletin of Spanish Studies* 92, no. 5 (2015): 771–90.

51. Friar Francisco is mentioned repeatedly in the "cartas de Consejo" sent to the Logroño Inquisition in 1635 and 1648. AHN, Inquisition, leg. 2220.96a, b, and c.

52. Juan Gomez de Mora, *Auto de la Fé celebrado en Madrid este año de MDC XXXII* (Madrid, 1632). Francisco's sentence can be found on p. 11v.

53. For more on these natives, see Nancy Parrott Hickerson, *The Jumanos: Hunters and Traders of the South Plains* (Austin: University of Texas Press, 1994); see also her article "The Visits of the 'Lady in Blue': An Episode in the History of the South Plains, 1629," *Journal of Anthropological Research* 46, no. 1 (Spring 1990): 67–90.

54. Colahan, *Visions of Sor María de Agreda,* report to Father Manero, pp. 121, 126.

55. Benavides *Memorial* of 1634, Ayer MS, p. 109.

56. *Tanto que se sacó de una carta,* in Palóu, *Evangelista del Mar Pacífico,* p. 311: "Y la primera vez que ha ido fué el año de 1620 y ha continuado siempre, hasta el año de 1631." Colahan, *Visions of Sor María de Agreda,* p. 107.

57. Benavides, 1630 *Memorial,* pp. 79–80, clearly states that "la santa"—as he calls the Lady in Blue—visits the Jumanos and helps them greet the missionaries sent in 1629. Jiménez Samaniego (*JSRV,* 136–37) claims that all the exterioridades ceased in 1623 but also relates that María saw Benavides and his friars at the San Antonio mission when she went there with the Jumanos (*JSRV,* p. 124). Benavides arrived at San Antonio in 1625 and departed in 1629.

58. *Tanto que se sacó de una carta,* in Palóu, *Evangelista del Mar Pacífico,* p. 314: "Desde el año 1620 hasta este presente de 1631." Colahan, *Visions of Sor María de Agreda,* p. 111.

59. Benavides, 1634 *Memorial,* Ayer MS, p. 108.

60. Benavides, 1634 *Memorial,* Ayer MS, p. 109.

61. Benavides, 1634 *Memorial,* Ayer MS, p. 109.

62. Benavides, 1634 *Memorial,* Ayer MS, p. 109.

63. Clark Colahan raises the question of whether Benavides asked the Jumanos "leading questions that encouraged them to give the answers he wanted." *Visions of Sor María de Agreda,* p. 95.

64. Benavides, 1630 *Memorial,* pp. 78, 80; *Memorial of 1634,* Ayer MS, p. 109. Jiménez Samaniego (*JSRV,* p. 119) says the image was shown to the natives because Luisa de Carrión was well known for her bilocations in Spain, and the friars suspected she might be the mysterious missionary.

65. Benavides, 1634 *Memorial,* Ayer MS, p. 109: "Porque vosotros no nos la aveis preguntado y entendiamos que tambien andava por aca."

66. Benavides, 1630 *Memorial,* p. 80; 1634 *Memorial,* Ayer MS, p. 109. Jiménez Samaniego simply says, "They were received with great demonstrations of piety and joy." *JSRV,* p. 119.

67. Benavides's 1630 *Memorial* (p. 80) mentions two crosses, but the revised text of 1634 mentions only one cross and says María had "helped them decorate" it (1634 *Memorial,* Ayer MS, p. 109).

68. Benavides, 1634 *Memorial* (Ayer MS, p. 110).

69. Benavides's 1630 *Memorial* (pp. 80–81) reports a crowd of 10,000 natives assembled to ask for baptism but does not mention any baptisms actually taking place at this time. In contrast, the 1670 hagiography (*JSRV,* pp. 119–20) says that the natives had learned so much from María that they needed no further instruction before being baptized and that so many received the sacrament that they could not be counted ("Fueron innumerables los que bautizaron").

70. Benavides, 1634 *Memorial,* Ayer MS, p. 110.

71. Benavides, 1634 *Memorial,* Ayer MS, p. 110.

72. Benavides, 1634 *Memorial,* Ayer MS, p. 111.

73. A compelling argument made by John Kessell in "Miracles or Mystery: María de Ágreda's Ministry to the Jumano Indians of the Southwest in the 1620s," in *Great Mysteries of the West,* edited by Ferenc Morton Szasz (Wheat Ridge, CO: Fulcrum, 1993), p. 127.

7. The Trouble with María

1. Question asked by the Inquisition in 1650. In Eduardo Royo, ed., *Autenticidad de la Mística ciudad de Dios y biografía de su autora,* vol. 5, María de Ágreda's *Ciudad Mística de Dios* (Barcelona: Herederos de Juan Gili, 1914), p. 421.

2. See Joaquín Pérez Villanueva, "Sor María de Ágreda y Felipe IV: Un epistolario en su tiempo," in *Historia de la Iglesia en España,* edited by Ricardo García Villoslada, 5 vols. (Madrid: BAC, 1979), 4:384.

3. See Andrew Keitt, *Inventing the Sacred: Imposture, Inquisition, and the Boundaries of the Supernatural in Golden Age Spain* (Leiden: Brill, 2005), pp. 1–12.

4. AHN, Inquisition, leg. 2220.96b, letter of June 6, 1635, signed by Isidoro de San Vicente.

5. AHN, Inquisition, leg. 2220.96 contains these letters, which were bound together haphazardly, with no regard for sequence, continuity, or chronology.

6. AHN, Inquisition, leg. 2220.96b, letter of October 6, 1635, signed by Isidoro de San Vicente. See also Clark Colahan, "María de Jesús de Ágreda: The Sweetheart of the Holy Office," in *Women in the Inquisition: Spain and the New World,* edited by Mary E. Giles (Baltimore: Johns Hopkins University Press, 1999), p. 160.

7. AHN, Inquisition, leg. 2220.96d, unsigned copy of letter of May 26, 1635: "Francisco de la Fuente declaró con la misma forma había sido llevado para el proprio effecto y tubo tan mal fín."

8. AHN, Inquisición, leg. 2220.96a, letter of December 1, 1648.

9. This correspondence can be found in an appendix to *María de Jesús de Ágreda, Correspondencia con Felipe IV: Religión y Razón de Estado* (Madrid: Castalia, 1991), pp. 247–52. For details on this doomed plot, see Ramón Ezquerra Abadía, *La conspiración del duque de Híjar, 1648* (Madrid, 1934).

10. Royo, *Autenticidad,* pp. 406–7 (Royo had access to the original documents and claims to quote directly from them).

11. Royo, pp. 407–11. Final remark on p. 411: "Que ellas vivan persuadidas á que no ha de haber en el mundo quien se acuerde de ellas."

12. Royo, pp. 411–13.

13. Unfortunately, the transcript of this inquest has vanished. Francisco Silvela, editor of the correspondence between Sor María and King Philip IV, claimed to have found it in the 1880s at the archive of the Dukes of Gor and so did Eduardo Royo in the early 1900s, but all subsequent attempts to find it have failed. The only access to it available now is an extract published by Eduardo Royo in volume 5 of his *Autenticidad,* pp. 416–37. This extract, in turn, is summarized by Pérez Villanueva in "Sor María de Ágreda y Felipe IV," vol. 4, chap. 3, pp. 361–418.

14. Letter 244, Sor María to King Philip, March 11, 1650. In Francisco Silvela, *Cartas de la Venerable Madre Sor María de Agreda y del Señor Rey Don Felipe IV,* 2 vols. (Madrid, 1886), 2:20.

15. Royo, *Autenticidad;* Pérez Villanueva, "Sor María de Ágreda y Felipe IV," vol. 4, chap. 3, pp. 361–418.

16. Royo, *Autenticidad,* p. 421.

17. Royo, p. 419.

18. Clark Colahan, trans., *The Visions of Sor María de Ágreda: Writing Knowledge and Power* (Albuquerque: University of New Mexico Press, 1994), report to Father Manero, pp. 120–21.

19. 2 Cor. 12.2–4: "I know a man in Christ who fourteen years ago was caught up to the third heaven. Whether it was in the body or out of it I do not know, but God knows. And I know that this man—whether in the body or out of it I do not know, but God knows—was caught up to Paradise. The things he heard were too sacred for words, things that man is not permitted to tell."

20. Colahan, *Visions of Sor María de Ágreda,* report to Father Manero, p. 121.

21. Colahan, *Visions of Sor María de Ágreda,* report to Father Manero, pp. 121–23.

22. Colahan, *Visions of Sor María de Ágreda,* report to Father Manero, p. 127.

23. Colahan, *Visions of Sor María de Ágreda,* report to Father Manero, pp. 121–23.

24. Royo, *Autenticidad,* p. 426.

25. Pérez Villanueva, "Sor María de Ágreda y Felipe IV," p. 387.

26. Colahan, *Visions of Sor María de Ágreda,* report to Father Manero, p. 127.

27. Colahan, report to Father Manero, p. 128.

28. Royo, *Autenticidad,* pp. 430–32. At one point she cites "San Eusebio (Homilia segunda de Deipara) y también San Idelfonso."

29. Royo, p. 432.

30. Royo, pp. 433–35.

31. Royo, "Mi interior," pp. 435–36; Pérez Villanueva, "Sor María de Ágreda y Felipe IV," p. 387.

32. Royo, *Autenticidad,* pp. 436–37. The final sentence reads: "Es católica y fiel cristiana, bien fundada en nuestra santa fe, sin ningún genero de ficción ni embeleco del demonio."

33. Letter 242, February 18, 1650, in Silvela, *Cartas,* 2:15.

34. Letter 243, February 26, 1650, in Silvela, *Cartas,* 2:17.

35. Letter 242, February 18, 1650, in Silvela, *Cartas,* 2:15.

36. For Philip's life, see Aurelio Musi, *Filippo IV: La malinconia dell'impero* (Rome: Salerno, 2021); Alfredo Alvar Ezquerra, *Felipe IV, El Grande* (Madrid: La Esfera, 2018); Eduardo Chamorro, *Felipe IV* (Barcelona: Planeta, 1998).

37. See R. A. Stradling, *Philip IV and the Government of Spain, 1621–1665* (Cambridge University Press, 1988).

38. See John H. Elliott, *The Count-Duke of Olivares: The Statesman in an Age of Decline* (New Haven, CT: Yale University Press, 1986).

39. See John H. Elliott, *The Revolt of the Catalans: A Study in the Decline of Spain, 1598–1640* (Cambridge University Press, 1963).

40. Text available in Luis Villasante, "Sor María de Jesús de Ágreda a través de su correspondencia con el rey," *Archivo Ibero-Americano* 25, no. 98–99 (1965): 149. Also available in Anna Nogar, *Quill and Cross in the Borderlands: Sor María de Ágreda and the Lady in Blue, 1628 to the Present* (University of Notre Dame Press, 2018), p. 47.

41. Nogar, *Quill and Cross,* p. 62n9.

42. *Mystica Ciudad de Dios, Milagro de su Omnipotencia y Abismo de la Gracia, Historia Divina, y Vida de la Virgen Madre de Dios, Reyna, y Señora Nuestra Maria Santissima, Restauradora de la Culpa de Eva, y Medianera de la Gracia. Manifestada en estos Ultimos Siglos por la Misma Señora a su Esclava Sor María de Jesús, Abadesa de el Convento de la Inmaculada Concepción, de la Villa de Ágreda* (Madrid: Bernardo de Villa-Diego, 1670) (hereafter *MCD*). I have used the Spanish 1807 Pamplona edition (P1807) because it is available online and is therefore accessible—at least for now—to anyone with internet access (https://academica-e.unavarra.es/handle/2454/12299).

43. See Ismael Bengoechea Izaguirre, "Vidas de la Virgen María en la España del siglo XVII," *Estudios Marianos* 49 (1984): 59–103.

44. For a listing of pre-twentieth-century editions and translations, see Zótico Royo Campos, *Agredistas y Antiagredistas: Estudio Histórico-Apologético* (Murcia: San Buenaventura, 1929), pp. 468–70. The most widely printed English translation of *The Mystical City* is that of Father George J. Blatter, who chose to publish it under the pen name Fiscar Marison (Charlotte, NC: TAN Books, 2006).

45. Rev. 21:9–27. The Heavenly Jerusalem was also known as the City of God, and the title of Sor María's book, *The Mystical City of God,* was an allusion to the intimate connection between the Virgin Mary and the Heavenly Jerusalem as co-redeemer of the human race along with her son Jesus, the divine ruler of that apocalyptic city.

46. *MCD* I.1.1.5 (P1807 1:27); Rev. 12.1–6: "A woman clothed with the sun, with the moon under her feet, and on her head a crown of twelve stars."

47. *MCD* III.6.21.1358 (P1807 6:402–4); Blatter, *The Mystical City of God,* para. 647.

48. *MCD* IV.8.5.458 (P1807 8:90).

49. *MCD* I.1.1.9 (P1807 1:32–33).

50. *MCD* I.1.1.9 (P1807 1:33).

51. See Benito Mendía, "En torno al problema de la autenticidad de la Mistica Ciudad de Dios," *Archivo Ibero-Americano* 42, no. 165–68 (1982): 391–430.

52. *MCD* I.1.1.10 (P1807 1:34).

53. *MCD* I, introduction, paragraph 12 (P1807 1:11–12).

54. *MCD* I.1.2.14 (P1807 1:36–37).

55. *MCD* IV.8.23, letter to sisters. 16 (P1807 8:419).

56. *JSRV,* pp. 301–6. T. D. Kendrick, *Mary of Ágreda: The Life and Legend of a Spanish Nun* (London: Routledge & Kegan Paul, 1967), p. 73, disagrees with Jiménez Samaniego on the date of the book burning, offering proof that it must have been 1646 rather than 1645.

57. *JSRV,* pp. 307–8. The hagiographer blames the second burning on the same confessor who ordered the first burning. Kendrick disagrees, attributing the second burning to María's fear of the Inquisition. Kendrick, *Mary of Ágreda,* p. 74.

58. Kendrick, *Mary of Agreda,* p. 77n2.

59. *MCD* IV.8.23.791 (P1807 8:403).

60. *MCD* IV.8.23, letter to sisters. 15–16 (P1807 8:417–18).

61. "Historical Notice," appendix to *The Admirable Life of the Glorious Patriarch Saint Joseph: Taken from the Cité Mystique de Dieu* (New York, 1860), pp. 320–21; English translation of José Jiménez Samaniego's *Life of the Venerable Mary of Jesus of Agreda* (Evansville, IN: Keller-Crescent Printing and Engraving, 1910), pp. 144–45.

62. This seemingly "impossible" miracle was relatively common throughout medieval and early modern times in the Orthodox and Catholic Churches, and the phenomenon has continued up until the present day. See Heather Pringle, "The Incorruptibles," *Discover* 22, no. 6 (June 2001): 66–71; and also the chapter with the same title in her book *The Mummy Congress: Science, Obsession, and the Everlasting Dead* (New York: Hyperion, 2001), pp. 242–68. For more on Saint Teresa's incorruptible corpse, see Carlos Eire, *From Madrid to Purgatory* (Cambridge University Press, 1995), pp. 425–45.

63. For a thorough Agredista summary of the polarization, see Benito Mendía and Antonio M. Artola Arbiza, *La Venerable M. María de Jesús de Ágreda y la Inmaculada Concepción: El proceso eclesiástico a la "Mística Ciudad de Dios* (Ágreda: Monasterio de la Concepción., 2004).

64. Mendía and Artola Arbiza, *La Venerable M. María de Jesús de Ágreda,* p. 66; Nogar, *Quill and Cross,* p. 252n15.

65. Nogar, *Quill and Cross,* pp. 55n75, 56n82.

66. See Luis Villasante, "La *Mística Ciudad de Dios* y el problema de la revelaciones privadas," *Scriptorium Victoriense* 19 (1972): 35–62.

67. Andrés Ivars, "Expediente relativo a los escritos de la Venerable Madre Sor María de Jesús de Ágreda," *Archivo Ibero-Americano,* 1917, p. 132.

68. On this point, see Villasante, "La *Mística Ciudad de Dios*."

69. Nogar, *Quill and Cross,* p. 57n90.

70. Quoted in Royo Campos, *Agredistas y Antiagredistas,* p. 327.

71. "Finalmente no puede atribuirse al demonio, porque desde el principio al fin no inspira ni respira otra cosa que humildad, paciencia, amor y sufrimiento de trabajos." *MCD;* P1807, vol. 1. The first seventy-two unnumbered pages of volume 1 of the 1807 Pamplona edition contain various approbations of *The Mystical City,* including those from the universities of Salamanca, Alcalá, and Louvain. The quote from Louvain cited here appears two pages back from the final unnumbered page.

72. See G. Calvo Moralejo, "El Escotismo de la Mística Ciudad de Dios y su influencia en el proceso de beatificación de la M. Ágreda," in *Giovanni Duns Scoto: Studi e ricerche nel VII Centenario della sua morte,* 2 vols. (Rome: Antonianum, 2008), 2:257–78; and Alessandro Apollonio, "The Decisive Contribution of Blessed John Duns Scotus to the Dogma of the Immaculate Conception: Objections, Old and New," in *Blessed John Duns Scotus and His Mariology* (New Bedford: Academy of the Immaculate, 2009), pp. 43–71.

73. Mendía, "En torno al problema de la autenticidad," p. 405.

74. Kendrick, *Mary of Ágreda,* p. 80.

75. For a very detailed but partisan summary of the controversies generated by Sor María over three centuries, see Royo Campos, *Agredistas y Antiagredistas;* also the more recent work of Fathers Mendía and Artola Arbiza, *La Venerable Madre Maria de Jesús de Ágreda.*

76. The findings of these reviews were published. See *Sacra Rituum Congregatio, Examen responsionis ad Censuram olim editam super libris misticae civitatis Dei* (Rome, 1730); *Synopsis observationum et responsionum super libris ven. abbatissae Mariae a Jesu de Agreda* (Rome, 1737); *Super examine operis a Maria a Jesu de Agreda conscripti* (Rome, 1747).

77. Eusebius Amort, *De revelationibus, visionibus et apparitionibus privatis regulae tutae ex Scripturá, Conciliis, Sanctis Patribus aliisque optimis auctoribus collectae, explicatae atque exemplis illustratae* (Augsburg, 1744). See Royo Campos, *Agredistas y Antiagredistas,* pp. 373–91.

78. See Eusebius Amort, *Controversia de Revelationibus Agredanis Explicate Cum Epicrisi Ad Ineptas Earum Revelationum Vindicias* (Augsburg, 1749); and *Nova Demonstratio de Falsitate Revelationum Agredanarum cum Parallelo Inter Pseudo Evangelia et Easdem Revelationes, Adita Nova Defensione Agredana a R. P. Dalmatius Kick* (Augsburg, 1751).

79. For examples, see Dalmatius Kick, *Revelationum agredanarum iusta defensio* (Regensburg, 1750); *Excussio novae defensionis agredanae* (Augsburg, 1751); and *Continuatio iustae defensionis revelationum agredanarum* (Madrid, 1754).
80. Mendía, "En torno a la autenticidad," pp. 417, 421.
81. Montague Summers, *The Physical Phenomena of Mysticism* (New York: Barnes and Noble, 1950), p. 61.
82. Nogar, *Quill and Cross,* p. 59n99.
83. Giacomo Casanova, *Histoire de ma Fuite des Prisons de la Republique de Venise, qu'on Apelle Les Plombs* (Leipzig, 1788), p. 40.
84. Casanova, p. 43.
85. Casanova, p. 42.
86. Casanova, p. 41.
87. María de Agreda and her *Mystical City* had a profound impact on Spanish America, especially colonial and postcolonial Mexico. For this dimension of the cult of Sor María, see the definitive study of this subject: Nogar, *Quill and Cross,* chaps. 3–6.
88. See Marilyn H. Fedewa, *María of Ágreda, Mystical Lady in Blue* (Albuquerque: University of New Mexico Press, 2009), pp. 258–73.

8. Tricksters of the Impossible

Epigraph: Testimony from Damian de Fonseca, onetime secretary to Luis de Granada: *Damiani a Fonseca Itinerarium,* cited by Alvaro Huerga, "La vida seudomística de la Monja de Lisboa," *Hispania Sacra* 12 (1959): 97n25.

1. Gospel of John 8:44.
2. The term "trickster" has multiple meanings. In everyday speech it normally refers to someone who can fool others. In the study of folklore and religion, the trickster is any being—usually charismatic—who deceives, plays tricks, ignores rules, defies convention, and creates mayhem, both constructive and destructive. Scholars have most often examined tricksters in ancient mythologies and tribal religions rather than in the major world religions, but their universality is undeniable. Anthropologist Victor Turner proposed that tricksters inhabit liminal spaces in society and ritual. Psychologist Carl Jung identified the "trickster" as one of the archetypes of the collective unconscious. All these meanings are applicable to the liminal "living saints" who are the focus of this chapter. See Victor Turner, *The Forest of Symbols* (Ithaca, NY: Cornell

University Press, 1967), esp. p. 99; Robert D. Pelton, *The Trickster in West Africa: A Study of Mythic Irony and Sacred Delight* (Berkeley: University of California Press, 1989), pp. 5–18.

3. William C. Christian Jr., "The Delimitations of Sacred Space and the Visions of Ezquioga, 1931–1987," in *Luoghi sacri e spazi della santità,* edited by Sofia Boesch Gajano and Lucetta Scaraffia (Università degli studi dell'Aquila, 2009), pp. 85–103; see also Carlo Ginzburg, "The Inquisitor as Anthropologist," in *Clues, Myths, and the Historical Method,* translated by John and Anne Tedeschi (Baltimore: Johns Hopkins University Press, 1989), pp. 156–64.

4. Anne Jacobson Schutte, *Aspiring Saints: Pretense of Holiness, Inquisition, and Gender in the Republic of Venice, 1618–1750* (Baltimore: Johns Hopkins University Press, 2001), pp. 201–4.

5. See Bernard McGinn, *The Persistence of Mysticism in Catholic Europe: France, Italy, and Germany, 1500–1675* (New York: Crossroad Publishing, 2020), pt. I, chaps. 1–5.

6. See Schutte, *Aspiring Saints;* and Pasquale Palmieri, *I taumaturghi della società: Santi e potere politico nel secolo dei Lumi* (Rome: Viella, 2010).

7. See Stuart Schwartz, *All Can Be Saved: Religious Tolerance and Salvation in the Iberian Atlantic World* (New Haven, CT: Yale University Press, 2008).

8. *Memorial de la política necesaria y útil restauración a la república de España* (Valladolid, Spain, 1600), fol. 25v; translated by John H. Elliott in *Spain and Its World, 1500–1700* (New Haven, CT: Yale University Press, 1989), p. 265.

9. *Tratado del examen de las revelaciones verdaderas y falsas, y de los raptos* (Valencia, 1634), pp. 344–47.

10. Marcelino Menendez Pelayo, *Historia de los heterodoxos españoles,* 3 vols. (Madrid: Librería Católica de San José, 1880–1881); facsimile edition, Madrid: Grandes Clasicos, 1992, 2:249–50.

11. "Un tiempo fideista," in José Antonio Maravall, *La cultura del barroco* (Madrid: Ariel, 1975), p. 44.

12. Stephen Haliczer, *Between Exaltation and Infamy: Female Mystics in the Golden Age of Spain* (Oxford University Press, 2002), p. 4.

13. Patrocinio García Barriúso, "El milagrismo: Sor Luisa de la Ascención, La Monja de Carrión, el Fr. Frolán Díaz, y el inquisidor Mendoza," in *HIEA,* 1:1089.

14. Teófanes Egido López, "Religiosidad popular y taumaturgia del Barroco (Los milagros de la monja de Carrión)," in *Actas del II Congreso de Historia de*

Palencia, edited by María Valentina Calleja González, 4 vols. (Palencia, Spain: Departamento de Cultura, 1990), 3:11.

15. José Luis Sánchez Lora, *Mujeres, conventos, y formas de la religiosidad barroca* (Madrid: Fundación Universitaria Española, 1988), pp. 456–57.

16. Fray Juan de los Angeles, *Diálogos de la conquista del reino de Dios* (1595), modern edition annotated by Angel González Palencia (Madrid: Real Academia Española, 1946), pp. 213–14.

17. Gaspar Navarro, *Tribunal de la superstición ladina, explorador del saber, astucia y poder del demonio* (Huesca, Spain, 1631), p. 28r.

18. For a superb introduction to this subject, see Andrew W. Keitt, *Inventing the Sacred: Imposture, Inquisition, and the Boundaries of the Supernatural in Golden Age Spain* (Leiden: Brill, 2005). The Inquisition in Venice preferred to use the term "pretense of holiness" (*simulata santità*) and other variations of it, such as *affetata, falsa, finta,* or *pretesa santità.* See Schutte, *Aspiring Saints,* preface, p. x.

19. See Carmen Soriano Triguero, "Inquisición, beatas y falsarios en el siglo XVII: Pautas del Santo Oficio para examinar visiones y apariciones," in *Disidencias y exilios en la España moderna: Actas de la IV reunión científica de la Asociación Española de Historia Moderna,* edited by Antonio Mestre Sanchis, Pablo Fernández Albaladejo, and Enrique Giménez López (Universidad de Alicante, 1997).

20. Keitt, *Inventing the Sacred,* p. 205.

21. Keitt, p. 7.

22. See María del Mar Graña Cid, "En torno a la fenomenologia de las santas vivas," in *Responsabilidad y diálogo: Homenaje a José Joaquín Alemany Briz,* edited by Xavier Quinzá Lleó (Madrid: Universidad Pontificia Comillas, 2002), pp. 415–53; and Gabriella Zarri, *Le sante vive: Cultura e religiosità femminile nella prima età moderna* (Turin: Rosenberg and Sellier, 1990); as well as her "Living Saints: A Typology of Female Sanctity in the Early Sixteenth Century," in *Women and Religion in Medieval and Renaissance Italy,* edited by Daniel Bornstein and Roberto Rusconi (University of Chicago Press, 1996), pp. 219–304.

23. See Carlos Eire, *Reformations: The Early Modern World* (New Haven, CT: Yale University Press, 2016), pp. 399–404.

24. *Cælestis Hierusalem Cives,* July 5, 1534.

25. Sor Juana has received considerable attention in the past three decades. See Jessica Boon, "Introduction," in *Mother Juana de la Cruz, 1481–1534: Visionary*

Sermons, edited by J. Boon and R. E. Surtz (Tempe: Arizona Center for Medieval and Renaissance Studies, 2016), pp. 1–33; Ronald E. Surtz, *The Guitar of God: Gender, Power, and Authority in the Visionary World of Mother Juana de la Cruz* (Philadelphia: University of Pennsylvania Press, 1990); Inocente García de Andrés, "Introduction," in *El conhorte: Sermones de una mujer; La Santa Juana,* edited by Inocente García de Andrés (Madrid: Fundación Universitaria Española, 1999); María Victoria Triviño, *Mujer, predicadora, y párroco: La Santa Juana* (Madrid, 1999); Daniel de Pablo Maroto, "La 'Santa Juana,' mística franciscana del siglo XVI español," *Revista de espiritualidad* 60 (2001): 577–601; María del Mar Cortés Timoner, *Sor Juana de la Cruz* (Madrid: Clasicas, 2004).

26. Her *sermones* were transcribed and archived. They are now available in García de Andrés, *El Conhorte.*

27. This phenomenon would also surface among "visionary" monastics in Italy. See Schutte, *Aspiring Saints,* pp. 154–74.

28. For a detailed summary of this development, see Isabelle Poutrin, "Les chapelets bénits des mystiques espagnoles (XVI–XVII siècles)," *Mélanges de la Casa de Velázquez* 26, no. 2 (1990): 33–54.

29. *Super virtutibus sanctae vitae et miraculis de sor Juana de la Cruz,* 1621, ASV, Congregazione dei Riti, n3076.

30. *Vida y fin de la bienabenturada virgen sancta Juana de la Cruz* (archived at the library of El Escorial, K-III-13); and *Libro de la casa y monasterio de Nuestra Señora de la Cruz* (archived at the BNE, MS 9661).

31. Antonio Daza, *Historia, vida y milagros, éxtasis y revelaciones de la bienaventurada virgen santa Juana de la Cruz* (Madrid, 1610).

32. Tirso de Molina, *La Santa Juana, trilogía hagiográfica, 1613–14,* edited by Agustín del Campo (Madrid: Castilla, 1948).

33. Pedro Navarro, *Favores de el Rey del Cielo hechos a su esposa la santa Juana de la Cruz* (Madrid, 1622).

34. When Juana's canonization process was restarted nearly a century after her death, Daza's *Historia, vida y milagros* was translated and published in French (1614), Italian (1618), German (1619), and English (1625).

35. For a brief summary of her case drawn from Inquisition files, see "Proceso de la monja Magdalena de la Cruz, que se finjió santa," in *Relación de las causas mas notables que siguió el Tribunal de la Inquisición, contra los que se decian brujos, hechiceros, mágicos, nigrománticos, y aliados con el demonio: Entre los que se refieren la del famoso mágico Torralba, Falso Musico de Portugal, Monja de Córdoba fingida santa, y otras de mucha nombradía* (Seville: El Porvenir, 1839), pp. 74–93.

36. "Muy preciada hija suya." Eyewitness testimony quoted in "Proceso de la monja Magdalena de la Cruz," p. 75 See also "Proceso de la santa fingida de Córdoba," in Gaspar Matute y Liquín, *Colección de los autos generales y particulares de fe celebrados por el tribunal de la Inquisición de Córdoba* (Córdoba: Santaló, Canalejas y Compañía, 1836), p. 183. A more recent edition (Madrid: D. Blanco, 1912), is actually harder to find. See also Geraldine McKendrick and Angus MacKay, "Visionaries and Affective Spirituality during the First Half of the Sixteenth Century," in *Cultural Encounters: The Impact of the Inquisition in Spain and the New World,* edited by Mary Elizabeth Perry and Anne J. Cruz (Berkeley: University of California Press, 1991), p. 95.

37. Jesús Imirizaldu, ed., "Testimony of Francisco de Encinas," in *Monjas y Beatas Embaucadoras* (Madrid: Editora Nacional, 1977), pp. 37–38.

38. Henry Charles Lea, *A History of the Inquisition in Spain,* 4 vols. (New York: Macmillan, 1907), 4:82.

39. Matute y Liquín, *Colección,* pp. 189–90.

40. Excerpt of letter from Zapata, in Imirizaldu, *Monjas,* p. 33. On the battle of Pavia, see Jean-Marie Le Gall, *L'honneur perdu de François Ier: Pavie, 1525* (Paris: Payot, 2015); and Angus Konstam, *Pavia 1525: The Climax of the Italian Wars* (Oxford: Praeger, 1996).

41. "Una reliquia andante." Ana Cristina Cuadro García, "Tejiendo una vida de reliqua: Estrategias de control de consciencias de la santa diabólica Magdalena de la Cruz," *Chronica Nova* 31 (2005): 308.

42. *Proçesso a Madalena de la Cruz,* BNF, MS 354, fol. 252v. See Cuadro García, "Tejiendo una vida de reliqua," p. 308n1.

43. BNF, MS 354, fol. 257v.

44. "Sentencia de Magdalena de la Cruz," I, in Imirizaldu, *Monjas,* p. 53. The crucifixion was incomplete because she had no way of nailing the hand she had used for nailing her other three extremities.

45. "Sentencia," IX, in Imirizaldu, *Monjas,* p. 55.

46. BNF, MS 354, fol. 264r; "Sentencia," VIII, in Imirizaldu, *Monjas,* p. 55.

47. Matute y Liquín, *Colección,* p. 185.

48. BNF, MS 354, fol. 253v; "Sentencia," XXIX, in Imirizaldu, *Monjas,* p. 59.

49. "Sentencia," XIII and XXIV, in Imirizaldu, *Monjas,* pp. 56, 58.

50. Matute y Liquín, *Colección,* p. 186; and "Sentencia," V, in Imirizaldu, *Monjas,* p. 54.

51. See Poutrin, "Les chapelets bénits des mystiques espagnoles," pp. 33–54.

52. BNF, MS 354, fols. 251v–252r.

53. "Sentencia," XXIX, in Imirizaldu, *Monjas,* p. 59.

54. *Obras del Venerable Maestro Juan de Ávila,* 9 vols. (Madrid, 1759), 2:127–28. See also Rady Roldán-Figueroa, *The Ascetic Spirituality of Juan de Ávila* (Leiden: Brill, 2010), p. 82.

55. Pedro de Ribadeneyra, *Vida del Padre Ignacio de Loyola, fundador de la Religión de la Compañía de Jesús* (Madrid, 1583), bk. 5, pp. 277–78.

56. Cuadro García, "Tejiendo una vida de reliqua," p. 309; "Sentencia," XV, in Imirizaldu, *Monjas,* p. 57.

57. "Las críaba en su celda": Rafael Gracia Boix, ed., *Autos de fe y causas de la Inquisición de Córdoba* (Córdoba: Diputación Provincial de Córdoba, 1983), p. 16.

58. BNF, MS 354, fol. 257r.

59. BNF, MS 354, fols. 253v–254r.

60. BNF, MS 354, fols. 252r, 265v.

61. BNF, MS 354, fol. 251v.

62. BNF, MS 354, fol. 259r.

63. BNF, MS 354, fol. 253r, 262r–262v; Cuadro García, "Tejiendo una vida de reliqua," pp. 310n4, 319n39.

64. BNF, MS 354, fols. 262r–262v; "Sentencia," XXVIII, in Imirizaldu, *Monjas,* p. 59.

65. BNF, MS 354, fol. 251r.

66. Letter written in early 1544 by a nun from the Santa Isabel convent in Córdoba, in Imirizaldu, *Monjas,* p. 44.

67. "Letter," in Imirizaldu, *Monjas,* pp. 44–45.

68. "Letter," in Imirizaldu, *Monjas,* pp. 47–48.

69. "Sentencia," V, in Imirizaldu, *Monjas,* p. 54.

70. "Sentencia," IX, in Imirizaldu, *Monjas,* p. 55.

71. "Sentencia," XIII, XXIV, XXIX, XXXV, in Imirizaldu, *Monjas,* pp. 56, 58, 59, 60.

72. "Sentencia," XIV, in Imirizaldu, *Monjas,* p. 56.

73. BNF MS 354, fol. 260v. Cuadro Garcia, "Tejiendo una vida de reliqua," p. 323, argues that Magdalena's extreme inedia claims were her "Achilles' heel."

74. For a perceptive analysis of the social dimension of Magdalena's downfall, see María del Mar Graña Cid, "La Santa/Bruja Magdalena de la Cruz: Identidades Religiosas y Poder Femenino en la Andalucía Pretridentina," in *Actas del III Congreso de Historia de Andalucía,* vol. 2: *Las mujeres en la historia de Andalucía* (Cordoba: Publicaciones Obra Social y Cultural CajaSur, 2002), pp. 103–20.

75. Montague Summers, *The Physical Phenomena of Mysticism* (London: Rider and Company, 1950), p. 218.

76. "Sentencia," XXXVI, in Imirizaldu, *Monjas,* pp. 60–61.

77. Magdalena's case would receive constant attention internationally in texts on feigned sanctity and demonology, such as Juan de Horozco y Covarrubias's *Tratado de la verdadera y falsa prophecia* (1588); Jean Bodin's *De la démonomanie des sorciers* (1580); and Richard Baxter's *The Certainty of the Worlds of Spirits* (1691). In 1939, French jurist and polymath Maurice Garçon would turn Magdalena's story into a historical novel, *Magdeleine de la Croix, abbesse diabolique* (repr., Grenoble: Éditions Jérome Millon, 2010).

78. Francisco de Encinas, in Imirizaldu, *Monjas,* p. 38.

79. On the development of this physical phenomenon of Christian mysticism, see Carolyn Muessig, "Signs of Salvation: The Evolution of Stigmatic Spirituality before Saint Francis of Assisi," *Church History* 82, no. 1 (March 2013): 40–68.

80. Agustina Bessa Luís, *A Monja de Lisboa* (Lisbon: Guimarães Editores, 1985).

81. The convent of the Annunciation housed over sixty nuns. See Alvaro Huerga, "El Proceso Inquisitorial de la 'Monja de Lisboa' y Fray Luis de Granada," *Hispania Sacra* 12 (1959): 334n6.

82. María could have read about Catherine's spiritual marriage in Raymond of Capua's fourteenth-century hagiography *The Life of Saint Catherine of Siena,* pt, 1, chap. 11.

83. *OCLG,* vol. 17, *Historia de Sor María de la Visitación* (hereafter *OCLG* 17), pp. 66–67.

84. Letter to Archbishop Juan de Ribera, March 1584, in *OCLG,* vol. 19, *Epistolario* (hereafter *OCLG* 19), p. 124; *OCLG* 17:147, 171.

85. *OCLG* 17:40, 47–48, 171.

86. *OCLG* 17:129, 169, 175–86.

87. *OCLG* 17:145. On this theme, see María Echaniz Sans, "El cuerpo femenino como encarnación de Cristo: María de la Visitación, la monja de Lisboa," *Revista d'etudis feministes* 9 (1995): 27–45.

88. *OCLG* 17:146.

89. *OCLG* 17:146–47.

90. *OCLG* 17:148, 193.

91. María could have read about Catherine's invisible stigmata in Raymond of Capua's fourteenth-century hagiography, *The Life of Saint Catherine of Siena,* pt. 2, chap. 5.

92. *OCLG* 17:146. The wounds on her head bled a little, constantly, and produced horrific headaches every Thursday evening that would last twenty-four hours and make every Friday a painful ordeal for María.

93. *OCLG* 17:157, 193.

94. *OCLG* 17:164.

95. *OCLG* 17:151.

96. Alvaro Huerga, "Vida seudomística," 46n41. The "nails" that protruded from these wounds were fleshy but were irregularly shaped and gave the appearance of being made of rusty iron.

97. Letter of Luis de Granada to Juan de Ribera, March 1584, in *OCLG* 19: 124. See Ramón Robres Lluch, "La monja de Lisboa. Sus fingidos estigmas. Fray Luis de Granada y el Patriarca Ribera," *Boletín de la Sociedad Castellonense de Cultura* 83 (1947): 182–214, 230–78.

98. See Urbano Alonso del Campo, *Vida y obra de Fray Luis de Granada* (Salamanca: Editorial San Esteban, 2005); John A. Moore, *Fray Luis de Granada* (Boston: Twayne, 1977); and Luis Muñoz, *Vida y virtudes del venerable varon Fray Luis de Granada* (Madrid, 1639), esp. chaps. 9–13, on his involvement with the Nun of Lisbon.

99. Cited in Ramón Robres, "La Monja de Lisboa según nuevos documentos romanos con una carta de Fray Luis de Granada," *Boletín de la Sociedad Castellonense de Cultura* 28 (1952): 523. For the correspondence with Ribera, see Ramón Robres and José Ramón Ortolá, *La monja de Lisboa: Epistolario inédito entre Fr. Luis de Granada y el Patriarca Ribera* (Castellón de la Plana: Sociedad Castellonense de Cultura, 1947).

100. *Relación de la vida y milagros de la priora de la Anunciata* (Paris, 1586).

101. *OCLG* 17:12–13.

102. *The Fugger News Letters: Being a Selection of Unpublished Letters from the Correspondents of the House of Fugger during the Years 1568–1605,* edited by Victor von Klarwill, translated by Pauline de Chary (New York: Putnam, 1925), p. 119.

103. Huerga, "Vida seudomística," p. 62.

104. "Examen de fr. Luis de Granada y fr. Gaspar d'Aveiro," app. 5.2, in Huerga, "Vida seudomística," pp. 88–89.

105. Report of Luis de Granada, Juan de las Cuevas, and Gaspar d'Aveiro, December 1587, app. 5.1, in Huerga, "Vida seudomística," pp. 85–86.

106. Report of Luis de Granada, Juan de las Cuevas, and Gaspar d'Aveiro, December 1587, app. 5.1, in Huerga, "Vida seudomística," p. 88.

107. Huerga, "Vida seudomística," p. 76.

108. Daniel A. Mortier, *Histoire de maîtres généraux de l'ordre des frères prêcheurs,* 8 vols. (Paris: Picard, 1903–1920), 5:645–46n1.

109. Mortier, *Histoire de maîtres généraux,* 5:646n2; Huerga, "Vida seudomística," p. 96n20.

110. Huerga, "Vida seudomística," p. 77.

111. Astrologer Guillén de Casaos, AHN, Inquisition, leg. 312, no. 2, fol. 5, Casaos to Alonso de Mendoza, Madrid, November 19, 1588, cited in Richard Kagan, "Politics, Prophecy, and the Inquisition in Late Sixteenth-Century Spain," in *Cultural Encounters: The Impact of the Inquisition in Spain and the New World,* edited by Mary Elizabeth Perry and Anne J. Cruz (Berkeley: University of California Press, 1991), p. 119n49.

112. Testimony from Damian de Fonseca, one-time secretary to Luis de Granada: "Non est vera sanctitas huius monialis, quae populum commovet et rebus politicis sese immiscet." *Damiani a Fonseca Itinerarium ac gesta ex variis relationibus eiusdem per me Io. Baptismam Reggianum, eius amanuensem, collecta,* AGOP, Santa Sabina, Rome, sec. 13, MS 460, fol. 131r., cited by Huerga, "Vida seudomística," p. 97n25.

113. A full description of this investigation can be found in the sentence eventually issued by the Inquisition in November 1588, which can be found in Imirizaldu, *Monjas,* pp. 179–97.

114. "Sentencia," in Imirizaldu, *Monjas,* pp. 181–87.

115. "Sentencia," in Imirizaldu, *Monjas,* pp. 187–93; and "Relacion sumaria de las cosas de Maria de la Visitacion, prioresa que fue del monasterio de la Anunciada de Lisboa" (1588), app. 7, in Huerga, "Vida seudomística," pp. 94–95.

116. "Sentencia," in Imirizaldu, *Monjas,* pp. 192–93.

117. "Sentencia," in Imirizaldu, *Monjas,* p. 193.

118. The official statement signed by Cardinal Archduke Albert, who was also inquisitor general, is at the BNE, MS. 11.077, fols. 12r–38v.

119. "Sentencia," in Imirizaldu, *Monjas,* pp. 196–97; also in Huerga, "Vida seudomística," pp. 124–25.

120. Richard Kagan emphasizes the political dimension of María's condemnation in his essay "Politics, Prophecy, and the Inquisition," pp. 118–20.

121. Huerga, "Vida seudomística," pp. 86–87.

122. For a very perceptive analysis of this response in relation to María's spectacular fall from grace, see Freddy Dominguez, "From Saint to Sinner: Sixteenth Century Perceptions of 'La Monja de Lisboa,'" in *A New Companion to Hispanic Mysticism,* edited by Hilaire Kallendorf (Leiden: Brill, 2010), pp. 297–320.

123. Some of María's devotees, such as Margarita de Agullona, were devastated by her fraudulence. See Jaime Sanchiz, *Relación breve de la vida, virtudes, y milagros de la humilde sierva del Señor sor Margarita Agullona* (Valencia, 1607), p. 95.

124. "Copia de una carta que el padre fray Luis de Granada escribió a la Majestad de la Emperatriz sobre la causa de María de la Visitación." *OCLG* 19:182–87.

125. "Sermón contra los escándalos en las caídas públicas," *OCLG* 17:207–56. On the writing of this sermon, see Muñoz, *Vida y virtudes,* chap. 13.

126. "Sermón," *OCLG* 17:216.

127. "Sermón," *OCLG* 17:237.

128. "Sermón," *OCLG* 17:257.

129. Cipriano de Valera, *Enjambre de los falsos milagros, y ilusiones del demonio con que María de la Visitación priora de la Anunciada de Lisboa engañó a muy muchos: Y de como fue descubierta y condenada en el año de 1588* (London, 1594). I have used this edition: *Los dos tratados del papa i de la misa* (Madrid, 1851), pp. 554–94.

130. De Valera, *Enjambre,* pp. 586–88, 591–94.

131. For more on Valera, see Paul J. Hauben, *Three Spanish Heretics and the Reformation: Antonio Del Corro, Cassiodoro De Reina, and Cypriano De Valera* (Geneva: Librairie Droz, 1967).

132. De Valera, *Enjambre,* p. 582.

133. The two definitive biographies on Sor Luisa by Father Patrocinio García Barriúso are extremely difficult to find outside Spain: *La monja de Carrión: Sor Luisa de la Ascensión Colmenares Cabezón* (Zamora, Spain: Ediciones Monte Casino, 1986) and *Sor Luisa de la Ascensión: Una contemplativa del Siglo xvii* (Madrid: self-published, 1993). The most thorough listing of all the extant manuscript sources on the life of Sor Luisa can be found in his *Monja de Carrión,* pp. 5–13.

134. Various visionary "living saints" of the seventeenth century were Spanish Franciscan nuns, and quite a few had run-ins with the Inquisition. See Francisco Luis Rico Callado, "La Inquisición y las visionarias clarisas del siglo XVII: El caso de sor Luisa de la Ascensión," *Bulletin of Spanish Studies* 92, no. 5 (2015): 771–90. And these Franciscans were part of a larger phenomenon: see María Laura Giordano, "Al borde del abismo: 'Falsas santas' e 'ilusas' madrileñas en la vigilia de 1640," *Historia Social* 57 (2007): 75–97.

135. See Patrocinio García Barriúso, "La Monja de Carrión Sor Luisa de la Ascensión y Sor María de Jesús, la Monja de Ágreda," *Verdad y Vida* 49 (1961): 547–52.

136. See Barriúso, *Monja de Carrión,* pp. 193–222. For samples of her poetry, see the appendix on pp. 509–19.

137. Pedro de Balbás, *Memorial informativo en defensa de Sor Luisa de la Ascensión, monja professa de Santa Clara de Carrión* (1643), p. 153r.

138. Alonso de Benavides, *Memorial a la Sanctidad de Urbano VIII nuestro señor açerca de las conuerçiones del Nueuo Mexico hechas en el felicissimo tiempo del govierno de su pontificado, 1634,* Congregatio de Propaganda Fide, Vatican Archives, Rome; Ayer MS, p. 111.

139. Alonso de Benavides, *Memorial que Fray Juan de Santander de la Orden de San Francisco, Comissario General de Indias, presenta a la Magestad Catolica del Rey don Felipe Quarto, nuestro Señor. Hecho por el Padre Fray Alonso de Benavides, Comissario del Santo Oficio, y Custodio que ha sido de las Provincias y conversiones del Nuevo Mexico. Tratase en el de los Tesoros espirituales, y temporales, que la divina Majestad ha manifestado en aquellas conversiones y nuevos descubrimentos, por medio de los Padres desta serafica Religion* (Madrid: Imprenta Real, 1630), pp. 78, 80; Ayer MS, p. 109; *JSRV,* p. 119.

140. Balbás, *Memorial,* pp. 158r–158v.

141. In the first denunciation of Sor Luisa made to the Inquisition, her accusers charged that her reputation as a saint rested mainly on the claim "que a diez y seis años que se sustenta sin comida o con tan poca, que se tiene por milagro." AHN, Inquisición, leg. 3708, caja 1, cited in Barriúso, "Milagrismo," *HIEA,* 1:1096.

142. AHN, Inquisición, leg. 3704, caja 3, fol. 166v; Fray Luis de Granada, *Relación de la causa de Soror Luisa de la Ascención, monja del convento de Santa Clara de Carrión, que se da para calificar* (1633), p. 92r.

143. AHN, Inquisición, leg. 3704, caja 1, fol. 531–32; AHN, Inquisición, leg. 3704, caja 2, fol. 32v; Barriúso, "Milagrismo," *HIEA,* 1:1094; de Granada, *Relación de la causa,* pp. 32r–37v; Balbás, *Memorial,* p. 40r.

144. Balbás, *Memorial,* pp. 20v–22r.

145. De Granada, *Relación de la causa,* pp. 37v–39r. See also Barriúso, *Monja de Carrión,* pp. 260–63.

146. De Granada, *Relación de la causa,* p. 10v: "Fray Antonio Daça y fray Alonso de Prodo testifican averla visto tan pegada a la Cruz, como si estuviera clavada."

147. Balbás, *Memorial,* pp. 12v, 13v, 14r–15v, 17v, 19r.

148. De Granada, *Relación de la causa,* p. 102r.

149. *Relacion berdadera de las mercedes que la hermana Luysa de Colmenares a recibido de la mano de Jesucristo el año 1604,* cited by Barriúso, "Milagrismo," *HIEA,* 1:1096; Balbás, *Memorial,* pp. 59v–65v.

150. BNE, MS 8540 contains 215 folios full of signatures of the initial members. Barriúso, "Milagrismo," *HIEA,* p. 1094.

151. De Granada, *Relación de la causa,* pp. 85r–96r. According to the *Catechism of the Catholic Church* (New York, 1995), p. 464, no. 1667, sacramentals "are

sacred signs which bear a resemblance to the sacraments. They signify effects, particularly of a spiritual nature, which are obtained through the intercession of the Church. By them, men are disposed to receive the chief effect of the sacraments, and various occasions in life are rendered holy."

152. Traditional iconography of the Immaculate Conception depicts the Virgin Mary's triumph over the devil and sin by showing her feet firmly planted on a snake, in reference to Gen. 3:15 and Rev. 12:1-2.

153. Balbás, *Memorial:* on purgatory, p. 124r; on resurrections: p. 161r. For an incisive analysis of Sor Luisa's miracles, see Egido López, "Religiosidad popular y taumaturgia del Barroco," 3:11-39.

154. Balbás, *Memorial,* fol. 142r.

155. One document describes the process of their creation as follows: "She would bring the crosses and beads, etcetera, and other things, and place them on the altar in her hermitage, and she would ask God interiorly to bless them, and she would go into ecstasy, and then she would see how Our Lord showered them with His blessing." De Granada, *Relación de la causa,* p. 126v.

156. AHN, Inquisición, leg. 3704, caja 2, fol. 146, Barriúso, "Milagrismo," *HIEA,* pp. 1095-96. The text lists six other "powers," including one "over all temptations, and especially those related to marital infidelity and sins of the flesh."

157. They were Inés Manrique, Jerónima Osorio, Susana Reinoso, María del Prado, María de Los Rios, and Constanza Alvarez. AHN, Inquisición, leg. 3708, caja 1. See Vicenta Maria Marquez de la Plata y Ferrandiz, *Mujeres pensadoras, místicas, científicas y heterodoxas* (Madrid: Castalia, 2008), pp. 28-29.

158. AHN, Inquisición, leg. 3708, caja 1. Text available in Marquez de la Plata, *Mujeres,* pp. 37-40.

159. AHN, Inquisición, leg. 3704, caja 3, fol. 165r-165v; Marquez de la Plata, *Mujeres,* pp. 44-45.

160. For more on the failed "Spanish Match," see Jean-Luc Nardone, ed., *The Spanish Match: Le mariage manqué du prince de Galles et de l'infante d'Espagne* (Toulouse: Presses Univeritaires du Midi, 2020); Alexander Samson, ed., *The Spanish Match: Prince Charles's Journey to Madrid* (Farnham, UK: Ashgate, 2006); and Glyn Redworth, *The Prince and the Infanta: The Cultural Politics of the Spanish Match* (New Haven, CT: Yale University Press, 2003).

161. De Granada, *Relación de la causa.*

162. "Copia de la carta que el licenciado D. Francisco Vallejo de la Cueva, Corregidor de Carrión escribió a S.M. en su Consejo Real de Castilla, en 3 de abril de 1635," in *Memorial Histórico Español* (Madrid: Real |Academia de la Historia, 1961), 13:158. The full text is available in Barriúso, "Milagrismo," *HIEA,* pp. 1098-99.

163. Balbás, *Memorial*, fols. 7r–8r. See Rico Callado, "La Inquisición y las visionarias clarisas del siglo XVII," p. 788.

164. De Granada, *Relación de la causa*, fols. 1r–4r.

165. AHN, Inquisición, leg. 3704, caja 2, fols. 204–422, cited in Barriúso, "Milagrismo," *HIEA*, p. 1099.

166. Francisco Silvela, ed., *Cartas de la Venerable Madre Sor María de Ágreda y del Señor Rey Don Felipe IV* (Madrid, 1885), 1:176–79.

167. Barriúso, "Milagrismo," *HIEA*, pp. 1098–99.

168. Teófanes Egido López lists only five miracles in 1635–1636: "Religiosidad popular y taumaturgia del Barroco," 3:18.

169. Barriúso, "Milagrismo," *HIEA*, pp. 1101–2; Marquez de la Plata, *Mujeres,* pp. 64–66.

170. Written testimony at AHN, Inquisición, leg. 3705/3; oral testimony at AHN, Inquisición, leg. 3704, caja 2, cited in Marquez de la Plata, *Mujeres,* p. 69.

171. Text in Marquez de la Plata, *Mujeres,* p. 67.

172. AHN, Inquisición, leg. 3705, fols. 19–944, cited in Marquez de la Plata, *Mujeres,* p. 68.

173. Balbás, *Memorial.*

174. Text in Marquez de la Plata, *Mujeres,* p. 72.

175. AHN, Inquisición, leg. 3708, caja 2. Text in Marquez de la Plata, *Mujeres,* p. 73.

9. Protestants, Deviltry, and the Impossible

1. Affidavit signed by Thomas Thornton and William Hudson, Boston, January 1693, sent to Cotton Mather, published in Robert Calef's *More Wonders of the Invisible World* (London, 1700), p. 23.

2. For a concise survey of the premodern devil, see the introduction written by Richard Raiswell for his edited collection of essays, *The Devil in Society in Premodern Europe*, with Peter Dendle (Toronto: Centre for Reformation and Renaissance Studies, 2012), pp. 23–68.

3. Stuart Clark, *Thinking with Demons: The Idea of Witchcraft in Early Modern Europe* (Oxford: Clarendon Press, 1997), p. 168.

4. Douglas Alchin, "Monsters and Marvels: How Do We Interpret the Preternatural?," *The American Biology Teacher,* November 2007, p. 565.

5. See Harman Bhogal, "Miracles, Cessationism, and Demonic Possession: The Darrell Controversy and the Parameters of Preternature in Early Modern English Demonology," *Preternature: Critical and Historical Studies on the Preternatural* 4, no. 2 (2015): pp. 152–80.

6. Michelle Brock and David Winter, "Theory and Practice in Early Modern Epistemologies of the Preternatural," in *Knowing Demons, Knowing Spirits in the Early Modern Period,* edited by Michelle Brock, Richard Raiswell, and David Winter (London: Palgrave Macmillan, 2018), p. 8.

7. "Ningun fundamento tienen sobre la palabra de Dios, sino sobre sueños, falsos milagros . . . I sobre ilusiones del demonio, que se finjia ser no menos que Christo." Cipriano de Valera, *Enjambre de los falsos milagros, y ilusiones del demonio con que María de la Visitación priora de la Anunciada de Lisboa engañó a muy muchos: Y de como fue descubierta y condenada en el año de 1588* in *Los dos tratados del papa i de la misa* (Madrid, 1851), p. 581.

8. "Verdadero milagro, pero de aquellos que haze Satanás para engañar los hombres." De Valera, *Enjambre,* p. 589.

9. "Et ea sunt opera diaboli; nos autem corporibus et rebus subiecti diabolo, panis quo vivimus, et totum quo vivimus in carne, est sub imperio eius." *WA* 40/1:314, *Galatervorlesung* (Commentary on Gal. 3:1).

10. See Erich Klingner, *Luther und der deutsche Volksaberglaube* (Berlin: Mayer und Müller, 1912); and Heiko Oberman, *Luther: Man between God and the Devil* (New Haven, CT: Yale University Press, 2006).

11. *WAT, Tischreden* [Table talk], vol. 6, passage 6811. Many of Luther's most revealing statements about the devil can be found in his *Tischreden*—that is, in transcripts of his conversations during meals with colleagues and students. The most revealing cluster of demon tales can be found in *WAT* 6:6808–35.

12. *WAT* 6:6816. For another account of the nuts, see *WAT* 5:5358b.

13. *WAT* 6:6832. "Es ist aber nicht ein seltsam unerhört Ding, das der Teuffel den häusern poltert und umhergebet."

14. *WAT* 2:1429; *WAT* 3:3601. According to Luther, this is the lesson to be learned here: "Videte, tanta est potentia Sathanae in deludendis sensibus externis; quid faciet in animabus?"

15. *WAT* 4:4040.

16. *WAT* 6:6814. "Gläube ich, dass de Affen eitel Teufel sind." For more on this, see A. Adam, "Der Teufel als Gottes Affe: Vorgeschichte eines Lutherwortes," *Luther Jahrbuch* 28 (1961): 104–9.

17. *WAT* 6:6815.

18. *WAT* 5:5358b. For a list of Luther's demonic encounters, see Jeffrey Burton Russell, *Mephistopheles: The Devil in the Modern World* (Ithaca, NY: Cornell University Press, 1986), p. 39.

19. *WAT* 3:2982b. "Et ego infirmitates meas non esse naturales, sed meras fascinationes puto." See also *WAT* 6:6819.

20. *WAT* 6:6813.

21. *WAT* 3:2829.

22. *WAT* 3:3841. "Prussia est plena Daemonibus."

23. *WA* 29:401.

24. *WAT* 6:6819. See also *WAT* 6:6813.

25. *WAT* 2:1252. Luther regarded Satan as both the instrument and the enemy of God. See his commentary on Psalm 2: *LW* 14:335. For more on this point, see Carter Lindberg, "Mask of God and Prince of Lies: Luther's Theology of the Demonic," in *Disguises of the Demonic: Contemporary Perspectives on the Power of Evil,* edited by Alan M. Olson (New York: Association Press, 1975), p. 95.

26. See Kathryn Edwards, "Magic and the Occult in Luther's World," in *The Oxford Research Encyclopedia of Religion* (Oxford University Press, 2016), accessed July 3, 2021, https://oxfordre.com/religion/view/10.1093/acrefore /9780199340378.001.0001/acrefore-9780199340378-e-504.

27. *WAT* 1:491: "So will ich sie in ars *weysen, da* gehort er hin." An alternate version of this line has Luther using an even more aggressive verb, substituting "show" (*weysen*) with "shove" or "throw" (*werfen*): "So will ich sie in Ars *werfen.*" *WAT* 1:217.

28. *WAT* 2:2059. "Cognito autem Satana, quod Satanas sit, facili verbo superbiam eius confundimus dicentes: Leck mich im arss, vel. Scheiss in die bruch und hengs an den halz."

29. *WAT* 5:5744. "Sihe da, Teufel, da hastu einen stab, gehe hin gen Rhom zu deinen abgott."

30. *WAT* 1:469. "Wenn das argumentum nit hilft, quod christianus est sine lege et supra legem, so weyse man yhn flugs mit ein furz ab."

31. *WAT* 1:812. See also *WAT* 6:6817.

32. *WAT* 6:6827. "So hab ich auch geschmissen und gepinkelt, daran wische dein Maul und beisse dich wol damit!"

33. On this point, one can safely ignore Mikhail Bakhtin's musings on Carnival and Lent in *Rabelais and His World,* translated by Helene Iswolsky (Cambridge, MA: MIT Press, 1968).

34. *WAT* 6:6827.

35. See Peter Morton, "Lutheran Naturalism, Popular Magic, and the Devil," in Raiswell, *Devil in Society,* pp. 409–38.

36. See Moshe Sluhovsky, "Calvinist Miracles and the Concept of the Miraculous in Sixteenth-Century Huguenot Thought," *Renaissance and Reformation/ Renaissance et Réforme,* n.s., 19, no. 2 (Spring 1995): 5–25.

37. "Merae sunt satanae illusions," *CO* 2.17. An English translation is available in *Institutes* 1:17–18, "Prefatory Address to King Francis."

38. *Institutes* 1:16:7; 1:13:13.

39. Bernard Vogler, "La Réforme et le concept de miracle au XVIème siècle," *Revue du l'histoire de la spiritualité* 48 (1972): 145; D. P. Walker, "The Cessation of Miracles," in *Hermeticism and the Renaissance: Intellectual History and the Occult in Early Modern Europe,* edited by Ingrid Merkel and Allen G. Debus (Washington, DC: Folger Shakespeare Library, 1988), pp. 111–24.

40. See Heribert Schutzeichel, *Die Glaubenstehologie Calvins* (Munich: M. Hueber, 1972), pp. 258–65; Ernst Saxer, *Aberglaube, Heuchelei und Frömmigkeit: Eine Untersuchung zu Calvins reformatorischer Eigenart* (Zurich: Zwingli-Verlag, 1970), pp. 44–45; and Vogler, "Réforme," pp. 145–49.

41. *Institutes* 1:8.5–6.

42. "Prefatory Address to King Francis," *Institutes,* p. 16.

43. "Prefatory Address to King Francis," *Institutes,* p. 17. Calvin cites Thess. 2:9–10: "The coming of the lawless one will be in accordance with how Satan works. He will use all sorts of displays of power through signs and wonders that serve the lie, and all the ways that wickedness deceives those who are perishing."

44. *Commentary on the Acts of the Apostles, O.C.,* 48.104.

45. "Hic enim finis est, ut mundus a Chrsto abductus ad sanctos transfugiet." *Commentary on the Acts of the Apostles, O.C.,* 48.104.

46. John Bale, *The Latter Examination of Mistress Anne Askewe,* in *Select Works of John Bale,* edited by Henry Christmas (Cambridge University Press, 1849), p. 236.

47. Saint Augustine, *De Doctrina Christiana,* bk. 2, chaps. 23–24, 30; and his *City of God,* bk. 8, chaps. 17–23. See also Lynn Thorndike, "The Attitude of Origen and Augustine toward Magic," *The Monist* 18, no. 1 (January 1908): 46–66; and *The Athlone History of Witchcraft and Magic in Europe,* vol. 3: *The Middle Ages,* edited by K. Jolly, C. Raudvere, and E. Peters (London: Athlone Press, 2002), 184.

48. Thomas Aquinas, *Summa Theologica,* I-II:92:1. "Superstitio est vitium religioni oppositum secundum excessum, non quia plus exhibeat in cultum divinum quam vera religio, sed quia exhibet cultum divinum vel cui non debet, vel eo modo quo non debet." For a masterful survey of these premodern developments, see Euan Cameron, *Enchanted Europe: Superstition, Reason, and Religion, 1250–1750* (Oxford University Press), esp. pp. 1–140.

49. Saint Augustine, *De Doctrina Christiana,* 2:20:30; 2:23:35.

50. Isidore of Seville, *Etymologies,* edited by Stephen Barney, W. J. Lewis, J. A. Beach, and Oliver Berghof (Cambridge University Press, 2006), bk. 8, pp. 173–90.

51. Aquinas, *Summa Theologica* II-II:96:2.

52. See Robin Barnes, *Astrology and Reformation* (Oxford University Press, 2016); Wayne Shumaker, *The Occult Sciences in the Renaissance* (Berkeley: University of California Press, 1972); Charles Webster, *The Great Instauration: Science, Medicine, and Reform,* 2nd ed. (Oxford: Peter Lang, 2002).

53. See Christopher I. Lehrich, *The Language of Demons and Angels: Cornelius Agrippa's Occult Philosophy* (Leiden: Brill, 2003); and Marc van der Poel, *Cornelius Agrippa: The Humanist Theologian and His Declamations* (Leiden: Brill, 1997).

54. Jean Gerson, "De Erroribus circa Artem Magicam et Articulis Reprobatis," in *Malleus Maleficarum* (Lyons, 1669), vol. 2, pt. II, p. 169. Cited in Cameron, *Enchanted Europe,* p. 131.

55. See Carlos Eire, *War against the Idols: The Reformation of Worship from Erasmus to Calvin* (Cambridge University Press, 1986), esp. pp. 8–53 and 166–94.

56. "In all probability those common juggling words of hocus pocus are nothing else but a corruption of hoc est corpus, by way of ridiculous imitation of the priests of the Church of Rome in their trick of Transubstantiation." Tillotson, Sermon II.xxvi.237 (1742), cited in *The Compact Edition of the Oxford English Dictionary,* 2 vols. (Oxford University Press, 1971), 1:314.

57. Session XXV: "On the Invocation, Veneration, and on the Relics of the Saints, and Sacred Images," in *Canons and Decrees of the Council of Trent,* original text with an English translation by Rev. H. J. Schroeder, OP (London: B. Herder, 1941), pp. 215–17.

58. Session XXII: "Decree Touching the Things to Be Observed and Avoided in the Celebration of the Mass," in *Canons and Decrees,* pp. 150–52.

59. For a longer list, see Joseph Wilhelm, "Superstition," in *The Catholic Encyclopedia,* 15 vols. (New York: Robert Appleton Company, 1907–1912), vol. 14, accessed January 29, 2023, https://www.newadvent.org/cathen/14339a.htm.

60. See Soergel, *Miracles and the Protestant Imagination* (Oxford University Press, 2012); and Julie Crawford, *Marvelous Protestantism: Monstrous Births in Post-Reformation England* (Baltimore: Johns Hopkins University Press, 2005).

61. See Richard Kieckhefer, "The Specific Rationality of Medieval Magic," *American Historical Review* 99 (1994): 813–36, and *Magic in the Middle Ages* (Cambridge University Press, 1989). For a monumental exploration of this subject, see Lynn Thorndike, *The History of Magic and Experimental Science,* 8 vols. (New York: Macmillan, 1923–1958).

62. See Laura Sumrall, "Natural Magic in Renaissance Magic," in *Encyclopedia of Renaissance Philosophy*, edited by Marco Sgarbi (Cham: Springer, 2019), accessed January 29, 2023, https://www.researchgate.net/publication/320645742_Natural_Magic_in_Renaissance_Science.

63. See Paola Zambelli, *White Magic, Black Magic in the European Renaissance* (Leiden: Brill, 2007).

64. For a magisterial summary and analysis of all these aspects of magic viewed from an English setting, see Keith Thomas, *Religion and the Decline of Magic* (Oxford University Press, 1971), pp. 25–50, 177–282.

65. Joseph Hansen, *Quellen und Untersuchungen zur Geschichte des Hexenwahns* (Bonn: Universitäts-Buchdruckerei, 1901), p. 38.

66. John XXII, *Super illius specula*, in *Witchcraft in Europe, 400–1700: A Documentary History*, edited and translated by Alan Charles Kors and Edward Peters, 2nd ed. (Philadelphia: University of Pennsylvania Press, 2001), pp. 119–20.

67. Bernardino of Siena, *Medieval Popular Religion, 1100–1500: A Reader*, edited by John Shinners (University of Toronto Press, 2006), p. 245.

68. For more on this text and its context, see Hans Peter Broedel, *The Malleus Maleficarum and the Construction of Witchcraft* (Manchester University Press, 2003).

69. Christopher Mackay, *The Hammer of Witches: A Complete Translation of the Malleus Maleficarum* (Cambridge University Press, 2009), p. 282.

70. See Otto Sigg, *Hexenprozesse mit Todesurteil Justizmorde der Zunfstadt Zürich* (Zürich: Offizin, 2012); Bruce Gordon, "God Killed Saul: Heinrich Bullinger and Jacob Ruef on the Power of the Devil," in *Werewolves, Witches, and Wandering Spirits*, edited by Kathryn Edwards (Kirksville, MO: Truman State University Press, 2002), pp. 155–79; William Monter, "Witchcraft in Geneva, 1537–1662," *Journal of Modern History* 43, no. 2 (June 1971): 179–204; Edwards, "Magic and the Occult in Martin Luther's World."

71. *Wahrhaftige und erschreckliche Thatten und Handlungen der 63 Hexen, so zu Wiesensteig mit dem Brand gerichtet worden* (1563). See H. C. Erik Midelfort, *Witch Hunting in Southwest Germany, 1562–1684* (Stanford University Press, 1972), pp. 88–90.

72. Monter, "Witchcraft in Geneva," pp. 179–204; statistics on p. 187.

73. *Hexenglaube und Hexenprocesse im Raum Rhein-Mosel-Saar*, edited by Franz Irsigler and Gunther Franz (Trier, Germany: Spee, 1995). Translated excerpts from the prosecutions in Trier are available in Kors and Peters, *Witchcraft in Europe*, pp. 308–17.

74. George L. Burr, ed., *The Witch Persecutions,* 6 vols. (Philadelphia: University of Pennsylvania History Department, 1898–1912), vol. 3, no. 4, pp. 18–19. Translated excerpts from the prosecutions in Bamberg, Würzburg, and Bonn are available in Kors and Peters, *Witchcraft in Europe,* pp. 348–53.

75. Brian Levack, ed., *The Witchcraft Sourcebook* (New York: Routledge, 2004), p. 201.

76. Wolfgang Behringer, *Witches and Witch-Hunts* (Cambridge: Polity Press, 2004), pp. 47–64 and tables 4.3 and 4.5.

77. Julian Goodare, "Witchcraft in Scotland," in *The Oxford Handbook of Witchcraft in Early Modern Europe and Colonial America,* edited by Brian P. Levack (Oxford University Press, 2013), p. 302. See also Brian Levack, *Witch Hunting in Scotland* (London: Routledge, 2008); and Christina Larner, *Enemies of God: The Witch-Hunt in Scotland* (London: Chatto and Windus, 1981).

78. See Malcolm Gaskill, "Witchcraft Trials in England," in Levack, *Oxford Handbook of Witchcraft*, p. 299; James Sharpe, *Witchcraft in Early Modern England,* 2nd ed. (New York: Routledge, 2019), esp. chaps. 2–3; Thomas, *Religion and the Decline of Magic,* chaps. 14–18; and Alan Macfarlane, *Witchcraft in Tudor and Stuart England,* 2nd ed. (Abingdon, UK: Routledge, 1999), esp. chaps. 3–4.

79. Raisa Maria Toivo, *Witchcraft and Gender in Early Modern Society: Finland and the Wider European Experience* (Farnham, UK: Ashgate, 2008).

80. Johann Weyer, *Witches, Devils, and Doctors in the Renaissance: Johann Weyer, De Praestigiis Daemonum,* translated by John Shea, edited by George Mora and Benjamin Kohl (Binghamton, NY: Medieval and Renaissance Texts and Studies, 1991), pp. 34, 310–12, 315, 522.

81. Joseph Glanvill, *Saducismus triumphatus: Or Full and Plain Evidence concerning Witches and Apparitions* (London, 1681). All page numbers cited here are from the London (1700) edition.

82. Glanvill, *Saducismus,* pp. 131–33.

83. Glanvill, *Saducismus,* pp. 63–66.

84. For more on this debate, see Thomas Harmon Jobe, "The Devil in Restoration Science: The Glanvill-Webster Witchcraft Debate," *Isis* 72, no. 3 (September 1981): 342–56.

85. Increase Mather, *Cases of Conscience concerning evil Spirits Personating Men, Witchcrafts, infallible Proofs of Guilt in such as are accused with that Crime* (Boston, 1693), p. 20.

86. Mather, *Cases of Conscience,* pp. 7, 15, 38.

87. Sarah Ferber, *Demonic Possession and Exorcism in Early Modern France* (London: Routledge, 2004), p. 153.

10. The Devil Himself

1. D. P. Walker, *Unclean Spirits: Possession and Exorcism in France and England in the Late Sixteenth and Early Seventeenth Centuries* (Philadelphia: University of Pennsylvania Press, 1981), pp. 14–15. Walker adds that since he "cannot demonstrate" the validity of this principle, all he can do is announce that he "shall try to conform to it."

2. "I will no longer talk much with you, for the ruler of this world is coming." John 14:30.

3. See Susanne Kord, "Ancient Fears and the New Order: Witch Beliefs and Physiognomy in the Age of Reason," *German Life and Letters* 61, no. 1 (2008): 61–78.

4. Stuart Clark, *Thinking with Demons* (Oxford University Press, 1997), pp. 687–726.

5. Julian "the Apostate," Epistolae, 19, in *The Works of the Emperor Julian,* translated by Wilmer Cave Wright, 3 vols. (London: Loeb Classical Library, 1930), 3:52.

6. Peter Burke, *Popular Culture in Early Modern Europe,* 3rd ed. (New York: Harper Torchbooks, 2004), p. 213.

7. See K. L. Roos, *The Devil in 16th Century German Literature: The Teufelsbücher* (Frankfurt: Peter Lang, 1972).

8. Charlene P. E. Burns, *Christian Understandings of Evil: The Historical Trajectory* (Minneapolis: Fortress Press, 2016), p. 102.

9. Huldrich Zwingli, "Acts of the Convention Held in Zurich 29 January 1523," in *Selected Works of Huldrich Zwingli,* edited by Samuel Macauley Jackson (Philadelphia: University of Pennsylvania, 1901), chap. 3.

10. *Institutes* I.15.13.

11. *Institutes* II.4.3; I.14.18.

12. See Alison Weber, "Saint Teresa, Demonologist," in *Culture and Control in Counter-Reformation Spain*, edited by Anne J. Cruz and Mary Elizabeth Perry (Minneapolis: University of Minnesota Press, 1991), pp. 171–95.

13. *Vida* 31.9, *O.C.,* p. 167.

14. Cited by Weber, "Saint Teresa, Demonologist," p. 182.

15. Pedro Ciruelo, *Reprobación de las supersticiones y hechicerías* (Salamanca, 1538). Quote from the English translation: *A Treatise Reproving All Superstitions and Forms of Witchcraft,* translated by Eugene A. Maio and D'Orsay W. Pearson (Rutherford, NJ: Fairleigh Dickinson University Press, 1977), p. 266.

16. *Rituale Romanum* (Paris: Lecoffre, 1885), pp. 486–87.

17. See Guido Dall'Olio, "The Devil of Inquisitors, Demoniacs and Exorcists in Counter-Reformation Italy," in *The Devil in Society in Premodern Europe,* edited by Richard Raiswell with Peter Dendle (Toronto: Centre for Reformation and Renaissance Studies, 2012), pp. 511–36.

18. H. C. Erik Midelfort, *A History of Madness in Sixteenth Century Germany* (Stanford University Press, 1999), p. 318.

19. See Robert Mandrou, *Magistrats et sorciers en France au XVIIe siècle* (Paris: Plon, 1968).

20. The principal source for this case is Jean Boulaese, *Le thrésor et entiere histoire de la triomphante victoire du corps de Dieu sur l'espirit maling Beelzebub, obtenue a Laon* (1578). For analysis of this case, see Sarah Ferber, *Demonic Possession and Exorcism in Early Modern France* (London: Routledge, 2004), chap. 2; Irena Backus, *Le Miracle de Laon* (Paris: J. Vrin, 1994); and Walker, *Unclean Spirits,* pp. 19–27.

21. See Anita Walker and Edmund Dickerman, "A Woman under the Influence: A Case of Alleged Possession in Sixteenth-Century France," *Sixteenth Century Journal* 22, no. 3 (1991): 534–54; Ferber, *Demonic Possession,* pp. 40–60; Walker, *Unclean Spirits,* pp. 33–42.

22. See Moshe Sluhovsky, "The Devil in the Convent," *American Historical Review* 107, no. 5 (December 2002): 1379–411.

23. See Jean-Raymond Fanlo, *L'évangile du démon—La possession diabolique d'Aix-en-Provence 1610–1611* (Paris: Champ Vallon, 2017); Anita Walker and Edmund Dickerman, "A Notorious Woman: Possession, Witchcraft and Sexuality in Seventeenth-Century Provence," *Historical Reflections / Réflexions Historiques* 27, no. 1 (2001): 1–26; and Ferber, *Demonic Possession,* pp. 70–88.

24. See Michel de Certeau, *The Possession at Loudun,* translated by Michael B. Smith (University of Chicago Press, 2000); Robert Rapley, *A Case of Witchcraft: The Trial of Urbain Grandier* (Montreal: McGill–Queen's University Press, 1998); Michel Carmona, *Les diables de Loudun* (Paris: Fayard, 1988); and for a collection of original documents, see Robert Mandrou, ed., *Possession et sorcellerie au dix-septième siècle: Textes inédits* (Paris: Fayard, 1979).

25. Nicolas Aubin [Des Niau], *The History of the Devils of Loudun, the Alleged Possession of the Ursuline nuns, and the Trial and Execution of Urbain Grandier, told by an Eyewitness,* translated by Edmund Goldsmid, 3 vols. (Edinburgh, 1887), 2:36–46. French original: *La veritable histoire des diables de Loudun, de la*

possession des religieuses Ursulines et de la condamnation d'Urbain Grandier, par un temoin (1634).

26. For a list of some of the accounts published in a single year, 1634, see de Certeau, *Possession at Loudun,* pp. 184–86.

27. *The cheats and illusions of Romish priests and exorcists. Discover'd in the history of the devils of Loudun: being an account of the pretended possession of the Ursuline nuns, and of the Condemnation and punishment of Urban Grandier a parson of the same town* (London, 1703).

28. As in the text *La demonomanie de Loudun qui montre la veritable possesion des religieuses Ursulines, et autres seculieres* (1634).

29. Pierre Yvelin, *Examen de la possession des religieuses de Louviers* (1643); *Récit véritable de ce qui s'est fait et passé à Louviers, touchant les religieses possédées* (1647); Daniel Vidal, *Critique de la raison mystique: Bénoit de Canfield, possession et dépossession au XVII siècle* (Grenoble: Jérôme Milion, 1990); Ferber, *Demonic Possession,* pp. 89–112.

30. *The Devils of Loudun* (1952), a novel by Aldous Huxley; *The Devils* (1961), a play by John Whiting; *Mother Joan of the Angels* (1961), a novel by Jaroslaw Iwaszkiewicz, turned into a film by director Jerzy Kawalerowicz; *Die Teufel von Loudun* (1969), an opera by Krzysztof Penderecki, based on Huxley's and Whiting's works; *The Devils* (1971), a film directed by Ken Russell, based on Huxley's and Whiting's works.

31. See Sluhovsky, "Devil in the Convent," pp. 1383–85.

32. Cotton Mather, "The Afflictions of Margaret Rule," in Robert Calef, *More Wonders of the Invisible World* (London, 1700), pp. 4–5.

33. Mather, "Afflictions," p. 7.

34. Samuel Aves, in Calef, *More Wonders of the Invisible World,* p. 22. Similar testimony was offered by Robert Earle, John Wilkins, Daniel Williams, Thomas Thornton, and William Hudson.

35. Affidavit signed by Thomas Thornton and William Hudson, Boston, January 1693, sent to Cotton Mather, published in Calef, *More Wonders of the Invisible World,* p. 23.

36. Testimony of Sister Isabel de Santo Domingo in *Procesos* 2:463. As mentioned in chapter 9, the same phenomenon was reported in one English demonic levitation case by Joseph Glanvill in *Saducismus Triumphatus* (1700), p. 133.

37. Calef, *More Wonders of the Invisible World,* p. 25.

38. Wallace Notestein, *A History of Witchcraft in England from 1558 to 1718* (New York: T. Y. Crowell, 1968), p. 328, admits in note 38 that the earliest source he

could find for this account was Alexander Chalmers, *The General Biographical Dictionary*, 32 vols. (London, 1812–1827), 25:248.

39. For this encore performance of the devil, see H. C. Erik Midelfort, *Exorcism and Enlightenment* (New Haven, CT: Yale University Press, 2005); and Gabriele Amorth, *An Exorcist Tells His Story*, translated by Nicoletta V. MacKenzie (San Francisco: Ignatius Press, 1999).

40. Martín de Castañega, *Tratado muy sotil y bien fundado de las supersticiones y hechizerías y vanos conjuros y abusiones* (Logroño, 1529), quoted in María Tausiet Carlés, "Religíon, ciencia y superstición en Pedro Ciruelo y Martín de Castañega," *Revista de Historia Jerónimo Zurita* 65–66 (1992): 141. See also David H. Darst, "Witchcraft in Spain: The Testimony of Martín de Castañega's Treatise on Superstition and Witchcraft," *Proceedings of the American Philosophical Society* 123, no. 5 (October 1979): 298–322.

41. Pedro Ciruelo, *Tratado en el qual se repruevan todas las supersticiones y hechizerias* (Barcelona, 1628), p. 45.

42. *On Witchcraft: An Abridged Translation of Johann Weyer's De Praestigiis Daemonum,* edited by Benjamin Kohl and H.C. Erik Midelfort (Asheville, NC: Pegasus Press, 1998), p. 96.

43. Reginald Scot, preface to *The Discoverie of Witchcraft* (1584; repr., London: Elliot, Stock, 1886), p. xx.

44. *Von Hexen und unholden, wider die schwarzen kunst, abergleubigs sägnen, unwarhaffts warsagen und andere derglychen von gott verbottne künst* (1571).

45. *Les Sorciers: Dialogue tres utile et necessaire pour ce temps auquel ce qui se dispute aujourd'hui des Sorciers et Eriges, est traité bien amplement, et resolu* (1574).

46. *De lamiis seu strigibus no inutilia scitu* (1572); *Repetitio disputationis de lamiis seu strigibus* (1578). See Charles Gunnoe, *Thomas Erastus and the Palatinate* (Leiden: Brill, 2011), pp. 339–74.

47. Hemmingsen, *Admonitio de superstitionibus magicis vitandis* (1575).

48. Paul Frisius, *Dess Teuffels Nebelkappen: Das ist kurtzer begriff dess gantzen Handels der Zauberey belangend* (1583), fols. Bvii, r–Cii, v; Ciii, r.

49. *Daemonologie: In forme of a dialogue, diuided into three bookes* (Edinburgh, 1597).

50. *The Demonology of King James I,* edited by Donald Tyson (Woodbury, MN: Llewelyn, 2011), p. 221.

51. Cotton Mather, *Wonders of the Invisible World: Observations as well historical as theological, upon the nature, the number, and the operations of the devils: Accompanyd with, I. Some accounts of the grievous molestations, by daemons and*

witchcrafts, which have lately annoy'd the countrey; and the trials of some eminent malefactors executed upon occasion thereof (1693).

52. *De la Démonomanie des Sorciers* (Paris, 1580); translated by Randy Scott as *On the Demon-Mania of Witches* (Toronto: Centre for Reformation and Renaissance Studies, 1995).

53. See Virginia Krause, "Listening to Witches: Bodin's Use of Confession in De la Démonomaie des Sorciers," in *The Reception of Bodin,* edited by Howell A. Lloyd (Leiden: Brill, 2013), pp. 97-115.

54. Jean Bodin, *Démonomanie,* in *Witchcraft in Europe, 400-1700: A Documentary History,* edited and translated by Alan Charles Kors and Edward Peters, 2nd ed. (Philadelphia: University of Pennsylvania Press, 2001), p. 302.

55. Peter Binsfeld, *Tractatus de confessionibus maleficorum et sagarum* (Trier, Germany, 1589).

56. *Daemonolatreiae libri tres: Ex ivdiciis capitalibus nongentorum plus minus hominum, qui sortilegij crimen intra annos quindecim in Lotharingia capite luerunt* (Lyon, 1595).

57. Nicholas Remy, *Demonolatry,* edited by Montague Summers, translated by E. A. Ashwin (London: J. Rodker, 1930), p. xii.

58. Pierre de Lancre, *Tableau de l'inconstance des mauvais anges et démons, ou il est amplement traicté des sorciers et de la sorcellerie* (Paris, 1612).

59. *La incredulité et mescréance du sortilège pleinement convaincue* (1622); *and Du sortilège* (1627), which was a rebuttal of Gabriel Naudé's *Apologie pour tous les grands personages qui ont esté faussement soupçonnés de magie* (1625).

60. Martín del Rio, *Disquisitionum magicarum Libri Sex* (1599-1600).

61. Martín del Rio, *Investigations into Magic,* translated and edited by P. G. Maxwell-Stuart (Manchester University Press, 1999), pp. 28-29.

62. Del Rio, *Investigations into Magic,* pp. 92-93.

63. *Compendium Maleficarum, ex quo nefandissima in genus humanum opera venefica, ac ad illa vitanda remedia conspiciuntur* (Milan, 1626), bk. 1, chap. 13, p. 69; translated by E. A. Ashwin as *Compendium Maleficarum: The Montague Summers Edition* (New York: Dover, 1988), p. 33.

64. *Canon Episcopi* (ca. 906), in Kors and Peters, *Witchcraft in Europe,* pp. 61-62.

65. Ulrich Molitor, "Transvection," quoted in *The Encyclopedia of Witchcraft and Demonology,* edited by Rossell Hope Robbins (n.p.: Girard and Stuart, 2015), p. 511.

66. Ulrich Molitor, *De Lamiis Et Pythonicis Mulieribus* (1489); *Von Hexen und Unholden* (1508); and *Hexen Meysterei* (1544). For an analysis of the ambiguities in the relation between text and image in various editions of Molitor's work,

see Natalie Kwan, "Woodcuts and Witches: Ulrich Molitor's De lamiis et pythonicis mulieribus," *German History* 30, no. 4 (2012): 493–527, esp. pp. 492, 509, and 511–13, and figs. 2, 12, and 13.

67. See Gerhild Scholz Williams, "Demonology," in *The Oxford Handbook of Witchcraft in Early Modern Europe and Colonial America,* edited by Brian P. Levack (Oxford University Press, 2013), p. 74.

68. *Vauderie of Lyon,* in *Origins of the Witches' Sabbath,* translated by Michael D. Bailey (University Park: Pennsylvania State University Press, 2021), pp. 89–103.

69. Martin Luther, *Decem praecepta Wittenbergensi praedicta populo,* in *WA* 1:406–10; translated by Edward Peters in Kors and Peters, *Witchcraft in Europe,* p. 264.

70. *The Sermons of M. John Calvin upon the Fifth Booke of Moses called Deuteronomie* (London, 1583), in Kors and Peters, *Witchcraft in Europe,* p. 264.

71. Lambert Danau, *A dialogue of witches, in foretime named lot-tellers, and now commonly called sorcerers* (London, 1575), chap. 4, originally published as *De venificis quos olim sortilegos, nunc autem vulgo sortarios vocant, dialogus* (Geneva, 1564).

72. *Compendium Maleficarum* (1626), bk. 1, chap. 13, p. 70, in Ashwin, *Compendium Maleficarum,* p. 34.

73. Wolfgang Behringer and Constance Ott-Koptschallijski, *Der Traum vom Fliegen: Zwischen Mythos un Technik* (Frankfurt am Main: S. Fischer, 1991), pp. 235–36, citing Brian Levack, *The Witch Hunt in Early Modern Europe* (New York: Longman, 1987), p. 40.

74. William Monter, "Witchcraft in Geneva, 1537–1662," *Journal of Modern History* 43, no. 2 (June 1971): 179–204; confession on p. 193, statistics on pp. 187, 204.

75. Bullinger, *Von Hexen und unholden, wider die schwarzen kunst* (1571). See Bruce Gordon, "'God Killed Saul': Heinrich Bullinger and Jacob Ruef on the Power of the Devil," in *Werewolves, Witches, and Wandering Spirits,* edited by Kathryn Edwards (Kirksville, MO: Truman State University Press, 2002), pp. 155–80.

76. Wolfgang Behringer, *Witchcraft Persecutions in Bavaria,* translated by J. C. Grayson and David Lederer (Cambridge University Press, 1997), pp. 212–321.

77. Lu Ann Homza, *Village Infernos and Witches' Advocates* (University Park: Pennsylvania State University Press, 2022), p. 6.

78. Homza's findings, cited in the previous note, are a major revision of previous studies of the Navarrese witch trials of the early 1600s and especially of the work of Julio Caro Baroja, *Las Brujas y su Mundo* (Madrid: Revista de Occidente,

1961), translated by Nigel Glendinning as *The World of the Witches* (London: Weidenfeld and Nicolson, 1964); and also Gustav Henningsen, *The Witches' Advocate* (Reno: University of Nevada Press, 1980).

79. See Jeffrey R. Watt, *The Consistory and Social Discipline in Calvin's Geneva* (University of Rochester Press, 2020), pp. 138–61; and his article "Calvin's Geneva Confronts Magic and Witchcraft: The Evidence from the Consistory," *Journal of Early Modern History* 17, no. 3 (2013): 215–44.

80. Bruce Gordon, *The Swiss Reformation* (Manchester University Press, 2002), p. 144.

81. Robert Scribner, "Incombustible Luther: The Image of the Reformer in Early Modern Germany," *Past and Present* 110 (February 1986): 38–68.

82. See Juan José Junquera, *The Black Paintings of Goya* (London: Scala, 2008): Valeriano Bozal, *Goya: Black Paintings* (Madrid: Fundación Amigos del Museo del Prado, 1999); Avigdor Posèq, "The Goat in Goya's Witches' Sabbaths," *Notes in the History of Art* 18, no. 4 (1999): 30–39.

83. Arthur Lubow, "The Secret of the Black Paintings," *New York Times,* July 27, 2003, https://www.nytimes.com/2003/07/27/magazine/the-secret-of-the-black-paintings.html.

84. See Janis Tomlinson, *Goya: A portrait of the Artist* (Princeton University Press, 2020), which is described by the publisher as "the first major English-language biography of Francisco Goya y Lucienne, who ushered in the modern era"; see also Rose-Marie Hagen, *Francisco Goya, 1746–1828: On the Threshold of Modernity* (Cologne, Germany: Taschen, 2012); Fred Licht, *Goya, the Origins of the Modern Temper in Art* (New York: Universe Books, 1979).

Epilogue

Epigraph: H. W. Turnbull, ed., *The Correspondence of Isaac Newton,* 7 vols. (Cambridge University Press, 1961), 3:241. See also William H. Austin, "Isaac Newton on Science and Religion," *Journal of the History of Ideas* 31, no. 4 (1970): 521–42.

1. For a brief introduction to his life, see Clément Duval, "Pilâtre de Rozier (1754–1785), Chemist and First Aeronaut," *Chymia* 12 (1967): 99–117. For a recent biography by one of his descendants, see Philip Buron Pilâtre, *Pilâtre de Rozier, un Lorrain d'exception, 1754–1785* (Metz: Éd. Serpenoise, 2006).

2. Jean-Paul Poirier, *Lavoisier, Chemist, Biologist, Economist,* translated by Rebecca Balinksi (Philadelphia: University of Pennsylvania Press, 1996), p. 146. Original French edition: *Antoine Laurent de Lavoisier, 1743–1794* (Paris: Pygmalion, 1993).

3. Charles Coulston Gillispie, *The Montgolfier Brothers and the Invention of Aviation, 1783–1784* (Princeton University Press, 2014), pp. 45–47.

4. Barthélemy Faujas de Saint-Fond, *Description des expériences de la machine aérostatique de MM de Montgolfier, et de celles auxquelles cette découverte a donné lieu* (Paris, 1783), pp. 25–27.

5. Mi Gyung Kim, *The Imagined Empire: Balloon Enlightenments in Revolutionary Europe* (University of Pittsburgh Press, 2016), p. 84. Charles Coulston Gillispie thinks that the story of the king's suggestion is "probably apocryphal." *Montgolfier Brothers,* pp. 38–39.

6. For contemporary accounts, see Faujas de Saint-Fond, *Description des expériences de la machine aérostatique;* Jean-Claude Pingeron, *L'Art de faire soi-même les ballons aérostatiques, conformes à ceux de M. de Montgolfier* (Paris, 1783); Marc Marie Bombelles, *Journal de Marquis de Bombelles,* edited by Jean Grassion and Frans Durif, 4 vols. (Geneva: Librairie Droz, 1977), vol. 1.

7. *La Correspondance littéraire, philosophique et critique* 13 (November 1783): 393–94. Also known as *Grimm's Correspondence,* this publication was a cultural newsletter distributed between 1753 and 1790 to elite subscribers. Friedrich Melchior, Baron von Grimm, was its founder and first editor.

8. Papers of Benjamin Franklin, Yale University, accessed January 29, 2023, https://franklinpapers.org/yale;jsessionid=nodeovqvc52553jzij76y8kpbqv5r40101248.nodeo?d=895503629&trans=true&vol=40&page=613.

9. Quoted by Andrew Stark, *The Consolations of Mortality: Making Sense of Death* (New Haven, CT: Yale University Press, 2008), p. 1.

10. Clément Villecourt, *Vie et Institut de Saint Alphonse-Marie de Liguori,* 4 vols. (Tournai, Belgium, 1864), 3:242; Augustin Berthe, *Saint Alphonse de Liguori,* 2 vols. (Paris: Victor Retaux, 1906), 2:591.

11. Christopher White, *Other Worlds: Spirituality and the Search for Invisible Dimensions* (Cambridge, MA: Harvard University Press, 2018), p. 5; see also his article "Seeing Things: Science, the Fourth Dimension and Modern Enchantment," *American Historical Review* 119, no. 5 (2014): 1466–91.

12. "Die Wohnungsnot ist für Gott eingetreten." David Friedrich Strauss, quoted in Karl Heim in *God Transcendent: Foundation for a Christian Metaphysic,* translated by E. P. Dicke, rev. Edwyn Bevan (London: Nisbet and co., 1935), p. 31.

13. Charles E. Hummel, "The Faith behind the Famous: Isaac Newton," *Christianity Today,* April 1, 1991. See Rob Iliffe, *The Religious Worlds of Isaac Newton* (Oxford University Press, 2017); and John Chambers, *The Metaphysical World of Isaac Newton: Alchemy, Prophecy, and the Search for Lost Knowledge* (Rochester, VT: Destiny Books, 2018).

14. Robert Boyle, *Works,* edited by Michael Hunter and Edward B. Davis, 14 vols. (London: Pickering and Chatto, 1999–2000), 11:429. See Michael Hunter, *Boyle Studies: Aspects of the Life and Thought of Robert Boyle* (Farnham, UK: Ashgate, 2015), pp. 184–85.

15. Quoted in Michael Hunter, *The Decline of Magic: Britain in the Enlightenment* (New Haven, CT: Yale University Press, 2020), p. 12. For examples of other early modern English scientists interested in the supernatural, see pp. 1–27. Hunter has written extensively on Boyle's religious interests in *Robert Boyle, 1627–91: Scrupulosity and Science* (Rochester, NY: Boydell Press, 2000), esp. pp. 230–31; and *Boyle: Between God and Science* (New Haven, CT: Yale University Press, 2009).

16. For more on Swedenborg, see Signe Toksvig, *Emanuel Swedenborg, Scientist and Mystic* (New Haven, CT: Yale University Press, 1948); Ernst Benz, *Emanuel Swedenborg: Visionary Savant in the Age of Reason,* translated by Nicholas Goodrick-Clarke (West Chester, PA: Swedenborg Foundation, 2002); and Lars Bergquist, *Swedenborg's Secret,* translated by Norman Ryder and Kurt Nemitz (London: Swedenborg Society, 2005).

17. For Kant's text, see *Kant on Swedenborg: Dreams of a Spirit-Seer and Other Writings,* translated by G. Johnson and G. E. Magee (West Chester, PA: Swedenborg Foundation, 2002). For a recent analysis, see Stephen R. Palmquist, *Kant and Mysticism: Critique as the Experience of Baring All in Reason's Light* (Lanham, MD: Lexington Books, 2019).

18. Letter to Moses Mendelssohn, April 8, 1766, in *Immanuel Kant's Sämtliche Werke,* edited by K. Rosenkranz and F.W. Schubert, 11 vols. (Leipzig: Voss, 1842), 11:8.

19. See Paolo Parigi, *The Rationalization of Miracles* (New York: Cambridge University Press, 2012); and Bradford Bouley, *Pious Postmortems: Anatomy, Sanctity, and the Catholic Church in Early Modern Europe* (Philadelphia: University of Pennsylvania Press, 2017).

20. White, *Other Worlds,* p. 13. For a blistering rejection of the "simplistic" views mentioned by White, see Brad Gregory, "No Room for God? History, Science, Metaphysics, and the Study of Religion," *History and Theory* 47 (2008): 495–519, and esp. p. 497n3, for a long list of books that counter those "simplistic" views.

21. Brad Gregory, *The Unintended Reformation: How a Religious Revolution Secularized Society* (Cambridge, MA: Belknap Press of Harvard University Press, 2015); Charles Taylor, *A Secular Age* (Cambridge, MA: Belknap Press of Harvard University Press, 2007). For two other significant interpretations, see

Alasdair McIntyrre, *After Virtue: A Study in Moral Theory* (University of Notre Dame Press, 1981); and Michael Gillespie, *The Theological Origins of Modernity* (University of Chicago Press, 2008).

22. Ethan Shagan, *The Birth of Modern Belief: Faith and Judgment from the Middle Ages to the Enlightenment* (Princeton University Press, 2018), p. 1.

23. Shagan, *Birth of Modern Belief,* p. 282: "A credulity is a framework of intellectual resources and assumptions that shapes religious knowledge and its relationship to other truth claims."

24. Shagan, *Birth of Modern Belief,* p. 282. Shagan refers to "credulities" as "spaces or conditions of believing."

25. See William Blake's poem "London," in *The Complete Poetry and Prose of William Blake,* edited by David Erdman (New York: Anchor Books, 1988), p. 26; on Weber, see Peter Baehr, "The 'Iron Cage' and the 'Shell as Hard as Steel': Parsons, Weber, and the Stahlhartes Gehäuse Metaphor in 'The Protestant Ethic and the Spirit of Capitalism,'" *History and Theory* 40, no. 2 (May 2001): 153–69.

26. "Remarks on the Proof of Miracles," paper 57, November 1875, in *The Papers of the Metaphysical Society, 1869–1880: A Critical Edition,* edited by C. Marshall, B. Lightman, and R. England, 3 vols. (Oxford University Press, 2018), 2:327.

27. Olivier Leroy, *La Lévitation* (Paris: Librairie Valois, 1928), pp. 106, 118.

28. See R. Laurentin and P. Mahéo, *Bilocations de Mère Yvonne-Aimée: Étude critique en réference á ses missions* (Paris: O.E.I.L., 1990); and C. Bernard Ruffin, *Padre Pio: The True Story,* 3rd ed. (Huntington, IN: Our Sunday Visitor, 2018).

29. On Carloni, see Didier Rance, *Maria-Teresa Carloni: Mystique au service des chrétiens persecutés* (Paris: Editions Salvator, 2020); and Vincenzo Speziale, *Maria Teresa Carlon: Stimmatizzata* (Udine: Edizione Segno, 2014). On Montella, see Cristina Siccardi, *La "Bambina" di Padre Pio, Rita Montella* (Prato: Città Ideale, 2003); and Aurino Arcangelo, *Suor Rita Montella, monaca agostiniana: Biografia, missione, carismi* (Prato: Città Ideale, 2019).

30. In addition to Friedkin's *The Exorcist* (1973), see Daniel Stamm's *The Last Exorcism* (2010) and Ole Bornedal's *The Possession* (2012). The diary of Raymond Bishop, the Jesuit priest who performed the exorcism in St. Louis, can be accessed at https://sensusfidelium.com/2019/10/19/the-actual-1949-diary -of-the-priest-who-inspired-the-1973-film-the-exorcist. See also Robert E. Bartholomew and Joe Nickell, *American Hauntings: The True Stories behind Hollywood's Scariest Movies—from* The Exorcist *to* The Conjuring (Santa Barbara, CA: ABC-CLIO, 2015).

31. See the work of Catholic theologian Herbert Haag, *Abschied vom Teufel: Vom christlichen Umgang mit dem Bösen* (Einsiedeln, Switzerland: Benziger, 1969);

translated into French as *Liquidation du diable* (Paris: Desclée de Brouwer, 1971); and the testy response from the future Pope Benedict XVI, "Abschied vom Teufel?," in Joseph Ratzinger, *Dogma und Verkündigung* (Munich: Wewel, 1973).

32. See the work of Gabriele Amorth, especially his *An Exorcist Tells His Story* (San Francisco: Ignatius Press, 1999) and *An Exorcist Explains the Demonic: The Antics of Satan and His Army of Fallen Angels* (Bedford, NH: Sophia Institute Press, 2016); see also Richard Gallagher, *Demonic Foes: My Twenty-Five Years as a Psychiatrist Investigating Possessions, Diabolic Attacks, and the Paranormal* (San Francisco: HarperOne, 2020); and Monsignor Stephen Rossetti, *Diary of an American Exorcist: Demons, Possession, and the Modern-Day Battle against Ancient Evil* (Bedford, NH: Sophia Institute Press, 2021).

33. See Griffin Paul Jackson, "Meet the Protestant Exorcists," *Christianity Today,* September 19, 2019. For recent examples of texts, see Jennifer LeClaire, *Deliverance Protocols and Ethics: A Handbook for Accurate Deliverance Operations* (Ft. Lauderdale, FL: Awakening Media, 2021); Alexander Pagani, *The Secrets to Deliverance: Defeat the Toughest Cases of Demonic Bondage* (Lake Mary, FL: Charisma House, 2018); John Eckardt, *Deliverance and Spiritual Warfare Manual: A Comprehensive Guide to Living Free* (Lake Mary, FL: Charisma House, 2014).

34. For a sample of essays in this tradition, see Gary S. Greig and Kevin N. Springer, eds., *The Kingdom and the Power: Are Healing and the Spiritual Gifts Used by Jesus and the Early Church Meant for the Church Today? A Biblical Look at How to Bring the Gospel to the World with Power* (New York: Regal Books, 1993).

35. A Pew Research poll in 2019 revealed the following about one of the central beliefs of the Catholic Church: "Nearly seven-in-ten Catholics (69%) say they personally believe that during Catholic Mass, the bread and wine used in Communion "are symbols of the body and blood of Jesus Christ." Just one-third of U.S. Catholics (31%) say they believe that "during Catholic Mass, the bread and wine actually become the body and blood of Jesus." Pew Research Center, "Just One-Third of U.S. Catholics Agree with Their Church That Eucharist Is Body, Blood of Christ," August 5, 2019, https://www.pewresearch.org/fact-tank/2019/08/05/transubstantiation-eucharist-u-s-catholics/.

36. See Traci Badalucco, "Stories, Traditions Keep Devotions to the Saints Alive," *National Catholic Reporter,* October 29, 2016.

37. Parigi, *Rationalization,* p. 28.

38. Bouley, *Pious Postmortems,* p. 6.

39. Agelli, p. 57; Bernino, p. 103; Pastrovicchi, p. 24.

40. Parigi, *Rationalization*, p. 14.

41. See Fernando Vidal, "Miracles, Science, and Testimony in Post-Tridentine Saint-Making," *Science in Context* 20, no. 3 (2007): 491.

42. For a perceptive analysis of Lambertini's ambivalent approach to Joseph's levitations, see Catrien Santing, "Tiramisù: Pope Benedict XIV and the Beatification of the Flying Saint Joseph of Cupertino," in *Medicine and Religion in Enlightenment Europe*, edited by Ole Peter Grell and Andrew Cunningham (Aldershot, UK: Ashgate, 2007), pp. 79–100.

43. See R. Messbarger, C. M. S. Johns, and P. Gavitt, eds., *Benedict XIV and the Enlightenment: Art, Science, and Spirituality* (University of Toronto Press, 2015), essays by Gianna Rebecca Messbarger, Gianna Pomata, Fernando Vidal, and John Heilbron, pp. 93–205; also Maria Teresa Fattori, ed., *Le Fatiche di Benedetto XIV* (Rome: Edizioni di Storia e Letteratura, 2011); and Giuseppe Cenachi, "Benedetto XIV e l'Illumismo," in *Benedetto XIV (Prospero Lambertini): Convengo internazionale di studi storici,* vol. 2 (Ferrara, Italy: Centro studi Girolamo Baruffaldi, 1982).

44. *Doctrina de servorum Dei beatificatione et beatificatorum canonizatione* (Bologna, 1734–1738).

45. Bouley, *Pious Postmortems,* pp. 54–56, 61–62.

46. See Carlos Eire, *From Madrid to Purgatory* (Cambridge University Press, 1995), pp. 425–45.

47. Bouley, *Pious Postmortems,* p. 133.

48. *Benedicti Papae XIV doctrina de servorum Dei beatificatione et batorum canonizatione, in synopsim redacta ab Emmanuel de Azevedo* (Brussels, 1840), p. 432.

49. Émile Durkheim, "The Rules of the Sociological Method," in *Classical Sociological Theory,* edited by C. Calhoun, J. Gerteis, J. Moody, et al., 3rd ed. (Hoboken, NJ: Wiley-Blackwell, 2012), pp. 204–5.

50. Taking Durkheim's insights further, Bertrand Méheust has argued that what any culture considers possible or impossible is largely determined, or "set up," by social practices. See his *Somnambulisme et Médiumnité,* 2 vols. (Le Plessis-Robinson: Institut Synthélabo, 1999), 2:271–72. Jeffrey Kripal has also expanded on the insights of Méheust and Durkheim in his *Authors of the Impossible: The Paranormal and the Sacred* (University of Chicago Press, 2010), p. 224.

51. Ten eloquent critiques of the functionalist approach can be found in Alister Chapman, John Coffey, and Brad Gregory, eds., *Seeing Things Their Way: Intellectual History and the Return of Religion* (University of Notre Dame Press, 2009).

52. Keith Thomas, *Religion and the Decline of Magic* (Oxford University Press, 1971), p. 5.

53. Parigi, *Rationalization,* pp. 55, 57. Stretching this functionalist analysis a bit further, Parigi, a sociologist, goes on to argue that "miracles and scientific explanations are thus both perfectly rational, in that they both rule out chance."

54. Parigi, *Rationalization,* p. 165.

55. For an introduction to this concept, see the essays in Philip Gorski, ed., *The Post-Secular in Question: Religion in Contemporary Society* (New York University Press, 2012), especially essays 1 and 7–10. See also Charles Taylor, "Western Secularity," in *Rethinking Secularism,* edited by C. Calhoun, M. Juergensmeyer, and J. Van Antwerpen (Oxford University Press, 2011), pp. 31–53; and John D. Boy, "What We Talk about When We Talk about the Post-Secular," *The Immanent Frame,* March 15, 2011, http://tif.ssrc.org/2011/03/15/what-we-talk-about-when -we-talk-about-the-postsecular/.

56. Exemplified most recently by Dale Allison's *Encountering Mystery: Religious Experience in a Secular Age* (Grand Rapids, MI: Eerdmans, 2022).

57. Luke Clossey, Kyle Jackson, Brandon Marriott, Andrew Redden, and Karin Vélez, "The Unbelieved and Historians, Part I: A Challenge," *History Compass* 14, no. 12 (December 2016): 594–602, https://doi.org/10.1111/hic3.12360; Clossey et al., "The Unbelieved and Historians, Part II: Proposals and Solutions," *History Compass* 15, no. 1 (January 2017): e12370, https://doi.org/10 .1111/hic3.12370.

58. Roland Clark, Luke Clossey, Simon Ditchfield, David M. Gordon, Arlen Wiesenthal, and Taymiya R. Zaman, "The Unbelieved and Historians, Part III: Responses and Elaborations," *History Compass* 15, no. 12 (December 2017): e12430, https://doi.org/10.1111/hic3.12430.

59. Editions Vues de l'Esprit, https://www.vuesdelesprit.org/.

60. Sylvain Piron, *Christine l'Admirable: Vie, chants et merveilles* (Brussels: Vues de l'Espirit, 2021), p. 110.

61. Piron, *Christine l'Admirable,* p. 148. For a review of Piron's book by Christine V. Bourgeois, see the *The Medieval Review,* May 18, 2022, https://scholarworks .iu.edu/journals/index.php/tmr/article/view/34542/37781.

62. Kripal, *Authors of the Impossible,* p. 224. See also Kripal's *The Flip: Epiphanies of Mind and the Future of Knowledge* (New York: Bellevue Literary Press, 2019).

63. Jeffrey Kripal, *Super-Humanities: Historical Precedents, Moral Objections, New Realities* (University of Chicago Press, 2022), pp. 217–18.

64. Archives of the Impossible, accessed 29 January 29, 2023, https://impossible archives.rice.edu/.

65. For more on Esalen, see Marion Goldman, *The American Soul Rush: Esalen and the Rise of Spiritual Privilege* (New York University Press, 2012); and Jeffrey J. Kripal, *Esalen: America and the Religion of No Religion* (University of Chicago Press, 2007).

66. Edward Kelley, Emily Williams Kelly, Adam Crabtree, Alan Gauld, Michael Grosso, and Bruce Greyson, *Irreducible Mind: Toward a Psychology for the 21st Century* (Lanham, MD: Rowman and Littlefield, 2007), p. xiii.

67. See the essays in Edward Kelly, Adam Crabtree, and Paul Marshall, eds., *Beyond Physicalism: Toward a Reconciliation of Science and Spirituality* (Lanham, MD: Rowman and Littlefield, 2015). See also Pamela Rae Heath, *Mind-Matter Interaction: A Review of Historical Reports, Theory, and Research* (Jefferson, NC: McFarland, 2011).

68. Nick Herbert, *Elemental Mind: Human Consciousness and the New Physics* (New York: Dutton, 1993), p. 3.

69. Michael Grosso, *The Man Who Could Fly: St. Joseph of Cupertino and the Mystery of Levitation* (Lanham, MD: Rowman and Littlefield, 2016), p. 174.

70. Grosso, *Man Who Could Fly,* p. 174.

71. "Whatever their personal beliefs, historians should not ask their readers to accept supernatural phenomena." D. P. Walker, *Unclean Spirits: Possession and Exorcism in France and England in the Late Sixteenth and Early Seventeenth Centuries* (Philadelphia: University of Pennsylvania Press, 1981), p. 15.

72. On "hard-edged alterity," see Stephen Nichols, "Modernism and the Politics of Medieval Studies," in *Medievalism and the Modern Temper,* edited by R. Howard Bloch and Stephen Nichols (Baltimore: Johns Hopkins University Press, 1996), p. 49; on the grotesque, see Paul Freedman, "The Return of the Grotesque in Medieval History," in *Historia a Debate: Actas del Congreso Internacional,* edited by Carlos Barros (Santiago de Compostela, Spain, 1995), pt. 4, pp. 9–19.

73. Dorian Llywelyn, SJ, "Millions of Pilgrims Travel to Lourdes Each Year. What Made It Such an Important Symbol of Hope and Healing?," *America: The Jesuit Review,* February 9, 2022, https://www.americamagazine.org/faith/2022/02/09/lourdes-hope-apparition-virgin-mary-242360.

74. On Germany, see David Blackbourn, *Marpingen: Apparitions of the Virgin Mary in Bismarckian Germany* (Oxford University Press, 1993). On Spain, see William A. Christian Jr., *Visionaries: The Spanish Republic and the Reign of Christ* (Berkeley: University of California Press, 1996). On France, see Ruth Harris, *Lourdes: Body and Spirit in the Secular Age* (London: Allen Lane, 1999). On Portugal, see Jeffrey S. Bennett, *When the Sun Danced: Myth, Miracles, and*

Modernity in Early Twentieth-Century Portugal (Charlottesville: University of Virginia Press, 2012).

75. Harris, *Lourdes,* p. 357.

76. In addition to William A. Christian Jr.'s *Visionaries,* see his *Apparitions in Late Medieval and Renaissance Spain* (Princeton University Press, 1981); *Person and God in a Spanish Valley,* rev. ed. (Princeton University Press, 1989); and *Moving Crucifixes in Modern Spain* (Princeton University Press, 1992).

77. Christian, *Moving Crucifixes,* pp. 16–19.

78. Bennett, *When the Sun Danced,* p. 3.

79. See Laura Ackerman Smoller, *The Saint and the Chopped-Up Baby: The Cult of Vincent Ferrer in Medieval and Early Modern Europe* (Ithaca, NY: Cornell University Press, 2014).

80. Definition number 7 of "suspended," adj. and n., *The Compact Edition of the Oxford English Dictionary,* 2 vols. (Oxford University Press, 1971), 2:3179.

Appendix 1: Seventeenth- and Eighteenth-Century Bilocators in America and Europe

1. See Doris Bieñko de Peralta, "El *impasse* de una beatificación. El proceso de sor María de Jesús Tomellín (1597–1637), monja concepcionista poblana," in *Normatividades e instituciones eclesiásticas en la Nueva España, siglos XVI–XIX,* edited by B. Albani, O. Danwerth, and T. Duve (Frankfurt: Max Planck Institute for Legal History and Legal Theory, 2018).

2. *Escrito por ella misma. Vida de la Madre Francisca de la Natividad (1630),* in *Monjas y beatas: La escritura femenina en la espiritualidad barroca novohispana, siglos XVII y XVIII,* edited by Asunción Lavrin and Rosalva Loreto López (Puebla: Universidad de las Americas Puebla, 2002), p. 50; see Magnus Lundberg, *Mission and Ecstasy: Contemplative Women and Salvation in Colonial Spanish America and the Philippines* (Uppsala: Swedish Institute of Mission Research, 2015), p. 195n45.

3. Lundberg, *Mission and Ecstasy,* p. 195n43. See also Doris Bieñko de Peralta, "Voces del claustro: Dos autobiografías de monjas novohispanas del siglo XVII," *Relaciones* 139 (Summer 2014): 157–94.

4. Alonso Ramos, *Los prodigios de la omnipotencia y milagros de la gracia en la vida de la venerable sierva de Dios Catarina de San Juan* (1690), edited by Robin Ann Rice, 3 vols. (New York: IDEA, 2016). See also a recent edition edited by Gisela von Wobeser (Mexico City: Universidad Nacional Autónoma de México, 2017).

5. Ramos, *Prodigios,* pp. 391–92.

6. Lundberg, *Mission and Ecstasy,* p. 198n52.

7. See Jeanne Gillespie, "In the Right Place and the Right (?) Time: Catarina de San Juan's Visions and the Jesuit Missionary Efforts," in *Women's Voices and Politics of the Spanish Empire,* edited by Jennifer Eich, Jeanne Gillespie, and Lucia Harrison (New Orleans: University Press of the South, 2008), esp. pp. 305–6.

8. Antonio de Siria, *Vida Admirable y Prodigiosas Virtudes de la Virgen Sierva de Dios D. Anna Guerra de Jesús, Sacada de lo que Ella Misma Dexó Escrito por Orden de sus Confessores* (Guatemala, 1716).

9. Ursula Suárez, *Relación Autobiografica,* edited by Mario Ferreccio Podestá (Santiago: Academia Chilena de la Historia, 1984). See also Kristine Ibsen, *Women's Spiritual Autobiography in Colonial Spanish America* (Gainsville: University Press of Florida, 1999); Manuel Durán, "Sor Ursula Suárez: Estrategias y espacios de poder," *Mapocho* 54, no. 2 (2003): 159–77.

10. *Jerónima Nava y Saavedra: Autobiografía de una monja venerable* (Cali, Colombia: Universidad del Valle, 1994). Prologue by Angela Inés Robledo, pp. 15–25.

11. Sebastián de Santander y Torres, *Sermón fúnebre que en las honrras de la Venerable Madre Iacinta María Anna de S. Antonio, religiosa de el monasterio de Sancta Catharina de Sena de esta ciudad de Oaxaca* (Oaxaca, 1720).

12. "Cartas de Francisca de los Ángeles," edited by Ellen Gunnarsdóttir, in Lavrin and Loreto, *Monjas y beatas,* pp. 224–62; see also Sarah Owens, "Journeys to Dark Lands: Francisca de los Angeles' Bilocations to Remote Provinces in New Spain," *Colonial Latin American Historical Review* 12, no. 2 (2003): 151–71; and Lundberg, *Mission and Ecstasy,* pp. 205–8.

13. Manuel Sanchez, *Vida de Madre María Manuela de Santa Ana* (1794), in *Sor Maria Manuela de Santa Ana: Una teresina peruana,* edited by Elia J. Armacanqui-Tipacti (Cuzco, Peru: Centro de Estudios Regionales Andinas, 1999), pp. 189–244; for context, see Constance Janiga-Perkins, "The Materiality of Meaning: Identity and Multiple-Authorship in Sor María Manuela de Santana's Spiritual Letters," *Textual Cultures* 10, no. 2 (Spring 2016): 28–50.

14. José Jerónimo Sánchez de Castro, *Vida de la Venerable Madre sor Antonia de la Madre de Dios, religiosa augustina recoleta* (Mexico, 1747).

15. See Helena Esguerra, *María de Jesús, una mística desconocida* (Bogotá: Editorial Kimpres, 2006); and Clara Herrera, *Las místicas de la Nueva Granada: Tres*

casos de búsqueda de perfección y construción de la santidad (Barcelona: Paso de Barca, 2013).

16. Carlos de Sigüenza y Góngora, *Paraýso occidental plantado y cultivado por la liberal mano de los muy cathólicos, y poderosos reyes de España nuestros señores en su magnífico real convento de Jesús María de México* (Mexico City, 1684).

17. *Epistolario de sor Dolores Peña y Lillo* (Chile, 1763–1769), edited by Raïssa Kordič Riquelme (Madrid: Iberoamericana Editorial Vervuert, 2008).

18. Lavrin, *Monjas y beatas,* pp. 354–55.

19. Isidro Sala, *Panegyrico piadoso en las honras, que a la Ven. Madre Sor Ursula Micaela Morata, fundadora y abadesa de este religionissimo Real Convento de los triunfos del SS. Sacramento de Capuchinas, hizo celebrar la Ciudad de Alicante* (Alicante, 1703); *Memorias de una monja del siglo XVII: Autobiografía de la madre Úrsula Micaela Morata, Capuchina,* edited by Vicente Benjamín Piquer Garcés (Alicante: Hermanas Clarisas Capuchinas de Alicante, 1999); Fernando Rodes Lloret, *Sor Úrsula Micaela Morata: Vida y Muerte* (Alicante: Universidad de Alicante, 2014).

20. José Rodríguez Moure, *Cuadros históricos de la admirable vida y virtudes de La Sierva de Dios: Sor María de Jesús de León Delgado* (La Laguna, Tenerife, 1911); *Domingo García Barbusano, Sor María de Jesús: La monja incorrupta del convento de Santa Catalina de La Laguna* (La Laguna, Tenerife: Artemisa, 1990).

21. Anonymous, *Compendium Vitae B. Joannis Josephi a Cruce* (Rome, 1839); P. Diodata dell' Assunta, *Vita di S. Gian Giuseppe della Croce* (Rome, 1839).

22. Anonymous, *Vita del Beato Angelo di Acri, Missionario Cappuccino* (Naples: Olivieri, 1825); *Abridgement of the life of the Blessed Angelo of Acri,* translated by W. G. (Thames Ditton, UK, 1828).

23. Venerable Monsignor Strambi, *The Life of the Blessed Paul of the Cross,* translated by anon. (London, 1853).

24. Vincenzo Ricci, ed., *S. Alfonso M. De Liguori maestro di vita spirituale* (Milan: Gribaudi, 1998); Frederick M. Jones, *Alphonsus de Liguori the saint of Bourbon Naples* (Barnhart MO: Luguori Publications, 1992); Jean Delumeau et al., *Alphonse de Liguori, pasteur et docteur* (Paris: Beauchesne, 1987).

25. Henri de Grèzes, *Vie du bienheureux Félix de Nicosie* (Clermont-Ferrand, France, 1888).

26. Eduard Saint-Omer, *The Wonder Worker of Our Days; Life Virtues and Miracles of St. Gerard Majella* (Boston: Mission Church, 1907).

Credits

Frontispiece. The Bowes Museum, Barnard Castle, County Durham, UK. © Bowes Museum / Bridgeman Images.

Figure 1. José Garcia Hidalgo, *Levitación de Santa Teresa y San Juan de la Cruz en la Encarnación de Ávila,* ca. 1675. Museo de Segovia. Fotografía: J. M. Cófreces.

Figure 2. Loreto Italian School, *The Ecstasy of Saint Joseph of Cupertino,* eighteenth century. Bonhams.

Figure 3. Author unknown, *Vita Beati P. Ignatii Loiolae Societatis Iesu Fundatoris,* vol. 2 (Rome, 1622), plate 74; artist, Peter Paul Rubens; engravers, Jean Baptiste Barbé and Cornelis Galle the Elder. Courtesy DigitalGeorgetown.

Figure 4. Chronicle / Alamy Stock Photo.

Figure 5. Sailko, CC BY 3.0 https://creativecommons.org/licenses/by/3.0, via Wikimedia Commons.

Figure 6. Albrecht Dürer, *The Ecstasy of Saint Mary Magdalen,* Metropolitan Museum of Art. Gift of Junius Spencer Morgan, 1919.

Figure 7. *The Death of Simon Magus,* from *Liber Chronicarum* (1493). Public domain, via Wikimedia Commons.

Figure 8. San Giovanni Bianco (1609–1679), *The Levitation of Saint Dominic.* Bonhams.

Figure 9. Vicente Carducho, *Vision of St. Anthony of Padua,* 1631. The Picture Art Collection / Alamy Stock Photo.

Figure 10. Vicente Carducho, *Stigmatization of St. Francis,* ca. 1610–1630. With permission of Hospital de la Venerable Orden Tercera de San Francisco de Asis, Madrid. Image courtesy of the Nasher Museum of Art at Duke University and the Museum of Fine Arts, Boston.

Figure 11. Giotto, *Ecstasy of St. Francis,* 1295. San Francesco, Upper Church, Assisi, Italy / Bridgeman Images.

Figure 12. Author unknown, *Vita Beati P. Ignatii Loiolae Societatis Iesu Fundatoris,* vol. 2 (Rome, 1622), plate 35; artist, Peter Paul Rubens; engravers, Jean Baptiste Barbé and Cornelis Galle the Elder. Courtesy DigitalGeorgetown.

Figure 13. Artist unknown, *Saint Ignatius Levitating,* engraving, 1693. Private collection / Tarker / Bridgeman Images.

Figure 14. Jeronimus Wierix, *Vita B.P. Ignatii de Loyola, fundatoris Societatis Iesu / Hieronymus Wierx inuenit, incidit & excudit* (Antwerp: Jeronimus Wierix, 1609), plate 3. Courtesy Saint Louis University Libraries Special Collections.

Figure 15. Adriaen Collaert and Cornelis Galle, *Vita S. Virginis Teresiæ a Iesv: Ordinis carmelitarvm excalceatorvm piae restavratricis, Apud Ionnem Galleum* (1630), plate 10. Courtesy Internet Archive via Sterling and Francine Clark Art Institute Library.

Figure 16. Adriaen Collaert and Cornelis Galle, *Vita S. Virginis Teresiæ a Iesv: Ordinis carmelitarvm excalceatorvm piae restavratricis, Apud Ionnem Galleum* (1630), plate 12. Courtesy Internet Archive via Sterling and Francine Clark Art Institute Library.

Figure 17. Adriaen Collaert and Cornelis Galle, *Vita S. Virginis Teresiæ a Iesv: Ordinis carmelitarvm excalceatorvm piae restavratricis, Apud Ionnem Galleum* (1630), plate 17. Courtesy Internet Archive via Sterling and Francine Clark Art Institute Library.

Figure 18. *Representacion De la Vida del Bienaventurado P. F. Juan de la Cruz Primer Carmelita Descalço. Por el R. P. F. Gaspar de la Annunciación Religioso de la misma orden. Scena Vite, B. P. F. Joannis a Cruce Primi Carmelite excalceati,* by Gaspar de la Annunciación; Gaspar Bouttats, engraving, 1678, p. 85, fig. 21. Women of the Book Collection, Sheridan Libraries, Johns Hopkins University.

Figure 19. Giambettino Cignaroli (1706–1770), *Ecstasy of St. Joseph of Cupertino.* Courtesy Il Ponte Casa d'Aste.

Figure 20. Chronicle / Alamy Stock Photo.

Figure 21. Gioan Antonio Lorenzini, *Saint Joseph of Cupertino.* Courtesy of Wellcome Collection.

Figure 22. © NPL—DeA Picture Library / Bridgeman Images.

Figure 23. The Picture Art Collection / Alamy Stock Photo.

Figure 24. Felice Boscaratti, *San Giuseppe da Copertino in estasi,* ca. 1762. Photo by Didier Descouens. Saint Lorenzo Church in Vicenza CC BY-SA 4.0, https://creativecommons.org/licenses/by-sa/4.0, via Wikimedia Commons.

Figure 25. Giambettino Cignaroli, *San Giuseppe da Copertino e la Vergine Immacolata,* 1757. Rita Guglielmi / Alamy Stock Photo.

Figure 26. Chronicle / Alamy Stock Photo.

Figure 27. Gallerie Nazionali di Arte Antica, Roma (MIBACT)—Bibliotheca Hertziana, Istituto Max Planck per la storia dell'arte / Enrico Fontolan.

Figure 28. Mariano Salvador de Maella and Pietro Leone Bombelli, *Retrato de María Jesús Coronel y Arana* (Rome, 1761). Courtesy Biblioteca Nacional de Espana.

Figure 29. José Félix de Amada y Torregrosa, *Compendio de los milagros de Nuestra Señora del Pilar de Zaragoza ...* (1680). Courtesy Biblioteca Nacional de España.

Figure 30. Giotto, *The Apparition at the Chapter House at Arles, 1297–99.* San Francesco, Upper Church, Assisi, Italy / Bridgeman Images.

Figure 31. Miguel Gamborino, *San Pedro Regalado,* 1793. Courtesy University of Navarra Library.

Figure 32. Author unknown, *Vita Beati P. Ignatii Loiolae Societatis Iesu Fundatoris,* vol. 2 (Rome, 1622), plate 76; artist, Peter Paul Rubens; engravers, Jean Baptiste Barbé and Cornelis Galle the Elder. Courtesy DigitalGeorgetown.

Figure 33. Artist unknown, *La morte di Mamma Franceschina.* With permission of Santuario San Giuseppe da Copertino. Photo courtesy La Pro Loco di Copertino, https://www.prolococopertino.it/.

Figure 34. Juan Francisco Leonardo and Hendrick Verbruggen, *Retrato de María Jesús Coronel y Arana,* between 1601 and 1700. Courtesy Biblioteca Nacional de España.

Figure 35. Antonio de Castro, *La Ve. Me. Maria de Iesus de Agreda. Predicando a los Chichimecos del Nuebo-mexico* (Mexico: Joseph Bernardo de Hogal, 1730), frontispiece.

Figure 36. Cristóbal de Villalpando, *Mystical City of God,* 1706. G. Dagli Orti / © NPL—DeA Picture Library / Bridgeman Images.

Figure 37. Joseph Glanvill, *Saducismus triumphatus, or, Full and plain evidence concerning witches and apparitions in two parts ...* (London: J. Collins and S. Lownds, 1689), frontispiece. University of Nottingham, Manuscripts and Special Collections, BF1581.G5.

Figure 38. Joseph Glanvill, *Saducismus triumphatus, or, Full and plain evidence concerning witches and apparitions in two parts ...* (London: J. Collins and S. Lownds, 1689), frontispiece. University of Nottingham, Manuscripts and Special Collections, BF1581.G5.

Figure 39. Joseph Glanvill, *Saducismus triumphatus, or, Full and plain evidence concerning witches and apparitions in two parts ...* (London: J. Collins and S. Lownds, 1689), frontispiece. University of Nottingham, Manuscripts and Special Collections, BF1581.G5.

Figure 40. Joannes Nys, *Vita et miracvla S.P. Dominici, prædicatorii ordinis primi institvtoris ...*, illustrated by Théodore Galle (Antwerp: Apud Theodoru Gallæum, 1611), plate 27. Courtesy Internet Archive via Sterling and Francine Clark Art Institute Library.

Figure 41. Adriaen Collaert and Cornelis Galle, *Vita S. Virginis Teresiæ a Iesv: Ordinis carmelitarvm excalceatorvm piae restavratricis* (Antwerp: Apud Ionnem Galleum, 1630), plate 7. Courtesy Internet Archive via Sterling and Francine Clark Art Institute Library.

Figure 42. Cotton Mather, from *The Wonders of the Invisible World* (Boston: printed by Benj. Harris for Sam. Phillips, 1693). Pictorial Press Ltd. / Alamy Stock Photo.

Figure 43. Albrecht Dürer, *The Witch,* ca. 1500. Metropolitan Museum of Art, Fletcher Fund, 1919.

Figure 44. Ulrich Molitor, from *De lamiis et pythonicis mulieribus* (Strassburg: Johann Prüss, ca. 1489). The Picture Art Collection / Alamy Stock Photo.

Figure 45. INTERFOTO / Alamy Stock Photo.

Figure 46. Hans Baldung Grien, *The Witches' Sabbath,* woodcut, 1508–1510. Reproduced in Hermann Schmitz, *Hans Baldung, gen. Grien* (Bielefeld, Germany: Velhagen and Klasing, 1922), p. 44.

Figure 47. Wilhelm Gottlieb Soldan, Max Bauer, and Heinrich Heppe, *Geschichte Der Hexenprozesse* (Munich: G. Müller, 1912). Reproduction from Peter Binsfeld, *Von Bekanntnuss der Zauberer und Hexen* (Munich, 1591). Courtesy of Hathi Trust.

Figure 48. Francesco Maria Guazzo et al., *Compendium Maleficarum in tres libros distinctum ex pluribus authoribus* (Milan: Apud Haeredes, 1608). Courtesy Hathi Trust.

Figure 49. Francisco de Goya y Lucientes, *Las Brujas,* 1798. Museo del Prado, Madrid / HIP / Art Resource, NY.

Figure 50. J. Collyer, after J. Russell, *Jean François Pilâtre de Rozier,* stipple engraving, 1786. Courtesy of Wellcome Collection.

Figure 51. Claude-Louis Desrais, *Vue et perspective du jardin de Mr. Réveillon fabriquant de papiers, Fauxbourg St Antoine ...,* engraving, 1783. Courtesy Bibliothèque nationale de France.

Figure 52a. Alinari Archives, Florence / Bridgeman Images.

Figure 52b. Artist unknown, *Mother Yvonne-Aimee de Malestroit.* History and Art Collection / Alamy Stock Photo.

Figure 53. Bartolomé Esteban Murillo, *The Angels' Kitchen,* 1646. Louvre, Paris, France / Bridgeman Images.

Index